INSTRUCTOR'S GUIDE TO

THE RIVERSIDE
ANTHOLOGY
OF LITERATURE

INSTRUCTOR'S GUIDE TO

THE RIVERSIDE
ANTHOLOGY
OF LITERATURE

MELODY RICHARDSON DAILY   DOUGLAS HUNT   W. RAYMOND SMITH

UNIVERSITY OF MISSOURI

Houghton Mifflin Company   Boston

Dallas   Geneva, Illinois   Palo Alto   Princeton, New Jersey

Printed in the U.S.A.

ISBN: 0-395-44634-1

COVER: Woodcut by Michael McCurdy

PREFACE

Perhaps in a properly constituted world every literature teacher would have a companion who would assist him or her by reading the textbooks, offering opinions on authors and works, running off to the library to do research, and developing questions for class discussion and writing. In *this* world, however, most of us have to do what we can for ourselves, assisted by casual discussions with colleagues.

This instructor's guide is intended to be the next-best thing to that invaluable and unavailable companion. In it you will find for each story, play, or selection of poems a brief overview and questions for discussion and writing. Each question is followed by an "answer" that is not presented as a model of a student response but as a teacher-to-teacher exploration of the pedagogical opportunities the question opens. In addition to these author-by-author "work-ups," there is for each genre a summary of connections between works that may help you when you are building your syllabus.

Three of us labored through a long summer to complete the guide. Often an entry will reflect indirectly the circumstances under which we worked. Melody Daily's entry on "To Room Nineteen," for instance, was shaped partly by a delightful and unresolved three-way argument over lunch. We talked long and hard over some of the pieces in *The Riverside Anthology,* but decided at last that a work-up should be offered as a private view rather than an averaged-out response. Accordingly, you will find at the end of each of them a set of initials.

Melody Richardson Daily (–M.R.D.)
Doug Hunt (–D.H.)
W. Raymond Smith (–W.R.S.)

Contents

POETRY

Common Forms and Subjects in the Poetry Section   185

SHORT FICTION

THEMES AND NARRATIVE TECHNIQUES
IN THE
FICTION SECTION

THEMES

1. *Men and Women*

Hawthorne, "Rappaccini's Daughter":
> Among other things, Hawthorne's encounter with the ancient theme of woman as the bane of man.

Poniatowska, "A Little Fairy Tale":
> A distinctly post–Freudian story in which men are the bane of women.

Atwood, "Rape Fantasies":
> A sometimes hilarious tale with the serious underlayer you would expect from the title.

Joyce, "Araby":
> Certainly one of the classic stories about adolescent infatuation.

Oates, "Where Are You Going, Where Have You Been?":
> A thrill–seeking suburban adolescent gets picked up by a man who may be the devil himself.

Chekhov, "The Lady with the Pet Dog":
> A natural contrast to "Araby" because it begins with a disillusioned womanizer and shows his gradual discovery of love.

Parker, "Here We Are":
> A rather cynical look at how little a young married couple have to offer each other.

Gallant, "The Remission":
> The disintegration of a marriage, the death of a husband, and a wife's beginning life anew with a man none of her friends or family approve of.

2. *Families*

Kafka, "The Metamorphosis":
> The surrealistic expression of a young man's rejection by his family.

Faulkner, "Barn Burning":
> A boy's unpleasant discovery of what his father really is.

Gallant, "The Remission":
> A middle–class family unraveling under the pressure of the father's prolonged illness.

O'Connor, "A Good Man Is Hard To Find":
> The Southern grotesque end of a family that embodies (and almost parodies) the tensions of family life.

Donoso, "Paseo":
> A glimpse through the eyes of a young boy at a family essentially untouched by love until his aunt goes through an almost magical transformation.

Munro, "Circle of Prayer":
> A slice of the life of a woman who has not only her own life to think of, but the lives of an adolescent daughter and a wayward husband.

Walker, "Everyday Use":
> An uneducated black woman from the rural south is visited by a daughter who has been educated almost into incomprehensibility.

Wilson, "The Raising":
> A southern town's self–appointed advisor on family life comes acropper when faced by a problem child.

3. *Some Views of Women*

Gilman, "The Yellow Wallpaper":
> A now–classic story about neurasthenia caused by lack of productive work and exacerbated by the medical profession's dim–witted view of the female constitution.

Wharton, "Roman Fever":
>   The story of a life–long rivalry between two ladies of visible rank
>   and invisible passions.

Steinbeck, "The Chrysanthemums":
>   A portrait of a woman denied motherhood by nature and other
>   productive occupation by society.

Lessing, "To Room Nineteen":
>   The decline into depression and suicide of a woman who discov-
>   ers that her self is vanishing under the pressure of her role as
>   wife and mother.

Adams, "Return Trips":
>   A woman's attempt to come to grips with her past, and particu-
>   larly her relation to her mother.

O'Brien, "Sister Imelda":
>   The story of a adolescent girl's fascination with a nun who seems
>   to live on the borderline between the worlds of the spirit and the
>   flesh.

4. *Some Views of Men*

Faulkner, "Barn Burning":
>   A picture of a particularly unpleasant sort of masculine pride that
>   expresses itself in rebellion against anything stronger.

Hemingway, "A Clean, Well–Lighted Place":
>   The gentler side of Hemingway's code, a story about sympathy
>   and dignity in the face of direness.

Hammett, "Fly Paper":
>   A "hard boiled" detective who does not wear his heart on his
>   sleeve.

Williams, "Jean Beicke":
>   Compassion mixes with brusqueness in Williams' doctor just as it
>   does in Hammett's detective.

Atwood, "Rape Fantasies":
>   A prolonged and comic meditation on the question of whether
>   men are beasts or sympathetic fellow humans.

5. *Obsession*

Hawthorne, "Rappaccini's Daughter":
>One of the earliest stories in the genre of scientific obsession.

Poe, "The Fall of the House of Usher":
>One of Poe's many tales in which the protagonist destroys himself by becoming prey to his fantasies. Poe is probably the most influential practitioner of the obsession genre.

Flaubert, "The Legend of St. Julian":
>A saint's life that leaves one with the uncomfortable feeling of having been told that there is a close link between sainthood and other obsessions.

Gilman, "The Yellow Wallpaper":
>A story that appears to be deliberately in the Poe tradition, but is based on autobiographical circumstances.

Woolf, "Solid Objects":
>A Member of Parliament becomes so keenly interested in little bits of the physical world around him that he is lost to the world of politics and human affairs.

Lessing, "To Room Nineteen":
>The protagonist's desire to be in control of her life eventually leads her to spend hours alone in a hotel room, and finally leads to her suicide.

Mishima, "Swaddling Clothes":
>A tale of a woman's conviction (based on traditional Japanese values) that a terrible price must be paid for the insult done a child in the hour of his birth.

Donoso, "Paseo":
>A middle–aged woman's attachment to a stray dog becomes an obsession for a life (or death) that takes her away from her well–ordered existence.

Godwin, "Dream Children":
>A childless woman begins to be visited by a child conjured either through psychic forces or an overheated imagination.

6. *Art and Artists*

James, "The Real Thing":
> An artist's discovery that he cannot work successfully with models who actually *are* what they seem to be.

Forster, "The Eternal Moment":
> A novelist discovers that by writing about an unspoiled Italian village, she has made it into a tourist center she abhors.

Borges, "The Aleph":
> A typically Borgesian story that confuses levels of reality to such a degree that we come to question the relation of the fictional to the factual.

Yourcenar, "How Wang–Fo Was Saved":
> A fable about an artist whose work improves upon reality, a devoted admirer whose life is changed by that work, and an emperor who wants to punish the artist for having made the empire seem drab.

Keillor, "The Tip–Top Club":
> A story that very lightly raises the serious issues of the artist/entertainer's relation to his audience by comparing a popular and mindless talk–show host with his sincere but inept successor.

Woolf, "Solid Objects":
> Shows how separate the practical and aesthetic realms are by having its protagonist's obsession with the appearance of physical objects destroy his Parliamentary career.

7. *The South*

Poe, "The Fall of the House of Usher":
> Southern Gothic by the master, a good way to help students see the evolution of a tradition.

Faulkner, "Barn Burning":
> A portrait of Ab Snopes, Civil War veteran of dubious credentials and founder of the tribe that Faulkner used to summarize a Southern type.

Hurston, "Spunk":
> One of Hurston's transformed folk tales from Eatonville, Florida, complete with eerie suggestions of supernatural intervention.

Welty, "Livvie":
> A story set in a deeply isolated countryside near the Natchez trace, where a girl cut off from her family could be absolutely ruled by her aged husband.

O'Connor, "A Good Man is Hard to Find":
> An O'Connor classic, grotesquely humorous and frightening at the same time, and featuring the author's eye and ear for the Southern manner.

Adams, "Return Trips":
> Features a cosmopolitan woman's memories of and return to a small Southern town.

Walker, "Everyday Use":
> Cultural conflict between a rural, uneducated black mother and her highly sophisticated urban daughter.

Wilson, "The Raising":
> A story Southern in speech and gesture and in the author's relish for a brand of humor O'Connor would have recognized.

8. *Cultures and Subcultures*

Faulkner, "Barn Burning":
> The impoverished South of the years following the Civil War.

Hurston, "Spunk":
> A story probably based on tales told in Hurston's all–black, very rural hometown of Eatonville, Florida.

Bambara, "The Lesson":
> A poor, young black girl from the inner city learns about the outside world.

Walker, "Everyday Use":
> Cultural conflict between a rural, uneducated black mother and her highly sophisticated urban daughter.

Yourcenar, "How Wang–Fo Was Saved":
    A Taoist fable from the Far East.

Singer, "Gimpel the Fool":
    A tale of life in an Orthodox Jewish community in Eastern Europe.

Gordimer, "The Catch":
    A story about race relations in South Africa.

Mishima, "Swaddling Clothes":
    A story revealing the conflict of traditional Japanese values and Western values.

García Márquez, "A Very Old Man with Enormous Wings":
    A fantasy set in a realistically sketched Latin American peasant community.

Achebe, "Civil Peace":
    The story of a simple man's tribulations in the days following a civil war in Nigeria.

9. *Stories with Supernatural Elements*

Grimm, "The Juniper Tree"
Hawthorne, "Rappaccini's Daughter"
Poe, "The Fall of the House of Usher"
Flaubert, "The Legend of St. Julian the Hospitaller"
Kafka, "The Metamorphosis"
Borges, "The Aleph"
Hurston, "Spunk"
Singer, "Gimpel the Fool"
Yourcenar, "How Wang–Fo Was Saved"
García Márquez, "A Very Old Man with Enormous Wings"
Donoso, "Paseo"
Poniatowska, "A Little Fairy Tale"
Godwin, "Dream Children"
Oates, "Where Are You Going, Where Have You Been?"

10. *Humorous Stories*

Parker, "Here We Are"
Singer, "Gimpel the Fool"
Ellison, "Did You Ever Dream Lucky?"

García Márquez, "A Very Old Man with Enormous Wings"
Bambara, "The Lesson"
Atwood, "Rape Fantasies"
Keillor, "The Tip–Top Club"
Walker, "Everyday Use"
Wilson, "The Raising"

NARRATIVE TECHNIQUES

Pure examples of any technique are quite rare, of course. Omniscient narration tends to narrow occasionally to limited; objective narration usually breaks down at some point and becomes either third–person limited or omniscient. These lists only indicate that a story uses a technique sufficiently to support class discussion.

FIRST–PERSON NARRATION BY CENTRAL CHARACTER

Williams, "Jean Beicke"
Hammett, "Fly Paper"
Borges, "The Aleph"
Singer, "Gimpel the Fool"
Adams, "Return Trips"
Poniatowska, "A Little Fairy Tale"
O'Brien, "Sister Imelda"
Bambara, "The Lesson"
Atwood, "Rape Fantasies"
Walker, "Everyday Use"

FIRST–PERSON NARRATION BY PERIPHERAL CHARACTER

Poe, "The Fall of the House of Usher"
Doyle, "The Speckled Band"
Donoso, "Paseo"

FIRST–PERSON NARRATION BY CHARACTER WHO MAY BE CENTRAL OR PERIPHERAL, DEPENDING ON INTERPRETATION OF STORY

Melville, "Bartleby the Scrivener"

THIRD–PERSON LIMITED

James, "The Real Thing"
Maupassant, "The String"
Chekhov, "The Lady with the Pet Dog"
Gilman, "The Yellow Wallpaper"

Forster, "The Eternal Moment"
Joyce, "Araby"
Porter, "The Jilting of Granny Weatherall"
Faulkner, "Barn Burning"
Steinbeck, "The Chrysanthemums"
Hurston, "Spunk" (a story with a "chorus" of bystanders)
Wright, "The Man Who Was Almost a Man"
Welty, "Livvy"
Lessing, "To Room Nineteen" (a story in which p.o.v. slowly narrows)
Gordimer, "The Catch" (a story with p.o.v. limited to what a married
       couple sees)
O'Connor, "A Good Man Is Hard to Find"
Mishima, "Swaddling Clothes"
Berger, "An Independent Woman"
Munro, "Circle of Prayer"
Achebe, "Civil Peace"
Godwin, "Dream Children"
Oates, "Where Are You Going, Where Have You Been?"
Silko, "Lullaby"

THIRD-PERSON OMNISCIENT

Grimm, "The Juniper Tree"
Hawthorne, "Rappaccini's Daughter"
Flaubert, "The Legend of St. Julian"
Wharton, "Roman Fever"
Woolf, "Solid Objects"
Kafka, "The Metamorphosis"
Yourcenar, "How Wang-Fo Was Saved"
Gallant, "The Remission"
García Márquez, "A Very Old Man with Enormous Wings"
Keillor, "The Tip-Top Club"
Wilson, "The Raising"

OBJECTIVE OR DRAMATIC

Parker, "Here We Are"
Hemingway, "A Clean, Well-Lighted Place"

FRAME STORY

Ellison, "Did You Ever Dream Lucky?"

Jacob and Wilhelm Grimm
The Juniper Tree

"The Juniper Tree" may be a good story to start a semester with for at least two reasons. The first is that a good deal of higher education involves unlearning oversimplifications that students learn more–or–less osmotically from the society around them. In literature, one of the most dangerous osmotic half–truths is that the principal yardstick by which art is to be judged is its fidelity to external reality. Fairy tales exemplify in homely form art that has other fish to fry: allegiances to the internal realities of the psyche to the shapeliness of the work. The second reason for starting with this fairy tale is that it shows how artificial the distinctions between genres can be. Here is a work made to be recited, structured on a number of symbols and patterns of repetition, and advancing a plot. Shall we call it poetry, fiction, or drama?

Randall Jarrell says in the counterpointed selection at the end of the story that Grimm's fairy tales are "the root of all stories. Certainly it is easy to connect "The Juniper Tree" with the tales of Hawthorne and Poe, with such fantasies as "The Legend of St. Julian" "The Aleph," "How Wang–Fo Was Saved," "A Very Old Man with Enormous Wings," or "A Little Fairy Tale." Such stories as "The Metamorphosis," "Gimpel the Fool," "Paseo," "Dream Children," and "Where Are You Going, Where Have You Been?" are hybrids that combine utter realism with fairy tale fantasies and grotesqueries.

Your class might enjoy comparing "The Juniper Tree," which was transcribed verbatim from an oral account, with Zora Neale Hurston's "Spunk," which was based on folk material but written in more literary form.

QUESTIONS

1. Fairy tales often divide into parts separated by changes of scene and point of view. In "The Juniper Tree" each part starts with a character's plight and ends in a marvel that seems to resolve the difficulty. Divide the story into its parts and describe the structure and point of view of each.

Though others would answer differently, I see five parts, each worth a bit of class discussion.

1. The Tale of the Pious Wife. This story fills the first paragraph of the story. Once it is launched by a little narration, it is told strictly from the point of view of the pious wife, whose plight is barrenness, and whose deliverance comes through the magical conception of a

son. Folklorists would surely be able to distinguish some patterns in
this magic conception. The mixing of blood and snow to produce a
child with fair skin and a ruddy complexion, the connection of the
months of pregnancy with the years' cycle from dead of winter to
fullness of harvest, the association of pregnancy with eating a magical fruit, the connection of life and death with a tree—all these are
variants on ancient story elements that appeal to us poetically rather
than "realistically." Similar elements appear in Elena Poniatowska's "A Little Fairy Tale."

2. The Tale of the Beheading of the Son. This second sub–tale is told
from the point of view of the second wife and also moves from plight
to marvelous (or at least spectacular) solution. The second wife knows
that her stepson will always "stand in her way" when she attempts
to settle the whole of her husband's fortune on her daughter.
Tempted by the Evil One, she manages a perfect crime, ending with
a decapitated corpse tied rather niftily together by a handkerchief
(the handkerchief motif appears in Margaret Yourcenar's "How
Wang–Fo Was Saved").

3. Marlinchen's Tale. At this the story's point of view shifts and we
are with Marlinchen as she seems to knock her brother's head off
and then has to watch him be baked into a pie and eaten by his father. The motif of the father who eats his children is another of
those grisly universals; its most familiar occurrence is in Greek
mythology, where Atreus has the children of his brother Thyestes
served up. Marlinchen's plight is now that she believes herself to be
her brother's killer, and she must make the situation right.
Accordingly she gathers up his bones and puts them beneath the
magical juniper tree, where they are marvelously transformed into
a living bird.

4. The Tale of the Marvelous Bird. Now the bird/son confronts the
problem of being an agent of justice. He does this by the most unlikely possible means, but who at this point is going to complain
about the bird's flying off with a millstone that can barely be lifted
by twenty millers using a beam for a lever. What is interesting to
me here is the storyteller's use of point of view. We are with the citizens of the town now, looking at the miraculous bird as a goldsmith, shoemaker, and miller would. A similar interest in reactions to the miraculous rather than the miraculous *per se* can be
found in Kafka's "The Metamorphosis" and Gabriel García Márquez's "A Very Old Man with Enormous Wings."

5. The Resolution. Here the point of view shifts rapidly among the
evil wife, the husband, and Marlinchen, all of whom are by now
living in different worlds. The husband, blissfully ignorant of all
that has happened, sees the beautiful bird with the same delight the
townspeople have. Marlinchen, overcome by grief, is harder to
cheer. The wife, however, feels the approach of doom. In the end,
each gets a just reward.

Students naturally tend to think of the fairy story as an unsophisticated
narrative intended for an unsophisticated audience. If they will look at
the way "The Juniper Tree" is structured, they may have cause to change
their minds. Here is a story cunningly constructed of a series of nested
sub–stories. The point of view shifts drastically from section to section in a
way that might today be characterized as avant–garde, and the psycho–
logical truth of the characterization is sometimes striking. Marlinchen's
inexpressible guilt because she believes she has killed her brother and
because she cannot condemn her mother would seem eerily familiar to
some of today's child psychologists, and the mother's rising horror at
what she has done makes her a miniature of such characters as Lady
Macbeth.

2. How does the storyteller use parallel actions and images to knit the
story together?

There are so many examples to offer here that I won't try to offer an
exhaustive list. There is the red and white motif mentioned above, which
connects the complexion of the son with the appearance of blood on the
snow, and later connects the son's head with the red apples in the trunk
and the white handkerchief that will cover the cut. There is the repeti–
tion of the song three times before three different types of workmen offer
three types of gifts. There are three appearances by the Juniper Tree: once
to mark the boy's conception and birth, once to mark his rebirth as a
bird, once to mark his return to human form. There is the parallel be–
tween the dinner at which the boy is eaten and the dinner that he in–
terrupts to take his revenge. There is Marlinchen's crying into the pot
where her brother is being cooked into black–puddings and her crying
onto her empty plate. A diligent search would surely discover a dozen
such parallels. The impulse to make a pattern is common in oral story–
telling and links it strongly to poetry as well as to fiction.

3. What are the least realistic details in the story and what are the most
realistic? Does the storyteller seem aware of the effect of the mixture of
realistic and fantastic details?

Students will probably list the resurrection of the boy as a talking bird, his re–transformation to human form, and his flight with the millstone around his neck as the least credible portions of the tale. Some may add that the calmness with which the husband watches his wife (blameless in his eyes) crushed by a millstone makes no sense.

Side by side with these flights of fantasy, we have some surprisingly realistic touches. The goldsmith is so struck by the beauty of the bird's song that he rushes out of the house, losing one slipper in the process, and stands in the public street gawking, his apron still on, his pincers in hand, with one sock exposed. The shoemaker looks up at the bird and has to shield his face with his hand because of the bright sun. Most remarkably of all, one of the millers scruples to give the stone away because it is owned by a partnership. Eventually all of the partner–millers agree to give the stone away, and they hoist it just as they realistically should, using a beam for a lever.

Is the storyteller aware of how these fantastic and realistic details fit together? Undoubtedly. If she were not enjoying the contrast between the realistic and the fantastic, she would have settled for something smaller than a millstone to crush the stepmother with, or would have avoided the absolutely unnecessary detail of having the twenty millers strain at a beam to lift it.

The pleasure of creating a world in which birds can talk but goldsmiths can't keep their slippers on is one of the principal motives of the writer or storyteller.

–D.H.

Nathaniel Hawthorne
Rappaccini's Daughter

In this short story we find Hawthorne exploring, among other things, a theme he treated often: the idea that scientific investigation, untempered by considerations of the full consequences, imperils both the subjects and the experimenter. Signor Baglioni points straight to the heart of the matter when he says that "as for Rappaccini, it is said of him—and I, who know the man well, can answer for its truth—that he cares infinitely more for science than for mankind" (p. 28). Rappaccini, then, is that variety of doctor not concerned with healing the sick; he is instead a laboratory scientist so consumed by his science that "he would sacrifice human life, his own among the rest, or whatever else was dearest to him, for the sake of adding so much as a grain of mustard seed to the great heap of his accumulated knowledge" (p. 28).

This theme of science gone awry runs through nineteenth–century literature, particularly the works of the Romantics. Some students will

probably point out that *Faust* and *Frankenstein,* a tale of magic advanced to
the point that it is a science and a tale of a science advanced to the point of
magic, belong to this tradition. An age fascinated by the marvels produced through what could truly be called technology—steam engines, experiments in galvanism—was beginning to learn of the attendant costs
of those wonders. In any event, some may argue that "Rappaccini's
Daughter" has nothing to do with science as Hawthorne must have
known it or we know it—the "poisonous maiden" motif is a remnant of
folklore and a merely magical vestige of a much earlier system of belief.
But in all these types of fictions the distinction between science and
magic is muddled; for men and women of the nineteenth century, as for
us, magic and a technology advanced beyond our understanding are, in
the final analysis, indistinguishable. Alchemy and experiments in
superconductivity are all the same to most of us.

But Hawthorne, here as in "Dr. Heidegger's Experiment" and "The
Birthmark"—his most anthologized "science–without–counting–the–cost"
tales—investigates and reveals as well what Melville calls "Innate
Depravity" in the counterpoint and what Poe called the "imp of the perverse"—the darkness of the human heart. Giovanni Guasconti feels himself drawn by that which repels and frightens him; after seeing the sap
from Rappaccini's deadly shrub kill a lizard and Beatrice's breath destroy
a butterfly, he is overcome by "a wild offspring of both love and horror
that had each parent in it, and burned like one and shivered like the
other . . . Blessed are all simple emotions, be they dark or bright. It is
the lurid intermixture of the two that produces the illuminating blaze of
the infernal regions" (pgs. 31–2). While we know less of his
motivations, Rappaccini himself, a man of medicine, misuses his powers
and art in creating in his daughter a being unassailable and deadly.
When his daughter accuses him of inflicting a "miserable doom" upon
her, he replies:

> Dost thou deem it misery to be endowed with marvellous gifts
> against which no power nor strength could avail an enemy—mis-
> ery, to be able to quell the mightiest with a breath—misery, to be as
> terrible as thou art beautiful? (p. 45)

QUESTIONS

1. One could argue that Signor Pietro Baglioni acts as Giovanni': "good
angel," trying to keep him from the evil influence of Rappaccini. Do you
think this is a sensible reading? Why or why not?

My answer would be yes—with so many qualifications that it might as
well be a no. Hawthorne, who is not given to fuzziness in these matters,

describes him as *"apparently* of genial nature [emphasis mine]" (p. 28). Just how genial is in some doubt. As it turns out, Baglioni harbors a professional jealousy toward Rappaccini that may color our impression of his motivations for befriending and "saving" Giovanni from his rival.

> "This must not be," said Baglioni to himself. "The youth is the son of my old friend, and shall not come to any harm from which the arcana of medical science can preserve him. Besides, it is too insufferable an impertinence in Rappaccini, thus to snatch the lad out of my hands, as I may say, and make use of him for his infernal experiments . . . Perchance, most learned Rappaccini, I may foil you where you little dream of it!" (p. 33)

If Giovanni and Beatrice are to Rappaccini merely subjects for an experiment, to Baglioni they are the arena in his campaign against his enemy. It is interesting to note that in combating his professional rival, Rappaccini, Baglioni promises to use the tools of the art they share, the "arcana of medical science." His enmity toward Rappaccini is based less on a belief that his rival's experiments on human beings is wrong than a belief that his methodology is unsound; Rappaccini is "a vile empiric, however, in his practice, and therefore not to be tolerated by those who respect the good old rules of the medical profession" (p. 40). Whenever people insist on the good old rules of their professions, we are quite right in suspecting their motives.

Finally, we must examine the circumstances surrounding the death of Beatrice. As Rappaccini and Giovanni stand silent and wondering at their part in the experiment and the death of Beatrice, Baglioni calls out "in a tone of triumph mixed with horror to the thunderstricken man of science, 'Rappaccini! Rappaccini! and is *this* the upshot of your experiment!'" (p. 45). Baglioni may be acting as a sort of chorus, driving home the point of the tale when he cries out to Rappaccini (and us) at the end of the tale; regardless, to taunt even one's worst enemy at such a moment is evidence of a vindictiveness we might not have expected from an entirely genial old professor of medicine.

[Some students may suspect Baglioni of even worse. After all, he has surmised the nature of the experiment, and he does know of Beatrice's poisonous nature; is it not also possible that he knows the effect the antidote will have on Beatrice?]

2. Do our feelings toward Giovanni change over the course of the tale?

We know little of Giovanni before his entanglement with Beatrice except that he is given to melancholy as a result of the "tendency to heartbreak natural to a young man for the first time out of his native sphere" (p. 24). Perhaps this tendency to heartbreak lends Giovanni a romantic overreadiness; in any event, he questions his own senses as he observes Beatrice and her fatal encounters with the reptile and the butterfly. Our sympathies at this point lie with him, as they usually lie with young people ready for love.

After his first exchange with Beatrice, however, Guasconti begins to fall in most readers' estimations. We learn that he is frightened and fascinated by Beatrice, and we are told twice that his passion does not run deep; he may be only infatuated with Beatrice:

> he had not a deep heart—or, at all events, its depths were not sounded now; but he had a quick fancy, and an ardent southern temperament, which rose every instant to a higher fever pitch (p.31)

> Oh how stubbornly does love,—or even that cunning semblance of love which flourishes in the imagination, but strikes no depth of root into the heart,—how stubbornly does it hold its faith until the moment comes when it is doomed to vanish into thin mist! (p. 37)

At the end of the tale, Giovanni thinks only of his own preservation and scorns Beatrice:

> Giovanni's rage broke forth from his sullen gloom like a lightning flash out of a dark cloud.
> "Accursed one!" cried he, with venomous scorn and anger. "And, finding thy solitude wearisome, thou hast severed me likewise from all the warmth of life and enticed me into thy region of unspeakable horror!"
>
> . . . .
>
> "Yes, poisonous thing!" repeated Giovanni, beside himself with passion. "Thou hast done it? Thou hast blasted me? Thou hast filled my veins with poison? Thou hast made me as hateful, as ugly, as loathsome and deadly a creature as thyself—a world's wonder of hideous monstrosity? Now, if our breath be happily as fatal to ourselves as to all others, let us join our lips in one kiss of unutterable hatred, and so die!" (p. 43)

While Giovanni's horror is understandable, his cruelty to a woman who loves him and whom he professed to love is unforgivable; the narrator leaves us with this final judgment of him:

> O, weak, and selfish, and unworthy spirit, that could dream of an earthly union and earthly happiness as possible, after such deep love had

been so bitterly wronged as was Beatrice's love by Giovanni's blighting words! (p. 44)

Without stretching the point to the breaking point, I think one could argue that Giovanni Guasconti is as much a dabbler in another's life as either Baglioni or Rappaccini. Rappaccini cares so much for his science that he removes his daughter from human company; Baglioni cares so much for his professional prestige that he is willing to turn a love between two young people into a contest between himself and his rival; Guasconti cares so much for the sensation of being in love that he can care little for Beatrice, who, after all is said and done, is only the object of his desires.

3. How does the symbol of the garden affect our understanding of the tale?

Students familiar with the counterpoint to this tale (and even those who aren't) will no doubt have questions and answers about just what Hawthorne is doing here with the symbol of the Garden of Eden. While Hawthorne does not give us a serpent in the garden, he does give us "a small orange–colored reptile, of the lizard or chameleon species" (p. 30). He does allow Giovanni to ask, after seeing Rappaccini tending to the poisonous shrub, "Was this garden, then the Eden of the present world? And this man, with such a perception of harm in what his own hands to grow,—was he the Adam?" (p. 26). Beatrice says that her father "created" that same deadly shrub, and that he is "fearfully acquainted with the secrets of Nature" (p. 42).

Students reading Melville's commentary in the counterpoint concerning Hawthorne's interest in "Innate Depravity" and "Original Sin" may be tempted in light of the biblical allusions above to make the sort of equations in analysis of "Rappaccini's Daughter" that are so dangerous in dealing with Hawthorne's symbolism.

Giovanni and Beatrice = Adam and Eve
Rappaccini = Adam
Rappaccini = God
Rappaccini = the Serpent
Giovanni = the Serpent

These sorts of equations, as tempting as they are, are always unsatisfying in dealing with Hawthorne. Anyone willing to make the identifications above will be hard pressed to defend them to the exclusion of the others; the point here is that Hawthorne is a symbolist, not an allegorist, and his characters and images are deep and baffling and infinitely suggestive. They do not defy analysis; in fact, since he is often a moralist, they invite it, but one can never light on the "right" answer.

–W.R.S.

Edgar Allan Poe
The Fall of the House of Usher

Students who haven't read this short story but have heard of Poe (perhaps through that series of deliciously bad movies supposedly drawn from his works and now shown only very late at night or very early in the morning) sometimes wrongly regret their interest and your choice of this selection after the first page or so of "Usher." The sentences are long and florid, and just don't seem to nudge the action along.

A glance at Poe's aesthetic redeems this tale, and reveals just how his ideal of a unified effect is achieved here as in few of his works. I have often read the first sentence aloud in class, exaggerating the long syllables: "*During* the *whole* of a *dull, dark,* and *soundless day* in the *autumn* of the *year,* when the *clouds hung* oppressively *low* in the heavens, *I* had been *passing alone* . . ." (p. 46). I then ask, "What's Poe trying to do with us here? What unified effect is he attempting to achieve?" In "The Philosophy of Composition," of course, Poe tells us that the repetition of long syllables has a powerful effect upon readers and listeners. Your students, without resorting to the gloss from Poe's essay, will have the good sense to realize just how the reader is being manipulated here. What they might not realize, however, is the simple truth that for Poe the distinctions between poetry and fiction as works attempting a unified effect are blurry at best, and that Poe's *modus operandi* for this work of short fiction is largely the same as that he claims for "The Raven" in "The Philosophy of Composition."

Poe pulls out all of his trademark stops in *Usher.* He asserts, once again in "The Philosophy of Composition," that the death of a beautiful woman is the fittest subject for poetry—thus the fate and appearance of the Lady Madeline. He relies on creaky Gothic machinery—thus the donjon and the "black and lurid tarn." He depends on a deep–seated fear that he had played on earlier—thus the motif of the premature burial.

But there are some master strokes here. Poe forces us to examine the House of Usher closely. He is too careful an artist, even at his worst, to have told us for no reason twice within the first two hundred words that the windows were "vacant and eye–like." The juxtaposition of the description of the House, with its "barely perceptible fissure" and "fine tangled webwork" of fungi at the eaves, and the description of Roderick Usher, with a physiognomy "speaking . . . of a want of moral energy" and "hair of a more than web–like softness and tenuity" is not a subtle touch, but it is a good one. (More than one student in my classes has noted, by the way, that the description of Usher provides us with an accurate physical description of Poe himself. If you draw, you might have a student read the passage while you sketch out the portrait. [Representing Roderick/Edgar Poe's cadaverous complexion on a blackboard is a challenge few of us can resist.]) Even Roderick's reading–list is worth our attention; Machiavelli's *Belfaegor*, after all, is about a woman who, in essence, drags her lover down to hell.

QUESTIONS

1. What is the point of view employed in this tale? How would you describe the narrator? Is he a reliable narrator?

The first–person narrator is a cipher for most readers. Alternately gossipy and coldly analytic, he never becomes the wildly unreliable narrator we receive from Poe in "The Tell–Tale Heart," "The Cask of Amontillado," or "The Black Cat." Or does he? He attempts early in the narrative to provide a "rational" or natural explanation for the effects the oppressive gloom of the House have upon him and explains away the apocalyptic storm as "merely electrical phenomena not uncommon." He takes a clinical interest in Madeline's symptoms as well. That chilly detachment and assured positivism waver, it seems to me, more than once in the course of the narrative.

2. Why is "The Haunted Palace" *in* this short story?

It isn't terribly good poetry (Or is it? The last two lines are chilling.), but it does of course cry out to be recognized as a poetic chronicle of Roderick Usher's loss of reason. We have two luminous windows, a stage whisper from Poe we know how to respond to by now, and the radiant palace is in "the monarch Thought's dominion. As Roderick declines into madness, so too are the "spirits moving musically/To a lute's well–tuned law" replaced by "Vast forms that move fantastically/To a discordant melody."

3. Does Poe try too hard to manipulate us?

Is Poe, given what we know about his aesthetic, merely pulling strings that he knows will have a certain effect upon us? Is he to blame for preying upon our imaginations through the subliminal effects of the "music" he plays for us in his first paragraph? Does he depend on his equivalent of special effects too much?

I often leave movies these days feeling as if the director had pulled strings that were just too easy for him or her to grasp. We can see through bald attempts at manipulation, and, while we may have a visceral and unavoidable response to sudden shots of sharks leaping out of the water or certain types of music, the affect, we feel, is somehow cheapened and diminished. As Poe's contemporary, Keats, said, "We hate poetry that has a palpable design upon us." Poe, since he pulls out nearly all of what he considered sure–fire "special effects," is transparent here, and some of your students may find that his tale suffers for it.

–W.R.S.

Herman Melville
Bartleby the Scrivener

Some literary historians treat "Bartleby" as the first short story in America, but whether you find that convincing or not depends on the distinctions you are willing to make between the tale and the short story. If one compares any of the characters in Poe's tales to the narrator in "Bartleby." one finds that it is hard to imagine, say, the narrator of "Usher" as existing anywhere but in that story; the narrator of "Bartleby" is, on the other hand, a creation of sufficient psychological complexity for us to imagine him actually existing. In short, Melville has created a convincing consciousness and Poe has provided us with an obvious construct, and it is this difference (among others) that marks "Bartleby" as a short story and "Usher" as a tale.

This short story may afford you the opportunity to compare the tale and the short story in some detail. One way of making that comparison concrete is to examine the differences between the depiction of the narrator and Bartleby himself. In Bartleby we see a character that would not be out of place in the tale—in fact, some critics have argued that there are echoes of "The Raven" in "Bartleby the Scrivener." Bartleby, like the Raven, is a mysterious figure that haunts the narrator, inspiring guilt and confusion through repetition of a message of negation. More importantly for my purposes, in his portrayal of Bartleby, Melville shows not the slightest interest in mimesis; we are no more likely to meet the scrivener on the street than meet someone like Roderick Usher at the laundromat.

The narrator in "Bartleby" is a character both round and dynamic. Melville adds layers of complexity to his character by allowing the narrator to present himself in the classic before and after manner. In describing his surroundings and his employees, the narrator discloses more of his "pre–Bartleby" self—obliquely—than he might through direct confession. The result is that we have a scrimshaw–fine delineation of his character. As the story proceeds, he is revealed as having gone through a profound change, moving in the process from an eminently safe man to a man capable of exclaiming "Ah Bartleby! Ah humanity!"

A great many readers take "Bartleby" to be Melville's reaction to his treatment at the hands of the reading public. This is a likely possibility, but it is also true that the story is what its subtitle claims it to be: a story of Wall Street. Wall Street was then as now the center of commerce in this country, and it is in commerce in both its senses—buying and selling and social intercourse—that Melville has Bartleby prefer not to engage.

QUESTIONS

1. Who is this story about?

You may wish to ask a more sophisticated version of this question. Whatever form it takes, it is nonetheless an important thing to ask. The answer is, of course, "The narrator." It is the narrator's movement from man of business to sentimentalist that is the mainspring of this short story. Bartleby is merely a device; in this short story and elsewhere, Melville uses characters and objects to present ambiguities and conflicts that reveal the character of those grappling with those ambiguities and engaged in those conflicts. In that regard Bartleby is merely a prop; *Moby–Dick*, after all, is seldom about the whale itself.

2. How do Melville's depictions of Nippers and Turkey contribute to our understanding of the narrator's relationship to Bartleby?

Melville uses Nippers and Turkey as foils for the narrator. Both provide us with alternate ways of reacting to Bartleby's passive resistance to human commerce, and Melville has prepared us early for this implicit comparison. The narrator describes himself as

> . . . one of those unambitious lawyers who never address a jury, or in any way draw down public applause; but, in the cool tranquillity of a snug retreat, do a snug business among rich men's bonds, and mortgages, and title–deed. All who know me, consider me an eminently *safe* man. The late John Jacob Astor, a personage little given to poetic enthusiasm, had no hesitation in pronouncing my first grand point to be prudence; my next, method. (p. 62)

In short, the narrator is more of a solicitor than a barrister; he shrinks from politics or disputation. The repetition of "snug" in the passage cited above is no accident, for the narrator insists on remaining within the confines of his retreat of an office and letting his business come to him. Nippers, on the other hand, has shady dealings with collection–agents, bail bondsmen, and is "considerable of a ward–politician" (p. 65). He is, as the narrator says, a victim of "diseased ambition" (p. 65). Turkey, not *safe* at all, grows more choleric and imprudent as the business day wears on. Both react violently to Bartleby's behavior, one threatening to blacken his eyes and the other to kick him out of the office. The narrator, while he is angered by Bartleby's behavior, never himself resorts to violence or threatens to—he remains prudent and *safe*. But, though he never does physical harm to Bartleby, he nonetheless leaves his offices and abandons Bartleby to the not–too–tender mercies of the next inhabitant of his offices. The narrator's hands—though he takes pains to juxtapose his own reasonableness and compassion to the excesses of his clerks—are not entirely clean. Bartleby refuses to absolve him in their last encounter:

> "I know you," he said, without looking around—"and I want nothing to say to you." (p. 87)

3. What, if any, changes come over the narrator in the course of the narrative?

Perhaps the most economical way to make your class understand the change overtaking the narrator is to compare the narrator as he presents himself in the first two paragraphs of the tale to his appearance in the final paragraph. What sort of man, you might ask your class, honestly believes that scriveners—the nineteenth–century equivalent of the copying–machine—might "seem an interesting and somewhat singular set of men." What sort of person would mourn the lack of biographies of scriveners? What sort of person would take pleasure and pride in having prudence and a methodical turn of mind cited as his virtues? Why does the narrator love to repeat the name of John Jacob Astor?

The speaker of the last paragraph is a changed man, no longer the hard–headed man of business, but one capable of imagining Bartleby in his job as clerk in the Dead Letter Office and empathizing to the point of morbid and maudlin sentimentality.

> Dead letters! does it not sound like dead men? Conceive a man by nature and misfortune prone to a pallid hopelessness, can any business seem more fitted to heighten it than that of continually handling these dead letters, and assorting them for the flame? For by the cart–load they are annually burned. Sometimes from out the folded paper the pale clerk takes a ring—the finger it was meant for moulders in the grave; a bank–note sent in swiftest charity—he whom it would relieve, nor eats nor hungers more; pardon for

those who died despairing; hope for those who died unhoping; good
tidings for those who died stifled by unrelieved calamities. On
errands of life, these letters speed to death. (p. 89)

So in the narrator we have two opposing visions of life that Melville is
careful to point to symbolically throughout the short story; on the one
hand is the detached and demanding world of business; on the other is a
world capable of assimilating the Bartlebys of the world. Both worlds are
represented in the office on Wall Street: on the one hand we have the
dark wall (much like the one Bartleby dies beside); on the other, the
shaft of sunlight entering the building through the skylight. The narrator provides us, in describing the Tombs, with the best of metaphors for
what has happened to him:

But a soft imprisoned turf grew under foot. The heart of the eternal
pyramids, it seemed, wherein, by some strange magic, through the
clefts, grass seed, dropped by birds, had sprung (p. 88).

The most impermeable structure—and heart—can be penetrated in unexpected ways.

–W.R.S.

Gustave Flaubert
The Legend of Saint Julian the Hospitaller

This story, perhaps more than any other in this anthology, will make
readers wish that they could unearth the original intentions of the author. Flaubert's tone here is very difficult to characterize, but it is safe to
make at least this assertion: This is not merely a tale of simple piety.

The aesthetic of the hagiography will probably be unfamiliar to your
students. A casual but critical reader of saints' lives would no doubt be
surprised and perhaps dismayed to discover that the narratives are all
very much alike. This is, after all, not surprising, since saints' lives are
ordinarily lived in imitation of Christ, and hagiographers, since they
are rarely interested in what moderns might call historical accuracy,
rely on biblical motifs and legends in constructing their stories. Before
his conversion in the story, St. Julian indulges his senses in slaughter-
ing animals; a great many saints were notorious sinners before their
conversions. St. Julian succors a repulsive leper; any number of saints'
lives involve similar sacrifices in helping the unfortunate. But the saints'
lives are not all dry homilies; some are romances that happen to be about
ascetics, a notion not too startling when one considers that saints' lives

naturally involve the supernatural and often catalogue deeds that are both heroic and superhuman.

My point here is that Flaubert both transcends and transforms the form. We have, in "Saint Julian," a tale of the miraculous as told by the consummate realist. Instead of a tendentious tale of a man's or woman's piety and miraculous works, we have a fascinating psychological portrait of a man seized and overcome by deviant passions. Instead of the spare style common to most hagiographies, we have a story filled with rich detail.

> Inside the castle, the locks on the doors shone brightly; costly tapestries hung in the apartments to keep out the cold; the closets overflowed with linen, the cellar was filled with casks of wine, and the oak chest fairly groaned under the weight of money–bags. (p. 91)

Some students will find Flaubert's depiction of Julian a bit hard to swallow. Saints may be sinners before they see the light, but Julian's savagery makes it hard for us to believe that he could be a candidate for canonization. Some of your students will no doubt be reminded of Grimms' *The Juniper Tree;* like that ancient story, "St. Julian" combines the miraculous and the horrific in an often disturbing way.

QUESTIONS

1. Realism and the miraculous make for an uneasy mixture. Find some examples of the unbelievable treated realistically; what is the effect?

Your students should have no difficulty finding examples, but they may have trouble determining the effect, since it is hard to determine if and how far Flaubert's tongue is in his cheek. Take, for instance, the following, in which the stuff of romance or even fairy–tale is described in detail that only a realist might feel obligated to muster:

> On the opposite side of the valley, he suddenly beheld a large stag, with a doe and their fawn. The buck was black and of enormous size; he had a white beard and carried sixteen antlers. His mate was the color of dead leaves, and she browsed upon the grass, while the fawn, clinging to her udder, followed her step by step.
> Again the bow was stretched, and instantly the fawn dropped dead, and seeing this, its mother raised her head and uttered a poignant, almost human wail of agony. Exasperated, Julian thrust his knife into her chest, and felled her to the ground.

The great stag had watched everything and suddenly he sprang forward. Julian aimed his last arrow at the beast. It struck him between the antlers and stuck there.

The stag did not appear to notice it; leaping over the bodies, he was coming nearer and nearer with the intention, Julian thought, of charging at him and ripping him open, and he recoiled with inexpressible horror. But presently the huge animal halted, and, with eyes aflame and the solemn air of a patriarch and a judge, repeated thrice, while a bell tolled in the distance:

"Accursed! Accursed! Accursed! some day, ferocious soul, thou wilt murder thy father and thy mother!" (p. 97)

It is odd indeed to see this incident in the hands of the author of *Madame Bovary*; one just does not expect to encounter talking deer, least of all talking deer delivering imprecations, in the work of Flaubert. But Flaubert is staying within the bounds of the genre in which he has chosen to work; he adds, however, the filigree of detail that makes this scene more striking than it might have been in a conventional saints' life or romance.

2. This story is divided into three parts. Why do you think that Flaubert organized his narrative in this fashion?

I. Julian the Deviant

Exposition and Complication

In Part One Flaubert handles the conventions of exposition, the setting is described, and he depicts the birth of the protagonist and the circumstances surrounding that birth. Here we see Julian grow into the depravity that results in self–indulgent slaughter and the curse being laid upon him by the stag. Taking the curse to heart, Julian returns home, where he narrowly misses fulfilling the prophecy by nearly killing both father and mother. He leaves home.

II. Julian the Knight–Errant

Further Complication and Catastrophe

In Part Two we see Julian, in an attempt to avoid the prophecy, suffer privation and discomfort and then dedicate himself to killing only one species—his own—as he travels around the known world fulfilling the chivalric ideal through kindness to the unfortunate and bravery in battle. After winning an exotic wife, he renounces war. Soon, however, "his other desire" (p. 101) overcomes him and he leaves his palace to hunt. He is surrounded and pursued by animals he cannot kill; "animals failing him, he desired to slaughter men" (p. 104). He indulges this desire by fulfilling the prophecy and accidently murdering his parents in his bed and their sleep.

III. Julian the Saint

Falling Action—Abnegation, and Denouement—Salvation

In Part Three we see Julian on the road to the renouncement of the self that will lead to his salvation. In an attempt to escape his past and expiate his sin, he leaves his castle, wife, and dead parents to beg on the road. His self–hate impels him to risk his life in saving others; finally, he considers suicide, only to recoil at a vision of his father that turns out to be his own reflection. Still haunted by the murder of his parents, he builds and operates a ferry–boat. Here he encounters a leper. It is in this encounter that Julian reveals that instead of taking life he is capable of sacrificing his own. Julian's offer of his body to the leper differs from his other brushes with death in that here he acts out of selfless generosity; his climbs up castle walls and his forays into burning buildings to rescue paralytics are undertaken in order to escape the prophecy or to destroy himself.

3. What is the nature of Julian's sin? [Or, if you prefer, "What flaw in Julian's character must be corrected before his ascension?"]

While Julian repulses us when he kills man or beast wantonly, it is his enjoyment of the act that we feel most repugnant. Take, for instance, his killing of the pigeon on p. 94:

> The pigeon hung with broken wings in the branches of a privet hedge.
> The persistence of its life irritated the boy. He began to strangle it, and its convulsions made his heart beat quicker, and filled him with a wild, tumultuous voluptuousness, the last throb of its heart making him feel like fainting.

Here, at the outset of Julian's "career," is evidence of a carnality that most of us would find unnatural. Julian's deviance, if this passage is any evidence, is a kind of sensuality that manifests itself in seeking and savoring the deaths of other creatures. His passion for hunting and killing leads to his cursing by the stag.

4. What does its last line tell us about "The Legend of Saint Julian the Hospitaller"?

The last line of the short story demonstrates an incongruous self–con-sciousness on the part of the heretofore transparent third–person narra-tor. Here Flaubert violates his famous dictum: "The author, in his work, must be like God in the Universe, present everywhere and visible nowhere."

I think it is quite possible that this last line is a rather elaborate joke and a comment on the genre in which he has been operating. It would be impossible to represent the saint's life in stained glass in the detail that Flaubert provides. Narratives, when they are presented in stained glass, must necessarily be reduced to tableaux capturing crucial moments in the central figure's life—the manner of presentation is much like that of the written hagiography. [Perhaps a triptych? See Question 2.] Descriptions like those of Julian's hunting falcon (p. 95) or his wife (p. 100) or, for that matter, of his murder of his parents are for various rea-sons unlikely to appear in stained glass in a church. Such realistic im-ages are, despite the disclaimer in the last line, the creations of the imagination of Gustave Flaubert.

–W.R.S.

Henry James
The Real Thing

Had this short story been written eighty years later, critics could have dubbed it "metafiction," that is, fiction that is a self–conscious exploration of its own internal logic and conventions. As is usually the case, the term is relatively new and the idea relatively old; cartoon characters have for years stepped out of the frame and "addressed" their creators or readers and Shakespeare often has his actors refer to themselves as fictional cre-ations. While this short story is not as baldly "metafictional" as that, here James does self–consciously explore the relationship of art to artist and the processes of creation.

In describing the Monarchs' confusion when the real thing is just not good enough, James is contributing to a discussion at least as old as Plato's attack on poets, one with a straight line of descent through any number of sixteenth, seventeenth, eighteenth and nineteenth century duels over the moral implications of creating illusions for others' pleasure. Are poets liars? Is there something inherently wrong in lulling readers or listeners into suspending their disbelief? This might be the time to remind your students that the Anglo–Saxon word for poet, *scop*, is the root for our "shape."

QUESTIONS

1. What is it about Miss Churm and Oronte that makes them better models than the Monarchs?

Though Miss Churm is vulgar and one would think unlikely to be a model for, say, a Russian princess, she is more plastic than the Monarchs. Because they are "the real thing"—the Monarchs are what they are and that's all that they are—they cannot be anything other than handsome and themselves. To nearly homogenize a metaphor, with the Monarchs one can easily tell the dancer from the dance.

> When I drew the Monarchs I couldn't anyhow get away from
> them—get into the character I wanted to represent; and I hadn't the
> least desire my model should be discoverable in my picture.
> (p. 124)

Miss Churm, on the other hand, is never "the real thing but always the same thing" (See the description of Mrs. Monarch, p. 120). She has a kind of cleverness, as the narrator calls it, that we might call a lack of individuality, but, at least as seen through the narrator's eyes, she can take on virtually any identity.

Oronte has something of the same quality, *the sentiment de la pose;* the narrator offers him the highest praise when he says, "He was sallow but fair, and when I put him into some old clothes of my own he looked like an Englishman. He was as good as Miss Churm, who could look, when requested, like an Italian." I'm not sure one can be sallow and fair, and it is certainly a paradox that the narrator finds that the Italian can look like an Englishman and that the Englishwoman can look like an Italian. Both have the quality that good actors say comes naturally—the ability to lose oneself and become another person—or at least that is the perception the narrator has of them.

2. What comment does James have his narrator make about the nature of art and artists?

A dangerous question that invites platitudes, but well worth the asking. You may wish to refer your students to the Counterpoint to Joyce Carol Oates' "Where Are You Going, Where Have You Been?" where she talks about the artist's ability to transform reality. The narrator in "The Real Thing" is making the same observation that critics and artists from Sidney to Coleridge have made; the artist reshapes and recreates through the power of imagination, what the narrator calls the "alchemy of art" (p. 118).

The Monarchs, despite their breeding and refinement, lack the sensibility to see that their "realness" impedes this creative process; as the narrator says, he has

> an innate preference for the represented subject over the real one; the defect of the real one was so apt to be a lack of representation. [He likes] things that appeared; then one was sure. Whether they *were* or not was a subordinate and almost always a profitless question" (p. 115).

The Monarchs, literalists that they (and perhaps we) are, cannot understand why they are unfit as models.

3. What is your estimation of the narrator's character? Do you at any time question his reliablility as a narrator?

James is careful to make this short story more than a veiled essay on art and artists, just as he is careful to make his narrator more than a priggish aesthete; it is the story of two people as lost as Bartleby the Scrivener, told by a man who pities them. They are truly pitiable, because they are dismissed without the explanation they could never understand. Few things are quite as pathetic as people in genteel poverty—here are people blessed and cursed with a kind of natural nobility that renders them unfit for any life other than one they can no longer afford. And they take it so well and try so hard to please in capacities they are so unsuited for that it is heart–rending. The narrator keeps the Monarchs on at some personal expense though they have outlived their usefulness.

There is at least one other reading of the way James allows his narrator to present himself. Some students, I suspect, will be impatient with his artsy considerations. "Oh, come on. With as much talent and imagination as the narrator by implication has, why can't he transform the Monarchs as he does Miss Churm and Oronte?" Isn't this short story an admission of a failure of his creative faculties? It's very easy to lay his failure at the Monarchs' handsome and "real" feet. Why doesn't he just *try* a little harder instead of letting them go? This is not the objection of a Philistine, because the narrator may be guilty of some of the charges here; it is perfectly reasonable to finish this short story wondering whether the artist is the real thing—is he an artist or an artisan? Does he in this short story reveal himself as a hypocrite, churning out what he calls his "potboilers"—illustrations for bad novels and magazines—and inventing artistic scruples to hide his own inadequacy as an artist? This sort of ambiguity makes for the most interesting and useful of classes.

4. Must the psychological complexity of James'characters necessarily be represented in such difficult language?

James' style is often opaque enough to obscure his meaning for impatient readers. "One acquires a taste for James" is cold comfort for many
classes; students find it difficult to believe that people could have talked
and thought as James presents them. And this difficulty is precisely the
opposite of the one confronting us in Hemingway's work. In the
Counterpoint for "A Clean, Well–Lighted Place" (p. 333) Virginia Woolf
complains that ". . . although Mr. Hemingway keeps us under the fire of
dialogue constantly, his people, half the time, are saying what the author
could be saying more economically for them." Many of your students will
be left with the sense that James' narrators, or "central consciousnesses,"
cannot say anything more economically than anyone, that James is, as
one critic says, like "a hippopotamus mouthing a pea."

My answer to that charge is, that without employing the mechanism
of stream–of–consciousness that was in a sense not available to him,
Henry James presents characters and their thoughts with a subtlety and
completeness that few writing in English can muster. His characters,
when he allows them to be, are the "roundest" in literature; what we
know of the narrator and the Monarchs we know in fine detail. In fact,
we know so much of them that we are permitted the "bewilderment"
James speaks of in the Counterpoint for this story—they are mysteries to
us because, they are represented with such fidelity to detail that they come
close to making the leap from characters to *people*—and we can never
know other people quite completely.

                                                                    –W.R.S.

Guy de Maupassant
The String

You may want to assign this story early in the semester because it is
literally a textbook example of the classic short story form. Once your students are familiar with the traditional form, they will better appreciate
the variations they encounter in the other stories in this collection.

Your students should recognize that Maupassant's stories differ radically from those of that other great nineteenth – century short story
writer, Edgar Allan Poe. Poe's stories such as "The Fall of the House of
Usher" create a unity of effect by evoking in the reader a single overriding emotion. Maupassant's stories achieve unity by meshing plot and
character. In "The String" Maître Hauchecorne, an old man on his way
to market, stoops to pick up a piece of string. His actions are observed by
the harness-maker, a longtime enemy. When someone reports that a
pocketbook has been lost in that area, the harness–maker claims that he
saw Hauchecorne pick it up from the road. The tragic consequences follow
inexorably because the personalities of the people involved make their

actions inevitable. Maupassant never called himself a naturalist, but after reading this story, your students may be ready to attach that label.

If you want to contrast the short story form developed by Maupassant with the earlier fairy tale, you might assign Grimm's "The Juniper Tree" as a companion piece to "The String."

QUESTIONS

1. How does Maupassant's story differ from a fairy tale (such as "The Juniper Tree")?

I would probably assign "The String" and "The Juniper Tree" at the same time because that pairing allows your students to discover some of the differences between the short story and the tale for themselves. But even if you don't assign "The Juniper Tree," your students should be able to answer this question either by reading the introduction to fiction (pp. 4 –15) in *The Riverside Anthology* or by recalling any of the fairy tales they know.

Your students will probably list the following characteristics of the fairy tale: an unidentified and nonspecific setting that could be anywhere or nowhere (Once upon a time....); flat, stock characters whose motives are never explored (stepmothers, for example, who unaccountably delight in wickedness); a skeletal plot in which the action is pushed along by circumstances rather than by the desires and wishes of the characters;); a good deal of blood and gore (at least in the unexpurgated pre–Disney versions); the operation of the supernatural (from witches to fairy godmothers); and, often, a simple moral. (Frequently the lesson seems to be that evil will ultimately be punished and goodness and virtue rewarded.)

After you discuss those characteristics, your students won't need to be told that "The String" is radically different from the traditional tale. Unlike the otherworldly setting of a tale, the locale of "The String" is as concrete as possible. Maupassant begins his story by planting it firmly in the little town of Goderville on market day. Although the passage of time makes Goderville of the 1870s seem quaint and unreal to modern readers, to Maupassant's contemporaries, Goderville would have been as commonplace and believable as a shopping mall is to us.

The main character in the story, Maître Hauchecorne, bears little resemblance to the flat characters in most tales. He is certainly not a cardboard cutout created to play a role in a plot. When he is introduced to us in the fourth paragraph, we immediately learn that he has a lifelong habit of frugality, that he suffers from rheumatism, that he quarreled with the harness maker (and has a well–developed capacity for hatred), and that he is painfully concerned about other people's opinions of him.

Although we don't realize the significance of those revelations at the time, we later discover that it is precisely those characteristics (plus one other that is not revealed until almost the end of the story) that cause the story to develop as it does. In a Maupassant story character and plot are inseparable.

The plot, too, stands in dramatic contrast to that of the tale. If we analyze the structure of the story carefully, we discover that it is so perfectly plotted that we might expect it to seem artificial and contrived. But it does not, probably because every incident flows naturally from believable human choices and responses. You might want to illustrate the stairstep construction of the plot by drawing a diagram of the action on the board.

                                        Culmination:
                                        He realizes he cannot
                                        prove his innocence

                He is relieved when   Conclusion:
                    purse is found   He wastes away
                                                                 and dies
            He tries to convince
                villagers of
                his innocence

        He tries to convince
            magistrate of
            his innocence

        Hauchecorne
        is arrested

    Background
    Information

After setting the scene, Maupassant introduces conflict with Hauchecorne's arrest. The action rises as Hauchecorne struggles to prove his innocence. First he fails to convince the magistrate. Next he realizes his neighbors and friends think he is lying. For a brief period after the purse is returned Hauchecorne believes he has been exonerated, but the turning point (both of the plot and in revelation of Hauchecorne's character) occurs when he learns that other people view the return of the purse as a clever bit of trickery. "He went home ashamed, indignant, choking with anger and confusion, the more dejected for the fact that he with his Norman cunning was capable of doing what they had accused him of, and even of boasting of it as a good trick" (p. 135). Maupassant waits until almost the end of the story to reveal that Hauchecorne and all the villagers know he is the kind of man who would have taken the purse. Once the reader is also aware of that significant fact, we realize how futile his attempts to prove his innocence must be. In the inevitable conclusion, Hauchecorne, like a spider caught in his own web, exhausts himself emotionally and physically by his hopeless efforts to escape.

As for other differences between the fairy tale and this short story, "The String" has no goblins, giants, murder, or mayhem. Instead Maupassant gives us a terrifying glimpse of the far more frightening and equally destructive forces rampant in the real world—hatred, false pride, vengeance, and deceit.

2. Why does Maupassant center the story around a piece of string?

This question should elicit some imaginative responses. Here are a few possibilities:

In a way the story is a reverse parable. If your students mentioned earlier that most fairy tales have a moral of sorts, they may notice that Maupassant refuses to reinforce the platitudes we generally accept unquestioningly. Although there are numerous tales and proverbs extolling the virtues of frugality (the "Waste not, want not" motif), Maupassant designs this story so that it is Hauchecorne's frugal act of retrieving a piece of dirty string that causes all his later problems. Of course, that's an oversimplification; Hauchecorne's problems are the result of all the events that have made him what he is when the story opens. Maupassant isn't really condemning frugality as the cause of all of humanity's sorrows, but neither is he willing to praise it unthinkingly.

At the same time Maupassant is using the piece of string to illustrate his own lesson that any event, even a seemingly trivial and insignificant action such as picking up a piece of string, can have major repercussions.

Or perhaps Maupassant uses the insignificant piece of string to suggest the triviality of Hauchecorne's existence. That's rather bleak for my taste, but the view of life presented in Maupassant's stories is unrelentingly somber.

3. In the Counterpoint Maupassant argues that "the higher order Realists should rather call themselves Illusionists." Does Maupassant's handling of this short story qualify him as an illusionist?

My answer to this question would be a resounding "yes." I suppose arguments could be made to the contrary, but I can't imagine what they would be.

The key to answering this question is to focus on the conscious craftsmanship of Maupassant, on his choices to select, delete, reorder, and focus reality. I notice that students (indeed all readers) who look at a short story in its finished form find it difficult to imagine that the raw material for that story could have been arranged in any number of radically different shapes. I would get my students started on this question by asking them to note how many things Maupassant chooses not to tell us about Hauchecorne. The list is endless, but for starters, we don't get a detailed physical description, we don't know if he is married or single, and we don't know the details about his quarrel with the harness maker. If you then ask your students why Maupassant chooses to include precisely those characteristics he describes in paragraph 4, and why he chooses to withhold the information about Hauchecorne's well–known cunning until the turning point of the story, they should begin to realize how difficult it is to create the illusion of reality.

It is, of course, quite impossible to transcribe reality. Even the best of stream–of–consciousness writers can not capture the flood of emotions, thoughts, sensations, and external stimuli that overwhelm us in but a single moment of time. Realists like Maupassant do not attempt to record the chaos of reality, but to distill its essence.

–M.R.D.

Sir Arthur Conan Doyle
The Adventure of the Speckled Band

"The Speckled Band" was Conan Doyle's favorite tale of Sherlock Holmes, perhaps because here we see the famous detective demonstrating all his powers and virtues and few of his vices. However else Holmes may fail to fit the mold Auden has set up in the Counterpoint for "The Speckled Band," (see p. 156), he is at least "aesthetically interesting" and "instinctively ethical." No seven percent solutions of cocaine (Bernard Shaw, distressed as he often was at others' popular success, called Holmes a "drug addict ") or bouts of depression here; Holmes is less detached and acerbic than in almost any of the tales ordinarily anthologized. In this tale, Holmes not only aids a lady in distress, but confronts and defeats an antagonist nearly as brilliant and dangerous as himself or Professor Moriarity. In doing so, Holmes operates on one of the most exotic stages allowed him by Doyle, menaced as he is by baboons, cheetahs, a band of gypsies, a venomous snake, and a gentleman "who can twist steel pokers into knots." Holmes comes off an ethical and cerebral superman.

The detective story was not new with Conan Doyle. The *Memoirs* of Vidocq (see "Araby," p. 219) published in 1828, tell of the exploits of the first chief of Surete, who was a master of disguise and one of the first policemen to use impressions of footprints in solving crime. He fascinated Edgar Allan Poe, who can truly be said to be the father of detective fiction. Between Poe and Doyle lay Wilkie Collins' Sergeant Cuff and Emile Gaboriau's Inspector Lecoq. But Poe's influence upon Doyle is unmistakable and undeniable. "The Purloined Letter," one of the sources for "A Scandal in Bohemia," involves a letter stolen from unnamed royalty; the thief's lodgings are scoured with no result. The trick, of course, is that the letter is in plain sight of the investigators after all, and only

August Dupin has the vision to see it and the audacity to steal it back from under the villain's nose. "The Speckled Band" owes something at least to Poe's "The Murders in the Rue Morgue," in which murders are committed in a room where the victims must apparently have been alone. In that story, as in "The Speckled Band," it is an animal (an orangutan, in Poe's tale) that kills.

But Sherlock Holmes is not Dupin in a deerstalker cap (Baker Street Irregulars know that he seldom wears a deerstalker cap). When, in "A Study in Scarlet," Dr. Watson compares Holmes to Dupin, Holmes retorts, "Now, in my opinion, Dupin was a very inferior fellow. That trick of his of breaking in on his friends' thoughts with an apropos remark after a quarter of an hour's silence is really very showy and superficial. He had some analytical genius, no doubt; but he was by no means such a phenomenon as Poe appeared to imagine. Dupin relies upon ratiocination, an ability somewhere between reason and intuition, while Holmes depends instead upon his powers of observation and "rapid deductions, as swift as intuitions, and yet always founded on a logical basis, with which he unraveled the problems which were submitted to him" (p. 138).

QUESTIONS

1. What obstacles does Doyle place in the way of our understanding and solving the mystery as readily as Holmes? Does Doyle "cheat," that is, give Holmes clues that we are not privy to?

Let's call these stumbling blocks "misdirections," for we are often led to assume one thing and another is delivered by the author in the denoement. In the first place, Grimesby Roylott is so promising a villain that he simply cannot be the murderer. In addition, the dying words of Julia Stoner, "Oh, my God, Helen! It was the band! The speckled band!" lead us (and Watson) almost inescapably to the conclusion that the band of gypsies is somehow involved in the crime. And, finally, even if the gypsies are guiltless, and with no visible signs of violence or hints of poison, could it not be that Julia Stoner died of fright when threatened by the cheetah or the baboon, which even the unimaginative Watson mistakes for a deformed child. We are taken in, but not Holmes. The saucer of milk and the dog–leash, which might, until we see the adder and have things explained to us, still convince us that the cheetah is employed by the killer, are discounted by Holmes.

In solving this murder, Holmes has no special knowledge, as he has in other stories, of arcane tobacco–ash patterns or types of poison, for example, that we do not. Miss Stoner's description is as available to us as to Holmes. The oddities of the locked and shuttered room, the dummy bell–rope, the ventilator, and the nailed–down bed, are all described to us shortly after Holmes sees them for the first time. As Holmes says to Watson, "I imagine that you saw all that I did" (p. 151). Doyle, I would argue, does not "cheat," and we can only marvel at Holmes' powers of observation and deduction. [The same cannot be said of Doyle in this instance; it is my understanding that snakes are deaf, and so the adder could not have heard the whistle.]

2. From whose point of view is "The Speckled Band" told, and why?

The first half of this question is so easy to answer that few of your students will try. My bet is that the second half is so difficult to answer that even fewer will try. My answer is pretty conventional. Watson, though Nigel Bruce and others have played him as a dimwit (I recommend the Granada Television version of the Holmes stories on PBS highly; their production of "The Speckled Band" is excellent—show it to your class if you can) is in the position of most of Doyle's readers. He is an intelligent man, who is occasionally opaque and occasionally acute, in short, like most of us. He is a foil for Holmes' brilliance, but he is after all a doctor, not the village idiot. It seems unlikely that Doyle, himself a doctor, would have been happy with modern portrayals of Watson as rather slow of understanding.

In some of the later tales, Holmes is his own chronicler, and those tales are just plain bad. They are bad for a number of reasons—Doyle's jingoism and his weariness with Holmes among them—but they are also bad because Holmes revealed to us through his own eyes is smug, self–congratulatory, and egotistical. When Holmes the egotist and eccentric describes his own exploits, the results are seldom readable, and admiration for him is hard to muster. Doyle, whether he knew it or not, has Watson exceed Holmes at least as a narrator.

3. Why is Dr. Grimesby Roylott such a terrible and fascinating figure? How would you explain his association with the gypsies and his keeping a menagerie at his ancestral home?

Holmes is not just being clever and solving a murder. I do not think it is merely a contrivance to say that here he excises an evil sensed by many Englishmen of Doyle's time. For Doyle, India is always the heart of darkness. In "The Sign of the Four" or "The Adventure of the Crooked Man," India is a place of dark, murderous, men[*] and darker motivations, the land of *thugee* (a type of murder by strangulation practiced by a noto-

---

[*] On a visit to Vancouver in 1914, Doyle observed a shipload of Sikhs hoping to immigrate. He claimed that the Germans were undoubtedly behind this attempt by the Sikhs to "force themselves upon Canada." (*Conan Doyle: A Biographical Solution*, Ronald Pearsall [New York: St. Martin's Press, 1977], p. 141.

rious band of professional assassins) and Shiva, Hindu goddess of destruction and reproduction. Dr. Roylott, from one of the oldest Anglo– Saxon families in England, and like the deadly Colonel Moran of "The Adventure of the Empty House," has been corrupted by a lengthy stay in a place where power erodes morals and "ordinary" standards of behavior cannot be enforced. Already cursed with a vicious temper, in India he indulges it fully and kills his butler. He then brings as much of India home with him as he can through his menagerie and through associating with the band of gypsies, a race of course originally from India. That the murder weapon is a serpent is a suggestive detail your class might wish to discuss, but at the literal level the speckled band is, after all, the swamp adder, the deadliest snake *in India.* In defeating Roylott, Sherlock Holmes cleanses the English countryside of an imported evil.

–W.R.S.

Anton Chekhov
The Lady with the Pet Dog

One of the best ways to point to Chekhov's special virtues and concerns as an artist is to compare this short story with those short fictions conveniently called "tales." If, for example, Poe's "The Fall of the House of Usher" is compared to "The Lady with the Pet Dog," Chekhov's passion for realistic detail, particularly in delineating character, leaps out.

The issue here is not *what* we know—we know as much, I think, about the personality of the narrator of "Usher" as we do Gurov—but how we are given to know it. In "Usher" what we know of the narrator he himself reveals through his apprehensions and through his depiction of Roderick Usher. In "The Lady with the Pet Dog" the third person omniscient narrator, refusing to make judgments, gives us a character who demands little suspension of our belief. One can feel Chekhov the dramatist at work here; he refuses to tell us who and what Dmitry Gurov and Anna Sergeyevna are; he shows us, however, with enviable clarity:

> She laughed. Then both continued eating in silence, like strangers, but after dinner they walked together and there sprang up between them the light banter of people who are free and contented, to whom it does not matter where they go or what they talk about. They walked and talked of the strange light on the sea; the water was a soft, warm, lilac color, and there was a golden band of moonlight upon it. (p. 159)

This is straight, good, reporting, just the facts (almost) and nothing but the facts—no narrative pyrotechnics like Poe's inevitable unreliable first person or Hawthorne's coy yet moralizing third person narrators.

QUESTIONS

1. How do the three settings relate to the development of character and the advancement of the plot?

Yalta operates much as one of Shakespeare's "green worlds"; at the vacation resort ordinary ties and rules of behavior can be for a while abandoned. Without his wife, without his children, without the strictures, protocols and professional obligations of Moscow, Gurov enjoys a license he could not at home. Anna Sergeyevna has come to Yalta to escape a more oppressive marriage still. For her, however, the vacation is an avenue of escape that turns to the bitterest of shame. She is convinced that she is a "vulgar, vile woman whom anyone may despise."

All this is pretty tendentious stuff: his pursuits are stereotypical; a balding, middle–aged, and experienced seductor with a wife who doesn't understand him is eager for another conquest and another abandonment. His conquest is a woman desperate for any emotional outlet and inexperienced to the point of naiveté:

> "Believe me, believe me, I beg you," she said, "I love honesty and purity, and sin is loathsome to me; I don't know what I'm doing. Simple people say, 'The Evil One has led me astray.' And I say of myself now that the Evil One has led me astray." (p. 161)

When they part, both think it is for always, she believing that they "ought never to have met" (p. 163) and he feeling more than a little relieved to be rid of a woman who no longer presents a challenge or a diversion.

When he returns to Moscow, Gurov becomes absorbed in his old life; "his recent trip and the places he had visited lost all charm for him" (p. 164). But his old pattern of seduction and then oblivion is, against his will, disrupted. The memory of Anna comes back to him so powerfully that he must talk of it; when those attempts prove unsatisfactory, he goes to S_____ (you might wish to ask your students the effect of this ellipsis). And here he discovers, in the backward and provincial opera house, that he loves a woman he might have scorned a year earlier:

> She sat down in the third row, and when Gurov looked at her his heart contracted, and he understood clearly that in the whole world there was no human being so near, so precious, and so important to

him; she, this little, undistinguished woman, lost in a provincial
crowd, with a vulgar lorgnette in her hand, filled his whole life
now, was his sorrow and his joy, the only happiness that he now
desired for himself, and to the sounds of the bad orchestra, of the
miserable local violins, he thought how lovely she was.
(p. 166)

They can manage only furtive declarations of love in S_____.
   Back in Moscow and arranging rendezvous, Gurov becomes aware that
he must live two lives—an open one, "full of conventional truth and conventional falsehood, exactly like the lives of his friends and acquain-
tances" (p. 168), and a secret life involving Anna Sergeyevna. The end of
the short story makes clear the demands of his Moscow obligations and
the complications of her S_____ life—and provides no easy resolution:

   Then they spent a long time taking counsel together, they talked of
   how to avoid the necessity for secrecy, for deception, for living in different
   cities, and not seeing one another for long stretches of time. How could
   they free themselves from these intolerable fetters.

2. To what extent does the short story end on a note of affirmation?

At first glance, the short story seems to end in a minor key.

   And it seemed as though in a little while the solution would be
   found, and then a new and glorious life would begin; and it was
   clear to both of them that the end was still far off, and that what was
   to be most complicated and difficult for them was only just beginning. (p. 170)

Gurov and his lover face the complicated and difficult business of disen-
gaging themselves from their families; one could be left with the suspi-
cion that this is, after all, an extramarital infatuation and dalliance fated
to end on the stereotyped bitter note. Even Gurov admits that Anna
Sergeyevna's affection for him is based on a miscalculation of his character. "She had constantly called him kind, exceptional, high–minded;
obviously he had seemed to her different from what he really was, so he
had involuntarily deceived her" (p. 163).
   At second glance, though, we might see that Gurov, the womanizer
who detests women and cannot live without them, the world–weary sexual adventurer, has found a woman capable of inspiring in him the notion that "only now when his head was gray he had fallen in love, really, truly—for the first time" (p. 169). In spite of unfortunate marriages,
"it seemed to them that Fate itself had meant them for one another" (p.
169). In short, it is likely that despite the disquieting paradox of the last

paragraph, when the lovers find themselves confronted by a vision of a "new and glorious life" and a life "complicated and difficult," there is hope for Anna and Dmitry. Even if circumstances force them to part, it is better to have . . .

A third glance will probably deepen the ambiguity of the ending.

3. Is Dmitry Gorov ennobled or degraded by his love for Anna Sergeyevna? How so?

The ultimate answer to this question is, I believe, "ennobled". If we examine Gurov's character early in the short story, we find all the attributes your students will undoubtedly point out in answering questions 1 and 2. We watch him, an unsavory mixture of misognynist and seductor, take advantage of a woman "with something pathetic about her" (p. 159). He grows "bored with her; he was irritated by her naive tone, by her repentance" (p. 161); "in his manner, his tone, and his caresses there had been a shade of light irony, the slightly coarse arrogance of a happy male who was, besides, almost twice her age" (p. 163). When they part, he is relieved.

But just as he settles into his Moscow routine he is overtaken by love for her. He discovers that

> everything that was of interest and importance to him, everything that was essential to him, everything about which he felt sincerely and did not deceive himself, everything that constituted the core of his life, was going on concealed from others . . . Judging others by himself, he did not believe what he saw, and always fancied that every man led his real, most interesting life under cover of secrecy as under cover of night. (p. 168)

That secret life allows him in middle age a passion that turns him from the adroit seducter to a schoolboy snatching kisses in the provincial opera house in S_____. Many students will find Gurov ennobled in his movement from cynic to a romantic willing to risk disgrace and divorce for his grand passion.

Other students will remind their peers that Gurov is, after all, an adulterer. While he does discover that he is capable of loving another human, is that so great a thing? One could argue reasonably that he loves Anna Sergeyevna's idea of himself as much as he loves her: "She had constantly called him kind, exceptional, high–minded; obviously he had seemed to her different from what he really was" (p. 163), just as one could argue that he is in love with being in love.

–W.R.S.

Charlotte Perkins Gilman
The Yellow Wallpaper

After writing "The Yellow Wallpaper" in 1891, Gilman sent it to William Dean Howells, who recommended the story to Horace Scudder, editor of the prestigious *The Atlantic Monthly*. Scudder rejected it with the following explanation:

Dear Madam,
　Mr. Howells has handed me this story.
　I could not forgive myself if I made others as miserable as I have made myself.
　　　　　　Sincerely yours,
　　　　　　H.E. Scudder

Apparently Scudder did not believe the world was ready for a story with neither happy ending nor moral uplift. When the story was finally published in 1892, it received mixed responses. Some reviewers read it as essentially a horror story and praised it as equal to the best of Poe and Hawthorne. Other readers saw it primarily as a story about mental aberrations. One physician questioned whether a story that "hold[s] the reader in morbid fascination... should be permitted in print" while another commended it as a "detailed account of incipient insanity." The story was not interpreted from a feminist perspective until the 1970's when writers such as Elaine R. Hedges began to make "the connection between the insanity and the sex, or sexual role, of the victim...."

All three interpretations are valid. The story is a chilling account of a young woman's descent into madness, not the inexplicable and seemingly unavoidable madness of Poe's Roderick Usher, but the all too understandable madness of a woman destroyed by her society. Two other stories you might want to assign along with this one are Gail Godwin's "Dream Children" and Doris Lessing's "To Room Nineteen." Both portray women considered insane by the society that molded them.

QUESTIONS

1. What sort of case can be made that the husband is really trying to drive his wife insane? Does he have any defenses to that charge?

To modern readers, the husband's actions are likely to seem diabolical. John begins by moving his wife, who has "a slight hysterical tendency," into a mansion that looks like a "haunted house," a long untenanted house three miles from the nearest village. He forces her to live in a room she hates, an upstairs room with barred windows, "rings and things in the walls," ugly wallpaper that has been stripped off in great patches, and a gate at the head of the stairs. John refuses to let her Cousin Henry and Julia visit her, discourages her writing, and leaves her alone for long periods while he takes care of "serious cases" in town. When she protests that she is not improving and asks to go home, he insists that she is not as capable as he of making a determination about her health. "[Y]ou really are better, dear, whether you can see it or not. I am a doctor, dear, and I know" (p. 178).

John's treatment of his wife is so at odds with present medical knowledge that it almost seems that he is trying to drive her crazy. Readers today are not surprised that after several weeks of such treatment the wife, who craves "congenial work, with excitement and change" (p. 172), begins to see "a faint figure" behind the pattern of the wallpaper who seems "to shake the pattern, just as if she wanted to get out" (p. 177).

In John's defense, you may need to remind your students that the story was written long before scientific experiments demonstrated that anyone, no matter how mentally healthy, could be driven mad if deprived of all sensory stimuli. We know that volunteers who float in body temperature water in total darkness and silence soon hallucinate. John, however, could not know the effects of sensory deprivation. In fact, John's treatment of his wife is exactly what was recommended by the medical experts of his day.

As Gilman tells us in the counterpoint to this story (p. 184), she herself suffered from "nervous prostration" (probably post–partum depression) soon after the birth of her child. Although this story is not pure autobiography, there are similarities between Gilman's experience and that of the woman in the story. Gilman was treated for depression by Dr. S. Weir Mitchell (who is mentioned by name in the story—p. 175). Mitchell prescribed his widely acclaimed rest cure which required bed rest, inactivity, and isolation. He ordered her to devote herself to her domestic duties and the care of her child, to refrain from reading more than two hours a day and to "never touch pen, brush or pencil as long as you live." After a month of such treatment, her condition worsened dramatically. She recalls this period in her autobiography: "I made a rag baby, hung it on a doorknob and played with it. I would crawl into remote closets and under beds—to hide from the grinding pressure of that profound distress." Unlike the woman in the story, Gilman somehow found the strength to abandon the treatment. Eventually Gilman realized that, for her, mental health and her domestic role were incompatible. She divorced her husband and gave him custody of their daughter.

In addition to this external evidence that John probably was attempting to cure his wife, there is also at least one significant internal clue. At the end of the story when John sees his wife creeping around the room, he faints. That's the response I would expect from a man who loves his wife and is genuinely horrified when he discovers that she is insane.

2. In what ways does the image of the yellow wallpaper contribute to the story?

I want this question to help the students go beyond the obvious. First I would expect them to tell me that the wallpaper symbolizes the position of women in the nineteenth century who were imprisoned by the narrow roles society assigned them. In addition they may note that the wife's "escape" from the wallpaper is an escape from sanity. Perhaps the bars the woman shakes are also the bounds of reason.

But the paper has more than symbolic significance. It also serves to set the mood of the scene, reveal the characters, and advance the plot. The mood is established with an early description of the paper's ugliness: "The color is repellent, almost revolting: a smouldering unclean yellow, strangely faded by the slow—turning sunlight. It is a dull yet lurid orange in some places, a sickly sulphur tint in others" (p. 173), the perfect choice for a guest suite in hell. The paper becomes even more ominous when we learn that it has been stripped off in great patches around the head of the bed about as far as the narrator can reach (p. 173).

The paper also demonstrates the precise nature of the relationship between the narrator and her husband. She tells us, "At first he meant to repaper the room, but afterward he said that I was letting it get the better of me, and that nothing was worse for a nervous patient than to give way to such fancies" (p. 173). Clearly John intends to "cure" his wife by stifling both her imagination and her will.

The narrator's descriptions of the wallpaper reveal her rapid mental deterioration. At first she sees it as merely ugly. After two weeks she thinks of it as a "vicious influence" and sees in it "a spot where the pattern lolls like a broken neck and two bulbous eyes stare at you upside down" (p. 174). Following the Fourth of July, she begins to lie on the bed and stare at the paper, determined to "follow that pointless pattern to some sort of a conclusion" (p. 176). After nine weeks the pattern turns into bars with a woman behind them (p. 179).

Eleven weeks into the treatment the narrator notices the smell of the paper permeating the house and thinks "seriously of burning the house— to reach the smell" (p. 180). She also sees the woman shaking the bars and speculates that she gets out in the daytime because she sees her out all of her windows. On the final day of her three months the narrator helps the woman in the wallpaper "peel off yards of that paper" (p. 182). In the story, the wallpaper both aggravates the narrator's condition and reflects it.

3. What does Gilman achieve by allowing the wife to tell her own story?

The point of view forces us to empathize with the narrator, but also to doubt her reliability. At first she is perfectly sane, and we believe everything she writes. We don't necessarily agree with her [For example, I don't want her to consider herself "unreasonably angry" when she gets upset with John (p. 172)], but we accept her views as typical of a middle-class woman of the nineteenth century.

Our close identification with her causes us to recoil with horror when we realize that she can no longer distinguish between the real and the imaginary. You might ask your students when they first begin to suspect that the narrator is losing touch with reality and when they are absolutely sure. Readers will disagree. Some will begin to doubt her sanity as soon as she imagines the paper moving; others will not become alarmed until she tells us that she has caught John and Jennie several times *looking at the paper* (p. 179). Jennie explains that she is concerned about the yellow smooches she has found on the wife's clothes. (The narrator has not yet told us that she creeps around the room.) That strikes us as reasonable, but the narrator has a different response: "Did not that sound innocent? But I know she was studying that pattern, and I am determined that nobody shall find it out but myself."

It was at that point that I first realized I could no longer trust her perceptions. Jennie's explanation is far more probable than our narrator's. From then on, we are skeptical and we read our narrator's words with a dual purpose. We read to find out the state of her mental health; we also try to decipher her entries, to find clues about what is happening in the real world she has left behind. When she tells us about the smell of the wallpaper, we doubt whether that smell could be detected by anyone else. And when she tells us that she has considered burning down the house to destroy the smell (p. 180), we become seriously concerned about her mental health. Her statement that "John is so queer now" (p. 181) convinces us not that he is acting strangely, but that he is as worried about her behavior as we are. And we wonder what he has observed that she has failed to record.

–M.R.D.

Edith Wharton
Roman Fever

"Roman Fever" illustrates perfectly the relationship between plot and character articulated by Henry James (Edith Wharton's mentor and friend) in *The Art of Fiction*. "What is character but the determination of incident? What is incident but the illustration of character? What is either a picture or novel that is *not* of character?"

This is not a story that will immediately grab your students' attention, but after a few pages, most readers find themselves fascinated by this tale of intrigue, duplicity and revenge. (I promised my daughter that if she persevered for four pages, she would want to continue. She did.) At the beginning we are introduced to two wealthy middle–aged American women who are chaperoning their daughters in Rome. We learn that these women have been friends and neighbors for years and that twenty–five years earlier they, too, had been chaperoned by mothers who attempted to protect them from the "sentimental dangers" of Rome. Sitting on a balcony overlooking the Palantine and the Forum, the two, "who had been intimate since childhood, reflect how little they know each other." That situation soon changes, and by the end of the story, each has made shocking discoveries about the other.

QUESTIONS

1. What does Wharton achieve by the use of foreshadowing?

[If your students have read O'Connor's "A Good Man Is Hard To Find," you might rephrase this question: "How does Wharton's use of foreshadowing differ from that of O'Connor?"]

The first purpose of this question is simply to force the students to notice the foreshadowing. You might ask your students to mark every line in the story that somehow helps to prepare us for the ending. They will probably be surprised at how early Wharton hints that things are not as they seem. For example, this clue appears on the second page. Alida Slade looks out upon the Palantine and remarks, "After all, it's still the most beautiful view in the world."

"'It always will be, to me,' assented her friend Mrs. Ansley, with so slight a stress on the 'me' that Mrs. Slade, though she noticed it, wondered if it were not merely accidental, like the random underlinings of old–fashioned letter writers.'"

Your students will probably begin by answering that Wharton uses the foreshadowing to keep the reader from feeling tricked by the ending (à la O'Henry). That's true, but you will want your class to notice that Wharton goes about this in a rather unusual way. Ordinarily, foreshadowing prepares us for some development in the plot. For example, in O'Connor's "A Good Man Is Hard To Find," the family reads that a murderer, The Misfit, is "aloose from the Federal Pen and headed toward Florida," the state where the family will soon be vacationing. When the little son is asked what he would do if he met up with The Misfit, he responds that he would "smack his face." Not much doubt about who will stop to "help" that family after their car careens into a ditch beside a road that "looked as if no one had traveled on it for months."

Unlike O'Connor, Wharton doesn't actually prepare us for all the swift turns her plot takes at the end. Although we might be able to guess that Barbara was not fathered by Mr. Ansley [I didn't], none of the foreshadowing would enable us to predict either the letter's existence or its author until Alida and Grace confess their secrets. Wharton prepares us for the ending, not by planting clues that enable the astute reader to foretell precisely what must happen, but by revealing the personalities of the two principal players. The ending is credible, even though surprising, because Wharton has convinced us that Alida and Grace would act exactly as they do.

Ask your students if they enjoyed rereading this story. (I am assuming they had to read it a second time to answer this question.) I hope they will decide the second reading is even more interesting because the reader knows how to interpret the lines that are initially so baffling.

2. How accurate are the judgments the two women would have made about each other before this meeting in Rome?

You might want to direct your students' attention to the last paragraph on page 186 and ask them to contrast the "labels" Alida and Grace each "had ready to attach to the other's name" with what we know about the women by the end of the story.

Our narrator tells us that Alida, had she been asked, would have characterized Grace as a woman who "*had been* exquisitely lovely," and who still is "good–looking," "charming," "distinguished," "irreproachable," "exemplary." Alida would not say but would imply that Grace is boring, conventional, and unimaginative. Grace sums up Alida as "awfully brilliant, but not as brilliant as she thinks" (p. 188). Grace would have told anyone that as a girl Alida was "dashing" and had a "vividness" Alida's daughter lacks. She would have told no one that she "had always been rather sorry for [Alida]" (p. 188). At the end of Section One of the story, Wharton warns us that neither of these portraits is accurate, "So the two ladies visualized each other, each through the wrong end of her little telescope" (p. 188).

Your students should have no difficulty seeing how inaccurate Alida's assessment of Grace is. Grace, who had an affair with her friend Alida's fiancé, Delphin Slade, who bore his child after marrying another man, and who then lived across the street from the Slades for years without ever revealing her secrets, is far from boring, conventional, or unimaginative. In fact, Grace has a number of qualities Alida has never guessed. Grace is romantic (she still remembers every word of the letter—p. 192), courageous (She went to the Colosseum alone at night—p. 7), and vindictive (She tells Alida, "I had Barbara."—p. 192). But even though Alida has been wrong in her judgment, she has been correct in her emotional response to her friend. She has indeed had good reason to hate and envy Grace.

Your class will probably decide that Grace's assessment of Alida is more accurate. She seems to be correct in concluding that Alida is not as brilliant as she thinks. After all, it never occurs to Alida that Grace would respond to the letter Delphin sends (p. 194). Neither does Alida manage to answer her own question about Barbara's parentage—"how two such exemplary creatures as [Grace] and Horace had managed to produce anything quite so dynamic" (p. 189).

But it turns out that Grace has seriously misjudged Alida in one important way; she never imagined Alida's Machiavellian ruthlessness. Alida admits that, even though she had been frightened by the story of the young girl who caught the fever and died after visiting the Colosseum at night, she schemed to send Grace there. She knew Grace had "a very delicate throat" (p. 190) and hoped she would become ill. "I wanted you out of the way, that's all. Just for a few weeks" (p. 193). Although she adds, "Of course I never thought you'd die," neither Grace nor the reader believes that she would have cared.

3. Why is the story called "Roman Fever"?

Your literalists will refer you to pages 189 and 191 and remind you that Roman fever was a disease feared by the grandmothers of these women, a disease that killed Grace's great aunt. That's true, but it still doesn't answer the question.

If your students need help, ask them if the events that occur in the story could have happened anywhere else. I think they will say "no." After all, Alida and Grace have kept their secrets for twenty–five years, even though they traveled in the same small social circle and lived across the street from each other. When the story opens, we learn that it is merely coincidental that they are together in Rome. ("[T]hey had run across each other in Rome, at the same hotel, each the modest appendage of a salient daughter. The similarity of their lot had again drawn them together...."—p. 187.) Neither seems to have the slightest intention of telling all. It is only because the two women sit overlooking "the great accumulated wreckage of passion and splendor" (p. 189) that they are again infected with Roman fever, a fever that can make even prudent girls and women most imprudent.

Wharton, an American who spent most of her life in Europe, seems to accept the Jamesian view that Americans, who are apt to lead rather innocent and uneventful lives at home, often discover both adventure and evil on their journeys to the corrupt Old World.

4. To what extent have social pressures shaped the lives of Grace and Alida?

The modern reader is likely to be appalled by the narrowness of the lives Grace and Alida have led. Although both have intelligence, beauty, charm, and wealth, it seems that there have been only two significant events in their lives—finding husbands for themselves on that first trip to Rome and finding husbands for their daughters this time. Alida divides her adult life into two stages: during the first she defines herself as the wife of *the* Slade, famous corporation lawyer, and during the second she is *the* Slade's widow, a "dullish business" (p. 187). Grace seems to think of herself primarily as the mother of *the* Slade's daughter. Slade, who betrayed both women, strikes us as unworthy of such devotion. Perhaps he would have received different treatment if Alida could have chosen to become a lawyer rather than marry one. Perhaps Alida and Grace could have been real friends if they had not been compelled to channel all their energies into competing for a husband.

Wharton was keenly aware of the pressures exerted on the women of her social class. Her own decision to become a writer puzzled her husband and caused her such internal conflict that she was afflicted by a sudden "paralyzing melancholy." Apparently her condition was improved by Dr. S. Wier Mitchell's "rest cure." [See the comment to Charlotte Perkins Gilman's "The Yellow Wallpaper" for a description of that treatment.. Eventually she and her huband were divorced, and Wharton, who was delighted with her single state, celebrated her liberation by traveling, writing, entertaining, forging friendships with writers such as Henry James, and doing charitable work. She never remarried.

-M.R.D.

E. M. Forster
The Eternal Moment

In this story, as in *A Passage to India*, Forster raises difficult questions about the nature of human relationships. The story focuses on Miss Raby, a middle–aged English author, who, twenty years earlier, had written a novel based on her first visit to the small Italian village of Vorta. That novel, *The Eternal Moment*, "which had made her reputation, had also made the reputation of Vorta" (p. 198). When Miss Raby, accompanied by her friend Colonel Leyland, returns to the now prosperous tourist attraction for the first time, she is saddened by the town's transformation (including colored lights that illuminate the great hotel sign). "A great tenderness overcame her—the sadness of an unskilful demiurge, who makes a world and beholds that it is bad" (p. 211).

Distinguishing Forster's voice from that of his characters is tricky business, and some of your students may initially mistake Miss Raby's opinions for the author's. Closer reading will reveal that Miss Raby's vision is not necessarily Forster's. Your students will discover that in "The Eternal Moment," as in all Forster's work, there are no simple answers, no clear distinctions between right and wrong, good and bad, progress and decline. Forster once wrote that his task as a writer was to transmit "life's complexity, and the delight, the difficulty, the duty of registering that complexity and conveying it." With this story he accomplishes that task.

QUESTIONS

1. How will Miss Raby's and Colonel Leyland's actions in the final scene affect their relationship?

In the final scene, each friend betrays the other. Colonel Leyland's betrayal is straightforward. With his usual concern for social propriety, he attempts to excuse Miss Raby's outrageous actions by suggesting that she is slightly mad. "[H]e took Feo by the arm, and then quickly raised his finger to his forehead" (p. 218). Although it is possible to interpret his gesture as a misguided attempt to protect Miss Raby from scandal, it seems more likely that he has chosen to sacrifice his friend in order to protect the reputation of "The English People," a group he seems to view as a rather exclusive club which justifiably demands certain standards of behavior. ("He was saving her, for he liked her very much, and it pained him when she was foolish. But her last remark to Feo had frightened him; and he began to feel he must save himself"—p. 214).

Miss Raby's betrayal is less obvious, but equally devastating. Early in the story the two friends discuss her theory that "self-exposure [the willingness to "intentionally make a fool of yourself before your inferiors"] was the only possible basis of true intercourse, the only gate in the spiritual barrier that divided class from class" (p. 199). Miss Raby understands how uncomfortable that notion makes Colonel Leyland, and yet she proceeds to involve him in her long and embarrassingly intimate discussion with Feo. She traps him into a situation where he, too, is forced to make a fool of himself. She does not intend to hurt him; worse than that, she simply fails to think about him. ("She was looking at Colonel Leyland, and discovered that he too was discomposed. It was her

peculiarity that she could only attend to the person she was speaking
with, and forgot the personality of the listeners"—p. 217.) But even when
she does consider him, "she had no careful explanation, no tender pity"
(p. 217). Miss Raby, with the best of intentions, sacrifices Colonel
Leyland, Feo, and even herself for her ideal—egalitarianism.

Until this episode the two friends had agreed to disagree, had re-
spected each other in spite of their differences, and had given each other
the latitude necessary for such a relationship to flourish. At the end,
however, all that has changed, and we know their friendship cannot
continue.

In an essay titled "What I Believe" Forster wrote, "[I]f I had to choose
between betraying my country and betraying my friend, I hope I should
have the guts to betray my country." Although that sentence appears in a
specific political context, it seems to suggest that, in Forster's view, loyalty
to an individual is more important than loyalty to an ideal. I think it is
that view that causes us to feel disappointed by the actions of both Miss
Raby and Colonel Leyland.

2. This story asks two large questions: Do the changes Vorta has experienced represent progress? Should people from different social classes
simply pretend that class distinctions are nonexistent? How does Forster
answer those questions?

The point of this question is to make your students realize that it's extraordinarily difficult to know what Forster wants us to think. Some
writers give us a central consciousness, perhaps a narrator, perhaps a
protagonist, who seems to speak for the writer and lets us know where
we are supposed to stand. Forster simply refuses to do that.

Forster's two central characters answer the large questions differently,
and Forster doesn't tell us which, if either, is correct. The idealistic Miss
Raby worries that prosperity will ruin Vorta: "She was not enthusiastic
over the progress of civilization, knowing by Eastern experiences that
civilization rarely puts its best foot foremost and is apt to make the bar-
barians immoral and vicious before her compensating qualities arrive"
(p. 203). But there is a suggestion that Miss Raby has underestimated the
people's ability to cope with prosperity. She is surprised to discover they
have erected a campanile. "She had feared to return to the place she had
once loved so well, lest she should find something new. It had never occurred to her that the new thing might be beautiful" (p. 199).

Colonel Leyland has quite a different view of Miss Raby's effect on
Vorta because he doesn't buy her theory that Vorta was Utopia before the
book was written. While contemplating Miss Raby's concerns, he thinks
to himself, "You think you've written a book that has spoilt the place and
made the inhabitants corrupt and sordid. I know just how you think. So

you will make yourself unhappy, and go about trying to put right what never was right" (p. 202).

Perhaps the revelation (p. 217) that the land is slipping from underneath the campanile suggests yet another possibility—that the impact of Miss Raby's book is so transitory as to be insignificant.

The two friends also have quite different views about the proper relationship between different social classes. On the face of it, Colonel Leyland is a snob who is uncomfortable when he and Miss Raby engage in a "mixed conversation" with Miss Raby's maid Elizabeth (p. 197). And yet we feel that Colonel Leyland, like Samuel Johnson, simply accepts social hierarchy as he accepts military rank, not as an indication that some people are morally or intellectually superior, merely that some are luckier than others. Colonel Leyland likes a well-ordered society where everyone knows what is expected of him or her. We feel that he would be as uncomfortable chatting with the queen as with a maid.

Although Miss Raby professes to believe that everyone is equal, Forster suggests that Miss Raby actually believes in her own aesthetic and moral superiority. (For her, hotel signs in colored lights are per se ugly.) She does not think of Feo as her equal; she merely wishes that he had been given the opportunity to rise to her level. That is, of course, the opportunity she wishes to present his son. That scene, where she cavalierly suggests taking Feo's child, never doubting that she can offer him a life superior in every way, demonstrates her peculiar notions of equality (p. 215). Colonel Leyland's calm acceptance of "the system" would never allow for change. Miss Raby's refusal to admit the existence of social inequalities is no more helpful. In the story she merely succeeds in making everyone extremely uncomfortable. And if she could wave a wand that would magically end social distinctions, we are rather certain that everyone would be remade in her image.

3. What is the significance of the story's title?

The Eternal Moment is the name or Miss Raby's first novel, the one that brought carriage loads of tourists to Vorta. The novel "was written round the idea that man does not live by time alone, that an evening gone may become like a thousand ages in the courts of heaven..." (p. 202). Although Miss Raby later "declared that it was a tiresome, affected book," in this story she rediscovers the truth she had only glimpsed in her youth.

When she realizes that she had been (but is no longer) in love with Feo for all these many years, she suddenly understands that "the incident upon the mountain had been one of the great moments of her life— perhaps the greatest, certainly the most enduring.... A presumptuous boy had taken her to the gates of heaven; and, though she would not enter with him, the eternal remembrance of the vision had made life seem endurable and good" (p. 214).

Forster presents Miss Raby as a flawed and therefore human woman
who is wrong about a number of things, but in this instance she seems to
be correct. I still don't know how Forster manages to signal that, this
time, she's right.

–M.R.D.

James Joyce
Araby

It's been my experience that students, when Joyce's notion of epiphany
is explained to them, have one of their own (of the literary variety) at the
end of this short story and consequently have a better idea of how "Araby"
"works." In this short story, as with all of its neighbors in *Dubliners,* the
central character learns with clarity and suddenness a deep truth, often
about his or her place in the nature of things. This is certainly the case
in "Araby." In fact, we are brought up against that deeper truth through
the narrarator so sharply and effectively that this short story must rank as
one of the greatest in English.

One of the reasons that this short story is so powerful is that virtually
everyone has been in the position of the narrator. The emotions that
strike him are those that besot all of us during what we imagine is our
first love. The same, of course, could be said of a great many works—some
of them teenage romance novels—but this story gives off some special
resonances by means of the retrospective antiromanticism of the narrator
as an older and perhaps wiser man. That constant juxtaposition of the
sensibilities of the narrator as a young boy and as a grown man, maintained through the slightly acidic attitude of the older toward the
younger, creates a tension between past hopes and present cynicism that
is released only in the very last line of the short story: "Gazing up into
the darkness I saw myself as a creature driven and derided by vanity, and
my eyes burned with anguish and anger" (p. 223).

QUESTIONS

1. Who is the narrator of "Araby"? What is his attitude toward this early
love? How do you know? What does Joyce's use of this type of narration
add to the story?

[I ask this many questions in a row to avoid the impression in students
that merely determining that Joyce allows us to see the action through a
first–person omniscient narrator is enough. It is of course much more

important that they see *why* Joyce might have chosen the narrator that he did.]

The narrator of "Araby" is unnamed, but we can, through careful attention to the text, establish the following:

that he is reminiscing. The story, after all, is in first person and written in the past tense.

that he looks back upon this experience with little fondness. Merely speaking the name of Mangan's sister is "like a summons to [his] *foolish* blood" [emphasis mine], and his adoration of her is "confused" (p. 220). The hyperbole "But my body was like a harp and her words and gestures were like fingers running upon the wires" is more than a little wry. Is that a simile that the man who thinks that he was deluded and derided by vanity might use—at least without a self–conscious chuckle?

2. How does the first paragraph prepare us for the rest of the short story?

This might be, if yours is an introductory class, the time to make clear the difference between connotation and denotation. Words and phrases like "blind," "set the boys free," and "detached" are heavily loaded in this context. A blind alley is to Americans a dead end, and in either England or the U.S. a "blind alley" is an enterprise that is wrong–headed or not profitable. In "set the boys free" Joyce is giving vent to his anti–Catholicism, surely, but he is also foreshadowing his narrator's chafing at being confined in school while there are dragons to be fought, bazaars to attend, and young women to defend. "Detached" I am less sure about, but the personification of "the other houses of the street" as imperturbable leads me at least to believe that we are invited to compare the narrator, who exiles himself from his playmates, to the detached and uninhabited house. In short, this first paragraph is a good example of foreshadowing through setting.

3. What are we to make of the religious allusions in this short story?

This is a very difficult question, and I hope your students provide you with a better answer than I'm about to. Joyce has his narrator confuse the sacred and erotic. The priest, for instance, whose mention in the story I think is otherwise unaccountable, seems to prepare us for that confusion. The priest's books, or at least the ones that interest the narrator, *The Abbot*, *The Devout Communicant*, and *The Memoirs of Vidocq*, are an uneasy mixture of the jejune and the soberly pious. The calls of the shop–boys selling pigs' cheeks are "shrill litanies" (p. 220), the street–singers "chant" (p. 220) about O'Donovan Rossa; the narrator bears his "chalice" (p. 220) (presumably his secret passion for Mangan's sister) through the market-place, which is "most hostile to romance" (p. 220). Her name (which we never learn) springs to the boy's lips "in strange prayers and praises which I myself did not understand" (p.220). The night–time reverie in the dead priest's drawing–room is strikingly familiar to accounts of mystical experience: "All my senses seemed to desire to veil themselves and, feeling that I was about to slip from them, I pressed the palms of my hands together until they trembled, murmuring: 'O love! O love!' many times" (p. 220). When the boy finally gets to Araby, he finds in "a si lence like that which pervades a church after a service" (p. 222) two men counting coins on a salver—in other words, men counting money in what had become to him a sort of Temple.

Then there is the scene in which Mangan's sister is illuminated by the lamplight: "Her brother and two other boys were fighting for their caps and I was alone at the railings. She held one of the spikes, bowing her head towards me. The light from the lamp opposite our door caught the white curve of her neck, lit up her hair that rested there and, falling, lit up the hand upon the railing. It fell over one side of her dress and caught the white border of a petticoat, just visible as she stood at ease" (pp. 220–221). Here we have at once a transfiguration of the Virgin just like any in medieval and Renaissance art or stained–glass window, a tableau from a production of the balcony scene from *Romeo and Juliet*, and a demonstration of the fine eye for detail usually attributed to teenage boys and girls.

–W.R.S.

Virginia Woolf
Solid Objects

I'd be tempted to pair this short story with Maupassant's "The String," which holds a similar plot line up to an entirely different light. In both stories a man's life is changed markedly through an encounter with a homely object apparently harmless and inconsequential. But in "The String" it is largely circumstance that dooms Maître Hauchecorne; he has the misfortune to be seen picking up the string by an old enemy, and his reputation and character conspire to make him a likely suspect. In this regard Maupassant is operating within a tradition that relied on the Wheel of Fortune to explain the ebb and flow of men's lives.

In "Solid Objects," though, John is not caught up in "external" circumstance—he is frozen into an obsessive pattern of behavior through the workings of his own mind, and his end is as certain as

Hauchecorne's. It is not surprising, I think, that Virginia Woolf points to the mind as the agent of change in a life. One could argue, of course, that Maître Hauchecorne's quality of mind allowed him to be trapped by circumstance. We can, as well, say of John what Maupassant says of Maître Hauchecorne—that his "whole mind" is given over to his defense, and that "his mind . . . began to weaken" (p. 135). But the bottom line is that the author of John's change is John himself. Woolf is more interested in ganglia than Fortuna.

If you decide to pair "The String" and "Solid Objects," you may wish to have your students look closely at the opening passages of each. Maupassant sets his scene through an appeal to the senses. We are told graphically of all the sights, sounds, and smells of the market scene at Goderville. Maupassant's treatment of this busy scene, for all its painstaking attention to detail, is after all fairly conventional. The "eye" through which Maupassant allows us to view his tale focuses on blue smocks, a horse's trot, and a number of other fine details, and then pulls out for a panoramic view of the whole market square.

Virginia Woolf's opening scene has an entirely different effect; the "eye" through which we view the opening scene is stationary, and has the same limitations an ordinary eye might; when John and Charles are far away, they are indistinguishable as human beings; the "black spot" that we are allowed to see first moves, then appears to have four legs, then becomes two young men, then two young men engaged in debate, then two young men debating while one punctuates his points with a walking–stick. It is only when the young men sit on the pilchard boat that they are close enough to the eye for us to discover details such as what they are wearing. [Anyone making this comparison should be certain to allow no confusion between manipulation of perspective and point of view.]

QUESTIONS

1. What is the significance of the title?

This short story asks the same questions implicit in "Dream Children": How are we to determine what is "real" and what is not?

Woolf, like most great artists, asks the questions much more clearly than she answers them. The short story begins with a comparison between the animate and the inaminate: "Nothing was so solid, so living, so hard, red, hirsute and virile as these two bodies for miles and miles of sea and sandhill" (p. 224). Two young men, presumably at the height of their physical and mental powers, sit discussing politics beside an abandoned boat by the ocean. But one of these young men reaches into the sand and finds something that is not living but is harder and more solid than either he or his companion. John's notion of what is real, or at least what is tangible and important, changes markedly as he burrows into the sand and becomes in the process childlike and enraptured:

> As his hand went further and further beyond the wrist, so that he had to hitch his sleeve a little higher, his eyes lost their intensity, or rather the background of thought and experience which gives an inscrutable depth to the eyes of grown people disappeared, leaving only the clear transparent surface, expressing nothing but wonder, which the eyes of young children display. No doubt the act of burrowing in the sand had something to do with it (p. 225).

From then on his life is lost to solid objects like the green glass. The sea itself, earlier only a backdrop or something into which intense and living and breathing men throw slate, is now "vague" and the shore "hazy" (p. 225): all attention is focused upon the glass. John's "Politics be damned!" is no longer merely fashionable, for his life has been turned away from that world and into one of his own creation. At the risk of reducing an extraordinary short story to a single image, the tableau of the mantelpiece serves as a condensation of the major theme. Here bills and letters, the necessary detritus of adulthood, are literally inferior to the new business of John's life. We learn, as John's contact with the "real world" grows less and less frequent, that these bills and papers gradually disappear. Solid objects have replaced them.

2. Is John mad?

Virtually everyone in your class, I think, might say that to withdraw from humankind in order to collect objects that seem worthless to almost anyone else is evidence of madness. I would argue that viewed from a similar perspective philatelists, Trappists, fakirs, and saints must appear mad as well. It is the nature of his obsession as it shapes the manner of his withdrawal that is evidence of mental illness; I think it is no accident that Woolf has John move from translucent glass to china to solid, opaque, and most substantial iron. His obsession with solidity—as he appears to define it—marks him as mad.

3. What judgments of John are we to make at the end of this short story?

Your class's answer to this question will depend on their answer to the question immediately above. If John has been taken (or has taken himself) from a promising career in Parliament and is reduced by some sort of madness to collecting trash, then he is pathetic and to be pitied. If, on the other hand, he is happy in his new life's work and in rejecting the confusion and competition of what we've called elsewhere the "real" world, then he is to be admired and perhaps even envied.

Those in your class hoping that John will "snap out of it" as readily as he snapped into it should probably read the end of the story again. [This is also a terrific opportunity to demonstrate just how damaging confused pronoun references can be.]

> "What was the truth of it, John?" asked Charles suddenly, turning and facing him. "What made you give it up like that all in a second?"
> "I've not given it up," John replied.
> "But you've not a ghost of a chance now," said Charles roughly.
> "I don't agree with you there," said John with conviction. Charles looked at him and was profoundly uneasy; the most extraordinary doubts possessed him; he had a queer sense that they were talking about different things. (p. 228)

It seems likely on the basis of this passage that John's pursuit of a political career has been entirely replaced by his pursuit of solid objects. By "it" Charles means that political career; John quite obviously means by "it" his quest for solid objects, a quest likely to last the rest of his life.

–W.R.S.

Franz Kafka
The Metamorphosis

In "The Metamorphosis" a young man, Gregor, wakes up one morning to discover that he has been transformed into a giant insect who still has human feelings. The plot revolves around the reactions of Gregor's family to this vile creature who was their son. "The Metamorphosis," written in 1912, can be seen either as a story that was ahead of its time or as a throwback to the tale popular before the modern short story form was created by writers such as Poe and Maupassant. The theme of alienation and the realistic treatment of a fantastic occurrence make the story avant–garde, a piece we might have expected from the later Expressionists or Surrealists. At the same time, Gregor's sudden and unexplained transformation is the stuff of fairy tales. (See question 1 of Maupassant's "The String" for a discussion of the characteristics of the tale.) If your students have read Grimms' "The Juniper Tree," you can ask them to recall the murdered child's metamorphosis into a beautiful bird with red and green feathers. One way of approaching this selection might be to have your students decide how "The Metamorphosis" is or is not like the traditional story or the traditional tale.

Franz Kafka's work has so influenced twentieth–century literature and thought that the word "Kafkaesque" is now used to describe anything characterized by surrealistic distortion, a sense of alienation, and a mood of impending danger. Your students may be interested to learn that Kafka is not as well known in his native land as he is in the rest of the world. Even though he is undeniably Czechoslovakia's most important writer, only one of his books (a collection of short stories that includes "The Metamorphosis") is now sold in Prague, and that book is published in German, a language few Czechoslovakians read. No Czech translations of any of Kafka's works are currently in print in the country of his birth.

QUESTIONS

1. Flannery O'Connor says that in "The Metamorphosis" "a certain distortion is used to get at the truth. What is "the truth" Kafka presents in this story?

This question should force your students to think about why anyone would write a rather long story about a man who, for no apparent reason, is changed into an insect. One interpretation of the story which most students find reasonable is that Kafka demonstrates through exaggeration the alienation all of us experience. You might begin class discussion by asking your students to think of humans other than Gregor who find themselves trapped in bodies that fail to respond to commands or bodies that elicit strange responses from other people. Your students will probably mention people who experience paralysis, the loss of limbs, or senility.

With a little prompting, your class will realize that all of us, no matter how "normal," inhabit bodies that alienate us from each other because people respond, at least initially, to external appearances. I know that others consider my gender, age, race, and clothing, and then draw conclusions about the kind of person I am long before they know anything about the me who lives inside. I make similar judgments about them. And even after we get beyond first impressions, even when we sincerely try to communicate honestly with others, we fail. Insurmountable barriers isolate us, barriers such as the limitations of language and human understanding. In this story Kafka seems to suggest that the sorrow Gregor feels when he realizes that he can never succeed in making his family understand him is an emotion experienced to some degree by everyone.

2. In the Counterpoint O'Connor says that the concrete detail of this story is absolutely convincing. Find five examples of details that make this fantastic story credible.

Your students will have no trouble finding examples. Here are a few they may suggest:

Gregor awakens to discover that he has turned into an insect. What does he do? He decides to "sleep a little longer and forget all this nonsense," precisely what any right-thinking person would do. Unfortunately he can't get back to sleep because he is "accustomed to sleeping on his right side" and he can't manage to get his body rolled over (p. 230).

Gregor discovers that he can't get himself out of bed. What does he worry about? "The next train went at seven o'clock; to catch that he would need to hurry like mad and his samples weren't even packed up, and he himself wasn't feeling particularly fresh and active" (p. 231). Gregor's response will probably strike your students as absolutely believable. I sometimes suspect that no matter what calamity befalls us—death, disease, war, famine, or airline strikes—the first question we ask ourselves is, "But will it make me late to work?"

Gregor edges around the door and is seen for the first time by other people. The chief clerk "utters a loud 'Oh!'—it sounded like a gust of wind—...claps one hand before his open mouth and slowly backs away as if driven by some invisible steady pressure" (p. 237). Yet another realistic response to a bizarre situation.

3. When do the changes that Gregor experiences occur? In what ways does Gregor remain unchanged?

I think this story should have been named "The Metamorphoses" because it actually deals with a number of dramatic transformations. The most obvious, of course, is the overnight transmogrification of Gregor's outward form. Your students should also notice other metamorphoses, Gregor's internal changes, which are more gradual. For example, he slowly learns to control his new body. Initially he has no command over "the numerous little legs which never stopped waving in all directions (p. 232), but later his legs are "quietly obedient, as he noted with joy..." (p. 239), and eventually he learns that he can crawl crisscross over the walls and ceilings and hang suspended from the ceiling in almost "blissful absorption." Another change is his loss of some human attributes. Initially Gregor's voice is intelligible to others. When Gregor's father first calls to him, Gregor apparently makes himself understood when he says "I'm just ready" (p. 231). But by the time Gregor has crawled to the door, the chief clerk is saying, "That was no human voice" (p. 236). Gregor also loses his taste for the foods that had been his favorites (p. 241), he begins to feel apprehension in his lofty, empty room and finds comfort by "scuttling under the sofa" (p. 242), and he realizes that day by day things are "growing dimmer to his sight" (p. 246).

Eventually he loses even his human interests. When Grete decides to clear his room of furniture, he is delighted until he hears his mother saying that Gregor might feel forlorn if they took away everything he loved. Then he asks himself, "Did he really want his warm room, so comfortably fitted with old family furniture, to be turned into a naked den in which he would certainly be able to crawl unhampered in all directions but at the price of shedding simultaneously all recollection of his human background?" (pp. 248–249).

One metamorphosis does not occur: Gregor's emotional responses remain human. At first, when Gregor realizes how repulsive the sight of him is to his sister, his concern for her motivates him to arrange a sheet on the sofa so that he can hide himself when she comes into the room (p. 20). Later, after his family's treatment of him becomes shameful (The ash can and garbage are stored in his room; his father throws an apple at him and seriously injures him; and his sister pushes food into his room with her foot; his responses are less noble but still all too human— rage; sadness; and a "growing lack of consideration for the others.")

Gregor's human need for beauty and love remains constant. He is drawn to his sister's violin playing. "Was he an animal, that music had such an effect upon him? He felt as if the way were opening before him to the unknown nourishment he craved" (p. 258). Even his final moments are spent thinking "of his family with tenderness and love" and willing himself to "disappear" as his sister wishes (p. 262). If Gregor did not remain human, the story might be more comic than tragic.

4. What metamorphoses do the members of Gregor's family experience?

The other members of the family undergo metamorphoses as profound as Gregor's. When the story opens, Gregor is the sole support of his family. We learn that when his father's business collapsed five years earlier (p. 244), Gregor took on a job as a traveling salesman, a job he despises, so that he could meet the expenses of the entire family. Since then both the family and Gregor "had simply got used to" that situation. His father, who has done no work for five years, has grown rather fat and sluggish (p. 245). His mother has asthma which keeps her "lying on a sofa every other day panting for breath beside an open window" (pp. 245–246), and his sister, a child of seventeen, spends her days "dressing herself nicely, sleeping long, helping in the housekeeping, going out to a few modest entertainments and above all playing the violin" (p. 246)."

During the course of the story, all three become stronger and more self-sufficient. All find employment. The mother does "fine sewing for an underwear firm," the sister takes a job as a salesgirl, and the father apparently becomes a bank messenger (see description of his transformation on pp. 251–252). They also discover that they have some capital (a few investments that survived the failure of the father's business, plus money saved from Gregor's earnings—p. 245), and they decide to take in boarders to earn additional income.

At the same time, their feelings toward Gregor change markedly. At the beginning his sister is a compassionate, loving person who tries to find out what food he likes best and then "with fine tact" withdraws while he eats. The mother, after recovering from her initial shock, begs to enter Gregor's room: "Do let me in to Gregor, he is my unfortunate son" (p. 247). The father never seems particularly sympathetic to Gregor, but after he injures him by throwing the apple, even he recollects that Gregor is "a member of the family, despite his present unfortunate and repulsive shape, and ought not to be treated as an enemy, that, on the contrary, family duty required the suppression of disgust and the exercise of patience, nothing but patience" (p. 253).

By the end of the story all have lost patience with Gregor. Grete insists that they "must try to get rid of it," the father responds that "she is more than right," and the mother does nothing to come to her son's defense (p. 260). The parents allow Grete to lock Gregor in his room (p. 261), and when they discover that he has had the decency to die, they celebrate by taking a tram into the open country where they "canvass their prospects for the future" and find that they are not at all bad (p. 264). Ironically, Gregor's unwilling imprisonment has brought about his family's independence, something his willing sacrifice of himself had never accomplished.

Some of your students may conclude that the family's treatment of Gregor is monstrous. You can remind them that Kafka deliberately turns us against the family by telling the story from Gregor's point of view. No one in Gregor's family ever suspects that he can understand what they say or that he still has human emotions. Few people other than saints manage to love the unlovable, and the insect in this story, whose appearance, odor, and actions are disgusting, is far from lovable.

–M.R.D.

William Carlos Williams
Jean Beicke

Your students probably know William Carlos Williams as a poet. They may not realize that he was also a physician who doctored the people of his northern New Jersey community for more than 40 years. Eschewing a more lucrative practice, he devoted himself to working class families. Many of his patients were immigrants who lived in extreme poverty. In fact he sometimes returned home from house calls so covered with bedbugs that he undressed in the bathtub to avoid infesting his home with vermin. Throughout his long medical career he spent his days making house calls, making rounds at the hospital, and treating patients at his office at home. His duties as a doctor ended at 9:00 p.m. or after the last patient was seen. Then, while the rest of the world slept, he wrote.

Williams was frequently asked how he maintained such a superhuman schedule. His response: "[A]s a writer I have never felt that medicine interfered with me but rather that it was my very food and drink, the very thing that made it possible for me to write. Was I not interested in man? There the thing was, right in front of me. I could touch it, smell it. It was myself, naked, just as it was, without a lie telling itself to me in its own terms."

In "Jean Beicke," one of several of Williams' doctor stories, the doctor/narrator tells the story of an eleven–month–old child who dies even though the doctor does everything he knows how to do "except the right thing." It is the unsentimental account of a doctor who looks at his own fallibility, and at the injustice of life and death, and then continues his work.

QUESTIONS

1. Who is the audience addressed by this narrator?

It is difficult to identify the "you" the narrator addresses when he notes that Jean's arms came down to her hips and then adds, "They should come down to her thighs, you know" (p. 267). He does not seem to be engaged in a dramatic monologue with an unseen but identifiable listener (as is the case in Margaret Atwood's "Rape Fantasies"). That leads us to believe he must be talking to us, his readers, but certainly not in the "you, the gentle reader" style of nineteenth–century writers like Trollope who assumed a great gulf between the narrator and reader and occasionally paused to give us additional information or to reassure us about the future of certain characters.

This narrator never treats us condescendingly. He uses medical terms without defining them, apparently believing that we know the terms or that we are capable of using a medical dictionary or that we can understand the story even if we can't define all the terms. His attitude toward us is further illustrated by his refusal to apologize either for his failure to save Jean or for the harsh remarks he makes about the children in the ward. It is almost as if we are imaginary confidants, extensions of the narrator, intelligent human beings who will not confuse blunt truth with heartlessness. I end up feeling flattered that he treats me as an equal.

2. What is the narrator's attitude toward   Jean?

Some of your students may be put off by Williams' tough guy talk (which you might want to compare to that of the narrator in Dashiell

Hammett's "Fly paper"). He repeatedly refers to the children in the hospital as "brats," describes Jean as "one of the damnedest looking kids" he had ever seen (p. 267), and comments, "I had to laugh every time I looked at the brat after that, she was such a funny looking one..."(p. 268). Others may be distressed by his dispassionately clinical description of her cause of death: "The left lateral sinus was completely thrombosed and on going into the left temporal bone from the inside the mastoid process was all broken down" (p. 270).

And yet we feel that he cares deeply about Jean. He admires her spunk, her ability to eat and gain weight even when she is deathly ill (p. 268). He worries about the pain she experiences when she is touched and he tells us, "We handled her as gently as we knew how..."(p. 267). He admits to us, if not to the nurses, "We all got to be crazy about [her]" (p. 268). And when he describes his reaction to her dying, he writes, "Somehow or other, I hated to see that kid go. Everybody felt rotten" (p. 269).

Some of your students may notice that the narrator's public statements are somewhat different from his private opinions. In his public role as callous doctor he kids the nurses about their devotion to the children: "I look at some miserable specimens they've dolled up for me when I make the rounds in the morning and I tell them. Give it an enema, maybe it will get well and grow up into a cheap prostitute or something" (p. 267). To himself (or to his reader) he calls them "poor kids," and he worries about the wisdom of curing children without curing the society that allows them to suffer from poverty, filth, malnutrition, neglect, and abuse. "You really wonder sometimes if medicine isn't all wrong to try to do anything for them at all" (p. 267).

3. Who is the story really about?

Although the story is named "Jean Beicke," I think most of your students will conclude that it isn't really about Jean, a baby who is introduced on page 267 and dies on page 270. If this were the story of a dying child, we might expect a more dramatic presentation. (Ask your students to imagine how any soap opera would handle the topic.) We might expect a conflict between the doctor and the forces of nature with the doctor fighting for the child's life and the audience cheering for his success. We might even expect to have the outcome of the struggle concealed until the end of the story. But Williams does not employ the traditional pyramidal formula of rising action, climax, and falling action. (You may want to refer your students to the plot entry in the Handbook.) In fact, it's difficult to identify the climax of this story, but I think your students will agree that it isn't Jean's death.

So it seems that the story is really about the doctor/narrator and his efforts to deal with Jean's death. Like all doctors, the narrator walks an emotional tightrope. If he becomes so totally detached that his patients are merely cases, he destroys his own humanity. If, on the other hand, he becomes so personally attached to individual patients that he cannot perform his duties as a doctor, he destroys the people he has sworn to aid.

The narrator seems to succeed in this difficult balancing act. He allows himself to care about Jean, but not to love her as unreservedly as the nurses do. After all, nurses have the luxury of deciding not to attend autopsies. He does not let his feelings for Jean interfere with his obligations to future patients. Although he admits that he "can never quite get used to an autopsy" (p. 270), he nonetheless observes Jean's autopsy, learns that he could have saved her, accepts the responsibility for her death, and vows that in the future he will always take a culture of the pus in suspicious cases (p. 269).

4. What does the final exchange between the ear man and the narrator mean?

I don't know the correct answer, but I think your students will offer at least three readings of this conversation: (a) The narrator really is as heartless and uncaring as some of his earlier remarks indicated. (b) Williams the author uses the ear man's question to demonstrate that the narrator's flip comments are simply inadequate to address the issues before them. (c) No deep hidden meaning; Williams is merely recording a conversation he once heard.

–M.R.D.

Katherine Anne Porter
The Jilting of Granny Weatherall

Porter once wrote: "My whole attempt has been to discover and understand human motives, human feeling, to make a distillation of what human relations and experiences my mind has been able to absorb. I have never known an uninteresting human being, and I have never known two alike; there are broad classifications and deep similarities, but I am interested in the thumbprint."

In this particular story Porter explores the thumbprint and psyche of Granny Weatherall, an eighty–year–old woman on her deathbed who conforms to none of our stereotypes. She is not a serene wise woman, a childishly senile incompetent, a feisty oldster who enjoys shocking people with her candor, or a sweet little old lady. She is Ellen, a strong woman whose husband died young, leaving her to rear their children alone, a woman who once fenced in a hundred acres, a woman who still keeps her letters from George, the man who jilted her sixty years earlier. Using a stream–of–consciousness style, Porter allows us to follow Ellen through the memories, thoughts, perceptions, and fears of her last day.

QUESTIONS

1. In the Counterpoint Eudora Welty claims that Porter's stories have surprisingly little sensory imagery. Is that true of this story?

Your students will need to begin by rereading the story and marking all the images. They should notice that there are few visual images, and most of those distort reality. Doctor Harry seems to "float like a balloon around the foot of the bed" (p. 272), the Hapsy Granny envisions "melted from within and turned filmy as gray gauze and the baby was a gauzy shadow" (p. 276), and Granny's photograph of her husband "shows John's eyes black when they should have been blue" (pp. 277–278). The few auditory images are also deceptive. "She listened to the leaves rustling outside the window. No, somebody was swishing newspapers: no, Cornelia and Doctor Harry were whispering together" (p. 273). The paucity of visual and auditory images is consistent with the point of view. After all, the story is told from within the consciousness of a very old dying woman (possibly hard of hearing) who seldom opens her eyes.

But the absence of these particular images may also suggest something about the nature of truth. Ordinarily we want to find truth by consensus, and sights and sounds seem to allow us to do that. If we can all see a barn or hear a roll of thunder, it is easy to agree that those things exist. But Porter tells us the task is not that simple, that each person must determine truth for herself. To demonstrate that view, Porter presents Granny's world through tactile images. Tactile sensations, unlike sights and sounds, are private, not communal. One person may feel comfortable at a temperature that makes another shiver; neither can rely on the other to validate his or her perceptions.

Porter fills the story with tactile images. Granny feels the doctor "spread a warm paw like a cushion on her forehead" (p. 272), she notes that "[h]er bones felt loose and floated around in her skin" (p. 272), she feels the "pillow rise and float under her, pleasant as a hammock in a light wind" (p. 273), and she feels "her face tying up in hard knots" (p. 273). At the end of her life, Granny is enclosed in a world only she inhabits. Alone, she struggles to discover the meaning of her life.

Porter's choice of images also demonstrates her literary commitment. By focusing on the intensely personal she sets herself in a camp opposite from that of writers such as T.S. Eliot and William Carlos Williams who give us hard, clear visual images that speak for themselves.

2. Who is Hapsy?

This is not an easy question. We can say with certainty that Hapsy is
female and that Ellen is especially fond of her. When the children
gather round Ellen, she wonders, "Did you send for Hapsy too? It was
Hapsy she really wanted" (p. 276). We are relatively sure that Hapsy is
already dead. That would explain why, when Ellen realizes she is dying,
she consoles herself by thinking, "You'll see Hapsy again" (p. 279).
Earlier, however, Ellen thinks, "Cornelia, you're to have the amethyst
set, but Hapsy's to wear it when she wants"—p. 278. Does that sentence
mean that Hapsy is alive or that Ellen has temporarily forgotten about
Hapsy's death?

Theories about Hapsy's identity abound. Some readers believe Hapsy
was Ellen's and John's daughter, perhaps Ellen's favorite. Others speculate that Ellen was pregnant when George jilted her and that Hapsy was
the black servant and friend who acted as midwife when Ellen secretly
gave birth to her illegitimate child, a child she later gave up for adoption. Still others agree that Ellen was pregnant but argue that Hapsy was
the child fathered by George but legitimatized by Ellen's hasty marriage
to John. Your students should be able to find passages in the story to support each of these readings. Each theory, of course, leads to a different interpretation of the story's ending.

3. How do you interpret the story's ending?

You might want to refer your students to Matthew 25:1–19, a parable in
which salvation is compared to the arrival of a bridegroom. Jesus tells the
story of ten virgins [bridesmaids] who take their lamps to go meet the
bridegroom. The five foolish virgins fail to carry extra oil, and their
lamps go out. While the foolish virgins are away buying more oil, the
bridegroom arrives, takes the wise virgins with him to the wedding,
and shuts the door behind them. The parable concludes with this admo-
nition! "Watch therefore, for ye know neither the day nor the hour
wherein the son of man cometh."

The connection between that parable and this story is problematic. It is
difficult for me to cast Ellen in the role of foolish virgin. If, however, we
believe that Ellen became pregnant with George's child, then we could
assume that she feels guilt for some unidentified and unexpiated sin
[refusing to repent her illicit love?; giving up her illegitimate child?;
failing to forgive George?; continuing to suffer from wounded vanity?].
Perhaps it is her sin that prevents her seeing the bridegroom.

I prefer to think of Ellen as a wise virgin who has lived a good life and
feels easy about the state of her soul. "She had her secret comfortable
understanding with a few favorite saints who cleared a straight road to

God for her. All as surely signed and sealed as the papers for the new Forty Acres" (p. 277). But God disappoints Ellen, just as George did.

Ellen did everything she should have to prepare for her first wedding. She had "put on her white veil and set out the white cake" (p. 275). "But [George] had not come, just the same" (p. 275). When George jilted Ellen, he took away "[s]omething not given back (p. 277)," possibly her faith in people. Ellen also prepares for her death, for the bridegroom who will take her to heaven, but once again she is jilted. She pleads, "God, give a sign. For the second time there was no sign" (p. 279). At that moment Ellen loses faith in her religion. But just as she lived without George, she courageously decides to die without God. She refuses to forgive the bridegroom's tardiness or to wait for him longer. "She stretched herself with a deep breath and blew out the light....that was herself" (p. 279).

—M.R.D.

Dorothy Parker
Here We Are

The Counterpoint for this story is a real lever into what Parker attempts here. It seems at first that we have all the makings of a television sitcom: the nervous bride and groom, anticipating the wedding night, having their first quarrel. In less competent hands and from a duller mind than Parker's, this story might have been precious and predictable, the story is instead a dissection and a prediction, and neither is entirely pleasant. If Parker's reputation depended on this short story, she need not have worried as she did in the interview in the Counterpoint that she was fated to be known as a humorist. In "Here We Are" she is only occasionally a humorist, and when we laugh with her and at the couple ours is nervous laughter. Parker's story is told with wit and, as she says, "wit has truth in it. The truth here is that this couple is embarking on a marriage that promises to be hell for both of them. This is a short story, then, "built" entirely of foreshadowing, and, while no Misfit or falling House of Usher awaits the couple, what they face is the sort of soul-grinding life together that situation comedies are, after all, seldom made of.

QUESTIONS

1. When is this story amusing?

"Here We Are" is most amusing when the bride and groom dance around any mention of the wedding night. When she is asked how it feels to be an old married lady, she replies "Oh, it's too soon to ask me that . . . At least—I mean" (p. 281). He says shortly afterward, "Let's don't think about a lot of Chinese. We've got something better to think about. I mean . . . We know darn well what's going to happen next. I mean. I mean—well, we know it's going to be great" (p. 282). After a heated exchange over his treatment of his new in–laws, he explains her contentiousness on pre–nuptial jitters. "You know, lots of times," he said, "they say that girls get kind of nervous and yippy on account of thinking about—I mean." Later, when she complains of feeling strange and alone with him, he explains, "Well, you see, sweetheart . . . we're not really married yet. I mean. I mean—well, things will be different afterwards . . . Well, we haven't got much longer to wait now . . . I mean—well, we'll be in New York in about twenty minutes" (pp. 285–286). After she expresses a desire to spend her honeymoon night writing thank–you notes, he hopes that "we could go right up to the Biltmore and anyway leave our bags, and maybe have a little dinner in the room, kind of quiet, and then do whatever we wanted. I mean. I mean—well, let's go right up there from the station" (p. 286). Finally, as the trip ends, he attempts to reassure both his wife and himself with "Pretty soon we'll be regular old married people. I mean. I mean, in a few minutes we'll be getting in to New York, and then we'll be going to the hotel, and then everything will be all right. I mean—well, look at us!" (p. 287).

Parker, as we can see, is certain to provide us with the flag "I mean" whenever the eager husband utters anything in the least suggestive of the consummation of the marriage. The husband's verbal tic when he becomes aware of appearing overeager is the equivalent of a "running gag" throughout the short story.

2. How does the point of view affect our impression of the relationship between the newlyweds?

The point of view is dramatic almost throughout the short story. This results in a detachment and distancing that makes the combat between the newlyweds all the more disagreeable. We are *shown* through dialogue, rather than *told* through exposition (or other intrusive techniques) of the potential for disintegration of this brand–new marriage; this calculated restraint turns sitcom into the beginnings of what we are forced to feel will be a kind of domestic tragedy.

Only the first three short paragraphs and two sentences describing a lapse in conversation allow for any intrusion by the narrator; Parker makes the most of these opportunities. We are told that both are wearing new clothing, she looking "as new as a peeled egg" (p. 281) and in new shoes still bearing the price tag. The young man, desperate to do anything but face the awkward question that faces them now that they are alone, spends a lifetime adjusting their new luggage. Parker cannot resist the wry "eight minutes for the settling of two suitcases and a hat-box is a long time." The bride, with no luggage to fuss over, must be content to stare "raptly out of the window, drinking in the big weathered sign boards that extolled the phenomena of codfish without bones and screens no rust could corrupt" (p. 281). Parker archly has our heroine staring at a view that could only be enrapturing if the alternative were painfully awkward—which it is. On p. 286 Parker piques our curiosity when she witholds the details of a fleeting reconciliation: "He rose, balanced a moment, crossed over and sat down beside her . . . There was a silence with things going on in it. "

3. What, as a result of reading this story, are we to think of marriage in general?

I think the title provides us with the answer to this one. The second word, I think, might lead us to believe that Parker feels this battle of the sexes to be, if not a universal condition, then one that is extremely com mon. Human beings fall in love and bind themselves to other human beings in some fashion; Parker implies here and elsewhere in her work that this is of necessity a bond that means misery for at least one of the parties.

Your students might find it interesting to determine which is the more sympathetic character in "Here We Are." My candidate is the husband, who, though he is thoughtless and oblivious at times, is still not spoiling for a fight as is his bride. Still, his motives for peacemaking are suspect.

–W.R.S.

Dashiell Hammett
Fly Paper

You might find it useful to have your class read this story soon after you treat Doyle's "Speckled Band." The bare bones of the plots look similar; in both stories, a young woman seems to be menaced by a powerful, clever, and evil man. The detective is brought in to defeat that man and rescue the girl. But of course the stories differ to such an extent that it is difficult at first reading to consider them members of the same genre.

One of the differences between the two stories lies in the world–views each presents. The fictional reality set up in the adventures of Sherlock Holmes is stocked with doting housekeepers, Persian slippers filled with tobacco, a genial and adoring companion for the detective, a chemistry laboratory, and momentos of past triumphs. In contrast, the world of the unnamed detective in Hammett's story is a dark place, with guns that wound and kill, hard women of doubtful virtue, and spat–out teeth. In other words, though Holmes says in "The Speckled Band" that his is a "wicked, wicked world," the fictional reality Doyle creates is in comparison to the world of "Fly Paper" a rather cheery *Boy's Life* kind of place, where evil can at least be momentarily defeated.

But this of course is not the case in "Fly Paper." It is not surprising that the American examples of *film noir* hat spring to mind are almost always detective stories much like this one. In this story and in those movies, the jaded protagonist operates with mixed success in a world as jaded as he. Evil or at least corruption permeates that world; the detective must reconcile himself to that evil and learn to use it to his own ends.

QUESTIONS

1. Describe Hammett's prose style in this story. Why is that style appropriate to the character of the narrator?

The short story begins with a sentence that is characteristic of the rest of the narrative. It is short, clipped, and assumes an initiated reader, that is, the type of reader who knows what a "wandering daughter job" is. It is a style that one could certainly describe as "non–literary"—the narrator is not, in the formal sense, "telling a story"; he might just as well be talking about his day in the back of a speakeasy. The language that the narrator employs in the face of events most of us would find at least disquieting is detached and filled with that slangy shorthand that baffles us now and would have delighted the original intended audience of Hammett's pulp fiction: "At the first corner he stopped to squirt metal at me—three shots. I squirted one at him. None of the four connected" (p. 309). I suspect most us might describe this encounter in a different manner. In short, the narrator is a man who has shot and been shot at, a man who can describe corpses and beatings and murders and rubber–hose questionings dispassionately.

2. What might account for Hammett's choice of a title?

The metaphor of the flypaper serves as the central thematic and plot device of the story. The poisoners are poisoned, and Sue Hambleton and Holy Joe are metaphorically trapped in flypaper that they had hung up for another. Circumstances largely of their own making have turned against them so that like papered flies they are trapped and die. If the "Old Man" is correct, then Sue has attempted to render herself immune to arsenic poisoning so that she can rid herself and Joe of Babe McCloor—and died in the attempt.

We're given a useful clue about Hammett's use of the metaphor when he includes the detail that the poisoned flypaper is wrapped around a copy of Dumas' *The Count of Monte Cristo.* In that novel, Madame Villefort, guided in the use of poisons by the Count, poisons her stepdaughter. Confronted by her husband with her crimes, Madame Villefort poisons herself and her son Edward, for whom she had hoped to obtain advancement by murdering his stepsister. As Madame Villefort is hoist with her own petard, so is Sue Hambleton.

3. Are there clear rules of behavior distinguishing the detectives from the criminals?

The simplest answer to this question is no, but it may not be the right one. When Peggy Carroll is badgered into submission by a pack of detectives (private and police), our Mirandaized sensibilities are offended; when the narrator inspects Sue Hambleton's apartment before the police arrive and blackmails Holy Joe and Peggy we wonder about his character and his attitude toward the law. His ice–cold detachment regarding the murders and brutality around him makes him, in some fashion, a participant. He even demonstrates a grudging admiration for Babe McCloor, a mugger, a killer—and a fearsome adversary. Babe isn't, at least, a poisoner, and he does kill Holy Joe to avenge the death of his woman. He even takes his medicine and without a whimper:

"You sure devastated me, bo," he said when I came in.
"Sorry," I said, "but—"
"I ain't beefing. I asked for it."
(p. 310)

But the very important detail not given us explicitly in the story is that it is the narrator's testimony that convicts Babe McCloor, for the narrator is the only witness to the shooting of Holy Joe. Apparently, then, the narrator's admiration of McCloor does not extend to letting him escape the law. Why the narrator must do this is an indecipherable question, I think. Does he have a moral sense, or is he acting only as an agent for a monolithic and inscrutable institution, the law, that demands a death for a death?

4. Is "Fly Paper" "literature"?

I'm sure you'll get interesting answers to this question if you ask it. We cannot exclude "Fly Paper" automatically from that exclusive club merely because it was first published in a pulp magazine. There is violence, yes, but not the loving attention to gory detail we find, say, in Sam Peckinpah movies or even *Beowulf.* The style is sinewy and tough, appropriate to the action and themes—like Hemingway's prose. The characters are flat and hardly dynamic, but the same could be said, for example, of virtually any character in *The Canterbury Tales.* It is true that this is not a tale of kings, gods, and heroes, but they are not necessary to so–called belle lettres. In short, as fairy tales have been assigned to children, so detective fiction (at least of this variety) has been assigned, perhaps unfairly, to an audience wanting tough talk, plenty of action, and a clear explanation of the intricacies of the case at the end—an audience some might call the great unwashed. The tastes of *literati*, rather than sales figures or entertainment value, seem to determine what enters the canon and what is excluded.

I'd be tempted to play devil's advocate (much as I've done above) and, when your class suggests characteristics of "Fly Paper" that might disqualify it as high literature, suggest that those elements can be found in other works—some no doubt already covered in class—in "the canon."

–W.R.S.

William Faulkner
Barn Burning

Faulkner puts his narrator on the razor horns of one of the most fearful of dilemmas in this story. What happens when your blood–kin commits an act that forces you to question and renounce your familial loyalties? Some students will no doubt quickly point out that Hamlet is in an analogous—though much more complicated—situation, but there is at least one important difference. The narrator in "Barn Burning" is a child, and children more often than not have a belief in the infallibility of their parents that is eroded only (traditionally, at least) during adolescence. So Faulkner gives another turn to the screw in having a child come to the acrid and world–view–shattering conclusion that his father, though "He was brave! . . . He was in the war!" is a flint–hearted scoundrel. But the young Snopes does not move from unalloyed love to pure hatred over the course of the short story; his feelings are mixed throughout. At the beginning of the story, he laments his father's crime and hopes for his rehabilitation; at the end of the story, he cries for his father and tries to retreat into the memory of his father as a war hero.

The War Between the States is the backdrop for this story, as it is for so much of Faulkner's work. We learn a great deal about Abner Snopes through Faulkner's description of what we must call his "war record." We are told that Abner was a horse thief preying on both sides during the war, that he had been shot in the heel by a Confederate as he fled on a stolen horse, that his allegiance during the struggle was to himself. As he looks back at De Spain's plantation, his observation is typically defiant and self–interested:

> "Pretty and white, ain't it" he said. "That's sweat. Nigger sweat. Maybe it ain't white enough yet to suit him. Maybe he wants to mix some white sweat with it." (p. 320)

The sweep of the War fought to maintain both a genteel tradition and the cruelest of economic systems passed over Abner Snopes; for him the only issue at hand was how much profit could be wrung out of the combatants. While it is almost impossible to imagine such a man capable of consciously symbolic action (see the metaphor in the passage cited above, though) Snopes, in tracking the horse manure into the De Spain house on his wounded foot, demonstrates his view of a tradition he despises because he is excluded from it.

QUESTIONS

1. From whose point of view is the story told? How does Faulkner "use" passages not told from Sartoris Snopes' point of view?

The principal point of view is third person; the action is viewed primarily through the eyes of Sartoris Snopes. Those passages in italic print mark a sort of interior monologue in which the boy feels the tug of "the old blood which he had not been permitted to choose for himself, which had been bequeathed him willy nilly and which had run for so long (and who knew where, battening on what of outrage and savagery and lust . . .) (p. 325).

Faulkner, however, does not limit his reader to just that perspective. There is another consciousness in "Barn Burning" that provides background, commentary, and a view of the future—a kind of chorus. We learn from that consciousness the particulars of Abner Snopes' enterprises during the Civil War; it apparently cannot resist speculating on Snopes' reasons for building a niggardly fire (p. 317) and telling us that "twenty years later, he [Sartoris] was to tell himself, 'If I had said thay wanted only truth, justice, he would have hit me again.' (p. 318).

2. What do you think Faulkner intends our opinion of Abner Snopes to
be?

While one could hardly say that the treatment of Abner Snopes is
evenhanded, still Faulkner does not make the mistake of painting him
as merely a monster. His son imagines him to be cut out of tin, hard,
cold, and impervious. He strikes his son after the boy has leapt to his defense against a bigger oponent, treats his wife brutally, and, having
proven his skill at horse thievery, tries his hand at another mortal sin
in rural society, barn burning. He cannot be restrained by ordinary rules
of behavior because he does not acknowledge that such a thing might
apply to him. Treated "unfairly," he takes matters matters into his own
hands. [Your students may wish to compare his motivations with those of
the Misfit in O'Connors' "A Good Man Is Hard To Find."

To catalogue Abner Snopes' vices would be to recount almost the whole
story, but against our will and better judgment Faulkner has us admire
something in him. The voice in the short story that exposes Snopes as a
renegade and thief also tells us that

> There was something about his wolflike independence and even
> courage when the advantage was at least neutral which impressed
> strangers, as if they got from his latent ravening ferocity not so
> much a sense of dependability as a feeling that his ferocious convic-
> tion in the rightness of his actions would be of advantage to all
> whose interest lay with his (p. 317).

And there is something prepossessing about Snopes that captures our
interest and at times our sympathy (see Faulkner's remarks concerning
Satan in the Counterpoint). Abner's anger at "the man that aims to begin tomorrow owning me body and soul for the next eight months" (p.
318) is understandable, and we must watch with fascination his
"absolutely undeviating course" (p. 319) as he moves toward confrontation
with the De Spains and what they represent for him.

3. What happens to De Spain's barn? What is the fate of Abner Snopes?
Does Sarty Snopes return to his family?

The first of these questions is the one we can answer with most certainty. After the boy hears the shots (p. 327), he looks backward "over his
shoulder at the glare" (p. 327)—presumably the glare of De Spain's burning barn.

There is no internal evidence of Snopes' death or survival. It is easy to
jump to the conclusion, because the boy cries out as if in mourning for his
father and speaks of his father in the past tense "He was brave!" that Abner Snopes is killed by the gunshots heard by the boy. It is just as likely

that the boy calls "Father! Father!" because he regrets his terrible choice. "He was brave!" could be read as "He was brave before he became an arsonist!" and a final attempt to mitigate his father's guilt. One could argue, of course, that Sartoris does not return to his family because he fears that his father will be alive and waiting when he returns to the homestead. The bottom line is that our vision of the story from the point when the gunshots are heard to the conclusion is that of the boy's—and he either does not know what happens to his father or knows so surely that it is not "reported."

One could argue just as reasonably that Sartoris Snopes literally has nothing to return to except a constant reminder of his own duplicity if his father *is* dead, and so moves down the road; this argument presupposes that the boy is walking away from his family, an assumption that the text may or may not support.

–W.R.S.

Ernest Hemingway
A Clean, Well–Lighted Place

This short story is as much as anything about heroism and compassion in the face of a fear of old age and death. A dangerous assertion: one of the touchstones for assessing the nature of a character is how that character treats animals, idiots, children, and the old. One need only look at *The Sound and the Fury,* Jane Austen's *Emma,* or, in *The Riverside Anthology of Literature,* "Livvie" or "Barn Burning" to see this principle in action. The older waiter in "A Clean, Well–Lighted Place" encourages the younger to treat the old man with deference and understanding; whatever sympathies we have for the younger waiter when the old man keeps him from leaving ebb as he reveals himself to be intolerant and slow of understanding.

In contrast to the brash young waiter, the older waiter has the wisdom to recognize that in the face of a world that is alternately dangerous or tedious all that men have is a sympathy for their fellow men. "Each night I am reluctant to close up because there may be some one who needs the cafe" (p. 331). The older waiter, then, attracts our sympathies because he, like the old man, is one "of those who do not want to go to bed . . . those who need a light for the night" (p. 331); he has faced his need for order within disorder and provides and seeks a clean and well–lighted place.

QUESTIONS

1. How are we to react to the younger waiter?

Your students will probably not warm to the older waiter until they
consider one alternative as manifested in the younger waiter. The
younger man, piqued at being made late to return home, tells the deaf
old man, "You should have killed yourself last week" (p. 330), and then
proceeds to pour the brandy until it runs over the edge of the glass and
into a saucer: he asserts that "'An old man is a nasty thing'" (p. 330) and
then, "speaking with that omission of syntax stupid people employ when
talking to drunken people or foreigners" (p. 331), refuses to serve the old
man. The young waiter, as he is preparing to leave, describes himself in
terms usually employed only by professional wrestlers: "I have confidence. I am all confidence" (p. 331).

2. How does the older waiter differ from his companion?

The answers to this question may well lead to a definition of heroism
as it is often portrayed in Hemingway. One truism you may wish to steer
them from is the notion that for Hemingway keeping a stiff upper lip in
the face of a life that is nasty, brutish, and short is the best one can ask of
men and women. In this short story, Hemingway's notion of heroism is
much closer to that of Stephen Crane: life may often be nasty, brutish,
and short—or at least without apparent meaning—but there can be solace
in a sense of community.

3. Why does the older waiter place himself with "all those who do not
want to got to bed . . . With all those who need a light for the night" (p.
331)?

We cannot say that the waiter merely fears death.

> What did he fear? It was not fear or dread. It was a nothing he
> knew too well. It was all a nothing and a man was nothng too. It
> was only that and light was all it needed and a certain cleanness
> and order. (p. 332)

Instead, he fears the nothingness and chaos that we think of now as a
commonplace in modern literature; its antidote is seldom religion, "Our
nada who art in nada, nada be thy name thy kingdom nada thy will be
nada in nada as it is in nada" (p. 332), or "youth and confidence
although those things are very beautiful"(p. 331), but rather a clean,
well–lighted café and all that it represents in this story.

But it is important to note that the waiter cannot find such a café at the end of the short story and that his malaise is with him at the end:

> After all, he said to himself, it is probably only insomnia. Many must have it. (p. 332).

We leave this story with the sense that the waiter's association of himself with the old man does not bode well. The waiter's version of the Lord's Prayer and his attempt to deal with "the nothing he knew too well" gives the exchange at the outset of the short story a new and disquieting meaning:

> "Last week he [the old man] tried to commit suicide," one waiter said.
> "Why?"
> "He was in despair."
> "What about?"
> "Nothing."
> (p. 329)

–W.R.S.

Jorge Luis Borges
The Aleph

In the Counterpoint to this story, Argentine poet, essayist, and short story writer Jorge Luis Borges muses, "I wonder why a dream or an idea should be less real than this table, for example, or why Macbeth should be less real than today's newspaper." Borges forces us to ask similar questions about the nature of reality by creating a fictional world that mixes fact and fiction in such a way it is difficult for us to tell one from the other. For example, one Borges' short story, "The Approach to al–Mu'tasim," purports to be a book review and was originally published in a collection of essays. Even Borges' friends were fooled, and one attempted to order the non–existent book reviewed. (Borges had used the name of a real publisher in London).

Borges is often credited with freeing Latin American writers from their reliance on traditional realism and with reacquainting writers from the United States with the possibilities of fancy, wit, parody, and intellectuality. This story illustrates the Borgesian style that has been so influential.

In "The Aleph" Borges juxtaposes the commonplace and the fantastic to create a magical world. In a story so packed with realistic detail that it seems to be a memoir, the narrator (whose name is Borges) recalls go-

ing into a cellar to view an Aleph, "one of the points in space containing
all points." In spite of his skepticism, the narrator does indeed see the
Aleph, a tiny iridescent sphere two or three centimeters in circumfer-
ence which contains the universe. When he stares into the Aleph he is
able to see all the events of past, present and future simultaneously, all
occupying "the same point, without superposition and without trans-
parency."

QUESTIONS

1. One term associated with Borges' work is "magical realism." What
examples can you find that illustrate a juxtapostion of the fantastic and the
commonplace?

Such juxtapostion is best illustrated by the scene in which the narrator
sees the Aleph. To view this marvel Borges descends into a most ordinary cellar "barely wider than the stairs" where "cases with bottles in
them and some canvas bags cluttered one corner" (p. 341). He lies down
on the tile floor with his head on a canvas bag folded in half and placed
"exactly in a precise spot" (p. 341) and fixes his eyes on the nineteenth
step of the stairs. Carlos then lowers the trap door, leaving Borges in total darkness where, Carlos predicts, some rodent will probably scare
him. And in that prosaic setting, Borges views the wondrous Aleph.

The vision is shattered by Carlos' "hateful, jovial voice" (p. 343), and
Borges returns from his journey into omniscience as spiteful as ever: "It
was at that instant that I conceived my revenge" (p. 343). The Aleph is
believable because it coexists with the pettiness of these two men.

2. How does Borges challenge our traditional notions of the distinction
between the real and the imaginative?

Using one of his favorite techniques, Borges purposely blurs the
distinctions between his story, a fiction, and the real world. For the first
twelve pages Borges seems to be writing a memoir. He opens by describing what seems to be the real death of a real woman: "On the incandes-
cent February morning Beatriz Viterbo died, after a death agony so
imperious it did not for a moment descend into sentimentalism or
fear..." (p. 334). He sets his narrative in real time: "Beatriz Viterbo died
in 1929. From that time on, I never let a thirtieth of April [her birthday]
go by without a visit to her house. I used to arrive there around seven–
fifteen and stay about twenty–five minutes" (p. 335). He places the events
in a believable setting: "[T]he iron billboards in the Plaza Constitucion
bore new advertisements for some brand or other of Virginia tobacco" (p.
334). He further enforces the illusion that this is a memoir by having the

narrator refer to himself as Borges, thus destroying the usual distance between author and narrator.

Borges further confuses the issue with his matter–of–fact treatment of the magical Aleph. To accomplish this, Borges the writer uses Borges the narrator to demonstrate how an ordinary person (and thus the reader) would react to such an experience. When Carlos tells the narrator of the Aleph in his dining–room cellar (p. 340), the narrator has a logical explanation: "I was astonished not to have understood until that moment that Carlos Argentino was a madman" (p. 340). Both we and the narrator dismiss Carlos as mad. Later, when the narrator goes into the cellar, neither he nor the reader expects to discover an Aleph. In fact, we share his terror that Carlos may have entombed him. And when Borges finally does introduce the Aleph, the narrator reports his amazing experience as calmly as he describes the bottles and bags in the corner. "I closed my eyes; opened them. Then I saw the Aleph" (p. 341). The narrator never seems to be surprised by his experience or worried that we may doubt his truthfulness or his emotional stability. His only con-cern is that language is inadequate to "transmit to others the infinite Aleph" (p. 341). His focus becomes ours, and we forget to question the existence of the Aleph.

The fate of the Aleph also challenges our usual notions about reality. After convincing us that the Aleph exists (at least within the confines of this story) and can be seen by Carlos and Borges, the narrator calmly suggests that it has been destroyed. He tells us that the building in the Calle Garay was demolished and that Carlos' fortunate pen is "no longer benumbed by the Aleph" (p. 343). The logic of the real world compels us to challenge his assertion: Whether the Aleph is real or imaginary, it should be indestructible. If the Aleph is imaginary and exists only in the minds of the two men, it should survive the destruction of the building. And if the Aleph is what it's supposed to be—"the inconceivable universe"—it should be safe from bulldozers. To add to our bewilderment, the narrator declares that he has subsequently decided that the Aleph in Calle Garay was a false Aleph (p. 344) (personally, I can't understand how one could distinguish between a false and a true Aleph), and he speculates that the true Aleph exists within a stone column in the Mosque of Amr in Cairo where it is, of course, invisible. Once we find ourselves wondering which Aleph is "real," Borges has succeeded in destroying our preconceptions about reality.

3. How does the reliability of the narrator affect our reading of the story?

Yet another technique employed by Borges to force us to question the reality of the Aleph is his use of an unreliable narrator. Our narrator is hardly the average man on the street. [You might ask your students to compare the narrator of this story with the narrator of "The Fall of the

House of Usher."] Borges the narrator is an intelligent, highly educated writer who seems to have read everything, even Michael Drayton's *Poly-Olbion*. He is also a man obsessed with an unnatural passion for a dead woman. In fact, he seems to feel that Beatriz's death has improved his relationship with her. "[N]ow that she was dead, I could consecrate myself to her memory, without hope but also without humiliation" (p. 334). The narrator doubts the emotional stability of both Beatriz and her cousin Carlos (p. 340), and yet he chooses to devote himself to her and associate with him, hardly the acts of a rational man.

We have reason to question his veracity as well as his sanity. We learn that he has an enormous ego ("[I]ncredibly, my book *The Cards of the Cardsharp* did not get a single vote [for the National Prizes for Literature]"—p. 343). We realize that he lies without compunction. (He clearly enjoys telling us how thoroughly he deceived Carlos by promising to ask Alvaro to write the prologue to Carlos' book—p. 339.) We know that he is vindictive. (He refuses to admit to Carlos that he did see the Aleph; instead he suggests that Carlos needs a quiet rest in the country—p. 343.)

If the narrator is indeed a dishonest lunatic, his account of the Aleph can be interpreted in any number of ways: (1) He is telling what he believes to be the truth, but his vision of the Aleph was a delusion. (2) He invents the story of the Aleph to explain why Carlos wins the literary award. (3) He actually saw the Aleph and described it accurately, but he later invented the postscript (which suggests that the Aleph in the Calle Garay is false). The possibilities are infinite.

–M.R.D.

John Steinbeck
The Chrysanthemums

John Steinbeck is better known for his novels than for his short stories, and his works are more frequently concerned with the comradeship of men than with relationships between men and women. In "The Chrysanthemums," however, Steinbeck uses the short story form to focus on the problems faced by a woman who finds traditional female roles far too constricting.

Throughout Steinbeck's career he sympathized with and wrote about the oppressed. In his novel *The Grapes of Wrath* he told the story of the Joad family, Oklahoma farmers who lost their farm during the thirties and became migrant farm workers in California. And in *Of Mice and Men* he wrote about Lennie, a feeble-minded farmhand who could not survive in our society. So it is not surprising that Steinbeck would write about Elisa, a woman whose strength and energy far exceed the demands of her role. The story takes place in the Salinas Valley of California during the 1930s. As the childless wife of a rancher, Elisa finds only one outlet for her creative energy—her chrysanthemums.

There is an appropriate starkness about the whole story. The setting is a foggy winter day in the Salinas Valley. The plot is simple; there are only two major events, and both occur within a matter of hours. The three characters are developed through the physical descriptions and sparse dialogue. The point of view is essentially objective. Steinbeck does not offer answers, but his close observation of Elisa illuminates the problem that can occur when people are matched with roles on the basis of gender rather than ability.

QUESTIONS

1. How does Steinbeck use the details of setting to further the development of his characters?

Steinbeck is frequently praised for his skillful use of setting to enhance emotional effect, and he is particularly successful when his stories are set in his birthplace, the Salinas Valley of northern California.

This story opens with a description of the valley when it is closed off by the "high grey–flannel fog of winter." Steinbeck writes, "On every side it sat like a lid on the mountains and made of the great valley a closed pot." When we are later introduced to Elisa, the strong, energetic woman whose life is so limited by society's expectations for women, we realize how appropriate the domestic image of the closed pot is. Elisa too is shut in. But the statement that "It was a time of quiet and of waiting" suggests that Elisa may not be permanently reconciled to her condition as a shut–in.

The description of Elisa's house further suggests the nature of her dilemma. "Behind her stood the neat white farm house with the red geraniums close–banked around it as high as the windows. It was a hard–swept looking little house, with hard–polished windows, and a clean mud–mat on the front steps" (p. 346). Housekeeping is obviously not a sufficient challenge for Elisa. If her house is this clean early in the afternoon, how is she to fill the rest of her day?

If the house symbolizes the narrowness of Elisa's day–to–day existence, her chrysanthemums show her potential. As her husband remarks, "Some of those yellow chrysanthemums you had this year were ten inches across. I wish you'd work in the orchard and raise some apples that big" (p. 347).

In contrast to the symbols of Elisa's neat and orderly world are the images associated with the tinker. His "crazy, loose jointed" wagon has "crooked old wheels" and the round canvas top over the wagon is labeled with "clumsy, crooked letters" (p. 348). When he climbs out of the wagon his horse and donkey "droop like unwatered flowers" (p. 348).

2. Is Elisa developed into a believable person?

Although I like this story immensely, I have never found Elisa as real as, for example, Sylvia, the young girl who narrates Toni Cade Bambara's "The Lesson." When I finish reading "The Lesson," I find myself wondering what will happen to Sylvia as she grows up. When I finish "The Chrysanthemums," I wonder what Steinbeck meant by that final scene, but I don't think about Elisa as a person who continues to exist beyond the boundaries of the story.

One reason the reader is less likely to become as involved with Elisa is the point of view Steinbeck chooses. Technically, the point of view could be described as third person, limited to the thoughts of a single character—Elisa. But we are allowed so few glimpses into Elisa's head that the feel of the story is like objective narration. We are more Elisa's observers than her confidants. We know that she sees the dark speck in the road, that she realizes the tinker threw out the chrysanthemum seedlings, and that she understands that he couldn't throw them off the road because he wanted to keep the pot. But Steinbeck does not directly tell the reader what she thinks or how she feels at that moment.

Some of the dialogue reminds us that Elisa is a character rather than a person. The conversation between Elisa and her husband (p. 347) is particularly wooden and stilted. It seems to be there solely for the purpose of advancing the plot, and it reveals little if anything about Elisa's and Henry's personalities or about their relationship. "It's good to eat away from home" is reminiscent of the worst of Hemingway. In contrast, you might note the lively dialogue in "The Tip–Top Club." Not only does the conversation tell us a great deal about each speaker, but Keillor captures the idiosyncracies of each person's speech so accurately that we can immediately identify the speaker.

The final problem with Elisa as a fully realized character is that at times Steinbeck makes us so aware of Elisa's symbolic role that we lose sight of her as a particular woman. During the conversation with the tinker, for instance, there is a poignant moment when Elisa, who is kneeling on the ground, reaches toward him, almost touches the leg of his trousers but then drops her hand. It's a powerful scene, but then Steinbeck spoils it by adding, "She crouched low like a fawning dog" (p. 351). By reminding us of Elisa the symbol, the simile somehow destroys our visual image of Elisa the person.

3. What forces operate to confine Elisa to a traditional female role?

Elisa apparently believes that certain activities are off limits for women. When she talks with the tinker about his travels she says, "It must be very nice. I wish women could do such things" (p. 351). We see that in a sense she is limited by her own acceptance of the traditional view, but the real question is why she accepts that view.

Steinbeck is writing a short story, not an essay, and he doesn't give any clear answers to this question. One thing we can say with certainty is that Elisa is not restricted by physical weakness. She is described in terms more typically associated with masculinity than with femininity: "Her face was lean and strong...." "Her face was eager and mature and handsome; even her work with the scissors was over–eager, over–powerful" (p. 346).

Nor is she restricted by her husband, Henry, at least not directly. Henry is hardly a tyrannical ruler of the household. He may meet with the two men in business suits to sell cattle, but he immediately goes to Elisa to report the transaction (p. 347). He recognizes and appreciates both her talent and her strength. In one scene he actually encourages her to pursue a traditionally male occupation. After commenting on her ability to grow ten–inch chrysanthemums, he tells her that he wishes she would work in the orchard and raise some apples that big (p. 347). In a later scene he tells her that she looks "nice" and defines "nice" as "strong enough to break a calf over your knee, happy enough to eat it like a watermelon" (p. 353).

At other times Henry's suggestions that she depart from the norm are tentative. For example, he "puts on his joking tone" before he asks, "How'd you like to go to the fights?" And when she replies that she wouldn't like fights, he quickly explains that he was "Just fooling" (p. 347). Later, when Elisa tells him that she has read that the fighters "break noses, and blood runs down their chests," he seems shocked. He tells her, "I don't think you'd like it, but I'll take you if you really want to go" (p. 354). Naturally, she declines. Although Henry does not insist that she play a feminine role, neither is he courageous enough to help her resist societal expectations.

Elisa's encounter with the tinker illustrates two ways in which society attempts to keep women in their place. One is direct. The tinker warns that a life like his "ain't the right kind of a life for a woman," that it "would be a lonely life for a woman,...and a scarey life, too, with animals creeping under the wagon all night" (pp. 351–352). The direct threat fails. Elisa is challenged rather than frightened, and she emerges from the encounter stronger than ever.

But what the tinker fails to achieve directly, he accomplishes indirectly. After Elisa tells him that she has no work for him, he begins a conversation about her chrysanthemums. "The irritation and resistance melted from Elisa's face" (p. 349). He recognizes her vulnerability, flat ters her by asking for chrysanthemum seeds for "a lady down the road a piece," and succeeds in getting a job mending an old pan. Elisa does not realize that she has been manipulated until she sees that the chrysanthemum shoots have been dumped out in the middle of the road. She feels hurt, disappointed, rejected, foolish, and angry. For a moment she considers fighting back, at least vicariously, by attending a fight "where the men hurt each other...." But she rejects that response as inappropriate for a woman and consoles herself by deciding to have wine with dinner and by "crying weakly—like an old woman" (p. 354).

Through the tinker, society convinces Elisa that the qualities encouraged in women—trust, compassion, concern for others—make the male-dominated world too dangerous for her or for any woman. (Susan Brownmiller would say that those qualities are encouraged in women precisely because they make it difficult if not impossible for women to succeed.) In effect, some of Elisa's most admirable characteristics have been used to defeat her. Had she not been an unsuspecting and generous person, she would not have been deceived. At the end of the story she seems to be broken in spirit. It is as if she must admit to herself that she needs her husband to protect her from the real world as surely as she needs a wire fence to protect her flower garden from cattle and dogs and chickens.

The view presented by the story is bleak. Elisa seems to have only two options: She can continue to endure the frustration inherent in a role that offers no significant challenges or she can attempt to succeed in the world of men by becoming as callous as the tinker.

4. What does the story tell us about Steinbeck's opinion of the significance of work?

Steinbeck seems to believe that challenging work is something all human beings want and need. The lack of an occupation that is sufficiently rewarding seems to be the primary cause of Elisa's dissatisfaction. Because she has no children (so far as we know), motherhood, the one acceptable female role that might have afforded an outlet for all her creativity and energy, is closed to her, and she has no other occupation that is valued by the rest of the world. At the beginning of the story we see that Elisa derives a great deal of pleasure from her flower garden. Steinbeck uses images of strength to portray her when she is working with her chrysanthemums. But the carefully nurtured illusion that growing chrysanthemums is significant is shattered when the tinker carelessly discards the shoots she had entrusted to him. Without the illusion, Elisa suddenly becomes old and weak.

Another illustration of this point occurs when the tinker mends the pan Elisa gives him. Earlier the tinker is a rather pitiful creature, begging for work, his voice taking on a "whining undertone" (p. 349). But when Elisa hands him the saucepan, his manner changes. "He became professional....His mouth grew sure and knowing. At a difficult part of the work he sucked his under–lip" (p. 351). In this story—for both men and women—work is essential for human dignity.

–M.R.D.

Zora Neale Hurston
Spunk

Zora Neale Hurston was at various times a "maid, manicurist, raconteur, collector of folklore, student of voodoo, and the most competent female Afro–American author of her generation" (Darwin T. Turner in the Preface to Hurston's autobiography, *Dust Tracks on a Road*). Her interests in folklore and voodoo extended to her studies under Franz Boas, sometimes considered the father of modern anthropology.

Those interests are certainly manifested in "Spunk," a short story that suggests the operation of sympathetic magic and uses one of the oldest of storylines (and situations). Given the nature of her studies, it should come as no surprise that Hurston's work is filled with elements of folklore. If your students have the sense that they have heard this story—or ones like it—they probably have. It and stories like it are told around campfires or in darkened rooms all the time.

In all of her most–read works, Hurston presents characters caught up in elemental struggles, either with their own passions or those of others. Her characters have the hottest rages, the most primal loves and lusts, the deepest griefs, the profoundest humiliations. In this short story, Joe Kanty, Lena Kanty, and Spunk Banks are caught up in the conventional triangle with predictable results—Joe, overpowered by jealousy, and Lena and Spunk, overpowered by their love for each other, are bound to clash.

QUESTIONS

1. Who or what kills Spunk Banks?

There are a number of reasonable answers here. The simplest is that this is a ghost story, and that Spunk Banks is correct as he spits out his life on a sawdust pile. If this is a ghost story, then Joe Kanty's spirit, in revenge for all that Spunk had done to him in life, has pushed Spunk into the sawblade. Spunk is killed by a blade, just as Joe had intended in life. If this is a ghost story, and if we accept the workings of the supernatural as they are presented in the short story, then it is Joe who shows spunk. As Walter says,

'Lookit whut he done; took a razor an' went out to fight a man he knowed toted a gun an' wuz a crack shot, too,' nother thing Joe wuz skeered of Spunk, skeered plumb stiff! But he went jes' the same. It took him a long time to get his nerve up. Tain't nothin' for Spunk to fight when he ain't skeered of nothin'. Now, Joe's done come back to have it out wid the man that's got all he ever had. Y'all know Joe ain't never had nothin' nor wanted nothin' besides Lena. It musta been a h'ant cause ain't nobody never seen no black bob–cat.' (p. 358)

If we give credence to the notion that Joe has returned from the grave to finish off what he had begun with a larger, better–armed opponent, then this is spunk—with a vengeance.

But of course the ambiguities here allow for other interpretations. If one takes into account Hurston's interest in anthropology and voodoo, then it is perhaps more likely that she is presenting here a man whose conscience forces him into hallucinations and death. A man of simple beliefs who has done wrong and expects retribution is likely to seek his own punishment, and one could argue plausibly that this is the case with Spunk. If Spunk's guilt gradually forces him from the hallucination of the black bob–cat to believing that his nemesis has returned and pushed him into the sawblade, then this indirect study of his psyche makes the title fitting and proper.

2. How does Hurston's depiction of Elijah affect our perception of what happens in "Spunk"?

I think Hurston throughout the tale sets Elijah up as an unreliable narrator and thus undercuts the supernatural elements in the short story. At the outset, Elijah expresses admiration for a bold adulterer:

'But that's one thing Ah likes about Spunk Banks—he ain't skeered of nothin' on God's green footstool— *nothin'*! He rides that log down at saw–mill jus' like he struts' 'round wid another man's wife—jus' don't give a kitty. When Tes' Miller got cut to giblets on that circle–saw, Spunk steps right up and starts ridin'. The rest of us was skeered to go near it.' (p. 355)

As it turns out, of course, Spunk is afraid of some things, though they may not be of God's green footstool.

Elijah goads Joe Kanty into finally taking action against Spunk; he inquires about Joe's marriage and then approves when Joe promises violence: "Talkin' like a man, Joe.' Course that's *yo* family affairs, but Ah like to see grit in anybody" (p. 356). His response to "Spunk will sho' kill him" is pure sophistry: "Spunk wouldn't shoot no unarmed man" (p. 356). After all, Joe *is* armed. Elijah's admiration for Spunk is based entirely on Spunk's bravado and insistence on getting what he wants; his disdain for "that rabbit–footed colored man" is based on his assumption of Joe's cowardice.

It is Elijah—who enjoys considerable influence around the store—who tells (without corroboraton) the stories of Spunk's encounters with the bobcat and the sawblade. A man given to stirring up the conflict between Joe and Spunk may not be able to resist the sort of embellishments that local legends are made of.

3. How effective is Hurston's use of dialect?

In the first place, the dialect is perfectly appropriate to the setting and characters. There is little doubt that the story is set in the deep South in an area where the supernatural is believed to intervene in human affairs and where Spunk could be "laid . . . on the sawdust pile with his face to the East so's he could die easy" (p. 359). In the second place, the dialect rings true in every instance; it is plain that Hurston has an ear for the cadences of southern speech. Fiction writers who employ dialect tell us that it is extraordinarily difficult to maintain it convincingly over an entire work; Hurston seems to have succeeded, for the speech in "Spunk" is realistic and not once gets in the way of our understanding of her work. Your class may be interested in comparing Hurston's treatment of dialect with that of Eudora Welty in "Livvie" or Ralph Ellison in "Did You Ever Dream Lucky?"

–W.R.S.

Isaac Bashevis Singer
Gimpel the Fool

Isaac Bashevis Singer was born in Radzymin, Poland, in 1904 and moved to the United States in 1935. His father was a Hassidic rabbi, and both of his grandfathers were rabbis. As a youth Singer prepared to follow the rabbinical tradition, studying the Torah, the Talmud, the Cabala, and other religious writings.

Although Singer later rejected his family's orthodox views and chose to become a secular writer, he never lost his faith.

Singer's writing is difficult to categorize. He is an American writer who writes all of his stories in Yiddish, a language he recognizes as "dying from day to day." He lives in New York City, but sets his stories in the nineteenth–and early twentieth–century *shtetls* and city ghettos of Poland, communities that were destroyed by Hitler. He explores the dilemma of modern man struggling to find meaning in life, but he refuses to plumb the subconscious depths of his characters' minds. Singer once remarked, "When I tell a story, I tell a story. I don't try to discuss, criticize, or analyze my characters."

"Gimpel the Fool" is basically a Jewish saint's life. Gimpel is a simple baker who chooses to trust people. As a result everyone in town delights in deceiving him, even his wife, who confesses on her deathbed that not one of their six children is his. One night the Spirit of Evil comes to Gimpel and tempts him to avenge himself by deceiving the townspeople. The spirit suggests that Gimpel pour urine in the bread dough. "Let the sages of Frampole eat filth," he urges. Instead, Gimpel follows the advice a rabbi had once given him: "It is written, better to be a fool all your days than for one hour to be evil" (p. 362).

QUESTIONS

1. How does this story differ from others in which the real and the fantastic are mingled?

You might ask your students to compare this story with Kafka's "Metamorphosis," Borges' "The Aleph," or García Márquez's "A Very Old Man with Enormous Wings." In each of those stories the author jars us by juxtaposing the mundane and the incredible. In the first an ordinary salesman is transformed into a giant insect; in the second a man lies down on a cellar floor, stares up at the nineteenth step above him and sees the Aleph, a tiny sphere that contains the universe; in the third an angel falls to earth and is penned up in a chicken coop. In each story the "real" characters clearly recognize the incredible event as an anomaly.

In "Gimpel the Fool," however, the real and the fantastic are not so easily distinguished. Gimpel lives in a small Polish village, Frampole, that is much like the towns Singer knew in his childhood, and he describes the village and its earthy inhabitants with believable detail. For example, Gimpel recalls his first visit to the home of his future wife:

> I went to the clay house, which was built on sand.... I entered the house. Lines were strung from wall to wall and clothes were drying. Barefoot she stood by the tub, doing the wash. She was dressed in a worn hand–me–down gown of plush. She had her hair put up in braids and pinned across her head. It took my breath away, almost, the reek of it all (pp. 362–363).

In most ways the people of Frampole are familiar to us. They go to work everyday, they sing and dance at weddings, and they meddle in their neighbors' lives; they could be comfortable in any American neighborhood—except that they believe the world is inhabited by spirits.

The villagers know that "you don't whistle at night because it brings the demons out" (p. 368). And they are unruffled by events that would cause most of us to cut back on caffeine. When the Spirit of Evil appears to Gimpel and asks, "Why do you sleep?" Gimpel retorts, "What should I be doing? Eating *kreplach*?" Yet somehow the Spirit of Evil, a being "with a goatish beard and horn, long–toothed and with a tail" (p. 370), who urges Gimpel to seek revenge, seems more probable than Gimpel, a to tally good man.

2. How does the view of human motives and values presented by this story differ from what we learn in our society?

Our society teaches that it is difficult, if not impossible, to understand or judge human actions. Most of us agree that human motivation is incredibly complicated, that before we can explain why a person makes a particular decision, we need to know as much as possible about her chromosomes, her potty training and, perhaps, her astrological sign. Our approach to values is equally complex. Most of us are more comfortable with situational ethics, moral relativism, and values clarification than with concepts such as good and evil.

In striking contrast to that view, Singer presents a world where people are expected to recognize good and evil and to choose the good, which seems to be defined as that which harms no one. Gimpel perceives life as a series of either–or choices: He can believe people or he can distrust them; he can reject his son or he can celebrate his birth with the appropriate ceremonies; he can divorce his wife or he can treat her as a loving husband should; he can feed the town filth or he can bury the bread he defiled. He doesn't entertain the possibility of compromise. He would not, for example, decide to provide his son with food and shelter but deny him love.

In most instances, Gimpel knows what is right, but when he has doubts, he turns to his rabbi, not his analyst. Invariably Gimpel chooses the course dictated by love and by his concern for the welfare of others. When the oven bursts in the bakery one night and Gimpel returns home unexpectedly, he finds a man sleeping beside his wife. He is tempted to respond as most men would. "Another in my place would have made an uproar, and enough noise to rouse the whole town, but the thought occurred to me that I might wake the child. A little thing like that— why frighten a swallow, I thought" (p. 366). Gimpel quietly returns to the bakery. If your students have read the other saint's life in this collection, Flaubert's "The Legend of St. Julian," you might remind them of Julian's response to similar circumstances. When Julian discovers a man and woman sleeping in his bed, he murders both without pausing to notice that they are his parents.

Your students are likely to be amused, dismayed, or perplexed by Gimpel's approach to life. They are, after all, involved in an educational process that encourages them to question every assumption and to examine issues from multiple perspectives. For us the virtuous person is one who doubts the self–evident; Singer seems to be defining the virtuous person as one who chooses to believe the incredible.

It is difficult to know what Singer wants us to make of this story. Singer insists that his stories are not meant to teach or preach, merely to entertain. He explains, "Literature stirs the mind; it makes you think about a million things, but it does not lead you."

3. What does Singer accomplish by having Gimpel tell his own story?

If Singer had told the story from the perspective of anyone other than Gimpel, we would probably agree with the townspeople who consider him a fool. Our judgment that Gimpel is saint rather than fool is based, at least in part, on our realization that Gimpel knows that others deceive him but he nonetheless chooses to trust rather than doubt. Gimpel's philosophy is based on his profound insight that cynicism is ultimately self–destructive: "I resolved that I would always believe what I was told. What's the good of *not* believing? Today it's your wife you won't believe in; tomorrow it's God himself you won't take stock in" (p. 367).

To illustrate the effect of this particular point of view, you might ask your students to write a 150–word character sketch of Gimpel as he might have been described by any other character in the story. Elka, while living, would undoubtedly characterize Gimpel as a fool. She dies with a smile on her lips, and Gimpel imagines her saying, "I deceived Gimpel. That was the meaning of my brief life. After her death, however, Elka's assessment of him changes dramatically. The Elka whose face is turning black has redefined the word "fool." She appears to Gimpel and chastises him for defiling the bread. "You fool! Because I was false is everything else false too?" (p. 371).

Other viewpoints your students might want to explore are those of Gimpel's children (Gimpel divides his fortune among them, announces, "I saw your mother tonight. She's turning black, poor thing," and departs from Frampole—p. 371), the apprentice (He has a lengthy affair with Gimpel's wife, and later, when he sees Gimpel burying the bread, grows "pale as a corpse"—p. 371), and the rabbi (Surely Gimpel is the only person who actually lives by the precepts the rabbi teaches.).

–M.R.D.

Richard Wright
The Library Card

This work will no doubt cause difficulties for the teacher of fiction because "The Library Card" is excerpted from Wright's autobiographical *Black Boy*, its membership in the fiction club could be questioned. You may wish to have your students determine just how autobiography differs from "straight" fiction; how does Wright handle exposition, characterization, and setting?; do we have different expectations of autobiography than we have for fiction?

The short biography of Wright at the back of *The Riverside Anthology* is must reading for students unfamiliar with his life and work. Wright's ideology informs his work to such an extent that one cannot fully understand the latter without some knowledge of the former. But that is not to say that *Black Boy* is only a political document and that the narrator of "The Library Card" is a black Everyman suffering at the hands of a white supremacist culture, as worthy a subject as that might be. "The Library Card" is also the story of artistic development, and as Warren French has pointed out in *The Black American Writer: Fiction*,

> *Black Boy* is an outstanding account of a particularly sensitive type of artistic personality striving for identity, but it is as erroneous to read it as an account of the representative Negro experience as it would be to read Winston Churchill's memoirs as an account of the representative British schoolboy's "making his way."

QUESTIONS

1. Does "The Library Card" seem to you like genuine autobiography, that is, true to the life of the writer? Why or why not?

This question cannot be answered with any certitude. Wright, as far as I know, never spoke to the issue of the "accuracy" of *Black Boy*, and even if he did, authors are usually unreliable in such matters. I think, though, that whether or not the events are true is ultimately irrelevant; the fact is that the work is "true" in the sense that its depiction of the development of a sensibility is finely drawn and—to make my argument perfectly circular—rings true. It *is* the portrait of an artist as a young man. If it is autobiography, one could argue that it cannot be fiction, but any who have attempted autobiography can testify that the genre demands a kind of invention almost indistinguishable from that demanded of the writer of short stories. If it is not entirely autobiography, then portions of it must be fictional or borrowed, but who can tell what really happened and what is invented?

2. How does autobiography differ from fiction?

The lines between autobiography and fiction have always been blurry; fictions like *Clarissa* and *Great Expectations* "profess" to be a type of auto-biography.

It might be useful here to compare Wright's "The Library Card" to Charlotte Perkins Gilman's "The Yellow Wallpaper." Few of us, if we knew nothing of Gilman, would suspect at first reading that her story of madness was to any extent autobiographical. As it turns out, the halluci-nations, which strike most of us as unrealistic Gothic elements of the story, might have been drawn from the personal experience of the au-thor, who underwent the same type of treatment and presumably suffered the same symptoms as her protagonist and narrator. In short, whether or not "The Library Card" or "The Yellow Wallpaper" are autobio-graphical has little to do with our appreciation of the works—unless we are interested in Wright's and Gilman's lives. "The Library Card," like the autobiographical "The Yellow Wallpaper," is indistinguishable (for the most part) from "conventional" fiction narrated from first–person point of view. I say for the most part because in some instances the authors of stories narrated from first person point of view go to some pains to establish the unreliability of the narrator; it seems that the writer of an autobiography, if he or she is to fulfill the aim of autobiography—telling a life story—must maintain that credibility usually bestowed automatically to the autobiographer at all costs or wander into the neither–fish–nor–fowl world of the autobiographical novel.

3. Does Wright's polemicism dilute the force of "The Library Card"?

This question requires such a personal and potentially painful answer that few of your students may be inclined to answer it. Those inclined to say "yes" might well be reminded of this short story's similarity to Or-well's *1984*. In Wright's work, the narrator's fears of borrowing a li-brary card are much like Winston Smith's fears of doublethink; both characters fear reprisal from a monolithic and terrifying institu-tion/government.

Wright's fears that as a result of his reading he would be "filled with bookish notions, [and] act in a manner that would make the whites dis-like me" are much like Winston Smith's paranoia at reading what he should not read. "Dislike" is a euphemism; in an office populated with "Kluxers and sympathizers" (p. 374) one can imagine that the dislike of the whites in his office might have painful or deadly consequences—at the very least it could mean the loss of his livelihood. Wright's story, like Orwell's novel, is charged politically; his concern for individual freedom is stated no less forcefully than Orwell's. Students powerfully affected by the disutopian bleakness of Orwell's *1984* ought to find that

Wright's vision of the American south—where some people need to be careful what they read and think—is disturbingly familiar and that it quite literally hits closer to home.

Those students inclined to answer "no" might be jogged to respond to Howard Mumford Jones' criticism of *Black Boy* as theme–ridden melodrama. Jones claims that Wright "emphasizes an endless array of wrongs, but . . . he minimizes the development of his own personality. Jones is not alone in this criticism. Wright's work is avowedly autobiographical, and so "should be true"; Ellison, for example, says in the counterpoint that "there is more complexity in life" (p. 381) than Wright demonstrates in this work.

–W.R.S.

Eudora Welty
Livvie

This short story will seem to some of your students an extended poem in prose. Here, as in many of her works, Welty overwhelms us with the sensuousness of her imagery. It should come as no surprise to your students that Eudora Welty was a photographer; her visual sense gives this story at once a wealth of detail and an otherworldly quality.

In "Livvie" there is an odd mixture of the homely and the exotic. The house contains a "jelly glass with pretty hen feathers in it"; it is guarded by crepe–myrtle trees with bottles in the branches to ward off evil spirits. In fact, Solomon's dwelling at first glance is perfectly unremarkable—but it is a place where time seems to be slowed down. The old man himself lives without sustenance, lost in dreams and holding his watch, while his wife looks on:

> To look at him dreaming of her when he might be going to die frightened her a little, as if he might carry her with him that way . . . (p. 386)

Your students might be reminded of any number of narratives—most of them produced in the middle ages or Renaissance or set in those periods—that employ the same motif. In *The Merchant's Tale*, for instance, an old man takes a young wife and, for possessiveness' sake, encloses her in a garden. This December–May arrangement is usually given comic treatment, but in "Livvie" Welty does something a bit different. Despite the infectious exuberance of Cash McCord and the sense that Livvie is about to be freed from an unnatural arrangement, we should not forget that in this short story we have a young wife ripe for infidelity and a lover with his fist poised over a helpless and sleeping old man.

QUESTIONS

1. What change in the household of Solomon is signaled by the coming of Miss Baby Marie?

Though Livvie feels the stirrings of spring and grows restive in her captivity before her arrival, Miss Baby Marie brings with her a type of sophistication, or at least a kind of artifice that Livvie, in the static of Solomon's home, must be unfamiliar with. (Note, for instance, that Miss Baby Marie denies that her lipstick has "natural" ingredients like chinaberry flowers. If the saleswoman's visit demonstrates nothing else to us, it shows us how profoundly ignorant Livvie is of the ways of the world outside the house by the Natchez trace. She has no money—but there is a hint that Miss Baby Marie helps her see how it might be acquired. Miss Baby Marie, after being told that Solomon holds the purse strings in the house, asks to see the old man:

> They looked at him awhile so fast asleep, and then all at once they looked at each other. Somehow that was as if they had a secret, for he had never stirred...
> "Well! I'd certainly like to leave you with a lipstick!" said Miss Baby Marie vivaciously. She smiled in the door.
> "Lady, but I told you I don't have no money, and never did have."
> "And never will?" In the air and all around, like a bright halo around the white lady's nodding head, it was a true spring day . . . Livvie stood watching her go, and all the time she felt her heart beating in her left side. She touched the place with her hand. It seemed as if her heart beat and her whole face flamed from the pulsing color of her lips. She went to sit by Solomon and when he opened his eyes he could not see a change in her. "He's fixin' to die," she said inside. That was the secret. (p. 388)

There is more than a trace of wish–fulfillment in this passage; it is as if the visit of Miss Baby Marie has finally awakened Livvie to her imprisonment and her womanhood—and to the idea of removing the impediment to her living a complete life. Livvie touches her rouged lips, then her heart, and then announces, with little reason to believe it to be so, that Solomon is near death. Within two paragraphs Cash enters the short story.

2. Would you describe this story as realistic?

Your students, I suspect, will insist, given the insistence on almost photographic detail in this short story, that this is realism with a vengeance. How, then, do they account for the sense of reverie one gets from this short story? Perhaps the two directions the reader is tugged in can be accounted for by Welty's manipulation of point of view. When the perspective is purely dramatic or cinematic (or nearly so) the description is detailed but matter–of–fact:

> Going through that room and on to the kitchen, there was a big wood stove and a big round table always with a wet top and with the knives and forks in one jelly glass and the spoons in another, and a cut–glass vinegar bottle between, and going out from those, many shallow dishes of pickled peaches, fig preserves, watermelon pickles and blackberry jam always sitting there. The churn sat in the sun, the doors of the safe were always both shut, and there were four baited mouse–traps in the kitchen, one in every corner.
> (p. 383)

But when the narration becomes third person omniscient and we are privy to Livvie's thoughts, the world shimmers and becomes another place entirely.

> One day, climbing up the high bank, she had found a graveyard without a church, with ribbon–grass growing about the foot of an angel (she had climbed up because she thought she saw angel wings), and in the sun, trees shining like burning flames through the great caterpillar nets which enclosed them. Scarey thistles stood looking like the prophets in the Bible in Solomon's house. Indian paint brushes grew over her head, and the mourning dove made the only sound in the world. (p. 384)

We can see in this passage a different and highly imaginative sensibility at work; Livvie, as one might expect of someone deprived of "ordinary" stimuli, lives in a vividly painted world of her own making.

But we cannot attribute this otherworldly quality entirely to Livvie's fancy. It is also true that the circumstances contribute to our sense that we are dealing with a story much like that of Tennyson's "The Lady of Shalott," in which a character is held in a kind of suspended animation while the world wheels on around her. Livvie cooks and cares for Solomon, moving like a ghost around the house so that he will not be disturbed; the symbolism of his holding the watch and keeping her and the rest of his possessions out of time and out of touch with the rest of humanity will be lost on few of your students.

3. Are we to mourn Livvie's emancipation and Solomon's death?

I think this is liable to polarize your class into two camps. On the one hand, I suspect you'll find those students who feel that Solomon's temple is violated first by Miss Baby Marie, then Cash McCord. Cash is part peacock ("he wore a luminous baby–pink satin shirt . . . [a] wide platter–shaped round hat, the color of a plum(p. 389), part satyr ("then there was a noise like a hoof pawing the floor" (p. 390), part thief ("Cash must have stolen the money, stolen it from Solomon" (p. 390)), and part destroyer ("He even picked up a stone and sailed it into the bottle trees"(p. 390)). When Solomon says that "Young ones can't wait" (p. 392), he is pointing to the thoughtlessness and impulsiveness of youth, which can destroy a man's life–work and despoil his most valuable possessions.

Others will point out that Livvie is being kept from herself until she is freed by Miss Baby Marie, Cash McCord, and her own instincts. The December–May arrangement between Solomon and Livvie is unnatural; Solomon's death—since all must die—a good thing in that Livvie is no longer wasted on a comatose but still oddly domineering old man. And even he seems to recognize the unnaturalness of their arrangement and to forgive her and to sanction her awakening in his dying words:

> God forgive Solomon for sins great and small. God forgive Solomon for carrying away too young girl for wife and keeping her away from her people and from all the young people would clamor for her back. (p. 392)

                                                              –W.R.S.

Marguerite Yourcenar
How Wang–Fo Was Saved

"How Wang–Fo Was Saved," a Taoist fable translated and "freely developed" by Marguerite Yourcenar, is great fun to read. In addition, the story raises important questions about the power and purpose of art, questions that invite comparison with Robert Browning's "Fra Lippo Lippi," John Keats' "Ode on a Grecian Urn," and William Butler Yeats' "Sailing to Byzantium."

Wang–Fo is an artist, an old man who can "seize the dawn and capture the dusk." He and his disciple Ling renounce fame and fortune to wander through the Kingdom of Han exchanging paintings for rations of boiled millet. It is rumored that Wang–Fo has "the power to bring his paintings to life by adding a last touch of color to their eyes." One day Wang–Fo and Ling are arrested and brought before the Emperor to be punished for creating a world so much more beautiful than the Kingdom of Han that the Emperor is "filled with disgust at everything he owns,

and with desire for everything he shall never possess." The Emperor
tells Wang–Fo that he is going to burn out his eyes and cut off his hands,
but first Wang–Fo must complete an unfinished painting of the sea. Ling
attempts to save Wang–Fo but is beheaded. Then as Wang–Fo calmly
begins to "spread wide strokes of blue onto the unfinished sea," the
waters of that sea rise in the imperial palace and submerge the Emperor
and his courtiers. Ling, wearing a strange red scarf around his neck,
rows a wooden boat out of the painting. Ling helps Wang–Fo into the
boat, and they "vanish forever on the jade–blue sea that Wang–Fo had
just created."

Those of your students who have read Marguerite Yourcenar's historical novel *Memoirs of Hadrian* may be surprised by her shift from realistic
novel to fantastic tale. Different though the genres are, both works explore attitudes toward death. The novel, an account of Hadrian's final
months, sets out Hadrian's stoical acceptance of his impending death. In
the story Wang–Fo, who has just seen his disciple killed and believes he
is soon to be blinded and maimed, can so lose himself in his work that
he fails to notice the water rising about him.

QUESTIONS

1. Is Wang–Fo's talent a blessing or a curse for him? Explain.

Wang–Fo's artistic vision, like King Midas' touch, seems to be both
curse and blessing. Both men are granted the power to change the
world: Everything Midas touches turns to gold; everything Wang–Fo
looks upon is transformed into art. Such extraordinary power makes it
impossible for either man to experience the ordinary pleasures of life:
Midas cannot enjoy the embrace of his golden daughter; Wang–Fo cannot enjoy love or friendship because, for him, people are merely colors
and shapes to be captured on silk.

Consequently, Wang–Fo's only response to people is aesthetic. When
Ling's wife hangs herself, Wang–Fo does not feel sorrow; instead, he is
fascinated by the color of her face. "Wang–Fo painted her one last time,
because he loved the green hue that suffuses the face of the dead" (p. 395).
Even when Ling is killed and "his head falls from his neck like a cut
flower," Wang–Fo, "in despair, admired the beautiful scarlet stain that
his disciple's blood made on the green stone floor" (p. 399). Wang–Fo is
equally indifferent to his own fate. When the soldiers come to arrest
Ling and Wang–Fo, Wang–Fo "could not help noticing that the soldiers'
sleeves did not match the color of their coats" (p. 396).

Although we are repelled by Wang–Fo's callousness, we realize that
he cannot be blamed for being what he is. Midas wished for his magic
touch; Wang–Fo did not. Midas can compare the world he transforms to

the world he knew previously; Wang–Fo has never known a world other than that of "One Thousand Curves and Ten Thousand Colors" (p. 398). If Wang–Fo was fated from birth to love "the image of things and not the things themselves" (p. 394), he may be amoral, but he is not immoral.

It is impossible to know whether Wang–Fo's talent is a blessing or curse for him. Because we cannot imagine life on his terms and he cannot imagine it on ours, we simply cannot decide if one is better than the other.

2. Is Wang–Fo's talent a blessing or a curse for others? Explain.

For the Emperor, Wang–Fo's art is clearly a curse. Because the Emperor grows up isolated from the world outside his palace and surrounded by Wang–Fo's paintings, he imagines his kingdom to be as beautiful as the world within the paintings. When he finally encounters reality, he is digusted by its ugliness—"the coarse laughter of the soldiers," the vermin in the rice fields, and the mud and stones of the road (p. 398). Wang–Fo's art causes the Emperor to despise the Kingdom of Han and covet the empire created by Wang–Fo.

For Ling, on the other hand, Wang–Fo's art is a blessing. Before he met Wang–Fo, Ling had been afraid "of insects, of thunder and the face of the dead" (p. 394). Wang–Fo forces Ling to "admire the livid zebra stripes of lightning, and Ling, spellbound, stopped being afraid of storms" (p. 395). Wang–Fo "followed with delight the hesitant trail of an ant along the cracks in the wall, and Ling's horror of these creatures vanished into thin air" (p. 395). Wang–Fo paints Ling's dead wife, and Ling finds that mixing the colors requires "such concentration that he forgot to shed tears" (p. 395). Ling realizes that Wang–Fo has "presented him with the gift of a new soul and a new vision of the world" (p. 395), and he becomes Wang–Fo's disciple.

It is hard to know why Wang–Fo's art does not enhance life for the Emperor as it does for Ling, but, of course, that is a question we could ask about every artist's work. Why is Picasso's *Les Demoiselles d'Avignon* both loved and hated? At the risk of oversimplifying, I would suggest that Ling loves Wang–Fo's art for what it can do; the Emperor hates it for what it cannot do. If we use Western terminology to compare the two, we might say that Ling is of the art-for-art's-sake school of thought. He would undoubtedly agree with Browning's Fra Lippo Lippi: "If you get simple beauty and nought else,/You get about the best thing God invents:/That's somewhat...." The Emperor, in contrast, would reject the notion that "beauty is its own excuse for being"; he clearly demands that art serve some higher (but never precisely articulated) purpose. Perhaps he wants art to give him happiness; perhaps he expects it to transform the world (which he describes as "a mass of muddled colors thrown into the void by an insane painter, and smudged by our tears"—p. 398) into a better place. It fails to do either.

A Taoist reading of the story might suggest that the responses of the two men indicate the extent to which each has found the Tao (the way). The Tao is variously described as the ultimate source of the universe; the ineffable, transcendent, mystery of life; and the ultimate reality which can be known only through mystical insight. One Taoist epigram explains, "Those who know don't say, and those who say don't know." The Tao is also the ordering principle of the universe, the power that informs the physical world, creating the rhythms of nature. And finally the Tao is the way people should live to attain a harmonious relationship with the universe. Those who cultivate the proper mental state—*wu wei*—allow the power of the Tao to flow through them and direct their lives. They do not strive for money, power, or fame, and they attempt to live in tune with the natural world rather than to master and reshape it.

Wang–Fo seems to have found the way. He pays "no attention to pieces of silver" (p. 394), is unmindful of his own physical discomfort, and devotes his life to finding the reality behind external appearance. His ability to perceive what we might describe as the Tao is suggested when he examines the unfinished painting he had begun in his youth. Wang–Fo realizes that something is missing "because when Wang had painted it he had not yet looked long enough at the mountains or at the rocks bathing their naked flanks in the sea, and he had not yet penetrated deep enough into the sadness of the evening twilight" (p. 400). Ling finds the way through Wang–Fo's "gift of a new soul and a new vision of the world" (p. 395). Ling does not have Wang–Fo's talented hands, but he learns to rise "with the first rays of the sun" to pursue "timid landscapes hidden behind bunches of reeds" (p. 396).

The Emperor never finds the way. Because he focuses on the imperfections of the natural world, he cannot see its beauty. He complains to Ling, "The pebbles on the beach spoiled my taste for oceans" (p. 398). Rather than live in harmony with nature, the Emperor reshapes it in an artificial garden where flowers have no perfume, birds are not allowed, and high walls keep out the winds (p. 397). The Emperor never understands that he must relinquish personal power to gain the greater power of the Tao. He envies Wang–Fo because he mistakenly believes Wang–Fo "*reigns* peacefully over mountains covered in snow that cannot melt, and over fields of daffodils that cannot die" (p. 399). He fails to understand that Wang–Fo is art's servant, not its emperor. It is the Emperor's desire to control and possess that prevents his escaping, along with Ling and Wang–Fo, into what may be a higher plane of existence.

3. How is the world Yourcenar presents in this story like the world presented in Wang–Fo's paintings?

Your students should point out a number of similarities between the two. The story presents a world of impossible beauty and perfection: Ling's wife is a "woman of crystal–clear heart" who "never stops smiling" (p. 394). The doors of the Imperial palace swing on their hinges "with a musical note, and were placed in such a manner that one followed the entire scale when crossing the palace from east to west" (p. 397). Ling is a devoted disciple who jumps to one side when he is about to be beheaded "so that his blood would not stain his master's robe" (p. 399). Even when the story threatens real world ugliness—Ling is beheaded, the Emperor announces that he will have Wang–Fo's eyes burned out and his hands cut off, and we believe that the courtiers and the Emperor have drowned—art allows us to escape such calamities. At the end Ling is magically resurrected, he and Wang–Fo sail off into Wang–Fo's painting, and the submerged courtiers and Emperor forget that their sleeves were ever wet.

Yourcenar creates a world as vivid and colorful as Wang–Fo's paintings. I counted at least twenty–five references to color in the story. For example, Ling lives in a "house painted vermillion" and has a "plum tree that blossomed every spring with pale–pink flowers" (p. 394). Wang–Fo teaches Ling to notice "the brown splendor of roasts," and "the blush of wine stains," and Ling "discovers with surprise that the walls of his house were not red, as he had always thought, but the color of an almost rotten orange" (p. 395). The metaphors and similes of the story are equally colorful and vivid. Yourcenar writes that "Wang–Fo spoke as if silence were a wall and words the colors with which to cover it" (p. 395). She explains that the "pigtails of submerged courtiers rippled up toward the surface like snakes, and the pale head of the Emperor floated like a lotus" (p. 400).

–M.R.D.

Ralph Ellison
Did You Ever Dream Lucky?

Your students who have read *The Invisible Man* may be dismayed to find this short story, relatively speaking, "thin." By this I mean that for the most part the great issues of visibility and invisibility as Ellison defines them in his novel seem for the most part tangential to what goes on in this short story. But this short story is not only an *exemplum* about money as the root of all evil; it is interesting as an example of the humorous narrative, for its technical merits as a framed tale, because it demonstrates Ellison's interest in music, and finally because it suggests friendship as a consolation for invisibility.

The storyteller, Mary, and her antagonist, Portwood, are old and friendly opponents. Mary, for example, tells Portwood, "You got nowhere in this whole wide world to go—probably cause you make so much noise with your mouth" (p. 403). Portwood responds with "Now she's bound to lie. Mrs. Garfield, you done *guaranteed* she go' lie" (p. 404). This speech in the mouth of someone not an intimate would be insulting; coming from an old friend, it is the announcement that a ritual squabble is leading to a ritual storytelling.

> Mrs. Garfield smiled with gentle amusement. She'd been through it all before. A retired cook whose husband was dead, she had roomed with Mary almost as long as Portwood and knew that just as this was his way of provoking Mary into telling a story, it was Mary's way of introducing the story she would tell. (p. 403)

Ritual stories are often preceded by ritual warmups, and in "Did You Ever Dream Lucky?" the plot is impeded by the exchanges with Portwood (in fact, almost all of the dialogue seems superfluous at first reading) and with Mary's penchant for apparently tangential and irritating detail. This short story, then, has all the elements of the classic shaggy dog tale; the listeners and readers writhe with impatience as the narrator wades through minutia. Portwood will no doubt speak for some of your students when he grows impatient:

> ". . . Oh, such a commotion. Then all of a sudden all you can hear is Negroes' feet slapping the sidewalks . . ."
> "Never mind them feet," Portwood said, "what was it that flew out of there?"
> (p. 405)

The exchanges with Portwood, however, take on a new significance in light of the following passage:

> "Hush, Portwood!" Mary said. "What *green*?" She said singing full–throatedly now, her voice suddenly folk–toned and deep with echoes of sermons and blue trombones, "Lawd *I* was green. That what I'm trying to tell you. Y'all hear me? *I, Me, Mary Raaam–bo*, was green."

> "You telling me?" Portwood laughed. "Is you telling *me*?" Nevertheless he leaned forward with Mrs. Garfield now, surrendering once more to Mary's once–upon–a–time antiphonal spell, waiting to respond to her state theme: green. (p. 404)

Here Ellison is demonstrating his ever–present interest in the rhythms of black speech, song, and music; the exchanges between Mary and her audience remind us of the call and response antiphonal structure of the traditional black sermon—students unfamiliar with the flavor of such services will be interested in Mary's description of a "store–front" church on page 405.

QUESTIONS

1. Does this short story conform to Margaret Atwood's definition of American humor (p. 413)? Who is the dupe in this short story? The audience? The con–man or sharpie?

In the Counterpoint, Margaret Atwood describes the three roles usually available to American humorists: (1.) the con–man or sharpie, who fools (2.) the dupe, whose foolishness stands in sharp contrast to the cunning of the con–man in the eyes of (3.) the audience, who watches and admires the con–man's victory over the dupe. In short, those three roles are determined by the level of knowledge one has of the events unfolded in the narrative. The dupe, at the bottom level, doesn't know that he is dealing with counterfeit money or that the genuine Mexican plug is unridable; the con–man, at the next level, knows that the money is fake and that the horse is a nag—furthermore, he knows the depths of the dupe's ignorance. At the top level rests the audience, who knows some or all of the con–man's motives and takes delight at the difference in its knowledge and that of the dupe.

Ellison equips this short story with two audiences—Portwood/Mrs. Garfield, and us, and plays a variation on the structure Atwood describes in the Counterpoint. The two audiences are not given superior knowledge; in fact, the O. Henry–like ending drops Portwood, Mrs. Garfield, and us to dupe status in short order. The master touch here, if we continue to evaluate this short story in Atwood's terms, is that Mary plays the double role of con–man and dupe, and withholds the final vision of her younger self as "green" (read "dupe") until the end of the story.

2. What does Ellison gain by "framing" his tale?

You might wish to discuss the effect in general of the so–called "framed narrative," which allows the author and the narrator different audiences; the narrator is recounting the story to an audience composed of characters within the fiction itself but seldom involved in the action—the primary audience. The secondary audience is the reader himself or herself, and has what I call in the discussion immediately above superior knowledge of the action—sometimes. In a framed narrative like *The*

Canterbury Tales we know, for instance, of the rivalries amongst some of the pilgrims and of their ultimate destination— in short, Chaucer allows us to go "along for the ride" and to know as much as the narrator. In other framed narratives like *The Turn of The Screw* and "Did You Ever Dream Lucky?" the narrator's knowledge is superior to our own. What this means in this short story is that we are as surprised at the contents of the bag—because that knowledge is withheld from us—as was Mary and as are Portwood and Mrs. Garfield. In regard to the "tire chain" narrative, we are in precisely the same position as the primary audience.

3. What is meant by the term "green"? Why is this notion important to the narrative?

It is important to remember that the story of the tire chains is told ostensibly to demonstrate Mary's greenness when she comes to Harlem. By "green" Mary means not only the conventional "inexperienced" and "naive," but also wrong–headedness. Like the young people who have rushed out of the apartment to attend a dance where a car is the door prize, she longs for quick and easy money; experience has since taught her that one can only dream lucky: "They black and trying to get to heaven in a Cadillac" (p. 404). If there is a moral to Mary's story—and some students may maintain that "Did You Ever Dream Lucky?" because it is only a long joke, cannot contain a moral—it is that wealth will always elude some people.

I think some will find that Ellison is guilty of delivering a bleak message here. He is: the invisible are often fated to remain invisible. He leaves us, however, with more than this realization. Mary Rambo, Mrs. Garfield, and Portwood may be weathered by experience and living together out of necessity, but they are friends sharing warmth, food, wisdom, and each others' company. One bittersweet detail lost in my first reading is that Mary's story is told, after all, on Thanksgiving.

–W.R.S.

Doris Lessing
To Room Nineteen

"To Room Nineteen" is the story of a sensible couple who use their intelligence to create a good marriage complete with four children, big house, garden, charwoman, friends, and cars but later make the unsettling discovery that it somehow isn't enough, that life is far more complicated than they could have guessed when they were younger. The story focuses on the wife's attempt to escape the pressures of her role as wife/mother/mistress of the house, first through madness(?) and eventually through suicide.

Your students may by puzzled to find both insanity and suicide treated as understandable, perhaps admirable, reactions to an impossible situation. They may find it helpful to know that in two of her novels, *The Golden Notebook* and *Briefing for a Descent into Hell*, Lessing presents views similar to those of British psychiatrist R. D. Laing, who suggests that schizophrenia might be a more honest response to the horrors of life than normality. Like Laing, Lessing seems to believe that what the world calls insanity may be a truer vision of human existence.

You might want to assign this story along with two other portraits of women our society would label mad: Charlotte Perkins Gilman's "The Yellow Wallpaper" and Gail Godwin's "Dream Children."

QUESTIONS

1. In the Counterpoint Lessing complains that modern literature lacks "the warmth, the compassion, the humanity, the love of people which illuminates" nineteenth–century literature. Does "To Room Nineteen" demonstrate those qualities?

At first glance this short story seems to fall short of the demands Lessing makes of literature. Why does a writer who admires novels that are a statement of faith in man himself write a story about a woman who commits suicide?

One possibility is that Lessing is a product of the twentieth century herself, that she too has "accepted the condition of being uncertain and insecure," and, as a consequence, her writing suffers the same weaknesses she observes in the writing of others. Some of your students will undoubtedly make this argument.

I would, however, suggest that the story offers a world view much larger than that of its characters. The story opens with two people, Matthew and Susan, whose only goal is to build a balanced, sensible life characterized by "abstinence from painful experience" (p. 414). To that end, each is willing to make sacrifices. Susan gives up her job "because children needed their mother to a certain age" (p.416); Matthew continues to work for a newspaper he doesn't choose to read (p.415). Unlike the heroic figures in nineteenth century novels, Susan and Matthew choose life on a reduced scale.

To sustain their happy marriage, their four healthy children, and their large white gardened house, they consciously limit their existences ("...they used their intelligence to preserve what they had created from a painful and explosive world..." p. 416). To protect themselves from pain, they simply refuse to acknowlege the emotions evoked by the "great words like love, hate; life, death; loyalty, treachery...." Their determination to ignore irrational emotions is clearly illustrated by Susan's response to Matthew's sexual enconter with Myra Jenkins. Susan sensibly rejects the words "forgiveness," "confessed," and "faithful" as "stupid, all these words, stupid, belonging to a savage old world" (p. 417).

But by the end of the story, Susan, at least, has recognized and rejected the emotional sterility of her life. She decides that she cannot and will not become part of a "gallant civilized foursome" (p. 437), no matter how sensible and reasonable that course of action may be. She "dissolves in horror at them both, at how far they had both sunk from honesty of emotion" (p. 437). When Susan chooses death rather than hypocrisy, she has made her own "moral judgment." She has dared "to use words like good and bad."

Lessing doesn't follow Dostoevsky's lead by restoring order at the end of the story. She does, however, create a short story that can be read as Lessing believes literature should be read, "in order to enlarge one's perception of life."

2. Are Susan's actions comprehensible or incomprehensible? How does Lessing's use of point of view influence our response?

I'm sure that if we read a brief newspaper account of Susan's final months, we would quickly dismiss her as hopelessly deranged: WEALTHY SUBURBAN MATRON COMMITS SUICIDE IN DINGY HOTEL ROOM "Hotel proprietor testifies that Mrs. Matthew Rawlings, calling herself Mrs. Jones, stayed alone in room 19 every weekday from ten until five, that she always insisted on that room, and that she waited for it if it was engaged." And the newspaper reporter wouldn't even know that Susan saw a devil in her well-tended garden.

Lessing, however, forces us to think of Susan as more than a lunatic. She accomplishes that feat through point of view. Lessing begins the story light years distant from her characters. She tells us about "the Rawlings" without so much as giving either a first name until the fourth paragraph. By page two Lessing has moved in closer, close enough to let us see what the characters are thinking, but not close enough to reveal that the story will eventually focus on Susan. Throughout the first four pages Lessing treats the two characters as if they are one, as if they share every belief and thought. She uses the pronoun "they" ("They sensibly blamed neither themselves nor each other,") or she writes phrases such as "she knew, and so did he."

Not until the final paragraph on page four does Lessing allow Susan a separate thought. "Except, thought Susan, unaccountably bad-tempered, she [Myra Jenkins] was (is?) the first." At that point in the story the narrator separates herself from Matthew and merges into Susan. Lessing begins to present Susan's thoughts in first person. "The whole thing is

absurd—for him to have come home and told me is absurd.... For me to
care or, for that matter, not to care, is absurd...."

Although the narrator continues to make observations about the couple
as a unit ("...they put the thing behind them, and consciously knowing
what they were doing, moved forward into a different phase of their
marriage, giving thanks for past good fortune as they did so"—p. 417), it
becomes more and more difficult to distinguish between the narrator's
perceptions and Susan's. Even when Lessing writes that "Matthew never
was really struck, as he wanted to be, by joy...." (p.418), we suspect that we
are viewing Matthew through the eyes of his wife.

Eventually, we realize that we are seeing everything through Susan's
eyes. When Susan sees the devil in the garden, he is as real to us as he is
to her. Lessing does not write, "One day she thought she saw him."
Instead, she calmly observes, "Well, one day she saw him" (p. 425). And
we are as shocked and puzzled by his presence as Susan is.

Our identification with Susan makes it difficult for us to declare her
crazy. Even when she begins to question her sanity ("so I'm not crazy after all"—p. 425; "Miss Townsend, my four children and husband are
driving me insane..."—p. 426; "she knew quite well she was mad"—p.
427; "she said, with the cunning of a madwoman evading the real
point..."—p. 429), we feel that what the world calls madness is merely
her refusal to live a reasonable life, a life devoid of all emotion, emotion
which is, by definition, irrational.

Once I extricate myself from the story, I can honestly say that I find
suicide incomprehensible. But while I was reading, I saw that, from Susan's perspective, her actions were not only understandable but inevitable.

3. Is "To Room Nineteen" a story about women or about all people?

One of Lessing's greatest strengths is her ability to tell a story about
one specific woman while making a more general statement about the
condition of women and, indeed, of all people.

Certainly, on one level, the story is about the problems encountered by
a suburban middle–class woman when she tries to play the narrow roles
prescribed for her by society. Susan marries, becomes pregnant, gives up
her job, and moves with her husband to a large house in Richmond
where she dutifully resolves to care for Matthew, the children, the house,
and the garden until the children are old enough to go off to school and
she can "turn herself back into being a woman with a life of her own"
(p. 418). She accepts this "voluntary bondage" (p. 423), believing at first
that it is a temporary condition. But when the twins finally do go off to
school, she discovers that the "essential Susan," the self that has been "in
abeyance, as if she were in cold storage" (p. 419), has been permanently
misplaced. Susan is consigned to play her roles forever.

The essential Susan had been free to live her own life. The wife/
mother/mistress–of–the–house Susan can never be free. Susan "was
possessed with resentment that the seven hours of freedom in every day
[during weekdays in the school term] were not free, that never, not for
one second, ever, was she free from the pressure of time, from having to
remember this or that" (p. 422). In some ways the story is Susan's quest to
recapture her lost freedom. At first she seeks it in "Mother's Room."
(The description presages her failure.) Later she attempts to escape to
Wales but the "telephone wire holds her to her duties like a leash" (p.
428). Eventually she hires an au pair girl who allows her to "withdraw
herself spiritually" while she "looks for herself" (p. 434) in room nineteen. But Matthew searches her out and "the peace of the room" is gone.
In the end she can escape from her roles only by drifting off into the
dark river of death.

To the extent that women in our culture are the people most often required to sacrifice their own identities for the sake of their families, this
is very much a story about the problems of being a woman. But Lessing
doesn't allow us to explain away all the complexities of Susan with that
one simple explanation.

For one thing, Lessing insists that Susan's problems are not unique to
women. After Susan complains about her lack of freedom, Matthew reminds her that he is never totally free either (p. 423). Susan admits to
herself that the "good marriage, the house, the children depended just
as much on his voluntary bondage as it did on hers" (p. 423).

Lessing further suggests that Susan's problems are not shared by all
women. Although we can't be sure, we sense that both Mrs. Parkes and
Sophie find real satisfaction in the roles that destroy Susan.

4. What is the significance of the garden imagery?

You might begin by asking your students to note all the references to
the garden. (There are at least nine in the first thirteen pages of the
story.) It is in the garden that Susan is first "filled with tension, like a
panic: as if an enemy was in the garden with her" (p. 419). She decides
not to tell Matthew that she feels as if there were "an enemy there waiting to invade [her]," (p. 420) and she sits in the garden waiting "for the
demon to appear and claim her" (p. 422). Eventually he does just that.

Lessing invites us to compare Susan's encounter with her demon to the
biblical account of Eve's temptation by Satan. Susan is "standing at the
bottom of her garden" when she sees a man "with a reddish complexion
and ginger hair" who is wearing "a reddish hairy jacket, unpleasant to
the touch...sitting on a white stone bench...looking at her, and grin-
ning..." while tormenting a snakelike creature with a stick (p. 425).
Lessing never explains the nature of Susan's temptation, but immediately

after that encounter Susan decides to find a room. Perhaps, like Eve, Susan sacrifices Eden for knowledge—of herself and of the world beyond her garden, a world that admits the existence of emotion, however painful, as well as reason.

–M.D.R.

Mavis Gallant
The Remission

"The Remission," the only novella included in this anthology, will give your students an opportunity to compare the short story and the novel. Such comparisons are difficult because any rule we formulate to differentiate between the novel and the short story is inadequate. If we point out that a novel is longer than a short story, our students ask "How much longer?" Can a short story have seventy–nine pages? Can a piece of fiction with only forty–two pages ("The Remission") be a novella? If we claim that a short story merely reveals a character while a novel allows the character to develop, we can hardly classify Chekhov's "The Lady with a Pet Dog" as a short story. If we claim that short stories are distinguished by unity of effect, we have difficulty explaining why Henry James' *The Turn of the Screw* and Joseph Conrad's *Heart of Darkness* are not short stories.

If, however, we ask our students to examine a particular novella closely, they will quickly discover the characteristics that distinguish that genre. Justice Stewart once remarked that even though it is difficult to define pornography, he knew it when he saw it. After reading and discussing "The Remission," students will know a novella when they see one.

In "The Remission" Mavis Gallant presents the story of a father (Alec), mother (Barbara), and three children aged ten, eleven, and twelve who learn that Alec is terminally ill and consequently move to a small Mediterranean village where he wishes to spend his dying days. Instead of dying quickly, as he had anticipated, Alec goes into a remission that lasts far longer than the family's limited financial resources. Gallant observes that "Alec's remission was no longer miraculous—it had become unreasonable" (p. 455). While Alec lingers, his wife and children get on with their lives. Gallant presents this family, a unit often portrayed as monolithic, as an almost accidental grouping of heterogeneous entities, each of whom perceives and is affected by events differently. Through an omniscient narrator, Gallant presents a complex view of reality filtered, focused, mirrored, and refracted by multiple perspectives.

QUESTIONS

1. If you were required to rewrite "The Remission" as a ten–page story, how would you change it and why?

This question should demonstrate the restrictions imposed by the short story better than any theoretical discussion could. Your students will probably decide that the shorter version should be focused on the thoughts and feelings of a particular character, perhaps Barbara, Alec, or Molly. Gallant, of course, invites us into the minds of all three and also allows us an occasional glimpse of the world through the eyes of Will, James, Wilkinson, Mr. Cranefield, Mrs. Massie, the doctor, Genevieve (the governess), and Diana (Alec's sister).

After selecting a central character, your students will probably choose to tighten the plot (if there is indeed a plot to this novella) by examining the effect of the remission on that character and eliminating all the unrelated events. If, for example, this is to be a story about Molly, many incidents such as Barbara's telling Alec that "Eric has very kindly offered to stay at Lou Mas" (p. 461) can be omitted.

Your students may also decide to leave out some of the minor characters. Alec's sister could be dismissed by noting that she contributed the capital which permits "Alec's obstinate refusal to die on National Health" or by explaining that "Barbara called her sister–in–law 'the mouse'" (p. 443). Gallant, however, paints a miniature portrait of Diana, a forty–four–year–old woman who never married "though she was no poorer or plainer than most." Gallant tells us that Diana "had small brown eyes, was a vegetarian, prayed every night of her life for Alec and for the parents who had not much loved her" (p. 443). Gallant also gives Diana a cameo appearance at Alec's funeral (pp. 466–467).

2. How does the final event, when "every person in the room, at the same moment, spoke and thought of someone other than Alec," reflect the theme of the novella?

Even though it is impossible to sum up the meaning of this novella or any other in a single sentence, I would suggest that "The Remission" is primarily a comment on egocentricism. Gallant reminds us that although we play the starring roles in our own lives, we are, at most, supporting actors in the lives of others.

In scene after scene Gallant demonstrates that an event that is of crucial importance to one character has less or different significance for another. Alec's sister Diana makes "an impulsive gesture, perhaps a disastrous one" (pp. 443–444), by offering Alec half of the capital settled on her by a godparent. Diana might have expected her grand gesture to mark an epoch in everyone's life. If so, she is slated for disappointment. Alec accepts "in the same flat way he had talked about death" (p. 443) even though he "knew his sister had been sacrificed" (p. 444). Barbara spends Diana's money extravagantly, and experiences only one tiny twinge of guilt when she considers Diana's future: "I know, I know, but she can get a job, can't she" (p. 467).

In another scene, after Wilkinson gives Molly a ride, she asks him to come into the house, explaining, "I am not allowed to be in cars with men alone. In case someone happened to see us, would you mind just coming and meeting my mother? Just so she can see who you are?" (p. 456). For Molly the introduction is merely an attempt to avoid the possibility that her mother will be angry with her. For her mother the meeting is the beginning of a love affair that is "the last thing Wilkinson in his right mind should have wanted, and absolutely everything Barbara now desired and craved" (p. 457). Later Molly blames herself for "the disaster," because "she led the intruder home, let him in, causing Alec, always courteous, to remove himself first to the hospital, then farther on" (p. 469). Molly's guilt shows that she cannot understand how minor her role in the drama has been.

The funeral scene is the best example of the theme. Few if any of the mourners are thinking of Alec's death. Mrs. Massie composes her own obituary (p. 466), Mr. Cranefield considers how his novels are "likely to fare in the second half of the nineteen–fifties" (p. 468), James plans his revenge on the "people who had given him second hand clothes, thus (he believed) laying waste to his life" (p. 468), Molly imagines her return to the cemetery where she can confess her guilt (p. 469), Wilkinson feels ill because of his wrenched shoulder (p. 470), and Barbara begins "in the most natural way in the world to live happily ever after" (p. 470). At the end, Alec has ceased to be even an extra in the others' lives. He has made his final exit.

3. How does Gallant want us to respond to Barbara?

Your students will probably have a variety of reactions to Barbara. Some may agree with her "favorite brother" who calls her a "bitch, a trollop, a crook, and a fool" (p. 465). And that's his assessment of her before he learns that Alec signed his share of Lou Mas over to Barbara, and that Alec and Barbara revoked her brother's power of attorney.

I think, however, that most of your students will like Barbara better than they might have expected to like a woman who is happily having an affair with another man while her husband is dying in the hospital. Gallant evokes our sympathy for Barbara by portraying her as a woman more sinned against than sinning.

Barbara's brothers treat her shamefully. They assume she is dumb, and they feel safe making Barbara and Alec the registered owners of Lou

Mas because Alec is "entirely honorable and Barbara did not know a legal document from the ace of diamonds" (p. 442). Their attitudes toward Barbara are further illustrated by her brother's thoughts after receiving a letter from her. He wonders if this is "the sort of prattle poor dying old Alec had to listen to there in the south" (p. 444). Later when her wealthy brothers find a renter for Lou Mas, they have no qualms about turning her and her three children out of their home.

Alec's behavior toward Barbara is hardly more admirable. Before he became ill, he was, apparently, absolute ruler of his household. We learn, for example, that Barbara had wanted to name their children "Giles, Nigel, and Samantha, but Alec had interfered" (p. 447). After his illness, Alec becomes so self–absorbed that he ceases to care how his actions affect those who love him. Although he is leaving a wife and three children with no money, Alec decides to uproot his family and move to the Mediterranean to spend his final days (which stretch into years). "It did not occur to him or anyone else that the removal from England was an act of unusual force that could rend and lacerate his children's lives as well as his own" (p. 440). Neither does he consider the financial sacrifices others make on his behalf. Gallant reminds us that "Alec's obsti nate refusal to die on National Health" (p. 443) means that his sister and Barbara's brothers must somehow pay for his dying. We might like Barbara less if Gallant had allowed us to like Alec more.

We further sympathize with Barbara because others judge her so harshly. After Wilkinson moves in with Barbara, everyone condemns her, but "[n]o one could blame Wilkinson, who had his reasons" (p. 458). Her children reject her, Genevieve stops coming to see them, and Mrs. Massie concludes, "Alec is a gentleman and always will be, but Barbara...Barbara....If the boys were girls they'd be sluts" (p. 457).

Meanwhile Barbara continues to visit Alec every day, holding his hand, telling him stories, bathing him, combing his hair, and, with Wilkinson's help, changing his sheets (pp. 462–463). So far as we see, she never has an unkind thought about Alec, never blames him for her financial predicament, and never stops loving him. I think many of your students will conclude that Barbara deserves both title to Lou Mas and the happiness she finds with Eric.

–M.R.D.

Nadine Gordimer
The Catch

In "The Catch" white South African novelist and short story writer Nadine Gordimer explores the insidious effects of apartheid on the people—both white and "colored"—of her country. For the most part,

Gordimer does not write about the events that sometimes make headlines in American newspapers: demonstrations, strikes, boycotts, and the violent confrontations that so often accompany political protest. Instead, she focuses on the everyday lives of ordinary people, lives inevitably stunted by apartheid. In a recent interview Gordimer stated, "I think when you're born white in South Africa, you're peeling like an onion. You're sloughing off all the conditioning that you've had since you were a child."

"The Catch" is the story of a friendship that develops between a young white couple and an Indian fisherman who meet at the beach while all three are on holiday. They talk every morning and mostly they discuss "fishing, the sea, and the particular stretch of coast on which they are living." The young people like and respect the Indian who knows, "as magically to them as the diviner feeling the pull of water beneath the ground" where the fish will be on a given day. Sometimes the young man and woman forget that their friend is an Indian, and their memory lapse is an oddly liberating and exhilarating experience. But when three white friends from home arrive at the resort, the couple realize their white friends will never understand a cross–racial friendship. In a scene that is as uncomfortable for the reader as for the characters, the couple choose to deny their friendship with the Indian rather than attempt to explain it.

QUESTIONS

1. What is Gordimer's attitude toward the couple?

In the counterpoint Gordimer claims that she doesn't make judgments about people because "absolutely everybody has what are known as human failings." But her decision not to "write [people] off" hardly signals a willingness to ignore their faults. Her ability to be critical of human failings but sympathetic to the humans who fail is evident in her treatment of the couple in this story.

Gordimer does not portray the young man and the girl in the story as heartless monsters who glory in their racial superiority, but as likeable people who chafe under the constraints of their "preconceived ready–made roles": "The fact that [the fisherman] was an Indian troubled them hardly at all. They almost forgot he *was* an Indian. And this too, though they did not know it, produced a lightening of the heart, a desire to do conversational frolics with a free tongue the way one stretches and kicks up one's legs in the sun after confinement in a close dark room" (p. 473).

Neither does she deny the couple's racial prejudice, particularly that of the girl. When the Indian avoids answering her question about where he will sell the fish, Gordimer observes, "It irritated her, although she smiled, this habit of other races of slipping out of one's questioning" (p. 478). And when the young man wonders aloud how the Indian will carry the fish, his wife dismisses his concerns: "Oh, they're strong. They're used to it" (p. 478).

Gordimer understands how difficult it would be for the couple to escape "the song–and–dance routine" they undoubtedly learned as toddlers. Over and over she reminds us that they are incredibly attuned to the nuances of correct social behavior. When the Indian offers to sell them a fish, "[d]isappointment as much as a satisfied dig in the ribs from opportunist prejudice stiffened them momentarily....They shifted their attitude slightly" (p. 473). Then they realize he does not ordinarily sell his fish. "The girl felt the dismay of having mistaken a privilege for an imposition" (p. 474).

The couple's sensitivity to social (not racial) propriety pervades their relationship. They recognize that their growing friendship with the Indian requires a change in the quality of their talk, that "the simple question–and–answer relation that goes with the celluloid pop of a ping–pong ball and does so well for all inferiors, foreigners, and children" (p. 474) won't do. Their concern with doing the right thing even prevents them from learning their friend's name. "They did not know his name, and now, although they might have asked the first day and got away with it, it was suddenly impossible, because he didn't ask theirs" (p. 474).

Gordimer doesn't blame the couple for their cultural conditioning, for their automatic and unthinking responses. She does, however, fault them for cowardice, for allowing societal pressures rather than their individual consciences to rule. When the husband and wife see the Indian sitting beside the road with his fish, their hearts respond. The wife cries, "Les! It's him, with the fish!" (p. 479), and the husband stops the car to help their friend. But as soon as they stop, "someone from the back" asks "Who is it?" and all is lost. The young people realize that their friends will not understand their relationship with the Indian. The wife explains, "We've spoken to him on the beach," and the husband admits, "We know him well," but neither is willing to claim him as a friend.

Gordimer condemns the couple's treatment of the Indian by showing they are ashamed of their behavior. The husband drives in silence; the wife chatters nervously. When the Indian repeats her remark that "the catch was more trouble than it was worth," she feels "a stab of cold uncertainty, as if she herself did not know what she had said, did not know what she had meant, or might have meant" (p. 480). We feel that if the couple had been alone, they would have treated the Indian as a friend, but they lack the courage and imagination to play new roles before a hostile audience. We, like Gordimer, are ashamed of their actions. And yet we cannot help but ask ourselves if, under similar circumstances, we would have behaved more admirably.

2. How does the point of view influence our attitude toward the characters in the story?

Often a writer creates sympathy for a character by allowing us to view the world through that character's eyes [Gail Godwin's "Dream Children" and Franz Kafka's "The Metamorphosis" are two examples.] In this story, however, most of our sympathy is for the Indian, the only major character whose thoughts and feelings are never directly revealed to us. Gordimer does allow us to enter the consciousnesses of the young man and woman, but what we see evokes little sympathy. In fact, we might like the couple better if we were limited to viewing their actions, which are above reproach: The young people are polite, they engage in friendly conversations with the Indian, they trek down to the beach to photograph his trophy, and they graciously offer him a ride when he is too tired to carry his fish farther. Ultimately, we condemn them not for their deeds but for their failure to live up to their own vision of the way people, regardless of race, should treat each other. Gordimer does not excuse them as she excuses some white women in her society "because of their ignorance of what they have allowed themselves to become." Because we enter the minds of the young man and woman, we know that they are not ignorant. They understand how they should behave, and when they betray their friend, they are as disappointed in themselves and in each other as we are.

3. In the Counterpoint Gordimer explains how the physical descriptions of characters should be presented in a story. Does she follow her own advice?

In the Counterpoint Gordimer states "that physical descriptions of people should be minimal." In this story Gordimer never describes the physical appearance of the young man or the girl. She also states that when description is included, it should "come piecemeal at times when it furthers other elements in the text." That is precisely how she presents the description of the Indian. At first we, like the couple lying on the beach, hear the "sound of his feet thudding nearer over the sand," see his "thin strong bony legs" passing by at eye level and notice his "rolled-up faded trousers" (p. 472). Later they look up and we see his face—"a long head with a shining dark dome surrounded with curly hair...the beautiful curved nose...dark eyes slightly bloodshot from the sun, a wide muscular mouth smiling on strong uneven teeth..." (p. 472). Then, quite naturally given our vantage point, we observe his legs: "the dark, dull-skinned feet with the few black hairs on the big toe, the long hard shaft of the shin tightly covered with smooth shining skin, the pull of the tendons at his ankle..." (p. 472). We examine him again when he is staggering under the weight of the fish: "Long strands of grey curly hair blew over from the back of his head along his bright high forehead..." (p. 476). And when he poses for his picture, we focus on "his strong wide smile of pure achievement, that gathered up the unequal components of his face—his slim fine nose, his big ugly horse- teeth, his black crinkled–up eyes, and scribbled boldly a brave moment of whole man" (p. 477).

Later, when he is riding in the car, we notice only his clothes, so alien in this setting: "The sea–starched folds of his trousers made a slight harsh rubbing noise against the leather of the seat, his damp old tweed jacket smelled of warm wool, showed fuzzy against the edge of light" (p. 480). Our final glimpse of him beside the car shows a man bowed by the weight of betrayal. "He stood there as if his body still held the position he had carefully disciplined himself to in the car, head hunched a bit, hands curled as if he had had a cap he might perhaps have held it before him, pinned there by the blur of faces looking out at him from the car" (p. 481).

4. What is the effect of the metaphors in this story?

Throughout the story Gordimer uses metaphorical language to convey opinions and attitudes that are never directly expressed. For example, several similes both characterize and condemn the attitude of the couple toward the Indian. "He was 'their Indian.' When they went home they might remember the holiday by him as you might remember a particular holiday as the one when you used to play with a spaniel on the beach every day" (p. 474). Later Gordimer observes that "as an animal becomes more human every day, so every day the quality of their talk with the Indian had to change..." (p. 474). And when the husband watches the Indian struggling to carry the fish, Gordimer notes, "He was standing laughing proudly, like a spectator watching the winner come in at a race" (p. 476).

Other metaphors suggest the helplessness of the young couple whose lives are directed by forces beyond their comprehension. When the Indian catches the huge fish, "[i]nterest spread like a net, drawing in the few, scattered queer fish of the tiny resort..." (p. 476). Later the friends from home visit the resort, and "[a]s though the dam of their quiet withdrawal had been fuller than they thought, [the couple] found themselves toppling over into their old stream again, that might run on pointlessly and busy as the brook for ever and ever" (p. 478).

And, of course, there is the metaphor implied by the title. Just as the Indian finds that his "big catch is more trouble than it's worth" (p. 480),

the young white people decide that their catch, their friendship with the
Indian, is better in dream than in attainment.

                                                                                    –M.R.D.

José Donoso
Paseo

Two of Chilean José Donoso's most–treated subjects are childhood and
a disintegration of personality to the point of madness. We find both in
"Paseo," for in this story we see, through the eyes of an isolated and increasingly frightened child, a rigid personality crumbling into madness
under the burdens of civility and restraint.

We might regard civility and restraint as virtues in some, but in Gus-
tav, Armand, the narrator's father, and Mathilda, they are something
worse than a vice. The child in this story undergoes the sort of treatment
that Dickens' plucky orphans might complain of; instead of beatings and
deprivation, Donoso's narrator must endure (silently, of course) quiet tol-
eration and a loveless household. For entertainment, he must watch polite games of billiards; instead of outdoor childhood adventures, he indulges himself in bloodless "wanderings in and out of the empty sitting
rooms" (p. 489). One would expect, given that outline of the plot, that any
relief of this tedium would be a godsend; Donoso avoids the predictable by
providing an interruption of this sameness that turns out to be anything
but welcome. When affection enters this household, it does not come in
an altogether pleasant way—and it is not directed at the narrator, as one
might expect.

QUESTIONS

1. What does Donoso gain by using the narrator he does? How clearly
defined is the narrator as a character?

By choosing a first–person narrator of questionable reliability Donoso
preserves some useful ambiguities. When Aunt Mathilda first meets the
white bitch, the narrator tells us that she turned "in such absolute certainty of finding the bitch" (p. 489) following them that he "trembled" at
the mystery of her seemingly telepathic knowledge of the dog's
movements. Perhaps, he speculates, the look that passed between woman
and dog "contained some secret commitment" (p. 489). From the narrator's perspective, Aunt Mathilda's feeble attempt to shoo the dog away had
"the sound of something like a last effort to repel an approaching destiny" (p. 489). Blessedly, however, Donoso does not make the mistake of

having his narrator relate that his aunt felt the hackneyed gothic "sense of impending doom":

> It is possible that I am saying all this in the light of things that happened later, that my imagination is embellishing with significance what was only trivial. However, I can say with certainty that in that moment I felt a strangeness, almost a fear of my aunt's sudden loss of dignity in condescending to turn around and confer rank on a sick and filthy bitch. (p. 489)

Instead, since the first person narrator is a grown man looking back at the events of his childhood, he can express doubts about the accuracy of his perceptions, then turn around and say that nonetheless he felt "a strangeness." The effect is to defuse our own tendency to incredulity.

The question of what type of character the narrator turns out to be is a little complicated, then. He is, on the one hand, a boy starved for affection, inclined perhaps to perceive the adults around him as monsters of reserved civility, jealous of the dog that gets his aunt's affection, capable perhaps of imagining a sinister influence in the dog when one never existed. On the other hand, he is an adult objective enough to question the accuracy of his childhood perceptions *and still to believe them essentially accurate.*

2. How would you describe the world–view of Aunt Mathilda and her brothers?

Aunt Mathilda, before her adoption by the white bitch, always prefers the planned, the predictable; propriety is her principal characteristic; she sees suffering as an "error" and is intolerant of shirts that [are] not stupendously well ironed" (p. 485). Like her brothers, she enjoys the regularities of maritime laws and despises the disorder of actual ports and actual sailors (p. 486). Even death is the "final incision, clean and definitive, nothing more" (p. 486). Mathilda and her brothers seem almost disembodied and sexless, and prefer to deny their own animal needs and sensations; they move like ghosts in their house, never touching, never touched, refusing to venture into their garden "until the suffocation of the summer" (p. 492) forces them outdoors. This fastidiousness and a discomfort with natural functions come together comically when the brothers come unraveled at the sight of a puddle of urine on the floor (p. 493). The narrator can only now characterize their idea of order:

> I could not see that this order was in itself a kind of rebellion, constructed by them as a protection against chaos, so that they might not be touched by what can neither be explained nor resolved.
> (p. 487)

3. What does the dog represent?

This question is dangerous because it invites equations like "The dog represents Aunt Mathilda's animal nature." If your class has read "Rappaccini's Daughter," you might warn your students that Donoso in this story is like Hawthorne in that he is a symbolist, not an allegorist, and assigning finite and definite meanings to images and characters (animal or human) is a risky and imprecise business. The following readings may spark further discussion:

a.) The dog represents nature. Indeed, Donoso has written a story in which the dog must do so by default. If only one Martian appears on earth, it will have to become a symbol for all Martians. Nature has no other representative in the artificial world of the short story. Furthermore, Donoso draws our attention to this fact: "But animals for them existed only in the proportion in which they contributed to the pleasure of human beings. Which is to say that dogs, lazy as city dogs are, could not even dent their imagination with a possibility of their existence" (p. 488).

b.) The dog represents emotion, or perhaps we should say expressed, natural emotion. Once again, the symbolism is so natural that Donoso hardly has to insist on this. He has created a setting in which a cliche gains force. The boy grows up among cold people: "I wished that their confined feeling might overflow and express itself in a fit of rage, for example, or some bit of foolery" (p. 485). The dog is their antithesis: "Her whole body, from her quivering snout to her tail ready to waggle, was full of an abundant capacity for fun" (p. 492). She expresses emotion and provokes the aunt to express emotion. Particularly moving is the incident when Mathilda touches the dog as she has never touched the boy (p. 492), and when she laughs at the dog's behavior "as if unwound" (p. 492).

c.) The dog represents disorder, or to put it more strongly, the "chaos" of things that can "neither be explained nor resolved" (p. 487). She certainly represents this to everyone in the family. Once the bitch appears, Mathilda starts losing at billiards and can no longer remember the order of the shooters; she loses the "thread of order" (p. 491). One thing leads to another, Mathilda's center cannot hold, and the midnight strolls extend to her disappearance.

d.) The dog represents madness. Freudians will have a more precise picture, perhaps, and will say the dog represents the Id, the overly controlled family the Superego. There certainly is no balancing Ego here, nothing, unless it is the boy's own consciousness, that spans the gap between the spontaneous and emotional world of the dog and the rigid world of the story's adult. The boy is not amused by Mathilda's first laughter at the dog, perhaps because he already feels "the dark thing that had stirred it up" (p. 492). Of course, one need not base a reading of the dog as a representative of madness on Freudian psychology.

e.) The dog represents something else, some alternative to "that magnificent straight road that leads to death" (p. 486). We certainly can't be happy with the clinical and counter–intuitive answer that Mathilda is insane and her brothers just fine, and we really feel that Mathilda is exalted in the end when the boy sees her with "animation in her eyes" and an "excited restlessness" (p. 495) about her.

–W.R.S.
–D.H.

Flannery O'Connor
A Good Man Is Hard to Find

O'Connor forces most of us to take a wrong turn in this short story by tricking us into misaligned sympathies. Stanley Fish and others have exposed a similar ruse set up by Milton in *Paradise Lost*; we are apparently led by the poet to sympathize with Satan, who, after all, strives mightily against an implacable and placid adversary. And this sympathy can lead, of course, to misinterpretation by the most astute of critics. Blake, for example, was taken in to such an extent that he assigned Milton "to Satan's party." I think we are led to an analogous misunderstanding in "A Good Man Is Hard to Find."

The questions (or ones very much like them) below have been of help when I have taught "A Good Man is Hard to Find" in opening up a story that is a tough nut to crack.

QUESTIONS

1. How would you characterize the family in this short story? What details does O'Connor provide us with that lead us to that conclusion?

We are given a family so bland and yet so detestable that I must confess (as does at least one of my collaborators) that I smiled secretly as the black car approached the dazed but still pluckily insufferable family after the accident. I knew who and what awaited them (there is some rather heavy–handed foreshadowing on the very first page), and in a fashion they deserved him and it. Your class may have felt the same way. Doubtless some will disagree with these sentiments.

Let's look at that family. O'Connor leaves Bailey–boy largely undeveloped. What does strike us about him is his irascibility and ineffectuality. His wife's description, ". . . a young woman in slacks, whose face was as broad and innocent as a cabbage and was tied around with a green handkerchief that had two points on the top like rabbit's ears" (p. 497), leads us to believe that she has a cabbage for a head, and she says almost nothing throughout. Her baby is merely an appendage. The children are the sort of creatures found at family reunions in hell, if there are any. How often have we suffered at the hands of small tyrants much like June Star and John Wesley on vacations, at picnics, at parties? Consider John Wesley's braggadocio when asked what he'd do if confronted by the Misfit; consider June Star's treatment of Red Sam and his wife; visualize, if you can bear it, June Star's tap routine. The grandmother is manipulative, deceptive, and has a grating obsession not with *the* past—an obsession forgivable and often fascinating in the old—but with *her* past.

2. Do the Misfit's religious beliefs have any relevance to the story? How so?

To fully appreciate O'Connor's' sleight–of–sympathies here we have to look at the theology, if we can call it that, of the Misfit. He has, one could say, a terrifyingly literal Old Testament mentality. By that I mean merely that he takes "an eye for an eye and a tooth for a tooth" to its evaluative and vengeful extreme. As he says,

> "Jesus thrown everything off balance. It was the same case with Him as with me except He hadn't committed any crime and they could prove I had committed one because they had the papers on me . . . That's why I sign myself now. I said long ago, you get you a signature and sign everything you do and keep a copy of it. Then you'll know what you done and you can hold up the crime to the punishment and see do they match and in the end you'll have something to prove you ain't been treated right" (pp. 507–508).

> "Jesus was the only One that ever raised the dead," the Misfit continued, "and He shouldn't have done it. He thrown everything off balance. If He did what He said, then it's nothing for you to do but throw away everything and follow Him, and if He didn't then it's nothing for you to do but enjoy the few minutes you got left the best way you can—by killing somebody or burning down his house or doing some other meanness to him. No pleasure but meanness . . . (p. 508).

Every injury, no matter how small, must be avenged. In fact, since he is certain that the injustices done him must outweigh whatever he has done, he can kill and steal with impunity, assured that the ledger can never be equitably balanced. He demands heartsblood for a tooth, a life for the smallest imagined indignity.

And we find ourselves (or at least I found myself) practicing the Misfit's brand of sociopathy and religion. I smiled when that black hearse-like car approached because I knew that Bailey and his clan were going to be punished for being insufferable. I maintain that I am *not* inhumane; my disbelief not really suspended, I was finding satisfaction in the impending punishment of a poorly delineated pack of flat and non-dynamic characters, not fellow human beings.

3. Does our attitude toward the family change over the course of the narrative? Why or why not?

When they are led off to be slaughtered and the grandmother cries for her now–dead son and for herself and the nightmare quality of their execution comes all the way home, we realize what we and the Misfit have done. No one's death is cause for celebration. Bailey, his wife and children, and the grandmother in particular are most sympathetic when they are about to die; O'Connor's focus of the point of view upon the grandmother makes us feel a pity for her and a repugnance for the Misfit that we might have been incapable of feeling earlier in the narrative.

As Milton, then, has us admire Satan and participate in the original sin in doing so, so then does O'Connor have us loathe Bailey and Co. to discover that we have fallen into the same sort of madness demonstrated and practiced by the Misfit.

–W.R.S.

Yukio Mishima
Swaddling Clothes

I don't ordinarily believe that it's necessary to know about an author's life in order to understand his writings, but in this case I think it's helpful. It is, after all, difficult to separate artist from art when the writer consciously arranges for his suicide to occur on the very day he completes his major novel so that he can realize his "Bunbu–Ryodo" (a synthesis of the warrior arts and cultural arts).

Mishima, who was born in 1925 into a family of samurai nobility, spent his life following the samurai tradition. During World War II Mishima was bitterly disappointed when he failed his army physical and lost his opportunity to die for his emperor as a kamikaze pilot. He consequently vowed to develop his body into the physical ideal of the samurai, and he maintained that perfect condition throughout his life.

Although Mishima was a successful writer who prospered in post–war Japan, he came to hate the Westernization that he blamed for the demise of Japanese ideals. In 1963 he formed a private army of eighty–three university men dedicated to the goal of returning Japan to the way of the samurai. Apparently, Mishima decided that he could best advance his cause by his own suicide. In a letter to a friend, Mishima wrote, "After thinking and thinking through four years, I came to wish to sacrifice myself for the old, beautiful tradition of Japan, which is disappearing very quickly day by day."

In 1970, Mishima and four followers entered the Japanese military headquarters, took the commander hostage, and ordered that the soldiers be assembled on a parade ground. Mishima walked out on a balcony overlooking the 1200 men and exhorted them to rebel against the constitution, a constitution imposed by the Allies which robbed the emperor of his power and made Japan "spineless." When the soldiers heckled him, Mishima shouted "Long live the emperor," knelt on the floor and performed the traditional samurai ceremony of seppuku, a form of suicide reserved for the samurai warrior.

"Swaddling Clothes" dramatizes the concerns that shaped Mishima's work and his life: the conflict between Western and Japanese cultures, the vital importance of honor, and the nobility of self–sacrifice. It is a gripping story if you know nothing of Mishima's life; it becomes something more when you understand that its author was a man who both lived and died for the ideals he espoused.

QUESTIONS

1. Are the forces that compel Toshiko to go to the park so foreign to our culture that we as Westerners have trouble understanding the story?

I imagine that the initial response of your students will be that Toshiko is just plain weird, that it's one thing to be sympathetic to the baby boy born in her home, but it's quite another to feel so guilty that she knowingly seeks her own death. Your students may well claim that this is a story that could happen only in Japan. In a sense that may be true. But Toshiko is a complex character whose actions are more than a conditioned response to her culture's traditional notions of honor. Certainly the cultural element is present. While any of us would be upset and concerned about a birth under such circumstances, the focus of Toshiko's concern seems peculiarly Japanese. Her focus is not on the poverty and wretchedness the boy will endure but on the bloody newspapers, the symbol of the baby's dishonor. She cannot forget the shame enveloping the newborn wrapped in soiled newspapers and lying on the floor, a shame only she witnessed. "Blood stained newspapers. If a man were ever to hear of that piteous birth and know that it was he that had lain there, it would ruin his entire life. To think that I, a perfect stranger, should from now on have to keep such a secret—the secret of a man's whole existence..." (p. 513). Undoubtedly, one of the reasons she goes to the park is that her traditional Japanese values require her to do the honorable thing, to restore the child's lost honor by allowing him (or rather his symbolic counterpart) to destroy the only witness of his disgrace.

But there are other reasons for Toshiko's response. The narrator tells us that "Toshiko had been oversensitive [As I read the story "over–sensitive" is not to be disparaging, but your students may respond differently.] since girlhood: that was her nature. As the result of constant worrying, she never put on weight..." (p. 510). Toshiko's "delicacy of spirit" (p. 510) causes her to find the happening "horrifying" (p. 511). She is offended by the doctor's callous treatment of the newborn child (p. 511), and she is "shocked to find [her husband] entertaining friends with an account of 'the incident'" (p. 510). Toshiko, somewhat like Roderick Usher in Poe's "Fall of the House of Usher," seems to find a perverse pleasure in her own suffering. She does not attempt to put the incident out of her mind. At the nightclub, she sits "silently, thinking back on it" (p. 511). And later the narrator tells us, "No doubt Toshiko derived a certain satisfaction from her somber thoughts: she tortured herself with them without cease" (p. 512). On one level Toshiko's response is exactly what we might expect from a highly sensitive person who has been unhinged by a terrible event.

Still another explanation for Toshiko's decision to go to the park is a more universal one. The narrator makes it clear that Toshiko is bothered by the disparity between the social classes. We read that "Toshiko, whose own life had been spent in solid comfort, poignantly felt the wretchedness of the illegitimate baby" (p. 511). We learn that when she looks at her husband, she is "oppressed by the knowledge that their life together was in some way too easy, too painless" (p. 511). Your students should have no trouble understanding the guilt Toshiko feels because of her own prosperity. It is exactly what most middle–class Americans feel when they see homeless people living on our streets and in our subways. And just as we know that our contributions to charity don't begin to redress the inequities, Toshiko realizes that her loving gesture of wrapping the baby in swaddling clothes isn't sufficient atonement. "How strange that I should have this feeling of guilt! After all, it was I who took him up from the floor, swathed him properly in flannel, and laid him down to sleep in the armchair" (p. 511).

Toshiko, who has recently born a child herself, cannot help but contrast the future of her own son who will grow up to be "a fine, carefully educated young man" (p. 512) with that of the other boy "who has been sinned against" (p. 512). "Twenty years from now that wretched child will be in utter misery. He will be living a desolate, hopeless, poverty–stricken existence—a lonely rat" (p. 512).

Although "it would have been difficult for her to put her thoughts into words" (p. 511), Toshiko can visualize a kind of justice when she imagines the illegitimate child developing into a man who savagely stabs her own son. She is willing to allow such justice, but not to sacrifice her son. "No, when the time comes I shall take my son's place, she told herself suddenly" (p. 512).

2. What is the role of the husband in the story?

You might want to tell your students that the Counterpoint will offer some clues. In that selection Mishima suggests that many Japanese people have made a mistake by borrowing Western culture. He believes that such people are materialistic and wealthy and want nothing but to enjoy life without limitation, and that their lives are essentially "artificial."

Certainly Toshiko's husband (who is nameless in the story) fits that description. He lives in a house with Western–style furniture ("unhomely" in Toshiko's opinion—p. 510), wears an American–style suit (a "rather garish tweed coat"—p. 511), drives a Nash car (p. 511), and spends his evenings listening to jazz at nightclubs (p. 511).

In almost every way, he is Toshiko's opposite. She is quiet, refined and looks "more like a transparent picture than a creature of flesh and blood" (p. 510). He is an attractive actor with "a smiling face" and "strong white teeth" (p. 511) who "strides along the street" before dashing off to an appointment. Mishima portrays him as an insensitive lout. When the husband discovers that the new nurse they have hired is in labor, his only concern is "to rescue the good rug from the floor" (p. 510). Later he recounts the birth story for his friends' entertainment "as though it were no more than an amusing incident which they chanced to have witnessed" (p. 511). He is indifferent to the young woman's pain and dehumanizes her by describing her as "moaning like a cow" and "yelling like a stuck pig" (p. 510).

When Toshiko's husband is confronted with what Mishima calls "the raw stuff of life," he turns his head. First he leaves the house and then he trivializes the horror by turning it into an amusing story. In contrast, Toshiko stares unflinchingly at the "something 'raw' not only in our minds but in our history." Like Mishima she elects to "touch the fire." The first hint of Toshiko's inner strength comes when she "overcomes her disgust" at the scene of the birth and fetches a brand–new piece of flannel from her cupboard to swaddle the baby (p. 511).

Later, after she consciously decides to sacrifice herself for her child, she becomes fearless. First she decides "to go and view the blossoms by herself in the dark night" (p. 512). And although "as a rule when she walked in the traffic Toshiko used to cling fearfully to her companion, tonight she darted alone between the cars," (p. 512). When she sees the young man who seems to be "the embodiment of all her fears and premonitions," she has "an overmastering desire to get a glimpse of [his face]" (p. 513). Even when the young man seizes her, "she did not feel in the least afraid and made no effort to free herself" (p. 514).

In the final analysis, Mishima seems to be saying that the husband, whose outward appearance suggests strength and courage, is so corrupted by false Western values that he is afraid to face life. In contrast, Toshiko, who appears so frail, courageously searches for "the something genuine and pure" in life and accepts the consequences of her quest.

3. Why does the story seem tidier and more orderly than real life? Is that good or bad?

The purpose of this question is primarily to make your students realize that Mishima is not attempting to write a Maupassant story, that he isn't trying to create the illusion of reality. If this were a realistic story, the image of the young man on the bench "systematically covered with newspapers" (p. 513) might seem a bit contrived. But if the story is a poetic vision of the symmetry Toshiko both fears and seeks (the "fearful symmetry" of Blake's "Tyger"?), then all the carefully balanced images are absolutely true to the story's meaning.

Here are a few examples of balanced (but contrasting) images your students may note:

(a) the fake cherry blossoms decorating the front of the theater (p. 511) and the real blossoms in the park that form "a mass of solid whiteness" (p. 512),

(b) the descriptions of the husband's clothing (his "American–style suit"—p. 516) and the clothing of the young man on the bench (also Western but dirty and worn—p. 513),

(c) the infant lying on a parquet floor, his "frail body...wrapped in bloodstained newspapers" (p. 511) and the young man sleeping on the park bench "curled up on layers of newspapers, other newspapers covering him" (p. 513),

(d) the noise at the beginning of the story ("moans and groans from the nursery"—p. 510; the jazz orchestra at the nightclub braying—p. 511) and the silence at the end. "The forest of the Imperial Palace was pitch dark and utterly silent" (p. 514).

–M.R.D.

John Berger
An Independent Woman

As you might expect of a man who was once a teacher of drawing, John Berger has a talent for sketching complex subjects with a only a few

lines. In "An Independent Woman" he gives us an unforgettable portrait
of Catherine, a seventy–four–year–old French peasant whose spartan
physical existence has not deprived her of a rich emotional life.
Catherine has few material possessions, but she does have two lifelong
friends whose respect, love, and devotion give her life dignity and
meaning. The simple plot focuses our attention on the nature of the relationship of these three people: When the water to the *bassin* beside
Catherine's rural house stops flowing, her friends realize that without
that water source Catherine will have to carry buckets of water up frozen
slopes throughout the winter. Because they also realize that she is too
fiercely independent to ask for their help, they come to her aid unin-
vited.

You might want to assign this story and Steinbeck's "The Chrysanthemums" together. Steinbeck portrays an equally strong woman who is
stifled rather than encouraged by the men in her life.

QUESTIONS

1. How are the major characters in this story influenced by their social
environment?

The story seems to suggest that life in a simple rural community
forges a superior kind of person. When we read this story, it is easy to
forget that these strong, vigorous, vital people are old. Catherine, who is
seventy–four, is "just the eldest of the three" (p. 515). All three are a far
cry from the stereotypical notion of feeble old people. Each lives alone
and wrests a living from the land. The men are robust enough to spend
three days digging meter–deep trenches in snow–covered, rocky ground,
and Catherine carries buckets of water uphill from the spring to her
house across two fields during the months after the water to the *bassin*
ceases.

The two most admirable qualities of these people are their proud independence and their devotion to each other. Each is too independent to
ask for help. Catherine tells her brother that the water has stopped flowing and then "refused to mention the subject again" (p. 515). But in a
sense, each is able to be independent because all come to each other's aid
without being asked. Nicolas and Jean–François show up to dig the
trench; Catherine makes pastries for the tired men. The flashbacks show
us that this willingness to help their friends has been the pattern of
their lives: Nicolas and Jean–François came to cup Catherine when she
was ill, and when her brother Mathieu's wife died, Catherine left her
job at the doctor's house and came back to the village to spend the next
fifteen years bringing up her "two nieces like daughters."

Given his political persuasion, Berger probably believes that these peasants are better people than they would have been had they been corrupted by the evils of capitalism which are so inescapable in city life. Fortunately, Berger is too good a writer to be obtrusively didactic. He does, however, imply that people who live in cities are more class conscious, more concerned about money, and less concerned about treating other people as they should. It was while working in the city that Catherine "first heard the word 'peasant' used as an insult" (p. 517), that she was denied two months' wages when she left the doctor's house to care for her dying sister–in–law (p. 518), and that she formed her "lasting impression of the capital [as a place] where money continually changed hands. There, without money, you could literally do nothing. Not even drink water. With money you could do anything. He who could buy courage was brave, even if he was a coward" (p. 516).

Berger shows us that in a rural setting, with no money, Catherine, Jean François, and Nicolas became self–reliant, resourceful, courageous, and compassionate, and he makes us wonder what they would have been like if they had moved to the city. Yet Berger can hardly be accused of romanticizing the pastoral existence by suggesting that Catherine's life has been idyllic. He tells us that she never married because "each year of her life more men had left the valley, and she herself had inherited too little to propose to any of them that they should remain" (p. 516), and that when she thinks about dying, it is not an altogether unpleasant prospect: "On the other side I'd have no goats to look after, no potatoes to lift, no chickens to feed" (p. 520). We can't be certain that Catherine would have been less courageous if she had lived in a different society, but I'm inclined to believe that her knowledge that she has managed life under difficult circumstances makes her more confident that she can also manage death.

2. How effective is Berger's choice of point of view?

Berger writes the story in third person but allows us to see into Catherine's mind. This technique is effective for several reasons. First, it contributes to the suspense. Like Catherine, we wonder if the men will come back the third day, and like her, we do not know if they will succeed in finding the spring. Although Berger could have achieved the same effect by having Catherine narrate the story, it would have been hard for us to believe that Catherine, who is probably illiterate, would have written the story. And she is much too private to have related it to anyone.

The point of view is also successful in helping us to understand and admire Catherine. If this story were reported by an objective observer, most of us would probably think of Catherine as alien (and thus incom

prehensible), or we might pity her because of her poverty. By allowing us
to see into Catherine's mind, Berger demonstrates that both responses
are inappropriate. Berger shows us a woman who in many ways is exactly like the rest of us: Catherine laughs, jokes, curses, and cries. She
occasionally thinks about death, and she delights in the companionship
of her two friends. She differs from most people only in that she is surprisingly courageous. Catherine is a realist who refuses to squint when
she faces either life or death. Because she knows that old people die, each
night "she [lays] out her linen and stockings before climbing into bed,
so that Nicolas should know exactly how to dress her for the coffin" (p.
517). If she fears falling on the ice and lying there all day without being
found, it is not because she is afraid of death but because she prefers to die
in her house: "I want to see death come past the things I've lived with.
Then I can concentrate and not be distracted" (p. 520). Because we see
into Catherine's mind, we know she is not a woman who needs our pity.

The point of view effectively gives us a picture of reality much like that
presented by cubism, the revolutionary art form Berger so admires. Because cubists do not feel compelled to paint only what our eyes can see at
any given moment, a cubist may create a portrait of a woman that allows
us to see her face and the back of her head simultaneously. Berger, too,
refuses to be bound by a limited perspective. Berger reminds us that the
seventy–four–year–old woman we see today is merely one facet of Catherine, a complex woman who is a composite of a lifetime of experiences
still existent in her mind—Nicolas singing to cover the sounds of her
cries when she is being cupped (p. 519), the doctor's wife screaming for
help when Catherine picks up a poker (p. 518), her brother Mathieu saying he buried the pipe one meter deep (p. 515). The point of view selected
by Berger allows him to demonstrate that Catherine's emotional and
mental life is far more complex and varied than her daily activities
might suggest.

3. How do the flashbacks throughout the story reveal what has been significant in Catherine's life?

If we watched Catherine going about daily life in her isolated house—
carrying water from the spring, tending the goats, working in her
garden, we might imagine that she focuses her attention on the natural
world around her. On the contrary, the flashbacks indicate that virtually
all of her thoughts and memories concern her relations with people.
Only one paragraph is used to describe the valley where she has spent
most of her life (p. 520).

For Catherine, the most important part of life is human contact. The
story's title, which seems to suggest that people don't need others, turns
out to be ironic. Catherine may be too independent to ask for help, but
she needs and wants her friends' assistance and friendship. When

Nicolas and Jean–François arrive to dig for the pipe, she kisses them both and "the expression in her eyes was excited as though she had willed the two men to come" (p. 516). It is clear that Catherine's friendships with Nicolas and Jean–François have filled and enriched the lives of all three. C. S. Lewis once wrote that friendship "causes half of all the happiness in the world." Berger seems to agree.

–M.R.D.

Alice Adams
Return Trips

We seldom know how a particular story originates in the author's mind, but some stories, such as Dashiell Hammett's "Fly Paper," make us think the author began with a great idea for a plot and then invented characters to play the required parts. Authors such as Henry James seem to first imagine characters, then observe them to see what they do. Other writers apparently start with a fascinating idea which somehow becomes the nucleus of a story. Borges' "The Aleph" is a likely candidate for that category.

"Return Trips" suggests yet another point of origin. It is as if Alice Adams created one fully developed character, and then asked herself, "How did this woman come to be the person she is today?" In this story that character is the narrator, a "tall thin woman, graying, in early middle age" who teaches history, writes books about the Trotskyite movement, is involved in a "turbulent, difficult, and sometimes rewarding marriage," and regrets that her mother died "long before [their] war was in any way resolved." In an attempt to understand and perhaps resolve that war, the narrator eventually returns to Hilton, the southern town where her relationship with her mother "went so darkly and irretrievably wrong."

QUESTIONS

1. What is the significance of the title?

On one level, the title merely describes the trips the narrator makes [first in her dreams and later in reality] back to Hilton, the southern town her family lived in during her adolescence (p. 525), and the return trips to Greece and Yugoslavia that the narrator and her Greek husband Andreas plan for the following fall. On another level the title refers to trips that are even more significant to the narrator—her journeys through time that transport her from present to past and back again in an unending cycle.

The narrator presents a rather unorthodox view of the relationship between the past and the present. Most people would say that the present is shaped by the past; the narrator argues that the past is similarly shaped by the present. For her, past events are not chiseled in marble but typed on the screen of a word processor. She suggests her theory in this passage:

> A very wise woman who is considerably older than I am once told me that in her view relationships with people to whom we have been very close can continue to change even after the deaths of those people, and for me I think this has been quite true, with my mother, and in quite another way with Paul (p. 525).

It is the narrator's cycle of journeys between past and present that allows such relationships to continue to evolve. When the middle–aged narrator travels back to a previous experience, she is not the child or young woman who originally participated in that experience. Consequently, each return trip allows her to discover a past she could never have seen before. And just as her present perspective changes the past, her discovery of a "new" past changes her present. The woman who returns to the here and now is not the woman who left it moments or eons earlier.

If you ask your students to label every passage in the story to indicate whether it focuses on distant past, intermediate past, recent past, present or future, they should notice that the structure of the story reflects the narrator's concept of time. The story does not move forward in a linear, chronological fashion but instead spirals (forward?) between time periods.

2. What is the turning point of the story?

It is much easier to discuss the turning point of a story such as Maupassant's "The String" in which the writer introduces a conflict and then presents one unbroken chain of cause and effect that leads inexorably to a climax. Your students may conclude that there is no turning point in this story because the narrator simply relates events pellmell as they pop into her mind.

You may want to suggest that your students first attempt to identify the central conflict in the story and then look for a passage in which it is in some way resolved. I would suggest that the central conflict is the narrator's struggle to make peace with her past, which for her is symbolized by Hilton, the southern town where she lived during her teenage years. The narrator's ambivalence toward Hilton is suggested by her description of it as "the scene of our family's dissolution, and the heady start of my own adolescence" (p. 525), two separate events that are almost causally linked in her mind.

Hilton marks the beginning of the narrator's estrangement from her mother. For the narrator Hilton is "romantic and exciting," the scene of her "first overtly sensual experience" (p. 526). As she later realizes, her collisions with her mother were probably unavoidable: "Nearly adolescent, I was eager for initiation into romantic, sensual mysteries of which I had dim intimations from books" (p. 526). The narrator at twelve sees her mother as a barrier between her and happiness, an ogress who insists that she come back from her walks with "those lean, tall sweet-talking Southern boys" (p. 526) by ten. "[My mother] wept and raged, despairing and helpless as she recognized the beginning of my life as a sensual woman, coinciding as it probably did with the end of her own" (p. 526). The narrator later recalls, "My mother filled me with a searing discomfort, a longing to be away from her" (p. 527). None of those emotions are surprising. As a teenager, I often felt that my mother's primary purpose in life was to make me miserable. My daughters, who are now twelve and fifteen, sometimes have similar [and, I might add, unjustified] feelings about me.

In the normal course of things, the narrator, after surviving adolescence, would have established a non–adversarial relationship with her mother. Two events make that impossible. The first is the narrator's chance view of her father parked in the family car on the back road to her house "kissing someone; their bodies...blotted into one silhouette" (p. 528). She later recalls that she felt "burning rage, a painful seething shame" (p. 528). The experience would have been devastating under any circumstances; its impact is even greater because the narrator, immediately before seeing the car, had been kissing her date. Because she too finds Hilton "romantic and exciting" (p. 526), it is as if she is somehow unwillingly implicated in her father's betrayal of her mother. Perhaps the narrator would eventually have realized that she was not her father's accomplice. But before she has time to resolve her conflicts, her mother dies "most unexpectedly...in a senseless automobile accident" (p. 530) "long before the war [between mother and daughter] was in any way resolved" (p. 525).

Hilton, the symbol of that internecine warfare, becomes the focus of the narrator's nightmares and fantasies. In the nightmares she walks down the "long, intensely familiar hill" leading to her family's house in Hilton, but she never arrives at the house because it is so hot and she is "burdened with the most terrific, heavy pain" in her chest (p. 525). In some of her fantasies she imagines what her life would have been like if she had stayed in Hilton and married "one of those lean and sexy sweet-talking boys." She admits, "And often that seemed a preferrable way to have taken" (p. 531). In another fantasy she returns to Hilton, buys and renovates the house her family had lived in, spends her days doing re

search and writing books, and becomes "the sort of good daughter" to
Popsie Hooker that she "was so far from being" to her own mother (p.
532).

When she does at last return to Hilton, neither the nightmares nor
the fantasies come true. She begins "the long descent" toward her house
and smiles "inexplicably happy at just that moment—with no heat, no
pain in [her] heart" (p. 533). Her house is not, as she had imagined,
"neglected, needing paint, new gutters, perhaps even falling apart" (p.
532), but "repainted—all smartened up with bright white paint and long
black louvered shutters..." and four recent–model sports cars parked in
the driveway (p. 533). Popsie is "barely recognizable, so shrunken and
wizened had she become" (p. 534). The narrator, who is now a professor
like her mother and who is approximately the same age her mother had
been when they lived in Hilton, views Popsie much as her mother must
have and characterizes her as "that silly little person, my mother's
natural enemy" (p. 535).

The turning point occurs immediately after Popsie asks the narrator,
"Where did you get that beauty, do you think?" and then caustically remarks, "Your mother never was even one bit pretty ",p. 535). Without
hesitating, the narrator rejects Popsie as substitute mother by declaring
her allegiance to her long dead mother, "Actually I look quite a lot like
my mother" (p. 535). She fortifies her position by insisting that she
doesn't favor her father at all. The narrator leaves Hilton with "an unusual sense of well–being" (p. 535), having at last dealt with her "guilt,
and the sheer irresolution" of her connection with her mother (p. 530).

3. Using the terms *analytical* and *objective* as they are defined by Maupassant in the Counterpoint, explain why you might place this short story in
one category or the other.

Your students will probably classify Adams as a writer who chooses "to
flaunt psychology rather than conceal it." Certainly that description
would fit the narrator of this story, a woman who is given to introspec-
tion and who attempts to be as analytical as possible. She mentions that
she wanted to marry Paul, and then writes a paragraph explaining why
she wanted to be married (p. 524). She notes that both of her husbands
have been unlike Paul and "wearily" reflects on her "tendency toward
extremes and contrasts" (p. 536). She remembers her youthful anger toward her mother and explains, "Having no idea how much I pitied her,
I believed that I hated her" (p. 527). The narrator does her best to tell
"the why and wherefore of every impulse."

But Adams is not the narrator. Although Adams is undoubtedly interested in "all the secret motives of our every action," she, like Maupassant's objective writer, often reveals those motives by trying "to discover
the action or gesture which that state of mind must inevitably lead to in

that personage." Adams does not tell us why the narrator returns to Hilton. Instead, she shows us the return trip, lets us listen to the narrator's conversation with Popsie, and leaves us to puzzle out its significance.

–M.R.D.

Gabriel García Márquez
A Very Old Man with Enormous Wings

A place to begin with this short story is with the Counterpoint, in which García Márquez explains the "journalistic trick" he employs in "A Very Old Man with Enormous Wings":

> For example, if you say that there are elephants in the sky, people will not believe you. But if you say that there are four hundred and twenty-five elephants in the sky, people will probably believe you. (p. 543)

García Márquez provides us with the number and type of details that make the very old man with enormous wings a homely thing—no more an object of long-term curiosity than a three-legged pig. We first meet the angel when he is groaning and thrashing in the mud, and we soon learn that he is bald, has few teeth, and has "huge buzzard wings" (p. 538). The visiting priest notices that the angel is "much too human: he had an unbearable smell of the outdoors, the back side of his wings was strewn with parasites and his main feathers had been mistreated by terrestrial winds" (p. 539). In short, the angel ceases to become an angel for us and for Pelayo and Elisenda and becomes merely "a very old man with enormous wings." This journalistic trick of transforming the supernatural into the domestic produces an effect you may wish to call for convenience's sake "magical realism."

And we can see the trick of the impossible being turned into the plausible in microcosm throughout the early parts of the short story. Every magical event is brought down to earth with a thump and grounded in reality, sometimes in the same sentence. Take, for instance, "The world had been sad since Tuesday" (p. 537); in that one line are we raised up by the pathetic fallacy "The world had been sad," and asked to believe in the type of animism that fills the works of García Márquez—then we have to downshift our imaginations immediately for the "since Tuesday" at the end of the sentence. The same thing happens in the very next sentence: "Sea and sky were a single ash-gray thing and the sands of the beach, which on March nights glimmered like powdered light, had become a stew of mud and rotten shellfish." After the metaphor employing the sea and the sky, those beautiful sands become—suddenly—at the end of the sentence—a putrid stew. What García Márquez does at this level he does throughout the whole story: time and time again during the short story we are forced to compare the divine and the dungheap.

QUESTIONS

1. How does the very old man with enormous wings differ from the conventional Christian view of how angels look and act?

A simple question that demands a not–so–simple answer. You might find that reading the first two paragraphs of "A Very Old Man with Enormous Wings" and then reading the following passage from *Paradise Lost* (concerning another fallen angel) makes your point forcefully:

Thus Satan talking to his nearest mate
With head uplift above the wave, and eyes
That sparkling blazed, his other parts besides
Prone on the flood, extended long and large
Lay floating many a rood, in bulk as large
As whom the fables name of monstrous size,
Titanian, or Earth–born, that warred on Jove,
Briareos or Typhon, whom the den
By ancient Tarsus held, or that sea–beast
Leviathan, which God of all his works
Created hugest that swim the ocean stream:
Him haply slumbering on the Norway foam
The pilot of some small night–foundered skiff,
Deeming some island, oft, as seamen tell,
With fixed anchor in his scaly rind
Moors by his side under the lea, while night
Invests the sea, and wished morn delays:
So stretched out huge in length the arch–fiend lay
Chained on the burning lake . . .
(1.192–209)

Your students will be sure to see that García Márquez's fallen angel lying moaning on a beach of mud and rotten shellfish is far removed from conventional literary depictions of angels. And that is why García Márquez's view is so amusing; he has yanked the rug out from under our expectations. Even Milton's Satan is grander than the very old man with enormous vulture wings.

2. What judgments are we to make of Pelayo, Elisenda, and the other villagers?

García Márquez is poking good–natured (or perhaps not so good–natured) fun at human nature throughout. Pelayo and Elisenda, had the tale been set on another continent and in a different century, might be held up as examples of the Yankee, that hard–nosed and unflappable huckster with an eye for a buck. In short, characters like Pelayo and Elisenda have been with us at least since *Lazarillo de Tormes.* They are workaday folks with a sick baby and a house and yard full of crabs who just don't have the time or imagination to be astounded by the appearance of an angel. They are too soft–hearted to club the angel to death, as the wise neighborwoman suggests, but they are "magnanimous" to the extent that they are willing to put the sick angel on a raft on the open sea with three days of provisions and leave him to his fate. Hard–nosed utilitarian Pelayo, instead of treating the angel with the reverence one might be expected to offer to such a being, promptly pops him into the chicken coop with the rest of the poultry—and then exhibits him for profit. Elisenda, tired of having an angel underfoot, drives him out of the bedroom with a broom like the family dog (p. 541), and rejoices when the feathered stray flaps off like "a senile vulture" (p. 542).

When the miraculous and the mundane rub together a callus seems to be formed. It always amazes me, for instance, that children can sit deadpan through movies with special effects that make me dive under the seat despite the fossilized popcorn and congealed soda. My wife tells me that a constant barrage of the unbelievable is likely to dull one to its effects. The villagers seem to have that childlike capacity to approach the supernatural with a matter–of–factness that renders it anything but super. No one, for instance, doubts the angel's supernatural origins: the village wise woman proclaims him an angel come for the sick child, and that is that. But the villagers, despite their superstitious awe of the angel, are quick to turn to a more entertaining and less expensive form of entertainment when the "frightful tarantula the size of a ram and with the head of a sad maiden" (p. 540) hits town.

3. How is Father Gonzaga's reaction to the angel different from his parishioners'? Is he more or less gullible than they?

The parishioners' suggestions for what should be done with the angel are naive but always practical. The wise neighbor woman suggests that as a fallen angel he should be clubbed to death; another maintains that "in order to win all wars" he should be named a five–star general. Others suggest that the angel be put to stud in order to improve the gene pool. All the villagers, then, wish to put the angel to some *use.*

Father Gonzaga, who has a doctrinal if not monetary stake in determining the authenticity of the angel, attempts to speak to it in "the language of God" (p. 539), that is, Latin. He soon discovers that nothing in the captive "measured up to the proud dignity of angels," and makes *his* use of the angel by making the old man the subject of a brief sermon on "the risks of being ingenuous" and on snares set by the Devil (p. 539). Even though the angel fails the litmus test of responding in Latin, the priest agrees to rely on a higher authority, which turns out to be the slow–moving administrative mechanisms of the Church.

Pelayo and Elisenda cannot wait for the Pontiff's seal of approval and market their prize aggressively, filling their yard with pilgrims and their rooms with money. In the meantime, the good Father waits for guidance from his superiors:

> But the mail from Rome showed no sense of urgency. They spent their time finding out if the prisoner had a navel, if his dialect had any connection with Aramaic, how many times he could fit on the head of a pin, or whether he wasn't just a Norwegian with wings. (p. 540)

Here García Márquez has given over almost completely to satire. Rather than demonstrating the kind of excitement one might expect when an angel is discovered, the Church spends its time in bloodless academic discourse, leaving Father Gonzaga to deal with cripples seeking cures through the touch of parasite–ridden feathers. This is mere superstition! Fortunately for Gonzaga, yet another monstrosity, this time a pious and repentant spider–woman who by example does the work of God, appears:

> . . . she had sneaked out of her parents' house to go to a dance, and while she was coming back through the woods after having danced all night without permission, a fearful thunderclap rent the sky in two and through the crack came the lightening bold to brimstone that changed her into a spider. Her only nourishment came from the meatballs that charitable souls chose to toss into her mouth. A spectacle like that, full of so much human truth and with such a fearful lesson, was bound to defeat without even trying that of a haughty angel who scarcely deigned to look at mortals. Besides, the few miracles attributed to the angel showed a certain mental disorder, like the blind man who didn't recover his sight but grew three new teeth, or the paralytic who didn't get to walk but almost won the lottery, and the leper whose sores sprouted sunflowers. (p. 541)

The priest, whose faith must have been shaken by this inappropriate angel, ceases to suffer from insomnia when a creature that he can put to *use* as a moral example appears as the new main attraction in the village.

Gonzaga, then, is as guilty as Pelayo and Elisenda for demanding utility of the angel.

–W.R.S.

Alice Munro
Circle of Prayer

In the Counterpoint to this story Margaret Atwood asserts that the central theme of Canadian literature is survival. Although "Circle of Prayer" is not a tale of "those who made it back from the awful experience—the North, the snowstorm, the sinking ship—that killed everyone else," it is a story about "hanging on, staying alive." "Circle of Prayer" focuses on two ordinary days in the life of Trudy, a recently divorced woman in her mid–thirties. We see Trudy worrying about and arguing with her teenage daughter Robin, working the four–to–midnight shift at the Home for Mentally Handicapped Adults, helping her friend Janet make Kleenex flowers for a wedding, and—in her spare moments—trying to sort out her feelings for her former husband and make sense of her life.

QUESTIONS

1. How does Munro use (a) setting and (b) plot to reflect the disorder and confusion of her characters' lives?

In this realistic short story Munro shows life as anything but neat and tidy. The story is crowded with images of disorder—Robin's bedroom where clothes "old and new and clean and dirty were scattered on the floor" (p. 544), the lawn of the Home littered with soft–drink cans and beer bottles (p. 546), Genevieve's and Dan's chaotic household (p. 548), the noise and constant vibration of road construction (p. 552), ice cream dribbling down Marie's and Josephine's chins and arms (p. 555), and Dan's mother's vacant hotel with "old dead leaves and broken shingles on the roof" (p. 557).

The plot (or sequence of scenes) is also disorderly. Subplots abound— one about Robin and the jet beads, another about the cause of Dan's and Trudy's divorce, another about Janet and the Circle of Prayer, and yet another about Kelvin. Scenes from the various subplots are juxtaposed in the story just as they are in life. In one scene Trudy is looking at the mugs at the Home, in the next she is remembering her honeymoon, and in the next she is talking on the telephone with Robin (pp. 556–558).

Munro makes us feel that such disarray is appropriate in a world where fourteen–year–old girls die in senseless accidents and marriages end for no apparent reason.

2. How does Munro want us to feel about the people in this story?

In this story there are no saints and no villains. Dan, a man who deserted his wife and daughter, is a likeable fellow who "is good at everything" (p. 548), a man who "shops for bargains, cooks, looks after [his stepchildren], grows vegetables, and drives a taxi on Saturdays and Sundays" (p. 548) so his wife Genevieve can spend her time in the law library studying. Munro makes us believe that he probably didn't intend to fall in love with Genevieve (He met her in his auto–repair shop, not a singles bar), that he does indeed love both Genevieve and Trudy, that he despises himself for making Trudy unhappy, and that his life with Genevieve is not paradise. Although Dan insists that he has never been happier, Robin doubts him, and after reading her description of the "madhouse" in Richmond Hill (p. 548), so do we. [I concede that I may be biased because of my own experiences. When I started law school, my three children were five, eight, and eleven. I'm quite sure that during the three years I was a student, neither my husband nor I would have claimed that we had never been happier.] Munro presents Dan as a good man whose life gets muddled, not because he has some tragic flaw, but because that's just the way life is. Like Trudy, we understand Dan's dilemma and we sympathize with him.

Trudy, our heroine, is unlikely to be canonized. When she is angry, she hurls insults, obscenities, and pottery (pp. 552. 544). When Dan "ditches" his fiancée Marlene for Trudy, Trudy is oblivious to Marlene's suffering: "Trudy had no feelings for Marlene at all. Marlene was over thirty—what could she expect?" (p. 549). When her friend Janet suggests that Trudy join the Circle of Prayer, Trudy cruelly mocks her (p. 555). We overlook those incidents because we understand why they occurred, and Munro makes us believe that Trudy is essentially a good person who tries to do what is right—when she can figure out what that is and muster the strength to do it. She tells Robin she didn't throw the jug at her, she encourages Dan to go back to Genevieve (p. 553), and she apologizes to Janet and makes fresh coffee for her (p. 556).

Although the characters in this story sometimes make mistakes that hurt others, they are not evil and they do not enjoy the suffering they cause. They have nothing in common with the monsters depicted in stories such as Joyce Carol Oates' "Where Are You Going, Where Have You Been?" or Flannery O'Connor's "A Good Man Is Hard to Find." Munro seems to be telling us that if we knew why people act as they do, we would be unable to despise them. But, like Kelvin, we find our minds clouded by "a gentle head fog" that "doesn't obscure facts, just motives"

(p. 546), both our own and those of others. I suspect that if Munro had explained more about the people who tease Kelvin when he goes to town, we might even be sympathetic toward them (p. 556).

3 . What is the significance of Kelvin's statement, "If I was smart enough to know what to pray for, then I wouldn't have to"?

Kelvin's observation illustrates perfectly the central problem of Trudy's life, and—I suspect—of most people's lives. If Trudy knew that her prayers would be granted, she wouldn't be able to decide what to pray for. She could pray to get Dan back, but could she forgive and forget? Would he be happy? Would she feel guilty if she made Genevieve miserable? She could pray to turn back the clock and prevent Dan from meeting Genevieve, but could she be sure that Dan wouldn't fall in love with another young woman? She could pray that Dan would be different, that he would no longer be "a man who could change course quickly, see the possibilities, flare up with new enthusiasm" (p. 549). But would he still be the man she fell in love with?

Dan, Robin, and Kelvin are in equally confused states. Dan is in love with two women and is attempting to be a good father to his own daughter and Genevieve's children. Robin, struggling through the limbo that separates childhood and adulthood, loves her parents and hates them for complicating her life. Kelvin doesn't quite fit in anywhere. "Perhaps he shouldn't be in the Home at all, but where else?" (p. 546).

4. Identify the rituals described in the story and explain their significance.

If we define ritual as the acts prescribed by custom or authority as proper for a particular occasion, your students should find a number of examples:

♦ Trudy and Janet make five hundred roses out of pink Kleenex to decorate the car for Janet's niece's wedding (pp. 547, 555).

♦ Tracy Lee's family holds visitation at the funeral home (p. 549).

♦ Robin and her friends place jewelry in Tracy Lee's casket and sing as they file past the coffin (p. 550).

♦ When a member of the Circle of Prayer is in trouble, she calls another member and asks for the Circle's prayers. The member who received the call phones one other member who phones yet another until everyone has been contacted and they all pray together (p. 554).

◆ Janet and Trudy buy personalized mugs for the residents of the Home, and Kelvin buys mugs for Janet and Trudy (p. 556).

◆ Trudy makes fresh coffee to offer Janet when she comes to work (p. 556).

These rituals serve a number of purposes. They mark the significance of important events, provide a pattern for correct behavior, create a feeling of unity among the participants, and impose order on an otherwise chaotic world. Apparently Robin and her friends have never been to a funeral home and don't know what is expected of them, but they know that the death of a teenager has to be observed in a special way and they make up their own ritual: "It was like a religious ceremony. The girls behaved as if they'd been told what to do, as if this was what was always done on such occasions. They sang, they wept, they dropped their jewelry. The sense of ritual made every one of them graceful" (p. 550).

The importance of ritual is particularly evident when it is absent. When Trudy and Dan try to decide whether to part (p. 551), their confrontations are characterized by yelling, screaming, crying, drinking and wondering what to do next. Perhaps divorce rituals would have alleviated their pain.

5. Is the story ultimately optimistic or pessimistic?

I'm not sure why, but I think it's optimistic. The story doesn't close with a traditional happy ending: Tracy Lee is dead, Dan is married to Genevieve, and Robin and Trudy will continue to clash. And yet there is a sense of well-being. In the final scenes three people demonstrate their affection for Trudy. Janet accepts Trudy's apology and means it. "Sometimes you think they're your friend, and they are" (p. 556). Robin makes amends by asking if she can run over to the Home and ride back with Trudy (p. 558). Kelvin tries to cheer her up with his answer to her question about prayer. His halfway joke "radiates—expands the way some silliness can, when you're very tired. In this way, when she was young, and high, a person or a moment could become a lily floating on the cloudy river water, perfect and familiar" (p. 558). We feel that so long as Trudy has friends like Janet and Robin and Kelvin, she will continue to survive and—sometimes—to find moments of inexplicable happiness.

—M.R.D.

Chinua Achebe
Civil Peace

The Counterpoint to this short story and some assessments by critics might lead students to see Achebe's short story more as a lesson in cultural relativism than a work of fiction. The story stands strongly on its own two feet, though; if it is didactic, it teaches us something that passes rather easily over boundaries of race, culture, and nation: our lives may be interrupted by forces that seem to operate arbitrarily and murderously, taking from us what we hold dearest. "A Good Man Is Hard to Find" and "Where Are You Going, Where Have You Been?" rely for their successes on the same fears in us—the fear that drives some of us to keep baseball bats and shotguns in our closets. Blind circumstance and his own roving malice place the Misfit with Bailey–boy and family when they are completely at his mercy; Arnold Friend marks Connie for death at the drive–in because she catches his eye. In this story, Jonathan Iwegbu and his family find themselves in danger of losing their lives over *ex gratia*—"egg–rasher"—money to unknown and unseen desperados.

But despite the universality of this fear in us that Achebe knows and relies on, there is a great deal in the setting and in Jonathan's responses to the cards he is dealt that might strike Western readers as alien. Job, for instance, does despair and curse God; Jonathan, on the other hand, carries on his life amongst carnage and privation that would make most of us crawl onto our couches and pull the afghan over our heads (if we had couches or afghans and were allowed to keep our heads) or run screaming into the night. Indeed, Jonathan carries optimism to an extreme that most of us might consider escapism or madness, always buoyed by piety and the knowledge that events are shaped by a purpose he cannot fathom—nothing puzzles God.

QUESTIONS

1. Why does Achebe begin with a history of Jonathan's bicycle?

This short story is remarkable in the way that Achebe stacks details to create a unified effect. In fact, a glance at just the first page of the short story reveals a quantity and quality of detail that assures us that for Achebe less is more—that is, less overt sentiment results in a more powerful effect upon the reader. In the guise of giving us the history of a bicycle, Achebe delivers exposition and describes a setting that might be maudlin if presented "straight," that is, with predictable outrage at the conditions the Iwegbus must suffer. What follows in brackets is a sketchy accounting of what we learn in the process of being told about the survival of the bicycle.

"He had come out of the war with five inestimable blessings—his head, his wife Maria's head and the heads of three out of their four children . . . he also had his old bicycle . . ."

[There has been a war; Jonathan counts the survival of the majority of his family as a blessing—he has little else. That Jonathan and most of his family have their "heads" may be metonymy—but maybe not. His bicycle, with which he builds his "fortune," survives the war as well.]

". . . had he not had some doubts about the genuineness of the officer. It wasn't his disreputable rags, nor the toes peeping out of one blue and one brown canvas shoe . . ."

[Jonathan lives in circumstances in which an officer *might* be so disreputably dressed; he also lives in circumstances where men might have to rely on dangerous trickery (impersonating an officer in order to commandeer a bicycle).]

" . . . Jonathan . . . produced the two pounds with which he had been going to buy firewood which his wife, Maria, retailed to camp officials for extra stock–fish and corn meal, and got his bicycle back. That night he buried it in the little clearing in the bush where the dead of the camp, including his own youngest son, were buried."

[What we might consider staples are not taken for granted by Jonathan and his family. Their diet is a poor one. He is forced to bury his bicycle; nearby is the (presumably mass) grave containing the body of his youngest son.]

In short, in following the tale of the bicycle we learn indelibly something that the assertion in the first line might not have driven home: that for Jonathan Iwegbu "happy survival" is more than just a greeting. We learn as well that material things we might discount, paradoxically, have for him the greatest and the least value imaginable.

2. What point of view does Achebe choose? How does that affect our perception of the encounter with the bandits?

The narrator is third person limited omniscient. Quite plainly Jonathan Iwegbu is the central consciousness, for we often know what he thinks and feels. And when we hear and feel what Jonathan hears and feels during the assault on his home we feel his terror. His rickety door and house could serve as obstacles for only the most disinterested of thieves; we recognize when his attackers mimic his family's calls for help just how helpless they are. The head thief's irony is deadly serious: "My fren, why you no de talk again. I de ask you say you wan make we call soja? . . . Now make we talk business. We no be bad tief. We no like for make trouble. Trouble done finish. War done finish and all the katakata wey de for inside. No Civil War again. This time na Civil Peace . . ."(pp. 562–563). This banter does little to disguise the chilling possibilities: "Lookia my fren, no be play we come play for your house. If we make mistake and step for inside you no go like am–o" (p. 563). The bandit chief, perhaps because of the solemnity of Jonathan's oath but finally for reasons known only to him, calls off the siege—after Jonathan hands over the egg–rasher money.

3. Do you believe Jonathan when he says of his egg–rasher money that "I count it as nothing"? How do you interpret his final speech?

Most readers will probably take Jonathan at his word here, but there is slight evidence of rancor in his final speech. When he asks "Or is it [the ex gratia money] greater than other things that went with the war?" the answer must be no, but he did, after all, lose a son. His calmness in the face of the *ex gratia* pounds must not be interpreted as a bland indifference to the loss of money that might decide life or death for his family. When Jonathan says "let egg–rasher perish in the flames! Let it go where everything else has gone," we detect anger at having just one more possession taken from him by force and chance. The "Nothing puzzles God" at the end of the short story may not ring true for all your students.

Still, we are invited to compare Jonathan's loss of the egg–rasher money to that of the unnamed man whose pocket is picked in the ex gratia queue. That man collapses "into near–madness" (p. 561) and an "extremity of agony" (p. 561) when his twenty pounds is taken from him; Achebe is careful to point out that for Iwegbu and his family life after the loss of the twenty pounds goes on pretty much as usual, with Jonathan preparing his bicycle for the day's work, his wife cooking akara balls, and his son washing beer bottles soon to be refilled with palm wine.

–W.R.S.

Elena Poniatowska
A Little Fairy Tale

"A Little Fairy Tale" is unlike any fairy tale your students have ever read. If the scenes from this short story were presented in a series of paintings, they would bear a striking resemblance to the surrealistic visions painted by Salvador Dali. Weird and frightening images fill the story: Berta, a young girl in a white dress, walks through the forest gathering strawberries and is gored by a wild boar. The narrator, another young girl, goes to the windowless house of witchlike Madame Dot and is told that the boar killed Berta "for the black flower that grows between a woman's legs." Later, on the narrator's wedding night, her husband is transformed into a wild boar with "eyes glowing red" who charges his bride "head–on from his powerful tuxedo."

In the Counterpoint to this story W. H. Auden describes the fairy tale as "a projection in symbolic images of the life of the psyche," and he concludes that the tale can travel from one country or culture to another if "whatever it has to say holds good for human nature in both." This story, with its exploration of the fear and fascination evoked by the mysterious powers of sexuality, travels well.

QUESTIONS

1. What happens to Berta?

This question will demonstrate to your students how difficult it is to know what happens, even on the literal level, in this story. Berta's death is related by an unreliable narrator who may have been deliberately misinformed by other people. No wonder we don't allow hearsay testimony in the courtroom.

We can be relatively certain that Berta bled to death, that her father led the hunters, and that her fiancé fled drunk and crazed to Cahors (p. 566). Beyond that, all is conjecture. The narrator hears reports that Berta was killed by a wild boar that gored, or bit, or charged her. "Or who knows?" (p. 566). But because the narrator at that time is a young girl who must be protected from certain kinds of knowledge (she and Sofia are not allowed to see the dead Berta), we can't be sure that people tell her the truth about what happened. Madame Dot tells the narrator that the boar killed Berta "for her flower," which—if true—seems to mean that Berta's death was in some way caused by a sexual act. Perhaps Berta was raped and murdered, perhaps she died during a miscarriage, an abortion, or childbirth, or perhaps she was simply gored by a wild boar. This incident, like all the others in this nightmarish scenario, can be interpreted in any number of ways.

What matters is, that regardless of what actually occurred, the narrator, a naive and impressionable young girl, is convinced that death, brutality, and sexuality are inextricably bound. She is so frightened that she runs out of Madame Dot's house and doesn't stop running until she is twenty-three (p. 567).

2. Why does the narrator see her husband as a wild boar?

There are at least two explanations: It may be that the husband actually is a brutal beast whose assault of his wife forces her to remember the fate of Berta and to confuse the identities of the two attackers. On the other hand, it may be that the narrator was so traumatized by Madame Dot's story that she perceives any sexual encounter as threatening and any man, no matter how loving, a wild boar.

It is difficult to understand the narrator's attitude toward sexuality because the story is deliberately ambiguous. The early descriptions of the narrator as young girl digging in the damp earth of the forest are filled with sexual imagery. The narrator recalls, "I would stop to stroke the rough bark, to plunge my hands into the damp earth, to cut the stems of mushrooms with their fascinating texture; crack; I'd stroke them with my index finger for a long time, watching their skin stiffen like the leaves of certain plants that tighten and close on themselves" (p. 565). And she remarks that such digging still causes her excitement and satisfaction. These early scenes may suggest gentle, pleasurable masturbatory experiences. Or they may symbolize the young girl's search for answers to adult mysteries. Or they may represent nothing more than the typical childhood delight of playing in the dirt.

The narrator's account of her wedding night is equally ambiguous. Although she describes her husband as a wild boar, she is attracted as well as repelled by him, and her description of their lovemaking could suggest pain, or ecstasy, or both:

> I who had begun to caress the fascinating texture of mushrooms, to feel their damp beneath my fingertips, fell backwards; crack, crack, crack, and when he put his arms around me I fell down, down onto a steep path that descended to the deepest reaches of the woods. My screams must have pierced the thin walls of the hotel...."

Even the narrator's comment that "the same scream was heard again that night, but over the years it grew fainter and less frequent" (p. 568) is open to multiple interpretations. Did their lovemaking become less frequent? Less brutal? Less pleasurable?

At the end of the story the narrator, "whose hair has begun to turn white" (p. 568), dreams of returning to the forest to put her "hands into the earth, find the truffle and feel the little creatures that make their homes in the dense weeds" (p. 568). She says that if she could start over, she would hope to meet up with some other animal, perhaps a unicorn, or a tapestry lion, or a swan, or a deer—anything except the wild boar. Perhaps she wishes for romantic courtly love; perhaps she wishes for less frightening and brutal sexual experiences; perhaps she wishes for a return to the innocence of childhood.

3. How is the story similar to a fairy tale? How is it different?

This story seems to have all the characteristic ingredients of a fairy tale; a nonspecific time and place; a dark, mysterious forest where evil forces lurk; a witch (possibly evil or possibly good); the magical transformation of a human into a wild boar; and even a fairy godmother. What more could anyone ask? But if W. H. Auden's definition of the fairy tale as "a serious tale with a human hero and a happy ending" is correct, then this story is a deliberate perversion of the traditional fairy tale, a Black Mass recognizing though not celebrating the triumph of darkness, confusion, and fear.

Poniatowska echoes the language of fairy tales, but the echoes are distorted. Instead of "Once upon a time," she begins with "From time to time...," and she ends the story with a jumble of well-known lines:

> A fairy tale, yes, because it's late now and I don't have what it takes for all this jousting, and the little dog laughed to see such sport, right? and all I know is that they lived everly happily after and had many children and rode in a carriage, and all the king's horses and all the king's men do you want me to tell it over again?

Poniatowska further confuses us by establishing familiar patterns and then turning them upside down. We all know that the handsome hero is supposed to rescue the heroine from danger. But instead of saving his bride from a wild boar, this Prince Charming becomes a wild boar. "Beauty and the Beast" and "The Frog King" have led us to believe the love of a good woman can change an animal into a man; Poniatowska tells us that a wedding can turn a man into a beast.

–M.R.D.

Edna O'Brien
Sister Imelda

This is a short story that will, I suspect, spark more discussion than one might think at first reading. Among other things, it is "about" the tension between the sacred and the profane, "about" the examined life and the sort of life that most of us scorn—and live. We view Sister Imelda as the narrator does, and she seems a creature of infinite variety, as fascinating for her spirituality as her worldliness; in short, in a world as dull and oppressive as the convent school the sister becomes the focus for the longings, temporal and otherwise, of the young girl.

You might find it useful to compare this story with "The Legend of St. Julian the Hospitaller. The method of depicting another character torn between the sacred and the profane is entirely different. Julian is *not* infinitely various; in fact, his stints as butcher, then warrior, and then ascetic are relieved only by his passage into another obsession. While Flaubert's method of characterization may be appropriate to the depiction of a madman and saint, O'Brien's method is appropriate to the depiction of a living, breathing woman as seen through the eyes of a living, breathing, and adoring girl.

I think an even more valuable comparison is to be made between "Araby" and "Sister Imelda" because of the confusion between the amatory and the sacred. The boy in "Araby" associates his love for Mangan's sister with religious feelings just as the narrator confuses her feelings for Imelda as—pardon the distinction—bride of Christ and woman. The stories are also ripe for comparison in that both deal with a passion for what turns out to be the unattainable, and both passions have a sort of subterranean sexuality, being more crushes than grand loves.

This story affords a real opportunity to teach how characterization is shaped and limited by point of view. Since the point of view is not omniscient, we are not privy to the thoughts of Imelda; only dialogue and the descriptions given us through the eyes of the smitten narrator allow us glimpses of the nun.

QUESTIONS

1. Choose some words or phrases used to describe Imelda near the beginning of the short story. How do these affect our impression(s) of the sister?

[All from p. 570, unless marked otherwise.]

◆ "she was tall and limber"

◆ "Her pale, slightly long face I saw as formidable . . ."

◆ " . . . her eyes were different, being blue–black and full of verve . . ."

◆ "Her lips were very purple . . . They were the lips of a woman who might sing in a cabaret, and unconsciously she had formed the habit of turning them inward, as if she, too, was aware of their provocativeness."

◆ "It was amazing how her looks changed. Some days, when her eyes were flashing, she looked almost profane . . ."

◆ "She might have been a girl going to a dance, except for her habit."

◆ "Hasn't she wonderful eyes," I said to Baba. That particular day they were like blackberries, large and soft and shiny" (p. 511).

At the outset of the short story, the narrator stresses the physical at tributes of Sister Imelda; your students will no doubt mention that this physical description is followed by delicious speculations regarding Imelda's life before the convent. The fact of the matter is that Imelda is a striking and changeable woman ("trapped," we are given to believe, in the gloom and doom of the convent) and is liable to spark such gossip.

2. What is the source of the narrator's attraction for Imelda?

The easy answer here is that the narrator is romantically involved with Sister Imelda; a number of students in a class I visited recently said that in the early going the short story was so heavily charged that they were "waiting for it to happen." Some students maintained that Imelda, in an attempt to recruit the narrator to the sisterhood, toys with her affections and purposefully leads her on. This seemed to me a cynical reading (one worthy of Baba); I do think that any reader must be forced to admit that there is an attraction between Imelda and the narrator that at times borders on the erotic.

But there is more going on here. The same students who reported that this was a love story (after all, intimacy was forbidden by the Mother Superior for some reason) reported also that that element, as it were, "dropped out" of the short story; Imelda is for the narrator the object of an admiration based on the nun's physical attraction *and* her piety. After all, the following passage is as true of one's great teachers and spiritual advisers as it is true of one's loves:

> . . . I had no idea how terribly she would infiltrate my life, how in time she would be not just one of those teachers or nuns but rather a special one, almost like a ghost who passed the boundaries of common exchange and who crept inside one, devouring so much of one's thoughts, so much of one's passion, invading the place that was called one's heart (p. 571).

The Counterpoint to this story (p. 585) may dissuade students who believe that O'Brien's interests are primarily in the erotic. O'Brien says there that

I vacillate between states of certain love toward people, and paranoia. The times in my life when I have really been with another human being—a man or a woman or a child—and I have really looked at their faces and their necks and their eyelids and their whole being and what their faces say, apart from what their lips are saying, and have observed myself observing that state—I have, at those odd and very, very rare moments, felt that it is really possible to be very near another person. And there is then an extraordinary—it is very subtle—but an extraordinary glory.

3. What is Baba's reaction to encountering the nuns on the bus? How does it differ from the narrator's?

Baba is a perfect example of unredeemed worldliness in the face of what would undoubtedly be disapproval from the nuns. Baba argues for confrontation and insults in a situation that the narrator finds acutely uncomfortable. The early–story speculations about the escapades of the nuns by the girls in the convent were amusing; the heavily made–up Baba's suggestion that the two sisters "might be off to meet two fellows" and her vision of them "in the golf club getting blotto and hoisting up their skirts" (p. 584) is merely vulgar.

The narrator, on the other hand, is deeply disturbed by the encounter, mainly because of her sense of never having reached the standards of piety implicitly set by Imelda. And she fails Imelda in the way that most of us fail those whom we love and are separated from; there is no conscious decision to reject the Church and forsake Imelda—the narrator merely gets caught up in the World and drifts away. "'They know not what they do' could surely be said of us" (p. 583).

–W.R.S.

Gail Godwin
Dream Children

"Dream Children" is a psychological mystery. At the beginning we are introduced to a "cheerful neat young woman, a wife" and her husband (a television producer?) who seem to be like "so many ambitious couples moving to this Dutch farming village, founded in 1690, to restore ruined fieldstone houses and plant herb gardens and keep their own horses and discover the relief of finding oneself insignificant in Nature for the first time!" (p. 586). But we soon learn that something "out of the ordinary, predictable, auspicious spectrum of things that happen to bright attractive young women" (p. 586) has happened to this young woman. As the story unfolds, we first see the effect this "something" has had on her, and finally we discover what terrible thing has transpired.

"Dream Children" is one of several stories about obsession included in this book. (Poe's "Fall of the House of Usher," Maupassant's "The String," Charlotte Perkins Gilman's "The Yellow Wallpaper," and Lessing's "To Room Nineteen" are others.) In "Dream Children," by focusing on a young woman's obsession with her "dream child," Godwin creates a spellbinding story at the same time that she explores the mysterious realms of the subconscious and the paranormal.

QUESTIONS

1. Is the child the woman in the story sees a "real" child who can travel to her because the "race of children possesses magically sagacious powers" or does he exist only in her imagination?

Godwin never tips her hand on this one. Like Henry James' "The Turn of the Screw," this story is deliberately ambiguous. Perhaps our protagonist has paranormal experiences; perhaps she's insane.

Godwin gives us sufficient reason to think that the woman (who is never given a name) could be mad. The story opens with the observation: "The worst thing. Such a terrible thing to happen to a young woman. It's a wonder she didn't go mad." That's what our protagonist imagines other people saying about her. In the fourth paragraph we learn that her neighbors consider her reckless because she races her horse across the fields, disregarding the danger of woodchuck holes (p. 586). And later the farmer DePuy tells her husband, "It's madness, the way she rides" (p. 592). Her husband concludes that she "did not look mad" (p. 593), but people don't ordinarily make such observations about others unless they have first entertained some doubts. At the end of the story, after we have seen the horror of her childbirth experience, we can read the sentence "[I]t's a wonder the poor woman kept her sanity" and question whether she did.

Godwin offers us no objective proof that the child actually appears. No one except the young woman either hears or sees him. But then he never visits when anyone else is present in the house.

At the same time Godwin makes it possible for us to believe that in some way the child actually travels to the nursery in the woman's home. To make the paranormal more credible, Godwin lists the titles of books the woman has been reading, all of which deal with out–of–body experiences (p. 588). Godwin even includes a story about an out–of–body visit John Cowper Powys paid to his friend Theodore Dreiser (p. 588). Godwin also tells us about the woman's childhood sleepwalking experiences and, in a flashback, the child psychiatrist who once treated this woman presents a plausible explanation for both the sleepwalking and the present events: "Usually these journeys are quite harmless, because children are surrounded by a magical reality that keeps them safe. Yes, the race of children possesses magically sagacious powers! But the grownups, they tend to forget how it once was for them" (p. 590). [For a remarkably similar view, you might refer your students to the fifth stanza of Wordsworth's "Ode: Intimations of Immortality": "But trailing clouds of glory do we come/From God who is our home": and "The youth, who daily farther from the east/Must travel, still is Nature's priest".]

Godwin also gives us details that make the visits from the child seem real, details unlikely to be imagined by a grieving mother:

The child is two years old before he makes his first visit. [That fact makes me ask myself why she waited so long to imagine him. I answer my question by thinking that perhaps she didn't merely imagine him. Perhaps he is a real child who cannot make this journey until he is old enough to walk.]

He is a little cold and scared (p. 591). [I wouldn't choose to imagine that about my child.]

He wears hand–me–down pajamas (p. 591). [Wouldn't this woman assume a standard of living like her own?]

He is playing with coquina shells (p. 591) [She doesn't know what they are until she finds a picture in a child's nature book.] She knows that she can neither touch the child nor speak to him (p. 594). [If this is the wish–fulfillment fantasy of a mad woman, why set such limits?]

When she coaxes the boy outside to see her animals, her dog disappoints her by "whining and backing away in fear," but her horse "perks up his ears and looks interested" (p. 594). [Why does she imagine inconsistencies she can't explain?]

Godwin also makes the visits seem real by presenting them through the woman's eyes. We share her fear the first time she sees the "small dark shape in one corner, on the floor" and she feels "distinctly, every single hair on her head raise itself a millimeter or so from her scalp" (p. 591). We understand her excitement when she tries to explain to her husband that the miracle of television, a kind of time and space travel, suggests that there are other miracles not yet officially approved (p. 592). We read with her that "dream and reality aren't competitors, but reciprocal sources of consciousness" (p. 594), and we tend to believe her when she insists that she can recognize the difference in quality between a dream and "those truly magic times when, through his own childish powers, he somehow found a will strong enough, or innocent enough, to project himself upon her still–floating consciousness, as clearly and believably as her husband's image on the screen" (p. 593).

Godwin has carefully crafted the story so that either a psychological or a paranormal interpretation is possible. At the end, we are no more able to answer the question posed by the woman than she is: "Who can explain such things?"

2. Why does Godwin wait until nearly the end of the story to tell us about "the terrible thing that happened"?

I ask this question primarily to get the students to look carefully at the story's structure. They will notice that Godwin slowly gives us more and more information about the event the woman and her husband never discuss. In the opening italicized lines, we learn merely that it was "such a terrible thing." In the third paragraph we discover it was a "freakish" thing that we would never expect to have happen "in an

American hospital." DePuy's remark that the young woman needs children (p. 586) and the husband's anger when Victoria casually relates a childbirth horror story (p. 587) suggest what must have happened. Finally, the explanation of why she and her husband no longer have sex ("She had bled for a whole year afterward, until the doctor said they would have to remove everything") makes us realize both that she gave birth to a child who died and that there will be no other babies. We think we know the whole story.

Then the visitations begin. At first we assume she is seeing her dead child who is "exactly two years older than the only time she had ever held him in her arms" (p. 591). But there are unanswered questions. Why does a dead child appear in hand–me–down pajamas? Why does he have another mother, "a harassed woman with several children" who lives in Florida? (p. 593). Was our protagonist's baby stolen from her at the hospital?

Then in two of the most powerful paragraphs I've ever read, Godwin answers all our questions (p. 594). First she shows us the worst thing that could happen to a woman. Something goes wrong, and a presumably healthy baby is born dead. And before we or the mother can recover, an even more unimaginable horror occurs. An overworked nurse puts a baby in the woman's arms and says, "Here's your little boy." Just as the new mother "with profound religious relief" thinks, "So that other nightmare was a dream," the mistake is discovered and the baby is torn from her body for the second time.

Your students should note that the structure of the story accomplishes several things. Certainly it keeps us interested by forcing us to attempt to solve the mysteries. In addition, because the childbirth scene is replayed only after we have already become so fond of the young woman, we are more affected by the event than we would have been earlier. And, reflecting back on question 1, I think that if I had known the full extent of the woman's tragedy from the beginning, I might have been more likely to assume that she was (or should have been) mad.

3. Does Godwin suggest that the pure mental stuff of life (whether we label it imagination or paranormal experience) is more significant than what we ordinarily label the "real world"?

If your students focus on the main character, their answer to this question is likely to be yes. But if you ask them to examine the other characters in the story, they will see that Godwin seems to say that there is no simple answer that is equally true for everyone.

The main character is a woman for whom the interior life is the only one that matters.

At the other end of the spectrum, "oiling his tractor," is Mr. DePuy, "a kind distracted father and husband, a practical hardworking man who would never descend deeply into himself" (p. 595). Mr. DePuy is so firmly grounded in reality that he resents the young woman's refusal to take it seriously. "[H]e almost wished for a woodchuck hole to break that arrogant ride" (p. 595).

Somewhere between those extremes is the husband. He tells Virginia Darrow, "I think it's more a question of whether we want to face things as they are or escape into fantasies of how we would like them to be....I am a pragmatist" (p. 593). When he sees the titles of the books his wife is reading, "[s]omething revolted in him, he couldn't help it; he felt an actual physical revulsion at this kind of thinking" (p. 593). The wife understands that her husband would consider her experiences proof of insanity: "But if she told her husband that she, too, is in two lives, he would become alarmed; he would sell this house and make her move back to the city where he could keep an eye on her welfare" (p. 588).

The husband, unlike Mr. DePuy, concedes that most people need some form of escape, and he decides that it's better for his wife to read books about the occult than to turn to alcohol (p. 593). He chooses not to mention his wife's reading; he simply escapes into his own fantasy life in the city where he has a mistress and a job in the world of television.

Mrs. DePuy is the character who best understands the young woman. Mrs. DePuy can enter the imaginative world far enough to realize that the young woman rides recklessly because "[s]he has nothing to fear anymore" (p. 586). Mrs. DePuy feels the attraction of that state of existence, but her ties with the physical world constrain her. She continues to hang out "her children's pajamas in the backyard of the old Patroon farm" (p. 595), even though she watches "that other woman ride, a woman not much younger than herself, but with an aura of romance—of tragedy, perhaps" (p. 586). And the emotions she feels are both envy and pity.

–M.R.D.

Joyce Carol Oates
Where Are You Going, Where Have You Been?

One of the first things your class will need to know about "Where Are You Going" is that it is "true." By this I mean that the story they are about to discuss really happened, and the names and some of the circumstances have been changed to protect the innocent and dead and to hint darkly at the nature of the guilty. Arnold Friend seems to have been based on the murderous Charles Schmid of Tucson, Arizona, convicted of killing three teenage girls; Ellie on his friend and accomplice John Saunders; Connie is a composite, I think, of the three murdered girls. The side by side comparison that follows may be of help on two fronts:

(1.) It demonstrates that the nightmare quality of the fiction springs at least in part from the nightmare quality of the source of that fiction; (2.) It may provide fuel for your class's assessment of Oates' claim in the Counterpoint, in which she says that "Sartre is insisting that the materials of life cannot become translated immediately into the materials of art; the two belong to entirely different dimensions."

"Where Are You Going"

Life, 4 March 1964

He looked as if he probably did hard work, lifting and carrying things. Even his neck looked muscular (p. 602).

In high school Schmid was an indifferent scholar but a fine gymnast whose skill won him a state championship.

Then he seemed to become embarrassed, abruptly, and looked over his shoulder at Ellie. "Him, he's crazy," he said. "Ain't he a riot, he's a nut, a real character." He [Ellie] wore a bright orange shirt unbuttoned halfway to show his chest, which was a pale, bluish chest and not muscular like Arnold Friend's (p. 604). . . Ellie turned for the first time and Connie saw with shock that he wasn't a kid either—he had a fair, hairless face, cheeks reddened slightly as if the veins grew too close to the surface of a forty-year–old baby (p. 604).

As a baby, John Saunders had been so afflicted with allergies that scabs encrusted his entire body. To keep him from scratching himself his parents had tied his hands and feet to the crib each night, and when eventually he was cured he was so conditioned that he could not go to sleep without being bound hand and foot. . . Later, a scrawny boy with poor eyesight. . . (p. 82)

It was an open jalopy, painted a bright gold that caught the sunlight opaquely (p. 600).

He cruised in a golden car, looking for the action (p. 23).

One of his boots was at a strange angle, as if his foot wasn't in it. It pointed out to the left, bent at the ankle. . . "I thank you, sweetheart," he said, with a mock bow, but again he almost lost his balance. He had to bend and adjust his boots. Evidently his feet did not go all the way down; the boots must have been stuffed with something so that he would seem taller (p. 607).

He habitually stuffed three or four inches of old rags and tin cans into the bottoms of his high–topped boots to make himself taller than his five–foot–three and stumbled about so awkwardly while walking that some people thought he had wooden feet (p. 23).

His whole face was a mask, she thought wildly, tanned down onto his throat but then running out as if he had plastered makeup on his face but had forgotten about his throat (p. 606).

The face is his own creation: the hair dyed raven black, the skin darkened to a deep tan with pancake make–up, the lips whitened, the whole effect heightened by a mole he has painted on one cheek. . . At the time of his arrest last November, Charles Schmid was 23 years old. He wore face make–up and dyed his hair (p. 24).

"My sweet little blue–eyed girl," he said, in a half–sung sigh that had nothing to do with her brown eyes but was taken up just the same by the vast sunlit reaches of the land behind him and on all sides of him, so much land that Connie had never seen before and did not recognize except to know that she was going to it (p. 610).*

The dead lay hidden in the hard scrubby desert (p. 24).
. . . It is spooky country, dry and empty, the yellow sand clotted with cholla and mesquite. . . (p.82).

---

*This comparison is made more cogently in Tom Quirk's "A Source for 'Where Are You Going, Where Have You Been?'" *Studies In Short Fiction*, Fall 1981, Vol. 18, no. 4, pp. 413–19.

But this juxtaposition is not to imply that "Where Are You Going, Where Have You Been?" is a roman à clef. The short story permits, thanks to the transmutation the incidents go through in Oates' imagination, a number of interpretations.

QUESTIONS

1. Why is this short story frightening?

Although some readers insist on reading "Where Are You Going, Where Have You Been?" as a sordid story of teenage sexual experimentation, it is obviously a good deal more, primarily because of Oates' portrait of Arnold Friend. He is the archetypal demon lover. I, for example, was oddly sorry to discover the real–life facts behind the details in the short story, because when I first read this short story (before I knew of Charles Schmid) I believed I had landed upon the "right" reading. I said to myself, "Ah, here is another story of a young person encountering evil for the first time ("Young Goodman Brown," *Oliver Twist*, every *Bildungsroman* ever written, etc.). But learning the facts behind the story need not diminish the terror of the narrative. As a matter of fact, isn't Oates providing us with a rather hip version of the satanic? Why does Arnold Friend walk so strangely? Could Oates be suggesting—merely suggesting—that his feet are cloven within his boots? Who claims to be humanity's oldest "friend" in "Young Goodman Brown"?
In short, the interpretations of Arnold Friend as Satan or as Charles Schmid are not mutually exclusive, and I was neither entirely wrong nor entirely right in assuming before I knew of Charles Schmid that Oates was giving us another edition of the encounter–with–Old Nick story so popular in American literature ("The Devil and Tom Walker," "Never Bet the Devil Your Head," "The Devil and Daniel Webster," "Young Goodman Brown," *Damn Yankees*). Your class, I think, will discover finally that the truth about this story lies somewhere between a one to one equation of Arnold Friend with Charles Schmid *or* Satan.

2. Is Connie being punished for her promiscuity and disrespect for her
parents? Does this short story make any sort of statement about the culture
that produces relationships like that between Connie and her parents?

The article from *Life* cited above ended with an indictment of fast cars,
rock and roll, and permissive parents. It seems unlikely that "Where
Are You Going, Where Have You Been?" is a moral fabliau, or, if it is,
the didacticism is well–disguised. The title, however, may be drawn
from Bob Dylan's "A Hard Rain's Gonna Fall" (this seems likely, given
the dedication) and in that song a young man, in response to the questions "Where have you been, my blue–eyed son?/Where have you been,
my darling young one?" talks of being saturated by experience in a
world facing destruction.

3. Where is Connie going at the end of the story?

It might be interesting to poll your students on this issue. We are
given little if any internal evidence that she is killed by Arnold Friend,
so some might doubt that she is killed. Most readers, I'll warrant, are
convinced that she disappears forever into the desert. Her reactions to his
advances would indicate that she has a premonition that she will come to
harm, and Arnold does, after all, threaten to kill her family and in-
timates that he could burn down their house. You might wish to xerox
the two-column presentation of portions of the *Life* article and excerpts
from "Where Are You Going, Where Have You Been?" A comparison of
the last entry in both columns will indicate pretty clearly just what
happens to Connie.

–W.R.S.

Toni Cade Bambara
The Lesson

In this short story Miss Moore, a college-educated black woman, tries
to teach a group of children from a New York slum that "poor people have
to wake up and demand their share of the pie." After her lectures on
economics fail, Miss Moore loads the kids into a taxi and carts them off to
the wonderland of F.A.O. Schwarz. When the children look in the
window of the toy store, they are stunned to discover that a toy sailboat is
priced at $1,000, more money than any of their families spend on gro-
ceries for a year.

But this story is not depressing. The narrator, one of the girls who
participated in the expedition to Fifth Avenue, is a bright, articulate,
witty storyteller who refuses to label her childhood joyless. She remem-

bers the lesson, but she also remembers what fun it was to be a high-spirited and irreverent youngster who enjoyed mocking the adult world. Bambara's humorous treatment of a serious subject is consistent with the philosophy of writing she explains in the Counterpoint, "If I'm not laughing while I work, I conclude that I'm not communicating nourishment, since laughter is the most sure–fire healant I know."

QUESTIONS

1. How does the adult narrator feel about her younger self?

Bambara doesn't provide us with an easy answer to this question. Unlike Mary, the woman in Ralph Ellison's "Did You Ever Dream Lucky?" who tells a story about "how green" she was twenty years earlier, this narrator doesn't intentionally establish distance between herself and the child she was. In the first line the narrator suggests that many years have passed since the lesson took place: "Back in the days when everyone was old and stupid or young and foolish and me and Sugar were the only ones just right...." But after that sentence the adult Sylvia merges with her younger self and describes Miss Moore as young Sylvia would have: "[T]his lady moved on our block with nappy hair and proper speech and no makeup. And quite naturally we laughed at her..." (p. 611). By the second paragraph, when the story of the visit to the toy store begins, the adult Sylvia has disappeared completely. In her place is a much younger Sylvia who tells the story in present tense. "So this one day Miss Moore rounds us all up at the mailbox and it's puredee hot and she's knockin herself out about arithmetic" (p. 611).
Because the adult narrator never interrupts with commentary and doesn't reappear at the end of the story, we have no direct evidence of her attitude toward young Sylvia. But the structure of the story suggests that the adult narrator is somewhat amused by the inability of this bright young girl to figure out what Miss Moore is up to. The narrator causes us to dismiss Miss Moore initially, then change our opinion, then watch Sylvia change hers. After reading the description of Miss Moore that appears on the opening page, readers are likely to accept Sylvia's characterization of her as a manipulative do–gooder who doesn't know much about children. The trip to F.A.O. Schwarz, however, causes us to reevaluate Miss Moore and conclude that the woman is, if nothing else, a brilliant teacher. Part of the gentle humor of the story is accomplished by our watching young Sylvia struggle toward realizations we make more quickly than she does. Sylvia, much like some of Jane Austen's heroines, prides herself on how perceptive she is, but still misses the point. To the extent that we identify with Sylvia, we are amused not just by her predicament but by memories of similar incidents in our own lives.

2. Why does Sylvia "kinda hate" Miss Moore?

Sylvia, like any normal child, wants to spend hot summer afternoons at the pool or the show, not dressed up in a "pinafore scratching the shit outta" her listening to Miss Moore "knockin herself out about arithmetic" (p. 611). But there's more to Sylvia's animosity than that. Sylvia senses that Miss Moore is her adversary. Although Sylvia doesn't understand the nature of their struggle, she knows that she doesn't intend to lose. As she insists, "[A]in't nobody going to beat me at nuthing." In Sylvia's opinion, Miss Moore has already bested everyone else in the neighborhood, including the grownups who allow her to take responsibility for the young one's education even though she is "not even related by marriage or blood" (p. 611). Sylvia observes, "[W]hen she came calling with some sachet she'd sewed up or some gingerbread she'd made or some book, why then they'd all be too embarrassed to turn her down and we'd get handed over all spruced up" (p. 611).

Sylvia suspects that Miss Moore wants something from her, something Sylvia doesn't intend to give, and she fights Miss Moore at every step. When Sylvia asks Miss Moore how much a real boat costs, she explains that she wouldn't ordinarily question Miss Moore: "I never talk to her, I wouldn't give the bitch that satisfaction" (p. 614). Later Miss Moore asks Sylvia if she is angry, but Sylvia refuses to answer. "I'm mad but I won't give her that satisfaction" (p. 615). Near the end of the story, when Miss Moore asks, "Anybody else learn anything today?" and "[looks] dead at" Sylvia, Sylvia walks away (p. 616). Although Sylvia never concedes defeat, it is obvious to the reader that Miss Moore has won.

The pre–Miss Moore Sylvia was a happy child who was contented with her lot in life because she didn't know that she had other options. When Miss Moore tells the children they are impoverished, Sylvia disagrees. ("And then she gets to the part about we all poor and live in the slums, which I don't feature"—p. 612). But Miss Moore refuses to leave Sylvia in blissful ignorance. She forces Sylvia to ask herself, "Who are these people who spend that much for performing clowns and $1000 for toy sailboats? What kinda work they do and how they live and how come we ain't in on it?" (p. 615). Miss Moore teaches Sylvia a hard truth: "Where we are is who we are....But it don't necessarily have to be that way...(pp. 615–616). The lesson frees Sylvia from her past and makes her responsible for her future. For that, Sylvia both hates and loves Miss Moore.

3. How successful is Bambara in portraying Sylvia and her friends realistically?

Sometimes children in fiction seem to be untalented actors playing roles that could have been imagined only by adults. Surely there are no children as unrelentingly obnoxious as those in Flannery O'Connor's

"A Good Man Is Hard to Find." In contrast the children in this story are absolutely believable. While Miss Moore lectures them about "real money," Sylvia and Sugar lean on the mailbox "being surly," Flyboy "[checks] out what everybody brought for lunch," Fat Butt eats his peanut–butter–and–jelly sandwich, Junebug mooches potato chips, and Rosie Giraffe "shifts from one hip to another" (p. 612). Anyone who has ever observed a group of fifth graders waiting to go on a field trip will recognize this crew.

Bambara creates multidimensional children whose moods and actions change from moment to moment. Sometimes the children are rude to each other: "Who wants to know about your smelly–ass stationery?" Rosie asks Mercedes (p. 613). Sometimes they are rowdy and noisy: "Me and Sugar and Junebug and Flyboy hanging out the window and hollering to everybody..." (p. 612). Sometimes they are shy: "We all walkin on tiptoe and hardly touchin the games and puzzles and things" (p. 615). Sometimes they entertain each other by shocking adults. When they get ready to enter the store, for example, Sugar asks Miss Moore, "Can we steal?" (p. 612).

Another characteristic of these children that makes them believable is their abilty to observe, describe, and predict adult behavior (even if they can't understand it)—an uncanny ability apparently shared by all children (as anyone who has ever watched children mimic their teachers or parents can testify). This talent is demonstrated most clearly by Sylvia. She sums up Aunt Gretchen in a few short sentences: "She was the main gofer in the family. ... You got some ole dumb shit foolishness you want somebody to go for, you send for Aunt Gretchen" (p. 611).

Sylvia's observations of Miss Moore are particularly keen. After Sylvia tells Miss Moore that she'd rather "go to the Sunset and terrorize the West Indian kids" she notes that "Miss Moore files that remark away for next week's lesson on brotherhood" (p. 612). And we know Sylvia is right. Sylvia notices that when they get to F.A.O. Schwarz, Miss Moore presents it to them "in the voice she uses at the museum" (p. 612). She observes that when Miss Moore explains how the semi–precious stones were fused into a paperweight, "her hands [are] doing the mining and all the factory work." She remarks that Miss Moore responds "Not exactly" to a student's answer "when you warm or way off too" (p. 613). And she realizes that Miss Moore is feigning ignorance when she asks whether they have desks at home: "And she know damn well what our homes look like cause she noseys around in them every chance she gets" (p. 613). Sylvia can describe Miss Moore's expressions precisely: "Givin me one of them grins like she tellin a grown–up joke that never turns out to be funny" (p. 615).

Although Bambara gives Sylvia the sharp vision of a child, she does not invest her with understanding beyond her years. Sylvia describes the moment after the children have recited the price tag on the sailboat:

"We look at Miss Moore and she lookin at us, waitin for I dunno what"
(p. 614). By demonstrating that Sylvia can describe Miss Moore's actions
without understanding her motives, Bambara reminds us that even
though Sylvia is intelligent, she is still a child.

–M.R.D.

Margaret Atwood
Rape Fantasies

If someone had told me that a feminist like Margaret Atwood could
(or would) write a funny story called "Rape Fantasies," I would have questioned that person's sanity or sense of humor. But it's true. In the story a
wonderfully wacky narrator describes her imagined encounters with
very human would–be rapists who have problems of their own. One, for
example, an ugly fellow covered with pimples, gets his zipper stuck, starts
to cry, and decides to jump off a bridge. The narrator, Estelle, feels sorry
for him and sends him off to her dermatologist, assuring him that after
his complexion improves, he will be quite good looking and won't "have
to go around doing stuff like this" (p. 622).

The reason the story can be humorous is that it doesn't actually involve
rape. None of Estelle's fantasies end with rape. Instead, in each encounter something happens that causes the rapist to see his intended victim as a person. And once that occurs, it is unthinkable that he would
rape her. As Estelle says, "I think it would be better if you could get a
conversation going. Like, how could a fellow do that to a person he's just
had a long conversation with, once you let them know you're human, you
have a life too, I don't see how they could go ahead with it, right?" (p.
624). Now that's the ultimate rape fantasy.

QUESTIONS

1. What are the sources of humor in this story?

I am operating under the assumption that parts of the story are funny.
If your students are so offended by the topic that they don't find the story
humorous, you may have to rephrase the question: How does Atwood attempt to make the story humorous?
Most humor is based on the incongruous, the unexpected. In this story,
the author continues to surprise us. For example, the rapists conjured up
by Estelle offer a hilarious contrast to the stereotypical fantasy rapists
imagined by her coworkers. Greta, the blond who aspires to be a recep-
tionist, describes a man dressed in black and wearing black gloves who
climbs down a rope to enter her room on the eighteenth floor (p. 619).

The men Estelle imagines are less like Tarzan: one obligingly twists the top off the plastic lemon she then squirts in his eyes (p. 621); one has a "puffy nothing face" and gets his zipper stuck (p. 621), one has a bad cold and threatens "I'b goig do rabe you" (p. 622), and another accepts a vaccination mark as a sign from God (p. 623).

The outcome of the incidents Estelle narrates is also unexpected. Although the situations are potentially disastrous, they have surprisingly happy endings. One rapist is sent off to a dermatologist (p. 622), one accepts a Neo–Citran and Scotch and watches the Late Show with Estelle (p. 622), and another, after hearing that angel voices have told Estelle that she is to give birth to St. Anne, gets confused, apologizes and climbs out the coal chute again (p. 623). Even the one who is dying of leukemia has the good fortune to find the "one other person in the world who can understand what he's going through" (p. 623).

2. Who is Estelle speaking to in the story? How does that affect your reading of the story?

When the story begins, Estelle appears to be speaking directly to the reader. The story seems to be the equivalent of a lengthy aside.

But in the next–to–the–last paragraph we discover that Estelle has been talking to a person she has just met in a bar. "I'm not what you would call a drinker, but I like to go out now and then for a drink or two in a nice place, even if I am by myself....Like here for instance, the waiters all know me and if anyone, you know, bothers me....I don't know why I'm telling you all this, except I think it helps you get to know a person, especially at first, hearing some of the things they think about" (p. 624). We then realize that the story is actually a dramatic monologue exactly like Browning's "My Last Duchess." All of Estelle's remarks are made to a specific but unseen person.

There are a few early clues that the "you" Estelle adresses is not the reader. After Estelle reveals Darlene's age, she says, "[I]t's more or less confidential. But it's all right if I tell you, I don't expect you'll ever meet her, though you never know..." (p. 619). And later when she describes her vaccination mark, she says, "[Y]ou can see, it's sort of an odd–shaped one..." (p. 623). I'm relatively sure that her listener is male although Estelle doesn't tell us that directly. Here's my best circumstantial evidence. After Estelle talks about how hard it is to meet people in a city, she says, "But I guess it's different for a guy" (p. 622). And again, after she explains why she could never stick her fingers in a rapist's eyes, she wonders, "But maybe it's different for a guy" (p. 623).

If Estelle's audience is indeed a man she has just met in a bar, we have to look again both at her motives for talking about rape fantasies and at the tone of the story. (On to question 3.)

3. What is the tone of the story (the author's attitude toward the subject, the audience, and herself)?

This is a tough question. First your students will have to distinguish between the voice of the narrator, Estelle, and the tone of the writer, Atwood. When I first started reading the story and assumed that Estelle was talking to me, the reader, I would have described her voice as light-hearted and playful. After all, she tells me that "Sondra's head went round like it was on ball bearings" and that Chrissy is "pretty but cool as a cucumber, like she's been painted all over with nail polish" (p. 618). Those are intentionally funny images that Estelle obviously selects for their amusement value.

She also pokes fun at herself. She tells us about the time she did a Cossack dance under the table, hit her head and knocked herself out cold (p. 621). She describes herself in one fantasy rape scenario as "no object of beauty....[Y]ou'd have to be some kind of pervert to want to rape someone with a cold like mine, it'd be like raping a bottle of LePages mucilage the way my nose is running" (p. 622).

But at the end of the story, after I understand that Estelle is talking to a man she hardly knows, a man she might like to know better, I hear her voice differently. Now I see the levels of her conversation. On one level she is a sophisticated woman engaging in singles' chatter and making an effort to be an amusing conversationalist. At the same time, she is a frightened woman bravely whistling in the dark, hoping that this man who has just had a long conversation with her will know that she's human, that she has a life too, and that he will agree that under such circumstances he couldn't possibly rape her.

The author's tone is even more difficult to discover because Atwood never addresses us directly. There are no authorial comments to let us know what we should think. I would, however, argue that Atwood takes the subject of rape quite seriously. Early in the story she has the narrator Estelle remind everyone of the difference between rape and rape fantasies. "Rape is when they've got a knife or something and you don't want to" (p. 620). And Estelle again recalls reality when, immediately after her Kung–Fu fantasy, she says, "[I]n real life I'm sure it would be just a conk on the head and that's that, like getting your tonsils out, you'd wake up and it would be all over except for the sore places, and you'd be lucky if your neck wasn't broken or something" (p. 623).

Atwood deliberately rejects the customary treatments of the subject "rape fantasies." We have come to expect one of two equally serious approaches: (1) an argument that women really do have erotic rape fantasies that they are ashamed to confess or (2) outraged denial, an insistence that such fantasies exist nowhere except in the perverted male mind. Atwood upsets our expectations by showing us a warm, loving, funny, and all too vulnerable young woman who chatters blithely about the humorous encounters she imagines. Atwood's tone seems to be as light as Estelle's: "I mean, I don't see what's wrong with a little joke now and then. Life's too short, right?" (p. 620).

But with the closing paragraphs, the tone darkens. Atwood suddenly juxtaposes the fantasy world where Estelle always manages to prevent rape with the real world where a woman has to choose either solitary safety or sociable danger. Both Estelle and the reader recognize the risk she is taking by trusting a stranger. And yet, as Estelle laments, "You can't spend your whole life in the Filing Department or cooped up in your own apartment with all the doors and windows locked and the shades down" (p. 624). "[H]ow are you supposed to meet people if you can't trust them even that basic amount?" (p. 624). In the final sentence, Estelle's voice and Atwood's merge in bewildered sorrow, "I mean, I know it happens but I just don't understand it, that's the part I really don't understand."

–M.R.D.

Garrison Keillor
The Tip–Top Club

Most of your students will know Garrison Keillor as the creator, writer and host for the popular radio program "A Prairie Home Companion" or as the author of *Happy to Be Here* and *Lake Wobegon Days*. If so, they will expect an amusing story about ordinary small–town midwestern people. They won't be disappointed. This story chronicles the birth, life, and death of a radio club. The Tip–Top Club consists of radio talk–show fans dedicated to the notion that a talk show should be, above all else, cheerful. "Controversy was the very thing that distinguished 'The Tip–Top Club.' It had none" (p. 627). For eighteen years the club members call in to give each other helpful advice such as the "idea of pouring warm soapy water into overshoes and wearing them around the house to give yourself a relaxing footbath" (p. 625). Then their beloved host retires, and the club members have to deal with the unthinkable—change.

Like all Keillor stories, this one is more than an anecdote. Keillor is quite willing to entertain us, but he is not willing to let us read without thinking. In "The Tip–Top Club" Keillor asks us hard questions about the relationship of the artist (or of any individual person) to the community, questions worthy of discussion in a literature class.

QUESTIONS

1. Find examples of statements made by particular people in the story that could not have been spoken by anyone else.

Keillor has an amazing ability to reproduce the way people talk. The speech patterns of his characters are no more interchangeable than the people themselves. I might ask my students to write the examples they select on the board to see if the rest of the class could name the speakers. If you want to list your own examples, here are a few I would bet that your students can correctly identify:

 ◆ "Every foulmouth in town will be slobbering into his telephone for the chance to get on the air" (p. 628). [Roy Jr. the distrustful]

 ◆ "Well, I don't know. Let me know what *you* think" (p. 628). [Bud the self–effacing]

 ◆ "I was slapping them down like barnyard flies. We were up to our ears in crazies. Finally, my fingers got sore, and Alice pulled the plug on the switchboard and her and me set down and had a cup of coffee and left that poor dumb SOB sit and die by himself" (p. 634). [Harlan the profane pragmatist]

 ◆ "I appreciate your honesty, sir. I don't necessarily agree with that statement, but I think it's important that you feel you can be honest with me" (p. 633). [Wayne the psychobabbler]

 ◆ "The distinguished gentleman who spoke earlier on cats was very well–informed on most points, but I feel he may have over-looked the fact that cats will not shed if brushed regularly" (p. 630). [Tip–Top caller speaking to Bud—unfailingly courteous]

 ◆ "You make me absolutely sick. You're the biggest mistake they've made down there" (p. 633). [Tip–Top caller speaking to Wayne—unwaveringly cruel]

I can't distinguish among the voices of the Tip–Top callers (I don't think Keillor wants us to), but it's easy to identify their listener.

2. Does Keillor, who was himself the host for a morning "music and call–ins" radio program, seem to favor Bud's or Wayne's style of hosting?

Some of your students will base their answer on their knowledge of Keillor's style on "A Prairie Home Companion." They may, for example, point out that he read announcements of his listeners' birthdays, something we can imagine Bud doing. But they should be able to answer this question even if they've never listened to "A Prairie Home Companion."

I think your students will decide that even though Keillor seems to like both Bud and Wayne, he doesn't enthusiastically approve of either. Both have good intentions. Bud is a kind man who *never* asks his callers about their occupations, not after the first few times: the answers were always apologetic sounding..." (p. 631). But Bud is a host who allows his guests to usurp his role. The "listeners" become the hosts who choose the topics, do all the talking, and offer opinions on every uncontroversial subject from hobbies to housework. Bud becomes the listener, "the recording secretary" (p. 626), and if he has any opinions, he keeps them to himself. When a caller reports that Communists are trained "to insinuate their beliefs into a conversation without anyone being the wiser," Bud replies, "Appreciate your concern, sir, and believe me, we'll be on guard" (p. 629). After listening "to the same stuff" for eighteen years, Bud loses "whatever personality he had in the beginning." "A goddam ghost," Harlan said. "When he comes in, I don't even see him anymore. He don't really exist, except on the air" (p. 632).

Wayne is Bud's antithesis. Bud is a self-effacing fellow whose says, "Tell me about yourself" (p. 630); Wayne is unbelievably egocentric. (Ask your students to count the number of times Wayne uses the pronoun "I" in the third full paragraph on page 632. I find 18.) Bud's style of speaking is "warm and reassuring" and he always tries "to look on the bright side"; Wayne expresses doubts about his own abilities, and he discusses depressing topics like his divorce (p. 634). Bud identifies with his audience; Wayne feels alienated from and superior to the Tip-Top Club members. He tells them, "I've had a hard time relating to working-class people (p. 635).

But Keillor doesn't make Wayne despicable. Keillor forces us to admire Wayne's courage and his determination to "keep on trying." He makes us sympathize when Wayne is bombarded by abuse that surprises even Harlan. And he gives Wayne some lines that few of Keillor's readers are likely to dispute: "There's a lot of anger and violence out there—and I don't say people shouldn't feel that way, but I do feel people should be willing to change. Life is change. We all change. I've changed" (pp. 634–635).

Bud, of course, never insisted that his audience would have to change. For eighteen years he allowed them to stay in their comfortable patterns of thought. He screened the callers: "no kids, no foreign accents, and nobody who seemed unusually intense or determined to get on the air" (p. 629). He limited the topics of discussion: no politics, no religion, no criticism of others, and no promotion of products, services, clubs, fund drives, or events (p. 630). I think most readers will be inclined to agree

with Harlan's assessment: "What's left to talk about? Not a goddamn
helluva lot."

Keillor the radio show host is probably a combination of Bud and
Wayne, a man who can be interested in the hobbies of the Tip–Top Club
members and in Woody Allen movies, a man who is both attracted and
repelled by the notion of a homogeneous community willing to sacrifice
everything for cheeriness.

3. Is it going too far to say that this story is about the role of the artist (in
this case a radio talk show host) in society?

Some of your students will undoubtedly object that such a question requires a too serious approach to a lighthearted story, that this is an example of Keillor's "three pages sharp and funny about the lives of geese"
("Introduction to *Happy to Be Here*"—p. 635). Maybe. I agree that the story
is fun to read, and many of the lines make me laugh, but I don't think
the story is all that light. In fact, very few of Keillor's stories are merely
humorous. If you remind your students that Keillor wrote this story
while he was a radio show host, they may be willing to concede that this
is the kind of question that should have interested him.

In "The Tip–Top Club" Keillor gives us portraits of two artists: Bud is
an artist so closely aligned with his community that he is willing to accept all of its limitations. He allows his audience to remain static but
cheerful for eighteen years, and in the process he sacrifices his own
identity. He is loved, but we finish the story knowing that adulation isn't
enough.

Wayne is an artist so alienated from his audience that he is unable to
communicate with them in any meaningful way. They hate him, they
unite against him, and they refuse to hear anything he has to say.

The problem illustrated by Keillor's story is also discussed by Auden
in "Poetry Which Is at the Same Time Light and Adult" (p. 1057). (You
might have your students read that one–page Counterpoint before they
tackle this question.) Auden explains how difficult it is for a poet to
establish precisely the right relationship with society: "For if it is true
that the closer bound the artist is to his community the harder it is for
him to see with detached vision, it is also true that when he is too isolated, though he may see clearly enough what he does see, that dwindles
in quantity and importance." Keillor shows us Bud, who is too closely
bound, and Wayne, who is too isolated.

Keillor seems to agree with Auden that "[t]he problem for the modern poet, as for everyone else to–day, is how to find or form a genuine
community, in which each has a valued place and can feel at home."
Keillor doesn't articulate a solution to the problem. But he does give us a
glimpse of the future we face if we don't work out our own solution, a
bleak future where people simply abandon the attempt to communicate:

"[I]n July the station switched the Tip–Top slot to what it called a 'modified middle–of–the–road pop–rock format' with a disc jockey who never talked except to give time, temperature, and commercials. His name was Michael Keske, but he never said it on the air."

Keillor doesn't tell us how an artist should relate to his audience, but perhaps he demonstrates his answer through his relationship to us, his readers. Like Bud, Keillor identifies with and likes his audience; he assumes we have shared values and beliefs. He expects us to know without being told that the radio station's solution to the problem—a disc jockey who doesn't talk—should not be ours. Unlike Bud, Keillor is able to step outside our community (at least with one foot), satirize our failings (after all, we are the ones who have made the "modified middle–of–the road pop–rock format" a commercial success) and expect us to laugh at ourselves and then try to improve.

–M.R.D.

Alice Walker
Everyday Use

Your students probably know Alice Walker as the author of *The Color Purple*, a novel about Celie, a black woman who is abused first by her father and later by her husband. Eventually, Celie's friendship with another woman teaches her that the world offers love as well as misery, and Celie finds the strength to leave her husband.

"Everyday Use" also stars courageous black women who succeed in spite of the odds, but in this story Walker forces us to question our conventional definitions of success. The story focuses on a cross–cultural confrontation between two women who just happen to be mother and daughter. The mother is an independent woman who takes pride in her abilty to "[knock] a bull calf straight in the brain between the eyes with a sledge hammer and [have] the meat hung up to chill before nightfall." The daughter is a young woman whose fierce determination has enabled her to obtain an education and material prosperity. When the daughter comes home for a visit, dressed in African clothing and announcing she has changed her name from Dee to Wangero, the mother calmly, though with silent amusement, accepts her daughter's new identity. The conflict arises when Wangero, who has recently acquired an interest in her heritage, insists that her mother give her two quilts hand pieced by her grandmother, quilts promised to Wangero's sister Maggie. Wangero insists that she deserves the quilts: "Maggie can't appreciate these quilts! She'd probably be backward enough to put them to everyday use."

QUESTIONS

1. Does Walker want us to conclude that the quilts should be hung on the wall or put to "everyday use"?

I don't think Walker answers this question for us. Our sympathies lie with Maggie who, "like somebody used to never winning anything, or having anything reserved for her," tells her mother that Dee can have the quilts because Maggie "can 'member Grandma Dee without them" (p. 642). I imagine most readers are pleased by the mother's decision to give the quilts to Maggie. Yet Walker's readers, who are likely to be educated people who have more in common with Dee than with her almost illiterate mother, recognize that Dee is correct, that these irreplaceable, hand stitched quilts will be in rags after five years of everyday use.

Walker uses the quilts to symbolize the dilemma presented by this conflict of cultures tale. Dee has the education and leisure and wealth to "appreciate" the aesthetic value of such treasures, but for some reason she lacks the ability to understand their greater value as a legacy from women she should honor. Dee says that she wants the quilts because "[t]hese are all pieces of dresses Grandma used to wear. She did all this stitching by hand. Imagine" (p. 641). But we (and the narrator) suspect that Dee is more interested in impressing her friends with these "priceless" pieces of folk art than in recalling the dresses her grandmother once wore, the grandmother whose name Dee/Wangero has rejected (p. 639). Apparently the quilts would have less sentimental value if they had been "stitched around the borders by machine" (p. 641), and they have somehow acquired significance since Dee went away to college. At that time the mother offered Dee a quilt, but she refused it, telling her mother "they were old–fashioned, out of style" (p. 642). Ironically, Dee is willing to destroy her relationship with her mother and her sister in order to lay claim to an object that she incorrectly believes will establish a link with her ancestors. But the quilts cannot give Dee what Maggie already has—an understanding of her heritage based on a spiritual kinship with the women who made those quilts and taught Maggie to quilt.

Dee admires the objects made beautiful by everyday use, the kitchen bench impressed with "rump prints" (p. 640), the churn handle "with a lot of small sinks...where thumbs and fingers had sunk into the wood" (p. 641), but not the people who created and used those objects.

2. What makes the story humorous?

I hope your students will agree that the story has some wonderfully funny moments. Incidents that could make us sad or angry become amusing when we view them through the eyes of a narrator with a well developed sense of humor. The dream in which the narrator imagines her appearance on T.V. is a perfect example. The narrator is not embarrassed or unhappy because her real life appearance fails to meet her daughter's expectations. She is proud to be a "large, big–boned woman with rough, man–working hands" who can "kill and clean a hog as mercilessly as a man" (p. 637), and she chuckles when she pictures herself as Dee would want her, "a hundred pounds lighter," with "skin like an uncooked barley pancake," exchanging quick and witty conversation with a white man (p. 637). [You might ask your students why the notion of remaking parents, a possibility that provokes laughs in the movie *Back to the Future* and in Shel Silverstein's poem "Clarence," is currently so popular.]

The similes the narrator uses demonstrate her comic view of life. She describes her son–in–law as a short, stocky man with hair "all over his head a foot long and hanging from his chin like a kinky mule tail" (p. 639). She notes that when Maggie sees her brother–in–law, she sucks in her breath "like when you see the wriggling end of a snake just in front of your foot on the road" (p. 639). She explains that Dee's hair "stands straight up like the wool on a sheep. It is black as night and around the edges are two long pigtails that rope about like small lizards disappearing behind her ears" (p. 639).

3. What does Walker accomplish by having the mother narrate the story?

If this story were told by an objective narrator, we might be inclined to feel sorry for Maggie and her mother, two poor uneducated women who live in a three–room shack, and we would probably label Dee an unqualified success, a woman who has pulled herself up by her own bootstraps. But Walker forces us to reexamine our assumptions about "the good life." Because we view the narrator's life from the inside, we become convinced that her life is richer than we might have imagined and we find ourselves questioning Dee's (and thus society's) definition of success. Walker shows us the narrator's thoughts to demonstrate that the narrator is an intelligent, clear–sighted woman whose opinions are worth considering. Although the narrator may not be able to read books, she can certainly read people. She notices that Dee takes pictures of her and the house before she kisses her, that Asalamalakim looks down on her "like somebody inspecting a Model A car" (p. 640), and that "every once in a while he and Wangero sent eye signals over [her] head" (p. 640).

Because we are privy to the narrator's thoughts, we are aware of her doubts about the American dream. Her skepticism is first suggested in her dream about the T.V. show featuring Dee. When the narrator describes Dee as a "child who has 'made it'" (p. 636), the quotation marks around the phrase "made it" indicate that the mother may not accept the world's judgment of Dee.

Our insiders' view persuades us that the narrator's negative view of Dee is not based on resentment or envy. Dee's mother obviously loves her beautiful, successful, well-educated daughter. She is happy to have Dee visit, she makes an effort to pronounce Dee's new name correctly ("I'll get used to it. Ream it out again"—p. 640), she resists the temptation to ask Hakim–a–barber if he is a barber (p. 640), she prepares Dee's favorite foods, and she gives Dee the dasher and top from her butter churn (even though she still uses the churn and will have to replace those parts—p. 640). But she is not blind to her daughter's flaws. She remembers how Dee hated their house that burned, how she used to think Dee "hated Maggie too" (p. 637), how Dee forced education on Maggie and her mother ("She...burned us with a lot of knowledge we didn't necessarily need to know. Pressed us to her with the serious way she read, to shove us away at just the moment, like dimwits, we seemed about to understand"). The narrator knows that Dee can be selfish, thoughtless, and even cruel, and she is not taken in by any of Dee's ploys to acquire the quilts. The narrator notices that Dee first asks for the quilts, "sweet as a bird" (p. 641), then simply takes them: "She held the quilts securely in her arms, stroking them....Dee (Wangero) moved back just enough that I couldn't reach the quilts. They already belonged to her" (p. 641). And the narrator is not surprised by the anger Dee displays, "for she has a temper" (p. 642).

If we had not viewed Dee through the narrator's eyes, we could not appreciate the significance of the narrator's decision to keep the quilts. The point of view allows us to understand that it is not pity for Maggie, envy of Dee's success, or need for the quilts that motivates the narrator. We know that the mother who "[snatches] the quilts out of Miss Wangero's hands and [dumps] them into Maggie's lap" is rejecting Dee's conclusion that quilts should be hung ("As if that were the only thing you *could* do with quilts"—p. 642), and proudly proclaiming her right to think for herself and to make her own decisions about values.

–M.R.D.

Leslie Marmon Silko
Lullaby

In the Counterpoint to this short story, Silko tells her interviewer that she wishes her readers "would have a little bit better understanding of place...." "Lullaby" certainly gives us that. The story is told from the perspective of an old Navajo woman, Ayah, whose life has now "become memories." As Ayah recalls watching her grandmother "spinning a silvery strand of yarn around the smooth cedar spindle," we enter a world few of us have experienced firsthand.

Silko, who is of mixed native–American, Mexican, and Caucasian ancestry, has written a number of stories about the native–American culture of Laguna Pueblo, New Mexico. In this story she paints the portrait of a courageous woman and allows us to glimpse the culture that produced her. Silko also shows us the fear and pain that can result when two very different civilizations collide.

QUESTIONS

1. What do the metaphors in the story tell us about the old woman?

If your students need to review terminology, you can remind them to check the Handbook entry "Metaphor and Symbol." Then you might begin by asking them to list all the metaphors in the story. (They may note that most are actually similes.)Here are some examples they may find:

◆ "[The snow] came in thick tufts like new wool—washed before the weaver spins it" (p. 644).

◆ "The blankets her mother made were soft and woven so tight that rain rolled off them like birds' feathers" (p. 644).

◆ "She was frightened by the way they looked at the children, like a lizard watches the fly" (p. 645).

◆ "Snowflakes were flying inside like moths and melting into a puddle on the oiled wood floor" (p. 648).

◆ "They looked at her like she was a spider crawling slowly across the room" (p. 648).

◆ "The rags made his feet look like little animals up to their ears in snow" (p. 649).

◆ "[The clouds] were massive and full, crowding together across the sky. She watched them with the feeling of horses—steely blue–gray horses startled across the sky. The powerful haunches pushed into the distance and the tail hairs streamed white mist behind them" (p. 650).

Although this question requires close reading of the story and some hunting through the text, once your students see what all the metaphors have in common, the answer to the question is relatively simple. Your students will undoubtedly notice that all these examples employ vehicles drawn from the natural world. These natural images suggest the woman's close identification with the physical world around her. That leads us to the next question.

2. How would you describe Ayah's relationship to nature?

Ayah's harmonious relationship with her environment may cause some of your students to leap to the conclusion that this story is a modern pastoral. Tell them to look again. The natural world depicted in this story is definitely not an idyllic paradise island where the temperature is pleasant and food abundant. The Navajos inhabit a harsh desert where life is fraught with hardship, danger, and pain. In the winter the snow falls so fast that Ayah watches it "fill in her tracks, steadily, until the direction she had come from is gone" (p. 644). In the summer "only a trickle of water" flows in "the wide deep creek bed" (p. 644), the old couple's few sheep must be herded to "dry sandy arroyos where sparse grass" grows (p. 649), and there has not been "enough rain for their garden in five years (p. 649). The natural world has inflicted the pains of birth (p. 645), death ("There had been babies that died soon after they were born, and one that died before he could walk"—p. 647), illness ("the old woman who died in the winter, spitting blood"—p. 646), and old age ("He smelled strong of woodsmoke and urine. Lately he had been forgetting"—p. 649).

But Ayah neither hates nor fears the natural world. She is part of a culture that has found accommodations in a seemingly inhospitable environment. Ayah's people use the gifts of nature wisely. From wool and natural dyes they create beautiful, functional blankets. ("Ayah remembered sleeping soft and warm on cold windy nights, wrapped in her mother's blankets on the hogan's sandy floor"—p. 644.) From deer and elk skins they fashion high buckskin leggings and elkhide moccasins. ("If the snow was dry or frozen, a person could walk all day and not get wet"—p. 644.) From the earth they dig the materials for building ("the old hogan with a dirt roof and rock walls where she herself had been born"—p. 649).

Two scenes in particular depict Ayah's harmonious relationship with the physical world. When she gives birth to her first child, she is not frightened, and she does not struggle against the powerful forces taking control of her body. Instead she studies those forces and labors with them:

She waited alone, learning the rhythms of the pains while her mother went to call the old woman to help them. The morning was already warm even before dawn and Ayah smelled the bee flowers blooming and the young willow growing at the springs (p. 645).

Even when her babies die, she knows how to respond. She carries them up to the top of a hill and buries them "in fine brown sand with round quartz pebbles that washed down the hills in the rain. She had endured it because they had been with her" (p. 647).

Ayah finds pleasure and solace in nature. In the opening scene when she is sitting outside in a snowstorm, she reaches out for the snow "like her own babies had, and she smiles when she remembers how she had laughed at them." On the April day that the white doctors first try to take her children, she grabs the children and hides in the hills. There "[t]he sun warmth relaxed her and took the fear and anger away" (p. 646).

In the final scene, which is deliberately ambiguous, we read that Ayah "recognized the freezing," but we don't know if that line means she and Chato will freeze to death before morning. Ayah knows whether they will survive, but we don't. Even if we assume Ayah is dying, we are not surprised when she welcomes death, which is merely a reunion with earth and with her babies, by singing a lullaby.

3. How do Ayah's encounters with white civilization compare to her encounters with nature?

Your students should point out that Ayah's encounters with white civilization cause her anger, fear, pain, and sorrow. She is convinced the white world offers nothing of value. Certainly the objects that symbolize white culture to Ayah stand in sorry contrast to Navajo blankets, buckskin leggings, and hogans sculpted from the earth: Jimmie's old army blanket ("[T]he green wool was faded, and it was unraveling on the edges"—p. 644), Ayah's black rubber overshoes ("old ones with little metal buckles"—p. 644), the shack provided by a white rancher until Chato was too old to work ("the gray boxcar shack with the paint all peeled off the wood; the stovepipe on the roof ...rusted and crooked"—p. 646).

In Ayah's opinion the sins the white world has committed against her are far worse than any blow nature has ever dealt. The white world steals her son Jimmie and her babies Danny and Ella. Ayah's culture has prepared her to deal with death, but not with these incomprehensible losses. She continues to mourn Jimmie: "It wasn't like Jimmie died. He just never came back" (p. 645). When she thinks about her babies, she decides that "[i]t was worse than if they had died: to lose children and to

know that somewhere, in a place called Colorado, in a place full of sick
and dying strangers, her children were without her....[S]he could not
bear this pain. She did not sleep for a long time after they took her
children....She carried the pain in her belly and it was fed by everything she saw..."(p. 647).

The Navajos have learned to live in harmony with nature, but they
have not worked out accommodations with the white culture. Chato tries
assimilation; Ayah opts for complete separation. Neither is successful.
Chato learns to speak English and Spanish, takes a job with a rancher,
accepts commodity foods, and picks up a pale blue government check each
month. But none of his efforts are rewarded. When he becomes too old to
work, the white rancher fires him and tells him to get out of the shack
by the next afternoon. "All of Chato's fine sounding English didn't
change things" (p. 647). His ability to speak Spanish is also of dubious
benefit: "The bar owner didn't like Indians in there, especially Navajos,
but he let Chato come in because he could talk Spanish like he was one of
them" (p. 648).

Ayah does her best to avoid the white world. She never forgives herself for letting Chato teach her to sign her name. "Because it was like
the old ones always told her about learning their language or any of
their ways: it endangered you" (p. 647). She attempts to hide her babies
from the white doctors, but she fails, just as she failed to keep Jimmie at
home. Ayah wants nothing from white culture except to be left alone. ("If
the money and the wine were gone, she would be relieved because then
they could go home again; back to the old hogan with a dirt roof and
rock walls where she herself had been born"—p. 649) But it seems that
she cannot escape from white civilization any more than she could escape
from the natural world that surrounds her.

4. Does the story suggest that white people are evil and knowledge is
dangerous?

If your class is composed primarily of white, middle-class students,
this story may make some a bit uncomfortable and defensive. So it's probably best to get this objection out on the table.

I would say that the story is not particularly biased against whites. It is
true that the story is told from Ayah's perspective. Silko thus engages our
sympathy for an old woman who has suffered much. At the same time,
Silko makes a conscientious effort to avoid labeling all whites "bad guys."
The author's assessment of the situation seems to be summed up perfectly
by the famous line from *Cool Hand Luke*: "What we have here is a failure
to communicate."

You may need to remind your students that in each scene that involves
an unhappy encounter between the two worlds Silko makes it clear that

white people, as well as Navajos, are puzzled and sometimes frightened by a way of life they can't understand.

When Chato told the military man who informed them of Jimmie's death that "they could keep the body if they found it,...the white man looked bewildered" (p. 645). When the "thin white woman" brought the children home for a visit, she "was nervous and kept looking at a dainty gold watch on her wrist....[S]he was worrying about the unpaved road. She was frightened by what she saw inside too...(p. 648). When Ayah entered the bar, the men "were afraid; she could feel their fear" (p. 648).

Ayah believes that her knowledge of white culture hurt her, that if she had not learned to write her name, she would not have lost her babies. Ask your students if they agree. I think they will quite sensibly respond that if either Ayah or the white doctors had known more, if either had been able to speak the other's language, the tragedy might have been prevented. Even Chato, who knows more about white culture than Ayah, doesn't know enough about it to object that a form signed by a woman who can't read English is not enforceable.

Perhaps Silko's message is not that knowledge is dangerous, but that people from different cultures inflict harm on each other because of ignorance. I think she would agree with these lines from Alexander Pope's *An Essay on Criticism*:

> A little learning is a dangerous thing:
> Drink deep, or taste not the Pierian spring;
> There shallow draughts intoxicate the brain,
> And drinking largely sobers us again.

—M.R.D.

Leigh Allison Wilson
The Raising

It is appropriate that Flannery O'Connor provides the Counterpoint for this short story, because Wilson is obviously indebted to O'Connor's view of a South "rich in contradiction, rich in irony, rich in contrast, and particularly rich in speech" (p. 664). In addition to sharing an interest in that which is uniquely and peculiarly southern, O'Connor and Wilson deal with universals of the human condition—the characters in their fiction as it is represented in *The Riverside Anthology* are often rendered grotesque by their obsessions and hypocrisy.

The characters in this short story are, no mistake, vulgar and cheesy— and often as not, deformed. Wilson forces us to see Hawklenville through Diane Arbus' lenses:

Laura Jane turned her head in the direction of Mrs. Talley, squint-
ing her eyes, and the cat, as though synchronized puppetlike to her
movements, turned its head around and squinted at the women
with two uneven green eyes that matched the color of the Jell–O.
One of its eyes had an ugly yellow pustule on the rim, making the
whole eye look like an open wound in the act of rankling . . . At
the door she stopped, facing the room, and caught Mrs. Eastman's
eye. There was an expression of malignancy on her face. She
dropped the thumb and the hand wandered with a will of its own to
the side of her face where it started to scratch a cheek. It might have
been a large, pink spider dropped incredibly there to spin a cobweb.
(p. 603–4)

Mrs. Eastman, with a voice "like a foghorn in the midst of a desert"
(p. 652) and sporting a beehive hairdo, is "a formidable personage, stout
and big–boned and not unlike the bouncer in a hard–bitten country bar"
(p. 652). The social worker wears "a pink polyester pantsuit that clung to
her legs and gave the appearance of a second skin shedding off from the
waist down" (p. 661). The retarded cabdriver who runs off with Buddy
Ruth Quarles has a wart on the corner of his eye that "puckered and
bobbed every time he opened his mouth" (p. 658).

Wilson forces us to ask the same question about her characters as
O'Connor does in "A Good Man Is Hard to Find": What happens when
bad things happen to insufferable people? Your students, I suspect, will be
as torn at the end of this short story as they are at O'Connor's.

If you treat this short story late in the semester, and if your readings
have included "Livvie," "Barn Burning," "The Library Card," and "A
Good Man Is Hard to Find," then your students may observe that the
South and southerners don't fare too well in modern southern literature.
It is, oddly enough, a regional prejudice more in contemporary southern
writers than the editor of this anthology. By this I mean that one must
look to the nineteenth century—or at least earlier in this century—to
find a tradition of baldly celebrative "southern" literature. You may wish
(particularly if your students are likely to have strong feelings in the
matter) to determine if Wilson has fallen into the Erksine Caldwell
syndrome; that is, if she is indulging in the now time–honored representation of a south where bigotry and incest underlie church socials and
genteel tradition. Your students may be hard pressed to draw the line
between social criticism and stereotype in "The Raising."

[In fact, you might wish to evaluate Wilson's accomplishment in light
of O'Connor's claim in the Counterpoint that

There is nothing worse than the writer who doesn't *use* the gifts of
the region, but wallows in them. Everything becomes so Southern
that it's sickening, so local that it is unintelligible, so literally re-

produced that it conveys nothing. The general gets lost in the particular instead of being shown through it.]

QUESTIONS

1. How are we prepared for the coming of Daryl?

Wilson handles a good deal of the exposition in her description of the bridge party. There, Mrs. Eastman is established as "a specialist in armchair mothering" (p. 652). She is also established as an inveterate gossip who delights in cataloging the failures of others as parents. Her comeuppance is all but inevitable.

Mrs. Eastman takes an inordinate pride in a child she has never seen and is smugly satisfied that she has the talent and will to shape him to her ends and ambitions. "Smart as a *whip*," she claims, certain that "she would make a lawyer out of him, distill the taint of his blood like meltwater. She would recreate the boy in her own image and watch him tower among men in her old age" (p. 653). One has the sense from the beginning of the short story that such aspirations, based on pride and mean–spiritedness, are doomed to failure.

All of part 3 of the short story is devoted to a portrait of Daryl, who has lived in nine orphanages, "one of which burned down mysteriously" (p. 660), who knows "the appetites of a very old man" (p. 660), and is "of conspicuous unknown origin" (p. 660). We see in his tyranny of the other urchins in the orphanage just what lies in store for the Eastmans.

> Each little boy had a scar of some kind on some part of his body, and each boy loved Little Daryl with a passion that drew blood. He had seen to that. (p. 660)

Wilson also foreshadows the effects of Daryl's entry into the Eastman household through the incident involving the eight mongrel dogs he brings home. The Eastman's home is turned to a chaos of dog fur and dogfights, and "eventually, one by one, the dogs skulked emphatically from the premises and trotted off westward" (p. 655). Daryl's kin, the Melungeons of Goins Hollow, will remind most of us of mongrels in breeding and behavior:

> Brown–eyed and maize–colored, they wedlocked themselves, cheated on themselves, coalesced with abandon, and produced either geniuses or idiots. They had no in–betweens. They loved each other or they killed each other . . .(p. 659)

Daryl, brought home for much the same reasons and in much the same manner as the dogs, takes what he can and trots off much like the dogs. Her glee at describing the Quarles' valuables being taken away in a U–Haul (p. 658) can only be matched by her horror at having her belongings stolen by Daryl.

2. What is Mrs. Eastman's view of motherhood?

For Mrs. Eastman, motherhood, or "raising," is largely a matter of exhibiting one's probity, intellect, and social standing through the behavior of one's children. The simpleton Mrs. Cowan, because by having shrewd children she has violated the "superior parents–superior children" dictum Mrs. Eastman holds dear, is "the most wicked woman of her [Mrs. Eastman's] acquaintance" (p. 653–654). Mrs. Eastman mangles the conventional marriage vow in describing her obligation to her new son; Daryl "is a responsibility. He's a responsibility for bad and for worse, for sickness and disease, forever and forever, till the dead do us part" (p. 659). Paradoxically, if "raising" means to educate in the ways of the world, then it is she who is "raised," when she encounters a child who might make a Snopes run for cover.

3. Is Daryl's appearance in any sense a punishment for the Eastman's? Why do/don't you think so?

Given Mrs. Eastman's character, it would not be surprising if any of your students claimed that Daryl is her just desserts. I would only remind them that whatever her motives for adoption, Mrs. Eastman's main ambition in life has been blunted and destroyed, and surely that must count for something.

But whatever sympathy we have for her is likely to vanish at her treatment of her husband, an otherworldly lawyer, who, when pointing out the beauties of Hawklenville to his new bride, had been jarred into the realities of his situation with her blank "Do tell." Our stay at the bridge party with Mrs. Eastman and her cronies has made us feel for him; we understand the visceral effect she has upon her husband:

> Mr. Eastman said nothing and sat tight, as if he were just hanging in a closet without any insides; he wanted to pat his wife kindly on the cheek or else smack her very hard in the middle of her face. But he did nothing at all, could have been dead except for the heart pounding madly between the places he breathed. (p. 658)

Disappointed by his marriage and where it has brought him, he retreats into his warren of an office and seems desperate for some sort of buffer between himself and his overbearing wife, who "didn't know shit from apple butter" (p. 657). That buffer is to be his new son: "This boy, this Little Daryl, would be his new salvation" (p. 657). One suspects that Eastman's motives for adopting Daryl are not the purest; they undoubtedly have more to do with diverting his wife's attention from himself to a fresh victim. If we chuckle at the image of Daryl walking away from the Eastman home, his pockets stuffed with jewelry and food, we repent at reading the last paragraph:

> When Mr. Eastman come home all he could hear were his wife's screams, and all he could see was a brown figure in the distance, the plumes of a rooster sticking out like an exhaust under its arms, and all he could think would be forever silent. (p. 664)

–W.R.S.

POETRY

COMMON FORMS AND SUBJECTS
IN THE POETRY SECTION

The decision to gather poems by the same author in one place in *The Riverside Anthology* comes from a conviction that we are unlikely to understand a poet well if we look at a single instance of his or her work, however cleverly it may be juxtaposed to the work of another writer. Nonetheless, the anthology invites author–to–author comparisons in several ways. Counterpointed poems following Shakespeare, Donne, Marvell, Blake, Whitman, Owen, and Cullen create small units on the pure lyric, the poem of wit, the carpe diem poem, the hymn and anti–hymn, Whitmanism, the war poem, and the protest poem. In addition, you may want to exploit in your syllabus the large collections of sonnets, dramatic monologues and dialogues, poems on the role of art, poems tied to mythologies and history, and poems centering on seasons, animals, and plants.

FORTY–TWO SONNETS

Petrarch/Surrey,	"The soote season that bud and blome furth brings"
Shakespeare,	"When in disgrace with fortune and men's eyes"
	"That time of year thou may'st in me behold"
	"Not marble nor the gilded monuments"
	"Since brass, nor stone, nor earth, nor boundless sea"
	"When my love swears that she is made of truth"
Donne,	"Death be not proud, though some have called thee"
	"Batter my heart, three–personed God"
Milton,	"On the Late Massacre at Piedmont"
	"Methought I saw my late espoused saint"
Wordsworth,	"The world is too much with us late and soon"
	"Composed Upon Westminster Bridge"
Tennyson,	"The Kraken"
Baudelaire,	"A Phantom" (three linked sonnets)
	"By Association"
	"Correspondences"
Rossetti,	"An Artist's Studio"
	"They Desire a Better Country" (three linked sonnets)

Hopkins,	"The Windhover"
	"Pied Beauty" ("curtal" sonnet)
	"God's Grandeur"
	"The Sea and the Skylark"
	"Thou Art Indeed Just, Lord"
Yeats,	"The Folly of Being Comforted" (sonnet in couplets)
	"Leda and the Swan"
Robinson,	"The Sheaves"
Rilke,	"Archaic Torso of Apollo"
Millay,	"Love Is Not All"
Rimbaud,	"The Sleeper in the Valley"
Albizzi,	"Prolonged Sonnet: When the Troops Were Returning from Milan"
Cummings,	"the Cambridge ladies who live in furnished souls"
Cullen,	"Yet Do I Marvel"
	"From the Dark Tower"
	"Black Majesty"
Shelley,	"Ozymandias"
Neruda,	"Never, forever . . . they do not concern me"
	"Lost in the forest, I broke off a dark twig"
Auden,	"Luther"
	"The Sphinx"
Bishop,	"The Prodigal" (linked sonnets)
Lowell,	"Night Sweat" (linked sonnets)
Wilbur,	"Praise in Summer"

SEVENTEEN DRAMATIC MONOLOGUES AND DIALOGUES

Blake,	"The Chimney Sweeper"
	"The Little Black Boy"

Tennyson,	"Ulysses"
Browning,	"My Last Duchess" "Fra Lippo Lippi" "Andrea del Sarto"
Housman,	"Terence, This Is Stupid Stuff" "Is My Team Plowing?"
Yeats,	"Crazy Jane Talks to the Bishop"
Frost,	"Home Burial"
Eliot,	"The Love Song of J. Alfred Prufrock" "The Journey of the Magi"
García Lorca,	"The Faithless Wife"
Auden,	"The Unknown Citizen"
Bishop,	"Crusoe in England"
Jarrell,	"The Woman at the Washington Zoo"
Brooks,	"The Chicago Defender Sends a Man to Little Rock"

THIRTY-SIX POEMS ON THE ROLE OF ART

Shakespeare,	"Not marble, nor the gilded monuments" "Since brass, nor stone, nor earth, nor boundless sea"
Keats,	"Ode on a Grecian Urn"
Browning,	"My Last Duchess" "Fra Lippo Lippi" "Andrea del Sarto"
O'Hara,	"Why I Am Not a Painter"
Baudelaire,	"Correspondences" "The Albatross"
Dickinson,	"I died for beauty"

Housman,	"Terence, This Is Stupid Stuff"
Yeats,	"Sailing to Byzantium"
Turner,	"Hymn to Her Unknown"
Brecht,	"A Film of the Comedian Chaplin"
Stevens,	"Study of Two Pears" "Anecdote of the Jar"
Rilke,	"Archaic Torso of Apollo" "Duino Elegies: IX"
Raine,	"Statues"
Fuertes,	"Painted Windows"
Williams,	"The Yellow Flower"
Moore,	"Poetry"
Montale,	"Little Testament"
Cullen,	"Epitaph for a Poet"
Brooks,	"The Chicago Picasso"
Wilbur,	"Praise in Summer"
Clampitt,	"Beach Glass" "Man Feeding Pigeons"
Bly,	"Words Rising"
Kumin,	"At a Private Showing in 1982"
Rich,	"Aunt Jennifer's Tigers" "Love in the Museum" "Diving into the Wreck"
Hass,	"Santa Lucia" "Heroic Simile" "Meditation at Lagunitas"

SIXTEEN POEMS TIED TO MYTHOLOGIES

Milton,   from *Paradise Lost*

Wordsworth,   "The World Is Too Much With Us"

Tennyson,   "The Kraken"
                           "The Lotos Eaters"
                           "Ulysses"

Yeats,   "Leda and the Swan"
                           "The Second Coming"

Rilke,   "Archaic Torso of Apollo"

Eliot,   "The Journey of the Magi"

Millay,   "An Ancient Gesture"

Bogan,   "Medusa"

Auden,   "Musée des Beaux Arts"
                           "The Sphinx"
                           "The Shield of Achilles"

Merwin,   "The Judgment of Paris"

Glück,   "The Triumph of Achilles"

SEVENTEEN POEMS TIED TO HISTORY

Whitman,   "The Wound–Dresser"

Frost,   "The Gift Outright"

García Lorca,   "Ballad of the Spanish Civil Guard"

Cullen,   "Black Majesty"

Brutus,   "Nightsong: City"

Revard,   "Discovery of the New World"

Neruda,   "The Danger"

Auden,	"Spain, 1937" "Luther" "Voltaire at Ferney"
Brooks,	"Riot" "The Chicago Defender Sends a Man to Little Rock"
Lowell,	"For the Union Dead"
Wilbur,	"After the Last Bulletins"
Clampitt,	"The Burning Child"
Hass,	"Meditation at Lagunitas" "Pala Alto: The Marshes"

FIFTEEN POEMS TIED TO SEASONS

Shakespeare,	"That time of year thou may'st in me behold"
Petrarch/Surrey,	"The soote season that bud and blome furth bringes"
Hardy,	"Weathers"
Bécquer,	"Will Not Come Back"
Wordsworth,	"Tintern Abbey"
Keats,	"To Autumn"
Housman,	"Loveliest of Trees"
Frost,	"Stopping by Woods on a Snowy Evening" "Nothing Gold Can Stay"
Williams,	"The Botticellian Trees"
Millay,	"Spring" "Oak Leaves"
Cummings,	"in just–spring"
Thomas,	"Poem in October"
Olds,	"Summer Solstice, New York City"

TWENTY–EIGHT POEMS INCLUDING ANIMALS

Donne,	"The Flea"
Blake,	"The Lamb" "The Tyger"
Smart,	"For I will consider my cat Jeoffry"
Eberhart,	"For a Lamb"
Baudelaire,	"The Albatross"
Dickinson,	"A bird came down the walk" "A narrow fellow in the grass"
Housman,	"The Windhover"
Rilke,	"The Panther"
Moore,	"Peter" "Elephants" "The Fish"
Cummings,	"r–p–o–p–h–e–s–s–g–r"
Montale,	"The Eel"
Bogan,	"The Dragonfly"
Neruda,	"Horses"
Bishop,	"The Armadillo"
Jarrell,	"The Snow Leopard"
Thomas,	"Over St. John's Hill"
Wilbur,	"Still, Citizen Sparrow" "The Death of a Toad"
Merwin,	"Noah's Raven"
Rich,	"Aunt Jennifer's Tigers"

Plath,	"Medallion" "Black Rook in Rainy Weather" "The Arrival of the Bee Box"
Glück,	"Horse"

SEVENTEEN POEMS INVOLVING FLOWERS AND PLANTS

Blake,	"The Sick Rose" "The Poison Tree"
Tennyson,	"Now Sleeps the Crimson Petal"
Williams,	"Queen Anne's Lace" "The Yellow Flower"
Montale,	"The Sunflower"
García Lorca,	"Song of the Barren Orange Tree"
Neruda,	"Lost in the forest, I broke off a dark twig"
Roethke,	"Big Wind" "Root Cellar" "Frau Bauman, Frau Schmidt, and Frau Schwartz"
Thomas,	"The Force that through the Green Fuse Drives the Flower"
Clampitt,	"Lindenbloom"
Merwin,	"The Last One"
Plath,	"Tulips"
Hass,	"Weed"
Glück,	"The Apple Trees"

THE ELEMENTS OF POETRY: NOTES TOWARD AN APPROACH

Obviously, a division of poets and their poetry into categories of technical elements will not yield complete justice—and the following listing is, as are all such lists, somewhat arbitrary. Nonetheless, those teachers who want to give their students a sustained introduction to the elements of poetry might consider the following arrangements. Consult the workup in this *Guide* for each poet for a close examination of the poet's reflection of the category in which he/she is placed.

SOUND
- Shakespeare
- Coleridge
- Keats
- Tennyson
- Robinson
- Wilbur
- Clampitt

FORM
- Shakespeare
- Tennyson
- Whitman
- Dickinson
- Rossetti
- Frost
- Cummings
- Merwin

TONE
- Donne
- Marvel
- Pope
- Keats
- Tennyson
- Robinson
- Jarrell

RHYTHM
- Donne
- Marvell
- Hopkins
- Hughes
- Auden
- Roethke

THEME
- Browning
- Rossetti
- Yeats
- Rilke
- Moore
- Owen
- Bogan
- Cullen
- Auden
- Thomas
- Brooks
- Lowell
- Rich

IMAGE
- Donne
- Milton
- Keats
- Baudelaire
- Hopkins
- Williams
- Eliot
- Millay
- García Lorca
- Hughes
- Roethke
- Bishop
- Bly
- Glück

RHYME   METAPHOR & SIMILE
  Blake   Shakespeare
  Dickinson   Donne
  Kumin   Milton
                                           Moore
SYMBOL   Kumin
  Blake   Plath
  Coleridge
  Hopkins
  Rilke
  Montale
  Neruda

William Shakespeare

The Shakespeare poems appear here counterpointed with a cluster of other lyrics that are far more musical than intellectual, and with a famous (or notorious) passage in which A. E. Housman says that poetry has nothing to do with the intellect. The position toward which all this pushes is extreme, of course, and may give class discussion a edge of controversy even while you are talking about a poet most students are more determined to admire than to understand.

If you are starting the study of poetry with Shakespeare, you have here an excellent opportunity to insist that students *listen* to the poems before they begin hunting too hard for messages. You may want your students to read the handbook entry on the "Sound of Poetry," especially, in conjunction with these selections. The imbalance created by putting so much emphasis on the ear and so little on the cerebellum can easily be redressed by taking a close look at the wit of Sonnet 138, or by comparing Shakespeare and Donne.

QUESTIONS

1. Reading through these poems *merely* for their sound, what passages of one to four lines are particularly effective, and why?

It might be a good idea to have students come to class with three passages that they are convinced would be "ravishing poetry" even if they were "nonsense." The rule that I would set for this game is that in each case the student should come with some "technical" explanation of what makes the passage work. Here are some lines that might rise to the surface under these circumstances.

◆ Sonnet 55: "And broils root out the work of masonry."

◆ Sonnet 65: "O, how shall summer's honey breath hold out
Against the wreckful siege of battering days?"

◆   "Come away, come away death
              And in sad cypress let me be laid
          Fly away, fly away, breath;
              I am slain by a fair cruel maid."

◆ "A Ballade":   ". . . that Buridan should steer
Sewed in a sack's mouth down the Seine?"

◆ "Volverán": "Dark swallows will doubtless come back killing
the injudicious night flies with a clack of the beak;"

◆ "Weathers": "And hill–hid tides throb, throe on throe"

Among the things that students acquainted with the "Sound of Poetry"
section of the handbook might be able to point out are these, noted passage–by–passage:

◆ Students will probably see that the line from Sonnet 55 makes
wonderful use of the repeated *r*-sound. Substitute "fights" for "broils"
and the effect is lost. They might also feel, as I do, that the line gets
three successive stresses at "broils root out," a good example of the
force of substitution.

◆ Students may note the relative euphony of the first line and the
relative cacophony of the second, particularly strong in the words
against, wreckful. They are less likely to note the breathless quality
given the first line by the repeated sound of the initial *h.*

◆ Some students will notice, and perhaps be able to describe, the
strong rhyme of the opening dactyls on the first and third lines.
Others might note that the four stresses in the second and fourth
tend to fall on syllables linked in sound (*sad* and *CYpress, slain* and
maid).

◆ The alliteration on the *s*-sound is obviously the main attraction
here, but notice in the second line the wonderful interplay of sounds
in "mouth down the Seine."

◆ The repeated cacophonous *k*-sound is the most obvious element
here, and suggests deliberate onomatopoeia. The alliteration on *dark*

and *doubtless* also does its work, and the linkage of sounds in "killing/the injudicious nightflies" makes it into one hum.

◆ Good heavens! A line so dense with echoing sounds that it would take a paragraph to list them. Also a line dense with stresses that choke its movement. Compare the corresponding line of the preceding stanza, which begins with three anapests and skips along lightly.

2. In what ways does the form of Shakespeare's sonnets add to their effectiveness? In what way does it hinder their effectiveness?

Your students will be better prepared to handle this question if they have first read the handbook entry on poetic forms, especially the section on the sonnet. The sonnets are a lightning rod for arguments between those who favor organic form and those who favor fixed form. In the introduction to *The Wedge*, for example, William Carlos Williams says that all sonnets say the same thing. They are, if I follow his argument correctly, exercises in imposing an order on the world, and while this imposition of order may be important, it eventually becomes tedious, particularly if it is the same order (iambic pentameter, rhyme) over and over. Robert Frost, however, turns naturally to a Shakespearean sonnet when he wants to talk (in "The Figure a Poem Makes") about the galvanizing effect that a poet's commitment to a fixed form can have, an effect analogous to the "fixed" commitments all people must make if they are going to be actively involved in life. In effect, Williams is saying that a poet who decides to write a sonnet is tying himself or herself to a machine. In effect, Frost is responding that a person who gets married, takes a job, or makes a friend is also tying himself or herself to a machine, and that to tie the knot with grace and pleasure is the thing.

But the question need not be answered at such an abstract level. Consider the practical advantages Shakespeare has in Sonnet 73. The conventional three quatrains have the advantage of being separate but related shelters within which the poet can nurture images he wants the reader to notice. In the first quatrain the poet gives us the image of a bare tree in winter. In the second, he gives us a fading sunset and the succeeding blackness. In the third he gives us a fire burned down to its last coals. This procession of images registers on us emotionally without Shakespeare's having to provide an explanation of their relation. The year dies, the day dies, the fire dies. A daytime scene, a twilight scene, a night scene. The solemn and inevitable progress to the end seems all the more solemn and inevitable for the form it is presented in. It is arguable that this expert juxtaposition of three images is the fruit of the discipline imposed on the sonnet: that the quatrains aren't just passive containers of the images, they also help create them. (Notice the comparable procession of images in 29 and 65, or the replacement of images by arguments in 138.)

Of course, the three expertly crafted, self–contained quatrains of iambic pentameter lines could become terribly predictable. One of the things that Shakespeare does to avoid monotony is to vary the meter occasionally (a bit too rarely for some tastes). Note, for instance, the enjambment of lines 2 and 3 of Sonnet 73 and the beginning of line 4 with three successive stresses and a caesura.

If I were teaching Sonnet 73, I would ask my students to look especially at the 13th line and to ask themselves where the logic of the poem demands a stress that runs contrary to the regular iambic meter. There might be two ways of looking at it. For three quatrains the poet has been presenting himself as decrepit, now he has to turn the poem around and say that it is precisely this decrepitness that makes him attractive to the person that loves him. Surely this is an extraordinary idea, and to carry it, we might place our emphasis on the unusual nature of the younger person:

U / U / U / / / U /
This THOU perceiv'st, which makes THY love more strong

THY, of course, breaks the iambic pattern. My own reading would put the stress on the surprising outcome of the lover's perceptions rather than on the lover himself or herself:

/ U U / U / U / U /
THIS thou perceiv'st, which makes thy love MORE strong

The stress on THIS is surely indicated by the inversion of the natural word order "thou perceiv'st this." It refers (rather vaguely, by the standards of school grammars) to "all this unpleasant—though highly poetic—stuff about my age"; the stress on MORE is for me the turning point of the poem.

3. Are Shakespeare's sonnets as similar in emotional content as they are in external form?

Every student will approach a question like this suspecting that he or she had better find a way to answer "no." The shortest way to such an answer is to compare 73 with 138. In both cases, the disparity in age is an issue, but 138 light–heartedly balances the poet's old age against the young lover's unfaithfulness. Students who tend to confuse Shakespeare with Bible camp may be surprised by the pun on "lie" in the 13th line of 138. Once they see it, they need to see how perfectly it captures the tone of the poem. Notice that this pun is actually introduced in the second line, where the poet knows that the lover who claims she is "made of truth" (is faithful), in fact, lies (here and there). Notice that it is matched by a pun in line 5, where the poet "vainly" thinks that she thinks him young. The poem is a wonderful combination of frankness and flattery—a thoroughly "adult" poem that takes disillusionment as part of the game. Finally, like 73, it gives an affecting picture of a relationship, but the tone is entirely different. Here the approach to the heart is distinctly through the head.

–D.H.

John Donne

To prepare your students to read Donne, you may want them to read the handbook entry on wit. Donne's combination of metaphysical wit and unconventional meter has kept his reputation in flux over the centuries. Coleridge's epigram goes to the heart of the matter:

> With Donne, whose muse on dromedary trots,
> Wreathe iron pokers into true love–knots;
> Rhyme's sturdy cripple, fancy's maze and clue,
> Wit's forge and fire–blast, meaning's press and screw.

Beyond wit and "dromedary" meter, however, students should learn to see the great struggle between Donne's worldliness and his religious devotion, expressed on the one hand in the combination of secular and religious imagery of the love poems (cf. "The Relic," "A Valediction") and on the other in the sometimes harsh and erotic imagery of the religious poems (cf. Holy Sonnet 14).

QUESTIONS

1. What images in Donne's poems or in the three twentieth–century poems that follow them embody the sort of wit that Housman disapproves of and Eliot approves of?

The most famous of Donne's "poetical anagrams" are probably the conceits in "The Flea" and "A Valediction: Forbidding Mourning." These are so familiar (and so teachable) that I will pass them by. You can generally start a discussion of these poems by asking students to explain the ingenious reasoning behind the conceits. Dugan's "Love Song," like "The Flea," extends its conceit (the comparison of the speaker's unhappy life to an ill–constructed house) from the first of the poem to the last. You might particularly ask your students how the swearing serves a dual purpose in the poem ("By Christ/I am no carpenter") by the standard of Christ, who is. Adrienne Rich's "Two Songs," like "A Valediction," moves through a series of ingenious shorter conceits to an extended final one: note how neatly everything in the moon–landing metaphor works, down to the use of different languages to signal the isolation of the lovers. Sandra McPherson's "7,22,66," like "The Sun Rising," expresses its wit not by conceits, but by the range of objects that can be brought into the poem and justified, each with its own application. It is almost as though McPherson had set herself the task of writing a poem that would successfully integrate Gideon Bible, soap, and stationery.

2. Why would some people object to the wit of poems like "The Flea" or "A Validiction: Forbidding Mourning"? How can this wit be defended?

The long and short of the objection is that Donne's style of wit is in bad taste, that it is merely showing off, that it replaces content with form. I suppose that Housman's comment about "poetical anagrams" is as clear a statement of the case against Donne as one could find: A surface that flashes with ingenuity cannot redeem a poem without a core of solid truth and feeling. Even novelty becomes old hat eventually, and by Pope's time the metaphysical conceit had fallen out of fashion:

> Some to conceit alone their taste confine,
> And glittering thoughts struck out at every line;
> Pleased with a work where nothing's just or fit;
> One glaring chaos and wild heap of wit.
> Poets, like painters, thus, unskilled to trace
> The naked Nature and the living grace,
> With gold and jewels cover every part,
> And hide with ornaments their want or art.
> True wit is nature to advantage dress'd:
> What oft was thought, but ne'er so well express'd.

No one would claim that the image in "The Flea" was one that was naturally on everyone's mind and was just waiting for a poet to express it clearly. It *is* outrageous.

In defense of outrageousness, however, we could begin by citing the contemporary poet W. D. Snodgrass: "... it is a poet's business to say something interesting. Something so interesting and so valuable that people should stop doing whatever it is they are doing and listen,... should stop thumbing through their order books, turning the dials on the TV, chasing the secretary around the desk." Donne's conceits are so startling that they force us to do a double–take, and a double–take is one sign that the poet has our attention, at least.

Of course, a double–take isn't worth much if our second look finds only a "glaring chaos, and wild heap of wit." You might want to have your students examine this embarrassing conceit describing Mary Magdalene's eyes in Crashaw's "The Weeper."

> Two walking Bathes, two weeping motions;
> Portable and compendious Oceans.

Here the second look isn't worthwhile.

Donne, however, improves on a second look, for reasons that lead us to a third question.

3. Isn't Donne's style of wit at odds with the emotion expected in love poetry?

Really, now! To court a woman by suggesting that making love is no more serious than being bitten by a flea! To woo her by talking about what you will look like when you are dug out of your grave! To assure your wife of your undying love by comparing her to a draftsman's tool! What ever happened to whispering sweet nothings?

One thing that happened, it seems to me, is that Donne broke away from the habit of seeing the beloved as an intellectual lightweight incapable of holding in mind any notion more complicated than "gather ye rosebuds while ye may." The Woman (regard her for now as a collective figure) to whom Donne's poems are addressed is not a simple shepherdess or a dweller among untrodden ways. She is expected to know something about Church history ("The Good Morrow," line 4), alchemy (line 19), and Ptolemaic astronomy ("The Sun Rising," line 30). She is expected to be comfortable with the world of maps, courtiers, coins, huntsmen, and goldsmiths. There is a compliment here that is surely preferable to Robert Herrick's

> Fain would I kiss my Julia's dainty Leg
> Which is as white and hair–less as an egge.

Of course, it might be objected that Donne is not addressing any woman or women at all, that the woman in the poem is merely a convention that allows the poet to show off his learning and his wit. "The Flea" is so "smarty–smart" a poem, as a student once told me, that it supports this hypothesis. If Donne *is* addressing a woman, the argument goes, he is using her really as a stage prop while he winks at the audience. Other poems, however, strike me very differently. "A Valediction," as C. S. Lewis once pointed out, is one of the few great poems about *married* love, and if we read it closely, we see that its extraordinary images replace the references to nubile limbs, soft lips, and shining eyes that ordinarily dominate love poetry. Donne's cleverness allows him to be honest: the love he feels is not the love of a new affair. It would be very worthwhile, by the way, to have your students compare the imagery of "A Valediction" to that of McPherson's "7,22,66." One discusses married love in images that suggest permanence: the movement of the Ptolemaic spheres, gold in the hands of a skilled craftsman, the gigantic compass that always draws a

true circle. The other discusses married love in images that suggest root-
lessness: objects that can be taken from motel rooms, the tides washing
below the motel, the undecipherable key to the next anonymous room.

4. Compare Donne's Holy Sonnet 14 with Shakespeare's Sonnet 73. What
does the comparison show about the difference in technique between the
two poets?

Students should note that Shakespeare's sonnet uses three neatly defined
images drawn from the natural world or the domestic world close to
nature (tree, sunset, hearth fire). None of the images seems jarringly
unlikely in a poem about aging and death. Donne's images, on the other
hand, are harder at first to define because they are not always introduced
by a formula that tells us a metaphor is coming ("In me thou see'st"). In
the first quatrain, the verbs suggest the actions of a goldsmith or silver-
smith. In the second, the simile explicitly compares Donne to a captive
town besieged by its rightful ruler. In the third, and in the couplet,
Donne is compared to a woman betrothed to the wrong man and hoping
to be ravished by her true lover. All three images have some tradition behind them, but collectively they seem jarring in this poem of religious
devotion. Notice that the images, unlike Shakespeare's, are not those
likely to appear on greeting cards. The first, like many of Donne's, comes
not from the natural world but from the world of human contrivance: his
system of imagery repeatedly points us to smiths, cartographers,
musicians, alchemists. The third involves a level of violence nowhere
paralleled in Shakespeare's sonnets. The violence comes, one feels, from
Donne's impatience with his intellect, the weak or untrue Viceroy of the
second quatrain. We know that throughout his life he struggled with
religious doubts, and prayer here is to have God overwhelm these doubts by
whatever force is necessary.

The violence of the imagery is paralleled by a violence in language and
meter. Notice how much the first lines vary from regular iambic pentameter

    / ∪ ∪ /   / / ∪ / ∪ /
Batter/ my heart,/ three–per/soned God/ for You

    ∪ / ∪ /   /   / ∪ / ∪ /
As yet/ but knock,/ breath,/ shine,/ and seek/ to mend;

We can see here why Housman complains that metaphysical verse was
"generally inharmonious, and apparently cut into lengths and tied into
faggots by deaf mathematicians." There are ten syllables to the line here,
but the extraordinary irregularity, and the monosyllabic feet combined to
do violence to the regular meter. Shakespeare's occasional substitutions,

diereses, and enjambments can't compare to Donne's explosiveness. In defense of Donne, it can surely be said that he captures the rhythms of the impassioned voice, not only in this poem, but in the very colloquial passages of "The Sun Rising" and "The Canonization."

–D.H.

John Milton

Nothing is harder than to give students a sense of the grandeur of Milton's poetry in an introductory course where they can read him only in snippets. The selections in *The Riverside Anthology* are chosen to emphasize two aspects of his verse: the organ music, as Amy Clampitt calls it, which can best be discovered by reading aloud and which, frankly, defies analysis; and the use of figurative language to provide both enlarged meaning and fresh imagery. The handbook entries on imagery and metaphor might be assigned in conjunction with Milton.

QUESTIONS

1. *Paradise Lost* is a highly embellished telling of a very familiar story. The embellishment comes largely in the form of imagery, often introduced by figures of speech. After reading through the selection from Book IX return to two passages—lines 425–456 and lines 1099–1133—and study how the imagery enhances the story.

These two passages, discussed in full, would provide more than can be talked about in a class hour. Hitting some of the high points, however, will give students a sense of the density of Milton's fable and the richness of its appeal to the senses as well as the intellect. Some observations on the first passage:

◆ We start with synaesthesia—a cloud of fragrance so dense it veils Eve from Satan's sight.

◆ We move to a description of the roses that has both lush sensory appeal and symbolic significance. Note the stress on colors in 429, but note also that the roses' variegated heads are drooping on their slender stalks. Roses are, of course, a fixed symbol for beauty and innocence, and Milton makes these a symbol for weakness as well. Even if he had not called his shot by the explicit metaphor in 432–34, we would probably have seen the connection with Eve.

◆ The allusions to Adonis, Alcinous, Laertes' son, and the sapient king will mean very little to your students. You might want to explain that Adonis, according to Greek ("feigned") myth, was killed by a boar but is revived each spring as bed of *briefly* blooming blood–red flowers. The mythical garden of Alcinous enchanted Odysseus ("Laertes' son"). Apparently Odysseus' love of gardens was inherited, since Laertes gave up his crown to devote his life to gardening. The "sapient king" is Solomon, whose love of Sheba led him to disobey Jehovah. All of this provides both foreshadowing and elevating association with great myths and Bible stories. The flower that blooms so briefly foretells the passing of the garden; the king who gives up power to enjoy the innocent garden contrasts with Satan; Solomon's being led into sin by Sheba foreshadow's Adam's sinning for love of Eve.

◆ The heroic simile in 445–56 introduces a wealth of imagery, principally olfactory (more evidence of Milton's use of non–visual imagery). It also reminds us that Milton belongs to a period when pastoral tradition is very alive: Hell is a city, the Garden is like the English countryside idealized.

◆ The effect of the simile is to help us understand Satan's temporary change of heart on seeing Eve. It may be worth taking your class through the result (lines 456 to about 475) to *listen* to the verse. Particularly note the caesura after the metrically and meaningfully surprising phrase "Stupidly good" (465). The verse seems to pull up in surprise as Satan pulls up, and it moves haltingly through the next line. Note the way that it regains momentum in line 467, huffing energetically through the alliterated *h*'s.

In the second passage note:

◆ As Coleridge mentions in the Counterpoint, the image of the Malabar figtree with its "echoing walks" is partly auditory, but it is also tactile (coolness amid heat), and visual.

◆ Both the Malabar figtree and the American Indians about to be introduced are typical of the eclectic imagery of the English Renaissance, which imported its imagery from all corners of the globe. It seems almost that as soon as a thing is discovered, the Renaissance poet wanted to work it into a poem.

◆ The image has great symbolic importance. Just as the figtree becomes the ancient center of a ripple of succeeding generations, so Adam and Eve are the epicenter from which humanity will spread.

And their sin, original sin, will also be an epicenter from which generations of sin will take root.

◆ The storm in 1121–1126 echoes the danger of storm to the roses of 425 ff., and the rain brought on by Adam's eating the apple in 1000–1004. Such correspondence between inner and outer weather is just the sort of thing that Ruskin criticized as the pathetic fallacy. Pathos is partly beside the point here, though. We are dealing with an event of supernatural importance; Nature has cause to tremble.

If you can arrange your questions in class so that students uncover some of the importance of Milton's imagery for themselves, you will have done as much as can be done with him in an introductory class.

2. How convincingly drawn are the characters of Satan, Adam, and Eve?

Space prevents my commenting much on this question, but it could produce good class discussion. Satan's pride is, of course, notoriously convincing and must come partly from Milton's knowledge of his own character. Feminists will be quite understandably outraged by the idea that Eve's vanity makes her a fit representative for all women. The bickering of Adam and Eve at the end of the chapter, however, and the overheated nature of fallen sexuality may strike some students as being impressionistic representations of what everyone learns about their own internal lives.

3. How are Milton's sonnets different from those of Shakespeare or Donne?

Apologies to those of you who are teaching Milton without having taught the other two. You might nonetheless refer your students to Shakespeare's Sonnet 73 (a good standard), and perhaps to Donne's Sonnet 14. Milton's sonnet is in the Italian form, which means that its natural "fulcrum" is not between the last quatrain and the couplet, but between the octave and sestet (your students should get this much information form the handbook entry on sonnet form).

But the first thing to notice is that Milton's verse rides over the natural divisions of the sonnet far more impatiently than either Shakespeare's or Donne's. In "When I Consider," the first quatrain is enjambed in the second, and the second is enjambed into the sestet, which can be said to begin after the semicolon in line 7. From that semicolon forward enjambment becomes the rule rather than the exception: not till 13 do we get an end–stopped line. Competent critics (like Samuel Johnson) with ears accustomed to more regular rhymed verse, have found Milton's sonnets barely tolerable: and indeed there is something ungainly about Milton's attempt to sqeeze his gargantuan poetry into a glass slipper. The transition between lines 6 and 7, for instance, is terribly difficult. Unless we are willing to make a major pause in the middle of a quatrain (we are, of course), it is hard to tell who is chiding whom in line 7. Those who read Milton's sonnets with pleasure read them, I suspect, almost as if they were blank verse, attending to the rhymes and line endings only distantly, as they would in, for example, Browning's "My Last Duchess."

It is probably worth pointing out that Milton's stresses depend largely on syntax and rhetoric, and are not much constrained by metrical regularity. (In this Milton is closer to Donne than to Shakespeare.) "Lodged," for instance, gets a strong stress because it is a verb separated from its subject, "talent." The series of relatively short sentences in the sestet, because their word order is normal and they are not filled with qualifying phrases and clauses, seem to move very quickly, and the enjambment adds to the feeling of speed. This makes the pause after line 13 more effective.

Like Donne's poetry, Milton's compresses and compounds the worlds of personal experience, theology, and learning. After your class discussion has established what this poem is about on a personal level—the struggle between bitterness and resignation brought on by Milton's mid–life blindness—you may want to ask your students if they recognize any allusions behind

- ◆ "my light is spent"
- ◆ "one talent which it is death to hide"
- ◆ "day–labor"

The allusions are to the parable of the wise and foolish virgins ("our lamps are gone out"—Matthew 25), the parable of the talents ("But he that received one talent digged in the earth and hid his lord's money"—Matthew 25) and the parable of the laborers in the vineyard ("And when he had agreed with these laborers for a penny a day, he sent them into his vineyard."—Matthew 20). *Someone* is likely to recognize the second, at least. Why does Milton make these allusions? Probably you will have to read some relevant passages before it becomes clear that all three parables are about God's harsh judgment. The foolish virgins whose lamps expire are shut out of the house by the master. The cautious servant who buries the talent is "cast into outer darkness." The day laborers who complain that their master is unjust are rebuked: "many be called, but few chosen." All to involve the coming on of darkness. These parables become fused in Milton's opening lines, and to those who share Milton's deep immersion in the scriptures, they raise deep feelings: resentment of God's treatment of man and fear of a darkness deeper even than Milton's blindness if that resentment leads to damnation. Both the surprising comparisons and the intense religious devotion of the poem remind us that Donne and Milton were poets of the same century.

If your students find Milton hard going, you might want to give them a reward by comparing "When I Consider" with Countee Cullen's far more accessible "Yet Do I Marvel." They will then see that their knowledge of Milton can make them better readers of the many poets who have admired him.

–D.H.

Andrew Marvell

Marvell is a great deal more fun to teach than many poets who outrank him in the canon. "To His Coy Mistress" never fails; "A Dialogue Between the Soul and Body" is a very teachable example of metaphysical wit deployed on a serious subject; "Bermudas," "Eyes and Tears," and "The Definition of Love" all have the feel of minor classics that we can relish simultaneously for their virtues and their peculiarities. The Counterpoints here are probably among the most directly useful in the book, each pointing clearly to a line of discussion in class.

QUESTIONS

1. Eliot's Counterpoint attributes a certain sort of wit to Andrew Marvell. How is this wit different from metaphysical wit? What examples can you find of each sort of wit? (You might refer your class to the handbook entry on wit.)

This longish question is not so dull as it seems, if only because Marvell's metaphysical conceits are sometimes outrageous enough to bring us to the edge, at least, of an outright smile. Here are my favorites:

◆ "Eyes and Tears," second stanza: the tear as a surveyor's plumb bob.

◆ "Eyes and Tears," second stanza: Mary Magdalene's tears as liquid chains.

◆ "The Definition of Love," throughout: the lovers as poles on which the globe turns, and their union as the reduction of earth to a planisphere!

◆ "To His Coy Mistress," lines 11 and 12: love as a plant (perhaps a watermelon, my gardening experience suggests) grown "vaster than Empires."

It really is hard in these four cases to tell how much to attribute to deliberate humor, how much to Marvell's having what Housman calls an "engrossing preoccupation" with metaphor and simile. Of course, the conceits are sometimes very much on point:

◆ "Eyes and Tears," sixth stanza: the earth as a flask in which liquid is distilled each day by the sun's heat, but being only water (tears) falls back again as rain. This image, like Donne's famous "twin compasses," blows a human implement up to gigantic proportions. The result is to *reduce* the earth to a simple and heartbreaking thing, a closed container in which tears fall, evaporate, and fall again.

◆ "A Dialogue Between the Soul and Body," first stanza: the soul as a prisoner locked in the dungeon of the body, an extraordinary extended metaphor.

◆ "A Dialogue Between the Soul and Body," lines 41–44: the comparison of the soul to architects who "square and hew" the natural trees of the forest. The implication here is that the body would be innocent if only there were no soul in it to create sin. Blake might have liked this idea. The Victorians, who were fairly certain that the body was a source of evil, would probably not.

If you begin your discussion by concentrating on this sort of metaphysical wit, then you can isolate it for a time and try to find the "tough reasonableness" that Eliot believes is the heart of Marvell's particular wit. This wit is far harder to isolate, but we seem to see it in these places among others:

◆ "To His Coy Mistress," throughout: Archibald MacLeish's "You, Andrew Marvell" exactly identifies the bedrock underneath the tough reasonableness. If we blow away the delightful froth, we find a frightening awareness of the "always coming on/The always rising of the night." *Marvell, however, does not blow away the froth.* He is capable of concentrating simultaneously on the grimness of time's "slow–chapped power" and the playfulness of the hyperbolic images in the first half of his poem. "There is here," as Eliot says, "an equipoise, a balance and proportion of tones . . ."

◆ "A Dialogue Between the Soul and Body," lines 9 and 10. Here at the end of the powerful extended metaphor, filled with the gravest significance for a man of Marvell's religious conviction, we get a beautifully turned, self–denigrating wisecrack: "vain head, and double heart." I suspect, by the way, that the head is "vain" both in today's sense of self–adoring and the etymological sense of "empty" (from Latin *vanus*, "empty"), a meaning very alive to literary men of the seventeenth century. Perhaps, too, the heart is double because it is fickle, but also because it has two chambers (bad anatomy, I know, but

Marvell's may have been imperfect). See also in the same poem line 29, which appears to be both a complaint by the soul that being cured is unfortunate because it leaves one in a body, *and* a glancing blow at the nastiness of seventeeth–century medical practices.

◆ "Eyes and Tears," particularly stanzas 7 and 14. I cite these not because they exemplify the wit Eliot is talking about, but because they go so far in explaining its basis. Marvell was a Puritan with a vision of sin and sorrow very like Milton's: at bottom there are "weeping eyes, seeing tears." He was also a cultivated gentleman who knew the pleasures of life and did not despise them. To "maintain the proportion" must have been as difficult an accomplishment in his life as it was in his art.

2. Which of the counterpointed poems share the sort of wit Eliot detects in Marvell?

Moving from toughness to lyricism, I would put the poems in this order: "The Flaw in Paganism," "To the Virgins," "A Late Aubade," "You, Andrew Marvell," and "Question." I have no confidence in this being the "correct" order; although all the poems at least touch the *carpe diem* tradition, we are clearly comparing apples to oranges. Nonetheless, the attempt to arrange some of the poems on such a spectrum can help your class locate the quality Eliot describes.

"The Flaw in Paganism," like many of Dorothy Parker's poems, is pure deflating wit, tough but not lyric, since it doesn't fully accept the emotion it deflates. "To the Virgins" is obviously closer to Marvell, but less tough, since it is "comparatively poor in shades of feeling to contrast and unite": we don't get the contrast between the grisliness of the graveyard worms and the playfulness of "I would/Love you ten years before the flood." "A Late Aubade" certainly has urbanity, but has less to be tough about, since boredom rather than death and decomposition is the worst thing its world has to offer. "You, Andrew Marvell" and "Question" face the reality of death squarely, but without the mixture of emotion that is the essence of the sort of wit Eliot praises in Marvell. Of course, this ranking says nothing directly about the quality of the poems: only the most doctrinaire critic would insist that a poem must be tough (or tender) to be good.

3. What makes "Bermudas" unlike Marvell's other poems?

Bliss, surely. There are few poems in the language that capture innocent delight the way this one does. Your class should probably discover the rhythm of the poem first, and experiment with it a bit. Once the song starts in line 5, you can read the poem in exaggerated iambs:

> What SHOULD we DO but SING his PRAISE,
> That LED us THROUGH the WAT'ry MAZE.

And, indeed, the poem is, by the standards of more restrained and serious verse, excessively iambic, with lots of diaresis and few substitutions. But I think that the song rhythm is even stronger than that of a regular iambic beat. Note that the typical line has a caesura after four syllables:

> What should we do // but sing his praise,
> That led us through // the wat'ry maze.

The result is to create a subunit four beats long. Now the rhythmic question becomes shall this half line beat with about the same force every second syllable in a regular iambic meter? Or shall it have one particularly strong syllable per half–line, as a song has one particularly strong beat per measure?

> What should we DO // but sing his PRAISE,
> That led us THROUGH // the wat'ry MAZE.

Or shall we put our one stress in the middle of the measure:

> What SHOULD we do // but SING his praise,
> That LED us through // the WAT'ry maze.

My own feeling is that the further we get into the poem, the more strongly this last pattern asserts itself, so that if you ask your class where the oars pull in the final four lines, they will say they pull in the middle of the measure.

> And ALL the way, to GUIDE their chime,
> With FALLING oars, they KEPT the time.

But I would not insist that all students buy this reading. Someone who wants to beat on WAY, CHIME, OARS, TIME can make a case. (Though IN, BOAT, AND, NOTE in the two lines preceding seems a bit unlikely.)

Obviously, a whole (and amusing) lesson in metrics could be done with the poem. (See Maxine Kumin's "Morning Swim" for an opportunity to reinforce this lesson.) But there is, besides the cheerful meter, a series of cheerful images of God's benevolence in creating in the Bermudas what almost amounts to a new Garden of Eden. See lines 13–14, 18–20, and, perhaps best, 17–18:

> He hangs in shades the orange bright,
> Like golden lamps in a green night.

Here is a conceit born in euphoria, and of course to the English Puritans who landed in the Bermudas there was cause enough to be delirious with joy.

But what has become of "tough reasonableness" and "balance of proportions and tone"? They show, I think, just twice: in the parentheses of lines 29 and 35. In the midst of all this buoyancy, there is just the slightest reminder that the Puritans might smile at their own pride and remember that their songs may not, really, rebound off the vault of heaven.

–D.H.

Alexander Pope

Teaching Pope's poetry requires meticulous preparation because, like most satire, it is highly topical and assumes a knowledge of the details of the social life it is sending up. The selection in *The Riverside Anthology* is intended to keep the range of topical knowledge reasonably narrow but still give a sense of Pope's relation to the social scene. The selection from *An Essay on Criticism* can be read intelligently by someone who knows next to nothing about neoclassicism. "To a Young Lady" explains itself fairly well, and the city/country contrast it turns. "Timon's Villa" is harder going, but I include it because those teachers who know Pope well and want to discuss the bases of neoclassical taste have in it an excellent springboard. *The Rape of the Lock* is represented by a passage that definitely depends on a cultural peculiarity of the eighteenth century—the voguishness of card games, and particularly of ombre. But Pope, delightfully, *treats* ombre as a peculiar game and so sets it up as a focus for class discussion. The teacher who learns as much about the rules as is given in the footnotes and who comes to class with a deck of cards can turn the need for special knowledge to his or her advantage.

QUESTIONS

1. Pope's reputation was made largely by his satiric wit and his cleverness at compressing a witticism into a single line or couplet. In what lines or couplets do you find this capacity for compact satire at work?

I use this as a lead–off question because students will like Pope for his humor if they are to like him at all. Many of my own favorites come from *Essay on Criticism*, which reads in places like a very sophisticated joke book. The "Sound and Sense" passage is dense with gags:

> While expletives their feeble aid do join;
> And ten low words oft' creep in one dull line. (10–11)

If your students don't know that *do* is an expletive in the first line, they will miss the point, but anyone who will read the second aloud is bound to catch on. Most students should immediately see how clever the couplet at 16–17 is:

> If crystal streams *with pleasing murmurs creep,*
> The reader's threaten'd (not in vain) with *sleep.*

Threatened both by the word, and the thing itself, of course. Students who are not accustomed to the idea of poetry that satirizes poetry may respond instead to Pope's political and social satire. In the "Game of Ombre" passage, for instance, we have one of his great couplets:

> The hungry Judges soon the sentence sign,
> And wretches hang that Jury–men may dine. (21–22)

The humor here is grim, of course, but that brings us to a second question.

2. Besides the cleverness of the well–turned phrase, what is the source of Pope's humor? What is it that he finds funny? How is this related to Housman's complaint that Pope and his contemporaries were not poets?

Like all satirists, Pope draws his humor from the discrepancy between the grand things that people imagine themselves to be and the puny things they actually are. We can see the pattern most clearly in "Timon's Villa," when we meet the occupant of the certainly grandiose and supposedly grand estate:

> Who but must laugh, the Master when he sees,
> A puny insect, shiv'ring at a breeze! (9–10)

In Pope's satire, humans are never much more than pretentious insects. Timon at his grand estate, the ladies and gentlemen making so much of their game of ombre, the country squire in the third paragraph of "To a Young Lady," all these shrink in Pope's verse. The brilliant humor of *The Rape of the Lock* depends on a sort of shrinking by inflation; describing the actions of the essentially trivial characters in mock–heroic verse shows us how far they are from heroic. You might have your class look at the heroic simile in lines 81–86 and ask them what its effect is on the way we view the game of Ombre. A comparison between a card game and a battle in which the soldiers fall "heaps on heaps," if seriously proposed, would be morally outrageous. In a comic poem, it becomes a comment on the outrageous seriousness Belinda attaches to her trivial pursuits.

Eighteenth-century humor seems sometimes to amount to endless retellings of a single joke, the punchline to which is expressed in lines 101–102 of the "Game of Ombre":

Oh thoughtless mortals! ever blind to fate.
Too soon dejected, and too soon elate!

It is this excessively reasonable attitude that drives Housman to dismiss
the whole century as one in which "man had ceased to live from the
depths of his nature." If we include dejection and elation in poetry only in
order to deflate them, we have excluded some, at least, of poetry's deepest
themes.

3. Pope's statement that "True wit is nature to advantage dress'd/What oft'
was thought but ne'er so well expressed" implies that he will use his verse
to "dress up" or "decorate" familiar ideas. Does this seem to be true?
Where do you find him "dressing" his ideas most elaborately?

The "Game of Ombre" is certainly one of the best–dressed passages in
English literature. Your class can get a sense of how much dressing there
is if you first have them (or help them) reconstruct the actual action of the
game. The game is played in nine tricks, and can be summarized as follows:

◆ Belinda, Ace of Spades; Baron, low spade; Third hand, low spade.
◆ Belinda, Deuce of Spades; Baron, low spade; Third hand, low spade.
◆ Belinda, Ace of Clubs; Baron, low spade; Third hand, X.
◆ Belinda, King of Spades; Baron, Jack of Spades; Third hand, Jack of
Clubs.
◆ Belinda, King of Clubs; Baron, Queen of Spades; Third hand, X.
◆ Baron, King of Diamonds; Belinda, X; Third hand, X.
◆ Baron, Queen of Diamonds; Belinda, X; Third hand, X.
◆ Baron, Jack of Diamonds; Belinda, Queen of Hearts; Third hand, X.
◆ Baron, Ace of Hearts; Belinda, King of Hearts; Third hand, X.

This is the frame on which lines 25–100 of Pope's poem are stretched.
The decoration comes largely from the description of the cards in terms
appropriate to epic heroes. You might point out lines 66–74, where the
Queen of Spades and King of Clubs are personified, and the King described in some detail. Modern decks usually continue the practice of representing the king holding an orb and wearing a "pompous robe," but
they no longer represent the face cards at full length, so that we don't see
the "giant limbs." (It would be worthwhile to bring a deck to class for
comparison's sake.) The personification of the cards as nations at war is
extraordinarily clever, but it is not witty in the metaphysical sense. Pope is
not bringing together ideas previously unjoined; the deck of cards was
originally designed to represent precisely what Pope describes it as representing, and everyone who has played cards will have recognized the
analogy to war. Here, indeed, we have an example of something that "oft
was thought, but ne'er so well express'd."

Lines 30–39 of the "Sound and Sense" passage might be cited as another example of a commonplace generalization ("the sound must seem an echo to the sense"). As it turns out, though, Pope's brilliant exposition of the idea turns it into something a bit more controversial than it sounds. Innumerable pages have been written on these four lines:

> When *Ajax* strives, some rock's vast weight to throw,
> The line, too, labors, and the words move slow.
> Not so when swift *Camilla* scoures the plain,
> Flies o'er th'unbending corn and skims along the main.

Can the poet really control the pace of a line so precisely as Pope suggests? Samuel Johnson thought not. He dismissed the supposed ponderousness of the Ajax line and the supposed speed of the Camilla line as "technical and nugatory," and argued that the sense of the passage would determine how the line was read. But Ajax does seem to be slowed down both by the closeness of the stressed syllables and by the difficulty of enunciating distinctly the separation where one word ends with a consonant (particularly an *s*) and the next begins with the same sound or a closely related one:

> /　　/　　　/　/　/　　　/
> When Ajax strives, some rock's vast weight to throw

Camilla skims through her twelve syllables faster than Ajax labors through his ten because the stresses are more widely distributed and the tongue–twisting consonants are avoided:

> /　　　　/　　/　　/　/　　/
> Flies o'er th' unbending corn and skims along the main.

Even those who share Housman's reservations about Pope's poetry should be able to appreciate the brilliance of execution in lines like these.

–D.H.

William Blake

In for a penny, in for a pound. There really is no way to teach Blake cautiously. Unless you can get your class to see the importance of his revolt "against the centralized tyranny of the intellect," they will have no way to understand why they should be interested in a collection of poems that on the face of it are simple hymns or songs for children. This puts a teacher in an odd position: to stand in front of a college classroom and plead for the importance of undiscipline and unreason while your students dutifully take notes is awkward. Nonetheless it may be the only way.

One way to approach the question is to try to give students an admittedly over–simple picture of the negative side of the Age of Reason and the Industrial Revolution. If we assume that the human spirit is made up about equally of reason and passion, work and play, order and disorder, judgment and imagination, we can get a sense of the dangers created by a society that always favors the first term over the second. In the second half of the eighteenth century, the factory system was developing in England, forcing rural workers used to the natural rhythms of days and seasons into industrial towns and cities where they were forced to work according to the unnatural rhythms of the clock and sometimes in horrifying conditions. A tiny, privileged, educated, landowning class continued to be politically and socially dominant, ruling England as high–handedly as England ruled its colonies. In literary and artistic circles, neoclassicism held sway: Dr. Johnson and Sir Joshua Reynolds were kings in this realm. One believed that "human life is everywhere a state in which much is to be endured and little to be enjoyed," and that a wise person was one reconciled to this truth. The other believed that the source of beauty was a correct averaging of the proportion of natural objects. I don't know how to convey the horror that the Romantics felt for the Age from which they sprang. Perhaps it is enough to have students imagine a world in which every aspect of their life is designed, supervised, and monitored by an industrial engineer. But of course this will be someone's notion of bliss.

It is not everyone's notion of bliss, and the eighteenth century ended in a series of rebellions, most significantly the American and French revolutions. Blake was present on June 6, 1780, when a mob, irritated beyond reason and restraint, burned Newgate prison to express a general hatred of authority.

If you can get the picture of the "centralized tyranny of the intellect" clearly established, then you have laid a foundation that will help your students understand something of Blake's importance. If they *don't* get it, you might insist that they try again. The *Encyclopaedia Britannica*, not given to overstatement, says that Blake's poems "were as formative for the culture of the 20th century as the Bible and *The Pilgrim's Progress* had been for an earlier age." An inability to understand Blake's struggle will cut students off from a great deal of modern literature and thought.

QUESTIONS

1. How do hymns like Charles Wesley's "Gentle Jesus" fit into the world view of the Age of Reason? How are Blake's poems like and unlike Wesley's hymns?

Your students are not likely to think of Charles Wesley as a rebel, but if they will think about the implication of this and most other Wesley hymns, they will see that Wesley and Watts' lyrics are diametrically opposed to the general tenor of the Age of Reason. The Age exalted an adult skepticism about human motives and about the possibility of pure joy in life. Wesley and Watts exalt the child, trust, and love. The Age was industrial and urban in its outlook, and sought for the improvement of life to come through increasing sophistication of taste and technology. The hymns are pastoral: their images of lambs and shepherds have no place in the daily life of London, or in a literary scene that battened on disillusionment. Even the form of the hymns is at odds with the Age. The short lines and obvious rhymes are remarkably childish compared to the heroic couplets of Pope.

Watts and Wesley seem to have identified and strengthened an element in the imaginative and emotional life of the mass of English people. I suspect that if we could shake off a bit of bookish snobbishness we would be willing to call them great popular poets of their age. Blake builds on their foundations, but sees more clearly the implications of the exaltation of innocence, trust, and emotion.

The obvious poem to compare with the hymns is "The Lamb." In it Blake deliberately adopts "Wesley's hammerheaded iambics."

    /   /   /   /
    Lov/ing Je/sus, gen/tle Lamb.

     /   /   /   /
    In/ Thy gra/cious hands/ I am.

      /   /   /   /
    He/ is meek/ & he/ is mild,

      /   /   /   /
    He/ became/ a lit/tle child.

The deletion of the last syllable in Blake's refrain

    Little Lamb, who made thee?

makes it scan as trochees. But this is a very slight change. Far more important, though your students may not think so at first, is a change in speakers. Wesley and Watts have speakers who talk *to* the child, and despite their exaltation of innocence, to some degree talk *down to* the child. In Blake's *Songs of Innocence*, the child speaks, and what we learn about the world is measured by the purity of the child's vision.

This change in perspective alters everything. It is one thing to praise the innocence of children in the safety of the nursery. It is quite another to hold the adult world up to the standard of childhood, to present a vision of life as pure, childish delight (" The Lamb"), to condemn the rationally structured economic and political system because its fruits are ugly compared to a child's dreams (" The Chimney Sweep"), to suggest that a boy born in Africa and told that the essence of life is joy may be more correct than all the dour philosophers who pronounce life "a state in which much is to be endured and little to be enjoyed." Blake took very seriously Jesus' statement, "Except ye become as little children . . . ye shall not enter into the kingdom of heaven" (Matthew 18:3). In fact, Blake supposed madness comes largely from his close reading of the Sermon on the Mount, which led him to oppose private property, reject the established church, deny the authority of government, and oppose war and violence.

2. How do the *Songs of Experience* differ from the *Songs of Innocence?*

It is probably easy to make too much of contrast between innocence and experience in Blake. Eventually the reader learns that embracing contraries is one of Blake's great accomplishments, that innocence and experience are not opposite states. In general, though, we can say that the narrator in *Songs of Innocence* is a child living in nature (" The Lamb") or spiritually near enough to nature not to have lost its innocent vision even in ugly surroundings (" The Chimney Sweeper"). In *Songs of Experience*, the speaker is in the city not just physically, but spiritually. He retains the vision of innocence (he has not succumbed to Reason, or Urizen), but the vision is darkened.

One way to get at the difference is to contrast "The Lamb" and "The Tyger." The Lamb is made, so to speak, the old–fashioned way, by the hands of a benign creator whom Blake significantly identifies with Christ rather than with Jehovah. The Tyger is "framed" with hammer and chain in the heat of a furnace by an immortal blacksmith strong enough to "twist" its sinews. "Did he who made the Lamb make thee?" is a haunting and difficult question, one you may want your students to try to answer. They will soon learn that the Tyger is a free symbol and that the class will have different notions of what it represents. If it is a symbol of reason and repression, surely the answer is no. If it is a reflection of the real world in which innocence and experience combine in "fearful symmetry," then the answer is "yes, and no."

The poems in *Experience* are filled with frightening images. "The Poison Tree" is built on one where the meaning seems closely controlled: the tree is wrath. "London" has images that can be explained: the chimney sweeper's cry "Every blackning Church appalls" and the soldier's sigh "Runs in blood down Palace walls" because Blake wants to place the blame for things where he thinks they belong—with a church that countenances brutality and a state that thrives on violence. Even where these images can be "explained," however, they cannot be explained away. Perhaps because of their synaesthesia, they have the weight in our imagination of free symbols rather than controlled metaphors. They seem to go directly to the subconscious, like the image of the worm in "The Sick Rose," a symbol that will not be tied down: it seems to represent every evil that destroys innocence—debased sexuality, corrupted religion, calculating self-interest.

3. "Auguries of Innocence" is a series of epigrams that states Blake's philosophy. Choose a half-dozen examples and explain their meaning.

I'm not sure that all can be explained, but a discussion of them leads in interesting directions. Here are four of my favorites:

> A dog starvd at his Masters Gate
> Predicts the ruin of the State

> He who the Ox to wrath has movd
> Shall never be by Woman lovd

> The Bleat the Bark Bellow & Roar
> Are Waves that Beat on Heavens Shore

> He who shall teach a Child to Doubt
> The rotting Grave shall neer get out

The first connects miserliness and cruelty to helpless creatures with self-destructive public policy. The second suggests that a man capable of beating an ox has a sadism in his soul that is inconsistent with sexual love. The third connects wildness with heaven, and also (because we can't know who is bleating, barking, etc.) may connect us with the animals. The fourth could be the slogan of the Romantic revolution. Blake's epigrams are not witticisms like Martial's, Pope's, or Dorothy Parker's. They turn on the paradoxes of a mystic's mind. Their logic of reversals is closely related to that of the Sermon on the Mount.

–D.H.

William Wordsworth

In teaching Wordsworth, as in teaching Blake, it is important to establish in your class's mind a vision of the Age of Reason against which the Romantics were rebelling. For a highly biased view of that age, see the comments on Blake in this manual. I think it is useful to remind the class that Wordsworth was in France for more than a year in the heady days of the Revolution, after the monarchy tumbled, but before the guillotine became the symbol of the Terror. That he fell in love and fathered an illegitimate daughter during this time might seem a merely personal detail, but it is an important hint of what the times were like. For many people of Wordsworth's generation the early days of the French Revolution seemed to be the beginning of a new era of humanity, one in which it was no longer necessary to think of man as a creature born in sin and needing to have his depravity curbed by church, state, social hierarchy, and conventional morality. The Wordsworth of 1791 and the Blake of the same period had a great deal in common. The Wordsworth of 1798, whom we meet in "Tintern Abbey," was "chastened and subdued": The Revolution had become the Terror, and his high animal spirits had declined somewhat. Still he felt an impulse to overturn the aristocratic and neoclassical emphasis on man as a creature naturally feeble, erring, and tasteless until he acquires the trappings of urbane (and urban) culture. Now, however, he attempted to overturn this emphasis not by external acts, but through an alteration in consciousness. In *Romantic Ideology*, Jerome McGann says that this attempt to use poetry or consciousness to "set one free of the ruins of history is the grand illusion of every romantic poet."

Wordsworth's great success comes partly from his ability to reject the old formulas of the Age of Reason without seeming to embrace unreason. This ability surely comes from his preoccupation with embracing two other entities who were both revolutionary and stabilizing: nature and his own mind. It is hardly an exaggeration to say that Wordsworth was the inventor of the Romantic dogma that exposure to nature makes men more moral, or restores to them their native morality. (Blake saw uncorrupted human nature an unspoiled external nature as symbolically related, but he never seems to have shared Wordsworth's faith in Nature as a tonic.) It is also very nearly true that he was the first secular poet to believe that there might be an audience waiting to hear him explain his internal life. If we eliminated all the poetry from *The Riverside Anthology* that follows either of these two Wordsworthian leads, the volume would be considerably thinner.

QUESTIONS

1. In the preface to *Lyrical Ballads*, Wordsworth says that "painful feeling . . . will always be found inter–mingled with powerful descriptions of the deeper passions." What evidence is there in "Tintern Abbey" of these painful feelings?

Obviously, the same question could be asked of any number of Wordsworth poems, including especially the Intimations Ode.

I find Wordsworth hard to teach until students come to grips with the melancholy that underlies his optimism and gives his best poetry its balance and subdued dignity. As Coleridge points out, Wordsworth is often at his greatest when he is at his least revolutionary in both language and outlook. In "Tintern Abbey" and the Intimations Ode, he has one foot in the melancholy rationality of the eighteenth century: he knows and dreads the inevitability of change and death, and he feels the vanity of human wishes as strongly as Samuel Johnson did. In "Tintern Abbey," he mentions "hours of weariness" (28) "in lonely rooms, and 'mid the din/Of towns and cities" (26–27). He talks about the "heavy and the weary weight/Of all this unintelligible world" (40–41). There could hardly be more cheerless lines than

> In darkness and amid the many shapes
> Of joyless daylight: when the fretful stir
> Unprofitable, and the fever of the world,
> Have hung upon the beatings of my heart (53–56)

or

> . . . hearing oftentimes
> The still, sad music of humanity,
> Not harsh or grating, though of ample power
> To chasten and subdue. (92–95)

or

> . . . greetings where no kindness is, nor all
> The dreary intercourse of daily life. (133–34)

What is the source of all this melancholy? The poem does not fully specify, but seems to assume that anyone who has thought deeply about the human condition will find cause enough for sorrow. It is worth considering, of course, that Wordsworth has returned as a *changed* man to an unchanged landscape: he cannot feel in his twenty–eighth year what he felt in his twenty–third. The sense, as he puts it in the Intimations Ode, "That there has passed away a glory from the earth" is the ground bass of the poem.

2. How does Wordsworth counteract this pain with "an overbalance of pleasure"?

This is a difficult question for students to answer—impossible for them to answer well unless they have felt the aesthetic pleasures the poem offers. They might at least see that the poem has a consoling theme: That Nature can

> . . . so inform
> The mind that is within us, so impress
> With quietness and beauty, and so feed
> With lofty thoughts . . .

that the receptive mind, absorbing the sublimity of nature, will have grown strong enough to face undisturbed the harsh realities of life. Frankly, one difficulty your students may have with the poem is that they simply do not believe this doctrine to be true. It would be worth pausing in class discussion to decide what *they* believe to be the sources of strength that allow a person to endure "evil tongues," "rash judgments," "sneers," and the other bitternesses of life. Some will say religion; some will say friendship. Some may say art; some may say jogging and proper diet. Very few will say exposure to natural beauty.

Fortunately, the pleasures of the poem do not depend on the reader's sharing Wordsworth's beliefs about the power of the landscape. The cause of Wordsworth's remarkable tranquillity in the face of a troubled world is less important than the *fact* of the tranquillity. When we read the poem we get a sense of great poise, great enough to allow the poet to move confidently between opposing states: hope and doubt, energy and tranquillity, joy and sorrow. He will carry us quickly from the openness, movement and energy of "little lines/Of sportive wood run wild; these pastoral farms/Green to the very door" (15–17) through the imagery of smoke to the stillness of a hermit sitting alone in his cave by the fire (21–22). He will, between lines that mention "the din/Of towns and cities" (26–27) and the "fretful stir/Unprofitable, and the fever of the world" (54–55) make us feel the contrary state in which the breath and even blood almost cease to move (44–46). These movements between contradictory states are done so masterfully that we hardly realize how audacious they are, but they register on us and give us a pleasant sensation of being led by a steady hand. You might direct your students' attention to the long sentence that begins in line 36 and stretches to line 47 (or, if you will, 50). Here the steadiness of Wordsworth's hand and his mastery of the rhythm of blank verse are most apparent.

Nor less, I trust To them I may have owed another gift,	Prosy in its guardedness, the verse here builds suspense. What gift?
Of aspect more sublime; that blessed mood, In which the burthen of the mystery,	The language richens, and we feel more suspense. What mystery?
In which the heavy and the weary weight Of all this unintelligible world,	The line moans, and *heavy* and *weight*, added to burthen, make us feel that the "unintelligible world" (heavy with syllables) is surely about to crush us.
Is lightened—	A surprising release.
that serene and blessed mood, In which the affections gently lead us on—	But a return to the previously suspended thought. What gift? What mood?
Until, the breath of this corporeal frame And even the motion of our human blood Almost suspended,	Another long suspension of a thought and grammatical construction.
we are laid asleep In body, and become a living soul;	The carefully prepared–for climax

The long sentence winds us up like a spring. Its grammatical complexities, its parallelisms that lead us back rather than forward, its often highly irregular and enjambed lines prepare us to feel the exhilaration of the last line and a half—regular iambs, sweetly put together by the repeated sounds of the *l*'s and *s*'s and the alliterated *b*'s. The word *soul* has rarely been so well prepared for.

3. Wordsworth is known as a poet who contrasts contrary states—hope and doubt, energy and tranquillity, joy and sorrow. Where do you find such contrasts best used?

This question might lead students to talk about any number of passages from "Tintern Abbey" or the Intimations Ode or "Resolution and Independence." It might also, however, lead to a good discussion of the sonnets. Certainly "The World Is Too Much With Us" turns in line 9 from sorrow and doubt to an energetic affirmation of what joy and hope should

be like. "Westminster Bridge" depends on the contrast between the expected image of London's bustle and the image Wordsworth presents of
London when its "mighty heart is lying still." The most remarkable example, however, is probably "There Was a Boy." Here Wordsworth creates
(again, by the crafting of a long blank verse sentence that builds up to an
effect) a chaos of energetic sound, "halloos and screams, and echos loud."
The sudden silence that follows is naturally full of anticipation; we all
hang listening like the boy, and we understand how in such a moment
quieter impressions can "enter unawares into his mind."

4. How does "Resolution and Independence" embody some of the ideas
mentioned in Wordsworth's letter to John Wilson? How does it go beyond them?

This should be a fairly easy question for your students to answer. Many
of Wordsworth's justly neglected poems ("The Idiot Boy," for instance)
seem to be clumsy pieces of propaganda for his anti–aristocratic views. In
this poem, as Margaret Drabble says, "it is not the thought that counts, for
the thought is trite enough." Eventually one can foresee that in a
Wordsworth poem, the last will always (and a bit too automatically) become the first: the meek, the uneducated, the decrepit, the unintelligent,
even, will speak with wisdom and power. Sympathetic as we may be with
Wordsworth's views, we eventually find such poems a bit formulaic.
"Resolution and Independence" certainly adheres to the formula. It is a
clear instance of "looking out of ourselves towards men who lead the simplest lives, and those most according to nature; men who have never
known false refinements, wayward and artificial desires, false criticisms,
effeminate habits of thinking and feeling . . ."
The formula works so well here partly because Wordsworth's imagination carries him beyond both the facts of the case and a narrow didactic
purpose. Your class may be interested in Dorothy Wordsworth's factual
account of the meeting with the leech gatherer:

When Wm and I returned from accompanying Jones we met an old
man almost double, he had on a coat thrown over his shoulders above his
waistcoat and coat. Under this he carried a bundle and had an apron on
and a night cap. His face was interesting. He had dark eyes and a long
nose. John who afterwards met him at Wythburn took him for a Jew. He
was of Scotch parents but had been born in the army. He had a wife 'and a
good woman and it pleased God to bless us with ten children'. All these
were dead but one of whom he had not heard for many years, a sailor. His
trade was to gather leeches, but now leeches are scarce and he had not
strength for it. He lived by begging and was making his way to Carlisle
where he should buy a few godly books to sell. He said leeches were very
scarce partly owing to this dry season, but many years they have been
scarce—he supposed it owing to their being much sought after, that they

did not breed fast, and were of slow growth. Leeches were formerly 2/6 [per] 100; they are now 30/. He had been hurt in driving a cart, his leg broke his body driven over his skull fractured. He felt no pain till he recovered from his first insensibility. 'It was then late in the evening, when the light was just going away.'

This old man is simultaneously a representative of "men who lead the simplest lives," an embodiment of nature, and an echo of the magician who appears suddenly in a tale of chivalry or romance. He is compared to a huge stone, a sea beast, and a part of the landscape, neither alive nor dead. He carries a long grey staff, is "motionless as a cloud," and "cons" the water "as if he had been reading a book." His eyes ("sable orbs") flash, he is associated with religious men, and he is said to be

Like one whom I had met with in a dream;
Or like a man from some far region sent,
To give me human strength by apt admonishment. (111–13)

In "Resolution and Independence" as in the Lucy poems, we get rather trite thought (someone is worse off than I; those who live close to nature are virtuous) transformed by a powerful imagination. If we read the poem one way, the leech gatherer is an allegorical figure representing resolution and independence. If we read it another, he is a symbol in which the power of the landscape, moral force, and magical power are all concentrated and combined.

–D.H.

Samuel Taylor Coleridge

Coleridge is a delight to teach because his range of styles gives something both to students who are engaged with serious poetry and to those whose closet favorite is Robert Service. "Kubla Khan" is such a familiar crowd–pleaser that I will bypass it in the questions below. "The Rhyme of the Ancient Mariner" may seem dauntingly long to some of your students, but they will quickly find themselves caught up in it. They will learn a great deal if you set them the task of finding connections between it and the more meditative "Frost at Midnight."

QUESTIONS

1. Explain the pattern of rhythm and sound in the stanzas of "The Rhyme of the Ancient Mariner" and give examples of stanzas you find particularly effective.

If your students consult the Sound of Poetry entry in the handbook section of *The Riverside Anthology*, they will find this a relatively easy question to answer. Though Coleridge avoids monotony by introducing some irregularities, he writes essentially in ballad stanzas: alternating lines of iambic tetrameter and iambic trimeter, rhymed abcb. The tetrameter lines ordinarily have a strong caesura in the middle, dividing the line into two half–lines and producing the singing rhythm discussed in the handbook entry on dipodic meter. Sometimes Coleridge (who is clearly having a good time with his metrics) will add internal rhyme and alliteration to make the half–lines mirror each other:

    /   \\   /   \\
In mist or cloud, on mast or shroud

    /   /   /
It perched for vespers nine;

       /   \\   /   \\
Whiles all the night, through fog–smoke white,

    /   /   /   /
Glimmered the white Moon–shine. (75–78)

Some individual lines are worth noting for their sound effects:

This body dropped not down (231)

And the sails did sigh like sedge (319)

The thick black cloud was cleft . . . (322)

The poem begs to be read aloud, with gusto, and if you can persuade your class to read some of the bravura passages, they will enjoy both the poem and themselves. The Rhyme, even to those who miss its better qualities, has at least the appeal of "Casey at the Bat" or "The Cremation of Sam McGee."

2. Does reading "Frost at Midnight" help us find meaning in "The Rhyme of the Ancient Mariner"?

Coleridge's famous comment on "willing suspension of disbelief" might fruitfully be brought into play in a discussion of the meaning of the Rhyme. Students are often inclined to treat the search for poetic meaning as a matter of code cracking, and so might be inclined (as, frankly, many professional critics are inclined) to make the poem into an allegory: Albatross=Nature, Mariner=poet, etc. Coleridge's own statement that his aim was "interesting the affections by the dramatic truth of such emotions, as would naturally accompany such situations, supposing them real" changes the meaning of poetic meaning. The Rhyme means what it makes us feel.

What we feel is registered (and partly shaped) by the reactions of the Wedding Guest, who learns that beneath the cheerful and gregarious surface of life lies the possibility of isolation and terror. I suppose that we could say the poem means isolation and terror.

But in the "willing suspension" passage from *Biographia Literaria* Coleridge says that his poems about the supernatural get their "human interest and semblance of truth" by transference "from our inward nature." In other words, the emotions of isolation and terror have to exist in us without the rather artificial stimulants of albatrosses, ghost ships, and revived corpses. These devices become symbols of something within. If your students read "Frost," they will get a better idea of the "inward" basis of the Rhyme's emotion. "Frost" was written while Coleridge was at work on the Rhyme, and I think that your students will see a few similarities between the poems at once. In "Frost" the poet is in "solitude, which suits/Abstruser meanings" (5–6); in the crucial portions of the Rhyme, the Mariner is rather emphatically "Alone, alone, all, all alone" (232). In "Frost" the night is windless and there it is "calm indeed! so calm, that it disturbs/And vexes meditation with its strange/And extreme silentness" (8–10). In the Rhyme, the Mariner's ship is becalmed, "As idle as a painted ship/Upon a painted ocean" (117–18). Most important, it seems to me, is the fact that both the poet and the Mariner observe joy at a distance, as something others may have. The Mariner passes "like night, from land to land" (586) to tell his story, and is indifferent to the pleasures of the marriage feast. The poet, himself "reared/In a great city, pent 'mid cloisters dim" (52–53), hopes that his child, raised among the beauties of Nature, will live a joyful life. Lines 64–65 of "Frost" are critical: the lonely poet, his meditations apparently vexed by an inner as well as an outer calm, hopes that God will mold his son's spirit by giving it joy "and by giving make it ask." The curse on the poet is failure to ask, to want, or to hope—ennui or dejection.

Now, if your class has come to grips with the emotional content of "Frost," they are in a better position to understand the emotional meaning of the crucial events of the Rhyme: the shooting of the Albatross, the becalming, the blessing of the serpents. It may be accurate enough to say that the Albatross represents Nature or the imagination, but it is probably more important for your students to realize how gratuitous the killing of the bird was. It is an act of indifference, not of love or hate. The crew reacts to the killing not out of love or hate for the bird, but out of self–interest: there is a grim humor in lines 91–102, where the sailors at first condemn the killing because they are afraid it will take away the south wind, then praise it because it seems to clear away the fog. The becalming of the ship, lines 111–138, is surely the heart of the poem. Here we get a series of images that (like those in Eliot's "Hollow Men") are "objective

correlatives" of dejection: the bloody sun apparently fixed directly above the
mast, the motionlessness of "a painted ship/Upon a painted ocean," the
parching planks of the ship, "Water, water, everywhere,/Nor any drop to
drink," the slimy sea crawling with slimy creatures, the speechless
tongues "withered at the root." This is a nightmare vision of the emotional state described in the other poems, a dejection so deep it seem
impossible to escape from it. When the escape does come, it is triggered by
an event beyond the control of the Mariner's conscious mind: he sees *and*
feels the beauty of the serpents.

> A spring of love gushed from my heart,
> And I blessed them unaware:
> Sure my kind saint took pity on me,
> And I blessed them unaware.

The dejection passes away as unaccountably as it comes on. Suddenly the
Mariner can pray, the Albatross falls off and sinks like lead, the wind
freshens, the corpses are filled with blessed spirits and begin to sing. All
this is joyful enough, but it leaves us, like the Wedding Guest, more
"stunned" than delighted. Like "Frost," the Rhyme suggests that we are
not in control of our fates, that we are condemned to be moved to sorrow or
joy by emotions we do not understand.

3. Of what is the Aeolian harp a symbol, and why does Coleridge seem to
flee from the implications of the symbol in the last 15 lines of the poem?

One can answer this question very briefly if one avoids thinking too
deeply about it. Coleridge tells us in lines 35–49 that the harp makes him
think of the possibility that every human mind is an instrument framed
to receive and articulate the inspiration of what Emerson later called the
Oversoul. He then shuts off this line of thought because Sara (his wife), a
devout soul, objects to the "unhallowed" nature of this sort of "vain
philosophy."

If we think more deeply about the situation, we wonder what is behind
it. We could turn to biography and talk about the unhappiness of Coleridge's marriage, to which he seems to have been driven more by a sense
of obligation than by love. We can see the pattern of Coleridge's relation
with Sara in the poem: his restlessness with the narrowness of her views,
his guilt about leaving her behind in his spiritual quest.

But we shouldn't hastily conclude that it is only Sara that holds Coleridge back. A side of him may have joined Sara in her disapproval; and
we should ask what there is to disapprove of. The image of the soul as Aeolian harp suggests a passive reception of inspiration, a willingness to
loosen the reins of the psyche, assuming that the urges one opens oneself
to are to be trusted. It is a notion more consistent with the outlook of Eastern mystics than with that of Western Protestant theologians. Certainly it

is inconsistent with the idea of fallen humankind, always on the brink of being ensnared by the flesh and the devil.

Early and late in his life, Coleridge espoused fairly orthodox Western religious views and tried to find a safe harbor in the church. In the middle years, he indulged himself in the "Bubbles that glitter as they rise and break/On vain Philosophy's aye–babbling spring." The result, as we know, was not always happiness: the mind at sea suffers both from storms and calms. The impulse to cling gratefully to traditional values, "Peace, and this Cot, and thee," is certainly understandable.

–D.H.

John Keats

In one of his letters, John Keats gives this remarkable picture of himself:

Talking of pleasure, this moment I was writing with one hand, and with the other holding to my mouth a nectarine. Good God! how fine! it went down soft, pulpy, slushy oozy—all its delicious embonpoint melted down my throat like a large beatified strawberry.

Sensuousness is the overwhelming quality of Keats' verse; until students learn to appreciate it, they will have no reason to want to read him. One way to get at that sensuousness is to confront them with passages where content cannot be an issue and have them appreciate them as beatified strawberries.

It might be best to whet your students' appetites, therefore, with a couple of particularly sweet passages. Before they begin to read Keats on their own, I like to read students the thirtieth stanza of *The Eve of St. Agnes.*

And still she slept an azure–lidded sleep,
In blanched linen, smooth, and lavender'd,
While he from forth the closet brought a heap
Of candied apple, quince, and plum, and gourd;
With jellies soother than the creamy curd,
And lucent syrops, tinct with cinnamon;
Manna and dates, in argosy transferr'd
From Fez, and spiced dainties, every one,
From silken Samarcand to cedar'd Lebanon.

Without the text in front of them, students have no idea what some of the lines mean, and so are forced to deal with the poetry as a surface of sound. Ask them to identify what lines they particularly like the sound of and why, and you will get them involved with one level of Keats' sensu-

ousness. The line "jellies soother than the creamy curd" is delicious–
sounding even if we had no idea what the words mean: I remember one
student explaining the appeal of the line simply by prolonging the sounds
of sooother and creeeamy. The line "silken Samarcand to cedar'd
Lebanon" is almost a song unto itself, with its interplay of sibilants (*s*–
sounds), and labials (*m*'s and *n*'s). Ask them to think about Keats writing
these lines with a nectarine held to his mouth. They'll get the picture.

QUESTIONS

1. Where in the selections from Keats do you find the strongest appeal to
the senses? Explain.

The imagery in Keats is so strong everywhere that your students should
come to class with any number of examples. A good one is the second
stanza of "Ode to a Nightingale." Here the primary appeal is logically to
the sense of taste, but notice that Keats manages to bring us a sense of the
coolness of wine cellars in line 12 and the contrasting heat of Southern
France in 14 (*sunburnt*), 15, and 16 (where *blushful* suggests the warm rush
of blood to the cheeks). Our sense of movement (our kinaesthetic sense) is
appealed to in the mention of both delving (12) and dancing (14). The
contrast of the greens and reds mentioned or implied in lines 13 (*green*),
14 (*sunburnt*), 16 (*blushful*), 18 (*purple*), and 20 (*forest dim*) appeals to our
vision. The "beaded bubbles winking at the brim" appeals to our sight and
also to our sense of internal pressures. The way that Keats brings all these
images to bear on the central image of taste is typical of his brand of
synaesthesia, which is often quite different from Baudelaire's. In Keats it
is not so much that an appeal to one sense is translated into an appeal to
another. Instead, the images seem to crowd together so closely that they
become entangled.

2. What emotions are common in Keats' poetry, and how are they related
to the appeal to the senses?

Keats' melancholy can hardly escape your students' notice, but I'm
afraid that poetic melancholy (partly because of Keats' influence) has become a cultural cliché, and can easily be mistaken for a pose. It would be
good to have your students think about the plain prosaic basis of Keats'
gloom. There are, of course, the biographical details: the death of his father when he was 8, the death of his mother when he was 14, the death of
his brother Tom when he was 23, his falling in love with Fanny Brawne
in the same year that tuberculosis began to kill him.
More important than the biographical details, however, is the view of
life produced by Keats' nature and by the influence of Romanticism. Keats
seems to have lived without traditional religious faith and without the

neoclassical vision of a continuity of culture more significant than the life of the individual. Like Blake and Wordsworth, he had turned away from the old forms. But while Blake had a mystical vision of the "everlasting gospel" to sustain him, and Wordsworth had a mystical belief in the spirit of Nature and the immortality of the soul, Keats had only his senses and a *feeling* of mystery that they inspired. He was alone in what he calls "the Chamber of Maiden Thought." Those acute senses therefore became a torment, since every beautiful thing brought with it a reminder that the beauty would pass away irrecoverably.

The constant grieving for life shows everywhere in Keats, of course. "La Belle Dame sans Merci" is an example particularly worth discussing because it appeals directly to the heart and the subconscious without any of the logical surface of "When I Have Fears" or "Grecian Urn" or "Melancholy." I have had good luck asking my class what the beautiful fairy represents (not as in an allegory, but as in a dream). Some will say Fanny Brawne, some will say Beauty, some will say Life: all good, all worth discussing. Now what does the dream of pale kings mean? One student floored me by citing Macbeth: "And all our yesterdays have lighted fools/The way to dusty death." Neither the student nor I could articulate the connection between these quotations very well, but there is a strong emotional tie between the world—weariness of Macbeth and the melancholy of Keats.

3. How is the imagery varied in the three stanzas of "To Autumn"? Is there any sense of progress from stanza to stanza?

I am not sure at all that there is "progress," actually, but the suggestion that there is one may cause your students to look more closely at the remarkable imagery of the poem. The first stanza is dominated by images of weight

". . .load and bless/With Fruit the vines . . ."

". . . bend with apples . . ."

and fullness

". . . fill all fruit with ripeness . . ."

"To swell the gourd and plump the hazel shells
With a sweet kernel; to set to budding . . ."

". . . Summer has o'er—brimmed their clammy shells."

The appeal here is not to the traditional five senses, but to senses that belong to our muscles or even our internal organs. The sense of internal pressures is particularly unusual: things swell and plump and bud and finally brim over.

The second stanza, with its personification of Autumn, would seem to appeal primarily to the sense of sight, mentioned in the first line, but its visual images are relatively faint and teasing: the blowing hair of the personified figure on the granary floor is vaguely connected with blowing chaff; the "laden" head of line 20 vaguely suggests both the seed–head of a stalk of wheat and the bent head of a gleaner. What is more striking is the number of images of slowed or stopped motion. Autumn's hair is not *blown* by the wind from the winnowing fan, it is "soft–lifted." The half–reaped furrow stands untouched while Autumn is sound asleep "Drowsed by the fume of poppies," the poem's most conspicuous olfactory image. Autumn stands steady by the brook and immobile, apparently, watching the slow oozings of the cider press.

The imagery of the third stanza is largely auditory, though it has strong visual images in lines 25–26. Gnats wail, lambs bleat, crickets sing, a robin whistles, and "gathering swallows twitter in the sky." Your students can hardly miss this sudden chorus of sounds, but you might want to ask them why it is delayed until the last stanza. The question may cast a retrospective light on the "progress" question.

I would assume that the chorus of sounds is delayed till the last stanza because in fact, on a warm day in Autumn, sunset suddenly brings all these sounds to life. An hour or two before sunset, in the heat of mid–afternoon, the landscape may be very hushed, as in stanza 2. In stanza 1, before the heat has burned off the mists (line 1), we have the energy of morning. It seems wrong–headed to insist that the imagery progresses mechanically from morning through afternoon to evening, but it is worth remembering that Keats wrote the poem under the influence of a long Sunday walk. It seems to reproduce the rhythm of the day he walked in, and perhaps the rhythm of the walker himself.

–D.H.

Alfred, Lord Tennyson

Tennyson is a rare example of an undeniably great poet whose greatness was widely and immediately recognized in his lifetime. This popular acclaim has in some ways been a curse. It produced in Tennyson himself a tendency to try to write long, philosophical poems, a vocation he was never truly equipped for. In the half–century following his death, he inevitably fell into a disfavor among those who had anti–Victorian axes to grind. Today he is emerging as a figure both more *interesting* and less *major* than his nineteenth–century reputation might have suggested.

The major poetic influence on Tennyson was Keats, whom he resembles in mood and technique. This may mean as a practical matter that you will not want to treat both poets in detail, but to have your students concentrate on one or the other. You may want to teach Tennyson with Browning ("Ulysses" and "My Last Duchess" make a good lesson on uses of the dramatic monologue). Or you might pair Tennyson and Christina Rossetti together to contrast his large, aimless spiritual malaise with her more sharply focused spirituality.

QUESTIONS

1. The Victorian period was generally a period of industrial and technological progress and faith in the perfectability of human life. Do the poems collected here seem to fit this Victorian view?

One could, of course, find more optimistic poems among Tennyson's work, but the enduring ones, as a critic once observed, tend not to picture life at a promising beginning or a prosperous middle, but at the "penultimate moment." "Ulysses" involves the hero's final voyage, made in anticipation of impending death: "something ere the end,/Some work of noble note, may yet be done" (51–52). "The Lotos Eaters" (though the *Odyssey* tells us that the crew will be made to sail on) has the air of a final stop. The Kraken is waiting to rise at the end of time. Mariana is waiting, without hope, for Angelo or for death. The weeper in "Tears, Idle Tears" thinks of "days that are no more."

Tennyson often writes from the perspective of someone whose life is essentially over, who waits with great melancholy for the end. T. S. Eliot's comment that Tennyson is "the saddest of all the English poets . . . the most instinctive rebel" is exactly on point here. The quasi–official progressivism of the age left a part of Tennyson untouched. His poems look to the past for joy and triumph, to the present for melancholy, to the future for death. Eliot's argument that Tennyson's ear made him a rebel seems farfetched. A wrenching family history and the death of his friend and emotional supporter Arthur Hallam in 1833 seems a more likely explanation.

2. Is Tennyson's "Ulysses" essentially an optimistic or a pessimistic poem?

"Ulysses" is generally seen as a statement of Victorian optimism, or at least Victorian courage. If your students look at it carefully, though, they will find the "instinctive rebel" present. Tennyson says that he wrote the poem with the thought of Hallam's death very much on his mind. There are several notes sounded that seem inconsistent with easy optimism:

◆ The poem starts out with a statement that Ulysses' "idle" life is a burden to him. The images here might come from Eliot's "The Hollow Men": a cold hearth, "barren" crags, an old wife who will

bear no more children, subjects with the appetites of greedy animals
(1–5). Ulysses knows that if he stays in Ithaca, he will "rust
unburnished" (23).

◆ The image of experience as an arch leading to a constantly
receding horizon (19–21) seems a perfect symbol of futility, as does
the image of knowledge as a sinking star (31).

◆ The work that Victorians should find important, the improvement
of human life, is unappealing, and is left to Telemachus (33–43).

◆ The ship in the harbor is described in some of Tennyson's more
mournful–sounding lines. Notice the lifeless and sinister verbs:

> There lies the port; the vessel puffs her sail;
> There gloom the dark, broad seas . . . . (44–45)

No freshening breezes and dancing pennants here. Tennyson assumes
an audience that knows Ulysses will die on this voyage, and he gives the
setting a funereal atmosphere:

> The long day wanes; the low moon climbs; the deep
> Moans round with many voices . . . . (55–56)

Of course, if we concentrate too much on the melancholy passages of the
poem we miss its point. One has the feeling that Tennyson is facing his
melancholy squarely, putting himself a hard case. What if the best part of
life *is* over? What if he hasn't the talent or disposition to do the practical
work of making society better? What if the world he is living in is loveless and hopeless? What then? Only if we see how formidable the element of despair is can we appreciate the heroism of the poem:

> 'Tis not too late to seek a newer world.
> Push off, and sitting well in order smite
> The sounding furrows . . . (57–59)

Finally, I think the poem is neither optimistic nor pessimistic. It has a
sort of existential courage about it, a determination to go on without hope
on the chance that there may yet be something good in life.

3. What might the land of "The Lotos Eaters" symbolize?

I hope that your students will see that "Ulysses" and "The Lotos Eaters"
are complementary poems. In both "Ulysses" represents the active
principle, the urge to take arms against a sea of troubles. The melancholy

music in the background of *Ulysses* and the power of the lotos are part of that "abyss of sorrow" that Eliot finds at the bottom of Tennyson's work.

It might interest your class to know that Tennyson knew a good deal about the effects of depressants and opiates. His father was an alcoholic, his brother was an opium addict, and he himself struggled throughout his life to resist a dependency on opium (then a commonly prescribed drug). In addition, the family seemed predisposed to depression: Tennyson feared that he had inherited "black blood." "The Lotos Eaters" is a more interesting poem if we see it not only as a reworking of a classical subject, but also as a poem in which Tennyson gives expression to a side of his personality that he fears. Tennyson was all his life a prodigious worker. He wrote more poetry than he should have, perhaps, and he kept himself on a rigorous schedule of self–improvement, including prescribed hours for exercise and study of languages and science. But there was always a side of him that seemed to say

> Surely, surely, slumber is more sweet than toil, the shore
> Than labor in the deep mid–ocean, wind and wave and oar. (171–72)

4. Where do you find examples of Tennyson's famous virtuosity at sensuous description and appealing sound?

Tennyson's technical accomplishment is so remarkable that you could find remarkable lines by closing your eyes and running your finger down the page. For physical description, you might look at "Mariana," where Tennyson begins with images that objectify Mariana's despair—the moss-encrusted flower pots and rusted nails of the first stanza—then begins to develop a series of images that show us the world through the eyes and ears of a recluse with heightened sensibilities, who cannot bear the light of day (stanza 2). Note that the sensory images become objectively smaller and subjectively more alarming as the poem progresses. The night noises in the third stanza might disturb any light sleeper. By the fifth stanza, Mariana is being troubled by a shadow cast by the moon. By the sixth, she is disturbed by the *shrieking* of a mouse behind the wainscot!

You might look at the seventh ("Dark House") lyric from "In Memoriam" for another remarkable effect of matching sound and emotion. The oncoming of the light after a night standing in the rain outside Hallam's house is marked by a line full of harsh *t*'s and *k*'s and alliterated *b*'s: "On the bald street breaks the blank day." Once again the interruption of melancholy by light and motion and the "noise of life" seems painful.

"The Lotos Eaters" is a remarkable display of virtuosity, and you might want your students to scan a stanza or two and make notes on the rhyme scheme. The opening Spenserian stanzas (iambic pentameter, rhymed ababbcbcc) are among the greatest in the language, and both here and in the choric songs, Tennyson manages to use the repetitiveness of the rhyme to suggest monotony and languor, while at the same time introducing variety in his rhythm and imagery. The stanzas of the choric song are a remarkable series of inventions, each different from the other, each intricately rhymed and ingeniously varied in meter. You might have your students look at 3 and 4, especially, which develop the contrast between the active and the passive life and are closely related to each other (and to the sonnet) in their formal structure. (It might be worth discussing, by the way, how close these stanzas come to making the same statement about life that Jesus makes in the Sermon on the Mount. Tennyson may want to cry "Courage!," but he gives the lotos flower its due.)

Perhaps the best–known example of Tennyson's brilliant ear for the music of the language is the conclusion of "Come Down, O Maid":

> . . . the children call, and I
> Thy shepherd pipe, and sweet is every sound,
> Sweeter thy voice, but every sound is sweet;
> Myriads of rivulets hurrying thro' the lawn,
> The moan of doves in immemorial elms,
> And murmuring of innumerable bees.

The onomatopoeia here is remarkable: the lines, too, moan and murmur. It would be worthwhile having your students trace all the sound echoes in the last three lines, or at least to read them aloud as Tennyson surely would have, humming and chanting.

–D.H.

Robert Browning

Some of your students will find Browning difficult to read, so it is best to come to class equipped to admit gracefully that he *is* difficult, and that readers have always found him so. The most famous statement of his difficulty comes from Browning himself, who wrote in 1868, "I can have little doubt that my writing has been, in the main, too hard for many I should have been pleased to communicate with; but . . . I never pretended to offer such literature as should be a substitute for a cigar, or a game of dominoes, to an idle man." My favorite statement comes from an anonymous wit who said that Browning's translation of Aeschylus' *Agamemnon* (1877) could be understood quite easily by referring to the Greek.

As Eugenio Montale points out, Browning could produce lyrics ("Meeting at Night" and "Two in the Campagna" are good examples) good enough to find their ways into volumes of best–loved poems, but finally the lyric Browning is far less interesting than the lyric Tennyson or the lyric Christina Rossetti. The dramatic monologues continue to intrigue readers because they follow the movement of alert minds that shuttle quickly between honesty and sophistry, between special pleading and large philosophical statements. Unfriendly critics say that the philosophy of Browning's characters is never very deep, but this criticism misses the point. It is always deep enough that we can imagine a person living by it. Browning can take us into the maze of a character's thinking and show us every twist and turn. Mazes are never easy, of course, but they are what we must expect if we accept the unstated premise of the dramatic monologue— that everybody is constantly composing a justification for his or her life.

QUESTIONS

1. Explain the implied setting and circumstances of Browning's "My Last Duchess." How do these details affect our reading of the poem?

"My Last Duchess" is probably the best starting point for a discussion of the dramatic monologue because it is so extraordinarily compressed. Studying it, your students will see how much work Browning leaves to the reader, but also how much help he offers in this work. The single word "Ferrara" after the title gives your students a place and gives anyone with a background in Renaissance history an atmosphere. (Browning does assume such background in his readers. Most of us learn to rely on an encyclopedia.) Ferrara was in the Renaissance one of the little Italian city states grown prosperous by trade. It flourished in a period of political intrigue—think of Machiavelli's *Prince*—and its wealth, concentrated in the hands of the Duke, was lavished in conspicuous consumption. In Browning's century and even more in our own, art is often confused with effeteness or civic–mindedness. Browning enjoys writing poems that put art in a hot–blooded context, and a Renaissance duke can plausibly be presented as avaricious, dangerous, double–dealing, and passionate about art. (Perhaps museum curators can be so characterized, but not in 57 lines.)

City and period established, you can turn to the question of who is addressing whom and under what circumstances. The Duke (that much is established in the first line) addresses a stranger (7), who is in the service of a count (49) whose daughter (52) the Duke intends to marry. That much is clear, but I would push further and ask your students *why* he is talking to this man. Students who have read the poem attentively will realize from lines 48–53 that the Duke and the Count's man have been arranging a marriage: "as I avowed/at starting" is the giveaway. At starting of what? At starting, apparently, of a part of the negotiation of a marriage contract.

And now I like to ask my class to tell me as exactly as possible what the physical situation is, where in the palace the two men are talking (the gallery?), and in what postures (the Duke standing, having just drawn the curtain aside; the count's underling seated). Once all this is settled, we are ready to discuss what the Duke reveals about himself, both deliberately and unintentionally. The astonishing arrogance of the man shows most clearly only to students who realize that he is deliberately revealing the murder of one wife to a man who represents the interests of the next. The odd combination of pride and groveling is only apparent to students who know that the Duke is revealing his secrets to, employing his unctuousness on, a man who is not only a stranger but his social inferior. "I choose/Never to stoop," he says, while he attempts simultaneously to bully and to butter up a functionary who may help him squeeze a greater dowry out of the Count.

2. How well does Andrea del Sarto know himself?

Sometimes I start a class discussion by converting a question of this kind to multiple choice. How well does he know himself?

    a. hardly at all
    b. a bit less than the average person knows himself or herself
    c. a bit more than the average person knows himself or herself
    d. well
    e. almost perfectly.

Once students have committed themselves to an answer by show of hands, I call on them to explain their choice.

My own choice is d. Andrea is not a man we admire, but he knows himself not to be admirable. He blames Lucrezia for failing to inspire him (119 and 127, for example), but he also knows that incentives come from the "soul's self" (135). He sees himself the judgment history will make on him, that he is a brilliant technician who hasn't the true "light of God" in him (79). He knows that his decision to leave his work for Francis (his opportunity for brilliance) was perfectly characteristic of him, that there is something in him that fears brilliance as a bat fears light (169–171), that in art and in nature he is a man of the gray middle tint and the twilight (34–35, 40, 46–49). He knows that settling for Lucrezia's superficial perfections despite her stupidity and infidelity is the perfect symbol of his compromise with life (260–68). All this shows more insight into his own character than most of us have into our own.

What does he not know about himself? There are some small things. For instance, he presents himself as someone untouchable by praise or blame ("What does the mountain care?"—96), though he obviously is affected by flattery (65, 159–60, 185–95). There is also, I think, one overwhelming thing, best expressed in lines 195–198:

    . . . and indeed the arm is wrong.
    I hardly dare . . . yet, only you see,
    Give the chalk here—quick, thus the line should go!
    Ay, but the soul! he's Rafael! Rub it out!

One feels that Andrea has a moment here, representative of many moments, when he might have broken out of his limitations, but that he refused to see it. Within half a dozen lines, he has shrunk back to size and is pitifully attempting to extort gratitude from Lucrezia because he has sacrificed his art for her.

3. What sort of art—visual or literary—would a philosophy like Fra Lippo Lippi's produce?

You might have to caution your students about two aspects of this question. First, we are talking about Browning's Lippo Lippi, not the historical one. Unless they have learned to see them in the context of early Renaissance painting, they are likely to find Lippo's own paintings rather tame by comparison to Browning's descriptions. Second, Lippo's "philosophy" has to include his personality and attitude toward life as well as his aesthetic theory.

Still, the theory is worth talking about. It is perfectly expressed in lines 301–305:

> For don't you mark? we're made so that we love
> First when we see them painted, things we have passed
> Perhaps a hundred times nor cared to see;
> And so they're better, painted—better to us,
> Which is the same thing.

It is surely worth noting that the clash between Lippo's philosophy and the Prior's (176–199) encapsulates a conflict between the medieval and Renaissance world views. The Prior says that the purpose of art is to set men to praising God, to prepare them for the next world, and that art needs "no more body than shows the soul." Lippo, too, is interested in the soul: lines 157–58 and 214–19 show this. He just can't buy the idea that soul and body are separate, or that this life is nothing more than a preparation for the next. Things represented by art are "better to us" not because they take us out of this world, but because they engage us with it.

"Love calls us," as Richard Wilbur says, "to the things of this world." And this leads us to a distinction much larger than the medieval/Renaissance distinction. There are artists whose call is mystical and whose motion is away from the world—from the external world—toward a world of internal experience. They seem to chasten the flesh, to offer "no more body than shows the soul." Rilke, Plath, and (in his melancholy lyrics) Tennyson all have on their hair shirts. Other artists turn outward, lending their minds out, as Lippo says (307) so that others can see the world. Auden, Wilbur, Williams, and (in a way so extreme as to be almost unrecognizable) Bishop seem to me to do this, and so occasionally are accused of soullessness or cleverness: mere doodling in the

antiphonary's marge (131). Browning distinctly belongs to the external-
izing school.

Of course, great artists always transcend such easy dichotomies, and one
of the interesting things about Browning's personae is that they are such
personal creations, and so revealing of the author's inner life. One feels
in reading both "Fra Lippo Lippi" and "Andrea del Sarto" that by assuming a mask, Browning has been able to silence one part of his personality
to let another side speak more passionately. "Less is more," as Andrea
says. Less internal for Browning may ultimately have meant more ex-
pressive.

–D.H.

Walt Whitman

Whitman's influence on twentieth-century poetry has been enormous,
but very unevenly distributed. Among those profoundly influenced by him
are Hart Crane, William Carlos Williams, Wallace Stevens, and Allen
Ginsberg. Ezra Pound, that transmitter of poetic influence, admired
Whitman's work; and, of course, Whitman's very American voice was
welcomed abroad by Yeats, Neruda, and others. On the other hand, admiring Whitman is hardly a requisite to admiring or producing poetry.
Richard Wilbur admits that he will read Whitman only as an assigned
duty, and Louise Bogan says that she admired him a good deal until she
grew out of her adolescence.

When you teach Whitman, therefore, you may be doing no more than
helping your students see what the stir is all about. Those inclined (almost
congenitally, it seems) to take to him will do so; others should at least
understand why enthusiasts are enthusiastic.

Part of the enthusiasm has to do with Whitman's ability to convert the
here and now, the democratic and the unhallowed, into poetry that makes
it epic. He renames the land and all that is in it, often in catalogues that
are reminiscent of Homer and in cadences that remind us of the Bible.
Part of it has to do with his all–accepting attitude toward the world, the
flesh, and the soul. If you want to give your students a sense of how much
Whitman's attitudes can differ from those of another poet, have them read
section 5 of "Song of Myself" side–by–side with Marvell's "A Dialogue
Between the Soul and Body." In Marvell the soul and body are opposed; in
Whitman they are joined.

QUESTIONS

1. W. S. Merwin says that *Leaves of Grass* (which includes "Song of My-self") is "emotional propaganda about an emotional approach to a historical moment." What is it propaganda for?

You might have to set your students up to answer this question by having them consider the date of publication and what it implies. Whitman was writing "Song of Myself" in an era when America was (in every sense) in an expansive mood. To be young then amid the complexity and bustle of New York City, or in the still unspoiled countryside of Long Island, and to feel to the west a continent of epic proportions opening, must have been very heady stuff. In 1855, neither America nor Whitman had had to come to grips with history. The past had been pushed aside to make a fresh start. By 1865 ("The Wound Dresser"), both America and Whitman had a history that could not be ignored. (Wordsworth's young manhood in the early years of the French Revolution comes to mind as a parallel.)

In this atmosphere, Whitman became more deliberately, proudly, defiantly, and perhaps chauvinistically American than most twentieth–century Americans can imagine being. To be American meant to throw off the shackles, to believe in democracy not just as a political system, but as an assertion that at the core all people had the makings of greatness in them. When Whitman says in Section 32 of "Song" he admires the animals because "Not one kneels to another nor to his kind that lived thousands of years ago," he is sounding a note that belongs to a "historical moment," as Merwin says. Merwin (and most of us) are aware that that moment served as a prelude to the exploitation of the continent and the native Americans who inhabited it, but as a moment it positively glowed. The "emotional approach" Whitman took to it was essentially to bask in the glow and feel an enormous sense of well–being and power. The citizen didn't have to kneel before the ruler, the worker before the boss, the libido before the conscience, the body before the soul, the impulsive before the diligent, the weed before the flower: All, Whitman felt, could live together on equal and friendly terms. Your students will find many illustrations of this view of life in the sections from "Song."

Are the poems emotional propaganda? We will never know, of course, but the question is worth considering. It poses a dilemma. Most of us have our moments of Whitmanesque acceptance only at intervals, amid many moments of doubt, guilt, fear, terror, disgust, and fatigue. It is possible that Whitman was genuinely unlike us. This is Randall Jarrell's view: that Whitman did "see the green earth . . . as she was seen by the sources of Time."

But perhaps he did feel what we feel and deliberately pretend that he did not. We know that Whitman saw himself as a public poet shaping the consciousness of future generations of Americans. Did he decide to assume a stance, as Merwin says? This just raises another problem for your students to consider. Must a poet report all sides of his or her experience?

2. Whitman was among the first users of free verse. Why do his poems not sound like prose?

"Sound like prose," is, of course, a bit dangerous. William Carlos Williams, one of Whitman's great admirers, says that poetry ought to "come up like prose, only better." Still Whitman's language is clearly patterned, and if you will set your students the task of trying to explain the pattern in one or two of the poems, they will begin to understand the rhythms Whitman uses.

Section 11 of "Song" is a good place to start. If you ask students about the purpose of the internal divisions in the poem, they should quickly see that the "stanzas" emphasize the shuttling back and forth between the sight of the men and the thoughts of the woman. Within these subunits of the poem, repetition and parallel construction hold the verse together. Students can hardly miss the repetitions of "twenty–eight" "young men," "and all so" in the first three lines. It might be worth having them mark the comparable repetitions in subsequent lines. They should note, too, the patterns that do not involve literal repetition. In the first three lines, for instance "young men" is balanced by "womanly," and "friendly" by "lonesome." All this is fairly obvious, but it works. By the time we get to lines 13–16, we find it natural that the streams of water that pass over the bodies of the young men should become the hand of the woman "descend[ing] tremblingly from their temples and ribs." The syntax leads naturally to the metaphor, and the metaphor seems less a figure of speech than a physical experience.

Similar analysis can be done of any of Whitman's poems. He is, as Jarrell says, "more coordinate and parallel than anybody." Some of your students will notice that his structures and cadences are reminiscent of the Bible. You might particularly want to point out the sixty–third psalm or the second or fourth chapters of the Song of Solomon.

3. What affinities are there between the poems by Berryman [or Ginsberg, or O'Hara] and Whitman's poems?

Students are likely to see at once that Ginsberg's poem starts in the expansive, accepting mood of "Song of Myself," but turns in line 21 to something darker. There is an echo here (whether intentional or not) of Whitman's own development from early optimism to later concerns about America's becoming a materialistic, vulgar society. The O'Hara poems are pure celebrations of life, and, in the case of "Steps," American life. You may want to ask your students whether O'Hara answers the question of why he is not a painter, by the way. I *think* that he does, by saying that Mike Goldberg's "Sardines" at least has the letters left, while his

"Oranges" never mentions an orange: the poem is absolutely a–historical, rootless, capable of turning itself to anything; the painting *almost* is.

The Berryman poems, intended as parts of a twentieth–century *Song of Myself*, are the easiest to contrast with Whitman. By dividing the speaker's personality into parts—I, Henry, and Mr. Bones—Berryman introduces a divided consciousness very unlike that of "Song," where Whitman seems never to have second thoughts (there are second thoughts in "The Wound Dresser"). Berryman is full of second and third thoughts. In Dream Song 4, Henry experiences lust; Mr. Bones sees the situation's comedy; "I" feels the agony of having to be both Henry and Mr. Bones. In 14, Henry (who seems to be the part of the personality nearest the surface, first to engage with the world) seems to live his own life, leaving "I" (the watcher of everything, including Henry) quite behind. All this division might seem un–Whitmanesque, and is, but Berryman *accepts* the division and even enjoys it in much the same way that Whitman enjoyed and accepted apparently contradictory things.

–D.H.

Charles Baudelaire

You may want to point out to your class that the "Writing About Literature" section of *The Riverside Anthology* focuses on a prose poem by Baudelaire.

Baudelaire, even in an era of X–rated movies, still has the power to shock. "To the Reader," particularly, which is not at all softened in the Lowell translation, may make some students (and teachers) uncomfortable. Both its language and its appraisal of the human situation are deliberately brutal and unnerving—excursions into "the disorderly circus of our vice." Some twentieth–century readers of Baudelaire, including Louise Bogan, have felt that there are two Baudelaires, the one that wants to shock us with his showman's tricks (as in "To the Reader") and the one who gives us the memorable pictures of the life of the urban poor in Paris in mid–century (as in "The Little Old Women." Bogan believes the second to be the truly valuable Baudelaire.

I am inclined to think that the two Baudelaires are best seen as one. There was for a time a lively body of criticism that presented Baudelaire as a devout Catholic, writing about the sinfulness of the human condition because inside him was an alternative vision of a beatific state. As devout Catholic, almost as primitive Christian, he was naturally concerned about relations between the degenerate state of the rich and the wretched state of the poor: Think of the story of Lazarus and Dives. I believe that this school of criticism has waned somewhat from lack of biographical substantiation, but it points to a valuable truth. There is a kind of inverted idealism in Baudelaire's poems. For all his dandyism, he was never quite the "man of the world," never able to look equally on vice and injustice. The boredom he writes about and wraps himself in is not something he enjoys: "Tears have glued its eyes together."

QUESTIONS

1. What is unusual about Baudelaire's appeal to the senses?

Your students should notice at least two things. One is synaesthesia, something of a trademark among Baudelaire and the symbolists who followed him. "The sounds, the scents, the colors correspond" ("Correspondences, 8") is virtually a definition of synaesthesia, and the stanza in which the lines appear are its classic justification: that the correspondences among the various senses imply a "deep and shadowy unison," as if these impressions were all pointing to the same thing in the psyche. The impressions become symbols, and the symbols (human products, after all) seem to be looking in on us "with accustomed eyes."

The third stanza of "Correspondences" gives familiar examples of synaesthesia: scents like children's bodies, sweet as flutes, green as grass. Notice that the lines 12–14 do not present examples of synaesthesia, but say that scents like musk and incense create a world of impressions. "By Association," while it doesn't present as classic an instance of synaesthesia, is synaesthetic to the core: it is a catalogue of sights and sounds suggested by a scent.

The second thing your students should notice is the presence in Baudelaire of a great deal of olfactory imagery. "Correspondences," "By Association," and "A Phantom" all appeal strongly to the sense of smell. It may be that Baudelaire uses such imagery because it is somewhat impolite in western society, a too–strong reminder of our animal nature:

> and from discarded underclothes
> still fervent with her sacred body's
> form, there rose a scent of fur.
>   ("A Phantom," 26–28)

2. What images best characterize Baudelaire's view of the human condition?

This question is not easy to answer, since it requires students to decide what Baudelaire's view of the human condition was. The evidence from Baudelaire's journal, however, should help them see that Baudelaire believed himself to be living in a time of degeneracy, particularly among the middle class (from which he himself came, though he was often very poor). One of the most striking images in "To the Reader" reflects this view of the decay of human nature in modern times:

> The devil, watching by our sickbeds, hissed
> old smut and folk–songs to our soul, until
> the soft and precious metal of our will
> boiled off in vapor for this scientist.
>
> (9–12)

The images in the stanzas that follow are more disturbing still: men eating toads and walking to hell along a road crowded with rotting corpses, the man trying to arouse his sexual interest by an encounter with an old prostitute. These images are similar to others in poets we do not think of as decadent: Milton's Satan, "squat like a toad," whispers venom into the ear of Eve in *Paradise Lost*, Book IV; the corpses crowding the road to hell and the substitution an old woman for a young lover would not seem out of place in Bunyan, Dante, or another writer of allegory. Here they are particularly disturbing because they are not part of an allegory, but part of a direct statement of what our lives are like.

The images of the decadence and disease are thicker in Baudelaire's poetry than they are even in *Hamlet*. Boredom smokes and looks forward to a guillotining ("To the Reader," 38–39). The poet grills his heart and eats it ("A Phantom," 8). The speaker in "The King of the Rainy Country" is so far gone that he cannot be revived even by his old pleasures—watching falcons rip doves apart, hearing his starving subjects groan, seducing the ladies of the court, taking baths in human blood. "The Little Old Women" shrink year by year until they can be buried in caskets the size of those made for children.

If your class has read Whitman before Baudelaire, it might be worth having them consider how different the imagery in the two poets is. Both of them were accused of immorality and tastelessness in their day, and might still be today. But Whitman is, relatively speaking, a walk in the sunshine. His love of life includes a love of the frankly sensual; Baudelaire often finds the life around him, including the life of the flesh, disgusting. Even the beauty of a beautiful young woman is presented unpleasantly as a contrast between "the unstudied grace of a marmoset" and the superficial frame of civilization that separates her from "mere nature" ("A Phantom," 29–42).

3. How is it possible to reconcile the attitude toward the poor taken in "King of the Rainy Country" with that taken in "The Little Old Women"?

At one level this is a very simple question; at another a fairly complex one. On the simplest level, we can reconcile the two poems by remembering that the poet and the speaker in the poem are not often (or ever) identical. "King" can be seen as a dramatic monologue spoken by someone so caught up in his own melancholy that he has no compassion for the poor and would be content to have them die of starvation if their groans would make him happy. (It might be interesting to have your students compare it with Tennyson's "Ulysses" and Browning's "My Last Duchess," by the way.) The speaker in "The Little Old Women," one might argue, is an entirely different person, perhaps more closely identifiable with Baudelaire himself.

A more complex way of looking at the question is to assume that the poems express the same view of the world. Disillusionment and outrage are at work in both poems. In both life is cruel. It can satisfy neither the rich nor the poor: the rich, young, and sound–limbed live with unsatisfiable desires (or, worse yet, the desire for desires); the poor, old, and infirm live "under God's undeviating paw" ("Women," 84). The principle difference between the two poems is that none of the amusements offered in "King" amuse, but the sight of the suffering old women gives the speaker (Baudelaire?) "secret pleasures you cannot suspect!" Why? I think because the Old Women still have a capacity for *genuine* suffering and a desire for genuine pleasure. Their eyes are "cisterns fed by a million tears" (33), but they are "gimlet–sharp . . . the eyes of a child, a little girl who laughs/in sacred wonder at whatever shines" (18–20). The eyes can come to life "like some old eagle's brightening beneath the absent laurel on her marble brow!" (59–60).

Baudelaire's compassionate pictures of the life of the poor sometimes surprise people who think of him solely as a dandy and a decadent. We should remember that for him "dandyism" did not mean fine dress and self–indulgence, but a deliberate refusal to indulge in middle–class optimism or self–delusion. In theory, the dandyism of Baudelaire should have let him see untroubled the handbasket the world is going to hell in. In fact, the handbasket seemed to trouble him a great deal.

–D.H.

Emily Dickinson

In *The Oxford Companion to American Literature,* James D. Hart makes an observation about Dickinson that is so useful that you may want to read it to your students:

> Her mind was charged with paradox, as though her vision,
> like the eyes of birds, was focused in opposite directions on the two
> worlds of material and immaterial values.

A good starting point for the study of Dickinson is the notion that Dickinson saw these worlds more distinctly and more separately than most of us do, and that she therefore was able to bring them together with a more brilliant wit.

The prose Counterpoints by Bogan and Wilbur are particularly good for giving your students some sense of the mystical and religious dimensions of Dickinson's poetry. For a glimpse into her technical virtuosity, you might want to refer them to the introduction to the poetry section of the anthology (p. 677).

QUESTIONS

1. Where do you find a poem that is successful despite the fact that we cannot understand what it means on the literal level? How does it succeed?

Many of Dickinson's poems might be so described. In this collection, students might fasten on ("Wild Nights"), ("It was not Death"), ("I died for Beauty"), ("Because I could not stop for Death"), or ("My life closed twice"), all of which seem to refer (obliquely) to events and relationships that are not specified. ("Of Bronze—and Blaze—") might also seem to refer to an unknown event, but we know that the reference is to the aurora borealis.

My own example would be ("My Life had stood—a Loaded Gun"). Many questions here are unanswerable from the poem itself. Who is the master? If the poet is speaking in her own voice, how is she like a loaded gun? Who are the enemies on whom she can lay an emphatic thumb? Confronted by such mysteries, we can turn detective and try to find biographical referents (in which case the Reverend Charles Wadsworth will loom large in our interpretation of the poem) or else we can take the poem as we find it, in the manner of the new critics.

If we take the poem as we find it, it becomes an extended metaphor for a life of service or servitude: the reader will have to decide which. We can avoid a narrowly biographical reading if we assume that the persona of the poem stands for us all. The poet presents all of us as an object without a will or purpose until a Master puts us to our proper use. Then we become joyful (the "Vesuvian face" metaphor, complex in a typically Dickinsonian way, tells us this: the underlying tenor is the joyful human face; the vehicle is the muzzle of a rifle, glowing with fire; this vehicle becomes tenor for a second–level vehicle, Mt. Vesuvius). We also become powerful (the "Yellow Eye" and "emphatic Thumb": one suggesting both the flash of the gun barrel and a basilisk–like power to kill by a glance, the other suggesting that the servant becomes so powerful that the master's enemies are like insects).

Through line 20, then, we have a poem that could be fit into one or both of two recognizable traditions: religious poems like Donne's Holy Sonnet 14 or Milton's Sonnet 19 that show how the devout person gains freedom by becoming a servant, and love poems (I think of Elizabeth Barrett

Browning's) in which the lover gains the same sort of freedom by submission to the beloved. It is possible, of course, as in Donne's sonnet, for a poem to allude to one kind of submission as a symbol for another. And I think it is possible that in Dickinson's poem *both* kinds of submission are subsumed in something that is psychologically larger than either. T. S. Eliot sometimes argued that (theology laid aside for a minute) life cannot be psychologically satisfactory until we commit ourselves to something outside ourselves. Dickinson's loaded gun would be an apt metaphor to illustrate Eliot's observation.

But what can we do with the last stanza, the most mysterious in the poem? Does it mean that even though the object of devotion dies, it (he?) will continue to live in the heart of the devotee, whose devotion is her life? Does it mean that the devotee becomes immortal because of the devotion? Does it mean that the devotee is living a death–in–life and wishes for the power to die (comparable to "The privilege to die" in ("The Heart asks Pleasure First")? We don't know. As Richard Wilbur points out, Dickinson always redefines the largest spiritual questions and makes them personal and pressing. We don't know whether this is a poem about salvation or damnation, about human or spiritual love, but we see all these things more freshly when we read the poem.

2. Comment on the importance of oxymoron in Dickinson's work.

I'm not sure many of us are up to commenting very sensibly on this subject, but your students should notice some examples:

> homely Anguish ("I like a look of Agony")
> Dimity Convictions ("What soft—cherubic creatures—")
> a transport/Of cordiality ("A narrow Fellow")

Dickinson's formidable wit, in both the seventeenth–century sense of the word and the contemporary sense, shows in these phrases. Dorothy Parker could have—might have—enjoyed "Dimity Convictions." John Donne might have written about the "homely Anguish" that strings beads on the face of a dying person. There are often phrases in Dickinson that do the work of oxymoron, but that might not be identified as such. The impossibility of a "Vesuvian face" ("My life had stood") makes the image striking. "And strut upon my stem" is effective in ("Of Bronze— and Blaze") precisely because a flower on a stem cannot strut. The impulse toward oxymoron in Dickinson is related to the impulse toward hyperbole: in ("It was not Death"), for instance, "siroccos" crawl on her flesh and her "Marble feet/Could keep a Chancel, cool." These statements, at once precise and outlandish, give us the sense of an energetic mind straining against the limitations of conventional language and conventional thought.

3. How does Dickinson use poetic form as a way to surprise the reader?

Richard Wilbur's contrast of Dickinson and Isaac Watts comes to mind here. Watts might be a "fine versifier" (see "A Cradle Hymn," p. 747), but he is not an inventive one. Dickinson is endlessly inventive and finds within the form of the traditional hymn unexpected opportunities. That she is working in this traditional form is a point you can make by having your students imagine themselves singing ("Because I could not stop for Death") or ("A narrow Fellow in the Grass") to the tune of "Amazing Grace" or, if you want to stay non–sectarian, "The Yellow Rose of Texas."

Part of what surprises us in Dickinson's use of the form is the rhyme. Because English is a rhyme–poor language, and because the association of ideas in most hymns and songs are predictable, a rhyme scheme usually makes word choice fairly predictable. I'll wager that your students could fill in the following blanks without looking at Watts' "A Cradle Hymn":

Hush, my dear be still and slumber
Holy angels guard thy bed!
Heavenly blessings without
Gently falling on thy _____.

Sleep, my babe, thy food and raiment,
House and home thy friends provide;
All without thy care or _____.
All thy wants are well _____.

Though Dickinson is sometimes predictable, she sometimes surprises us, as in the last stanza of ("I died for Beauty"):

And so, as Kinsmen, met at Night—
We talked between the Rooms—
Until the Moss had reached our lips—
And covered up—our _____—

There is no predictable sentiment that tells us what word Dickinson will end this poem with, no stock phrase in the offing, and given the freedom of her rhymes and half–rhymes, any number of words suggest themselves: *tombs, wombs, glooms, hymns, homes, rhymes. Names* is a surprise because the association with *Rooms* had led us to expect something more physical. But, of course, the name can be perfectly physical here—the moss–covered name on the tombstone is a metonymy for the individual identities of the two "Kinsmen," for their lives in the memories of the living, and for their poetic reputations. It is a brilliant word choice, and its appearance within the rhyme scheme is just unexpected enough to make us feel the brilliance.

Another particularly brilliant use of the unexpected rhyme word comes in ("It was not Death"). Dickinson has just given a series of images death:

the lying down, the night, the consuming fire, the cold of sculpted sepulchres with "Marble feet" that could cool a chancel (borrowed, perhaps, from Keats' "Eve of St. Agnes"). Having prepared us by saying that "it" was none of these, she goes on:

> And yet, it tasted, like them all,
> The Figures I have seen
> Set orderly, for Burial,
> Reminded me, of _____.

Though it is not quite logical, I suspect most of us feel the word *them* to be likely here. The rhyme of *m* and *n* (two nasals) is close enough for Dickinson to use (compare *refined/ashamed* in ("What soft—cherubic creatures—"). The syntax of the final line seems clearly to lead to a noun or a pronoun in objective case. *Mine,* so right, is so unexpected that it forces a double take. Its unexpectedness reinforces our surprise at the perspective: Dickinson seems to be looking at a row of corpses among them.

Dickinson's virtuosity with rhyme and stanzaic patterns allows her to create effects a competent versifier like Watts would never have attempted. In ("A narrow Fellow in the Grass"), for example, we have a series of approximate and half rhymes (e.g., *rides/is, seen/on, corn/noon*) and one delightfully idiosyncratic full rhyme (*me/cordiality*) in the first five stanzas. At the fifth stanza, when Dickinson ends a series of clever observations and settles down to a direct statement of elemental fear, we have a full rhyme (*alone/Bone*) as effective as an electric shock. In 303, she sets up a contrast in each stanza between long lines and short. In the first stanza the predominantly iambic lines have 10, 4, 8, and 4 syllables; in the second 10, 4, 9, 4; in the third 9, 2, 9, 2. The important difference here is the shortness of the short lines in the last stanza. They are very clipped and hard, and seem to imitate the sense of the verse:

> I've known her—from an ample nation—
> Choose One—
> Then—close the Valves of her attention—
> Like Stone.

–D.H.

Christina Rossetti

Rossetti certainly grew up in one of the most interesting families in England. Daughter of a distinguished Italian emigré and Dante scholar, she had one sister (Maria, another Dante scholar and an Anglican nun devoted to social work), one scholarly brother (Michael, also devoted to Dante), and one poetic brother (Dante Gabriel, a poet in his own right and also a brilliant translator of Italian poets and a painter). Like her siblings, Christina was perfectly bilingual: she wrote poems in Italian and English and did her own essays on Dante.

Dante, one would gather, was a great influence on Christina Rossetti. Like him, she was a poet who combined the spiritual and the lyrical. Like him she explored (particularly in such poems as "They Desire a Better Country") the relation between earthly and divine love.

QUESTIONS

1. Virginia Woolf suggests that Rossetti's religion may account for "the fixity and sadness" of her poetry. Explain the role of religion in the poems.

The somber religious side of Rossetti should not be hard for your students to find. It is certainly present in "Good Friday," the only overtly meditative poem in this selection from Rossetti, and a poem that could be fruitfully compared with Donne's Holy Sonnet 14. Both poets attempt to turn their minds by main force, so to speak, to a proper emotional state— one in which they can *feel* the bases of their faith, the grandeur of God for Donne, the horror of Christ's innocent suffering for Rossetti. In both cases the poem moves through a succession of metaphors: the poet's heart in Donne is like a chalice or other object that needs to be melted and re-formed by a smith, like a town occupied by enemy forces and withstanding siege, like a woman betrothed to the wrong man waiting to be ravished by her true love. Rossetti's images are less violent. She is like a stone, when she should be like a sheep (an obedient and affectionate member of the flock). She is not like (negative metaphor) a series of things that begin with devotion and move outward toward the lifelessness: the women of the gospel story who wept for Jesus (Luke 24:27), Peter who wept bitterly because of his denial (Luke 22:62), the thief on the cross beside Jesus who had a change of heart (Luke 24:40–43), the sun and moon (which, though lifeless, reacted to the crucifixion by an eclipse, hiding their faces as if to weep—Luke 24: 44). She is a rock. In the end, her prayer that Christ will "smite a rock" is precisely parallel to Donne's plea that God will

> Divorce me, untie, or break that knot again,
> Take me unto you, imprison me, For I
> Except you enthrall me, never shall be free,
> Nor ever chaste, except you ravish me.

Freudian critics would have no trouble connecting the untied knot with the smitten rock, I suppose, but the rock also has its definite meaning in biblical lore: Moses, leading his thirsty people in the wilderness, "smote the rock twice: and the water came out abundantly" (Numbers 20:11). Christ, surely, greater than Moses, can get some water (some tears) from *this* rock.

It is not only in "Good Friday" that the alternative to brute insensibility is tears. L.E.L., who appears to be an alter–ego for Rossetti, stands as a stark figure in the middle of much gaiety. She seems singled out for grief:

> All love, are loved, save only I; their hearts
> Beat warm with love and joy, beat full thereof:
> They cannot guess, who play the pleasant parts,
> My heart is breaking for a little love.

But being singled out for grief in the end is being singled out for glory. The angel of the last stanza does not appear to those "who play the pleasant parts"; it is to the sufferer that he appears to say that the tables will be turned. "True best is last, true life is born of death." This is the logic of the Sermon on the Mount: "Blessed are the poor in spirit: for theirs is the kingdom of heaven. Blessed are they that mourn, for they shall be comforted. Blessed are the meek, for they shall inherit the earth" (Matthew 5:3–5).

It is easy enough to do a biographical reading of this poem, since Rossetti had, in fact, turned down two proposals of marriage from men she loved because they did not share her religious views. A narrow reading of the poem might say that Rossetti looks forward to the vindication of these renunciations in the greater love of heaven. I think, however, that this is too narrow. The "little love" L.E.L. craves is probably a love that could never be satisfied on earth. Consider the theme of "By the Sea": the ocean, symbol of inhuman nature cut off entirely from heaven, can be filled with creatures that "Are born without a pang, and die/Without a pang, and so pass by." These creatures can be perfect in their own way—"sheer miracles of loveliness." Humans, Rossetti implies, to whatever extent they are spiritual beings and outside of nature, *must* feel a pang. A part of them will always be longing.

2. Does Rossetti's poetry have any qualities that would appeal to readers who do not share her religious beliefs?

Woolf, certainly no renouncer of the world and the flesh, finds life in the "sensual Pre–Raphaelite intensity" of Rossetti's imagery and in the spiritedness of her poems ("You pulled legs; you tweaked noses").

The imagery of many of Rossetti's poems is, frankly, predictable (see especially "Song"), but it is usually energetic. In "L.E.L.," for example, we get what we would expect in a spring poem: birds pairing, leaves peeping out, nests in the grove, rivulets running golden in the sun, lilies budding, behives whirring, the rabbit thinning his fur (this is fresh), green lavender, rosemary, and myrrh. We get it, however, catalogued in some detail and put into a context where the liveliness of spring shows more dramatically against the backdrop of the deadness of L.E.L.'s spirits. "Life and Death" contrasts some predictable spring imagery in the first stanza with more impressive autumn imagery in the second: "shrunk leaves dropping in the wood," "the blackened beanfields." "Passing and Glassing" contains a series of autumnal images, the most striking of which to me is "the fallen peach,/Unlovely . . . ." Those who have seen fallen peaches in various states of decay will appreciate the understated force of that image. It is characteristic of Rossetti that her autumnal imagery should be much more interesting than her vernal.

As for "pulled legs and tweaked noses," there are no poems here that feature absolute hijinks, but there is an occasional irony. "In an Artist's Studio" is one poem if we look at it as a comment on the model, another if we see it as a comment on the artist. If we concentrate on the model, as Dolores Rosenblum does, we might see her as a woman "vampirized by art," killed as a living personality by the artist who "feeds on her face" and yet denies that she has a particular identity. If we concentrate on the artist, however, the poem is about his inability to see what is in front of him or to take his art seriously as anything but a way to fathom the beauty of his model. His state is pitiful, and sad, but it also has an almost cruel humor about it: ". . . every canvas means/The same one meaning, neither more nor less." Coming from an art critic, this would not be a pleasant comment. One wonders how Christina Rossetti, herself sometimes a model for the Pre–Raphaelite painters, felt about their obsession with the beauty of Elizabeth Siddal who served as a model for several of their paintings.

There is also a dense irony in "Passing and Glassing." You might ask your class what they would guess the poem to be about if they read only the first two lines. Surely we begin with a stereotyped picture of female vanity, with the idea that women want to see themselves reflected everywhere: in shop windows, in pools of water, in the eyes of men. When the looking glass turns out to be the decaying things of the world, the sterotype is turned on its ear. "Song" has the same cliché–turned–over sort of irony about it. The word "forget" in line 8, though the rhyme prepares us for it, is unexpected. Women thinking of their death are not supposed to be so indifferent to whether they are remembered.

It isn't imagery or irony, though, that makes Rossetti so memorable a poet, but lyricism, which will be the subject of our next question.

3. Woolf says that Rossetti's poems "sing like music in one's ears." Comment on the musical quality of Rossetti's poetry.

Rossetti is as committed to formal verse as it is possible to be, and writes poems in which meter and rhyme are major attractions. You might want your students to look especially at "'They Desire a Better Country,'" a poem

in three stanzas, each of which is a Miltonic sonnet, or "Life and Death,"
where the nine–line stanzas have only two rhymes each.

Rossetti's lines are so regular metrically that an occasional inversion,
as in the trochaic openings of the first and tenth lines of "Life and
Death," has great force. They are usually end–stopped, so that the metrical
and stanzaic patterns are very apparent. Inside the lines, the sounds are
very tightly knit. Consider these samples from "'They Desire a Better
Country'":

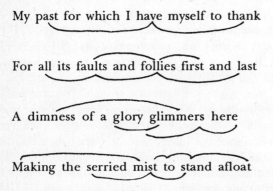

My past for which I have myself to thank

For all its faults and follies first and last

A dimness of a glory glimmers here

Making the serried mist to stand afloat

Even when these lines are not important in themselves, they have a
hypnotic effect that helps create the unity of emotion Rossetti's poems depend on. Like Keats and Tennyson, Rossetti finds a music that perfectly
expresses her deep melancholy.

–D.H.

Gerard Manley Hopkins

Harold Bloom says that Hopkins' poetry "stems directly from Keats and
the Pre–Raphaelites, especially Christina Rossetti." The observation is
certainly correct, but it is more useful in raising questions than in giving
answers. In Keats we have the most sensuous of poets, the most involved
with the beauty of the world as an end in itself. In Rossetti we have a poet
who subordinated art to religious purpose and who (both in life and art)
renounced the physical world in favor of the spiritual. To "stem directly"
from two such sources is no mean feat.

Perhaps the clearest way to think about Hopkins' relation to his poetic
predecessors and contemporaries is to say that he came into poetry (like
most of the Pre–Raphaelites) as a follower of Keats, but that under the influence of his Catholic faith and of Christina Rossetti's example, he strove
to write poetry that would reconcile sensuous delight with spiritual purpose.

In the process, he coined two terms that have kept scholars busy for several decades: "inscape" and "instress." "Inscape" (to put it very amateur-

ishly) seems to be the underlying pattern that unites apparently diverse things. We can think of the "inscape" of a biological species as the underlying resemblance that makes individual variations on a theme. But "inscape" can extend beyond a single species and beyond living things, so that Hopkins can, for instance, look down from a cliff on the waves playing on a beach and try by contemplation to find the underlying pattern of this great movement. Individual things, too, have their inscape: they are more than a collection of parts. Perhaps the clearest idea of what Hopkins' notion of inscape meant can be found in the following journal entry:

> The ashtree growing in the corner of the garden was felled. It was lopped first: I heard the sound and looking out and seeing it maimed there came at the moment a great pang and I wished to die and not see the inscapes of the world destroyed any more.

Had Hopkins been less devout, he might have related inscape to the local gods of ancient pantheism. Certainly he believed that God not only created nature but was expressed by nature. The force, the "instress," that creates "inscape" is an aspect of God's presence in the world. The discovery of the inscape is an act of worship, a meditation on God's nature.

The philosophy of "inscape" and "instress," then, helped Hopkins reconcile his Keatsian attraction to the beauty of nature with his Rossettian desire to glorify God. To find and celebrate the inscape was both a joy and a duty.

QUESTIONS

1. How is the sound and meter of a Hopkins poem like that of Ezra Pound's translation of "The Seafarer"?

Pound's translation is, of course, notably faithful to the Old English metrical system, which essentially required

◆ Stresses that follow the logical and grammatical force of the words rather than the "lexical accent" we find in dictionaries;

◆ Lines that include four such stresses;

◆ A caesura that divides the line into two half–lines with two stresses each;

◆ Alliteration to link one or both of the stressed syllables in the first half–line to one or more of the stressed syllables in the second half-line.

Among the lines you might want to point out are 4–7:

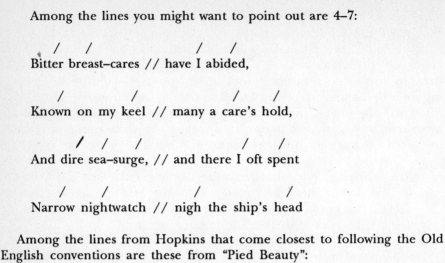

Bitter breast–cares // have I abided,

Known on my keel // many a care's hold,

And dire sea–surge, // and there I oft spent

Narrow nightwatch // nigh the ship's head

Among the lines from Hopkins that come closest to following the Old English conventions are these from "Pied Beauty":

For skies of couple–colour // as a brinded cow;

For rose–moles all in stipple // upon trout that swim.

Fresh–firecoal chestnut fall; // finches wings;

Landscape plotted and pieced // —fold, fallow, and plough

And all trades, // their gear and tackle and trim.

The similarities here are obvious, but so are some differences: Hopkins uses five stresses to the line. He uses an elaborate rhyme–scheme, and makes the network of sound still denser by assonance (couple–colour; rose–mole; in stipple; fold, fallow) and consonance (listen to the *l*'s in "rose–moles all in stipple"). The sound of a Hopkins poem, compounding as it does the powerful rhetorical and alliterative stresses of Old English poetry and a Keatsian denseness of phonemes singing each to each, can be overwhelmingly rich.

2. What does Hopkins mean when he says that "The world is charged with the grandeur of God"? How does his poetry embody this meaning?

The word "charged" is dense with associations. In Hopkins' day more than our own it would have been associated with "charging" a firearm:

ramming home the powder and ball that would later "flame out." It carried then, as it carries now, an association with electricity, and with emotional energy (the Victorians might describe an argument as emotionally charged; today the sports fan may describe a team as charged up). It generally signifies both the filling of a thing and the energizing of a thing. The image of the grandeur of God filling the world as an electric charge fills a storm cloud, or coal fills a furnace, or black powder fills a gun barrel, or emotion fills an impassioned person is *itself* charged: it is rammed full of meaning and feeling and it "*will* flame out."

One of many ways that Hopkins' poetry embodies this sense of the world "charged" is by repeated imagery of fullness, of internal pressure, internal heat, internal beauty. "There lives the dearest freshness deep down things," he says in "God's Grandeur," and his poems give us several images of this freshness:

> . . . blue–bleak embers, ah my dear,
> Fall, gall themselves, and gash gold–vermillion.
>
> > "The Windhover"

> It gathers to a greatness, like the ooze of oil
> Crushed.
>
> > "God's Grandeur"

> . . . and pour
> And pelt music, till none's left to spend.
>
> > "The Sea and the Skylark"

We should remember two things at this point. First, that Hopkins was an admirer of Keats, who had an acute sense of internal pressures (compare "To Autumn"). Second, that Hopkins used the term "instress" to name the force that creates "inscape." There is always a sense in Hopkins of things building themselves up from the inside, and of pressures building up in the poet and in the receptive reader.

Some of the pressures built up by the poem come from the sound and stress patterns discussed in the first question. One sometimes feels that a Hopkins poem is the aural equivalent of a Volkswagen filled with football players. Some of the pressures are built up by the difficulties of making literal sense of the sound–surface. "The Sea and the Skylark," for example, involves no subtle thought. Its paraphrasable content is very near that of Wordsworth's "The World Is Too Much with Us." At first reading (or, better, listening), however, the octave is a wall of cascading sounds that seem to be put together without any intention of making a meaning. That is, Hopkins puts his audience in the position of the poet: just as he must listen to the sounds of the sea and the skylark and try to find the "inscape" of them (it has to do with the freshness of primeval things), so his readers must listen to his song and try to find its underlying sense (which is also a "rash–fresh re–winded new–skeined score": the same old song become new again). I think that Hopkins is deliberately creating difficulties for the reader, a surface opaqueness ("blue–bleak embers") that can suddenly, when the reader *gets* it, fall away to reveal the meaning ("gash gold–vermillion"), a "charge" that will be released in a sudden flash of understanding.

3. Paraphrase "The Windhover" in 100–150 words.

The ambiguities of the poem are notorious, and the main purpose of this question is to bring them to the surface. One summary might be

> I saw a falcon this morning outlined against the dawn. He rode on the air, hung there almost motionless, braking himself with his wings, then shot off on a long glide, fast and effortless, like the glide of a skater sweeping through a loop of a figure–eight, defying the wind's efforts to control him. I was moved by the artistry of the flying. Beauty, courage, pride, feathers, and air all came together. And the spiritual fire that breaks from you, Christ, is lovelier and more dangerous still. None of this is a wonder in a world where the most plodding object can reveal a flash of beauty: the ploughland shines when the share cuts through it, and dark embers break open to reveal a golden flame.

This summary is almost exactly the same length as the poem and leaves a great deal out. In the process of writing it, I was forced to learn things about the poem I had never noticed. I also realized that I simply could not be sure about the meaning of such phrases as "rung upon the rein of a wimpled wing" and "sheer plod makes plough down sillion shine." I could *feel* them.

4. What does the word *buckle* mean in the tenth line of "The Windhover," and why is the way that we interpret it crucial to our understanding of the poem?

Concentrating on this word may open up a general discussion of the poem and Hopkins' meaning in other poems. The first thing students will have to notice is that buckle is here a verb. Hopkins very often likes us to encounter a word in a context where its grammatical function is momentarily unsettled: compare the use of *achieve* in line 8. Here, after the long list of nouns, we at first may see *buckle* as a noun, but we soon call it a verb and so bring the kaleidoscopic sentence into focus.

But what does the verb mean? It might mean buckle in the sense closest to the meaning of the noun: to fasten or connect, as a belt buckle does. It might mean to crumple, as metal does under pressure or heat. If we accept the first meaning, then the point of the sentence is that the falcon combines disparate qualities—"brute beauty and valour and act, oh, air, pride, plume"—into one thing: a reading certainly consistent with Hopkins' notion of inscape. If we accept the other reading, then all these grand qualities crumple (almost as if bending their knees) before the "chevalier" (Christ) of line 11. The choice between these readings is the crux of much critical debate, including a debate over whether we *must* choose. Perhaps it is possible to say that the buckle means, in effect, "come together and, great as they are, are humbled by" the chevalier.

(I am ignoring the possibility, suggested by Jerome Bump, that the Windhover may "buckle" by pulling in his wings and plummeting as if for prey.)

It is surely wrong to insist that students in an introductory poetry class solve the riddle posed by *buckle*, but in the process of discussing it, they will probably be led to discover the underlying logic that connects the description of the falcon with the mention of the chevalier Christ. Surely whichever reading of *buckle* we choose, we will conclude that the grandeur of the falcon is introduced as a point of comparison. If the falcon has such grandeur, how much the more so Christ. "How much the more so" is one of the standard movements of biblical logic: compare Matthew 6:26–29,

> Behold the fowls of the air: for they sow not, neither do they reap, nor gather into barns; yet your heavenly Father feedeth them. Are ye not much better than they . . . . And why take ye thought for raiment? Consider the lilies of the field, how they grow; they toil not, neither do they spin: And yet I say unto you, That even Solomon in all his glory was not arrayed like one of these. Wherefore, if God so clothe the grass of the field, which to–day is, and to–morrow is cast in the oven, shall he not much more clothe you, O ye of little faith.

–D.H.

A. E. Housman

Housman's reputation is built on a small group of poems, most from *A Shropshire Lad*, that are so alike in form and theme that they lend themselves to parodies like Kingsmill's and Pound's. This narrow range keeps him from being one of the greatest names in poetry, but it also makes him a good poet to teach and to learn from. We see what he is up to quickly enough that we can spare some attention for how he does his work.

"Terence, This Is Stupid Stuff" is, whatever highbrow objections can be raised to us, one of the delights of English poetry. I have had two professors—one in classics, one in biology—recite it to me verbatim with great gusto. It is a pleasure to teach.

QUESTIONS

1. What weaknesses in Housman's work do the parodies of Kingsmill and Pound justifiably make fun of?

Kingsmill perfectly captures the predictable pattern of a Housman poem, which bangs away at its iambic tetrameter (or sometimes trimeter) with only occasional variation and is rhymed with more accuracy than inventiveness. The pattern, of course, is that of English ballads, but it has rarely been used so regularly in poem after poem. Eventually it seems like a parody of itself. How easy is it to pick the imposter among passages as alike as these?

> And silence sounds no worse than cheers
> After earth has stopped the ears
>   ("To an Athlete Dying Young," 15–16)

> And malt does more than Milton can
> To justify God's ways to man
>   ("Terence, This Is Stupid Stuff," 23–24)

> But bacon's not the only thing
> That's cured by hanging from a string.
>   ("What, Still Alive," 7–8)

> And while the sun and moon endure
> Luck's a chance, but trouble's sure.
>   ("Terence," 45–46)

The proverbial wisdom, colloquial speech, and quotable despair can seem a mere mannerism.

It is impossible to miss the posture that Housman assumes as a poet. Here he subdues the thirty–five–year–old professor who could wield a footnote like a dagger and becomes Terence, the twenty–year-old Shropshire lad for whom mortality seems to be a new and fascinating discovery. "What, still alive at twenty–two?" is a brilliant question to aim at a poet who seems a remarkable case of arrested development.

Pound's parody occasionally touches on the particulars of Housman's form and diction; like Kingsmill, he takes a dig at the chipper rhythm and the chummy use of "lads" that often accompany the worst of news:

Some lads get hung, and some get shot.
Woeful is the human lot.

Principally, though, it is the predictability of the theme that Pound lampoons: "Oh, Woe, woe, woe, etcetera . . . ." It is perhaps worth noting that Housman only wrote poetry when he was ill.

2. What elements in Housman's work do the parodies fail to do justice to?

It is hard in Kingsmill's parody to tell whether he is laughing with Housman or at him when he writes the characteristically understated

Like enough, you won't be glad,
When they come to hang you, lad.

In general, though, the parodies don't do justice to Housman's poker-faced sense of humor. This humor shows best when the irony is thickest, as in "Is my Team Ploughing?" When the dead friend asks about his girl, he innocently uses the expression "And has she tired of weeping/As she lies down at eve?" Terence replies,

Ay, she lies down lightly,
    She lies not down to weep:
Your girl is well contented.
    Be still, my lad, and sleep.
        (21–22)

The double meaning is in every line, but particularly in the litotic "lies not down to weep." My guess is that most readers miss the humor until they read the poem a second time and have been alerted by the heavier-handed irony of the poem's last two lines. There is a similar understated humor in this passage from "Terence":

Oh I have been to Ludlow fair
And left my necktie God knows where,
And carried half–way home, or near,
Pints and quarts of Ludlow beer.
        (29–32)

The intent, we assume, was to bring the beer home, but Terence drank as he walked. The characteristic humor in "Terence," however, is wit in the Neoclassical style:

And malt does more than Milton can
To justify God's ways to man.

The couplet is like one of Pope's epigrams. It is funnier, of course, to those who have bruised their brains reading *Paradise Lost*, Milton's attempt to "assert eternal providence,/And justify God's ways to man."

Housman is capable, too, of extracting some humor out of his verse form:

> The world, it was the old world yet,
> I was I, my things were wet.

The combination of truism, monosyllables, and a rhyme on trivial words makes this passage appropriately limp and silly. Earlier in the poem, we get a parody of Terence's verse:

> The cow, the old cow, she is dead;
> It sleeps well, the horned head.
>   (7–8)

After the perfect regularity of the preceding lines, the seventh seems to sputter like a badly tuned engine. You might have your students scan it. Its stresses seem to fall on *cow, old, cow, she,* and *dead.* This "moping, melancholy, mad" verse sounds to me more like a parody of Tennyson than of Housman himself, but I don't doubt that Housman is here doing his version of "Woe! woe, etcetera."

3. How is Auden's attitude toward Housman different from Kingsmill's or Pound's?

Auden takes the man with the poet and sees a sad story in Housman. I think one biographical detail slips his notice and he substitutes Cambridge for Oxford in the first line. It was at Oxford that Housman fell unhappily in love with a fellow student, Moses Jackson, and—apparently for this reason—failed his examinations. The examination system at British universities is merciless, and the failure ought, in the normal course of things, to have ended Housman's scholarly career. But Housman went to work in the British Patent Office by day and for ten years spent his nights on the most meticulous scholarship ("Deliberately he chose the dry–as–dust"). Eventually his publication record was overwhelming, and he became a professor first at University College, London, then at Trinity College, Cambridge. It is as though, in the years following the emotional and professional trauma of the affair (manifest or latent) with Jackson and the resultant academic failure, Housman became two men. Emotionally, he kept his "tears like dirty postcards in a drawer"; professionally, he pursued a career which consisted largely of attacking others who pursued the same career ("He timidly attacked the life he led").

The emotional life that had no other outlet shows in the subjects of his poetry: the passing of youth, the pain of loss, the inevitable end of love and friendship, "The uncritical relations of the dead." Auden, with his unflagging interest in the causes of art, seems to see fairly clearly into the dilemma of Housman.

–D.H.

William Butler Yeats

One of the distressing effects of graduate–level education in literature can be a phobia about teaching W. B. Yeats. His indisputable greatness has made Yeats scholarship into an academic industry, filled with contentious debates between heavyweights like Richard Ellmann and Harold Bloom. His mythological system seems simultaneously complex and simple–minded, and we wonder if we have to present it to our class (or put up with it ourselves) in order to understand the poems. Most of this nervousness can be dispelled if we bear three things in mind: (a) first that Yeats' poems have a great immediate appeal to those who know nothing about "gyres" or Blake's prophetic books; (b) next, that the simplified version of Yeats' mythological system can be presented in about three minutes; (c) last, that Yeats himself made less of his mythological system than some of his academic critics have. The "circuits of sun and moon" that he so carefully worked out to explain human history came from the same source of inspiration as did the poems, but their intricacies are largely irrelevant to the poems. Yeats says that some of his wheels within wheels are "plainly symbolical" and that if he sometimes in a bout of inspiration took them literally "my reason soon recovered . . . ."

Here, then, is my three–minute drill on Yeats' view of life and history, adequate to introduce students to the poems collected in *The Riverside Anthology*. From his youth Yeats was very religious but could not stay comfortable within the bounds of traditional Christianity. He began to "worship" (though the word seems wrong) an "infallible church of poetic tradition," assuming that the inspired artist must be describing a reality deeper than the surface flow of everyday events. Influenced by Blake, Yeats found his own deeper reality involved the struggle in the world between two great forces: the outward-looking force of reason, science, and practical action, and the inward–looking force of emotion, instinct, and imagination. Yeats saw the history of Western civilization divided roughly into epochs of 2000 years: from the birth of Greco–Roman civilization (2000 B.C.) to the birth of Christ, the outward force held sway; from the birth of Christ the inward force has held sway, and will continue to do so until about 2000 A.D., when a new cycle will begin. Each era can be said to begin with an encounter between the natural and the supernatural world. The New Testament provided Yeats with one such encounter: the birth of Christ from the union of Mary and the holy ghost. Classical mythology provided a parallel encounter: the birth of Helen of

Troy from the union of Zeus and Leda. The nature of the third encounter is yet unknown, of course.

A cycle begins, then, in a miraculous birth that causes cataclysmic changes in the course of human history, but the course of history moves away from this central event in a gyre, getting further and further from its core.

Much more could be said about the mythological system, of course, but this is probably sufficient.

In teaching Yeats, it is important not to let this system overwhelm the more immediately accessible appeal of the poems. Yeats is a great love poet and a great poet on the uneasy marriage of flesh to spirit. If your students learn to appreciate these things, the gyres will take care of themselves eventually.

QUESTIONS

1. Why would the sentence from Pater on page 901 be particularly appealing to Yeats?

This question is just to sharpen your students' eyes to the Yeatsian motifs. Notice that Mona Lisa is presented as a mysterious force associated with both the births that initiate cycles in Yeats' mythological system. Notice, too, that she is an agelessly beautiful woman, unlike Maud Gonne, the love of Yeats' life, whose aging is the subject of "The Folly of Being Comforted." Pater's praise of a painting that seems to capture something more permanent than human events anticipates Yeats' golden bird in the fourth stanza of "Sailing to Byzantium."

2. If we look at Yeats' poems in the order of their composition, what can we say about his changing attitude toward nature?

Technically, this will point students to Yeats' imagery, which begins (to oversimplify in a way that will alarm Yeats scholars) with the Romantic embrace of nature and ends at the opposite pole. In "The Lake Isle of Innisfree" we find nature associated with the peaceful heart: Yeats, "on the roadway, or on the pavements gray" hears the sounds of Innisfree's waters "in the deep heart's core," just as Wordsworth "in lonely rooms, and 'mid the din/Of towns and cities" remembers "With tranquil restoration" the beauteous forms observed near Tintern Abbey.

As Yeats grew older, his images of nature began to change. "The Folly of Being Comforted," written when both he and Maud Gonne were in their mid–thirties, is a tangle of unresolved tensions. The "one that is ever kind" (probably Lady Gregory) seems to be offering a Wordsworthian consolation: age may ruin the beautiful face, but it will bring the philosophic mind. "Heart" (not head) cries that she is *more* beautiful now than ever before. But the closing couplet, addressed to Yeats' heart, is ambiguous:

> O heart! O heart! if she'd but turn her head,
> You'd know the folly of being comforted.

Does this mean, "You'd know that Lady Gregory doesn't need to try to comfort you because age cannot take from Maud Gonne's beauty"? Or does it mean, "You'd know that it is foolish to attempt to be comforted since there is no comfort possible for such a loss"? Both meanings are possible, and Yeats, who knew the power of reconciling contraries, may have intended both. Maud is more beautiful to the heart because she is less beautiful to the eye, because her inevitable aging and passing make her more precious. If she turns her head, her face will move him more passionately than ever.

The split between the flesh and the spirit, "the fire that stirs about her when she stirs," is established before Yeats is forty and becomes increasingly important in the later poetry. There are flashes of the old worship of youth and natural beauty in poems Yeats published when he was in his early fifties ("The Scholars," "The Cat and the Moon"), but increasingly, he seems to stand outside of nature, as in "The Wild Swans at Coole."

"Wild Swans" was written when Yeats was fifty–one and had returned to a place of great natural beauty he had visited years before. It is, therefore, natural to compare it to "Tintern Abbey." Yeats' return, however, has an added poignancy: his first visit came after his first rejection by Maud Gonne, this after his second. Apparently he feels, like Wordsworth, a loss of emotional power. The swans'

> . . . hearts have not grown old
> Passion or conquest, wander where they will,
> Attend upon them still.

But Yeats feels his own heart aging, and in the final stanza the image of his awaking and finding that the swans have flown away to delight other men's eyes suggests that he fears he will eventually lose all "passion and conquest."

In the later poems, the images of nature are far less pleasant than anything we would expect in the Romantics. In "Crazy Jane Talks with the Bishop" we have the unpleasant truth that ". . . Love has pitched his mansion/In the place of excrement," and in "Sailing to Byzantium" we have Yeats' image of himself as an aged man, "A tattered coat upon a stick" (10), a spirit "fastened to a dying animal" (22). In "Among School Children," he doubts that a woman would go through the pangs of childbirth if she knew what her child would look like in sixty years (stanza 7). Nothing could be further from the romanticism of the early Yeats.

3. Comment on the role of art objects in Yeats' poems.

This question is designed to draw your students' attention to the gold mosaic in the third stanza of "Sailing to Byzantium," the golden bird in the fourth, and the religious images in the seventh stanza of "Among School Children." As nature becomes less attractive, art becomes more so. And for Yeats, the most attractive art is very artificial, stylized, heavy with significance. Most of your students probably have a vague notion that Byzantine mosaics and religious icons are inferior forms of art: we seem to teach people whom we teach very little else that the Renaissance was a great breakthrough because it broke the back of religion (translated as superstition) and replaced it with realism (translated as science). Yeats had a different view. In *A Vision* he wrote:

I think if I could be given a month of Antiquity and leave to spend it where I chose, I would spend it in Byzantium a little before Justinian opened St. Sophia . . . . I think I could find in some little wine–shop some philosophical worker in mosaic who could answer all my questions, the supernatural descending nearer to him than to Plotinus . . . maybe never before or since in recorded history, religious, aesthetic and practical life were one . . . architect and artificers . . . spoke to the multitude and to the few alike . . . .

If your students have read Browning's "Fra Lippo Lippi," they may want to consider the conflict between Lippi's view of art and Yeats'.

It might be worth pointing out to your students, apropos of artifice, that both "Sailing to Byzantium" and "Among School Children" are written in rhyme royal, a pattern formal as a mosaic.

4. How do "Leda and the Swan" and "The Second Coming" fit into Yeats' mythological scheme? How important is a knowledge of this scheme to a proper appreciation of the poems?

This question will be such old hat to you that I won't belabor it. Clearly these poems gain much of their energy from Yeats' envisioning one as the moment when classical culture with its "knowledge and power" came into existence, one as the moment when Christian culture, with its spiritualism and compassion degraded to anarchy, comes to an end.

On the other hand, they would be great poems if no reader had ever heard of Yeats' scheme. The remarkably convincing portrayal of the impossible event "her thighs caressed/By the dark webs, her nape caught in his bill" is shocking and powerful enough, as is the juxtaposition of rape, knowledge, and power. The first eight lines of "The Second Coming" so graphically convey an emotion common to the twentieth century that they are quoted by people of every political persuasion who have only the vaguest idea of who Yeats is. They have become part of our common literary heritage, like the Bible. There are surely good reasons in Yeats' mythology for the beast in the second coming to be a sphinx (lion's body and head of man) with a blank gaze and "slow thighs." In an introductory course, we can leave these reasons to the scholars, though. What counts is the effect of this image, and the effect is heart–stopping.

–D.H.

Edwin Arlington Robinson

Robinson once defined poetry as "a language that tells us, through more or less emotional reaction, what cannot be said." I'm afraid that many readers today, seeing Robinson's rhymed stanzas and willingness to point to a moral, will conclude too hastily that they *know* what the man is saying, that he is a simple poet. "Richard Cory," they will conclude, says that even the fortunate can be unhappy; "Miniver Cheevy," that we should live in the real world rather than in dreams; "Eben Flood," that it is dangerous to brood on the past; and so forth. When students get beyond these simple formulas, they will find that Robinson is much deeper and much sadder than this, and they will learn a valuable lesson about the difference between the paraphraseable content of a poem and its meaning.

QUESTIONS

1. Explain what Frost meant about Robinson's "never having let a grief go further than it could in play" by analyzing some of the poetry. Is this playfulness a virtue?

Let's begin by looking at the easy cases, the poems to which Frost's dictum most obviously applies. "Miniver Cheevy" is certainly a poem about grief—a grief Robinson must have shared in; he, too, in his later years turned to tales of chivalry as an escape from the narrowness of contemporary life, producing long poems on the Arthurian legends. Humor permeates the poem, though. In addition to the fourth "thought" that Frost points out, there is

♦ the protagonist's name, which one critic says "could only belong to a man whom fate had sentenced never to be taken seriously"

♦ the verbal juxtaposition of Romance and modern life in such expressions as "Priam's neighbors" and "the medieval grace/Of iron clothing" (23–24). The effect of the juxtapostion is to deflate Romance.

♦ the use of double rhymes on the first and third lines of each stanza. Double rhymes often sound so strained as to be comic, and Robinson here uses them to underscore the deflating humor.

There are things about "Miniver Cheevy" that make me smile every time I read the poem. "He wept that he was ever born/And he had reasons" is one: the juxtapositon of Cheevy's histrionic state and Robinson's deadpan comment on it is perfectly set up by the double rhyme (*seasons/reasons*). I particularly enjoy the way that the meter in line 23 makes us decide to give *medieval* its four syllable, hippety–hop, double–iambic pronunciation, and the rhyme of *seen one* and *been one* tempts us to give *been* the unlikely pronunciation my third grade teacher attempted to inflict on her class.

"Mr. Flood's Party," as sad a poem as any, contrasts Flood's happy past when "many friends" would open "many doors" to welcome him. The poem is full of heart–rending gestures: "He set the jug down slowly at his feet/With trembling care, knowing that most things break" (27–28). But it is also a comic poem. The name Eben Flood captures both the tragic and comic sides of the poem: on one hand, it reminds us of the ebb and flood (or flow, as Matthew Arnold says) of human misery; on the other it sounds like a good name for a drinking man. The elaborate conversation Flood has with himself shows the glimmerings of a wit in ruins, and Robinson's commentary is sometimes downright funny:

> . . . he lifted up his voice and sang,
> Secure, with only two moons listening. (46–47)

Even when there is nothing we would call humor in the poems, there is an irony that borders on grim humor. The miller's statement that "there are no millers any more," for instance, is both an explanation of his suicide and an announcement of it. The closing lines of the second and third stanzas of "Eros Turannos" are so indirect in their comment on the man's venality and the woman's self–delusion that they seem to be delivered tongue–in–cheek.

As for the effect of Robinson's humor, no one could describe it better than Robert Frost, who said that "style is the way the man takes himself; and to be at all charming or even bearable, the way is almost rigidly pre-scribed. If it is with outer seriousness, it must be with inner humor. If it is with outer humor, it must be with inner seriousness." Robinson's charm, and his courage, shows in his ability to experience grief and humor simultaneously.

2. How does Robinson use sound to knit his poems together?

Robinson's inventiveness as a technician shouldn't be overlooked. The stanza form in "Eros Turannos," for instance, is ingenious and demanding. Each stanza rhymes ababcccb, with double rhymes on the "b" lines. It is a wonder that the poem doesn't collapse under the strain, but the actual effect of the formal structure is to treat powerful motion with some sense of distance and some compensatory pleasure, as Wordsworth says, "from the sense of difficulty overcome." It may be, too, that Robinson slows down and speeds up the pace of his lines to suit their sense in this poem. We are inclined to read lines 45–49 with increasing acceleration:

> Though like waves breaking it may be
> Or like a changed familiar tree,
> Or like a stairway to the sea
> Where down the blind are driven.

Part of the reason for this acceleration, as Ellsworth Barnard points out, is an effect like that Pope creates in the "Sound and Sense" passage from *An Essay on Criticism*. Line 45 is slowed down by long vowels in all but two syllables and by the necessity of enunciating slowly the transition between "waves" and "breaking." Line 46 moves faster because its vowels are shorter, but is slowed up by "changed," one of the longer syllables in the language. Line 47 "has nothing to stop the rush of words, until in the last line they pause to measure the heavy footfalls of Fate."

It is possible, as Dr. Johnson says, that these changes in pace are figments of the reader's imagination, or at best "technical and nugatory," but no one could deny the presence of assonance and consonance in the poems.

It would be worthwhile to have your students mark first the principal assonances, then the principal consonances in the following passage.

> Alone, as if enduring to the end
>
> A valiant armor of scarred hopes outworn,
>
> He stood there in the middle of the road
>
> Like Roland's ghost winding a silent horn.
>
> Below him, in the town among the trees,

Where friends of other days had honored him,

A phantom salutation of the dead

Rang thinly till old Eben's eyes were dim.

Alone, as if enduring to the end

A valiant armor of scarred hopes outworn,

He stood there in the middle of the road

Like Roland's ghost winding a silent horn.

Below him, in the town among the trees,

Where friends of other days had honored him,

A phantom salutation of the dead

Rang thinly till old Eben's eyes were dim.

These tight relations among sounds make Robinson's poems among the most memorable (literally) in the language. They have the effect, too, of drawing together ideas that are dense with apparent contradictions. "A valiant armor of scarred hopes outworn": can scarred hopes really be an armor? is outworn hope better or worse than new hope as an armor? is there really valor in having worn hope out? or is the valor in still, somehow, wearing the hope despite its being scarred and worn? Robinson's compactness, partly stemming from his form and certainly compounded by the auditory links among words, is one of the pleasures and difficulties of reading him.

–D.H.

Robert Frost

Frost's undeniable greatness as a poet and his accessibility make him a good subject in an introductory poetry course. A colleague of mine tells the story of having a flat tire deep in a thinly populated region of the Ozark mountains. As he was starting to jack the car up a bearded man in a pickup stopped to help and to talk. My colleague, not knowing just what

English professors and Ozark farmers have in common, made a few awkward comments about how nice it was to be outdoors in the early spring. The farmer agreed, and within a few sentences was reciting Frost's beautiful lyric "Nothing Gold Can Stay." Rarely has an American poet enjoyed this sort of popularity.

The popularity can be a disadvantage if your students have absorbed the notion that Frost is just a cheerful nature poet, slightly cornball. The Kinnell poem is present partly because it so accurately identifies the side of Frost that has least to do with his popular image.

QUESTIONS

1. Do Galway Kinnell's observations in "To Robert Frost" square with what we read in Frost's poems?

This is a large question, large enough to produce many pages or much discussion. The Kinnell poem is a remarkable combination of tribute, criticism, and thought about the role of the poet. It deserves serious study in its own right, but is so thoroughly meshed with Frost's own work that studying one soon becomes studying the other.

Kinnell sees (behind the garrulous old man at Ripton) a huge, mythic figure who lived close to a dark truth about life and death, "Who dwelt in access to that which other men/Have burnt all their lives to get near" (86–87). Kinnell's view is that Frost felt more strongly than most of us the presence (even the attraction) of oblivion, of nature that is unconcerned with man and time that undoes all human effort:

> The dark trees, for which no saying is dark enough
> Which mask the gloom and lead on into it,
> The bare, the withered, the deserted. (61–63)

What "turned" Frost from oblivion was "Love,/Love of things, duty . . ." (72–73). This love and duty make a person run backward against the stream of oblivion to make order (Kinnell, lines 77–79: the idea permeates Frost's poetry; the particular image comes from "West Running Brook").

Now if your students will hold this vision of Frost in mind, I think they will find it easier to see to the heart of "Stopping by Woods," "Home Burial," "The Wood Pile," "Acquainted with the Night," and "Neither Out Far nor In Deep." Let's take "Home Burial" as our example. The encounter between husband and wife becomes an encounter between two ways of facing death: the wife's grief over the dead child takes the form of an absolute gloom "for which no saying is dark enough"; she wraps herself in her sorrow and refuses to be consoled. What we discover, with some surprise, is that grief for the dead child is not the whole of it:

> The nearest friends can go
> With anyone to death, comes so far short
> They might as well not try to go at all.
> No, from the time one is sick to death,
> One is alone, and he dies more alone. (102–106)

Beyond grief for the child is grief for herself and for everyone who must die alone while others go about the business of life, hardly noticing. In Tennyson's "In Memoriam" (stanza 35, line 16) personified Love says that it is "half–dead to know that [it] shall die." Amy, the wife, feels much the same thing. In the face of death, she finds no consolation: ". . . the world's evil," she says. She speaks for a side of Frost's character that Kinnell has perceptively identified, the side that brooded on "the obscure/Pouring of this life to the sea" (Kinnell, 80).

The husband speaks for the white wave that "rides in place" on the surface of the stream of oblivion (Kinnell, 78), ignoring the inevitable end as much as it can. What are we to make of Amy's accusation that he could dig his child's grave, lean his spade up against the wall, sit at the kitchen table and talk about how "Three foggy mornings and one rainy day/Will rot the best birch fence a man can build"? It might be callousness, but it is also courage. He is not unaware of death; he is "wonted" to it (23). It is, as Kinnell says, "Love/Love of things, Duty" that keep his grief reined in. Faced with the certainty of death, he puts life into what order he can, takes and offers what comfort he can. "Broad-shouldered little slabs there in the sunlight" (28), "the best birch fence a man can build" (88), "I will find out now—you must tell me dear" (12). The man is, like the mysterious stranger in "The Wood–Pile," "Someone who lived in turning to fresh tasks" (35).

The two impulses that Kinnell identifies as the heart of Frost's greatness are represented here in their classic juxtaposition: the deep, solemn pull of oblivion in the wife's attitude; the answering (less solemn, sometimes trivial or hectoring, but courageous) pull of commitment to life in the husband's.

2. Where in Frost do we find the "recklessness" of elaborate commitments to poetic forms? How effective are these formal poems?

The interlocked stanzas (aaba/bbcb/ccdc/dddd) of "Stopping By Woods" are not more ambitious than the single–rhyme tercets of "Provide, Provide" or the terza rima of "Acquainted with the Night." How effective are they? I think one needs to concede from the outset that they are perfect— conspicuously perfect. Frost creates an obstacle of enormous difficulty and then surmounts it with no apparent effort. Neither meter nor rhyme strains the absolute naturalness of his speech. Every line seems inevitable. There is surely a note of awe and envy in Kinnell's apostrophe to Frost: ". . . you who nearly foreknew/The next lines of poems you suddenly dropped."

The question is whether this perfection is a large or small thing: a technical trick or a great artistic accomplishment. The case for great accomplishment depends on Frost's view that poetic form is "an epitome of the great predicament." In light of the blank truth that "One is alone, and he dies more alone," all entanglements in the world are "alien entanglements": we *choose* them, and our choosing is a great act of faith in the teeth of the evidence. A sestina royale is arguably a greater act of faith than a career in politics or science, since its rules of arbitrary grace don't mask the existential emptiness in which it must be performed. Many of Frost's best formal poems are performed on the very brink of chaos. Certainly the three poems we are looking at here approach perfect bleakness: the poet longs for the "dark and deep" woods, outwalks "the furthest city light," and reminds us that nothing "keeps the end from being hard." To treat these themes with such formal control and musicality is a testimony to something noble in human nature. Hemingway was thinking of the same sort of nobility in "A Clean, Well–Lighted Place" when he has the older waiter point out that the old customer "drinks without spilling. Even now, drunk."

3. What is the theme of "Provide, Provide"?

Students sometimes assume that this poem means what it says, but here is a place where Frost clearly enjoys the "pleasure of ulteriority." The speaker in the poem recommends a philosophy, but the poem itself does not. If I read the poem right, the theme is not "Die early and avoid the fate" or "Make the whole stock exchange your own!" It *may* be "Too many fall from great and good/For you to doubt the likelihood." How we should "provide" against this likelihood is a problem posed by the poem rather than answered by it, though. "Provide, Provide" is a good poem to reinforce the truth that, since the eighteenth century at least, poetry has not often been in the business of providing advice.

4. Frost tells us that "saying one thing and meaning another" is at the heart of poetry. How does "Departmental" say one thing and mean another?

The obvious way that the poem says one thing and means another is that it uses the metaphor of the anthill to describe human behavior. It is an ancient trope, but Frost manages it particularly well. When the first ant passes the dormant moth, he ignores it and is "off on his duty run":

> Yet if he encountered one
> Of the hive's enquiry squad
> Whose work is to find out God
> And the nature of time and space,
> He would put him onto the case.

Here we realize what the game is, and that Frost's comment is on the specialization that can reduce the range of human emotion and curiosity. But Frost plays the game with a wonderfully deadpan humor: "Ants are a curious race."

The other way that the poem says one thing and means another is in its form. Its form declares it to be light verse: it is a rhymed beast fable written in short (three–stress) lines. The rhymes are sometimes very funny (*any/antennae*) and often double (*Formic/McCormic*). The form keeps us smiling, but the theme (or *a* theme) is very similar to a theme in "Provide, Provide" and "Home Burial": that we all die alone—

> Nobody stands round to stare.
> It is nobody else's affair.

–D.H.

Rainer Maria Rilke

My three words of German hardly allow me to comment on the problem of reading Rilke in translation. The motive for wanting to include him was embarrassment that so many American anthologies are profoundly insular, ignoring figures like Rilke whose stature in the literature of the Western world is very great. The key that allowed me to include him was the high quality of Stephen Mitchell's translations: I'm sure that those who have more German than I will say that the poems are not the same in Mitchell's English, but I think they are very great and surprisingly accessible. If you have not read the Mitchell translations, you might look at "The Panther" and "Archaic Torso of Apollo" to get a sense of how well they work.

QUESTIONS

1. What does Rilke mean by "transformation" in line 71 of the Ninth Elegy, and how does the idea of transformation connect the elegy with "Evening" and "Archaic Torso of Apollo"?

The idea of transformation in Rilke is related to the idea of inscape in Hopkins. It involves going so deeply into things that they reveal their inner nature, or we *create* their inner nature by articulating it. In an era when every freshman is a logical positivist, this idea of transformation is likely to meet with a cool reception. Your students may warm to it if they begin with "Evening" and work their way through "Archaic Torso" on their way to the Ninth Elegy.

"Evening" is a relatively simple lyric on our divided nature, half earthbound, half spirit. It offers no way of reconciling the division, but says (beautifully and sadly) "it is alternately stone in you and star." Here is something we have all felt.

"Archaic Torso" is a poem more charged with energy, one which raises the possibility that stone might become star. The command to "change your life" at the end of the poem comes from a vision of the possibility of transformation. Rilke wrote the poem in a period when, under the influence of the great sculptor Auguste Rodin, he was turning away from direct descriptions of emotion, and investigating things in their thinginess (*Dinglichkeit*). Certainly it is a remarkable observation of the statue itself (apparently Rilke studied it in the Louvre): "a smile . . . where procreation flared" is an exact visual image of the curve of the abdomen over the pelvic girdle; the analogy between the play of light on the patina of the stone and the glistening of a "wild beast's fur" is striking and precise. The comparison with Hopkins comes naturally to mind when we look at this poem: there is the same receptiveness to things, and the statue's "brilliance from inside" reminds us of Hopkins' inscape.

But the internal brilliance of Rilke's statue is not the same as Hopkins' "dearest freshness deep down things." Hopkins is a great *nature* poet; the statue is manmade and stands, as all manmade objects do, in opposition to nature. Its order, its bodying forth of beauty, power, sexual and animal energy, come from artifice—the internal light is that of the (little *c*) creator.

And it is this sense of the *made* object—like Yeats' golden bird in "Sailing to Byzantium"—that brings the subjective element of the poem to the fore and connects it with the idea of transformation. Even as he is contemplating the statue objectively, Rilke feels the spirit of the ancient sculptor challenging his own spirit. I am reminded of the passage in *Pauline* where Browning apostrophizes Shelley's spirit ("The air seems bright with thy past presence yet . . .") or of the passage in "Little Gidding" where Eliot encounters the "familiar compound ghost" of Yeats/Tennyson/Dante. However "objective" the poem may be, it turns out to be a subjective encounter between an artist and an ideal of creation.

The encounter, like that between the Magi and Christ in Eliot's "Journey of the Magi," causes pain because it reveals a new possibility. The thought that rushes in upon Rilke as if spoken by the statue is "You must change your life," but there is no indication of how change is possible. The German word "andern" might be translated "change," "remould" or "transform." Rilke might mean "you must improve the way that you live," but he might also mean "you must take the material of your life and transform it." Either interpretation suggests the possibility that the stone of "Evening" might be transformed into a star. But how is this miracle to be accomplished?

This question brings us squarely to the Ninth Elegy, a poem that announces Rilke's turning of a spiritual corner. The elegy starts on a note that might have been sounded by "Evening":

> . . . why then
> have to be human—and, escaping from fate,
> keep longing for fate?
>
> Oh *not* because happiness exists . . .

Our human situation, if we examine it in itself, is essentially tragic, and our lives unsatisfying, purposeless. But if we escape ourselves, we can discover our role as artists who can, by "saying," *transform* the things around us (the stone) into something spiritual (the star).

> . . . Perhaps we are *here* in order to say: house,
> bridge, fountain, gate, pitcher, fruit–tree, window—
> at most: column, tower . . . . But to *say* them, you must understand,
> oh to say them *more* intensely than the Things themselves
> ever dreamed of existing. (32–36)

Articulating the inner spirit of *things* is what reconciles the star and the stone. The Angel in line 53 is a pseudonym for God throughout the elegies. Here at last, our mortal life gives us something to offer the Angel: "Tell him of Things. He will stand astonished" (57).

The exuberant note on which the Ninth Elegy ends is that of a person who has found his life's purpose: to make the transient things around him "invisible" (70), spiritual, beyond time. The conception is deeply religious. Mystics seem periodically to discuss the possibility of redeeming the world and making it fit to carry before the throne of God.

2. What might "The Panther" symbolize?

Whenever I ask students a question of this sort, I caution them that "symbolize" does not mean "mean." The circumstances in which this poem was written can help reinforce that point. Rodin had suggested to Rilke that he ought to visit the Paris Zoo so that he could learn to see things with fresh eyes. In those days, painters and other artists were issued a special ticket that allowed them to visit the Jardin des Plantes from 8:00–11:00 AM, before the general public was admitted. For several years Rilke went regularly.

"The Panther," then, comes from direct, deliberate observation, and might be compared with the sketches of Paris street life that Maupassant had written thirty years earlier under the direction of Flaubert.

As in "Archaic Torso," the accuracy of objective observation is impressive: "powerful soft strides . . . like a ritual dance" captures something in the striding of great cats in their cages that we have all seen without seeing; so too is the way that the panther periodically freezes with tensed muscles looking at something that has caught his attention. So why does "The Panther" have to symbolize anything? Why can't it simply be an accurate sketch? The principal reason is the perspective. From the first line forward, we are not only looking at a panther, we are looking out at the world from inside a panther. The feeling of lost freedom is so strong that it attracts symbolic interpretation. For some readers this particular panther in this particular cage becomes a symbol for all animals "scanted in a dull cage," as Hopkins puts it. For others this ripple expands further: man is an animal, and cages need not have bars. The poem becomes a symbol for all forms of confinement: cats in cages, people in unhappy marriages or jobs or families, souls trapped in bodies.

–D.H.

Wallace Stevens

A logical point of departure for reading Stevens is his agnosticism, and the dilemma that agnosticism creates. If your students have read Wordsworth and/or Coleridge, they will be able to see this dilemma as related to the dilemma faced by the Romantics. Once a person rejects the idea of order imposed on the world by religious belief, what does he or she have to replace it with? Perhaps, as in the case of Wordsworth, one has a consoling sense of harmony with the natural world and a "philosophic mind" that can sustain one when the "visionary gleam" begins to fade. Perhaps, as in the case of Coleridge, one finds no adequate consolation. Perhaps one constructs a personal mythology, as Blake, Yeats, and (to some degree) Dickinson do, and so returns to religious ritual patterns by the back door.

In the case of Stevens, none of these things happened. Instead, he turned to the philosophy of what he called the "Supreme Fiction." Like Yeats' mythology, Stevens' philosophy, taken in large doses, may so distract your students from the poems themselves that they lose all sense of proportion, but they probably need to know a little about it. Essentially, it is concerned with the psychology of perception, with the relation between the external world and the person who is viewing it. We can reduce the philosophy to two axioms:

(1) that external reality is *everything*, the ground of all knowledge; everything else is merely fiction, and

(2) that external reality is *nothing* until we imaginatively impose on it some order, some fiction.

Stevens was able to hold these contradictory notions in his head simultaneously while maintaining a monumental sanity; "the final believe," he said "is to believe in a fiction, what you know to be a fiction, there being nothing else. The exquisite truth is to know that it is a fiction and that you believe in it willingly."

QUESTIONS

1. What do "Study of Two Pears" and "Anecdote of the Jar" show us about Stevens' philosophy of seeing?

Perhaps all of Stevens' poems can be arranged on a continuum ranging from those that celebrate "things that in being real/make any imaginings of them lesser things" ("Bouquet of Roses in Sunlight") to those that testify to the transforming power of the mind, "the terriblest force in the world" (Saint John and the Back-Ache). "Study of Two Pears" seems to be near one extreme of this continuum, and "Anecdote of the Jar" near the other. "Study" will make more sense to your students if they take seriously the implications of the first line. This poem is a lesson in seeing: the equivalent of a teacher's leaning over a student's shoulder and issuing instructions while he or she attempts to paint a still life. The sections of the poem might almost be a numbered list of instructions to students.

What do these instructions do? They tell the student of seeing first of all not to be distracted by metaphor; not to expend energy finding ingenious analogies for what the pears are like. They tell the student last of all not to think that they can make of the pears whatever they will: no sympathy for expressionism here. Sections (instructions) 2–5 tell the student that the pears can be seen as a composition of large yellow forms touched with red, that they are not flat surfaces with outlines, that if we look closely we will see that the color is not simply yellow and red but contains shadowings of blue, that the yellow is not simply yellow but contains many colors. I suspect that someone who knows painters better than I would find in this an affirmation of the notions of Cézanne, Renoir, and Pissarro, a rejection of the art of Manet. Certainly Stevens was very sympathetic with the Impressionist view that objects when "not seen/as the observer wills" are never simple units, but compounds of sense impressions.

At any rate, we can say that the general drift of "Study" is toward fidelity to the external world. "Ancedote of the Jar" takes us somewhere

else. Here the dazzling variety of forms offered by the external nature—
"the slovenly wilderness"—is subordinated to a man–made form deliberately placed in the landscape. The result is order: to the person who placed
the jar, or to any person whose idea of order is *human* ordering of things,
the jar naturally takes "dominion everywhere." Nature is "seen/as the
observer wills" whatever "Study" may tell us. The order may be high or
low, pleasing or displeasing, but it is inevitable.

The tone of "Anecdote" is a puzzle to critics, by the way, some arguing
that the jar is the ruination of nature, some arguing that it gives significance to nature, some seeing the whole thing as a slur on the character of
a great state.

There is, at any rate, a tension between the way of seeing that we find
in "Study" and the way we find in "Anecdote." One insists that we respect
the external world, one shows that we inevitably transform it into
something it is not. The tension, however, is not a downright inconsis-
tency. Transforming the world in a way that does not debase it is one of
the themes in Stevens' poetry.

2. Paraphrase "The Emperor of Ice Cream" and comment on its meaning.

This is an absolutely horrible question that could get good results if you
pose it as an informal writing assignment, and then read out (or have
students read out) some of the results. You might get something like this
(I model it on an actual student response):

Call the big, crude man who rolls cigars and have him whip up some
ice cream for the funeral. Let the common women hang around for a
while in their street dress, and let the boys who bring flowers bring
them in old newspapers rather than elaborate vases. No use dressing the
situation up. Cover the corpse up with a sheet she once embroidered with
images of birds. You'll find it in that cheap dresser there. Don't worry if
her feet show. Let the lamp shine on her for everyone to see. No reason to
make a fuss. When you're gone, you're a goner. There is no God to care.

The poem seems to mean that with no God and no soul, a funeral has
no meaning.

Imperfect as this response may be, you will very likely have worse. Students very often miss the meaning of the third line entirely or fail to see
that we are talking about a funeral. If you can get a response this good, it
gives you a basis for class discussion: What is the significance of the embroidered fantails? (To show that the corpse had been a woman with more
imagination and sense of beauty than her mourners?) Is the poet in
sympathy with the voice that gives these rather depressing orders for how
the funeral should be organized, or is he creating a resistance in us,
getting us to say, "No, no. We can do better than this. Life is not so value-
less?"

3. How do "Page from a Tale" and "Disillusionment at Ten O'Clock" re-inforce Stevens' notion that each viewer sees a different reality?

If your students attempt to answer this question, they will have to spend a good deal of time (productive time) trying to figure out what is literally happening in the poem. I *believe* that what we have is a scene in which Hans, sitting by his fire of driftwood on the shore, is subjected at the same time to several stimuli: the sound of cracking ice on the sea, the sound of the blowing wind, the sound of Yeats' "Lake Isle of Innisfree" passing in memory through his head, the sight of the ice–locked ship, the sight of bright stars, the sound of the fire dying, the increase in cold, the sight of lights on the steamer. Even though this sounds like a vision of apocalypse, Hans views it, as Marianne Moore says, with a "spiritual happiness" that makes him open to experience.

Then, at line 26, we move from Hans' present perspective to speculations on what Hans will next see: men who will climb out of the boat and "march single file, with electric lamps, alert/For tidal undulations un-derneath" the ice that is creaking and moaning around them like a liv-ing thing. They will be walking through what they had assumed to be dawn, but what will be (I think) the aurora borealis. How will they view the aurora? Will it be for them a terrifying experience, as if it were a dawn coming from hell with a host of demons in tow? Or will they fail to notice the brilliance around them, blinded by the light thrown by their electric lamps. They will not, we can be sure, experience what Hans experiences a few hundred feet away.

"Disillusionment" puts the women in white nightgowns (and pre-sumably their husbands and families too) in somewhat the same position as the men marching single file with their electric lamps. Their imagi-nations are so constricted that they cannot break from the predictable pat-tern even in dreams. Only the drunken sailor, freed from the pressures of respectability, can see in dreams a sight comparable to the one Hans sees.

4. How does "Sunday Morning" deal with the problems created by lack of religious faith? How confident does Stevens appear to be that he has solved them?

Once again, your students will have to struggle with the literal level of the poem a bit before they know what to make of it. They should, with little prompting, discover that the poem is something like a dramatic monologue, comparable to the "The Love Song of J. Alfred Prufrock," for instance. They should be able to see that the woman who is sometimes the speaker, but very often a character observed, is sitting in her dressing gown eating oranges and drinking coffee in a sunny room with a rug that features a bright green cockatoo. This seems comfortable enough, but it is Sunday morning, and—though she can stay away from church—she cannot stay away from thoughts of religion. She thinks of Christ, and resists the thinking.

The poem is a struggle between two visions of life: it might be compared to Coleridge's "Aeolian Harp" in this regard. In effect, the woman's position is that "Divinity must live within her self" and that in the rich experience of the world, she can know the sublime. But she feels, too, the emotional calms when that sublimity passes away (compare Coleridge's "Frost at Midnight" or Bogan's "Zone"), and feels "The need of some imperishable bliss" (62). Remarkably, the poem shifts in the fifth and sixth sections to a line of thought that Keats would have responded strongly to: "Death is the mother of beauty"—it is the very fact that experience is so transient that makes it so vital. If the fruit hung eternally on the tree in perfect ripeness, we would cease to see it as beautiful. If we could see an infinite number of springs, we would know neither the excitement nor the pathos of the season.

Having traveled this far, the poem returns to religion and finds a sympathy with even its most primitive forms. Those who worship the sun do so because they are part of "the heavenly fellowship/Of men that perish." Their worship will transform the world they experience, making it a "Supreme Fiction."

The magnificent final section begins with a voice that announces not that Christ is risen, but that he is unrisen, and that we are living in "the old chaos of the sun," where we must die, and so are free to know the beauty of the world. There is hardly a more moving passage in English verse than the final six lines. The closing image of pigeons that "sink,/Downward to darkness, on extended wings" captures the combination of sorrow and beauty that permeates the poem.

Does the poem seem a triumphant statement of Stevens' resolution of the problem living without faith? No. What it seems instead to be is an expression of painful beauty of a life without hope of immortality.

–D.H.

William Carlos Williams

"Williams is a writer to whom writing is the grinding of a glass, the polishing of a lens by means of which he hopes to be able to see clearly": so said Wallace Stevens. Stevens also said, in his preface to Williams' *Collected Poems*, that a Williams poem was "a little sentiment, very little, together with acute reaction" in the form of the "anti–poetic." The more I read Williams, the more useful I find these observations.

The questions below are, therefore, essentially "lens," "sentiment," and "anti–poetic" questions.

Williams is one poet whose work ought to be approached with some biographical knowledge: at least students should be aware that he was a practicing physician among the poor in Paterson, New Jersey, and that he was also profoundly interested in the visual arts and a friend of modern painters. It might also be worth having your students read Williams' very short story "Jean Beicke" (266-271) as a way of understanding more about the consciousness of the writer.

QUESTIONS

1. What does Williams make us see, feel, or taste in such poems as "The Red Wheelbarrow," "Young Woman at the Window," and "This Is Just to Say"? What circumstances make us see these things more clearly in Williams' poems than we would if we set out deliberately to see them ourselves?

In class discussion, it might be worth beginning with the second half of this question and telling the story of the circumstances under which Williams is said to have composed "The Red Wheelbarrow." He was in a house where a small girl he was treating was hanging between life and death when he looked out the window to see the scene the poem describes. Even if the particular story is apocryphal, its general tenor is right. Williams wrote a great deal of his poetry and prose in minutes stolen from a demanding medical practice. Many of his best early poems have the feeling of being snatched: they are moments of clarity, order, pattern suddenly come into focus despite (or, more likely, *because of*) Williams' involvement with a disorderly and sometimes ugly world.

In the case of "The Red Wheelbarrow," we have ordinary objects presented simply, so simply that they seem to glow. A great deal of effort has been expended trying to make these objects stand for general truths. The editor of a college literary magazine, for instance, sent Williams the following explication:

> So much depends upon
> The ovum and the sperm (chicken)
> Man's ingenuity (wheel)
> His labor (barrow)
> And the elements (rain)

The temptation to this sort of explication is created by the lens of the opening phrase: behind the phrase "so much depends/upon" all those objects look so large, so significant, that we want to make them more than they are. Williams enhances this effect by presenting each object in a separate stanza, and giving each noun a separate line: barrow, water, chickens. Each thing is seen fresh, one at a time, but with the relation between images made clear.

The same sort of separation and joining of images is seen in "Young Woman at the Window," a poem that directs the eye downward from the mother's face to the child's with a series of connections like those that connect figure to figure in a Renaissance painting. The movement, as in the painting, makes us notice the juxtaposition of figures: the woman crying and self-absorbed, the child, indifferent to her tears, pressing his face to the window to see what is happening outside. Once again, we are catching a fleeting glimpse of things through a window and trying to find what "depends" on these things, how they are connected to each other and to life.

Reed Whittemore points out that the sense of stolen glimpses, stolen experiences, runs through many Williams poems and is most perfectly expressed in "This Is Just to Say." Here Williams literally filches some fruit, probably from his own icebox, and writes a poem that could be a note of explanation to his wife, left on the kitchen table. The plums have a special savor, one feels, because they were *not* eaten for breakfast, as planned. Because they were eaten irregularly, on impulse, at an odd time, they could surprise the senses with their sweetness and coldness.

It is the nature of glimpses that one cannot set out deliberately to see them. Williams avoids any impression of deliberation.

2. How does Williams' use of the line affect our reading of "To a Poor Old Woman"?

The most spectacular effect comes in the repetitions of the same sentence in the second stanza. Because the line break creates a slight pause and gives extra emphasis to the initial word of the next line, we get a slightly different focus each time: first on the plums, "*They* taste good to her"; then on the old woman, "They taste good/*to her*"; then on the goodness, "They taste/*good* to her." "Comforted," hanging as its own line, also gets a special emphasis. And the effect of using the title both as a dedication and a first line is to plunge us immediately into the poem, slightly off guard.

Some of your students may be inclined to think that Williams and other free verse poets are merely writing prose and hacking it arbitrarily into lines. In "To a Poor Old Woman" the effects created by the lineation are plain enough that your skeptics can see them.

3. Explain the major images in "The Botticellian Trees" and "Queen-Ann's-Lace." How are they used in each poem? How are they related from poem to poem?

Many Williams poems avoid metaphor entirely and concentrate on the thing in itself, but here are two poems that are extended metaphors. "The Botticellian Trees" begins with a simple visual comparison: bare winter trees look like handwriting against the sky. Williams elaborates the metaphor with almost Metaphysical thoroughness. Lines 7–12 convert the

images to that of decorated letters in an illuminated manuscript. Lines 15–
24 shift the metaphor into the realm of grammar, where the straight
branches are like main clauses ("stript sentences") now being
"modified/by pinched–out/ifs of color, devout/conditions." I don't think I
am being entirely idiosyncratic when I think of diagramming sentences
here: the sentence diagram is very like a branch sprouting smaller
branches, such as *if*–clauses. In lines 25–30, the metaphor shifts and the
branches move as a woman's limbs move under a dress: a wonderful simile that captures the delayed swaying bounce of both leaves and skirts. In
31–33, it shifts once more, and the leaves are like a song above the words
written by the limbs.

In "Queen–Ann's–Lace," it is much harder to tell what is tenor and
what is vehicle. Is Williams describing a woman by comparing her to a
field taken over by wild carrot, or is he describing the field by comparing
it to a woman? The easy and standard answer is that the field is the vehicle and the woman (or the woman's desire) is the tenor. The poem may
be better, though, if we assume that "Her body" from the beginning refers
at least as much to the flower as to a woman. The exact visual detail about
the purple spot in the center of each hand–span–sized flower clearly starts
with an impulse to describe the flower. The idea of a purple blemish
where a man's hand has touched a woman's flesh is disturbingly erotic,
but never erases the primary picture of the flower. Call it tenor or call it
vehicle, the image of the flower is the magnetic part of the poem, and it
becomes a symbol of desire, nature, hardiness, and Williams' anti–poetic
sensibilities.

Stevens says that Williams ("This will horrify him") is a Romantic
poet. Certainly the imagery in these two poems and many others by
Williams is romantic; the budding and flowering might be compared to
what we find in Keats or Tennyson.

4. Can Williams' poems be defended against Robert Bly's charge that
they have "no inward life"?

I should say at the outset that Bly's attack on Williams is primarily an
attack on Williams' followers, and that the charge of "no inward life" is
displaced from them to him. But let's look at the case that Bly himself
chooses: "Between Walls." In a "poetic" world, a doctor would look out of
a hospital window, see a beautiful green lawn, and be unsurprised, un-
moved—though perhaps comforted. But in this "anti–poetic" world, the
doctor looks out on cinders and sees the broken pieces of a green bottle. "So
what?" your students may ask. The poem *can* be interpreted as a heartless
snapshot with the poet as "an immovable eye." We are not inclined to
interpret it this way for several reasons: the very fact that Williams wrote
the poem means that he felt moved to write; our experience with other
Williams poems leads us to suspect that he will find beauty and meaning
in unpoetic things; and the diction of the poem very subtly tells what
Williams is seeing. The spot is one "where/nothing/will grow"; the

pieces of grass are "green" and they "shine." There is hint enough here to allow us to reconstruct the Williams' moment of vision: One looks out the window expecting grass, realizes that the window opens on a cindered area between walls, and sees flashes of shining green every bit as satisfying to the eye as the grass would have been— more satisfying because less expected. It is precisely the "inward life" that makes a broken bottle in this poem better than a manicured lawn, equal to the flower of the wild carrot, and makes the flower of the wild carrot more beautiful than the rose.

If students will look at "The Yellow Flower," they will find a poem with "inward life" that Bly would surely acknowledge:

> I have found no cure
> for the sick
> but this crooked flower
> which only to look upon
> all men
> are cured.

Typically, the yellow flower is not a strapping rose raised in a sunny climate on a diet of bone meal and composted manure. It is a puny struggling thing (compare "Jean Beicke"). Beauty for Williams usually comes from the struggle of life to assert itself in strangling circumstances. (It might be worth noting that Williams wrote the poem in January, 1953, after suffering a stroke and in the grips of depression, typing it out painfully with one hand because the other was partly paralyzed.) Williams' comparison of the yellow flower to Michelangelo's *Slaves* gives us a perfect symbol of his own art. If you can bring a photo of these remarkable sculptures to class, your students will see the point quickly. The slaves are in no conventionally beautiful pose: their "beauty" comes from the tension of their struggle to escape.

–D.H.

Marianne Moore

Few poets have as definite a profile as Marianne Moore. We read many of her lines and think that only she could have written them. The call, for instance, for "imaginary gardens with real toads in them" is perfectly characteristic: the presence of an animal, the linkage of formality and freedom in the notion of a garden, the love of paradox. Perhaps her most distinctive characteristic is the precision of image that William Carlos Williams discusses in the Counterpoint. Each image is laid out like a white disc on a black table, with "almost no overlaying at all." Moore might be taught side–by–side with other poets (Williams, Eliot, and

Stevens, for example) who were affected by the imagist movement. It might be more interesting, however, to contrast her with other poets who have written about animals, including Christopher Smart, Dickinson, Hopkins, Frost, Rilke, Bogan, Neruda, Jarrell, Thomas, Wilbur, Bly, and Plath.

QUESTIONS

1. Moore has a reputation for the sort of precise detail we might expect to find in an article on natural history rather than in a poem. Where do you find this sort of detail?

This question appears merely as a way to draw students' attention to such expressions as

> the detached first claw on the foreleg corresponding
> to the thumb, retracted to its tip
> > ("Peter," 4–5)

> his eyes bisected by pupils of a pin's width
> > ("Peter," 21)

> . . . his forty–pound bough dinner
> > ("Elephants," 9)

> electrified alternate edges
> > oppositely charged . . .
> ("Four Quartz Crystal Clocks," 19–20)

Sometimes Moore's poetry sounds like an eccentric soundtrack of a nature film that she might have viewed at the Museum of Natural History. Imagine, for example, these sentences in a film: "Of the crow–blue mussel shells, one keeps adjusting the ash heaps; opening and shutting itself like an injured fan. Pink rice–grains, ink–bespattered jellyfish, crabs like green lilies, and submarine toadstools, slide each on the other." I suspect an audience would be mildly surprised by "keeps adjusting the ash heaps" but would they think that they had been exposed to poetry unaware?

2. What separates Moore's poetry from prose?

Here is a question that might grow out of the previous one. The most obvious answer and perhaps the weakest is the presence of meter and rhyme. Moore's meter, when she uses one, is syllabic: she counts the number of syllables to a line and ignores the stresses, a system so idiosyncratic that to ears trained to other meters, it hardly counts as a meter at all. Her rhymes are interesting. Elizabeth Bishop, who knew her well, reported that Moore was "against rhyme in principal" but that she was delighted, for instance, by Ogden Nash's

> I love the Baby Giant Panda;
> I'd welcome one to my veranda.

She used a rhyming dictionary, called it "indispensable," in fact, but her most characteristic rhymes are not likely to be found in such a dictionary:

> time/proxime/crime ("Four Quartz Crystal Clocks," 44, 46, 48)
> full/eagle ("The Frigate Pelican," 35–36)
> swiftness/crevices ("The Fish," 13–14)
> (can) live/revive ("The Fish," 38–39)

Her rhymes are sometimes on exotic words, sometimes on unstressed syllables ("light rhyme"), sometimes half–rhymes.

In a poem like "Peter," neither metered nor rhymed, the richness of sound is something that we don't find in most prose. The same lines that we cite for prosaic detail we might cite for meshing of sound:

> the detached first claw on the foreleg corresponding
> to the thumb, retracted to its tip

Here we have alliteration (*f*irst, *f*oreleg; *c*law, *c*orresponding), consonance (re*t*rac*t*ed to i*t*s *t*ip), and combination of assonance and alliteration in adjacent words (*foreleg corre*sponding). In

> his eyes bisected by pupils of a pin's width

we have abundant assonance and consonance, and in lines like

> To leap, to lengthen out, divide the air, to purloin, to pursue (43)

sound almost seems more important than sense.

But the sound effects of Moore's poems really don't lie much outside the range of normal prose. The more considerable poetry is in her imagery, and particularly her metaphors. Again, let's concentrate on "Peter." In lines 4–10 alone, we have five metaphors: eyebrows like fronds or like katydid legs, whiskers like shadbones or porcupine–quills, a body flattened by gravity as seaweed is flattened by the sun.

3. What is the effect of the metaphors in "Elephants"?

One effect (I hope your students will come up with others) is to blur the line between humans and elephants. Elephants are compared to knights

templar (10), gray pilgrims (28), temples (33), prisoners (42),
philosophers (47, 60), and soldiers (59). People are compared to frogs (18),
elephants (21), and gnats (36). In one intricate passage (47-51), an
elephant is compared to Sophocles and Sophocles is compared to a bee. All
of these metaphors can be seen as illustrations of the theme stated in lines
57-58: "These knowers 'arouse the feeling that they are/allied to man' and
can change roles with their trustees."

4. What is the theme of "Four Quartz Crystal Clocks"?

The poem is peculiar enough to make a straightforward question about it
an interesting contrast. I think the concluding lines ". . . that punctual-
ity/is not a crime" come close to being a statement of the theme, though
the poem expands "punctuality" to include many other forms of precision,
particularly precision in language in lines 27–35. Moore enjoys herself
immensely in this poem: parading out exotic zoological names that might
have come out of Lewis Carroll (*aye–aye, angwan–tibo, potto, loris*), and
managing to drag in two spoonerisms (*bell–boy/buoy balls; glass
eyes/eyeglasses*). About one of these, Elizabeth Bishop tells a story that shows
us something about Moore's habit of filling a poem with bright images
and sounds gathered almost at random:

> I had been asked by a friend to bring her three glass buoy–balls in
> nets, sometimes called "witch balls," from Cape Cod. When I arrived
> at the old hotel where I lived, a very old porter took them with my
> bag, and as I watched him precede me down the corridor, I said to
> myself, "The bellboy with the buoy–balls." I liked the sound of this so
> much that in my vanity I repeated the phrase to Marianne a day or so
> later.

The humor of having "the sea/–side burden" (a play, I think, on *burden*
as *load* and as *theme*) "embarrass" (*disconcert* and *complicate*) the bell–boy
with the buoy–bells gets us into a deep linguistic thicket, but even Moore's
ambiguities are precise, so it is not surprising to find that she has written
a poem in defense of precision.

5. What are some examples of Moore's talent for aphorism?

Moore's ability to chisel a phrase shows in such expressions as these:

When one is frank, one's very presence is a compliment.
                                                                ("Peter," 36)

an animal with claws should have an opportunity to use them
                                                                ("Peter," 40)

Who rides a tiger can never dismount;
Asleep on an elephant, that is repose.
                ("Elephants," 63–4)

. . . imaginary gardens with real toads in them . . .
                ("Poetry," 31)

"Silence" is a poem largely about aphorism and made up of examples of the ability to make the generalization precise that is so characteristic of Moore. It is characteristic of Moore, too, that a poem about masterful speech should be called "Silence."

–D.H.

T. S. Eliot

Like Blake and Yeats, Eliot writes poetry that involves a symbolic system that most of your students will not be particularly familiar with. The difference is that Eliot's symbolic system is not a personal mythology, but the Western literary, religious, and cultural tradition embodied in such writers as Virgil, Dante, and St. John Perse. The density of Eliot's allusions to great writers of the past presents a potential problem to the teacher, since a thorough understanding of the underpinnings of a poem like "The Hollow Men" or "Journey of the Magi" would require a short course in the humanities. Even the apparently simpler "La Figlia che Piange" has its share of complexities: the epigraph from Virgil is Aeneas' address to Venus; "La Figlia che Piange" is the name of a Greek stele Eliot had tried to find in a museum in northern Italy in 1911; the reader who knows these things sees the encounter of the man and woman as imaginary, Eliot's posing of a model in a classical stance. But the reader who does not recognize the allusions will not see the poem the same way.

The best way through this difficulty in an introductory class may be that a professor of mine used in teaching "The Waste Land." He said that he hoped some of us would eventually spend many rewarding hours uncovering the layers of allusion in the poem, but that we should *begin* by viewing it as a brilliant collection of images that speak for themselves.

QUESTIONS

1. Paraphrase "Animula" in a way that clearly shows the psychological stages the soul passes through. How is this psychological development typical of Eliot's view of human life in other poetry? [And, if your students have read Wordsworth, how does it compare with his views?]

The poem can be divided into nine parts:

1. Lines 1–3 give us the world of the infant, unable yet to interpret the data of his senses and to assemble it into objects with three dimensions.

2. Lines 4–10 give us the world of the toddler, moving under tables and chairs, responding to objects and people, easily frightened, easily reassured, well attuned to the pleasures of the natural world.

3. Lines 11–12 give us the world of the child just developing an aesthetic sense and a curiosity about patterns.

4. Lines 13–15 give us the world of a child who can respond to language and story, and for whom the magic of language is unhampered by any need to check for objective truth. Line 15 ends a description of childhood's unsullied pleasures.

5. Lines 16–20 give us the world of schooling, formal or informal, in which the child is forced to distinguish truth ("is") from wish or appearance ("seems"), to learn to obey, and to learn to suppress desires.

6. Lines 21–23 give us the world of adolescence, where the child, becoming aware of the gulf between dreams and reality, escapes into the world of books, of impersonal knowledge.

7. Lines 24–31 give us the end of life, the world of late adulthood, senescence, and death.

Your students should notice two things at this point. First, the pattern is symmetrical. For 15 lines, the soul gains strength and capacity for delight; for 15 lines, it declines until it leaves "disordered papers in a dusty room." Then it begins a second life after the viaticum. The second thing your students should notice is that all of young adulthood is left out of the cycle, all the world of productive work and action. Therefore,

8. Lines 32–36 give us the alternative to this cycle, lives of action, speed, power, greed, violence, danger, and premature death (Hence, the echo of the traditional prayer, "Pray for us *sinners* now and in the hour of our death.")

9. Line 37 can be read two ways, at least. If the birth is the second birth (into eternal life—compare line 31), then it may mean the same thing as the traditional prayer. In the hour of death we finally come to life: a very Eliotish notion. If the birth is the first birth (my own interpretation) then the line must be read in a way that contrasts "us" with Guiterriez and the

others. Mary can intervene for *them* at the hour of *death*; she must "Pray for
US in the hour of our BIRTH."

Obviously, "Animula" has in it the major themes of all of Eliot's poetry.
There is the interest in the psychology of, as Yeats says, "men and women
that get out of bed or into it from mere habit." There is the contrast of
"lost/violent souls" ("Hollow Men," 15–16). There is the inversion of life
and death. It is perhaps worth pointing out to your class that it is
characteristic of Eliot to start out with the paraphrase from Dante, one of
his principal touchstones in the world of letters.

The comparison to Wordsworth can be made most completely by a look
at the Intimations Ode. Wordsworth has a more theological explanation
of the disorientation of the infant and the young child (they are souls
filled with the more perfect knowledge of eternity, blinking in this
strange, imperfect world). He notes much the same decline in joy, though
it descends later and is more amply compensated for by the philosophic
mind. Eliot is (if I may say this without seeming to denigrate) always
pushing a thesis opposite to that Whitman pushes: he is always trying to
show us that neither the external world nor the psychological world can
satisfy us until we commit ourselves to some basis of belief.

2. The critic Leonard Unger once compared an Eliot poem to a series of
slides projected on a screen, each slide "an isolated, fragmentary image,
producing its own effect, including suggestions of some larger action or
situation of which it is but an arrested moment." Discuss "The Hollow
Men" or "The Love Song of J. Alfred Prufrock" in light of this comment.

"The Hollow Men" is so filled with images of futility that one could
start almost anywhere. Let's focus on one image that has been brilliantly
explicated by Helen Gardner:

> The eyes are not here
> There are no eyes here
> In this valley of dying stars
> In this hollow valley
> The broken jaw of our lost kingdoms
>   (52–56)

The eyes in the poem are a troublesome image, probably related to
Canto XXX of Dante's *Purgatorio*, where Beatrice recalls her influence on
Dante's youth: "I led him, showing him my youthful eyes,/Along with
me upon the proper path." Let's let them stand for now as a symbol of
redemption and concentrate on that metaphor within a metaphor, the
comparison of the valley to "the broken jaw of our lost kingdoms. Gardner
points out that the image suggests

♦ the deadness and dryness of life
♦ the inability to communicate, or the lack of things to say
♦ the separation of our life (the jaw) from participation in the life of
the universe (the whole body)
♦ the problem of trying to reconstruct the whole life (our lost kingdoms) from the evidence of this one bone, just as the paleontologist
must reconstruct the whole creature from a fossilized fragment.

Having your students try similar interpretations of such images as the
dried voices (5), rats' feet (9), broken column (22), crossed staves (33), and
stone images (40) may lead to some irresponsible speculation, but will give
you a good chance to guide their reading of Eliot.

In teaching Prufrock, you will find equally pregnant images in

the etherized patient (3)
the insidious streets (8)
the cat–like fog (14)
the insect on a pin (57)
the ragged claws (73)
the eternal Footman (86)
the attendant lord (113)
the mermaids (125)

You may be able to stir up a good class discussion by having students explain how these images help convey the speaker's mental state, though I've
found that it is best to start by asking students to characterize Prufrock.
Teaching the poem can be a great pleasure: I've never had it fail or seen it
fail in a class filled with reasonably bright and eager students. The key is
to let students know that here, if anywhere, Yeats' characterization of Eliot
as a satirist is valid. The very name J. Alfred Prufrock is something that
might have come out of Dickens: it is a splendid label for a character who
combines pomposity and lack of imagination. Once students see the
comedy in the poem, they are ready to appreciate both its underlying seriousness and the brilliance of its imagery.

4. Is "Journey of the Magi" essentially an optimistic or a pessimistic poem?

I think this is another way of asking the question, "Is the spiritual state
of the protagonist better than that of the hollow men, or worse?" Eliot's
most optimistic poems are not exactly giddy, of course: a critic once
observed that even when Eliot seems most confident of the salvation that
awaits him as a Christian "nearly every line is written while looking
into the eyes of the demon."

Those who want to argue that the poem is pessimistic will point out that
all of the three landscapes presented are somehow wrong. In their native
land, the Magi have summer palaces, sherbets, and silken girls—all very

civilized, but very self–indulgent—and the people clutch their gods like possessions. In the hard lands between the Magi's home and Bethlehem we find something like the dry landscape of "The Hollow Men," and the natives are unfriendly thieves, self–indulgent without civilization. In Bethlehem, the first sight we see are three trees that presage the three crosses on Calvary; the first people, six ruffians gambling as the soldiers at the foot of the cross will eventually cast dice to divide the garments of Christ. And when the Magi finally find Christ, they experience his birth as a death. The only effect of knowing that the divine event has occurred is to make them feel more wretched than before, worse off for living the old life with an impotent awareness that somewhere there should be a new life. In fact, one could argue that the effect of this long winter journey was to take men with adventurous spirits and great courage, and turn them into Prufrocks. The speaker is now, like the hollow men, living in a premature death and longing for a real death.

Of course, I think this argument is finally wrong–headed. The descent into the valley around Bethlehem is a descent into the new life. The Magi come from the barrenness of an idol–worshipping culture, through a dry, cold, bitter land. When they arrive at the valley, they find it temperate, wet (water and life are often linked in Eliot), verdant. The three trees remind us of Calvary, but Calvary can be a symbol of triumph rather than defeat, and the white horse may remind us of the one Christ rides in triumph in the book of Revelation (chapters 6 and 9). The ruffians are there, of course: Bethlehem is part of the real world. The speaker may long for death, but in line 33 he says the crucial words "I would do it again."

Very often in Eliot we find characters who seem to have no purchase on life, nothing firm that they can plant their foot on. Prufrock wonders whether it would have "been worth while . . . To have squeezed the universe into a ball/To roll it toward some overwhelming question" (91–94). The Magus may not know how to live in the new dispensation, but he knows it would be worthwhile. He points the way to something greater, a way out.

–D.H.

Edna St. Vincent Millay

Millay's great popularity in her lifetime has not been followed by a great deal of recognition from the literary establishment. To some degree this is because of weaknesses in her poetry that Louise Bogan notes in the counterpointed review. But I have a feeling that the Millay underground following is large enough to force some reappraisal. Several friends, when I mentioned my inclination to put in a cluster of her poems, told me rather breathlessly that they hoped I would. They had been closet ad-

mirers of her for years, they said, and then began to name their favorite
poems.

I suspect that the uneven state of Millay's reputation comes from a tendency for her poetry to strike a posture. Millay was in her generation a
symbol of the liberated woman: "the female Byron." She was active in the
literary, theatrical, and political life of Greenwich Village, bold and open
about her personal life, quite incapable of being bowled over or swept away.
Very often her poems manage to combine tenderness with a tough, ironic
stance. One feels sometimes that she writes with a consciousness that she
is defining a new type of American woman.

QUESTIONS

1. What is Millay's chief virtue as a poet?

Some of your students may admire Millay's ability to build to an effect
in the last line that simultaneously snaps the poem shut and opens out its
meaning. She certainly manages this effect in "Love is Not All," where
the poem's long resistance to clichés makes the understated "I do not
think I would" stronger than an Elizabethan hyperbole. "Recuerdo" lulls
us to sleep with its predictability until the last line gives us a gesture both
unexpected and credible. Others end just as strongly. Some of your students
may like the rhythms of one or two of the poems or, if they are aware of
the often servile tone of women's love poetry before Millay, the relative
toughness of her attitudes.

My own nominee for chief virtue is the frequency with which a sharp
image, tactile as often as visual, gets introduced without being obscured by
poetic diction:

>   . . . the redness
> Of little leaves opening stickily
>   ("Spring," 3–4)

> The sun is hot on my neck as I observe
> The spikes of the crocus
>   ("Spring," 6–7)

> . . . lazily fondled the fingers of their alert enemies
>   ("Modern Declaration," 5)

> . . . in the wood knee–deep with snow the only
> colored thing
>   ("Oak Leaves," 12)

> Your arms get tired, and the back of your neck gets tight
> ("An Ancient Gesture," 5)

2. Which poems seem most subject to Louise Bogan's criticism that they are "childish" or "charming"? Which suggest a sturdier "spiritual fibre"?

The point of this question is certainly not to insist that your students accept Louise Bogan's frame of reference, but that they attempt to come to grips with it, something they will find easier to do if they take time to look at Bogan's own poetry. Bogan is one tough customer, ready to express a grief (to use Frost's distinction from page 908), but not a mere grievance. If we compare her "To My Brother" with Millay's "Spring," we get a sense of the difference between the two poets.

The problem from Bogan's perspective (if I understand her correctly) with such poems as "Spring," "Recuerdo," "Modern Declaration," and "Love is Not All" is that they are too prettily posed, too rhetorical. They have a sense of deliberate rhetorical flair about them. A prolonged apostrophe to Spring, for instance, complaining that it cannot defeat death seems a bit slender from a twentieth–century poet. So, too, do love poems that express only two things about the poet's thought and personality: I am in love, and I'm alert enough to know that that brings me to the edge of cliché, so I'll be clever. These are surely the sort of poems Bogan had in mind when she praised Millay's lyrical ability but found she lacked depth.

Among the poems Bogan singled out for praise when she reviewed *Wine from These Grapes* were "From a Train Window" and "Oak Leaves." What I think Bogan saw in them was a decreased cock–sureness of attitude and an increased attention to the inner life. Both sound like the work of someone who has stopped complaining about death and is trying to see whether there is in her soul and in the external world any evidence that the fact of mortality might be endurable. It was easy at one point for Millay to pronounce Spring a blind idiot, perhaps because she was young enough and strong enough not really to feel what despair should lie behind that conclusion, but now she wants to consider the possibility that "the earth might know what it is about." "From a Train Window" gives us a world of long, unhurried rhythms, one in which things take care of themselves impersonally. One is reminded of the third chapter of Ecclesiastes: "To every thing there is a season, and a time to every purpose under the heaven. A time to be born, and a time to die. A time to plant, and a time to pluck up that which is planted." "Oak Leaves" could be an answer to "From a Train Window," a poem that resents death, but not with quite so green a gesture as "Spring." In "Oak Leaves" Millay admits that she is a "ten o'clock scholar" in learning to deal with death, that she identifies with the leaves that have boasted "that they would never die,/Never even grow old," that cling onto the tree all through the winter, "the only coloured thing." There is something of the old posing here, but there is also more thoughtfulness. (I think, by the way, that "Spring" is a more successful lyric; as Housman points out a gain in thought is not necessarily a gain in poetry.)

"An Ancient Gesture" is a more mature poem still, but I save it for question 3.

3. Which of the poems collected here shows Millay at her best? Which shows her at her worst?

I'll give my worst first, with the caveat that I wouldn't have included the poem if I didn't like it. "Recuerdo" seems to me to be a one–line poem: that is, the very patterned and ingeniously rhythmic early lines are frothy and without interest. "And YOU ate an APple, and I ate a PEAR": She CAN write in ANapests, WHY should we CARE? The final line, which skips along lightly on four stresses, gives the poem a brightness because of the unexpected and thoroughly right gesture of two lucky people giving all their money away, but remembering to hold back their subway fares.

I think "An Ancient Gesture" the best of the Millay poems, because it uses her strength with last lines but doesn't rely on it excessively. Here almost every line gets us somewhere interesting. "Penelope did this too" connects three millennia of women's lives (and human lives) without fuss or fanfare. "And more than once" gives us a sense of perspective: Penelope was a woman who endured something extraordinary, worse than most of us will ever know. The physical fatigue of the weaving and undoing is an unexpected and worthwhile detail. That string of words— "authentic, antique,/In the very best tradition, classic, Greek"—applied to so homely a gesture surprises and convinces us simultaneously. The distinction between Ulysses' rhetorical tears and Penelope's real ones is precisely the distinction between Millay's weak poems and her strong ones, and we feel the weight of experience behind it. Formally, the rhyme scheme works superbly. The rhyme of "cried" with "implied" is not telegraphed by an absolutely regular rhyme scheme, but it is prepared for. And how well it contrasts a disingenuous use of an emotion with the emotion itself.

–D.H.

Wilfred Owen

Though recent scholarship has somewhat dimmed Owen's high reputation, he is still the seminal English–speaking poet of protest against the horrors of twentieth–century warfare, and a great influence on such later figures as W. H. Auden and Stephen Spender. The pattern of an Owen war poem is typically a contrast: the horrors of war set against man's unwarlike nature or the hollowness of military and patriotic rhetoric. Predictable as it is, it can be terribly effective: "Arms and the Boy," "Dulce et

Decorum," and "Anthem for Doomed Youth" are among the most familiar poems in the language.

It is arguable that these poems exhaust the subject, that the gas warfare
of "Dulce et Decorum" and the multiple amputation of "Disabled" reveal
all the horror that our nervous systems can absorb. But if we look at the
collection of war poems assembled here, we see surprising range and
variation: war, like death, seems an inexhaustible topic.

QUESTIONS

1. How are Owen's "Dulce et Decorum" and Albizzi's "Prolonged Sonnet"
alike, and how are they different?

The poems are surprisingly similar to have been written 600 years apart
and in different countries and languages. The pattern is certainly not
created by any familiarity (Owen would never have read the obscure
Albizzi) but by a sad truth about wars in all centuries: that they raise up
armies of hopeful young men and often return them ruined. This sad
truth lends itself to the rhetorical pattern both poets use: if the soldiers and
their friends, families, and lovers knew *then* what they know *now* . . .
Both poets devote most of their poems to a graphic description of the state of
unhappy soldiers. In fact, the first eight lines of Owen's poem can be
compared very precisely with Albizzi. There is the same weariness of
footsoldiers stumbling past the point of exhaustion: "Men marched asleep
. . . Drunk with fatigue," says Owen; and "men march throughout the
night,/stumbling, for hunger, on their marrowbones," says Albizzi.
There is the same loss of equipment and clothing: "Many had lost their
boots/But limped on, blood–shod," says Owen; and "nothing on their
backs, or heads, or feet," says Albizzi. To this point, the soldiers might
almost have been in the same battle.

The horror of the gas attack is the principal difference between the two
poems, of course. Here is a genuinely novel horror of war, and Owen presents it in graphic images: the green sea of gas, the white eyes writhing,
the jolt of the wagon that brings the bitter blood gargling from the lungs.
Owen doesn't let up; he makes us see it, feel it, taste it.

This difference your students will quickly see. They may be slower to see
a difference in tone between the two poems, but I think it is there, and
reflects another historical change. Both poems have an ironic tone, but
Owen's irony is dark and humorless. The tone of Albizzi's sonnet is not
cheerful, but there is an element in it that approaches humor. The soldiers
are a sight worth reporting to Albizzi's "fair brother," but they are not
"we." Albizzi does not either identify closely with the soldiers or address
his poem bitterly to the people who sent them off to war by telling them
"The old Lie." When he supposes that "They [now] thought their haste in
going [off to the war] all too fleet," he seems to be smiling at their
naiveté. To finish the poem by saying that each soldier is "as silent as a

man being shaved" is to add a comparison both exact and rather light–hearted. War in Albizzi's time (and to some degree in Rossetti's) may have been terrible, but it was a terror generally visited on small armies of volunteers or mercenaries: not everyone needed to be caught up in it. Owen was writing in a new era of warfare, where men would be conscripted or shamed into service in such numbers that no one could stand on the sidelines and feel uninvolved.

2. How are "Arms and the Boy" and "More Light! More Light!" alike?

Once again the similarity is rhetorical: both poems use contrasts. Owen's contrast is between the grim implements of war and the body of a boy. The contrast is extraordinarily well crafted. The supple fingers of the boy are matched with the cold steel of the bayonet–blade. His teeth, "for laughing round an apple," are matched with the "fine zinc teeth" of the cartridges in their belt. Clearly this body is not made to come into contact with these implements. If God had intended it (so the logic of the poem goes), the boy would have claws, talons, antlers: at least the weapons He gives to animals made to fight.

Hecht's poem does not appeal to natural law, but instead contrasts states of civilization and barbarism. The first twelve lines allude to any (or all) of several incidents in which men were executed with astonishing brutality because of their religious beliefs. Chidiock Tichborne, hanged, drawn, and quartered at age 18 after writing his famous elegy "with his own hand in the Tower before his execution" comes to mind. So do the Protestant martyrs Latimer and Ridley, burned to death in 1555. Latimer's dying words were "Be of good comfort, Master Ridley, and play the man: we shall this day light such a candle by God's grace in England as I trust shall never be put out." Having contrasted English barbarism with the courage and faith of English martyrs, Hecht turns to Germany. There he tells of an incident that, he says elsewhere, he read about in Eugen Kogon's *The Theory and Practice of Hell.* The incident happens at Buchenwald, within a few miles of Weimar, long associated with the great poet Goethe. It is no more terrible than the execution of Latimer, but as terrible, and the contrasts are similar. The Pole matches Ridley's saintliness ("But he did refuse"); Goethe more than matches the civilization of Raleigh and Tichborne.

By joining incidents from two countries and two centuries, Hecht's poem, surely the stronger of the two, makes us feel the universality of the struggle between violence and peace, barbarism and civilization.

3. How does the approach taken by Rimbaud and Davidman differ from that taken by Owen, Hecht, and Levertov?

Owen, Hecht, and Levertov all overwhelm us with poems that present the horrors of war dramatically and graphically. In the case of Owen and

Hecht, this directness is cushioned somewhat by the formality of the verse; Levertov gives us undiluted horror and unabashed rhetoric. Rimbaud and Davidman are more subtle; they try to make us feel the violence at one remove. Rimbaud does this by presenting an idyllic scene spoiled at last by the fact that the only person in it has two red holes in his right side and is dead. Davidman's poem, written in reaction to the Nationalist bombings of Madrid in 1937 (bombing of cities was then a new tactic), keeps the violence still more removed. The bombs never appear in the poem, and so the reader is forced to supply them.

Your class may get into a worthwhile discussion of whether restraint or excess is preferable and whether any of the poems we are looking at goes too far in either direction.

4. What is the tone of "Channel Firing"?

Your students will see at once that the tone of Hardy's poem is much different from the tone of Levertov's or any of Owen's. Hardy disengages himself enough to play with what was surely a cliché in his time as it is in ours: "making enough noise to wake the dead." And what would the dead say, and what would God say back? This sounds at first like the stuff of which stand-up comedy is made. I would encourage my students to see the comedy. It is definitely present in the parson's comment that if *this* is what people are going to behave like after all the sermons he preached, he wishes he'd have "stuck to pipes and beer." But the poem becomes more serious in the last stanza, when time opens up and we think of Stourton tower, Camelot, and Stonehenge—each a symbol of an earlier military power, an earlier invasion. The recurrence of war and its ultimate futility now come into the poem in earnest.

–D.H.

E. E. Cummings

Cummings' use of typography is so interesting that I have put in as Counterpoints poems that will allow you to open up a discussion of the concrete appearance of the poem on the page. None of these poems are merely sight-gags, of course, and all can lead to good discussions.

At the same time, I've tried to avoid reinforcing the too-common impression that what makes Cummings interesting is newfangled packaging. In some ways, it is his commitment to traditional lyricism that makes him unusual among the poets of his generation. He did not intellectualize or temper his exuberance or his contempt or his anger. He frankly loved the formal: old forms or new. In all this he might remind one of a sixteenth-century poet rather than a twentieth-century innovator.

"i sing of Olaf glad and big," not discussed in the questions below, is a
poem that will pump adrenaline into any class.

QUESTIONS

1. How many patterns can you discover in "All in green went my love
riding"?

Surely among the purest lyrics in the book, "all in green" is a nested
set of sound patterns. Conscious study of these patterns may help your students understand the unconscious appeal of the poem. The first thing students need to do is to recognize the stanzas, which are longer units than
the spacing of the poem would indicate. Essentially, we have three stanzas
of 10 lines, followed by a half–stanza of 5. This makes the proportions of
the poem identical to that of a Shakespearian sonnet (10/10/10/5 versus
4/4/4/2). Using L to indicate an alliterated syllable, A to indicated an assonance, X to indicate an unpatterned syllable, and upper case to indicate
stress, we can describe the base pattern for the stanzas this way:

L x L went my LOVE RIDing

X x x X x DOWN

INto the SILver DAWN

four lean hounds crouched LOW and SMILing
[see comment below on stress in this line]

the X (x) X (x) RAN beFORE   [or SANG be FORE]

Xer be THEY than L x L

the L L DEER

the L L DEER

four X X at a X X x

the A x A x SANG beFORE

Obviously the second and third stanzas (lines 11–30) are closer to the
base pattern than the first stanza or the last half–stanza, but even these are
very close. In addition to repetitions of elements in the pattern, there are
patterns within elements. The line "four lean hounds crouched low and
smiling" is a beautifully knit collection of liquids (*l*- and *r*-sounds), labi-

als (*n*'s and *m*'s), semi–vowels (the *w*–sound in *crouched* and *low*), and variations on the *o*–sound. In fact, "lean hounds crouched low" is so inter-connected with sound that it becomes a unit (hence difficult to scan or even to parse; crouched could be a verb or a participle): the aural blending makes this team of smiling hounds particularly menacing, a destructive machine. Compare "four thin dogs running in a crouch and panting."

Another way of looking at the poem is to put the fixed pattern in the background and attend only to the foregrounded variations, assuming that they are the "content" of the individual stanzas:

All in green/[on a great] horse of [gold]///merry deer/Fleeter . . . dappled dreams/swift sweet/red rare/red roebuck . . . white water/cruel bugle.

Horn at Hip/echo///level meadows/Softer . . . slippered sleep/lean lithe/fleet flown/fleet does . . . gold valley/famished arrow.

Bow at belt/mountain///sheer peaks/Paler . . . daunting death/sleek slim/tall tense/tall stags . . . green mountain/lucky hunter.

All in green/[on a great] horse of [gold]///my heart [fell dead]

The content pattern here is

equipped thus/riding over this///riding toward this/simile with deer as tenor/adjectives/adjectives/repetition of first adjective from previous line, plus a synonym for deer, plus a color and a landscape/the hunter or a metonym for him.

Before leaving the "content" pattern it might be worth noting how one stanza is linked to another. The last element of the first stanza is the cruel bugle, and the next stanza begins with the word *horn* and concentrates on sound throughout. The last element of the second stanza is the famished arrow, and the next stanza begins with the word *bow*, and concentrates on images of death. The last element of the third stanza is the hunter, giving us a sense that the variations have run their course.

Having your class work out some of the patterns can help students see and admire the intricacy of Cummings' poem and hear things they might otherwise have missed. It may also strike some of them as a bit of pedantry, so you might want to round the discussion of this poem out by playing for them Peter Schickele's setting of this poem to music, which you can find on Joan Baez's *Baptism* album. Here all those wonderful sound patterns come to life and everyone gets a clearer sense of the relation be-tween lyric poetry and song.

2. How is Cummings' use of typography in "r–p–o–p–h–e–s–s–a–g–r" different from his use of typography in "In Just–" and "Buffalo Bill's"?

In "In Just–" and "Buffalo Bill's" the typography is used to indicate the stress and pace of the voice. It is analogous to musical notation. The effect is most obvious when Cummings uses speedups and slowdowns in close proximity:

> the queer
> old balloonman whistles
> far and   wee
> and   bettyandisbel come dancing
>
> from hop–scotch and jump–rope and
>
> it's
> spring
> and

Your students might want to consider here the relative duration of some four–syllable passages: "far and wee/and," "bettyandisbel," "and/it's/spring/and." The speed of "bettyandisbell" tells us at once that where you find one girl you find the other: their names have grown together in the talk of the neighborhood. The speeding up and slowing down imitates the speech of a child so excited that he is breathless, and occasionally overwhelmed by it all, so that the refrain "it's spring" breaks in wide–eyed on a train of thought. Still, it is probably wrong to assume that the poem is a literal imitation of speech: like "All in green" it is a pattern with variations.

In "Buffalo Bill's," too, the typography is used to establish the pace and emphasis of speech. The way that lines 6–8 rattle through the clay pigeons and then pause for emphasis on "Jesus" is as precise a score for reading as one could imagine.

In "r–p–o–p–h–e–s–s–a–g–r" we have something entirely different. Now the point is not to imitate the rhythms of lively speech, but to impede them. "Straightened out" the poem might be

> Grasshopper
>
> who, as we look, [is] now gathering up
>   into a (the) leap, leaps!
> arriving to become, rearrangingly,
>   grasshopper.

The translation misses everything important about the poem, which in the original version reproduces the jumpy movement, energy, and akimbo anatomy of the creature, plus the uncertainty of our vision of it when we are trying to bring the pieces of our impression together. It would be worth some class time to have your students try reading this poem as it is written. It is impossible, of course, to do so. The attempt may reveal that some of the rearrangements of the word *grasshopper* produce sounds like the dry rattle of a grasshopper in motion, but for the most part it will create pure frustration until the reader gets to the last line and at last can see and say the word completely. This impression that our sense of the creature only gets fully organized after some struggle is what gets lost in translation.

3. How does "Somewhere i have never travelled, gladly beyond" reveal both Cummings' traditionalism and his innovativeness?

Sometimes because of oddities of typography and syntax, students see only innovation in Cummings. In many ways this poem is a very traditional love poem, directly descended from Petrarch and company. Certainly the connection of spring with love or the lover with an opening rose is hardly innovative, and such oxymorons as "intense fragility" are common enough in poems about love, which has its own contradictions (compare the "sweet moan" in "La Belle Dame sans Merci"). What is unusual in this poem is not the typography or the grammar, but the complete abandon with which Cummings personifies nature. The flower imagining "the snow carefully everywhere descending" is a personification imagining a lovely personification. The astonishing last line has us imagining a raindrop with tiny hands that can open rosebuds, and then imagining a lover with smaller hands still.

–D.H.

Eugenio Montale

Despite Montale's great stature in twentieth–century literature (symbolized by his Nobel Prize in 1975), he is not a figure with whom every literature teacher is familiar. Here is the briefest of briefings for those of you who may be coming to his work without much background in the Italian literature of this century. Montale appeared on the Italian literary scene when Gabriele D'Annunzio (1863–1938) was clearly the predominant force. D'Annunzio, an ardent nationalist and militarist, wrote sweeping and enormously popular lyric poetry, considered himself a sort of superman, and (not surprisingly) was a favorite of Benito Mussolini. Tennyson might be the English–language poet who most closely approximates the sort of popularity D'Annunzio enjoyed; the poets are also comparable for the lushness of their verse and their tendency to write confident "public" poetry (think of *Idylls of the King* or "The Charge of the Light Brigade" rather than *In Memoriam*).

Montale's spirit was in almost every respect opposed to D'Annunzio's. He was never a nationalist in politics or literature. He generally avoided public pronouncements on affairs of state: his brief period of political activity in post–war Italy ended in disenchantment with both the Communists ("red clerics") and Christian Democrats ("black clerics"). His poetry explores the spiritual dimension of his private life in a way that some (desiring more rhetorical poetry for a politically turbulent era) attacked as incomprehensible, "hermetic."

Montale was an admirer of T. S. Eliot, and like Eliot attempts to connect the private life with the large symbols of the culture. Dante looms largest in Montale, and for the purpose of reading the poems collected here, we can get tremendous mileage out of one image in *Purgatorio* XXX: that of Beatrice with her "youthful eyes" putting Dante "upon the proper path." For Montale as for Dante, earthly love was an emblem of divine love. Montale's poems present several women who occupy the role of Beatrice, but the most important is Clizia, an idealization of the American Dante scholar Irma Brandeis, whom Montale met in Florence before World War II. Irma Brandeis's last name can be divided into parts meaning (in German) a flaming torch (*brand*) and ice (*eis*). Montale, following the practice of the troubadours of thirteenth–century Provence, includes in his poems "senhals," signs referring to the name and character of the beloved: flames, flashes, and gleams often announce the spiritual presence of Clizia/Brandeis. The name Clizia also has an association with brilliance: in classical mythology she is a woman beloved of the sun who is eventually transformed into a sunflower. Connected with Clizia as a symbol is the *iride*, a word that in Italian can mean "iris" (the flower) or "iris" (the eye) or "rainbow." If your students will learn to watch in Montale's poems for the appearance of the signs of Clizia, they will find that the poems take on new meaning.

QUESTIONS

1. Explain the meaning of the last three lines of "The Wall."

Or, to put it another way, "How is life like following a wall lined with the shards of broken bottles?" If you don't live in a community where the tops of fences are lined with broken bottles, you need to explain that it is fairly common in Europe to set broken bottles, sharp side up, in a layer of concrete at the top of a fence instead of using a strand of barbed wire to serve the same purpose. Montale pictures himself standing in the shadow of such a wall, surrounded by the sounds and sights of nature, but not (as Wordsworth might have been) inspired or consoled. He is "absorbed and pale" and in the end feels "melancholy wonder" rather than joy. Why?

Surely because the wall is unclimbable and apparently endless: "life and its travail is in this following a wall." What is on the other side that he should be so anxious to get to it? That is, of course, the unanswerable question. Students who want to tie every word of a poem down to a concrete meaning will be frustrated by this little poem, whose meaning is an emotion, really. Montale, like T. S. Eliot, was a searcher for the "objective correlative"—the "set of objects, a situation, a chain of events which shall be the formula of . . . [a] particular emotion." In this early poem, Montale comes up with a formula for the emotion of longing for something beyond what life has to offer, something we are barred from, but he doesn't define what that thing is.

2. What do we gain by knowing whether "The Sunflower" was written before or after Montale met Irma Brandeis?

In a sense, this question is a trap set to allow you to warn your students about the dangers of naive biographical interpretation, particularly of a poet who, like Eliot, saw the poet's relation to the poem as distant and indirect.

Let's begin with what the flower would naturally symbolize in the absence of any knowledge of Brandeis: the striving of all matter ("These dark things") toward God, or perfection, or consummation, or heaven ("the source of all brightness"). The poem works very well on this level: it compares favorably with William Carlos Williams' "The Yellow Flower" or William Blake's "Ah, Sun–Flower":

> Ah, Sun–flower! weary of time,
> Who countest the steps of the Sun,
> Seeking after that sweet golden clime
> Where the traveller's journey is done;
>
> Where the Youth pined away with desire,
> And the pale Virgin shrouded in snow,
> Arise from their graves and aspire
> Where my Sun–flower wishes to go.

You might point out that Montale's sunflower does not suggest to us the possibility of escape to a "sweet golden clime." Its ardor and passion are ends in themselves: "Thus to burn/Is consummation, of all ends the end." Assuming for the sake of argument that Brandeis and Montale had met before the poem was written, how would the biographical information affect our reading of the poem? Not a great deal. The symbolic importance of the sunflower as a symbol for the yearning soul is so strong that the association with a person would only add a slight interest. In fact, since the poem was written at least six years before Montale met Brandeis, we can see that she was integrated into Montale's system of symbols rather than being the inspiration for the whole system.

3. Comment on the symbolic importance of the glimmers of light we find in "The Eel," "La Belle Dame sans Merci," "Little Testament," and "The Motets."

All of these poems were written after the meeting with Brandeis, so we could say that the following images are signs of Clizia:

> The eel in "The Eel," described as a "flickering thread" kindled by "a flare from falling chestnuts," a torch, an "arrow of Earthly Love," a "spark proclaiming that everything begins only/when it is burned out," rainbow or iris or gleaming eye (*iride*).

> "This thing" in "Little Testament," variously described as marshlight, "pearl necklace snail's trail," "ground glass diamond sparkle," rainbow (*iride*). The negative descriptions are important here, too: *not* a lamp tended by a black cleric or red cleric, "an heirloom or charm/that can tranquillize monsoons," or "the fizzle of a wet match."

> In "The Motets," the squirrel beating its "torch–like tail," the flash of lightning, the "pale mass/writhing in the water," and the "two beams of light/that cross."

> In "La Belle Dame," the "suffocated fire" and the "flash of a lighter."

I think your students will soon realize that calling these images signs of Clizia does not exhaust their meaning. Instead it makes us ask ourselves what Clizia is a sign of. Irma Brandeis is clearly only part of the answer. Other parts may be

> Love, which "penetrating ever deeper the core/of stone . . . looks for life where only drought and desolation gnaw."

> Faith, which is the only thing that can sustain us in the face of despair, "the torch bearing Lucifer . . . rotating his hard coal wings."

> Poetry, the legacy Montale leaves us in "Little Testament."

> Inspiration, which comes like the "flash of lightning" in the tenth motet.

> Salvation, which eludes Montale when he is separated from Clizia ("Now hell is certain" in the first Motet)

Clizia, whatever she represents, is not an easy mistress. Frequently, as in "The Sunflower," we encounter images that equate her devotion (or devotion to her) to a complete burning of the self: "an autobiography can only survive in ashes,/persistence is extinction" ("Little Testament"); "everything begins only/when it is burned out" ("The Eel"). In his later poetry and prose (including the Counterpoint on page 997), Montale often presents himself as a comic or pathetic figure, no longer capable of this exacting service. Thus in "La Belle Dame," his inspiration dwindles from a consuming passion to "the flash of a lighter."

–D.H.

Louise Bogan

Bogan's comments on Dickinson, Millay, Cummings, and (indirectly) Olds give your students an opportunity to see what her commitments were in poetry. She was consistently drawn to mystical poets or those whose perceptions of reality (as in the case of the French symbolists) were at odds with what she plainly believed to be the narrowly channeled and over-safe perceptions of the rosy-cheeked suburbanite who will "meet forever Jim home on the 5:35." At the same time, she rejected any rhetorical posing and never played the rebel. She felt that women might have a special role in the world of literature, keeping open the channels of human emotion and avoiding the sometimes arid exercises the male Anglo-American of her time tended to produce. At the same time, she avoided, as Roethke says, "unabashed caterwaul."

Bogan would teach well in conjunction with any of the poets she comments on in *The Riverside Anthology*. I think she would also teach well with Blake (a poet who influenced her a good deal) or with Lowell (whose poetry involves the same sort of rigorous self-scrutiny) or with Donne (another influence).

Bogan's translation of Charles d'Orlean's rondel "The Castle of My Heart" appears and is discussed in the introduction to the poetry section (pp. 680–81). "The Dragonfly" (one of her finest poems) is discussed in the Handbook section on Metaphor and Symbol.

QUESTIONS

1. How is "Medusa," one of Bogan's earliest poems, typical of her work? How is it atypical?

This is a hard question, I know—really an impossible one to answer adequately. It is a fairly good way to force your students to try to read all the poems in light of the other poems, however, and it should bring out some useful generalities. First, it is (typically) a poem that is only indirectly about its author. Like Tennyson's "Ulysses," Millay's "Penelope," or Browning's "Fra Lippo Lippi," it raises up a figure from the past to embody the writer's emotion and thought. Bogan's figure is (typically) anonymous and unheroic: not Perseus, but one of the nameless victims of Medusa. This is a poet more interested in psychological states than in personalities.

The same sort of indirectness can be seen in "Evening in the Sanitarium," where Bogan does not appear at all (contrast Lowell's "Waking in the Blue"), and in most of the other poems. Only in "The Dream" and "To My Brother" does Bogan explain her feelings directly: once in the guise of dream–thoughts, once in a very subdued elegy.

The indirectness does not keep us from understanding the emotional state the poem evokes, however. Life has stopped. Something terrible rises suddenly and turns us to stone. A similar state of helplessness is evoked in "Zone," where we find ourselves "keel or reef"—in a situatation where we must capsize or shorten sail to let the terrible winds pass over us. A similar feeling that life contains mysteries that can destroy us is present in "Evening at the Sanitarium."

The poem is atypical, I believe, in its one–sidedness. It evokes a single emotional state and presents that state dramatically rather than meditatively. The emotion is not, to use Wordsworth's language, recollected in tranquility: it is immediately present. In "Zone," on the other hand, there is a sense of perspective. "We" (the shift to plural may remind us that the experience is widespread; it may also make the sailor and the ship—the soul and the body—one thing) have run aground. The ill winds that blow in the rigging may shape words "of fear and woe," but we know that this is "one short segment's arch/Of the zodiac's round." This is the poem of a more mature woman, who has "learned how to bear" a great deal. Among the things she learned how to bear, by the way, were periods of severe depression which led to hospitalizations in 1934. A biographical reading of "Zone" would surely equate going "keel or reef" in the "expected latitudes" with her periodic depression and would note the courage of a person who could face it so calmly. The tranquility of "Zone" is typical of the contemplative quality of the later poems.

2. What attitude toward life is expressed in "Evening at the Sanitarium"?

Some of your students may think of *One Flew Over the Cuckoo's Nest* or *King of Hearts* when they read this poem and conclude a bit too hastily that "Evening" is a poem about the superiority of so–called madness to so–called sanity. The poem is much more complex than that, and much more troubling.

As an aside, let me advance a perhaps quirky personal theory that the poem alludes in its first line to one of Wordsworth's sonnets:

It is a beauteous evening, calm and free,
The holy time is quiet as a Nun
Breathless with adoration; the broad sun
Is sinking down in its tranquility;
The gentleness of heaven broods o'er the Sea:
Listen! the mighty Being is awake,
And doth with his eternal motions make
A sound like thunder—everlastingly.
Dear Child! dear Girl! that walkest with me here,
If thou dost appear untouched by solemn thought,
Thy nature is not therefore less divine:
Thou liest in Abraham's bosom all the year;
And worship'st at the Temple's inner shrine,
God being with thee when we know it not.

Wordsworth's poem asserts (some would say a bit condescendingly) a harmony between the soul of his sister Dorothy (presented here as a total innocent) and the "calm and free" evening. This harmony, this lack of conflict and even of thought, is presented as the highest good.

In Bogan's poem, the "free" evening takes it course outside the decorative grills and drawn shades of the sanitarium, where patients are sent who *don't* lie in Abraham's bosom all the year: the befuddled former academic, the manic–depressive, the paranoiac, the girl gone euphoric after the birth of a child, the rejected older wife, the future suicide, the alcoholic grandmother. They are in the institution to become well–adjusted, to become "untouched by solemn thought," to return to a state of mind where they can be perfectly content arranging fruit salads, petting cats, tending gardens. In Bogan's poem, however, this adjustment is clearly not freedom: it is a cosmetic arrangement like the decorative grill on the windows and the soft carpet on the floors. It will make "the fathers feel justified; the mothers relieved," but it ignores the truth that there may be *cause* to feel emotions Wordworth would not like to attribute to Dorothy. The young mother's inordinate euphoria may be an essential part of her; the older wife may feel unwanted because she *is* unwanted. The narrow range of acceptable emotions may not be enough to accommodate all that the world throws at us, and no amount of ferocious knitting "on safe bone needles," no number of "deadly" games of chess can absorb the frantic energies created by a world that contains Medusas and typhoons. Adjustment is a specious goal; it inevitably breaks down, as it does for Mrs. C. and Miss R. at the poem's end.

But Bogan is not saying that Mrs. C. and Miss. R. are just fine and that it is the people outside the sanitarium who are crazy. She is ready to admit the truth of mental illness. It is the equation of wellness with decorum and lack of strain, with trivial pastimes and fruit salads, that disturbs her. The naive assumption that "Everything will be splendid" (18) once the mental hygienists have done their work is what galls her. It is not enough that the patient be made average: "as normal and selfish and heartless as anybody else" (15).

3. What interpretation can be placed on "The Dream"?

The symbols in dreams are always ambiguous, and Bogan's dream horse is (happily) impossible to pin down. She herself aligns it with fear and retribution, carried with her from childhood, but it is not clear what causes these emotions. A Freudian critic might see the horse as a sexual symbol like the boar in Elena Poniatowska's "A Little Fairy Tale." I certainly couldn't disagree, though saying this much about the symbol hardly exhausts its meaning. The horse might also be a symbol of life, or the world, "The terrible beast, that no one may understand." The woman who intervenes in the dream might be Bogan's alter ego, or perhaps a real woman from waking life. We will never know. What I think we can tell is that the poem is a moving story about trust, about things coming right. The woman in the dream in effect advises Bogan to surrender to her fate, to give the beast a token, as a woman might give a man a token of love. And the beast is tamed.

Such a simple poem works partly because it is technically perfect. You might have your students scan a few lines and note how rarely they achieve a regular iambic beat until the three successive iambs of "put down his head in love." You might also ask them to note the rhyme scheme. I think that the last stanza's rhyming abba after a series of abab stanzas introduces a new kind of tension that makes us lean forward in our seats, so to speak, waiting for the word that will rhyme with "glove." "Love" then comes fresh and unexpected.

–D.H.

Federico García Lorca

The selection from García Lorca is long enough to give some idea of the range of his major periods and works. If you don't know his work well and don't want to make him a major part of your syllabus, you might concentrate on "The Faithless Wife," "Lament for Ignacio Sánchez Mejías," and the counterpointed discussion of the *duende*. Students who respond to these three pieces will have a sense of the energy that is at the heart of García Lorca's work and can discover for themselves the way that the other works are related to it.

Part of García Lorca's great technical accomplishment is lost in translation, of course, but as he says in the Counterpoint, what counts is not the form but "the marrow of forms." Reading the translations, we get a sense of the intensity of sorrow, joy, and passion that makes many twentieth–century American poets turn to García Lorca and other Spanish–language poets as an alternative to the more cautious (or inhibited) figures like Eliot and   Williams.

QUESTIONS

1. What attitude toward life is expressed by "The Faithless Wife," and how does the imagery of the poem reinforce that attitude?

Some of your students, when they come to understand García Lorca's attitude toward life, will find it very disturbing. He raises the figure of the gypsy to mythical proportions because gypsies embody for him a vitality that the mainstream of society has lost. They keep their old tribalism intact, love and hate strongly, are unafraid of violence but incapable of the sort of politically organized violence represented by the Civil Guard. They also have, at least in García Lorca's poem, a code of personal ethics preferable to the killing influence of the written law. They are, we might say, specimens of unfallen humanity (though García Lorca's point is hardly that they are pristine). They are, as a student of mine once said, making the word seem to encompass all virtue, "sexy."

The English, by the way, do not share this view of gypsies. The typical anthology of English literature is full of poems arguing that some maiden or another should seize the day. This poem does not pause to argue, but instead shows a frank and unapologetic scene of mutual seduction. The gypsy is deceived in thinking the woman is a virgin, but he is not repentant; we doubt that the woman is much troubled by remorse, and she probably likes the sewing basket.

The imagery in the poem is thick with appeals to the senses, often synaesthetic. The image of the woman's breasts, opening suddenly "like spikes of hyacinth," is visual, tactile, and olfactory at once. When the starch of the woman's petticoat sounds "like a piece of silk/torn by ten knives" we get a complex sense of textures, coarse and smooth, a sound, and a violent visual image all at once. The most remarkable images are so sexually explicit that some teachers will have difficulty discussing them in class. In lines 32–35, we have the woman's thighs escaping the man's grasp "like startled fish,/half full of fire/half full of cold"—an image that expresses both her state of excitement and the contrast between the part of her flesh heated by contact with his body and the part cooled by contact with the cool sand. In the lines immediately following, we have the same explicitness in a thin gauze of metaphor: it is hard to miss the tenor of the image of a man riding on a smooth road on a mare made of mother–of–pearl.

This frank pleasure in the flesh may offend some of your students, but they should compare it to the denial of the flesh in the "Ballad of the Spanish Civil Guard."

2. How does the imagery in the "Ballad of the Spanish Civil Guard" contrast with that in "The Unfaithful Wife"?

Actually the imagery in "Civil Guard" is not of a piece, but full of contrasts. The "city of gypsies" is apparently viewed in a festival season, full of movement and color: bright red banners, green lanterns, pendants with suns and arrows, citizens dressed up as the Virgin and St. Joseph, as the Magi. Against this kaleidoscope of bright images we have the dominant image of the poem: the Guardsmen in their black capes.

Consider how the Guardsmen are presented to the senses. To the eyes, of course, they are black like the night, the only variation in hue being the dull gleam of "stains of inks and of wax" in their capes and the grayness of their faces. (The faithless wife shines brighter in the moonlight than crystals would.) Tactilely, they are associated with lead, patent–leather, hard rubber, serge—dry, hard substances. (The faithless wife is associated with several textures, some included to contrast with the essential softness and smoothness: flowers of the hyacinth, starchy petticoats, silk on a knife's edge, a salve, the skin conches and fish, mother–of–pearl). Audibly, they are associated with silence, then with screams and the clatter of guns. (The faithless wife is associated with a number of more natural sounds: the cry of the crickets, the rustle of petticoats, the barking of dogs in the distance.) The Civil Guards are associated with no smell. (The faithless wife is associated with hyacinth.)

The contrast of the Guards with the gypsies is a contrast of life against death. It is not surprising that the gypsy in "The Faithless Wife" is a marvel of healthy, generous sexuality, while the Civil Guards are sadistic mutilators and probably rapists (see lines 99–105).

Students will find in "New York: Office and Denunciation" another poem which suggests the perverseness that can come on people who are cut off from the natural pleasures and natural forces that can keep them healthy. In the symbolic world of García Lorca's poems, the Guardsmen in "Ballad of the Spanish Civil Guard" might be the inhabitants of a hellish city like New York, with its trains of "handcuffed roses/for the merchants of perfumes" and its river "that gets drunk on oil."

3. How does "Lament for Ignacio Sánchez Mejías" become something larger than a statement of personal grief for the loss of a friend?

The power of the "Lament" clearly comes from a personal loss rather than from merely abstract admiration for bullfighters. Nonetheless, particularly from section 2 forward, García Lorca moves away from the particular details of one man's death and presents Mejías as the perfected type of matador. He invokes, for example, the archaic stoic figures of the bulls of Guisando (in Castile) and, some lines later, a secret voice rising across all the ranches "shouting to celestial bulls." Then we get, in lines 104–123, a very beautiful passage beginning, "there was no prince in Seville/who could compare with him." In this passage are glimpses of centuries of Spanish heraldry, history, and character: swords, lions, marble torsos reminiscent of the Roman past, peasants in the mountains, riders with hard spurs, dewy mornings, fiestas, and, of course, bullfights. García Lorca presents Mejías as the Torero, and the Torero as a summary of all that is noble in the Spanish (or perhaps Andalusian) character.

A part of this character involves a keen awareness of the links between apparently contrary things: history and the present, suffering and joy, death and life, art and blood. The torero embodies a point where such contraries meet. The bullfight is simultaneously a bloody spectacle and theatrical event in which the death of the bull is celebrated simultaneously with the torero's life and grace and courage. It is violence controlled by a series of classic poses. García Lorca's comment (in the Counterpoint) that the cry of "Ole! Ole!" may finally be the same as the cry of "Allah! Allah!" shows how strongly he feels the deep metaphor of the bullfight. The elegance of the great torero, as he says in the "Lament," is more than a personal accomplishment:

> For posterity I sing of your profile and grace.
> Of your signal maturity and your understanding.
> Of your appetite for death and the taste of its mouth.
> Of the sadness of your once valiant gaiety.

An appetite for death and a desire to kiss it in life are the accomplishments not of ordinary athletes but rather of mystics and martyrs. Few nations have given the world as many as Spain has.

–D.H.

Langston Hughes

Hughes was one of the first black writers in America to make his living exclusively with his pen. In the process, he helped to fuel the Harlem Renaissance, a movement (or perhaps more properly a moment in literary history) that included Countee Cullen and Zora Neale Hurston. When I read the writers of that renaissance or read about it, I am stunned to realize that it could have happened in a country that could also produce the tragedy of the Scottsboro boys. Hurston and Hughes, particularly, seem to have arrived at a stage of "racial health" (as Alice Walker calls it) that allowed them to see the lives of black people as fascinating and diverse. They never forgot the racism around them, but somehow it seemed to leave no scar on their souls.

When Hughes came to Harlem in the twenties, it was the thriving capital of black American culture, a place whose prosperity would surprise most of its present inhabitants. Hughes found there an endless source of fascination: the people—their talk, their music, their dash, their clothes, their attitudes. More than one critic has remarked that the gusto with which Hughes absorbed Harlem and turned it into art is reminiscent of the gusto of Whitman.

QUESTIONS

1. Comment on the imagery in "Harlem Sweeties" and "Harlem." What "statement" do the images make?

About twenty-five years after Hughes published "Harlem Sweeties," the slogan "Black is Beautiful" became popular. His poem can be seen as a manifestation of the sort of black pride behind the slogan, but it is also an elaborate variation on the theme. Not black alone is beautiful, but a whole spectrum running from "Rich cream-colored/To plum-tinted black," from "walnut-tinted" to "blackberry." The cataloguing here might remind us of Whitman or Hopkins: there is the same joy in the variety of life. The gusto of the poem comes partly from racial pride, partly from a sensibility that delights in variations and overtones. It is worth noting that none of the skin colors mentioned is simple black or brown: Hughes is not working with the sixteen-color crayon box. Often there is a suggestion that the skin tone is actually mixed or layered: "plum-tinted" brings to mind certain dark plums which can seem simply black until we look closely and see a purple sheen. Of course, the palate is engaged by Hughes' imagery as well as the eyes. Your students should notice that there is a spectrum of tastes as well as colors: the sweetness of caramel, the sourness of persimmon, the spiciness of cinnamon or clove, the bitterness of coffee.

"Harlem Sweeties" does not trouble itself with overt racial messages; it is not a slogan poem. In describing the beauty of skin, it goes beyond messages to joy.

In "Harlem," the remarkable thing about the imagery is that it works so hard. The series of similes proposed for the dream would be powerful if the poet were white and the dream had no reference to race. With a black poet the meanings multiply and the images become more intense. The raisin in the sun is not only an image of the drying up of the spirit, but a picture of a small black face wilting in front of a huge white one. The syrup crusted over with sugar could be a representation of the dream becoming cloying self-deception, but it also becomes a symbol of the defensive good humor that helped create the stereotype of the naturally happy Negro. Certainly the notion of a dream as a sagging, heavy load makes sense without reference to race, but there appears to be a reference here to another stereotype—the shuffling, shiftless Negro. Festering and running, stinking like rotten meat: the images, applied to human beings, are almost too disgusting to bear. Hughes lets these images of black humanity crushed by the "dream deferred" build intolerable tensions in the reader, then suggests a response that we would now characterize as black rather than Negro: the white–hot anger of "does it explode?"

2. Translated to a thesis for a composition–class essay, what is the theme of "Theme for English B"? Explain the argument that supports it.

On one level this poem is a sardonic comment on English teachers—a subject my students usually warm to. The instructor gives one of those astonishingly nebulous questions for which we are notorious: write a page about yourself. Hughes (or Hughes' persona), sharper than his teacher, sees the implied world view: "If you write an honest page, you will reveal your identity."

Hughes' answer (his thesis) is, in effect, "I don't have <u>an</u> identity; I am made up of many things, not all of them perfectly reconciled." His support for the assertion begins with geography: he is partly Winston–Salem, partly Durham, partly Columbia, partly Harlem, partly New York generally. He is black, but this is not a comprehensive statement of identity: whites, too, "eat, sleep, drink, and [are] in love." He listens to music, but too eclectically for him to be neatly pigeonholed—"Bessie, bop, and Bach."

And, of course, the "identity" of the paper that is to reveal Hughes' identity is an enormously complicated matter: "it will be/a part of you, instructor." Here is the sort of insight into rhetoric that the instructor may labor all semester to impart to other students (and may have imperfectly grasped himself). The audience shapes the text; Hughes' will not be a letter home or a diary entry. It will be shaped by the expectations of a white instructor at a prestigious and overwhelmingly white school. To "be true" under these circumstances is an extraordinarily complicated business.

Yet Hughes does not find that writing to meet the expectations of a white instructor is automatically false:

You are white—
yet part of me, as I am part of you.
That's American.
Sometimes perhaps you don't want to be a part of me.
Nor do I often want to be a part of you.
But we are, that's true.

The rhetorical situation is merely another microcosm of the puzzle of "identity," including racial identity. The reason it is not false for Hughes to write "white" is that included in his complex makeup is a great deal of white culture. The reason that he can also write "black" is that the instructor ought to have an equally complex makeup including a good deal of black culture.

As I learn from you,
I guess you learn from me—
although you're older—and white—
and somewhat more free.

So much is implied in that "somewhat."
Having started with what appeared to be a dim–witted question and a somewhat truculent reply, the "page for English B" saves the situation. The student's reply is so good that it makes the question good. The page does come out of Hughes, and it is true in a more complex way than anyone had a right to expect.

3. How does Hughes use the rhythm of blues in his poems?

"The mood of the Blues," as Hughes says, "is almost always despondency, but when they are sung, people laugh." Here is a stanza from the traditional "Southern Blues":

I went to the gypsy
To have my fortune told,
I went to the gypsy
To have my fortune told,
She said, "Dog–gone you, girlie,
Dog–gone your hard–luck soul!

You might ask your students to work out the metrical pattern. Typically a blues singer would hit two stresses to a line:
i WENT to the GYPsy
to have my FORtune TOLD
i WENT to the GYPsy
to have my FORtune TOLD
she said, "dog–GONE you, GIRLie,
dog–GONE your hard–luck SOUL

Among the variations available to the singer are the addition of extra stresses and/or extra unstressed syllables:

well, i WENT to the GYPsy
just to HAVE my FORtune TOLD
. . .
dog–GONE your HARD–luck SOUL

We might state the metrical pattern as this: the standard line has two stresses, one of which is on the last or next–to–last syllable; variant lines can contain more stresses. It would be possible, then, to have a blues line just two syllables long or one eight syllables long: the pattern is accentual rather than syllabic.

The pattern of rhyme and repetition is obvious, and Hughes wrote a number of poems that follow it fairly strictly, including the famous "Bound No'th Blues."

In "Same in Blues," the four–line stanzas are blues stanzas with the repetition omitted. Their strong rhythms stand in contrast to the inter-posed three-line stanzas, which are arranged with a single stress in the first and second lines. It is, by the way, only the change in lineation that breaks up the blues rhythm:

> There's a certain amount of trav'lin'
> In a dream deferred

would fit the blues rhythm perfectly. By breaking the lines to avoid the blues rhythm, Hughes establishes two voices in the poem. We have a blues singer in the quatrains and the analytic commentator of "Harlem" in the alternate three–line stanzas.

The result is a poem that makes its strong emotional statements in blues form, a form set aside for strong emotions. After each such statement we get an almost parenthetical comment. The blues singer's voice sings about his baby leaving; the commentator says that this sort of instability comes with the dream deferred. The blues singer says that Leonard won't give Lulu a goddamn thing; the commentator says that having nothing and getting nothing to give is part of a dream deferred. And so forth. In the last quatrains the two voices seem to come together: the form is bluesy, but the language is at least half that of the commentator.

The fusion of the two personalities in "Same in Blues" is characteristic of Hughes' best work, which is simultaneously emotional and restrained, immersed in black folk tradition, but distinctly literary.

–D.H.

Countee Cullen

"Protest poems" by various authors are attached as Counterpoints at the end of the Cullen. These appended poems are among the most interesting in the book, but they should not lead your students to view Cullen as a protest poet exclusively.

In fact, Cullen's career illustrates the complex tensions that a black poet in America may be subject to. Like Gwendolyn Brooks (and unlike Langston Hughes or Lucille Clifton), Cullen was strongly influenced early in his career by traditional literary forms and standards. In Cullen's case, the predominant influences were Keats, Tennyson, Housman, and Robinson. Many of his poems are distinctly in the Romantic tradition and have nothing to do with race, but others graft the traditional literary forms to his experience growing up in a segregated society. His first collection, *Color*, published while he was an undergraduate, contained many accomplished lyrics defining the relations of truth, beauty, goodness, and mortality, but it was poems like "Yet Do I Marvel" that attracted the most attention. Readers who preferred to see Cullen primarily as a poet writing on racial themes were disappointed by his later volumes and must have been very puzzled by his publication in 1935 of a translation of Euripides' *Medea*.

When we look at Cullen's poems we are presented with a quandary. On the one hand, we have to agree with Cullen that being black should not limit a poet's attention to racial themes or cut a poet off from the long tradition of English verse. There is no reason to think that a separate–but–equal doctrine in poetic tradition is sounder than a separate–but–equal doctrine in education. On the other hand, we may be uneasy about poetry that draws constantly from the old wells and seems unaffected by a central fact of the poet's experience.

QUESTIONS

1. In what ways are "To John Keats" and "Yet Do I Marvel" clearly poems in the English tradition? Does its traditional nature make "Yet Do I Marvel" more or less effective as a poem on a racial theme?

"To John Keats" is so traditional in many respects that it is tempting to dismiss it as "merely conventional." The association of poetry, spring, and beauty is entirely expected, and I find it distressing that a poet a few years out of DeWitt Clinton High School and attending New York University should compare himself to a "lamb that bleats/To feel the solid earth recoil/Beneath his puny legs." Unaffected, apparently, by the life of the city around him, Cullen can concentrate on the dogwood petals that drift like snow on the breast of Mother Earth. The imagery in the third stanza is more striking: Keats becomes part of the earth rising up the "sap road" of a maple tree so that the leaves "Grow music as they grow." His fingers still produce the "Vision Splendid," though now they must push up "as grass in the hush/Of the night on the broad sweet page of the earth": the image of growth in the night suggests Keats' pervasive influence on Cullen and other poets, and the extra foot in the last line gives a feeling of how broad the influence has become. Striking as the third stanza is, though, its imagery is hardly new: it is a commonplace of the English elegy. We see it in *In Memoriam* when Tennyson describes the Yew which wraps its roots around the bones of Hallam and in its branches bears flowers. We see it parodied in Rodgers and Hammerstein's musical

Oklahoma! when Curley pretends to lament the passing of his enemy, the unsanitary Jud Fry:

> Pore Jud is daid, Pore Jud Fry is daid!
> His friends'll weep and wail fer miles around.
> The daisies in the dell
> Will give out a diff'runt smell
> Becuz pore Jud is underneath the ground.

Your class may divide on whether "To John Keats" is an entirely successful poem. They will almost certainly see "Yet Do I Marvel" as a stronger one. The poem is, however, absolutely as conventional as "To John Keats," and it is probably worthwhile to have your class enumerate the conventions followed. It is, first of all, a sonnet: its abab/cdcd/eeffgg rhyme scheme is a hybrid between the English and Italian forms. It is, furthermore, a sonnet complaining about God's apparent injustice, so that it has very precise literary precursors in Milton's "When I Consider How My Light is Spent" (perhaps alluded to by the reference to the blind mole) and Hopkins' "Thou Art Indeed Just, Lord." It is also a sonnet, like Wordsworth's "The World Is Too Much with Us," that draws its imagery from classical mythology. To the classical allusions, Cullen adds an allusion to Blake's "Tyger": the "awful brain" that compels "His awful hand." It is hard to imagine a poem more thoroughly in the white, English poetic tradition.

This association with the tradition does not weaken the poem, but gives it enormous power. Cullen acknowledges the whole literary canon contemplating the "problem of evil" and then he makes his fresh contribution to it: "To make a poet black, and bid him sing!" seems yet another ingenious form of divine torment.

I hope your students will see how brilliantly this sonnet summarizes the whole of Cullen's endeavor to be both a poet in the tradition and a poet enriching the tradition with a new racial consciousness. Why is it so "curious" to make a poet black and bid him sing? Because blacks are stereotypically non–literary singers? Because blacks are separated from the tradition of poetic song? Because blacks have been given so much more reason to shout than to sing? All these things seem implied by a poem that solves the problems even while it names them.

2. What is the theme of "Only the Polished Skeleton"?

Questions about theme can be dangerous unless they are hard to answer. This one is. My own reading is that the poem is a variation on the theme of life's inadequacy. Cullen asserts that while we are alive, the world offers us no real satisfactions that can satisfy us; we live by being fooled, indulging in specious hopes. But in death, if we could look back at all, we would discover that even the actual ("despised") events of life were worth more than we ever knew.

This general interpretation of the poem makes the intepretation of the second stanza very difficult, however. Where is the deceit—inside or out? The first stanza seems to suggest that deceit is inside us, that we fool ourselves. In the second stanza, however, logic "brutal and unkind" is fending off "subterfuge and fraud," which are the "onslaughts of the dust." Here we have (I believe) a grim picture of the mind (our innermost inside) pitted against the body and the body's false promise of life (compare "life that opens death's dark door" in "To John Keats").

Both the enigmatic nature of the poem and its success in reminding us of our mortality connect it with Louise Bogan's "The Engine," a poem with similar images.

3. Poems of protest are always "rhetorical" in the broad sense: they are intended to influence the thoughts or actions of the audience. Sometimes they are rhetorical in the narrower senses of (a) sounding like oratory or (b) craftily constructed to create a special effect. Do "From the Dark Tower" and "Incident" fall into either category a or category b?

My own answer would be that "Dark Tower" is fairly clearly type a and "Incident" fairly clearly type b. The "a"–ness of "Dark Tower" is obvious enough; your students will see at once that it sounds like a speech delivered to rouse a sympathetic audience. It might be worth pointing out that "The Dark Tower" was also the name of Cullen's column in *Opportunity* magazine; the poem has the feel of an editorial.

"Incident" strikes me as being type b. It starts out with every evidence of being light verse: the once–upon–a–time opening and the playful trotting meter (most notable in "i SAW a BALtiMOReAN") make this sound like a children's poem. When the word *nigger* is spoken at the end of line 8, the tone suddenly changes and the final stanza is subdued, adult, and sad. One of the difficulties in finding one's own tastes in poetry is deciding how to evaluate this sort of rhetorical flair: should we dismiss it as a "trick" beneath the dignity of true poetry, or shall we say that it is a part of poetry's legitimate function of taking readers aback and forcing them to see things from a fresh perspective?

4. Many of the poems collected on the pages following the Cullen poems are "type-b" rhetorical poems. Arrange them in order from least tricky to most, and discuss how the trickiness of the poems is related to their effectiveness.

"Nightsong: City" is arguably the least rhetorical of the poems, its trick amounting only to a brilliant extended metaphor that is discussed in the "Figures of Speech" section of the Handbook. The success of the poem depends largely on how well the image of the police car as a giant cockroach engages our feelings of disgust and loathing.

I would place "Ozymandias" next; the ambiguity of the eleventh line is one of the most famous examples of irony in the English language, and some would say that it is the rather pyrotechnic effect upon which the whole poem is built. Our detection of the ambiguity gives us a feeling of superiority to Ozymandias, and suggests the general inferiority of brute force and megalomania.

Soyinka's "Telephone Conversation" is essentially a humorous yarn (humor tinged with great bitterness, of course) that builds up to a punch line. The success of the poem depends on Soyinka's ability to make us feel contempt for the woman who will be the butt of the insulting joke that ends the yarn.

"Cinderella" turns on a reversal of the values of the familiar fairy tale story. Now the stepmother and stepsisters are the sympathetic figures and Cinderella is "a woman co-opted by promises." The cultural feminist slant here is clear; men are portrayed as evil influences in a way that parallels the portrayal of women as temptresses through the centuries. The effectiveness of the poem depends on our seeing embedded in the traditional story some sinister implications: it is not solid virtues that raise Cinderella above her sisters, but beauty, small feet, a joyful heart, and a willingness to defeat her half-sister in a contest for wealth and influence in a world dominated by men.

"Discovery of the New World" is probably the most spectacular of all these poems in its "special effect": narrating from an alien's perspective an account of the invasion of earth by aliens. The effectiveness of the poem depends upon the reader's seeing the parallel between the values of the alien and the values of white colonists in America, who saw the Indians as virtually their "lawful food and prey and slaves." Part of the trick is the thoroughness with which the poet maintains the alien's point of view. By forcing readers to discover the implied analogy, he turns what might have been a moral lecture into a science fiction/mystery story.

–D.H.

Pablo Neruda

Neruda is a poet whose importance in world literature is hard to overestimate. He, Jorge Luis Borges, and Federico García Lorca—born within five years of each other in Chile, Argentina, and Spain—helped make Spanish-language literature a major influence on the literatures of all languages in the twentieth century. It would be worthwhile to impress on your class the cultural and historical stage on which these men acted.

All three were born before World War I, but came to maturity after it. That is, they were born in an age where the values we associate with

Victorianism held sway. Commerce and industry might look forward, but literature and the arts tended to look backward, to define themselves by their adherence to a tradition that stretched back (at least in the imagination of many writers) to the classical past. We might cite Tennyson's "Ulysses" or "The Lotos Eaters" as great expressions of this old order in literature. The personal emotions of the poet were made universal by being shaped into a recognized literary form and being tied to allusions familiar to readers who had been schooled in the reading of Greek and Latin texts.

After World War I, the myth of an unbroken cultural tradition reaching back to Homer held less and less appeal, as we can see in the tone of Owen's "Dulce et Decorum Est." Poets after Owen were, with some very influential exceptions (including Eliot and Montale), inclined to see the old order as falsely assured, artificial, and academic, and they began an earnest search for a new order (or new disorder).

Neruda, Borges, and García Lorca are very different artists, but we can see in all three some characteristics of the great Spanish–language writers who emerged in the postwar years. Classical allusions are either gone, or are mixed (as in Borges) into a whirlwind of symbols, none of which have the authority Tennyson attaches to Ulysses. Metaphor ceases to play a carefully controlled minor role in the work and becomes instead a force in itself. Description becomes less important than suggestion, and adjectives very often are used not to refine an image, but to add unexpected dimensions to the nouns they modify. Poets like Neruda who pursued these new directions were to some extent at odds with poets in the Anglo–American tradition (Eliot, Moore, Williams) who tried to build a new poetic order on the precision of images. American poets of a later generation who rebelled against the "thinginess" of the Anglo–American modern poetry often saw Neruda and García Lorca as mentors.

QUESTIONS

1. Although "Here I Love You" makes no classical allusions, its elements are at least as old as the Roman poet Catullus: passion, grief, the loneliness of the separated lover. What makes the poem seem fresh?

"Here I Love You" is one of the *Twenty Love Poems and a Song of Despair*, a volume that has sold well over two million copies. What makes the volume so popular is largely Neruda's success in conveying in a direct, simple, dignified style the truths of young love (Neruda was twenty years old when the poems were published). One has the impression in reading the poems that Neruda is not following Catullus, but living through what Catullus lived through. We know in fact that the *Twenty Poems* tell the story of two of Neruda's love affairs, one with a country girl from the south of Chile, one with a more sophisticated woman from Santiago.

Writing from passion rather than from literary models, Neruda seems to discover in his own experiences associations that are deeper than literature, that go to the collective subconscious. The sound of wind in the pines and the sight of the moon setting on the ocean, images that would have been familiar to Neruda from his childhood, here suggest at once beauty, pleasure, sorrow, and loneliness. It is natural that in a port everything should be damp, but Neruda makes the dampness psychological as well as physical: "I get up early and even my soul is wet." It is natural that a port should be associated with parting, but Neruda makes the association concrete: "Sometimes my kisses go on those heavy vessels/that cross the sea towards no arrival." It is natural that the lover should be associated with nature, but Neruda makes the lover permeate nature: the stars are her eyes, and the pine needles want to sing her name. The imagery here is simultaneously familiar and surprising. A pine tree that sings the lover's name might seem like a Victorian image. Let it sing with leaves like wire and we have richer associations: the imagery is now aural, visual, and tactile, and we think not only of the beauty but of pain.

I suspect that it is Neruda's ability to elicit in a few images the range of contradictory emotions lovers feel that makes his love poems so popular. This ability never abandoned Neruda. In "Love" he comments explicitly on the mixture of the lover's emotions:

> . . . love has to be so,
> involving and general,
> particular and terrifying,
> honoured and yet in mourning,
> flowering like the stars,
> and measureless as a kiss.

"I am moved by the sight of you sleeping," he writes, and everyone who has been in love knows how emotionally rich and complex this sight is.

2. How does "Love Sonnet VI" illustrate Robert Bly's point that Neruda's poetry often moves "in the underworld of consciousness"?

It might be worthwhile to compare this poem with Baudelaire's "By Association." Baudelaire goes from the scent of the lover's breasts to the sight of the Malabar coast, to bodies of the natives, to ripe fruit, to a harbor scene, to the smell of tamarinds and the chanteys of sailors. The associations may move us, but they are distinctly his, reflections of his personality and exotic imagination.

When Neruda breaks off the dark twig it sets off a stream of associations often conveyed metaphorically. The twig whispers like a tiny human: its voice is like the rain, a cracked bell, a torn heart. It is like a shout hidden in the earth, "muffled by huge autumns." It sings under the tongue, another personification, but it sings for "the land I had lost in my childhood." The associations have less to do with the peculiarities of the poet's personality and more to do with the collective subconscious. Conscious trees are a commonplace of myth and folk story: think of the Grimm brothers' wish–granting Juniper Tree or the tree that bleeds and speaks when Dante tears a limb from it. Perhaps the similarity of body types (trunks and limbs) makes us inclined to give trees human characteristics. At any rate, it is not surprising in the world of dreams and stories to have trees speak, and it seems "natural" that a twig should only whisper. The roots of trees reach down below the surface, into things long buried, and so it is "natural" that the roots should be associated with things "deep and secret to me, hidden by the earth."

Beyond the symbolic appeal of the tree to the subconscious mind, there is the appeal of poetic justice. The poet, wandering in the forest, injures a tree by breaking off a twig. In return, he is "wounded by the wandering scent" of the tree and the memories it brings of his childhood.

3. How do "Ritual of My Legs" and "Sweetness, Always" give us a picture of Neruda's attitude toward life?

Once again, Tennyson comes to mind as a poet to contrast. Tennyson's "Ulysses" is built on a choice between the life of domestic and civic duty (to which Telemachus is suited) and the life of danger and adventure. Pleasure doesn't figure. In "The Lotos Eaters," pleasure does figure, but only as a thing to overcome. Certainly Tennyson could produce poems devoted to the pleasures of the senses (see "Come Down, O Maid"), but he did so rarely.

Neruda, on the other hand, never seems to doubt that life should be as filled with pleasure as possible, and that pleasure comes from the earth and the flesh. His call in "Sweetness, Always" for "eatable sonnets" and for attention to the "joyous/love–needs of our bodies" could not be clearer. His statement that

> Vanity keeps prodding us
> to lift ourselves skyward
> or to make deep and useless
> tunnels underground

might be written in the margins of any number of over–intellectual modern poems.

"Ritual of My Legs" is certainly not "The Waste Land." It is as straightforward a celebration of the body as one can imagine. Only a poet who finds the flesh important in itself, as metaphor for nothing else, could begin a poem by telling the reader that it panics him to spend time alone in bed and that he staves the panic off by considering the wonders of his

own body. Occasionally the poem states a position that reminds us of
Neruda's affinity with Walt Whitman:

> People cross through the world nowadays
> scarcely remembering that they possess a body and a life within it,
> And there is fear, in the world there is fear of the words that desig-
>   nate the body

I'm sure that some people would argue that such a statement was more
true in Chile in 1933 than it is in America in the 1980s, where seventh
graders don't hesitate to use words that designate the body or the things
we can do with it, and the local video store rents movies that remind a
large cross–section of the population that humans have bodies which can
do truly remarkable things.

There is, however, a considerable difference between the usually guilty
pleasure allowed by our "permissive" society and Neruda's enormous and
guilt–free appetite for the body and the sensuous world.

–D. H.

W. H. Auden

Auden combines two qualities that seem antithetical. He had an ear for
the musical qualities of the language as good, perhaps, as Milton's or
Tennyson's. In this respect, he could be called one of the most lyric poets of
the twentieth century, and he spent a good deal of his late career writing
what were quite literally lyrics: librettos and stanzas for music. In another
respect, he is the least lyric of poets. He does not switch off his analytic
intelligence and write from his heart. Instead, he seems always to be
puzzling out the world in which he finds himself, its politics and history
no less than its more poetic features.

He is a good poet for students to encounter whose vision of the poet is a
person with cape and plume, writing by candlelight in a rapture of self–
pity. Even those whose ears are deaf to his music can become engaged with
the intelligent view of life and history that we find in poems like "Musée
des Beaux Arts" and "The Shield of Achilles."

QUESTIONS

1. How does Auden's poetry differ from the poetry of the Romantic poets, as
he characterizes their work in the prose excerpt on page 1057?

Perhaps the key words in his characterization of the Romantics and
their relation to society are "bewildered," "horrified," and "uncertain."

In essence, he says that the Romantics made their great discoveries about private, subjective reality because they were forced to retreat from an objective reality that had become incomprehensible and threatening. Randall Jarrell once made a similar observation, saying that all poetry since the Romantic revolution has been spinning away from its communal center like galaxies spinning away from the big bang. Each poet becomes a specialist in his or her perceptions, and learns to emphasize the way these differ from the perceptions of other people.

Auden, more than any poet of comparable stature, has actively set himself against this trend. His statement that "the private world is fascinating, but it is exhaustible," sounds simultaneously like good sense and heresy.

The result of this attitude is poetry that centers on the public world, often the political world, and that is often concerned with public figures, living or dead. "Voltaire at Ferney" is written in praise of a man whose philosophy was antithetical to everything romantic and, some would say, everything truly poetic. He is "perfectly happy" and "very great" (and correspondingly egotistical) not because of the exquisiteness of his perceptions, but because he is building a hospital, planting trees, fighting injustice and prejudice. He is not bewildered or uncertain or horrified; he is the consummately reasonable, moderate, pleasure–loving person. Voltaire knows he will die working for the public good and, if I read the poem right, this makes him like the "uncomplaining stars" that compose "their lucid song." (They do not sing for him, of course, but he knows this.) Auden's "Voltaire" is not a projection from his inner life, like Tennyson's "Ulysses," not a vehicle for the poet's emotions. It is something plainer and (in the world of modern poetry) more surprising. It is a study of a person the poet admires and finds interesting, not as an alter–ego, but as a co–worker.

You might ask your students to look at the stanzaic pattern of this poem, by the way. It is, as one might expect in a poem about putting things in order, wonderfully orderly.

Distance, perspective, calm understanding, and attention to public issues and the public good: these very unromantic qualities are characteristic of Auden's poetry. "Musée des Beaux Arts" returns to the Old Masters for a lesson that might have come from Pope or Johnson: that our private disasters don't make the world stand still. It might be worthwhile to have your class compare this poem with Keats' "Ode on a Grecian Urn" and Rilke's "Archaic Torso of Apollo." Keats looks at a work of art and finds in it a mirror of his lyric and elegiac emotions. Rilke looks at a work of art and finds in it a reproach aimed at his way of life. Auden looks at a work of art and sees nothing personal in it at all. The universe is not centered on any person: the "dreadful martyrdom must run its course" while "the torturer's horse/Scratches its innocent behind on a tree."

2. What is Auden's view of the function of the poet?

Auden's view that the poet's function is somehow to serve the community rather than to explore his or her private consciousness only leads us to another question: How can the poet serve? Your students will find a number of statements that seem to contradict each other. Auden's Voltaire sees poetry as a tool in the long political and philosophical struggle between the forces of reason and the forces of superstition:

> And still all over Europe stood the horrible nurses
> Itching to boil their children. Only his verses
> Perhaps could stop them . . . .
> > (33–35)

But this may be Voltaire's egotism speaking, and in "In Memory of W. B. Yeats" we get the often–quoted opposite view:

> Now Ireland has her madness and her weather still,
> For poetry makes nothing happen: it survives
> In the valley of its saying where executives
> Would never want to tamper . . . .
> > (35–38)

Another way of framing the question is this: Does Auden believe that poetry can improve the human situation, or does he think that "poetry makes nothing happen"?

In the prose passage on page 1057, we get a direct statement of what Auden believes the poet's work to be:

> The problem for the modern poet, as for every one else to–day, is how to find or form a genuine community, in which each has his valued place and can feel at home. . . . Virtues which were once nursed by nature must now be recovered and fostered by a deliberate effort of the will and the intelligence.

I think that if your students will read Auden closely, they will see that he consistently uses his poetry to help his readers "find or form a genuine community." A genuine community is created by shared attitudes, beliefs, convictions, and faiths, and a good many of Auden's poems are frankly didactic. "Luther," "The Sphinx," and "Voltaire" are chalk–talks telling us how right–thinking people in the community he wants to create should view fanaticism, optimism, and meliorism.

"The Unknown Citizen," of course, warns us of the dangers of an efficient society that is *not* a community, but a beehive. JS/07/M/378 and his mates are clearly neither happy nor free, although "each in the cell of himself is almost convinced of his freedom" ("W. B. Yeats," 27).

In the closing quatrains of "In Memory of W. B. Yeats," Auden tells us
that the poet is a teacher who trains the emotions as well as the intellect:

> Follow, poet, follow right
> To the bottom of the night
> With your unconstraining voice
> Still persuade us to rejoice;
>
> With the farming of a verse
> Make a vineyard of the curse,
> Sing of human unsuccess
> In a rapture of distress;
>
> In the deserts of the heart
> Let the healing fountain start,
> In the prison of his days
> Teach the free man how to praise.

In poems like "Spain, 1937" and "The Shield of Achilles," Auden ful-
fills this function of the poet, showing the "bottom of the night" that
opened up in Europe with the Spanish Civil War and stretched into mid–
century. He teaches how to praise the volunteers who "came to present
their lives" in the Loyalist cause and how to value "any world where
promises were kept/Or one could weep because another wept" ("Achilles,"
58–59).

3. Auden's interest in music eventually led him to write librettos for operas. What examples can you find of particularly musical passages in his
poetry?

"In Memory of W. B. Yeats" is a *tour de force*; it shows Auden's metrical
virtuosity to advantage because it contrasts three verse forms. The free verse
of the first section is knit together by parallel constructions like
Whitman's:

> The provinces of his body revolted,
> The squares of his mind were empty,
> Silence invaded the suburbs,
> The current of his feeling failed . . . .

and by the echo of vowel and consonant sounds

> When the brokers are roaring like beasts on the floor of the Bourse.

The second section is written in iambic hexameter, gracefully varied, with half and full rhymes. The third is written in the "hammer–headed" (that is, begun with a stressed syllable) iambic couplets of Blake.

The contrast of rhythms between Thetis' thoughts and descriptions of the shield in "The Shield of Achilles" is also remarkable. Thetis' thoughts are in ballad stanzas (alternating four–stress and three–stress lines) that are fairly elastic and are sometimes lightly rhymed. Each of her four parts comprises two such stanzas, and ends with the thud of a line that crowds three stresses into five syllables:

/   /   /
And a sky like lead

/   /   /
Quite another scene

/   /   /
But a weed–choked field.

/   /   /
Who would not live long.

The unity with variation of these lines is typical of Thetis' other lines. The twentieth–century world portrayed on the shield marches more mechanically in iambic pentameter lines locked into a strict stanzaic pattern: rhyme royal. One suspects that Auden enjoyed the irony of presenting dreadful modernity in a rhyme scheme associated with Chaucer's *Troilus and Criseyde.*

Among the most musical lines in all of Auden, and among the most moving, are those that stretch from line 33 ("And the poor in their fireless lodgings dropping the sheets") to line 70 ("Our fever's menacing shapes are precise and alive") of "Spain, 1937." The pattern here seems to be long lines of five strong stresses regularly interspersed with short lines of three. But it is the test of the ear rather than the test of the finger that counts. To my ear, this passage gains momentum as the best passages from Whitman and Milton do.

–D.H.

Theodore Roethke

I was introduced to Roethke's poetry by a friend who could recite "I Knew a Woman" in a way that did both its double entendres and its music full justice, and so at first attempted to read him consistently as a smiling poet. Longer acquaintance shows that the poet, like the man, is subject to darker moods. Students may be better able to interpret Roethke's imagery if they know that his father and uncle were co–owners of a large greenhouse operation in Saginaw, Michigan. His father was a hearty masculine floriculturalist whom Roethke apparently idolized, but who sold his greenhouses, developed terminal cancer, and committed suicide when Roethke was in his early adolescence. One has the feeling that Roethke's greenhouse poems are written out of the psychological necessity to return to a way of life violently interrupted, never lived out to its conclusion. This is not to say that they are returns to an entirely idealized childhood, but they seem to show an integrated world, one where all of life's pleasures and pains can be compassed in a few images.

QUESTIONS

1. How much of the symbolic importance of Roethke's greenhouse and root cellar imagery is inherent in the subject? What is added by Roethke's treatment of the subject?

I hope this question will encourage students to discover that Roethke's imagery is far from arbitrary or idiosyncratic. A greenhouse is literally a place where delicate growing things are protected from a hostile environment. It is hardly a step into private mythology to make the greenhouse into a place where life and beauty are nurtured despite the hostility of the world. The root cellar is literally a place where roots and bulbs are kept cool and dark for storage purposes, but where they inevitably begin to sprout as the winter wears on. It is not surprising that these entombed roots should become symbols of all life's mysterious and secret (and not altogether polite) stirrings. The workers in the greenhouse literally assist nature in making things grow; they are inevitably symbols of whatever forces—human or divine—favor life over death. Roethke's statement in the Counterpoint that certain words are "drenched with human associations" is the clue to a large part of his poetry's appeal. He cites "hill, plow, mother, window, bird, fish" as examples. Surely *rose, glass, storm, sunlight, ditch, snake,* and *witch* could be added to the list. The words and images have a power of their own.

Usually Roethke's poetry intensifies the fixed and ancient "human associations" rather than altering them. Contrast, for example, "Big Wind" with Donne's "The Flea" or "A Valediction: Forbidding Mourning." Donne begins with a situation (courtship or parting) that is certainly drenched with associations all humans share, but he links the situation to an image that is new and startling. Roethke, on the other hand, rarely introduces a metaphor that takes us entirely by surprise. The comparison of a greenhouse in a storm to a ship on a stormy sea is almost a double dose of the same idea; and the comparison of three weathered old women to witches is hardly a surprise, especially if the women are associated with nature, growth, and fertility.

Typically, Roethke finds the impulse of the "human association"—the archetype, we might say—and extends it in its natural direction. By comparing the greenhouse to a ship in a storm, he adds drama to the struggle between human ingenuity and the hostility of the environment. The details of draining the manure machine and driving the pressure in the old pipes into the danger zone intensifies the conflict, so that by mere intensity it begins to attract interpretation. Isn't this just like every other desperate effort to foster beauty in a harsh world? Isn't it like the situation of a poet in a society indifferent to poetry? Isn't it like the conflict between all those who live for love or beauty in a society attuned to the values of cash, status and power? We ask these questions naturally, without much need of intellectual dexterity, because Roethke is using symbols we all understand.

Like the greenhouse, the root cellar is an image with inevitable associations: What could it "stand for" but the tenacity of life? Roethke improves on the natural meaning of the symbol by making the imagery very intense. We see and smell more in his eleven lines than we often do in a comparable passage from the Romantic poets. We also get repeated images of touch and texture: "dank as a ditch . . . pulpy stems . . . leaf mold . . . slippery planks." And, of course, we get those remarkable images of tumescence, internal pressure—more striking even than those in Keats' "To Autumn." That the imagery in the poem suggests sexuality and that the root cellar can be equated with the Id is hardly surprising. A lesser poet could have thought of such an idea, but Roethke gives it force.

2. What is the effect of unpleasant imagery in Roethke's poems?

Obviously, students will have to start by deciding what to call unpleasant, and they may disagree a bit with each other on this point. The images most on my mind are those that would seem impolite in dinner table conversation or in Victorian poetry: the mention in "Big Wind" of pumping fluid from the manure machine into the boilers of the steam plant, the painfulness of the horseplay ("At every step you missed/My right ear scraped a buckle") in "My Papa's Waltz," the leathery skin and the snuff–laden breath of "Frau Bauman, Frau Schmidt, and Frau Schwartze," and unsavory descriptions of "Root Cellar":

Shoots dangled and drooped,
Lolling obscenely from mildewed crates,
Hung down long yellow evil necks, like tropical snakes.
And what a congress of stinks!

Among the effects your students may attribute to images in these passages are the following:

◆ They keep the positive images of the poem from seeming merely pretty and ideal. A greenhouse as a symbol for the protection of life and beauty might be the cliché of a suburban architect who knows very little about the working of actual greenhouses. By introducing the manure machine, the burlap, and the hissing at the seams of the steam plant, Roethke gives us, as Louise Bogan says, "a close recording of the actual."

◆ Beyond avoiding a too–pure *presentation* of the positive things of life, these images correct our simple–minded tendency to confuse goodness with simple purity. In Roethke's poems (as in Hopkin's "Pied Beauty"), the most praiseworthy things may be those that are not immaculate, sterile, simple, clearly defined. A "congress of stinks" may be preferable to the air of a climate–controlled office complex. Three old women with callused hands and snuff–laden breath may be more fascinating than three fashion models. I'm sure that Roethke's idea of the good life must have included the texture of leaf mold and the odor of well–rotted manure, both excellent things to those who have learned to appreciate them, neither pleasing to those who are disgusted by the every thought of feces and decay. The father's roughness of "My Papa's Waltz" will also alarm tender sensibilities, who may feel that it shows a drunken brute abrading his son's ear with a belt buckle and pounding him on the head with a dirt–caked hand. It is surely more true to say that it shows a man who is hard–working, exuberant, and affectionate. His very roughness, though it causes pain, is part of his "pied beauty."

◆ The unpleasant images may also suggest that deep in the heart of things there is an essential unpleasantness, even when there is much good. If Frau Bauman, Frau Schmidt, and Frau Schwartze are in some ways like the three graces or the muses or three nature goddess, they are nonetheless three underpaid, over–worked, ugly old women leading lonely lives ("nurses of nobody else"). If the "root cellar" is a symbol of life's power, it is also a symbol of life's unseemliness and "obscene" passions. If the Child on Top of the Greenhouse is experiencing a moment of ecstasy, he is also experiencing a moment of guilt: everyone shouts and even the chrysanthemums look like accusers. Guilt, ugliness, decay and even obscenity are entangled in even the beautiful parts of life.

Though it may be illogical to think that all three of these effects can exist concurrently, they surely do.

3. How are the meters of "My Papa's Waltz" and "I Knew a Woman" suited to their subjects?

This question gives you a good opportunity to review some material from the Sound of Poetry section of the Handbook. Students should quickly discover that the underlying meter is iambic trimeter. You might read the poem according to its metrical stress, to establish the basic rhythm:

> the WHISkey ON your BREATH
> could MAKE a SMALL boy DIZzy;
> but *I* hung ON like DEATH:
> such WALTZing WAS not EASy.

We never lose track of the "ground beat," as Roethke calls it, and so always have the idea of the dance reinforced. Some students may see in Roethke's three–beat line an analogy to the three–four time of the waltz; I confess I quickly find myself over my head in attempting to trace analogies between meter and measure. There are, of course, many lines where the metrical stress and the rhetorical stress differ somewhat, and it might be worthwhile to have your class decide whether we should read lines like 13 and 14 with or against the meter, giving the impression of the dance's rhythm overriding everything or giving the impression that the rhythm breaks down.

The iambic pentameter of "I Knew a Woman" is not regular to the point of monotony, but it is far more obvious than it is, for example, in Milton's blank verse. One reason is that the lines are plainly bracketed by being end–stopped and rhymed lines: the pattern is easier to discover when we can hear the beginning and end of each repetition. Roethke also reinforces the meter by frequent use of repetition and of alliteration on stressed syllables ("She played it quick, she played it light and loose"). That the poem should be so rhythmic is obviously right; its themes are pattern, motion, and rhythm—roundness of hips, roundness of breasts, the sway of both hips and breasts when the whole body moves. You might ask your class why the rhythm should involve longer lines here than in "My Papa's Waltz." Surely a part of the answer is that the shorter lines could never give us the sense of lush, unhurried motions necessary to "I Knew a Woman."

–D.H.

Elizabeth Bishop

Elizabeth Bishop's reputation is growing steadily, but she is not yet truly popular and probably is underrepresented even in university poetry classes. The reason may be that her directness is somehow mistaken for obscurity. As the fine critic Helen Vendler points out, many of Bishop's poems either take the perspective of a child or have a childlike simplicity of speech and imagery.

I think your class will appreciate Bishop's work more readily if they think a bit first about the relationship between childhood and exploration. Children are natural explorers. The can give complete attention to an object that attracts them by the novelty of its color, taste, texture, or sound. This capacity for rapt attention, for wonder, engages children with the physical world, but—as every parent knows—it does nothing for their manners and can sometimes lead them to harm. We would like to think that children eventually learn to live in the world by acquiring wisdom. In fact, most of us get no further than "common sense," which keeps us sociable and sanitary and relatively free of strain by checking our exploratory impulses. Eventually, we lose our curiosity about the taste of things, stop staring at or sniffing strangers, and stop asking about things we don't understand. Unfortunately, as Henry David Thoreau points out, this sort of common sense can mean no more than that we have reduced our perceptions to conform to a sort of least common denominator. In order to stop sniffing and staring, we may stop smelling and seeing. "The commonest sense of all," Thoreau says, "is the sense of men asleep, which they express by snoring."

Some writers (perhaps all great writers) reach adulthood without having entirely shed the child's fascination with exploring the world. As a result they may be uncomfortable neighbors, always seeing things we haven't noticed, indifferent to some things common sense teaches us to value, apparently eccentric or difficult. Thoreau was certainly this way. A group of his Concord neighbors once found him immersed to the neck in a pond, naked except for his hat, oblivious to everything but the frog he was watching. Emily Dickinson, too, despite a life of rigid propriety, seemed constantly to be exploring landscapes no one had noticed: the small external sights of her garden, the internal mazes of her personality.

Bishop's range of physical exploration was much greater than either Thoreau's or Dickinson's, and her poems include landscape features from Nova Scotia, Brazil, and many points between. Sometimes the alienness of these landscapes helps the reader feel what every serious explorer comes to know: that the world is in fact alien, and cannot be made domestic by the coziness of an armchair and a hearth. To a poet like Bishop, the world is full of unexpected sights, pleasures, ironies, and terrors. It is never the comfortable, stable place "common sense" tries to make it.

QUESTIONS

1. Explain the experience Bishop describes in "In the Waiting Room" and tell how it is related to the themes and subjects of her other poems.

What this poem recreates is a tension between two ways of experiencing the world. One is the way of undivided attention, the sort of attention most of us experienced more often in childhood than we can now, and I think the sort that the Romantics viewed with almost religious awe. We are caught up for a time so completely in the thing we are seeing that we have no significant awareness of ourselves or of the passage of time. We are all eyes, all ears, all senses and imagination. As time goes by, we lose this capacity for undivided attention and can watch nothing without watching ourselves watching it, without thinking we are having (or are not having) a good time, without thinking of what we will have to do this afternoon, or about how we are getting older by the minute.

Apparently the poem recreates the moment when Bishop first felt the second consciousness ("shades of the prison house," as Wordsworth puts it) close in on her. Suddenly she is aware of herself as a person, another Aunt Consuelo:

> But I felt: you are an *I*,
>
> You are an *Elizabeth*,
> you are one of *them*.
> Why should you be one, too?

Part of the shock comes from the realization that her body really is like the bodies of those around her, and that she is stuck with it:

> What similarities—
> boots, hands, the family voice
> I felt in my throat, or even
> the *National Geographic*
> and those awful hanging breasts—
> held us together
> or made us all just one?

This passage reminds me of Marvell in "A Dialogue Between the Soul and Body":

> O, who shall from this dungeon raise
> A soul enslaved so many ways
> With bolts of bones, that fettered stands
> In feet, and manacled in hands.

But the underlying discovery is that she is not unique. Pinned to a body and a history, she is like the other people around her. How "unlikely," as she says, that the consciousness she has experienced everything through should be concentrated in just another body, so like all others.

Bishop's critical themes are here: the search for truly fresh experience; the avoidance of the second hand and the mass produced. We see them again in "Questions of Travel," where she pronounces it worthwhile to travel to a different hemisphere to hear "the sad, two-noted, wooden tune/of disparate wooden clogs" that have not machined to an identical pitch. We see it in "Crusoe in England," where Crusoe half–regrets leaving his desert island with "one kind of everything" and one knife that "reeked of meaning" because it was irreplaceable.

2. Bishop's interest in unique images makes her poems seem like an interesting album of photographs or a long home movie. What images are particularly interesting?

If this question seems to degenerate into a scavenger hunt, it probably should. We want students to forget about the poems as cultural experiences for the minute and instead to view them with the abandon that Bishop herself seemed to bring to William Carlos Williams' poetry: ". . . she admitted that for her the highpoint of the poem was the word that Williams invented to imitate the sea elephant's roar: 'Blouaugh.' It was music to her ears . . . ." Here are some of my favorite snippets from the Bishop album:

From "In the Waiting Room"

- ◆ the dead man slung on a pole and captioned "Long Pig" (25)
- ◆ the women with wire wound round their necks, "like lightbulbs" (30)

From "Questions of Travel"

- ◆ the unmatched wooden clogs (37)
- ◆ the bird singing above a gasoline pump in a baroque church made of bamboo (what a wonderful mishmash!) (43)

From "The Prodigal"

- ◆ the "glass–smooth dung" on the walls of the pig sty (4)
- ◆ the "pacing aureole" of the receding lantern reflected in the mud (23)

From "The Armadillo"

- ◆ *everything* about the appearance of the fire balloons
- ◆ the rabbit looking like ash "with fixed, ignited eyes" (36)

From "Crusoe in England"

- ◆ the high–domed turtles that hiss like teakettles (36)
- ◆ the waterspouts like flexible glass chimneys (51)

From "Filling Station"

- ◆ the "over all/black translucency" (4)
- ◆ the rows of cans that say "Esso–so–so–so" (39)

These are not, by and large, the things one finds listed in the Michelin guides. Bishop's perceptions are as sharp and cliché–free as if she had just landed on the planet.

3. How does Bishop suit her verse form to her subject?

Bishop seems equally at ease in metered forms and in poems that follow the cadences of natural speech. The free–verse poems are hard for students to discuss, but they might notice that she uses a shorter line in "Filling Station" and "In the Waiting Room" than she does in "Questions of Travel" or "Crusoe in England." We can speculate, very tentatively, that there may be good reasons for these choices. The short lines of "Waiting Room" lend themselves to phrasing that sounds plausible in the mouth of a child:

> It was winter. It got dark
> early. The waiting room
> was full of grown up people. (6–8)

> I said to myself: three days
> and you'll be seven years old. (54–55)

The short lines in "Filling Station" fit with its snapshot qualities. But "Questions" and "Crusoe" belong in the traditions of the ode and the dramatic monologue, and in them Bishop uses lines that are longer and more variable.

The metered and rhymed poems are so masterfully done that they seem effortless. Bishop once told an interviewer that she had tried to write villanelles before "One Art," but that this one had been a gift, coming to her almost fully formed. Certainly the shape of the poem, its repetitions with increasing meaning, is perfectly suited to the subject of increasingly serious losses. "The Prodigal," elaborately rhymed (abacdbcedfeggf/abacdbecffdfgg) in iambic pentameter, is really a pair of rearranged sonnets. It reminds me of the inventive choral songs of Tennyson's "The Lotos Eaters," but it may go Tennyson one better. Notice that the full rhymes seem to pull each line back into the poem, but that the closing half–rhyme (time/home) breaks the pattern, just at the point when the Prodigal decides to break away from his exile.

–D.H.

Randall Jarrell

Jarrell is very strongly represented in *The Riverside Anthology*. In addition to his poetry, we have his translation of and comment on *The Three Sisters*, his account of the composition of "The Woman at the Washington Zoo," and his comments on Grimm, Cummings, Stevens, and Wilbur: enough material that a clever student could eke out a research paper without seeing the inside of a library, certainly enough that students can by triangulation get a sense of where Jarrell stands.

Like Montale, Auden, Lowell, and Wilbur, Jarrell is a poet unreconciled to the consumer society that has developed in America in the last half of the twentieth century and spread itself across the world in a wave of advertising. In an essay called "A Sad Heart at the Supermarket," he tells us that the poet's mission is to recommend well–water and apples, but that this is very difficult when the public has been brought up on marzipan and ethyl alcohol.

If your students come to see Jarrell from the right angle, they will understand how strong his aversion to the artificial stimulants of twentieth-century society are and how firmly convinced he is that the purer life is available to those who can stay in touch with their bodies and with nature.

QUESTIONS

1. How are the themes of "The Woman at the Washington Zoo" echoed in Jarrell's other poems?

This question encourages students to look very closely at both "Woman at the Washington Zoo" (p. 1089) and Jarrell's discussion of it. I realize that teachers brought up in the strong trust–the–tale–not–the–teller tradition of New Criticism may be reluctant to place too much emphasis on Jarrell's commentary, but the particular case here argues for at least a temporary abandonment of the general rule. Jarrell's comment is a clear, frank, and fascinating account of the way that a poem becomes a magnet for the poet's deep concerns about the world around him. It gives students insight into the way that a very good and very representative twentieth-century poet thinks about his work. The themes that stand out in both the poem and the comment are

◆ a condemnation of the "many–levelled machine" in which the individual is reduced to an "aging machine part."

◆ a presentation of animal nature as an antithesis (perhaps an antidote) to the influence of the machine.

It is fairly easy to see the same themes appearing in other Jarrell poems.

The machine appears in "The Woman at the Washington Zoo" in the form of the bureaucracy, where a man can be called a Deputy Chief Assistant and see "nothing remarkable about the title," and where "no comment" is sometimes a form of protection and sometimes a sigh of relief. Jarrell's comment ties the poem to the Pentagon bureaucracy, surely among the largest human machines in the world. "The Death of the Ball Turret Gunner," however, shows the effect of a larger human machine still: "the state" militarized for global war and expending human life very efficiently—"When I died they washed me out of the turret with a hose." "The Snow Leopard" shows a human machine organized to another end: profit. The men who "trade to that last stillness for their death" are the "last cold capillaries" of a circulatory system whose heart is found in places like Wall Street of the Bourse. The "brute and geometrical necessity" or the market is bringing them into contact with a fate equally brute and geometrical. "Field and Forest" also shows the work of the market machine, here transforming the landscape. Heaven (not apparently averse to puns) asks the farmer "What's your field?" It a question to put to a specialized producer for the market system. The farmer answers with fields that "have a terrible monotony," analogous to the dull, null navy of "The Woman at the Washington Zoo."

"The Woman at the Washington Zoo" shows one of the odd truths about city life in the twentieth century: that we go to zoos to remember what it is like to be animals. The woman discovers that the caged animals are freer behind bars than she is, hedged by conventional behavior and inhibited from every display of joy in her body. "Oh, bars of my own body, open, open!" The sexual imagery is obvious, and it is characteristic of Jarrell to balance sex against the Pentagon bureaucracy. But Jarrell does not equate nature–in–humanity exclusively with sexual impulses. Sometimes, as in "The Death of the Ball Turret Gunner" and "The Snow Leopard," he simply shows what happens when the machine of society puts one of its parts into an environment hostile to the flesh. In one poem we are reminded that the warrior in his flight suit resembles a freezing, furry animal; in the other we are reminded that the trader, like the yak, is a "stunned universe/That gasps like a kettle for its thinning life."

"Field and Forest" shows man's affinity to nature as something deeper than the body. In effect, the farmer is two men in one. The machine man would "make farm out of all the forest" if he could, since the forest produces neither food nor dollars. But the natural man likes the forest much more than he likes the field. At night, with not only his pragmatism but his body laid aside, he wishes his ultimate wish: to return to the forest as the equal of a fox.

2. How does our knowledge of Jarrell's other poems help us understand "In Montecito"?

A poem that features "a scream with breasts" and a woman who disappears suddenly, leaving an empty girdle, might strike some students as too strange to bear interpretation. While the imagery is a remarkable combination of the literal and the surrealistic, I think readers familiar with Jarrell's themes can see them at work here. The contractors who are dismantling the scream are, again, parts of the machine that is always putting society into order without attending too much to the real demands of human nature. The scream might almost be the scream of "The Woman at the Washington Zoo," the scream of someone who has discovered she is trapped. Of course, Greenie Taliaferro is the most likely source of the scream. What we hear about her could allow us to conclude that she is a woman who reached late middle age convinced that what the machine gave her—a fancy car, money, cricket matches, an electric toothbrush, platinum hair—was enough. Suddenly it all gives way. Perhaps Greenie goes mad; perhaps she dies. Perhaps it is her scream that hangs in the air; perhaps it is the poet's scream on her behalf.

3. What is the tone of "Nestus Gurley"? How does the tone change as the poem progresses?

The tone of "Nestus Gurley" is so different from that of the other Jarrell poems collected here that your students may not catch it. You might ask them what they make of the third stanza (lines 20–29), how it fits with their expectations of poetry. It shouldn't be hard to find someone surprised by the triviality of ten lines devoted to Nestus Gurley's income, his hat, and the method of computing the monthly newspaper bill. Much of the poem is deliberately and delightfully trivial. In the first stanza, Jarrell hears "on the lawn,/On the walk, on the lawn" the sound of Nestus' footsteps: a reminder that the sound changes as he moves from grass to concrete to grass. In the sixth, we get a little picture of the appearance and habits of the cat Elsie. None of this would seem, in the cosmic scheme, to have the sort of weight we might assign to the shrinking forests of "Field and Forest" or the vision of the vulture in "The Woman at the Washington Zoo." Certainly Jarrell's thought of wearing the paper Nestus has folded into a "tricorne fit for Napoleon" is nothing more than an expression of high spirits: the poet leaping up into the air and clicking his heels.

The lightness of the poem shows in its characteristic repetitions and retractions.

> . . . a note or two
> That with a note or two would be a tune.

> Sometimes he comes with dogs, sometimes with children,
> Sometimes with dogs and children. (22–23)

> . . . "It's two–eighty."

"How could it be two–eighty?"
"Because this month there're five Sundays: it's two–eighty"
(27–29)

     . . . the boy Nestus
Delivers to me the Morning Star, the Evening Star
—Ah no, only the Morning *News*, the Evening *Record*

The play of statement and qualification here sometimes approaches the pure playfulness of Curley's comment on the pair of "snow–white" horses in *Oklahoma!*: "Well, one's like snow, the other's more like milk." It is surprising to find the author of "The Woman at the Washington Zoo" sounding so much like Oscar Hammerstein.

The pattern of repetition and qualification that at first establishes the light tone later helps the poem gain heft. The repeated motifs of sleeping and waking (lines 1, 11–12, 40, 44) and dawn and dusk (15–18, 20, 30–34, 39, 50–51, 64) build to the mention of our last sleeping and waking (death and the Last Judgment) in the final stanza. The motif of gold–leaf (31, 53) comes to represent the occasional beauty of this life, and the star (13–14, 33–34, 43–44, 49, 76) to represent our hopes. Nestus'

     . . . sound half song, half breath: a note or two
That with a note or two would be a tune.

appears first as a humorous comment. But we encounter it again in lines 66–67 and 79–80, and then we feel that it summarizes Jarrell's most optimistic view of the human condition.

–D.H.

Dylan Thomas

If your students read William Carlos Williams's comment on pages 1098–1099, they will find that it praises Thomas for qualities that seem to be antithetical. On the one hand, Williams says that the poetry can be called "drunken poetry, it smacks of the divine." On the other hand, he says that the "clarity of [Thomas'] thought is not obscured by his images, but rather clarified." I suspect that most readers starting fresh with Thomas will be at first inclined to agree with Williams' "drunken" statement to dismiss the assertion that the poems contain clear thought.

The accusation of being unclear haunted Thomas throughout his career. When he had published only a few poems, he received a rejection from an editor who admired the technical accomplishment of the poems, but felt that they had an unsubstantial, "dream–like quality," like the automatic writing of a person in a trance. Thomas, very upset by the note, wrote to his friend Pamela Hansford Johnson:

> Automatic writing is worthless as literature, however interesting it may be to the psychologist and pathologist. So, perhaps, after all I am nothing but a literary oddity, a little freak of nature whose madness runs into print rather than into ravings and illusions. It may be, too, an illusion that keeps me writing, the illusion of myself as some misunderstood poet of talent. The note has depressed me more than the usual adverse criticism. It shows not dislike, or mere incomprehension, but confession of bewilderment, and almost fear, at the method by which I write my poetry.

> But he is wrong, I swear it. My facility, as he calls it, is in reality tremendously hard work. I write at the speed of two lines an hour. I have written hundreds of poems, and each one has taken me a great many painful, brain–racking, sweaty hours.

In order to get students to do justice to Thomas, it will be necessary to get them to read the poems carefully for theme as well as for sound.

QUESTIONS

1. Explain the stanzaic pattern of "The Force that through the Green Fuse Drives the Flower"—both metrically and logically. Paraphrase one stanza.

This is a question I am not capable of answering completely and I don't expect students to answer it completely either, but the attempt should add to their understanding of the poem. Metrically the stanzas are made up of two lines of loosely iambic pentameter, a line of dimeter, and two more lines of pentameter. The rhyme scheme in the first stanza is *ababa* with weak rhymes (rhymes on unstressed syllables, "feminine" rhymes) in the *a*–position and half–rhymes in the *b*–position. The rhyme scheme disintegrates as the poem progresses, and in the last full stanza shows only in *sores/stars* (lines 18 and 20). The logical or rhetorical pattern appears to be this: each stanza begins by naming a force in nature, then shows the poet's relation to the force, then shows a contrasting force in nature and the poet's relation to it, then explains that the poet has no words to tell some object in nature what his relation to the object is. Like the rhyme scheme, the rhetorical scheme diffuses as the poem progresses, but it never quite vanishes.

Paraphrases of the stanzas are likely to vary widely from student to student: here are two creditable ones for the first stanza.

I am driven by the same natural force that makes the flower explode from the end of its green stem, and I will be killed by the same forces that dry up the roots of trees. And yet I cannot tell the rose that I am, like it, imperfect because I come partly from the fever of creation and partly from the chill of mortality and limitation.

The same force that makes water well up in a spring forces my blood through my arteries. Whatever dries up these babbling springs will eventually dry up my mouth, too. I cannot tell my veins that just as time will eventually drink dry the mountain springs, it will eventually drink them dry.

I'm sure you will find points to disagree with in each of these interpretations, an indication of how effective a paraphrase assignment on this poem ought to be in stimulating class discussion.

2. Is "The Hunchback in the Park" a poem about cruelty?

Here is a yes/no question that begs for a well–explained yes or (better, I think) no. I'm afraid that students who are used to having their emotions manipulated along fairly predictable lines may feel that their job when they are confronted by this poem is to be sympathetic with the hunchback and to be shocked by the cruelty of the children. Such a simple notion of the poem misses a great deal. It misses for one thing a plain bit of evidence: the "wild boys" are described in line 40 as "innocent as strawberries." More importantly, it doesn't deal with the role of imagination in the poem. What does the persecuted hunchback do in the park all day? What is his job? He creates

> A woman figure without fault
> Straight as a young elm
> Straight and tall from his crooked bones
> That she might stand in the night
> After the locks and chains

Psychologically, this woman is the perfect expression of the hunchback's desires: a beautiful woman who is (one presumes) his dream lover, and (more interestingly) an alter ego who is tall and straight and can defy the authorities who lock the park up every night. Certainly the cruelty of the boys and of the society in general must contribute to the man's misery and so lends intensity to his daylong fantasies, but I think Thomas's interest is in the redemptive, curative power of the imagination itself. Like Blake's chimney sweep or little black boy, the hunchback has a spirit that transcends physical and social limitations. The real man, so to speak, *is* that angel he creates.

The children, too, are preoccupied with imagination. When they are not persecuting the hunchback, they are imagining tigers and sailors in the woods.

3. What is the theme of "Over Sir John's Hill"?

If your class has read Hopkins's "The Windhover," they may enjoy comparing the two poems. In both, the image of a hawk, brilliantly depicted, becomes a vehicle for exploring the poet's view of life.

Thomas's view is very different from Hopkins's. While he has Hopkins's keen appreciation for the creation, he has no belief in a creator and so has to work out his affirmation of life within the context of a fairly dire Darwinian view. Put simply, Thomas's theme is that life (beautiful life) preys on life in a constant display of destruction. The hawk "hangs still" in his "fiery tyburn" and seems by his gaze to draw small birds to his "claws" and "gallows": the imagery shows he is ready to slaughter one of the innocent sparrows whose fall God is said to notice (Matthew 10:29); it also suggests that he is himself cued up for slaughter (a "noosed hawk"—ask your class to imagine what would happen to the swooping hawk in lines 10 and 11 if he were in fact noosed).

The only figures who seem to stand outside this world of carnage are the "fishing holy stalking heron" (11) and the poet. The heron, however, though his appearance makes him look like a holy man (compare "Poem on His Birthday") who "grieves on the weeded verge" (47), is quite as bloodthirsty as the hawk and just as surely doomed to die. His head is a headstone in line 12, and throughout the poem he is calmly sticking his sharp beak into the water to spear fish, even amid a shower of "snapt feathers" that drift down from the hawk's kill (50). The poet identifies himself with the heron:

> We grieve as the blithe birds, never again, leave shingle and elm,
> The heron and I,
> I young Aesop fabling to the near night by the dingle
> Of eels, saint heron hymning in the shell-hung distant
>
> Crystal harbour vale . . . .

And the identification ought to make us smile. For a carnivorous poet to write an elegy for the passing of sparrows swallowed up by hawks involves something like hypocrisy: Thomas is willing to face up to this with a bit of self–mockery.

Despite both the unsentimental picture of the food chain and the poet's wry admission that he is part of it, the poem is simultaneously a celebration of life and an elegy. The last four lines show the poet engraving "on this time–shaken stone" the notes of the tune he hears coming up from "the wear–willow river"; these notes are his dirge for the "slain birds sailing." If we look closely at the key phrases, we see that it is not merely the sparrows whose passing is lamented. The "slain birds sailing" suggests hawks at least as much as sparrows. The adjective "wear–willow" seems to imply both that the river is dressed in willows and that it wears them away as it passes. The "time–shaken stone" on which the poet writes might be a tombstone, but it might also be the earth itself. "Over Sir John's Hill" is finally a poem about the mutability of a well–loved world.

4. How are "Poem in October" and "Poem on His Birthday" related to such Romantic poems as Wordsworth's Intimations Ode or "Tintern Abbey"?

This question is so large that it may lead students in any number of directions. I hope that they will notice the poems are clearly in that meditative tradition Wordsworth established with "Tintern Abbey": a poet sees in the face of nature the inevitability of his decline and death, he approaches despair, but finds consolation. In "Poem in October," the poet at the "high tide" of his life climbs a hill overlooking the harbor and town and seems at first to be in harmony with nature and perfectly happy to look back on the spring and summer of his past. Then he remembers (as Wordsworth would) the "true/Joy" of "the long dead child" he once was. Now the thought of mortality is on him, and he looks down at the town "leaved with October blood" and can only hope (or pray) for another year of joy. "Poem on His Birthday," written five years later, develops the Wordsworthian pattern more fully. The poet is once again high above the sea. Through the first forty–three lines he contemplates life in the jaws of death and, therefore, naturally sees his birthday as another step toward inevitable destruction: he is the "rhymer in the long tongued room,/Who tolls his birthday bell." At line 44 the poem changes dramatically and becomes one of the most forceful affirmations of life in twentieth–century poetry: ". . . chains break to a hammer flame/And love unbolts the dark." The poem may have the sound of religious conversion to some ears, but Thomas does not accept any creed. He prays

> Faithlessly unto Him
>
> Who is the light of old
> And air shaped Heaven . . . .

Logically, he continues to recognize "The voyage to ruin I must run" (78), but the spirit feels something else:

> . . . the closer I move
> To death, one man through his sundered hulks,
>   The louder the sun blooms
> And the tusked, ramshackling sea exults (91–94)

Your students might notice that there is a stronger optimism here than in the Immortality Ode. It is not the mild consolation of the Philosophic Mind that Thomas feels, but a stronger inspiration as he nears his end.

–D.H.

Gwendolyn Brooks

It will be interesting to see what becomes of Gwendolyn Brooks' reputation over the next few years. It is hard to name a poet of comparable ability who has presented both academic critics and appreciative readers with such a conundrum. Brooks began writing poetry when she was seven years old, encouraged by a mother who wanted her to be "the *lady* Paul Laurence Dunbar." She had her first poem published when she was eleven, so that we can say she had been publishing for 21 years when she won her Pulitzer Prize in 1950, and she published steadily with Harper and Row through 1968. For thirty–eight of these thirty–nine years she was comfortable using in her poetry essentially the same technical tools used by, for example, W. H. Auden. That is, she wrote sonnets; invented her own stanzaic forms; adopted, varied, or abandoned the iambic pentameter line; mixed meters inventively within poems. She was, as Clara Claiborne Park pointed out in *The Nation* (September 26, 1987), "intellectual, disconcerting, subtle to the point of obscurity, all the things whites like and blacks [in the turbulence of the late 1960s] found unusable."

Under the influence of such black poets and editors as Don Lee (now Haki Madhubuti) and LeRoi Jones (now Imamu Baraka), Brooks began to reshape her poetic identity. She severed her connection with the sonnet and with metered verse. In 1972 she announced that her aim henceforward would be to write poems that would reach a specifically black audience, wherever they might be: ". . . in taverns . . . alleys . . . gutters, schools, offices, factories, prisons . . . pulpits . . . thrones." In fact, for whatever reason, she has become less accessible to white audiences and black ever since. She left Harper and began to publish with a series of smaller black publishing houses; her books, heretofore reviewed in *The New York Times Book Review, Saturday Review, Poetry*, and the other major literary magazines, are hardly noticed and essentially unavailable to the reader who does not live in Chicago or Detroit or on the campus of a major university with access to interlibrary loans.

In 1987, her career is getting a new appraisal, largely by black poets and critics, but in a climate more sympathetic with formalism, it is Brooks' early works that get the attention. The shift to free verse and direct rhetorical appeal, as scholars point out, did not make her poetry more black: Whitman is as white as Keats.

QUESTIONS

1. How marked is the difference in style and tone between "The Chicago Defender Sends a Man to Little Rock" and "Riot"?

"Little Rock" is a poem that shows the virtues that won Brooks her wide audience in the 50's and 60's. In tone, it is objective and compassionate. Apparently the newspaper would prefer a report full of rhetorical fire, a condemnation of Little Rock and its people. Instead the speaker finds that the "biggest News" is that the people of Little Rock "are like people everywhere," even though they spit at black schoolgirls and beat black schoolboys, even though they are filled with the "lariat lynch-wish." In this poem, Brooks is clearly writing as an "integrationist," someone whose deep impulse is to minimize the differences between the races. The term would later be leveled against Brooks as a criticism by more radical black writers.

The form of the poem is remarkable, as your students will see if they trouble to identify the rhyme pattern within each stanza: aaabbbb/aaa/aaaa/abbba/aaabcbb/abbccdcdec/abcbc/ aabbccdd/aabbccddee. This scheme is comparable in its inventiveness to something we might find in Tennyson (the Choric Songs in "The Lotos–Eaters") or Elizabeth Bishop ("The Prodigal"). The rhymes themselves are sometimes surprising: not everyone would have the nerve to rhyme on Lorna Doones, and Barcarolle/implacable/intellectual is surprising both aurally and intellectually. In lines 28–37, we get a passage "subtle to the point of obscurity" that might come from Wallace Stevens or T. S. Eliot: I *believe* that we are getting a comment on the Southern belle—her ability to soothe the male ego becomes entwined with her sense of fashion, so that

> The wispy soils go. And uncertain
> Half–havings are clarified into sures

may tell us that this reporter from Chicago, like all men, feels charmed in the presence of a beautiful and beautifully dressed woman who knows how to make him feel relaxed and confident. It might mean something entirely different.

Whatever the meaning of this passage, others are very clear. The speaker (and presumably Brooks) can't work himself up into a glowing hate. He even admires some things about the people of Little Rock: their culture (high and low), their sense of community (". . . it is our business to be bothered, is our business/To cherish bores or boredom . . ."). Yes, they do horrible things, but they are not the first or last: "The loveliest lynchee was our Lord."

"Riot," written early in Brooks' second career, is less "integrationist" in its tone. John Cabot "whitebluerose below his golden hair" is not viewed with any sympathy. A fictional figure amid the factual riots that broke out in Chicago after the assassination of Martin Luther King, he goes down crying, "Forgive these nigguhs that know not what they do." One feels the weight of "nigguhs" in a peculiar way. As a word used by a white speaker addressing a white or black listener, it would be (ordinarily) racist. As a word used by a black speaker addressing a black listener, it can be any number of things, including a parody of white racism. Here it is put into the mouth of a white character in a poem by a black poet. Does it make a difference whether her imagined reader is white or black? Yes. This word, more than any other, makes me feel the intended audience is distinctly black.

But it is a mistake to assume that the poetic style is as plain and direct as some representations of the two–career view of Gwendolyn Brooks would make us believe. "Little Rock" is a poem of ironies: the juxtapositions of daily kindness with hostility toward the school children, of striving for culture with the vulgarity of their violence, of churchgoing with the desire to lynch. In "Riot," the irony has not been replaced, but intensified and made more bitter. The contrast between the just anger of the poor and Cabot's concern for his Scotch, his restaurants, his galleries, and his Jaguar comes to a climax in the statement: "Que tu es grossier! " is presumably Cabot's comment on the crowd of rioters, but the reader will naturally apply it to him. Here is the old irony applied with new force.

2. Are the themes of "We Real Cool" and "The Chicago Picasso" related?

Here again, we have a poem from the first career and another that comes from Brooks' transitional period. I think, though, that the poems *are* on related themes. Discipline is the issue: "We must cook ourselves and style ourselves for Art," and there is a side of human nature that resists this discipline. In "Picasso" this resistant side is expressed by staying at home and having "the nice beer ready" and in belching, sniffing, and scratching. In "We Real Cool" the same side takes the form of endless hours posturing in the pool hall.

When you discuss "We Real Cool," you might want to ask your students to scan the poem and comment on the relation between form and content. The scanning will make them realize that the poem is like none other they have read: every syllable is stressed, and the only way I can think of to describe the meter is to assume that the basic foot is three stressed syllables, chanted. Brooks breaks her lines oddly—most of us would have put the We's at the beginnings of lines—so as to produce a sort of jive-talk countrapuntal rhythm. And, of course, she gives us a wonderful set of internal rhymes or alliterations.

Your students will surely notice that one effect of the strong rhythm of the poem is to make us feel the bump when it ends. Another, I think, is to make the words of the pool players sound simultaneously swaggering and childish.

3. What is the difference in tone between "A Street in Bronzeville: South-
east Corner" and "The Blackstone Rangers"?

Once again the difference in tone between the earlier and later Brooks
shows here. "Corner" is in several ways comparable to Frost's "Provide,
Provide!" There is the same theme of converting sexual attraction into
hard cash, and the same suggestion that "boughten" dignity is better than
none. Most important, there is a similar sense of detachment. The author
does not recommend a philosophy, but makes an observation. The extremely formal structure, by removing the poem from direct speech, keeps
it from sounding like speechifying. It is cool and ironic, and only says
that such things happen.

Your class might compare the neutrality and distance with which
Brooks discusses the Madam of "Corner" with the way that she becomes
engaged with Mary of "Gang Girls." She makes it clear that Mary is a
victim of her environment, "a rose in a whiskey glass." She gives us a
picture of Mary's life as an unvaried round of seasons in which a few
pleasures are stolen (often literally stolen, like the diamond) and sex, her
one power, has to be used with conscious calculation if she is to get out of
life even "the props and niceties of non–loneliness." In "The Blackstone
Rangers" a tough, compassionate involvement with people replaces the
subtler ironies of "Corner."

–D.H.

Robert Lowell

Ten years after Lowell's death, the question of his place in the history of
American literature is far from settled, partly because he was such a
commanding presence in his lifetime. Early in his career Lowell established himself as a master of formal verse and the sort of irony that delighted the New Critics. Later he came under the influence of William
Carlos Williams, and changed his spots dramatically. *Life Studies* (1959)
and *For the Union Dead* (1964) became banner books for poets who favored
freer forms and a less cautious exposure of the poet's emotions. In the late
sixties and the seventies, though his productivity decreased, Lowell's
"greatness" was so generally conceded that it is not surprising to find it
sometimes disputed today.

Some of his poems, however, are so indisputably great that there is no
way around them. "For the Union Dead" is one of these, and may be the
best possible introduction to his work.

QUESTIONS

1. How does "For the Union Dead" manage to be at once a poem about Lowell's personal life, American culture in the 1950s, and American history?

If you are Robert Lowell, descendant of such Lowells as James Russell, are already established as a poet of national importance, and are standing on Boston Common, it is perhaps easier than usual to see the connection between personality, culture, and history.

Nonetheless, we can see some particulars by which Lowell makes the connection. We can begin with the outermost circle of the poem: the historical. Because he is standing directly between the Statehouse and the memorial to Shaw and his Negro regiment, he is quite literally placed in the middle of a historical question. What has become of the Republic that "they gave up everything to preserve"? The answer is that the monument "sticks like a fishbone/in the city's throat." The dedication to the public life that Shaw represents is largely dead in Boston, and the emancipation for which he and his troops died has not yet come to pass: on television, Lowell can watch reports of the desegregation crisis in the public schools. It is not an accident that Lowell describes Shaw as "lean/as a compass needle" since his function in the poem is partly to show that the Republic has left its true course.

The historical level of the poem becomes a critique of contemporary culture not only on the desegregation issue, but on the other manifestations of life's increasing brutality and materialism. Boston Common is being excavated to create an "underworld" parking garage; it is perhaps surprising that the men who conceive of such a project would preserve the monument at all. As it is, both monument and Statehouse tremble (literally, and perhaps figuratively) because of the actions of the dinosaur steamshovels. Soon the Shaw monument will almost literally be a monument on a bubble, with nothing substantial to support it. The underground garage project seems a perfect symbol of a society willing to cut its historic roots out from under itself in the pursuit of utilitarian conveniences that Shaw would have despised. Equally striking is the advertisement on Boylston Street:

> . . . a commercial photograph
> shows Hiroshima boiling
>
> over a Mosler Safe, the "Rock of Ages"
> that survived the blast.

This is the only "monument" for the last war, and it chiefly symbolizes an avariciousness that is willing to profit from one of the great tragedies of history. It is hard to imagine a harsher condemnation of a society than a poem that ends with the lines "a savage servility/slides by on grease."

History and culture are taken personally throughout the "For the Union Dead," so that it is a bit false to distinguish between the public and private dimensions of the poem. Nonetheless, some passages point more clearly than others to Lowell's individual life. The theme here is mutability. Changes in the face of Boston remind Lowell of the passage of his life. In early middle age, he remembers his childhood visits to the aquarium, and compares himself unfavorably with the unaging "abstract Union Soldier" on war memorials who grows "slimmer and younger each year."

Lowell's success in knitting together the three levels of the poem comes largely from his having what Randall Jarrell calls "a thoroughly historical mind." Jarrell says that "His present contains the past—especially Rome, the late Middle Ages, and a couple of centuries of New England—as an operative skeleton just beneath the skin."

2. Poems like "The Neo–Classical Urn," "Night Sweat," and "Waking in the Blue" involve private memories that most of us would be reluctant to talk about even in a letter to a friend. Why do people who do not know the poet care to read such poems?

Some of your students may answer that *they* don't care to read them, or that people who do want to read them are compelled by little more than a prying curiosity. Yet Lowell's poems have appealed to a wide range of readers, and I think it is legitimate to ask students what qualities in the poems can account for their success.

One quality that I think they should learn to notice is humor. For Lowell, as for Sylvia Plath, humor is not inconsistent with even the direst of confessional poems. "The Neo–Classical Urn," for example, is about a memory that torments Lowell well into middle age (see the closing lines of "Night Sweat"), but the poem itself is partly parody. One feels that in lines 8–28 Lowell is "doing" Wordsworth with a twist. There is the same exuberance in childhood, "that season of joy," but the exuberance is hardly an illustration of close contact with heaven or nature: it expresses itself in the torment of turtles. The gathered turtles are dumped in an urn, and Lowell begins immediately to parody Keats' "Ode on a Grecian Urn": "Oh neo–classical white urn, Oh nymph,/Oh lute! The boy was pitiless who strummed/their elegy." "Waking in the Blue" has its ironies (the B. U. sophomore who is reading *The Meaning of Meaning* in a mental hospital) and its wisecracks (see lines 14 and 38–39), and it sketches Stanley, Bobbie, and Lowell himself with a Dickensian flair.

The humor sometimes makes us smile, but in both "Waking" and "Ode" it is clearly whistling in the dark: both poems end on a note that seems to wipe the smile off Lowell's lips and ours. This brings us to a second quality that makes the confessional poems so different from the artless

confessions we might get from other people who have suffered psychological traumas similar to Lowell's. Lowell is capable in the poems of
viewing himself with enough detachment to re–create himself as a character; in fact, the confessional poems in *Life Studies* and *For the Union Dead*
can be read almost as a novel that traces the descent of the character Lowell
into a dark night of the soul and shows his gradual re–emergence into
the light. Part of the equipment that seems to protect him from destruction
on the way down is his capacity for irony; but on the way up, this capacity
seems sometimes to be an encumbrance.

"Night Sweat" is the penultimate poem in *For the Union Dead*, and shows
Lowell with the armor of irony removed. Although it can be tied precisely
to a particular period in Lowell's particular life, it can surely be read as a
statement about Everyman's struggle to escape from the demon of isolation,
the panic of a creature dying alone in a body that is the spirit's funeral
urn. You might have your students look at its form closely. They will
discover that it is a double sonnet. The first shows in miniature the
descent characteristic of all the confessional poems. It begins with a look
back at the productive days before the spiritual and mental equipment
stalled, shows that the activity has ended, that Lowell now sleeps alone in
a "tidied" room in rising panic, preoccupied by death, sweating rather
than sleeping. The second sonnet begins with an act of will: "Behind me!
You!" Lowell says, echoing Christ's words to the tempter Satan. Day
comes, the room is flooded with light, his child explodes into the room
along with his wife, whose "lightness alters everything" and through
whom he seeks absolution for all his faults, including that childish tormenting of the turtles described in "Ode." Yes, there is much here that is
peculiar to Lowell's psyche and situation (including the identification of
his wife with the turtles). But there is also much that seems to come from
the collective subconscious and from the whole history of Western culture
and poetry. Certainly Dante, Donne, Jonathan Edwards, and T. S. Eliot
would have found the poem an open book.

–D.H.

Richard Wilbur

Randall Jarrell's comment that Wilbur always settles for six or eight
yards points directly to a quality in his work that some will see as a virtue
and some as a limitation. I would put it this way: no poet could be less exotic or mystical than Wilbur. He does not compel us to close our eyes with
holy dread; he hasn't fed on honeydew or drunk the milk of paradise. He
is closer in spirit to the Augustans than to the Romantics. One of his
virtues is a willingness to examine with a clear head and eye the world
we actually live in. Another is an astonishing ability to show that if that

world is not itself good, it is at least promising raw material that can be made beautiful and graceful by the tempered mind.

QUESTIONS

1. What is the artistic question raised by "Praise in Summer"? How does Wilbur answer it in this poem, and how does he seem to answer it in his other poems?

The question literally asked in lines 10 and 11 is "Does sense so stale that we must needs derange/The world to know it?" This is not a small question serving just to hang a poem on, but one of the major issues in Western art. Why can't the artists just *say* it, or paint it like it is? Why all this exercise in ingenuity? At first reading, the poem seems to argue against "uncreation." Certainly it begins with a series of metaphors so violently ingenious that they hardly seem fit for a poem praising the natural world: the earth and heavens are inverted so that moles become birds and trees becomes mine shafts cut into the air. It is the poet himself who wonders "why this mad *instead*/Perverts our praise . . . ." And then he asks what appears to be a rhetorical question: "To a praiseful eye/Should it not be enough . . ." to describe the creation unmetaphorically?

However, your better students will see that the last line is all metaphor. The sky is a blue ceiling swept clean by the flight of sparrows. Wilbur surprises us at last by suggesting that the answers to his questions are, "Yes, the senses *are* so stale that we must rearrange the world to see it; and no, it is not enough to say that trees grow green." The metaphors that begin the poem may be outrageous, but to say that the poet should avoid the outrageous is not to say that he should avoid the ingenious.

Ingenuity is everywhere in Wilbur. Among the cases that your students may cite are

◆ The comparison between the vulture cruising the sky and Noah cruising the ocean in "Still, Citizen Sparrow."

◆ The implied comparison in "The Undead" between self–absorbed people and vampires.

◆ The transformation of a crossword puzzle into a mystical nexus of the world's phenomena in "All That Is."

2. Discuss the way that Wilbur's poems appeal to the ear as well as to the mind.

"Praise in Summer" might once again be a good place to start. In addition to the sonnet's usual appeals of end–rhyme and meter, Wilbur finds

internal echoes for almost every line. Among the most obvious are those
in the first two lines:

> ObSCURELY yet most SURELY called
> As SOMEtimes SUMmer cALLs us ALL, I said.

This internal rhyming is not kept up at such a pace throughout, but assonance and alliteration are present to the last:

> That trEEs *gr*Ow *gr*EEn, and mOles *c*an *c*ourse in *d*ay,
> And *s*parrows *s*wEEp the *c*EIling of our day.

In the above lines the sound might be dismissed as merely decorative,
but there are certainly passages where sound and sense are carefully
matched. In "Death of a Toad," for instance, the toad's erratic movements
are echoed in an ingenious internal rhyme and a tongue–twisting of
aspirates: "with hobbling hop has got . . . ." The voice is forced to halt
between words and the *ob/op/ot*–rhyme marks each clumsy, unsym-
metrical hop.

In "Still, Citizen Sparrow," we get a remarkable bit of onomatopoeia:

>   . . . his saw
> Soured the song of birds with its wheezy gnaw
> And the slam of his hammer all the day beset
>
> The people's ears . . . .

Wilbur's delight in the sound of words gets its freest range in "All
That Is," where the crossword–puzzle conceit allows him to put together
lines that use sounds almost as freely as Jackson Pollock might use colors.
Listen especially to the vowels and liquids (*r*'s and *l*'s) in the following
passage:

> Is it a vision? Does the eye make out
> A flight of ernes, rising from aits or aeries,
> Whose shadows track across a harsh terrain
> Of esker and arete? At waterside,
> Does the shocked eeler lay his lampreys by,
> Sighting a Reo driven by an edile?
> And does the edile, from his running board,
> Step down to meet a ranee? Does she
> End by reading him from the works of Elia.

This is free play by someone equipped with a marvelous ear.

3. Can Wilbur be defended against the charge that his poetry is limited in significance, that it always settles for six or eight yards?

To answer this question well, your students will probably have to choose a poem that appears to have something substantial to say, and then examine it closely to see what its substance is. My own choice would be "After the Last Bulletins," a poem that certainly goes beyond eight yards. I think it goes "the whole way."

"After the Last Bulletins" is in some ways comparable to Lowell's "For the Union Dead." It is a poem in a cityscape: the objects are manmade (trash, railings, statues, gutters, subways) and so we are naturally invited to consider *humanity's* handiwork rather than God's or nature's. Some students, seeing that the principal handiwork presented is litter, will conclude too hastily that Wilbur has written a poem about, let's say, the ugliness of civilization by comparison to nature. While this is not a bad start, they will need to look harder.

It is not random litter in the alley; it is "the day's litter of news." While the citizens enjoy their submersion in "the thronged Atlantis of personal sleep," the city, too, is drowning in "a fierce noyade/Of all we thought to think." The litter of paper in the poem is only incidental to the more important litter of words and ideas. The flood of news has taken over everything: people retire to sleep only "after the last bulletins" and they wake to the sound of a "clear announcer's voice . . . like a dove." When they "return to life" it is "by subway–mouth" (yet another public mouth!) and "Bearing the morning papers." The tide of topicality, of public talk, of other people's ideas is hostile to the individual's contact with nature or with his (conscious) private life: the citizens leave the heart's "anarch and responsible" town for the regimented world of busy–ness early enough to "rouse . . . The songbirds on the public boughs."

This is the world we live in, and it is a hostile one to the human spirit. The tatters of newspaper "flail . . . at the tired patrolman's feet" like the Russian snow that seemed to say "Damn you! damn you!" when Napoleon rode over it.

Your students—denizens like all of us of the world created by the media—may wonder why Wilbur feels this world of public announcements to be so hostile. You may need to point out to them what the poem hints at, assuming an audience that needs only reminding. The world of the timely and the topical is at its core hostile to the enduring values that make the hero or the artist. The poet writes for the ages, not for the day, and a world littered with verbiage that is literally here today and gone tomorrow is not one where his enterprise is likely to prosper. Statues of heroes are erected because people assume (or once assumed) that heroism was not so much "newsworthy" as enduring: a quality of humankind that does not age or fade and can continue to inspire through generations. In "After the Last Bulletins" the "Unruly flights" of news–litter

> Scamper the park, and taking a statue for dead
> Strike at the positive eyes,
> Batter and flap the stolid head
>
> And scratch the noble name.

"Noble" here is perhaps a rare lapse in Wilbur's taste or judgment; it takes sides strongly, destroys the delicate balance that keeps the poet's ironies open. It is, however, just the sort of excess that Jarrell would like to see more of.

–D.H.

Amy Clampitt

Clampitt may prove to be one of the great poets of the last part of the century. She is certainly among the most unusual. For some years she wrote without any hope of publication, and she certainly has not attempted to follow poetic fashions. Most of the poets who come to mind in comparison are from the nineteenth century: she has the capacity for unexpected insights that we associate with Emily Dickinson, Gerard Manley Hopkins' love of oral effects, and the strong interest in nature that we associate with both. Among twentieth–century poets she might be linked with Eliot or Pound for her interest in the literary and religious culture of the past, with Louise Bogan and Randall Jarrell for her interest in psychoanalysis, and with Richard Wilbur for her interests in including in the poem the artifacts of daily life.

It may interest your students to know that one of Clampitt's favorite books is Charles Darwin's *Origin of the Species*. They may detect in her poetry a Darwinian picture of random flux that evolves toward a grand, unpremeditated pattern.

QUESTIONS

1. Comment on the importance of sound in Clampitt's poetry. Are there passages where the sound seems as important as the sense? Is this a strength or a weakness?

A good place to start may be with Swinburne, whom Clampitt mentions as an early influence later rejected as too mellifluous. You could give your students the following passage from *Atlanta in Calydon*:

> The ivy falls with the Bacchanal's hair
>   Over her eyebrows hiding her eyes;
> The wild vine slipping down leaves bare
>   Her bright breast shortening into sighs;
> The wild vine slips with the weight of its leaves,
> But the berried ivy catches and cleaves
> To the limbs that glitter, the feet that scare
>   The wolf that follows, the fawn that flies.

The patterns of sound here are so emphatic that we have to wonder if the sense exists primarily as a peg to hang phonemes on. Surely in the third and fifth lines, the vine is "wild" largely for the sake of its *w* to match that in "down" or "weight," its long *i* to match that in "vine," and its "l" to match that in "slips" or "slipping." The ivy in the sixth line is "berried" out of a similar phonetic convenience. "The wolf that follows, the fawn that flies" is a glissando of *w*, *l*, and *f* sounds.

If you show your students how much Swinburne seems to be driven by sound echoes, they should be able to detect parallel passages in Clampitt. When in "Lindenbloom" she calls the flowers "the in–mid–air/resort of honeybees'/hirsute cotillion," most of the pleasure is aural. "Hirsute" picks up the *h* of "honeybee," and is a rearranged echo of "resort." "Cotillion" rhymes with "million" five lines up and anticipates the sound of "milligram" one line down. The pleasure here is the pleasure of strange–sounding words placed in a setting where their sounds are refracted by surrounding words. Dr. Seuss, John Milton, Ogden Nash, and Richard Wilbur are filled with similar pleasures. A passage like

> . . . seraphs shaken
> into pollen dust
> no transubstantiating
> pope or antipope could sift
> or quite precisely ponder

is so much fun that some serious readers of poetry must wince when they read it. An

ANTIPoPe who TrANsuBsTANTIaTes

is audibly related to a Swinburne's

WOLF that FOLLOWs

or Clampitt's own sea

    playing cATCH or TAg/or TouCH–lAsT like a Terrier

in "Beach Glass."

It is easy to illustrate how echoic Clampitt's poetry is, and I think most readers will find many cases where the echoing is playful. It is harder to say whether it is a strength or a weakness, and worth provoking some argument about in class.

2. What is the effect of Clampitt's many cultural, historical, and literary allusions? Do they strengthen or weaken her poems?

You might assign students particular poems to consider in light of this question. "Beach Glass" and "Lindenbloom" are good candidates. Those who know Dante will also see an important allusion in "Man Feeding Pigeons."

The three "high culture" allusions in "Beach Glass" are to Cassandra (7), Murano (40), and Chartres (41). The first may, frankly, be superfluous—though it is amusing to think of Cassandra as a reef–bell. The second and third, however, are important to the poem. Clampitt introduces references to contemporary "low culture" in lines 29–33 by showing bits of glass from beer bottles, common wines, and ("no getting around it,/I'm afraid") Milk of Magnesia. When she mixes in the "treasuries/of Murano, the buttressed/astonishments of Chartres," she accomplishes several things. Murano, a part of Venice, was from 1292 the site of a great Renaissance glassware industry. Chartres Cathedral contains the most brilliant examples of medieval stained glass. The allusion to these places juxtaposes low and high cultures, contemporary and historical periods. Inevitably, the alert reader thinks about the implications. Is Clampitt ironically contrasting contemporary culture with the high culture of the past: their rose windows with our Milk of Magnesia bottles? Or is she, on the contrary, suggesting that if we learn to look at what is in front of us, the lapis of the Milk of Magnesia bottle is as beautiful as the blue glass of Chartres? Is the point continuity or discontinuity?

Or, better yet, is she reminding us that the few centuries that stand between us and Chartres are nothing compared to the age of the oceans that will eventually wear everything down to gravel and sand, including Chartres and Murano? She seems to accomplish all these things at once, at the same time creating an extended metaphor between the working of her companion's mind "turning over concepts/I can't envision" and the working of the sea: in both mind and sea the centuries produce interesting artifacts and juxtapositions.

Like "Beach Glass," "Lindenbloom" is named for the image that ties different places and times together. Here the sight of the tree in early ‑

spring unites fourteenth–century Avignon, contemporary Avignon, and (I believe) Central Park in New York City.

"Man Feeding Pigeons," though it is a beautiful poem even for readers who see no allusion, does insist twice that we stretch the secular present back to meet the religious past. First, Clampitt says that the common sidewalk pigeons glimmer (their feathers very literally do when they turn in the sun)

> . . . as though all the winged
> beings of all the mosaics of Ravenna
> had gotten the message somehow and come
> flying to rejoin the living . . . .

Pigeons as angels might be trite. Pigeons that glimmer like the angels on mosaics is fresher both because it adds a visual detail and because it suggests a spiritual flame like that Yeats sees in the mosaics of "Sailing to Byzantium." The image of angels leads to the grander allusion of the final line "the vast, concentric, paradisial rose." In cantos 31–33 of the *Paradiso*, Dante sees the congregation of white–robed saints as a "shining white rose" of many petals formed concentrically around the throne of God. Into the rose the winged angels descend "like a swarm of bees." Angels, roses, heavenly weeds, a congregation of winged beings, a man "convoked as he knelt on the sidewalk" and laid out a "benefaction" for "the unhoused and opportune/we have always with us": so much religious imagery and language is present that we see the common street scene Clampitt describes as an emblem of a spiritual state.

It seems superfluous to say that Clampitt's allusions in these poems strengthen them. Some poets may be weakened by reaching back into the cultural and religious past. Clampitt, like Milton (whom she greatly admires), grows stronger; she has the power of seeing past and present fused.

3. Discuss the role of time, change, and chance in one or more of Clampitt's poems.

"The Burning Child," "Dancers Exercising," "Beach Glass," and "Man Feeding Pigeons" all are remarkable for their images of constancy–within–mutability, which may be Clampitt's most significant theme. "Beach Glass," as we have seen, makes the unending erosion of the land by the sea into a symbol of both creation and destruction: objects come and go, but the sea's (and the mind's) "hazardous/redefinition of structures" is constant. "The Burning Child" explores the historical chances that have brought the poet and her companion to the present moment. In the process it presents a picture of waking life as a thing with no more structure than a dream or nightmare: the "minute particulars that build themselves/into a house that almost looks substantial" (25–26). And yet there is a constant:

life as the avoidance of both the tinder (the hellish side of life, the extermination camps, hell itself perhaps) and "the nurture whose embrace is drowning." (Psychoanalysts call the urge to crawl back into the womb and die the "thalassic regressive trend," linking it to the sea just as Clampitt does here.)

"Dancers Exercising" presents as a symbol for beatitude two dancers exercising in a mirror: "at the center/of that clarity, what we saw/was not stillness/but movement." Happiness lies in movement, improvisation, evolution apparently at random so that, like snowflakes, moments can be "no two ever alike." When we look closely at the poem, though, we find that Clampitt is not rejecting the still moment of insight or the persistence of memory. It may be that "the happier we are,/the less there is for memory to . . . come to a halt in front of," but the poem is an account of just such an arresting moment.

"Man Feeding Pigeons" perfectly balances the constant motion of life with its capacity to fall into a gesture of eternal importance. The paradisial rose the pigeons form is a thing of "unmanaged symmetry," and perhaps it is not a "thing" at all, "but the merest wisp of a part of/a process." Nonetheless it hangs there in the everyday air above an ordinary sidewalk and gives us an "inkling" of "states of being/beyond alteration."

–D.H.

Maxine Kumin

Maxine Kumin's poetry presents the reader with an interesting problem because it accurately portrays a life that is not ordinarily thought to be poetic. Rural poverty has long been a mainstay of poetry, even when the poet was in fact (like A. E. Housman) living a life far from the country. Bustling or impoverished city life, in the hands of Whitman, Williams, Hughes, or Brooks, has produced fine poetry. But the life of the comfortable middle class, in the city, country, or suburbs has not been thought poetic. Not even Richard Wilbur, who has labored hard at expanding the range of poetry to include much that is unpoetic, has managed (so far as I know) to work a garage–door opener gracefully into a poem.

Kumin writes about the life around her, and this is undeniably a comfortable life, one in which hardships must be voluntarily chosen if they are to exist at all. An interesting way to approach Kumin's work is to ask whether this middle–class life can be a subject for good poetry.

QUESTIONS

1. In the prose passage on page 1138, Kumin says that Antonin Artaud "invaded" her poem "In April, In Princeton" and "saved" it. Explain this statement. Is it true?

Students may complain that this is a hard question to answer without knowing more about Artaud. If you ask it in time for them to do a bit of library research, it will help. Even without knowledge of Artaud, however, the question is approachable.

What does the poem need to be saved from? Kumin describes it as "a very formal set piece" and as "a kind of ornament, an act of fealty for the semester I had spent so happily in that luscious, wealthy community." Without Artaud, what would this poem have to say? It would present a picture of what human intellect, wealth, and attention to detail can accomplish, how it set the diversity of the planet into order. Nature cannot resist this passion for order: even full-grown trees are uprooted and set in their proper places; dandelions and onion grass are rolled under new sod, artificially pure as carpet, but alive. Romantic notions of non–interference with nature notwithstanding, it works: the beauty is so complete that "it hurts." Nor can history or religion resist. The retreat route of Washington's army (in a less orderly day) is now part of the scenery, and in the Hillel Reading Room, Judaism and Hinduism mix effortlessly in a Yoga class.

Here is the middle–class poet's problem in spades. All this order, tolerance, pluralism, is a magnificent accomplishment—the sort of community that some of the best minds and hearts of the past several centuries (see Auden's "Voltaire at Ferney") have labored to achieve. Yet it is hard to praise it without seeming smug and shallow. A part of me reads about the Yoga class taken "lunchless" at noon and cringes: I mean *really*, from here it is only a step to poems about jogging, racquetball, vegetarian lasagna. Kumin sees all this clearly. It is her problem as a poet. And she is quite right about Artaud's saving the poem. Artaud would have doubted the stability of Princeton's accomplishment. He developed the theater of cruelty as a way of reminding the Parisians of his time that beneath the fair surfaces of civilization there were unpleasant passions, unpleasant histories. Eventually he went mad, almost as if to fulfill his own views of the precariousness of the ordering intellect.

Kumin, in lotus position, thinks of Artaud who could never sit this way for fear that his soul would fly out of his anus. It is an odd moment of identification, but it balances the optimism of the poem. It raises the possibility of the good order, the balance, coming undone. Notice the closing image of the magnolias that drop their porcelain petals, but do not (as they so easily might) shatter.

I believe that Artaud saves the poem *for Kumin,* and to some degree for others who know who Artaud is or will take the trouble to find out.

Whether he saves the poem for a significant number of readers is another question, one you may want to discuss with your class. Should the poet limit the range of his or her allusions out of consideration for the readers?

2. What images, similes, and metaphors tie Kumin's poems to her physical surroundings and her social and economic class? Do these images make you more or less receptive to her poems?

"The Longing to Be Saved" and "Making the Jam without You" are the poems most likely to attract attention in this discussion.

"The Longing to Be Saved" ties Kumin to a wardrobe large enough to include a "wrong negligee," a barn with horses, children who are doctors and lawyers, dimestore devil suits, the papery skins of late onions, and acetate cloth. These details disclose her age, her socio–economic status, and her physical surroundings: mid–life with grown, successful children, a country house, vivid experiences mothering (the devil–suit) and cooking (the onion) and perhaps sewing (the acetate). I think it is seriously worth discussing whether these images strike students as too tame and domestic to be of interest. It might be worth comparing the imagery used by Sylvia Plath or Lucille Clifton. Your best students should notice, however, that "The Longing" is not a poem about how satisfying the comfortable domestic life is. Without suggesting that there is anything wrong with such a life, Kumin suggests that there is something missing, that an interruption in the smooth surface would be welcome.

"Making the Jam" is (to stray from the question a bit) a particularly troublesome poem for me. It is dedicated and apparently addressed to Judy, the poet's nineteen–year–old daughter, who is off in Germany, but it is marred here and there by phrases that seem wrong either as comments to a nineteen–year-old or as internal musings. To whom can the comment that Judy speaks three languages (19–20) be addressed except an audience that doesn't know Judy? Isn't this just parental boasting? And the hyperbole "cracked the cupboards with our talk" (11) seems unlikely in a mother/daughter chat.

The images in the poem are distinctly prosperous and rural—middle-class modern pastoral, we might say. Ignore the purport of the poem and concentrate on the images, and you will get:

featherbed, eaves, turrets and towers, rain like bullets, kitchen a harem of good smells, stove top dancing with pots, crushing blackberries, white cocoon of seam, mountain, fat cows belled like a cathedral, ruins of a schloss, thicket with brambles soft as wool, buckets of plum–sized berries, mild hills of New Hampshire, heavy eyes of an honest dog, white unreconstructed kitchen, blood of berries, bric-a-brac of shelves, jelly glasses with sun driving through them, rubies, boy pale as paraffin, fresh baked bread, bright royal fur, a sliver, sweet stain of purple.

On balance, we can ask ourselves, what does this procession of images suggest about the writer. Clearly (unless she is assuming a persona, which she apparently is not) she is comfortably wealthy, familiar with the sights of the New Hampshire hill country (including cocoons, blackberries and brambles, and hounds). She is also filled with a delight in the sight and smell of things. It is the delight, finally, that makes the poem worthwhile. This is not, like "The Longing," a poem that suggests discontent. It is like a Rubens painting filled with jewels and fine cloth and the pink flesh of beautiful women. If we are going to enjoy such works we need sometimes to shut off the alarms set off by our feminist or egalitarian censors and revel for a while in the artist's reveling.

3. In the comment on page 1138, Kumin talks about writing formal verse with constraints and ornaments. Where do you find this formalism at work? What is its effect?

Since Kumin herself discusses the pattern in "In April, In Princeton," that would be a good place to start on this question. Here the main formal commitment is to stanzas made of three rhymed couplets. You might ask your students to try to scan the lines and evaluate the rhymes. What they will find is that the lines are not regularly metered, and may have three, four, or five stresses in their seven to thirteen syllables. Nor are the rhymes particularly reliable. There are full rhymes: of/love (6), unrolled/old (10), center/enter (24), floor/more (34). There are half-rhymes in the Dickinson manner: replete/light (14), noon/Room (20), disappear/air (28), perhaps/ cups (36). There is one comic double rhyme: asylum/phylum (32). And there are a number of rhymes so cryptic as to be nearly lost: Princeton/farms (8, a rough match of nasals), artery/army (4, a convenient overlooking of a syllable), Princeton/position (22, a mere consonance in an unstressed syllable).

The effect of all this is a poem that sometimes follows a form and sometimes merely alludes to it. Some of your students may feel that this is slovenliness on the poet's part, and may prefer the poetry that works *in* a form or *out*, but stay away from gray areas between. But there is a pleasure in watching a poet decide line by line how far the form should bend.

In "At a Private Showing" an occasional rhyme or partial rhyme seems always to be hinting at a deliberate system. Thus, in the first stanza, we have

details/tools (1, 3)
stake/sank (4, 7)
wheel/reel (5, 9)

There are similar hints of a rhyme scheme in the stanzas that follow, and in the final stanza, we get

soul/Hill (57, 62)
sight/night (58, 61)
Argentine/wine (59, 60)

This tight pattern of nested rhymes helps give the poem a sense of closure.

The most formal of the poems collected here is "Morning Swim," where all the rhymes are full but cloth/growth (8), and the meter is clearly iambic tetrameter. The meter, subject matter, and tone of this poem are so much like those of Marvell's "Bermudas" that Kumin must have intended a deliberate allusion (notice that Kumin's arms keep time to the rhythm just as the oars of the Puritans in Marvell's poem do; notice that the song is a hymn in both). If when you are teaching Kumin, you point your student back to Marvell, they will quickly discover these similarities themselves and will see the spirit and good humor of Kumin's poem.

–D.H.

Robert Bly

Robert Bly, like William Blake, has been influenced by the seventeenth-century German theosophist Jacob Boehme. Like Blake and Boehme, he objects that the scientific search for generalized, objective, publicly verifiable, rule–governed truth can blind us to other types of knowing. In Bly's case, the most important form of non–scientific knowing is what he calls "the discovery of hidden relationships" that can be found by examining our spiritual and emotional lives. One gets the impression from many of the poems that Bly wants to start with his present life and circumstances (in rural Minnesota) and search backward in time and downward in the psyche to find symbols of the sort one might associate with Grimms' fairy tales or even with the Lascaux cave paintings. Beneath the outer surface and shaping it, are the old atoms of experience: love, hate, anger, grief, earth, air, fire, water, growth, decay, desire.

The surrealism of Neruda and García Lorca has greatly influenced Bly's poetry. We sometimes see this influence in a startling image like "the setter of songs/who sleeps at night in his violin case," but usually Bly's images are less Dadaistic. They work because they seem ancient and inevitable. In "Mourning Pablo Neruda" (p. 1044), for example, Bly brings together grief, admiration, drought, water, granite, willow trees, and grasshoppers. All of these things belong naturally to the life of a Minnesota farm (as do car seats and faucets) and they form a perfectly comprehensible surface for the poem: Bly is thinking of Neruda as he does the daily chores. But the images—particularly the water escaping from the jar, seeping through granite, running underground to join the Minnesota, the Mississippi, and the sea—seem older and weightier than the poem in which they appear.

QUESTIONS

1. Where in the poems do we find images that seem to point to "true analogies" between our internal lives and the world around us?

This is a bear of a question, but one that Bly virtually demands us to ask about his poetry. Bly's images are sometimes so dense with suggested analogies that it takes many words to unpack them. Two examples may help your students get the general flavor.

In "My Father's Wedding, 1924," Bly first links physical limps with psychological weaknesses, then suggests that

> . . . If a man, cautious
> hides his limp,
> Somebody has to limp it! Things
> do it; the surroundings limp.
> House walls get scars,
> the car breaks down; matter, in drudgery, takes it up.

The analogy between the hidden personal flaw and the scars on the walls of houses or the mechanical problems with our cars is not capricious or arbitrary. It reminds me of the sort of cause/effect relations between moral and physical reality that Blake enumerates in "Auguries of Innocence":

> The Bat that flits at close of Eve
> Has left the Brain that won't Believe (25–26)

> The Beggars Dog & Widow's Cat
> Feed them & thou wilt grow fat (43–44)

> The Harlot's cry from Street to Street
> Shall weave Old England's winding Sheet (115–116)

Blake's aphorisms can sometimes be slowed down and reconciled with more scientific statements of a similar truth

> "Psychology tells us that one of the correlates of success is high self–esteem, and that self-esteem often depends on our perception of

ourselves as moral; therefore, the person who behaves morally by
helping the widow and beggar may in fact be increasing his chance
of prospering"

Bly's statement could be rationalized

"Psychology tells us that those who hide their defects may be filled
with subconscious feeling of self–reproach and unworthiness that
makes them 'accident prone.' Without knowing it, they manage to
make things go wrong around them—forgetting to add antifreeze to
the car for instance, so that the radiator bursts."

Psychology here is running far behind intuition, and Bly speaks for
intuition.

In "For My Son Noah, Ten Years Old," Bly contrasts the "undivided
tenderness" of the last stanza with images in the previous stanza of the
horse that "steps up, swings on one leg, turns its body," and the chicken
that "claws onto the roost, its wings whelping and walloping." I don't
think it is possible to explain the juxtaposition in an entirely rational
way, but it is a reminder that coexisting within all of us is the "kind
mind . . . calm and delighted" and another spirit whose rage animals
respond to instinctively, turning to avoid us or clawing their way onto the
roost as if to avoid a fox. The notion of the raging man contained within
the calm one appears again in Noah's picture of "a man with fire coming
out of his hair." Noah seems at some level to sense his father's rage and to
express it in the "true analogy" of rage and fire.

2. How is language related to "forgotten relations" and "true analogies" in
the poem "Words Rising"?

Anyone who has felt the etymologist's passion for pushing back toward
the roots of language will respond strongly to Bly's poem. Words come to
us from our remote ancestors bearing overtones of the contexts in which
they have been used and sometimes seeming to have some of their initial
impulse left. Notice that Bly carefully reminds us from the opening lines
that words are sounds—not the special property of scholars, but the
common property of the whole human race. You might have your students
look particularly closely at the rather mixed metaphor in lines 25–28:

We are bees then; our honey is language.
Now the honey lies stored in caves
beneath us, and the sound of words
carries what we do not.

The image implies at once the vast reservoir of human experience that is caught up in our language, and the relative insignificance of the individual user of words. But the next lines, abandoning the be metaphor, remind us that if the user depends upon the words, the words depend upon the user:

> When a man or woman feeds a few words
> with private grief, the shames we knew
> before we could invent the wheel,
> then words grow.

You might ask your class what these lines imply about the proper use of the language. They seem to me to say that a word prospers only when it is reinvested with its ancient emotion, another aspect of "forgotten relations."

You might ask your students to explain the historic or prehistoric associations Bly finds in his examples. "There are eternal vows/held inside the word 'Jericho'" (39–40) is probably the easiest to approach: even those whose knowledge of the Bible is vague will know immediately that our response to the word is far more emotional than geographic, that the name evokes Jehovah's covenant with his people. Those who know the Bible better will realize that the story of Jericho is indeed a story of "eternal vows." God promises Joshua:

> Every place that the sole of your foot shall tread upon, that have I given unto you, as I said to Moses. From the wilderness and this Lebanon even unto the great river, the river Euphrates, all the land of the Hittites, and unto the great sea toward the going down of the sun, shall be your coast. (Joshua 1: 3–4)

Joshua sends spies across the Jordan into Jericho, where they come to the house of the harlot Rahab, who hides them on condition that they swear "by the Lord" that when the Israelites take the city, she and her family will be spared. The spies promise "Our lives for yours, if ye utter not this business. And it shall be, when the Lord hath given us this land, that we will deal kindly and truly with thee." They give her a scarlet thread to hang in her window, and before the city is burned to the ground, Rahab is safely removed "and her father's household, and all that she had; and she dwelleth in Israel even to this day" (Joshua 6:25). All this (and the trumpets and shouts that bring down the city's walls, and the parting of the River Jordan so that the Israelites can cross dry–shod carrying the Ark of the Covenant before them) has become part of the word "Jericho."

And and *the* are words of a very different sort, so common most of use never notice them, but Bly imagines that they may have some of the deepest associations of all.

> The old earth fragrance remains
> in the word "and." We experience
> "the" in its lonely suffering.

And is, after all, the most universal of connectors: from prehistoric times it has been "sow and reap," "hunter and prey," "man and woman." Etymologically *and* comes from an Indo-European root meaning "in, " the closest relation of all. *The*, singular definite article, is closely related to the demonstrative pronouns *that* and *this*. The further we reach back the more closely the word seems to blend with a finger pointed to a singled-out object or person, an outcast with no *and*-ness.

More surprising even than the association Bly makes with *and* and *the* is this passage:

> We see a crowd with dusty
> palms turned up inside each
> verb.

The image is itself eloquent and evocative, but "each verb" is rather puzzling. You might ask your students what verb comes to mind when they consider the image. My nominee would be *give*. You might ask your students to speculate on what the *first* verb humankind invented would have been, when speech was little more than "growls from under fur." My nominee would again be *give*. The verb feels like the ancestor of all verbs and the analogue of all human relations.

–D.H.

W. S. Merwin

Like Robert Lowell, W. S. Merwin is a poet who early in his career showed himself a master of formal, ironic verse, but later found that he needed to break with closed forms and approach emotion more directly. The result has been poetry that is less complex in an academic sense, but by no means easier to approach. One of my friends *knew* that "The Different Stars" was an important poem for her when she first read it in 1970, though she couldn't fully understand what it was saying to her. She carried it, nonetheless, tucked into her wallet for almost seventeen years, finally realizing that it was in a way the story of those seventeen years. Because Merwin often expresses an emotional truth surrealistically, "getting" him will require different tools than "getting" a poet whose appeal is primarily intellectual. One of the most important tools is time.

There are two pointers that might help your students make a good beginning. First, they must avoid the pitfall of thinking of Merwin as a poetic rebel. It is true that he has broken with traditional formalism, and it is true that some of his poetry and prose are protests against racism, militarism, and ecological destructiveness. He is not, however, a rejecter of the past. In fact, his critique of American society is partly that it is too young, too brash, too cut off from world history. As a translator, Merwin is a champion of a longer and broader past. He would like us to see ourselves as heirs of not only an English tradition, but of French, Spanish, Latin, Portuguese, Greek, Chinese, and Japanese traditions as well.

Second, they should bear in mind the evocative power of an image found in every human culture: the image of the journey. Repeatedly, Merwin's poems return to the image of travelers who must leave things behind, encounter hardships among alien people, guide themselves by uncertain stars, sometimes be bewildered. Sometimes the journey seems to be the journey of the whole human race, and the fear is that the endpoint will be destruction.

QUESTIONS

1. Merwin is an advocate of "open form"; that is, he rejects the idea of the poet's starting out to produce verse that fits a set scheme of meter and rhyme. What sort of form do his poems have?

A good place to start on this question might be "The Judgment of Paris," a poem that could hardly be accused of formlessness. The encounters with the three goddesses follow a pattern: the goddess with eyes of a certain color speaks to Paris, Paris is dazzled, and the goddess urges him to take the gift she has to give, which he will lose anyway. A nineteenth–century poet might have put the poet in a fixed meter and in rhymed stanzas, but the result could hardly be more structured. And though the verse is not metrical, it is very far from prose. The euphony of the closing lines

> and Helen stepped from the palace to gather
> as she would do every day that season
> from the grove the yellow ray flowers tall
> as herself

> Whose roots are said to dispel pain

might be compared to Tennyson's famous closing of "Come Down, O Maid":

> . . . the children call, and I
> Thy shepherd pipe, and sweet is every sound,
> Sweeter thy voice, but every sound is sweet;
> Myriads of rivulets hurrying thro' the lawn,
> The moan of doves in immemorial elms,
> And murmuring of innumerable bees.

There is some of Tennyson's vowel music in Merwin's lines, and a similar succession of liquids (*r*'s and *l*'s). It would be harebrained to say that Merwin is imitating Tennyson, but sensible to assume that in this poem, in this mood, Merwin's "open form" instinctively draws near to Tennyson's "closed form."

Merwin always searches for forms suited to his particular subject, and he has been successful both in adapting and inventing. "The Last One," for example, borrows its form partly from oral storytelling patterns of children: the simple transitional, "well"; the series of short parallel sentences ("Well they shrugged . . . They cut . . . They laid . . . They shone . . . They exploded . . . They built . . ."). The poem's plot line is also reminiscent of the horror stories that are told at sixth–grade slumber parties: at first appearance the gothic element is just a bit odd; stage by stage, it grows to be terrifying. If your students compare the diction and the pattern of repetition in "The Judgment of Paris" and "The Last One," they will see how thoroughly Merwin is committed to his chosen form. Lines like

> They began to stomp on the edge it got their feet.
> And when it got their feet they fell down.
> It got into eyes the eyes went blind.

could not exist in the same poem with

> an apple as it is told
> discord itself in a single fruit its skin
> already carved
> *To the fairest*

The absence of punctuation might suggest that the same poet is at work, but to the ear, each poem seems to come from a different Merwin.

Another form students may notice is the circularity of "History," a poem that seems to chase its tail, the first line following naturally on the last. Undoubtedly, someone can name a poem similar in form written before 1986, but it is far more likely that Merwin reinvented the form in the process of writing than that he set out to write a poem that circles.

In most of the poems, it is far harder to make any abstract statements about the form. You must decide how to discuss with your class the possibility of truly organic form—form that cannot be abstracted from the content, but is apparent because all the parts of the whole work together and none seems superfluous. "For the Anniversary of My Death" could be a good poem to look at in this context. It starts with a metaphysical contemplation of the nothingness that follows death: a silence that carries like a sound, a star that shines darkness. It becomes in mid–poem an affirmation of things that exist in the world ("Surprised by the earth/And the love of one woman"), and we feel that it is coming up, all the way up, to a moment of celebration. The poem rises from gloom to exaltation ("bowing not knowing to what") in the same way as Shakespeare's Sonnet 29 and Patricia Hampl's "The Moment" (pp. 673–674 of *The Riverside Anthology*). Students need to consider whether such movement constitutes a "form."

2. What are Merwin's most important themes? Illustrate each theme by referring to one or more poems.

Mutability must surely be ranked among the most important themes. It is already fully developed in the early dramatic monologue "Grandmother Watching at Her Window," where the connection between loving and losing is so strong that the speaker assumes (in confusion or in wisdom) one to be the cause of the other:

> . . . God loves you so dearly
> Just as you are, that nothing you are can stay
> But all the time you keep going away, away.

If students will bear that last line in mind when they approach "History," it will help them understand this more ambitious and surrealistic poem. The speaker who leaves the farm at evening seems to walk into the farm's future, to see it in ruins, as it inevitably will be. The walk into the future is always a walk into the ruins of the present: "I was not going to be long," which ends the poem, takes us back to the start, "Only I never came back." Paradoxically, the circular shape of the poem serves to remind us that there is no turning back; when we leave the present it becomes a ruin. We can't come back to it any more than we can step into the same river twice. Only history carries the past into the present, and to us history is an unreadable language.
The importance of understanding the relation between past and present is another of Merwin's important themes. "History" suggests that the endless destruction we live in comes from our inability to find or read "a book full of words to remember," the thing that should have connected us to and preserved our pasts. "The Last One" shows ignorant men attempting to destroy in a day a forest much older than themselves and containing mysterious powers they know nothing of. "Emigré"shows in the plight of the immigrant an archetype of everyone's plight.

We move into the future as we do into a new country. Eventually we

> . . . come to the problem
> of what to remember after all
> and what is your real
> language

If we cling to the old, speak the language of the past, we cut ourselves off from our new present

> but if you rush to the new lips
> do you not fade like a sound cut off
> do you not dry up like a puddle

The dilemma is heartbreaking; finally, like the immigrant, we don't know whether to wish for the old country or the new, the past or the future. As Merwin says in "The Different Stars"

> oh if we knew
> if we knew what we needed if we even knew
> the stars would look to us to guide them

Some of your more capable students may point out that myth is an attempt to understand the relation of the past to the present and to "know what we need." In the Counterpoint, Merwin discusses the myths of Orpheus and Phaeton as myths of "harmonious interaction with the living world or envy and exploitation of it." It seems clear that "The Last One" is an extension of the Phaeton myth. "The Judgment of Paris," too, seems to be a myth of arrogation and arrogance: the goddesses, cutthroat competitors for the golden apple, tempt Paris as Satan tempts Faust, with offers of wisdom, glory, and possession of a beautiful woman. "Noah's Raven" is so striking a myth that I hesitate to bind it with any interpretation, but it is worth pointing out that the raven is the ultimate arrogator. He finds just enough land to accommodate *his* feet, so he claims it: he is the original inside trader, the totem–bird of me–first–ism.

–D.H.

Adrienne Rich

Rich's first book of poetry, published while she was still an undergraduate, won the Yale Younger Poets competition and the weighty endorsement of W. H. Auden. Like her contemporary W. S. Merwin, however, she turned away from the formal and rather academic poetry on which her early reputation was based and began to write poems more open in form and more manifestly committed to political and social goals. Her feminism, present in the earliest works, grew to a stronger and stronger commitment and has become her dominant theme. Her recent poems, she says, are about "sex, sexuality, sexual wounds, sexual identity, sexual politics . . . ." She also says that her "intention and longing" in everything she writes is to break down "the artificial barriers" between public and private life and between "the deepest images we carry out of our dreams and the most daylight events 'out in the world.'"

QUESTIONS

1. Several critics have noticed that Rich tends to distance herself from the subjects of her poetry. Discuss the use of detachment in one or more poems and describe its effect.

Rich herself can get students started on this question if they will look at the Counterpoint on page 1165. She tells us that "Aunt Jennifer's Tigers," published when she was about 22, was written with "deliberate detachment." Her aim was not the aim we associate with lyric poetry: not "the spontaneous overflow of powerful emotion." This is objective poetry, distanced and formal. The "girl who wrote the poems" is not merged with "the girl who was to define herself by her relation to men." We could say that the strategy is "double–distancing." The poet empathizes with the older women around her and understands the energies they must redirect into acceptable paths. Feeling the sense of entrapment herself, she *might* have written a dramatic monologue (a "Penelope" to match Tennyson's "Ulysses," let's say, or something like Jarrell's "A Woman at the Washington Zoo" or Bishop's "Crusoe in England"). This would have been "single–distancing," the adoption of a mask to speak through. Instead of taking up the mask and speaking directly through it, however, Rich keeps a greater distance; she *observes* Aunt Jennifer who is, in effect, a mask held at arm's length.

I think this observation from a distance has two effects. First, as Rich says, it allows the poet to handle highly charged subject matter: the distance (here aided by rhyme and meter) acts "like asbestos gloves." Take the gloves off and talk directly about the sense of entrapment and you create, as Wordsworth noted long ago, a poem that no one will want to read (or perhaps write) because the pain outweighs the pleasure of artistic performance: only a sadistic voyeur really wants to hear the moans of a person in agony, but we all have "enjoyed" an actor's imitation of agony.

The second effect can be, and in Rich often is, to make the emotion of the poem seem impersonal—the emotion of a type rather than the emotion of an individual. Aunt Jennifer is, let's face it, an idea: the idea of a trapped woman. If the poem makes us feel emotion, it is not Aunt Jennifer's emotion but emotion about the *idea* that there are Aunt Jennifers in the world. In the poems of Sylvia Plath or Lucille Clifton, on the other hand, we feel the emotion of the author radiating directly on us, not playing off an idea.

If we look at most of Rich's poems collected here (and I do not want to imply that they define the limits of her range) we will find that most have a considerable sense of distance about them, that they are poems of ideas. Certainly "Frame," a poem written 30 years after "Aunt Jennifer's Tigers," is very self-consciously a poem in which the emotion is focused outside the speaker, on a young girl who is the personified idea of women as victims just as surely as Aunt Jennifer is the personified idea of women as subordinates.

Your more perceptive students may notice that in most of the intervening poems—"Love in the Museum," "Orion," "Gabriel," somewhat less clearly "Planitarium"—an important motif is the projection of emotions on external objects: painting, stars, and imaginary messengers. Though Rich's comment on page 1165 might lead us to expect an increasingly direct expansion of emotion, displacement of emotion to something outside the self remains very common in her work.

2. Does Rich's feminist political intent damage her poetry?

This can be a hard and ugly question, but I think it is one that ought not to be avoided. My own feeling is that the political intent does damage some of the poems, but that the aesthetic damage may be in some ways one of the attractions of the poetry. Rich shows us in "When We Dead Awaken"—the essay from which our Counterpoint was taken—that a good deal of her poetic career has been an attempt to emancipate herself from the impersonal poetic agenda advanced by the overwhelmingly male poets of the generation that preceded hers. She wanted to be able to write poetry from a female rather than a "universal" (probably unconsciously male) perspective, and she wanted to be able to express herself without the protective armor of formalism. It is hard to deny that in "Frame" she accomplishes both, but the result, as we have seen, is now more direct statement of emotion. The distance that might have been imposed by formality and universality is not imposed by the presence of ideas as uncompromisingly correct as iambic pentameter could ever be. The poetry has become rhetoric.

It is surely good rhetoric.

You might have your class go back to "Aunt Jennifer's Tigers" once more and consider that it can be seen as a poem about art as well as a poem about sexual politics. Why are the needlepoint tigers that Aunt Jennifer creates invested with pride and courage, "sleek chivalric certainty"? Not, one feels, because Aunt Jennifer is using them with the fully conscious intent of fashioning them into a statement, but because she releases through them pent-up (and perhaps unacknowledged) emotions. They are like the visions of white bodies and green fields that visit Blake's chimney sweeper. They just come out spontaneously: "lyrics" so to speak, rather than statements. Or so Rich (like Blake) makes us believe. Often art is richer if the artist's emotions know more than his or her mind knows. When Rich writes on feminist topics, she faces the considerable problem of having a mind that tells her rationally why she feels what she feels. Sometimes the effect is to squeeze all ambiguities out of an image and to make the deepest level of the poem its ideology.

Robert Frost points out that a poem is most likely to prosper when it has the capacity to surprise both the reader and the writer. If the writer is too sure where she is going, the poem may suffer.

Still, to paraphrase Dr. Johnson, I cannot persuade myself to wish that Rich had been an Aunt Jennifer.

3. "Diving into the Wreck" is probably the most widely praised of all Rich's poems. What makes it so outstanding?

I wouldn't want to insist that students buy into the general critical opinion, and in my own opinion, both "Orion" and "Gabriel" are on the same plane as "Diving into the Wreck."

Still "Wreck" does stand out, largely because it puts all its chips on the power of images and so avoids ground where both Rich and the reader can know too confidently from the outset what is being said. You might ask your students what they believe the symbol of the wreck to represent. Among the possibilities are these:

◆ The past. A wreck on the ocean floor is always a sort of time capsule, and Rich declares her intention of exploring "the damage that was done/and the treasures that prevail." Certainly exploration of the cultural past (particularly the role of women as in "Planetarium") and the personal past (as in "Orion") is one of Rich's major themes.

◆ The subconscious. The images of descent into the sea, particularly in lines 35–51 ("I am blacking out . . . I have to learn alone/to turn my body without force/in the deep element"), make the poem seem to move to a different plane of perception. The surreal images ("the drowned face always staring/toward the sun") seem to come from whatever common source there is for dreams and myths. The fact that the speaker reads the book of myths before her dive reinforces both the historical and the psychoanalytic readings of the poems.

◆ The body. Several images connect the wreck with the body. The diver "stroke[s]" the beam of her lamp "slowly along the flank" of the ship, observes the "threadbare beauty" of the ship's "ribs," then dives into the hold full of rotting treasures and fouled instruments. Such passages bring to mind both the pleasures of the body and its inevitable decay.

◆ Our lives, taken as a whole. If we think about the exploration of the wreck as an exploration of our lives, then we see the poem as an extended metaphor explaining the poet's work. Her tools are the book of myths (literary heritage?), the camera (imagery?), and the knife blade (analytic intelligence?, utter frankness?). If your students have read "The Albatross," they will almost certainly see the similarity between Baudelaire's bird/poet hobbling along inhibited by his gigantic wings and Rich's poet/diver whose "flippers cripple" her until she is in the water.

Rich doesn't try to untangle these levels of symbolism and make an unequivocal statement with the poem; in fact, she frisks in her imagery, obviously enjoying seeing where the picture of the diver will lead her. In this respect the poem is like her "Two Songs" (p. 703) which frolics with the comparison of love making to plowing or landing on the moon.

–D.H.

Sylvia Plath

Plath is a poet whose artistic and personal lives are so intertwined that your students will have a difficult time understanding one without getting to know the other. To avoid a common misreading of "Daddy," for instance, they need to realize that Plath's father, a Polish immigrant, died when she was eight years old. He was certainly not a Nazi, nor was she a Jew: both were highly intellectual Unitarians. When World War II broke out Plath's father was a professor of biology and scientific German at Boston University. Plath told Alfred Alvarez that it was her father's death (not his character) that brought her such immense suffering. Like Roethke, Plath seems to have suffered the trauma of having her father die while he still seemed an immense, god–like figure. Her first suicide attempt came when she was nineteen.

Plath grew up with a self–discipline that we might associate with over–achievers, though it is hard to see how anyone with her talent and intelligence could be said to "over–achieve" it. She graduated from Smith *summa cum*, went to Cambridge as a Fulbright scholar, and there married poet Ted Hughes. Hughes reports that her early poems were written "very slowly, Thesaurus open on her knee . . . as if she were working out a mechanical problem." "Tulips" (1961) was written without a Thesaurus "at top speed, as one might write an urgent letter. From then on all her poems were written that way." In the months before her suicide, she wrote as many as three poems a day. The late poems, as Robert Lowell says, read like "controlled hallucinations, the autobiography of a fever."

QUESTIONS

1. How do Plath's earlier poems "Black Rook in Rainy Weather" and "Medallion" differ from her late poems "Daddy" and "Lady Lazarus"?

Ted Hughes' image of Plath working out the early poems as if they were mechanical problems fits with what we see in the poems themselves. They are highly disciplined, technically brilliant. Your students may not notice at first the elaborate rhyme scheme of "Black Rook": abcde/abcde/abcde, etc. The inventive half–rhymes and weak rhymes remind us that Plath was an admirer of Emily Dickinson, and that, like Dickinson, she could use rhyme to keep the mind unsettled. "Medallion" is written in half–rhymed terza rima: it would be a difficult accomplishment even if it were a worse poem.

Formally, the later poems seem to be wrecked versions of the earlier ones. The five–line stanzas of "Daddy" are like those in "Black Rook," but the rhymes have lost both their regularity and their half–rhyme subtlety. Now one full rhyme (*do/shoe/Achoo*, etc.) appears haphazardly and connects some of the most emotionally charged words: *you, Jew, through*. The three–line stanzas of "Lady Lazarus" disarrange the terza rima of "Medallion": there are generally two rhymes to the stanza and the second line often suggests the rhyme for the ensuing stanza, but the scheme is so irregular that it vexes our attention like a radio turned so low that we can tell it is playing music without quite being able to discern the tune.

The formal control of the earlier poems is consistent with their relatively restrained emotions. "Black Rook" hovers between hope and despair. It acknowledges moments of perception that remind one of Hopkins' visions of inscape:

> . . . I only know that a rook
> Ordering its black features can so shine
> As to seize my senses, haul
> My eyelids up and grant . . .

After the stanza break, however, we discover that what has been granted is not a beatific vision, but "A brief respite from fear/Of total neutrality." The greatest miracles that the poet has to hope for are "spasmodic/tricks of radiance" that will help her "Patch together a content/Of sorts." "Medallion" presents an object that might inspire horror or at least queasiness, but the poem's composure is so great that we seem hypnotized, willing to stare in fascination at the maggots coiled in the bruised flesh. Mixed with mention of maggots and innards are images of unexpected beauty like the description of the belly–scales: "Sunset looked at through milk glass." The result is not a feeling of white–knuckled horror but of chill: your class might want to compare the poem with Dickinson's "A

Narrow Fellow in the Grass," which has similar qualities, mixed with whimsy.

Both "Daddy" and "Lady Lazarus" abandon all restraint. The biographical distortions of the poems show that Plath will not be limited by fact in her dramatizing of emotion, nor will she try to balance that emotion with any glimmers of hope. She collects emotionally charged and melodramatic symbols one might expect to find in a wax museum or a B movie: Nazi atrocities, vampires, sadistic doctors. The poems are, as Richard Wilbur says, "free and helpless and unjust."

A third contrast that could be made between the earlier and later poems is their relation to the spoken voice. The early poems are musical: sound plays to sound in them in a way that we might expect from a poet well-trained in the English tradition and influenced by Roethke. They are not, however, poems written to match the rhythms of actual speech in the twentieth century, as your students can demonstrate to themselves by reading out portions of "Black Rook" and "Medallion." Plath herself said in 1963 that she could not read the poems in *The Colossus* (1960) aloud: "I didn't write them to be read aloud . . . . Now these very recent ones—I've got to say them . . . . Whatever lucidity they have comes from the fact that I say them aloud." Again your students will see the point if they read "Daddy" or (especially) "Lady Lazarus" aloud. The poems certainly don't sound like casual conversation, but they have the staccato rhythms of impassioned speech tinged with bitter irony:

> Dying
> Is an art, like everything else.
> I do it exceptionally well.
>
> I do it so it feels like hell.

2. Are the earlier poems or the later poems better?

This seems to be a question in dispute today. Ten or fifteen years ago, it was generally conceded that the late poems were the significant ones. Today, some readers are arguing that Plath's late poems are overrated and (though her tragic personal history makes one reluctant to say the word) bathetic.

At issue is the picture of Plath as a twentieth-century Cassandra, in touch, as Ted Hughes puts it, with "depths formerly reserved to the primitive ecstatic priests, shamans and Holy men." If she is a shaman, then a poem like "Daddy" cannot be measured for technical accomplishment against a poem like "Black Rook": it was written when the priestess was closer to the all-consuming fire and presents a vision of greater intensity (a vision in which "Daddy" is not Otto Plath, but the visionary embodiment of an evil loose in our century). If she is not a shaman, then a poem like "Daddy" documents the decline of a fine mind and talent.

Richard Wilbur's "Cottage Street, 1953" helps me think about this question by its contrast between Plath and Edna Ward. Are we to prefer the "grace and courage" that allowed Edna Ward to make "love" her last word, or the despair that led Sylvia Plath to take her life? As humans, we must choose Ward. And yet the poet's role is abandonment to whatever muse or demon calls most strongly. Wilbur implicitly acknowledges this:

> How large is her refusal; and how slight
> The genteel chat whereby we recommend
> Life

Plath's demon was despair, and I have to feel that her greatest poetry was produced when she gave into it most completely, abandoning restraint, technique, and taste. "Daddy" may be (as the formidable Elizabeth Hardwick says) a bad poem in many ways, but it is a *greater* poem than "Black Rook," which is a better one, morally and technically. Put it another way: we could conceive of another poet's giving us "Black Rook," but only Plath could give us "Daddy."

3. Comment on the role of metaphor in "Tulips," "The Arrival of the Bee Box" or "Cut."

The metaphors of Plath's later poetry are very effective and very disturbing, and your students should examine them closely. The assortment of metaphors that becomes attached to the tulips in "Tulips" is typical. They are, by the way, flowers of interest to those who collect literary anecdotes: they were sent by Theodore Roethke when Plath had an appendectomy in 1961. The flowers become the stimulus for a series of free associations, rather like the psychologist's inkblot. Because they are wrapped in white gift paper, they remind Plath of a baby in swaddling clothes: she had born her first child about a year before the poem was written. Because they are red, they "talk to" her own "wound" (39). The idea of talking wounds very possibly comes from Antony's funeral oration, where he imagines a tongue in every one of Caesar's wounds, crying out for vengeance (Act 2, scene 3). The idea of tongues brings us back to the flowers, which look like red tongues (41) or like red lead sinkers (42), or like—once sinking is introduced—"a sunken rust–red engine"—around which eddies swirl. Then we are back to the idea of tongues and wounds: the tulips open like "the mouth of some great African cat" (59). Then we are back to engines and wounds and blood: the tulips remind her of the red engine of her heart which "opens and closes/Its bowl of red blooms."
The associations here seem not to be checked by a premeditated scheme of meaning (such as that we seem to have in "Black Rook") or by an interest in visual fidelity (as in "Medallion"). Instead, the metaphors capture the state of Plath's mind in its agitated (and unwelcome) return from the passive near–death of anaesthesia and sedation. Plath appears in the late

poems to trust her instincts completely in introducing metaphors, assuming that her emotions are selecting them more effectively than her rational mind could.

–D.H.

Lucille Clifton

At their best, Clifton's poems strike very quickly, with such directness and so little superfluous technique that they almost defy commentary. She writes, as she once told an interviewer, out of the circumstances that surround her, the circumstances of a black woman who has known poverty and success. Nothing here is inaccessible, and almost everyone I have shown Lucille Clifton's work has liked it immediately. The problem here is not to appreciate her work, but to be able to talk about it sensibly. A scholarly paper might be got out of her relation to Whitman, whom she quotes frequently in *Generations*, her free–verse elegy–memoir on her family history; but the immediate problem in teaching her is to have students discover the way that she uses a few poetic tools powerfully.

QUESTIONS

1. Comment on the use of repetition and parallelism in Clifton's work.

The use of repetition might be one thing Clifton learned from Whitman, but it is more likely that they learned it from common sources—the Bible, the preacher, the public speaker. In "To Joan" it takes the form of parallel questions ("did you . . . did you . . . did you") and doubling for emphasis ("unreal unreal," "sister, sister," "my voices, my voices"). In "The Lost Baby Poem" it shows again in parallel questions ("what did i know . . . what did i know") and also a series of curses wished on her head ("let the rivers . . . let the sea . . . let black men . . . .") Rhythmic and rhetorical effects of this kind are pervasive in Clifton.

Somewhat different are the parallel constructions that bring together ideas we normally think of as separate. In "She Understands Me" we have "out of flesh, out of dictionaries," a juxtaposition that takes for granted that both creations are painful "blood and breaking." In "There Is a Girl Inside" we have

> she is a green tree
> in a forest of kindling.
> she is a green girl
> in a used poet.

Clifton works this metaphor hard throughout the poem, turning it this way and that to put it in a new light. In the first five lines, the girl inside is sexual passion trapped in a body that is waning. In these lines she is first a "green" (living) tree trapped in a dead forest that may burn down at any moment, then a "green" (innocent, presumably fresh–eyed and in–spired) girl trapped in the mind of a worn–out poet. The terseness with which Clifton's parallelisms and repetitions do their work is impressive.

2. Where is Clifton's diction most unusual, and what is its effect?

One part of Clifton's appeal is the colloquialness of her language, which on some occasions may take us somewhere dictionaries can't follow: most dictionaries, for instance, don't list the idiomatic use of "happen" ("For the Lame") to mean "it may happen that."

In general, though, Clifton's choice of words is not exotic until she has a special need, and then she lets us have a small surprise. In "The Lost Baby Poem," for instance, she needs to juxtapose the aborted child with the ones later born. She does so by single adjectives: the "almost" body, the "definite" brothers and sisters. There is something harsh about the labels, but this is an unblinking poem. Clifton did not almost destroy a life; she destroyed an almost life. She did a terrible thing, and the only mitigation is "almostness," that the baby was not quite real. Having clung to that thin distinction, she knows she must be doubly committed to the "definite."

Harshness of diction is common in Clifton. There is no trace of eu-phemism in "she is randy as a wolf" ("There Is a Girl Inside") or "the thing/drops out of its box squalling." These passages talk tough, and toughness is a good part of Clifton's appeal: consider "God's Mood."

3. What sort of images does Clifton use, and how are these related to her emotional content?

This question is so broad that it should net a number of answers. In the net somewhere, I hope, particularly if you have earlier discussed Keats' "To Autumn," will be images of internal pressures, of fullness. The most striking of these is the simile of the "shook bottle" in "For the Mute." Here is pressure that almost literally blows the lid off, used to represent the pressure of pent–up words in the mute person. "There Is a Girl Inside" is again about containment, internal pressure, to be released in "the sec-ond coming,/when she can break through gray hairs/into blossom." In "Perhaps" the eyes seem about to explode from the pressure of "seeing more than there is." In "She Understands Me," of course, there is "blood and breaking."

The images point to two features of Clifton's emotional content. First, there is always the sense of explosive energy. Second, there is a sense that that energy has been made more explosive by being contained. Clifton seems to chafe under any form of restraint—the restraint of self–doubt in "To Joan," poverty in "The Lost Baby Poem," weakness in "God's Mood," age in "There Is a Girl Inside." Clifton will not be contained, and even her remorse in "The Lost Baby Poem" becomes a cause for hyperbole: she will be "a mountain" for her living children.

–D.H.

Robert Hass

Hass has been devoting himself to translations lately, but his early books *Field Guide* (1973) and *Praise* (1979) were so remarkable that he seems likely to prove a major poet. His collection of essays, *Twentieth Century Pleasures,* from which both of our Counterpoints are taken, won a National Book Critics Award for Criticism, and is a gem: lucid and fascinating.

Like many mystical poets (Blake, Dickinson, Bogan, and—I believe—Clampitt), Hass is arrested by images that give the feeling that "what perishes and what lasts forever have been brought into conjunction." The image does not, however, make meaning: Hass is far from surrealistic. He locates meaning in the power of the mind to integrate images and make patterns until "a lot of different things are the same thing." An individual's identity is created by the patterns of identity he or she imposes on experience. As Hass shows in "Heroic Simile," the patterns may be very different:

> A man and a woman walk from the movies
> to the house in the silence of separate fidelities.
> There are limits to imagination.

One of Hass's projects as a poet is to make the "separate fidelities" more accessible, either by explaining (and he *will* explain) the patterns he discovers around him or by constructing and exploring another mind.

QUESTIONS

1. Paraphrase "Santa Lucia" by writing it either as a short letter addressed to a close friend, or as a paragraph that might appear in an essay about the relations of men and women.

This rather peculiar question might help your students concentrate on the way the poem works. It is a difficult poem because it combines the techniques of dramatic monologue and stream–of–consciousness narration with a series of allusions. A paraphrase assignment will reveal a wide variety of interpretations, some of them insupportable.

Whether your students use the letter or the essay form, we can hope that we will see certain themes emerge. The central one will be that there is a conflict between the eroticism that draws the man to the woman's door and the eroticism of the woman herself. The woman calls the man both "innocent" and "carnivorous." He bombards her with art objects because he is relentlessly after sex ("He wants to fuck": no one will miss that line). He is not, however, a wolf in sheep's clothing using art as a bribe or as a conscious disguise for lust. Instead, he is genuinely confused, poor man. He has absorbed art's standard views of the role of women: they might be temptresses (like Durer's "Eve" or Ingres' "Odalisque"), but the desire for them can be (think of Keats' "Ode on a Grecian Urn") an emblem of eternal beauty, a "flute" that plays *transcend, transcend.*

The woman, on the other hand, is tired of the old conjunction of desire, guilt, and false sublimity. She is tired of the paintings of naked women at the Louvre. She is not tired of, or put off by, sex. (I think she would agree with Adrienne Rich that "Lust, too, is a flower"—see the free association in lines 56–62.) She simply thinks that sex is usually somewhat beside the point, that the sublime if it comes is not likely to appear in sexual form; even "the erotic/is not sexual, only when you're lucky." The remarkable closing image of the poem expresses her image of the moment of transcendence:

> What I want happens
> not when the deer freezes in the shade
> and looks at you and you hold very still
> and meet her gaze but in the moment after
> when she flicks her ears & starts to feed again.

Somehow one imagines that her admirer's reaction to this view of transcendence would be blank incomprehension.

2. How do works of art, words, and natural objects acquire meaning in Hass's poetry?

The short answer here is "by association," sometimes very free association.

If, for example, your students have read William Carlos Williams' "Queen Anne's Lace," they will see in "Weed" a tribute to the power of the poem:

> . . . it is not the veined
> body of Queen Anne's lace
> I found, bored, in a spring classroom
> from which I walked hands tingling
> for the breasts that are meadows in New Jersey
> in 1933

But the effect of the poem is not precisely what Williams might have expected. Williams would have been happy to think that the poem made Hass's hands tingle for the feel of breasts, but one wonders whether he could imagine himself as creator of a myth that New Jersey, 1933, was a Never–Never Land where meadows grew breasts.

Just as the woman in "Santa Lucia" suggests that paintings at the Louvre can be seen either as expressions of sublimity or as women "naked & possessed," Hass suggests that anything to which we attach symbolic meaning may take off in an unexpected direction. Thus, in "Heroic Simile," the sight of the falling Samurai in Kurosawa's film suggests to Hass a falling tree (a standard heroic simile), the fall of Ajax in Homer (a standard point of reference for such a simile), chanted dactyls (a standard form), and then (far from standard) a whimsical fantasy about the woodcutters who find the tree. The simile (as some of Milton's nearly do) becomes so intricate that it detaches itself from the original story entirely and wanders off to new concerns: the way that the tree will be cut, the problem the men will have hauling the wood, the problem they will have existing only in a metaphor.

The vagaries of association in Hass are reminiscent of Stevens. There is the same insistence that the imagination makes a world unrecognizable to the unimaginative.

In most of Hass's poems both words (the ultimate cultural artifact) and natural objects acquire strong meanings that may be idiosyncratic. In "Meditation at Lagunitas," both the word *blackberry* and the body of the lover are "numinous" with associations. The "new thinking" would say that the word is less than what it represents: a mere abstraction of a rich experience, so that with the word standing between us and the blackberry itself, we can never again experience the berry whole, as an un–languaged child might. (This is, as Hass notes, rather like the old thinking of the Romantic poets on the fading of the visionary gleam.) Hass finds that the word itself is a rich experience, connected in the labyrinth of his consciousness with the small shoulders of his lover, which are connected in turn with his "childhood river/with its island willows, silly music from the pleasure boat," etc. Eventually the word becomes not a cause of loss, but an incantation against it. In "Weed" both a name ("horse–parsnip") and a natural object speak of "durable/unimaginative pleasures":

> reading Balzac,
> fixing the window sash, rising
> to a clean kitchen, the fact
> that the car starts . . . .

No one else would have made these connections. Hass makes them, and makes me, at least, find them as convincing as they are surprising.

3. Is Hass essentially an optimistic or a pessimistic poet?

In the first of the Counterpoints Hass, after saying that children have a natural love of the predictable, says that

> To see that power working on adults, you have to catch them out: the look of foolish happiness on the faces of people who have just sat down to dinner is their knowledge that dinner will be served.

Here is the same sort of undercutting of pretension that characterizes neoclassical humor, nineteenth–century Dandyism, and twentieth–century black humor. Often Hass's focus is on human limitation and weakness: the middle–class, unimaginative pleasures of "Weed," the rather pitiful confusion of art and lust in "Santa Lucia," the false cheer of the tennis whites in "Old Dominion," the fatuousness of "the new thinking" in "Meditation at Lagunitas," the protracted history of greed in "Palo Alto: The Marshes." In these scathing observations, Hass seems close to Baudelaire, a poet he apparently admires (he has written several prose poems like Baudelaire's).

In "Old Dominion," we get a direct statement that Hass has come to understand Jarrell's unhappiness about the human condition:

> . . . that in his art, like Chekhov's,
> everyone was lost, that the main chance was never seized
> because it is only there as a thing to be dreamed of
> or because someone somewhere had set the old words
> to the old tune: we live by habit and it doesn't hurt.

Yet one can't feel that Hass's final word is bleak. In "Old Dominion," the thought of life's unsatisfactoriness becomes a call to "take risks, not to stay/in the south, to somehow do honor to Randall Jarrell,/never to kill myself." The humor of "Heroic Simile" and "Weed" stave off despair, and "Meditation at Lagunitas" ends up with as beatific a vision of the possible harmony between human nature and external nature as one could hope to find.

–D.H.

Sharon Olds

Coleridge's comment that he would have recognized a couple of Wordsworth's lines if he had come upon them in the desert comes to mind when I think of Sharon Olds' poetry. There are critics who say that Olds is distinctly a follower of Sylvia Plath, and there are similarities in both the confrontation of painful relationships and the frequently tough wit. But Olds' view of life seems to me far more positive than Plath's, and her emphasis on simple universal experiences of the body—breathing, aging, touching—makes her poetry some of the most accessible now being written.

QUESTIONS

1. How does Olds make her poems talk about four levels of reality: the personal, familial, societal, and historical?

"Summer Solstice" is probably the best example to use in discussing this question, though similar techniques are used in most of the poems collected here. Most of Olds' poems begin with the family and expand to reach other levels. This poem starts with society: the way New York City deals with a man who threatens suicide. From the first words of the title, however, we get a sense of larger historical perspective. The summer solstice is an event that has been important to our species from prehistoric times: I think of Stonehenge and of the Mayan temple oriented to indicate the solstices and the equinox. (It might be worthwhile to begin your discussion of the poem by asking your class when they imagine humans first became interested in the solstice.)

When Olds says in line 6 that "the huge machinery of the earth began to work for his life," the apparent rhetorical excess (The NYPD as "machinery of the earth"!) reminds us of the celestial mechanics suggested in the title—the rolling of the earth around the sun and on its axis. *Time*, aided by the NYPD, manifested the motion of the planet, is now on the man's side. The allusion to astronomical observations as ancient as humankind prepares us for the remarkable concluding lines "campfires we lit at night/back in the beginning of the world."

The step up from society to history (or prehistory) is matched by a step down to the family. Notable examples are the cop who puts on a bulletproof vest to protect the "life of his children's father" (10), the safety net spread out "as the sheet is prepared to receive at birth" (22), and the thought that the cops are going to beat the man "as a mother whose child has been/lost will scream at the child when it is found" (31–32). Olds connects the different levels of reality by introducing multiple images, often via metaphor or simile, rather as Milton does in *Paradise Lost*.

The individual, particularly the individual in his or her body, does not figure as strongly in this poem as in many of Olds' others, but we are reminded of the sense-world in which the potential suicide lives—the hard iron stairs followed by the "soft, tarry surface" of the roof (2–3), the leg "hung over the lip of the next world" (18). Certainly the vulnerability of the individual is present: notice, for instance, the remarkable (perhaps not successful) mention of the fontanelle in line 15. Nothing better suggests the weakness of the flesh than the fact that we all have a hole in our heads.

2. Comment on the importance of breathing in "Sex without Love" and "The Race."

The effect in "Sex" is flashier—that panting in the ninth line that mimics the panting of those "who make love/without love." More significant is the breathing in "The Race." Your students will notice the father's breathing at the end of the poem, of course, and many will notice the contrast between the slow rhythmic breathing and the literally breath–taking rush of the poet on her way to the hospital. The verbs *rush* (2), *run* (12, 19, 23, 30, 34, 36, 40) and *race* (13, 23) dominate the poem, and part of the poem's rhythm is cardiovascular: note the deep breath in line 26 and the walk down the airplane's aisle in a "mist of gold endorphin light" (49). Your students may need a nudge to notice the way that Olds uses lineation, punctuation, and syntax to help create the breathlessness of the poem. Ask them how it would affect the poem if we had more end–stopped lines and more frequent punctuation:

> When I got to the airport,
> I rushed up to the desk.
> They told me the flight was cancelled.
> The doctor had said
> My father would not live through the night.
> And the flight was cancelled.
> A young man with a dark blond moustache
> Told me another airline had a non–stop
> Leaving in seven minutes.
> "See that elevator over there?
> Well, go down to the first floor.
> Make a right, get off at
> The second Pan Am terminal."

Olds' enjambments, run–on sentences, and omissions of quotation marks give the poem a feeling of speed and confusion.

The use of breathing in "The Race" is typical of two aspects of Olds' poetry. First, she reminds us that our bodies (the very things that seem to keep us separate) are our greatest common experience. Olds and her father, separated (if we allow ourselves an autobiographical reading) by a continent and some bad feelings (see "The Victims"), have at least one thing to unite them: they can be together quietly in a room, breathing. And she, so recently breathless, can appreciate the preciousness of the even rising and sinking of his chest. Compare the shared cigarette at the end of "Summer Solstice." The second aspect of Olds' poetry exemplified by the

breathing is the interest in the way events register themselves on the
body. "The Elder Sister" is full of such registering: the face elongated by
the pressure of birth, the clenched jaws and frown lines. "The Victims,"
too, connects the appearance of the body with the events of the life.

3. Some critics find Olds' imagery too ingenious, far–fetched, or unpoetic.
Where do you find imagery that might be so criticized? Can it be justified?

Your students might have a hard time seeing what this question is
driving at. Let's try to clarify it. Restraint is an article of faith with such
poets as William Carlos Williams, who never overstated and who used
figures of speech sparingly. Other poets (including, for instance, Donne)
introduce language and imagery that surprises and sometimes shocks us
because we don't expect to see it in the context. Olds is closer to Donne
than to Williams. Examples your students may notice are

> the pressure of Mother's muscles on her brain,
> the tight walls scraping her skin.
> Her face is still narrow from it, the long
> hollow cheeks of a Crusader on a tomb. ("Sister," 5–8)
>
>   . . . the white
> slugs of their bodies gleaming through slits in their
> suits of compressed silt, the stained
> flippers of their hands, the underwater
> fire of their eyes, ships gone down with the
> lanterns lit . . . .   ("Victims," 18–23)
>
>   Beautiful as dancers,
> gliding over each other like ice–skaters
> over the ice, fingers hooked
> inside each other's bodies, faces
> red as steak, wine . . . .   ("Sex," 2–6)

Dr. Johnson's objection that metaphysical wit consisted of
"hetrogeneous ideas linked by violence together" might be leveled against
Olds. Isn't it a bit much to move with such dexterity from birth canals to
Crusader tombs? Is the conceit comparing old men to marine creatures
and sunken ships an exercise in cleverness? Is the collection of images
describing "the ones who make love without love" so strangely mixed as to
be ludicrous? Someone should be willing to say so. On the other hand,
Olds' control of her images is impressive. "Sex without Love" is
deliberately ludicrous, and the move from the birth canal to the Crusader

tomb is practically an Olds signature: the juxtapostion of the beginning and the end, the explicitly sexual and the sublime.

–D.H.

Louise Glück

Louise Glück's poetry is not sunny and clear. It often seems to burrow underneath the apparently solid surface of family life and take us into regions where the light of reason and good cheer doesn't shine. Glück's confessional poetry doesn't come up for air as often as the poetry of Maxine Kumin, Sharon Olds, or Lucille Clifton, each of whom gives us a positive vision to balance her painful insights. It hasn't the intellectual wit of Adrienne Rich or Sylvia Plath. What it does have is tremendous gravity and compression: we feel that we are in the hands of a serious poet who might give us in a dozen lines a shock of insight that another writer might bury under a heap of transitions and explanations. Often the imagery in Glück's poems has the density, ambiguity, and power of the imagery of dreams.

A good match so show how Glück differs from a more optimistic poet like Kumin would be her "Still Life" (discussed and reprinted in the introduction to the poetry section, pp. 000–000) and Kumin's "The Envelope." The one takes the procession of generations to be a tragedy, the other takes it to be a blessing.

QUESTIONS

1. Comment on the way the passage of time is treated in Glück's poems.

In most of Glück's poetry, time present, time past, and time future exist simultaneously. The continuity of time clearly fascinates her, so that she is able to imagine herself (in "For My Mother") existing as a fully sentient being existing inside her mother's body before her own conception, watching the green moonlight filter through her mother's eyes and into her own bones. Or (in "Still Life") she is able to imagine herself standing where her mother stood, looking at herself (Louise) as a five–year–old.

To some extent, the motivating force behind these travels back and forth in time could be philosophy. Glück writes as a fatalist, a believer that time is a seamless web of causes and effects that link all events to all other events. From a fatalist's point of view, it is impossible to say when anything or anyone begins or ends. Before conception, Glück was destined to be conceived by this particular woman, so she is said to rest in her mother's body, just as in "Metamorphosis," the spot on her father's lung has always existed and as in "The Triumph of Achilles," the gods look on Achilles as "a man already dead."

Philosophical determinism is the minor partner here, though. Far more important is Glück's vision of the recurring cycles in human life. By far the most important is the cycle of reproduction and abandonment. Daughters grow up to abandon their mothers in order to have daughters of their own, who will abandon them: the cycle is unbreakable and (from Glück's perspective) tragic. The new–born daughter *is* the abandoned mother. Abandonment is inherent in the world of sex, conception, and fertility, which is the reason, I think, that Glück begins "To My Mother" with the notion that life was better before the act of sex that brought her into the world, and the reason that she ends the poem with an image of the "schools of spores" that seem to infiltrate the house and signal the changes (and losses) that will come to it over the next thirty years.

Men figure in "To My Mother" and "Still Life" only as agents of sex and corrupting time, like the spores. In "The Apple Trees," men are sim-ilarly sinister. The baby is always "your son," never fully accepted as part of his mother, a product of her body with the requisite number of "whittled ribs." Once again the issue is abandonment, harsher and more complete than the abandonment of daughters. Already she can see how the son will leave her; the lines on his palm are like a roadmap away. And not only will he leave her, but this leaving will be a pattern of his relation with women; men are mobile, women are "rooted to the river."

These poems might suggest an anti–masculine bias that could put off some of your students, but Glück knows that men are bound up in the cycles of time just as women are. In "Metamorphosis" the father becomes in his final illness like a child, and both the speaker and her mother become mothers to him. In "The Triumph of Achilles," Patroclus and Achilles are caught up in a cycle of love and mortality as inevitable, apparently, as the cycle of birth–motherhood–separation. In "these friendships" a Patroclus must always love, serve, and sacrifice, and an Achilles must always discover love and die.

2. Where in Glück's poems do you find one person standing in the place of another? Why does this happen?

This question is really another way into some of the material noted above. In the *Iliad*, when Achilles is sulking in his tent and the dis-heartened Greeks are being drubbed by the Trojans, Patroclus, Achilles' bosom companion, borrows his friend's armor and goes to battle. The ap-pearance of a substitute Achilles on the field turns the tide of battle until Patroclus meets Hector and is killed. Now the grieving Achilles gets new armor made by Hephaestos and goes to battle himself, but the return to battle seals his doom, since Paris has an arrow destined to penetrate Achilles' heel, the one part of him not magically protected. I give these details in case you are rusty and questions come up in class. The point we need to make here is that Patroclus and Achilles are interchanged in the story: they are shadow and substance, they stand in each other's places. Traditionally, we think of Patroclus as Achilles' shadow, since as a warrior, he is at best an imitation of Achilles. In Glück's poem, the roles are reversed. It is "the story of Patroclus," who always knew how to love and serve, that she is telling. The triumph of Achilles is his learning to love and to serve, to imitate Patroclus.

In "Still Life" the speaker, looking at the photograph, is literally looking at the world from her mother's perspective, and doing so at a time when she has reached the same stage in life that her mother had reached when the picture was taken. In "Metamorphosis" the speaker is in the same posture (nursing her father) in the third section that her mother is in at the beginning of the poem, the same posture that her mother often assumed in nursing the speaker and other children. She and her mother "wear the same armor," so to speak, just as Patroclus and Achilles do.

This reminder that people wear the same armor, strike the same poses, go through the same stages, is fundamental to Glück's poetry. She says in our Counterpoint passage that her poetry comes from what are "in the deepest sense, ordinary experiences." At her best, she can make us see how much our loves and losses are part of a larger human pattern.

3. What are some passages in Glück's poetry that you can't understand? Why are they difficult?

I ask this question because Glück is not always clear. Sometimes, frankly, I think she misses clarity by plain bad writing. In "Metamorphosis" lines 20–21 would not pass muster in a freshman essay:

> . . . the living circle us
> like so many tree stumps.

What does this mean? That there are other people in the room ("the living") who surround the dying man and his daughter as tree stumps might surround a tree about to become a stump itself? That "the living" (perhaps doctors and nurses) move around the father and daughter as if they were inanimate objects, or creatures already dead? The second interpretation seems more likely, but "so many" seems an odd expression to use when referring to two.

More often Glück's obscurity comes not from a defect in expression, but from the genuinely unsettled relations among her images. "The Apple Trees" works on the level of the subconscious or not at all. Why should the husband stand "among trees hung/with bitten apples"? Is this an allusion to the Garden of Eden (in which case it seems forced) or is it a dream–image that Glück herself could not pin down. Why does the air divide into panes of color? Is it because of the intervening window? Perhaps. Why does the baby held up for inspection appear as a heart on a blue stalk amid whittled ribs? Is it because Glück is remembering X–ray films? Does such an image come to mind because she doesn't find the boy quite real, because she has already foreseen the day that he will not be there? Why does darkness issue from the trees?

"Metamorphosis" is equally obscure to me in places. The mother who is apparently alive in the first section has been "lived without" for many years in the third. Are we to assume that she is an apparition in section 1? That she is lived without in section 3 only because the speaker manages miraculously to remember what her life was like when she and her mother were actually together in one body?

These sorts of questions are often on my mind when I read Glück, and I would want my class to know that if they find her poems occasionally obscure and difficult, they are no more lost than I am. Glück appears to be one of those poets whose virtue is keeping us lost, making us struggle to make sense of relations that defy conscious analysis.

–D.H.

DRAMA

THEMES LINKING
THE DRAMA AND FICTION SECTIONS

Those building syllabi that attempt to make thematic connections through the term may want to consider how the drama section echoes the themes listed for the fiction.

1. *Men and Women.*

Romantic love permeates *Twelfth Night,* a play made particularly interesting by Viola's disguise as a page. Lust and the attempts of law to control it are the mainsprings of the action in *Measure for Measure. The Three Sisters* and *Hedda Gabler* are both concerned partly with the vicissitudes of romance inside and outside marriage. *Fool for Love* shows passion wreaking havoc in three lives.

2. *Families.*

The Three Sisters and *Crimes of the Heart* both show the family as the center of a little society, and the love of three sisters as the force that holds the society together, at least temporarily. *Death of a Salesman* shows the disintegration of a family under the pressures of the salesman's ethic; it is a classic study of a father's relationship with his sons. *The Swamp Dwellers* shows a rural Nigerian family strained by the conflict between new ways and old. *Painting Churches* shows the struggle of an adult daughter to come to an understanding of (and with) her aging parents.

3. *Some Views of Women.*

Antigone provides one of the earliest examples in Western literature of a heroic woman; *Medea* contains stirring passages on the subordinate position of women in ancient Greece. Viola in *Twelfth Night* is a fine example of the Shakespearean heroine, witty and resourceful, capable of anything. *The Three Sisters* shows very attractive and capable women struggling to find a way to live with dignity and grace in difficult social and domestic circumstances. *Hedda Gabler* features a protagonist whose enormous energy and ambition are thwarted by the narrow roles that society offers her.

4. *Some Views of Men.*

It could certainly be argued that *Hamlet* is a portrayal of the Elizabethan ideal of masculine virtue—once Hamlet bestirs himself.
Angelo in *Measure for Measure* might be a portrayal of a distinctly
masculine villain. Part of the sadness of *Death of a Salesman* is its
presentation of an ideal of hardy, optimistic, omnicompetent
manhood breaking those who try to live up to it. The sangfroid of
the murderers in *The Dumb Waiter* is hardly less hyperbolic than
that we see in the hard-boiled detectives of American fiction. *Fool
for Love* presents an image of the manly man that will be familiar
to those who have lived in the West.

5. *Obsession.*

Krapp's Last Tape gives the clearest example of obsessive behavior in
the drama anthology, but several other plays feature characters
whose single-mindedness borders on obsession. In *Medea*, revenge
swallows up all other human feelings. *Twelfth Night* begins with a
picture of Orsino's love-sickness and gives us several other examples
of romance sweeping away reason. Those who read Chekhov closely
will discover that his characters tend to be controlled by a single
"humor," which often becomes compulsive. *Hedda Gabler* shows the
dangerous predominance of the protagonist's desire to control fate,
and *Fool for Love* shows love, jealousy, and manipulation carried to
extremes reminiscent of *Antony and Cleopatra.*

6. *Art and Artists.*

Both *Hamlet* and *The Real Inspector Hound* make use of the play-
within-a-play and so provide opportunities for the author to contrast
staged reality with "real" reality. *Painting Churches* revolves on the
difficulties of painting a true portrait of people as close to us as our
parents and is packed with both allusions to painting and thought
about how art works. And in Gardner Church it offers a study of the
artist in decline.

7. *The South.*

Crimes of the Heart!

8. *Other Cultures and Subcultures.*

Obviously, both *Antigone* and *Medea* can be used as inroads to Greek culture, and all three Shakespeare plays can be taught as products of Elizabethan England. *The Three Sisters*, like other Chekhov works, gives a useful picture of social stultification in pre-revolutionary Russia. Both *The Swamp Dwellers* and *Master Harold* give pictures of life in Africa; the first of Nigeria's conflict between tradition and modernization, the second of racial conflict in South Africa.

Sophocles
Antigone

One of the major difficulties of teaching this play is filling in all the background information. At the end of this entry you will find a genealogical chart of the House of Oedipus and a brief summary of the events that lead up to the opening of *Antigone*. You may want to copy those pages and distribute them to your students before they begin their reading. You might also ask them to read the handbook entries "Plot," "Protagonist," and "Tragedy" and the section on Greek drama in the text (pp. 1213-1216).

Although many of the issues introduced in *Antigone* are of universal concern, the play is also very much the product of a specific place and time—Athens in 441 B.C. American students who instinctively root for the underdog, especially when she is a Patrick Henryesque young woman who courageously defies a tyrant, are inclined to read this play as a clear-cut contest between good (Antigone) and evil (Creon). Students who understand something about Athenian attitudes toward the polis (a word we translate as "city-state" but which actually means much more) and toward drama will realize that the situation is far more complex.

In *The Greeks* H.D.F. Kitto explains that for Greeks the term *polis* meant "the whole communal life of the people, political, cultural, moral—even economic." Today we think of the state as an entity distinct from the individual; for Athenian Greeks such a notion would have been incomprehensible. We read *Antigone* and see a clash between two headstrong individuals; Greek audiences would have viewed Antigone's decision to disobey the laws of the polis and Creon's decision to ignore the laws of the gods by abrogating funeral customs as threats to the harmony of their society.

In the following passage, Kitto suggests another difference between ancient Athenian and contemporary societies, a difference reflected in our attitudes toward drama:

The Greeks thought of the polis as an active formative thing, training the minds and characters of the citizens; we think of it as a
piece of machinery for the production of safety and convenience.
The training in virtue, which the medieval state left to the Church,
and the polis made its own concern, the modern state leaves to God
knows what.

For the Athenians, drama was one of the most important training
devices employed by the polis, and the theater a place for educating as
well as entertaining the populace. Consequently, theaters were huge (the
one at Epidaurus seated 17,000 spectators), and dramatic festivals were
community events which have no modern equivalent. The yearly
Athenian drama festival, held in Dionysus' honor, was the most
significant. Playwrights submitted plays (three tragedies and a comedy)
to a board of judges who decided which four dramatists would be
permitted to compete in the festival. Although wealthy citizens were
required to underwrite the production costs, each patron could select the
dramatist he wished to sponsor and share the glory if his choice won
the competition. Although spectators paid a small charge for seats,
Athens paid the admission fee for those who could not otherwise afford
to attend. Thus, in 441 B.C. when *Antigone* won first place, Sophocles was
not merely presenting a play; he was communicating a message to the
entire population of Athens, a message regarding the proper
relationship among the gods, the polis, and the individual.

QUESTIONS

1. How does the opening scene prepare us for the rest of the play?

In less than 100 lines, Sophocles provides background information,
identifies the two actors on stage, reveals their personalities, sets the plot
in motion, and introduces the central theme of the play.
You might remind your students that before a Greek audience arrived
at the theater, they would have known the story of Oedipus and family.
Nevertheless, within the first fifty-five lines of *Antigone*, Sophocles summarizes all the significant events that occurred prior to the opening
scene: the deaths of Eteocles and Polyneices (13), the victory of Thebes
over the Argive army (15), the fate of Oedipus and Jocasta (49-54), Creon's
decision not to allow Polyneices' burial (27-34), and Creon's decree
sentencing anyone who disobeys his orders to death by public stoning
(35-37).
Sophocles immediately identifies the sisters by name and
relationship ("My sister, my Ismene..."—l; "Antigone"—ll), and

establishes sympathy for them (1-6). Beginning with line 37 he reveals the personalities of the two sisters as they discuss the consequences of disobedience. Ismene is fearful, cautious, and sensible. She recalls their parents' and brothers' tragic deaths, predicts that she and Antigone will also "perish terribly" if they "force the law" (59), and reminds Antigone of their inferior status as women. Antigone displays the pride and stubbornness that will prove her undoing. She glories in her opportunity to die heroically and boasts, "For me, the doer, death is best" (72).

In line 43 Sophocles suggests the conflict that will drive the plot when he has Antigone announce that she intends to bury her brother in spite of Creon's decree. In the ensuing conversation between Antigone and Ismene, Sophocles introduces the major question raised by the play—how to act when duty to the gods conflicts with duty to the state. Ismene decides her loyalty must be to the state: "So I shall ask of them beneath the earth/forgiveness, for in these things I am forced,/and shall obey the men in power" (65-67). Antigone decides to risk the "crime of piety." She explains, "Longer the time to please the dead/than that for those up here" (75-76). The rest of the play is a working out of the consequences of a conflict fully elaborated by line 76.

2. What is the role of the chorus in the play?

Students are sometimes put off by the conventions of Greek drama, especially the chorus, which may strike them as terribly artificial and intrusive. It often helps to remind students of the conventions modern moviegoers accept without question—background music, credits rolling across the screen, and an invisible camera zooming in for close-ups of people who think they are alone. Once students get used to the idea of a chorus, they are generally intrigued by the variety of functions it can perform. You might ask your class to mark each passage spoken by the chorus and identify its purpose. Here are a few possibilities:

Chorus as substitute for stage directions and setting. If you remind your students that the Greek audience has neither printed programs nor elaborate scenery to identify characters, time and place, they should understand the necessity of some of the Chorus's remarks. At one point, for example, the chorus identifies the character who has just walked onto the stage and suggests his mood: "Here is your one surviving son./Does he come in grief at the fate of his bride, in pain that he's tricked of his wedding?" (628-630). Later they describe what is happening to Antigone, "Now I am carried beyond all bounds./My tears will not be checked./I see Antigone depart/to the chamber where all men sleep" (804-807).

Chorus as prophet. Sometimes the chorus provides foreshadowing. After Teiresias prophesies terrible events, the Chorus adds, "And since the time when I first grew gray hair/his sayings to the city have been true" (1093-1094). Later the Chorus hints that the Queen may commit suicide, "This muteness may portend/as great disaster as a loud lament" (1251-1252).

Chorus as actor. Occasionally, the Chorus plays an active role in the development of the plot. It is the Chorus that finally convinces Creon to bury Polyneices and release Antigone (1090-1114).

Chorus as singers and dancers. Reading the play won't enable students to identify the passages that would have involved singing and dancing. More about that in the next question.

Chorus as speaker for the community. Because the Greeks saw drama as a forum for debating issues vital to the citizenry, this may be the Chorus's most significant function. At times the Chorus performs this role by listening to both sides of a discussion and then evaluating the arguments presented. This approach is illustrated by the Chorus's response to Creon's and Haemon's disagreement about Antigone's fate. The Chorus initially agrees with Creon's words (681-682), subsequently finds merit in Haemon's position, and finally advises each to learn from the other (724-726). At other times the Chorus simply proclaims the "correct" interpretation of events. At the end of the play, for example, the Chorus confidently explains the lesson to be learned from Antigone.

3. Which of the passages spoken by the Chorus would you guess were designed primarily to provide opportunities for singing and dancing? How are these passages related to the story?

Reading a Greek play is a little like reading an opera or a musical comedy—we miss a lot. Perhaps this question will encourage your students to imagine the music and pageantry Greeks considered essential to drama. You may want to provide a clue to this answer by telling your students that the chorus sang and danced during relatively lengthy passages called odes. Such odes generally consist of three stanzas: the "strophe" or "turn," the "antistrophe" or "counterturn," and the "epode" or "stand." The Greek chorus chanted the strophe as they moved across the orchestra, the antistrophe as they returned to their starting point, and the epode while standing in their original position.

Following is a brief summary of each ode's contribution to the play

With the *Ode of Entrance* (which begins with line 99) the Chorus, singing a triumphal song in celebration of Thebes' victory over Argos, enters the orchestra. [The structure of this ode is representative of the others in this play: Strophe I (99-116), Antistrophe II (118-133), Strophe II (135-147), and Antistrophe II (148-161).]

The *First Choral Ode* (334-372) praises the accomplishments of humanity. Then, with the warning that we must honor "the laws of the land and the god's sworn right," the Chorus foreshadows Creon's and Antigone's fates.

The *Second Choral Ode* (585-630) predicts the inevitable destruction of the House of Oedipus.

The *Third Choral Ode* differs from the others in that some of the lines are chanted by Antigone. In the first strophe and antistrophe (786-800), the Chorus, clearly reflecting on Haemon's statement that Creon "will not ever lay eyes upon [Haemon's] face again" (761-762), considers how love can defeat reason. The Chorus then attempts to console Antigone and to suggest the reason for her fall (801-877). This is the only ode in *Antigone* that ends with an epode (878-881).

The *Fourth Choral Ode* (946-984), in which the Chorus comforts Antigone by associating her fate with those of other noble figures such as Danae, reminds the audience of Antigone's heroic stature.

In the *Fifth Choral Ode* (1118-1151), a paean to the god honored by the Athenian drama festival, the Chorus pleads with Bacchus to save the city of Thebes and the House of Oedipus.

4. What is Antigone's tragic flaw? What is Creon's?

Throughout the play Sophocles suggests that both Antigone and Creon suffer from excessive pride, the frailty that has proved the undoing of prominent figures on and off stage. Creon's pride in his own judgment and his consequent refusal to consider the views of others is a recurrent motif. Haemon advises his father, "Then do not have one mind, and one alone/that only your opinion can be right" (705-706). Creon's response shows that Haemon knows his father well: "At my age I'm to school my mind by his?/This boy instructor is my master, then?" (727-728). Teiresias also accuses Creon of stubborn pride: "All men may err/but error once committed, he's no fool/nor yet unfortunate, who gives up his stiffness/and cures the trouble he has fallen in./Stubbornness and stupidity are twins" (1024-1028). Although Creon calls Teiresias a liar, he later confesses to the Chorus that he knows Teiresias' prophesies have always been true. He then admits that pride is the cause of his turmoil: "And my mind is torn./To yield is dreadful. But to stand against

him./Dreadful to strike my spirit to destruction" (1095-1097). Too late
Creon agrees "to come to counsel, and take advice" (1098).

Antigone, too, seems to have a case of exaggerated self-esteem. In the
Prologue, Ismene accuses her of being "hard of mind" (47) and claims
that Antigone has "a hot mind over chilly things" (88). Antigone
demonstrates the accuracy of Ismene's observations when she is brought
before Creon. Antigone arrogantly boasts that she deliberately disobeyed
Creon's order and adds, "And if you think my acts are foolishness/the
foolishness may be in a fool's eye" (469-470), a statement unlikely to inspire clemency. The Chorus concludes that Antigone's "self-sufficiency
has brought [her] down" (878), and that "[t]he same tempest of mind/as
ever controls the girl" (929-930).

Ironically, Creon and Antigone, who are blind to their own pride,
are acutely aware of it in others. When Antigone, justifying her actions,
states, "So not through fear of any man's proud spirit/would I be likely to
neglect these laws,/draw on myself the gods' sure punishment" (457-
459), she is clearly referring to Creon. Then Creon rails against
Antigone's pride:

> These rigid spirits are the first to fall.
> The strongest iron hardened in the fire,
> most often ends in scrapes and shatterings.
> Small curbs bring raging horses back to terms.
> Slave to his neighbor, who can think of pride?
> (475-479)

5. Why would the Athenians have considered pride a dangerous flaw?

The play suggests that such pride is dangerous because it can destroy
the delicate balance between individualism and the good of the
community. Athenian democracy was dependent on citizens reasoning
together to create a society in which each man could develop his
potential to the fullest. If individual pride prevented citizens from
respecting and learning from the views of others, wisdom could not
prevail and the polis would be destroyed. Sophocles suggests that pride
prevents both Antigone and Creon from thinking clearly. Antigone
refuses to listen to her sister Ismene or to believe Ismene loves her. Yet
it is clear to the audience that Ismene is speaking the truth when she
says, "But know this: you go/senseless indeed, but loved by those who
love you" (98-99). Antigone's warped view is further illustrated by her
response to the Chorus that is trying to comfort her: "Laughter against
me now. In the name of our fathers' gods,/could you not wait till I
went?" (839-840). Her self-delusion is even more apparent when she
laments that no one cares about her fate. Antigone claims, "I go, without

a friend, struck down by fate" (919), even though Ismene, the Chorus, and Haemon have all pleaded her cause.

Creon is as blinded by arrogance as Antigone, but Creon's powerful political position makes his blindness far more dangerous. At the time of this play, Athenian government was headed by Pericles, a general-in-chief elected by the citizens. The tyrannical views expressed by Creon in this exchange with Haemon should have frightened and angered an Athenian audience:

> Creon: Is the town to tell me how to rule?
> Haemon: Now there you speak just like a boy yourself.
> Creon: Am I to rule by other mind than mine?
> Haemon: No city is property of a single man.
> Creon: But custom gives possession to the ruler.
> Haemon: You'd rule a desert beautifully alone.

The moral of the play is expressed by the Messenger who announces Haemon's and Antigone's deaths: "So he has made it very clear to men/that to reject good counsel is a crime" (1242-1243). Pride makes both Antigone and Creon guilty of that crime, but because Creon as king wields enormous power, the consequences of his unreasonable refusal to listen to others are particularly devastating. Antigone may have caused her own destruction, but Creon is responsible for an offense against the gods, for political unrest, for the deaths of Antigone, Haemon, and Eurydice, and for his own moral, spiritual, and political fall.

6. Creon and Antigone disagree about whether a person owes primary loyalty to the polis or to the gods. Which is right?

Neither Creon nor Antigone is entirely right nor entirely wrong. Apparently, Sophocles would have us believe the Chorus is correct when they state: "When [a person] honors the laws of the land and the gods' sworn right/high indeed is his city..." (369-370). If the polis is in harmony with the gods as it should be, there is no conflict. But when that harmony is destroyed and polis and gods are set at odds, there is no correct course of behavior.

An Athenian audience probably would have agreed with Creon's conclusion that social order is based on respect for the law:

> There is no greater wrong than disobedience.
> This ruins cities, this tears down our homes,
> this breaks the battle-front in panic rout.

If men live decently it is because
discipline saves their very lives for them.
                                                (672-676)

Creon, a man who had just witnessed a long and bloody civil war
where brother fought against brother, cannot be faulted for trying to restore respect for the state. He is wrong, of course, in violating the laws of
the gods by commanding that Polyneices remain unburied, and his decree forces Antigone into an impossible situation: she is wrong if she
disobeys the state and even more wrong if she disobeys the gods. A
Greek audience would have approved the decision she makes, but not her
motives. As the Chorus notes, Antigone's need to defy Creon seems as
powerful as her desire to honor the gods: "You showed respect for the
dead./So we for you: but power/is not to be thwarted so./Your self-sufficiency has brought you down" (872-875).

An Athenian audience would have understood that there is no correct
answer to the question of whether a person owes primary loyalty to the
gods or to the polis. Something is seriously amiss when a person is
forced to make such a choice. Nevertheless, from the Athenian point of
view and within the context of the play, once Antigone is forced to
choose, she makes the right decision. Even Creon eventually admits that
she is right: "I've come to fear it's best to hold the laws/of old tradition
to the end of life" (1113-1114). He buries Polyneices, but discovers that the
penalty he must pay for sacrilege will be far greater than he realized.
The message for the Athenian audience was clear: "The gods must have
their due" (1349), and a polis that forgets that lesson will destroy itself.

7. How is the plot of *Antigone* structured?

Students who consider Antigone the protagonist of this play will answer this question differently from those who think Creon the protagonist. (For a discussion of both possibilities see the handbook entry
"Protagonist.") Everyone is likely to agree that the plot is divided into
the prologue, five parts, and the catastrophe, with choral songs
separating the sections.

Prologue (1-98), Chorus (99-153)
      Antigone announces her intention to defy Creon (43)

Part 1 (154-333), Chorus (334-372)
      Creon proclaims his edict, is informed that someone has buried
      Polyneices (245-247), and orders the guard to find the person who
      disobeyed him (326-328).

Part 2 (373-584), Chorus (585-625)
>   Antigone is arrested, admits her guilt, and is sentenced to death.
>   Ismene pleads for Antigone's life to no avail (568).

Part 3 (626-784), Chorus (785-801)
>   Haemon attempts to persuade his father to spare Antigone. When
>   he is unsuccessful, he threatens to kill himself (761-763).

Part 4 (802-945), Chorus (946-985)
>   Antigone appears on stage and Creon sends her to be entombed.

Part 5 (986-1117), Chorus (1118-1152)
>   Teiresias prophesies disaster, but Creon is unmoved. At last the
>   Chorus persuades Creon to bury Polyneices and release Antigone.

Catastrophe (1153-1345), Chorus (1346-1352)
>   The deaths of Antigone, Haemon, and Eurydice are announced,
>   and Creon assumes responsibility for their deaths.

If your students see Antigone as the protagonist of the play, they may
argue that the crisis (the incident after which her situation is certain to
improve or worsen) took place before the play began when she decided to
bury Polyneices. If that's the case, then every incident that occurs after
her decision is a part of the falling action that merely delays her
inevitable death. Others will contend that the turning point occurs in
Part 4 when Antigone is brought before Creon. At that moment she
could probably save her life by begging forgiveness. Instead she
infuriates Creon and guarantees her punishment by insisting that "the
wise will know [her] choice was right" (905). Those who nominate
Creon the protagonist will probably agree that the crisis occurs in Part 4,
but they are likely to focus on Creon's order to entomb Antigone, not
Antigone's defiant speech. After Creon sentences Antigone to a living
death, his downfall is as certain as hers.

                                                                                  –M.R.D.

The House of Oedipus

Many years before the events that take place in this play, King Laius,
the ruler of Thebes, and Jocasta, his queen, gave birth to a son. Because
the Oracle at Delphi prophesied that their son would someday kill his
father and marry his mother, Laius ordered one of his soldiers to take
the baby into the mountains, bind his feet, and leave him where he
would be eaten by wild animals. Laius never learned that the baby,

Oedipus, was rescued, taken to Corinth, and adopted by King Polybus
and Queen Merope. Oedipus grew up believing Polybus and Merope were
his natural parents. When the Oracle at Delphi told Oedipus that he
would kill his father and marry his mother, Oedipus attempted to escape
his fate by fleeing from Corinth to Thebes. On his journey Oedipus met
an imperious old man, Laius, who tried to force him off the road.
Oedipus became angry and killed him, not suspecting that he had just
fulfilled half the prophecy by murdering his father.

At that time the city of Thebes was being terrorized by the Sphinx, a
winged monster with the body of a lion but the head and breasts of a
woman. The Sphinx asked all travelers the same riddle, and when they
failed to give the correct answer, she devoured them. Oedipus sought out
the Sphinx who posed her riddle: "What goes on four legs in the morning, on two legs at noon, and on three legs in the evening?" Oedipus
replied, "Man. In childhood he crawls on hands and feet; in manhood
he walks erect; in old age he helps himself with a staff." The Sphinx reacted to his correct answer by killing herself. Thus Thebes was saved,
and the grateful Thebans made Oedipus their king. Not realizing that
the widowed Queen Jocasta was his mother, Oedipus married her and
unknowingly fulfilled the second half of the prophesy. Oedipus and
Jocasta had four children (Eteocles, Polyneices, Antigone, and Ismene),
and Oedipus ruled wisely for many years.

After Oedipus' children had grown up, a terrible plague visited
Thebes, and Apollo declared that the plague could be halted only by
finding and punishing Laius' murderer. Oedipus vowed to find the
murderer, and eventually discovered that he had killed his father and
married his mother. After that revelation, Jocasta killed herself.
Oedipus then stabbed out his eyes and spent his remaining years
wandering around the countryside, led by his daughter Antigone.
Jocasta's brother, Creon, became the regent of Thebes.

Just before the events of *Antigone* Oedipus' younger son, Eteocles, succeeded in becoming the king of Thebes and expelled his brother
Polyneices. Polyneices then led an Argive army against Thebes. After
many battles the two armies were deadlocked and agreed to decide the
matter with a championship combat between the two brothers. Each
killed the other, the battle was renewed, and Thebes was victorious.
Creon, who was again the ruler, declared that Polyneices, the traitor,
must remain unburied. Such vengeance horrified the Thebans. Because
they believed the souls of the unburied could never enter the kingdom of
death but were doomed to wander forever without rest, Greeks
considered it their sacred duty to bury even their enemies.

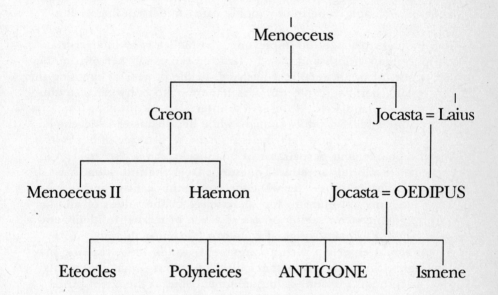

Euripides
Medea

It might be important to remind your students at the outset of a discussion of *Medea* that the aesthetic is somewhat different from that of more modern dramas. As the Introduction to the Drama section of *The Riverside Anthology* suggests, it is impossible to overlook the social nature of Greek drama and come to any sophisticated understanding of this play.

It is difficult to shake the impression that Medea is by modern standards more than a flesh and blood character expressing her own outrage at her treatment by an unfaithful husband. In the process of exposing the injustice done her, she explores issues important to everyone with children, husbands, and wives, to everyone interested in justifying the ways of men to the gods. So, oddly enough, while her character is developed to the extent that we know that she is a sorceress, betrayer of her own father and people, and perpetrator of infanticide, she is also an Everywoman exploring an ethical question: Does the individual have the right to seek justice no matter what the cost? Ethnocentric and literal-minded moderns unwilling to lose themselves in the values of another culture might insist on seeing *Medea* as a tale of marital infidelity and a custody battle; Euripides' original audience (assuming that any of its members would entertain such an argument) would insist that the play raises larger ethical and even theological questions—what judgments can we make upon someone acting inhumanly but as the agent of the gods in revenging a broken sacred oath?

Tradition has it that it is this perspective that may have infuriated the audience during the original production. Apparently the polis was moved almost to violence at the notion that Medea, despite her atrocities, had gained the approval of the gods signified by her triumph and *deus ex machina* escape at the end of the play. What behavior, after all, is receiving tacit approval at the end of this play? What attitude toward the gods' intervention in human affairs is implicit in *Medea*? Euripides' freethinking made him more popular in subsequent centuries than in his own.

Your students will then undoubtedly detect a change in attitude if they move to this play from Sophocles' *Antigone*. In insisting that her brother receive proper burial, Antigone is observing divine law in upholding the sanctity of blood-ties; her stance, then, in comparison to that of the coldly reasonable Creon, is pious, instinctual, and traditionally conservative. She is also, Sophocles would have us believe, regardless of her prideful motivations and other excesses, ultimately in the right. We cannot be sure of Medea's piety, and she seems to a larger extent than

Antigone seeking her own private ends in avenging herself on Jason. Euripides in *Medea* is more willing than Sophocles in *Antigone* to celebrate the exercise of will in the individual, and his emphasis on humanism is a marked departure from, for example, Homer, whose heroes found themselves compelled rather than impelled by the gods. Hera does not help Medea wield the sword that kills her children; Medea decides upon the course that *she* is choosing: "I know indeed what evil I intend to do" (l. 1078). Evil, as far as Medea is concerned, is not a matter of ignorance of what is right.

You may wish to give your students a more compressed version of the antecedent action than Euripides does in lines 1-33. The absolutely necessary details are that Jason, son of the deposed King Aeson of Iolcus, is set the task (in order to regain his kingdom) of bringing the sacred Golden Fleece back to his father's half brother, the usurper Pelias. Jason is aided in this seemingly impossible task by the Argonauts, a collection of heroes, and by Medea, the daughter of the keeper of the Fleece, King Aeëtes of faraway Colchis. Medea assists Jason with her magic in all the trials pressed upon him by her father; after the Fleece is seized, Medea kills her brother to create a diversion and flees with the Argonauts to Iolcus, where she uses her enchantments to trick King Pelias' daughters into killing him. The repercussions of his death force Jason and Medea to flee to Corinth, where the action of the play takes place.

[Your students may also find it of interest that *Medea* took the third prize in the Athenian dramatic competition of 431 B.C.; *Antigone* took first prize circa 442 B.C.]

QUESTIONS

1. How does the Nurse's speech (the prologue) prepare us to understand Medea's temperament and psychological state? What other use does Euripides put that speech to?

From line 20 on in the first speech of the play, the Nurse catalogues Medea's tribulations and describes her responses to Jason's cruelties. Medea "cries aloud on the/Vows they made to each other, the right hands clasped/In eternal promise. She calls upon the gods to witness/What sort of return Jason has made to her love" (ll. 20-23). Students of Greek drama will be quick to remind the rest of the class that oath-breakers usually fare poorly; it is a sin against both the *polis* and the god invoked. In lines 24-29 we learn that "she lies without food and gives herself up to suffering"—an inaction that ceases when she is forced to action by Creon. We are also prepared for the Chorus's inability to sway a resolute Medea when it is revealed to us that "No more than either a rock of surging sea water/She listens when she is given friendly advice." The nurse sympathizes with Medea's regret and guilt at betraying her country and father, and foreshadows the murders of the two children in describing Medea's desperation:

> She has turned from the children and does not like to see them.
> I am afraid that she may think of some dreadful thing,
> For her heart is violent. She will never put up with
> The treatment she is getting. I know and fear her
> Lest she may sharpen a sword and thrust to the heart,
> Stealing into the palace where the bed is made,
> Or even kill the king and the new-wedded groom,
> And thus bring a greater misfortune on herself.
> She's a strange woman. I know it won't be easy
> To make an enemy of her and come off best.

But the nurse, when guessing at what evil Medea might do, never considers the slaughter of the two children. The audience, familiar with the myth, would probably nod grimly and knowledgeably when, right after this speech, the children come on stage. The nurse does shortly afterward order the tutor to keep the children out of Medea's sight and mind.

2. How does the Chorus function in this play?

Early in the play and before the appearance of Medea, the Chorus, in conjunction with the Nurse and tutor, provides us with our first views of Medea's character. Like the Nurse, the Chorus perceives that Medea may be moved to desperate acts: "This passion of hers moves to something great" (l. 183). The Chorus attempts to console Medea and asserts that she is "in the right" when she complains.

Throughout the play the Chorus examines the circumstances in which Medea finds herself and provides pertinent and sententious conventional wisdom. When Medea seems overcome by passion, the Chorus utters this setpiece in praise of moderation:

> When love is in excess
> It brings a man no honor
> Nor any worthiness.
> But if in moderation Cypris comes,
> There is no other power at all so gracious.
> O goddess, never on me let loose the unerring
> Shaft of your bow in the poison of desire

Let my heart be wise.
It is the gods' best gift.
On me let mighty Cypris
Inflict no wordy wars or restless anger
To urge my passion to a different love.
But with discernment may she guide women's weddings,
Honoring most what is peaceful in the bed.

(ll. 627-641)

In response to Medea's earlier lament that she has been cut off from her homeland, an alien in an apparently xenophobic land, the Chorus sings:

O country and home,
Never, never may I be without you,
Living the hopeless life,
Hard to pass through and painful,
Most pitiable of all.
Let death first lay me low and death
Free me from this daylight.
There is no sorrow above
The loss of a native land.

(ll. 643-651)

After Medea wrings a promise for sanctuary out of Aegeus, she shares with the Chorus her intention of murdering her children; the Chorus (like us) is torn between commiserating with Medea and horror at what she announces:

Since you have shared the knowledge of your plan with us,
I both wish to help you and support the normal
Ways of mankind, and tell you not to do this thing.

That "normal ways of mankind" is extremely important here. The Chorus as representative of the polis, "supports the normal ways," that is, attempts to make Medea feel the restraints necessary to maintenance of the status quo.

But the Chorus refuses to take as active a part in the development of the plot as the Chorus in *Antigone*, which convinces Creon to release Antigone and bury her brother; instead, the Chorus wrings its hands as the action moves toward its grisly conclusion.

| Chorus: | Do you hear the cry, do you hear the children's cry? |
| | O you hard heart, you woman fated for evil! |

| One of the children (from within): | What can I do and how escape my mother's hands? |

| Another child (from within): | O my dear brother, I cannot tell. We are lost. |

| Chorus: | Shall I enter the house? Oh, surely I should Defend the children from murder. |

| A child (from within): | O help us, in God's name, for now we need your help. |
| | Now, now we are close to it. We are trapped by the sword. (ll. 1271-1278) |

3. Where does the action of the play reach a climax?

It may be difficult to mark the point of highest intensity in a play like *Medea*. In fact, you may discover that your students may gleefully run the risk—in insisting on a "right" answer to this question—of damaging the play by forcing it into a form that the author may not have employed in composition. A likely candidate, however, might be lines 178-180, when Medea cements her resolve to kill her children and the princess. In the long passage prior to this moment, Medea wavers when she sees the bright eyes of her children: "My spirit has gone from me/Friends, when I saw that bright look in the children's eyes./I cannot bear to do it" (ll. 143-145). She screws her courage to the sticking-place, however, and says

I know indeed what evil I intend to do,
But stronger than all my afterthoughts is my fury,
Fury that brings upon mortals the greatest evils.

From this point on, we know what Medea will do; all the complications begin to be resolved at this moment.

Some will find this argument unconvincing. There are two antagonists in this play, the state (represented by the house of Creon) and Jason, and Medea has private and public grievance to settle with both.

The state insists on expelling Medea because she stands in the way of the alliance of Jason and Creon; the king's distaste for Medea, however, is based as much on xenophobia as on the political inconvenience she causes. Jason has broken a marriage vow made before Themis and Zeus, and piety demands that he be punished; his conflict with Medea springs from the most personal of injuries, marital infidelity. If there are two antagonists and thus two conflicts and sets of complications, then the aforementioned scene when Medea hesitates before launching her revenge *and* the passage where Jason first refuses and then accepts the gifts that bring down Creon could be seen as equally significant. In fact, one could argue from this perspective that in the gift-giving scene (which precedes her scene with the children) Medea literally enters on a course of murders and revenge from which she cannot withdraw.

Still another argument could be made that the crisis or climax of the play occurs during those terrible moments when the Chorus stands outside the house of Jason and Medea and vacillates in deciding whether or not to save the children, who are calling out piteously. The force of this argument depends, of course, on the working definition of crisis that you and your class decide upon; if the crisis is the moment when the complications begin to be resolved, then your class might choose lines 1078-1080 (Medea wavers) or even lines 956-975 (Jason is gulled). If, however, you define crisis as that moment when the audience's pity and terror are at the highest pitch, then the answers to this question will surely include the murder of the children. Freytag, by the way, conflates these definitions in *Technique of the Drama.*

4. Are we to believe that Medea triumphs because her cause is just?

A "no" so qualified that it might be a "yes"—or vice-versa. The *deus ex machina* allowed the playwright to arbitrarily resolve conflicts that were perhaps unresolvable. When this device is employed, the resolution is not achieved through the internal logic of the drama, but rather through the intervention of the gods—ordinarily one could assume that the character preserved by the *deus ex machina* was receiving a rather ostentatious (in its archaic sense) sign of divine approval. One can easily understand how the audience during the Dionysian festival might have reacted with alarm at Euripides' handling of the end of *Medea*, when the murderess and regicide escapes with the aid of the gods.

On the other hand, it is so easy to detest Jason that one might— might—be moved to say that he deserves his fate. A smugger hypocrite is hard to imagine; he abandons his wife for the most mercenary reasons and in the most hard-hearted fashion. Medea has, after all, given or be-

trayed everything she holds dear for Jason, killing her brother, betraying her father, and leaving her homeland—a generosity her husband
denies:

> My view is that Cypris was alone responsible
> Of men and gods for the preserving of my life.
> You [Medea] are clever enough—but really I need not enter
> Into the story of how it was love's inescapable
> Power that compelled you to keep my person safe.
> On this I will not go into too much detail.
> In so far as you helped me, you did well enough.
> But on this question of saving me, I can prove
> You have certainly got from me more than you gave.
> Firstly, instead of living among barbarians,
> You inhabit a Greek land and understand our ways,
> How to live by law instead of the sweet will of force.
>
> (ll. 527-538)

Here Euripides gives the screw an extra turn by allowing Jason to tell
part of the truth. His version of the role Medea had in his success in
Colchis is hardly flattering to either of them. His characterization of
Medea as a barbarian who lives by the sweet will of force may be borne
out by the action.

Medea poses the same problem as *Hedda Gabler* or *Measure for Measure*:
How are we to evaluate character when there is no ethical yardstick, that
is, when no major character is genuinely admirable and provides us
with a measure against which we can compare the other characters?
One would think that Creon and Jason are surely disqualified to fit the
role; if we assume that Medea receives approbation from the gods because
she is the most admirable of the major characters, then Euripides has
presented us with a dark view of human nature indeed. We are, finally,
in the same position as audiences of *Tamberlaine* and some of the darker
seventeenth-century comedies and tragedies because, in the absence of a
genuinely admirable hero, we are forced to attach our sympathies to the
most successful or resolute villain, the cleverest rascal—who do we really
admire in *Volpone* or *Othello*, after all? Medea, despite the disabilities her
sex and nationality force upon her, defeats her opponents and dupes her
allies with wit and magic. Her manipulation of Aegeus by assisting him
in the interpretation of the Delphic oracle, the ploy of appealing to
Creon's love of his children in order to win an extra day in Corinth,
and her defeat of the man canny enough to bring the *Argo* home force
us, perhaps against our will, to admire her courage and knowledge of
human nature.

5. Where does Euripides use stichomythia? Why is it appropriate here?

Euripides employs stichomythia as a kind of verbal swordfight between characters, an audible battle of wits; Medea has a part in every duel in this play. In a culture where language and debate were so important, her prowess would have been noted and applauded, if her goals were not. Her first exchange is with Creon (ll. 324-329); he is convinced, against his better judgment, to allow her one more day in Corinth. She next takes on Aegeus (ll. 667-707), who in lamenting his own desire for children reveals himself to be vulnerable to Medea's promise to end his childlessness by drugs. In her final encounter with Jason (ll. 1361-1404), she gives better than she gets, inflicting punishment with a venomous economy and a shrewd knowledge of what will give him most pain:

Jason: Oh, I hate you, murderess of children.

Medea: Go to your palace. Bury your bride.

Jason: I go, with two children to mourn for.

Medea: Not yet do you feel it. Wait for the future.

Jason: Oh, children I loved!

Medea: I loved them, you did not.

Jason: You loved them, and killed them.

Medea: To make you feel pain.

As the nurse, who knows Medea best, tells us early in the play, "it won't be easy/To make an enemy of her and come off best" (ll. 44-45).

–W.R.S.

William Shakespeare
Twelfth Night

Perhaps no play of Shakespeare's gains so much by being heard and seen. A predictable suggestion: If it can be managed, show your class a production, almost any production.

The earliest performance of *Twelfth Night* that we are certain of took place in a London law school, the Middle Temple, in 1602, but its first and most famous performance is supposed to have taken place on Twelfth Night (the twelfth night of Christmas, for students who know at least the song) before Queen Elizabeth in 1600. This is conjecture, but reasonable conjecture, since the holiday is never mentioned in the text. It stands to reason that the title was derived from the great feast day on which the play was first given.

At least one scholar has claimed that in Malvolio's "I'll be revenged on the whole pack of you!" (5.1:378) Shakespeare first displays a genuinely dark side of human nature in his comedies and announces his intention to examine the tragic potential of comedy; from this point on, Shakespeare's comedy, specifically *Troilus and Cressida, All's Well That Ends Well,* and *Measure for Measure,* takes on a darker hue, and it is popular in some quarters to maintain that Shakespeare tired of frothy stuff and moved to a genre more suited to his mood. All this may or may not be true, and the real truth may be forever lost to us, but it is also likely that Malvolio, aware finally that he has been the butt of an elaborate joke, is giving vent to feelings we all might have in his place, and leaves in a huff.

One of the most profitable ways of examining the play is to look at the parties in opposition in the subplot. On the one side we have Malvolio, whose name means "bad wishes," and on the other side we have the riotous alliance of Sir Andrew Aguecheek, Maria, Feste, Fabian, and Sir Toby Belch, whose name is undoubtedly onomatopoeic. In Malvolio we find a man who despises revelry and dissolution; he hopes, since he doesn't like the taste, that there will be no more cakes and ale. He is the ultimate killjoy, the person who points out our foibles when we are happiest: we all know him or have been him. If he were content to remain a party of one, he might be tolerable; since he insists on proselytizing, he is intolerable. On the other hand, Sir Toby is the sort of rascal, like Falstaff, who somehow remains likable while demonstrating that he is a drunkard, a coward, and a sponger. If there were no Malvolio to represent his opposite principle, Sir Toby would be a much less sympathetic character.

One of the givens of the play is that Illyria is given over to the spirit of misrule symbolized by Sir Toby. In such a place characters burst into song with little provocation, food and drink are plentiful, and disguises one would think transparent are conveniently impenetrable. It is not surprising that this is the case, because the nobles of Illyria are ruled by excess as surely as are Sir Toby and his gang. Orsino begins the play with a speech demonstrating that he is a tiresomely Petrarchan lover too much in love with love, and his opposite number, Olivia, having spent the seven years preceding the action of the play in weepy mourning for her lost brother, develops an embarrassing passion for Viola in her disguise as Cesario. Like Malvolio after he discovers the love letter, both Orsino and Olivia are dominated by fancies that reduce them to caricatures.

QUESTIONS

1. What do the first fifteen lines tell us about Orsino's character?

Orsino is an epicurean of love, in love with love itself. Notice that he wants a "surfeit" of love, an "excess" of it—in short, he wishes to sate his appetite through excess. When he claims at the end of his first speech that "fancy . . . alone is high fantastical," he reveals very clearly his attitude toward the emotion that holds him. He is in love with the effect that love has upon him—that lyrical and imaginative frame of mind that he can achieve when he is under the influence of love. "Fancy," for the Elizabethans as well as for us, is not the same thing as love; it is, instead, a "passing" thing, impermanent and often whimsical. Shakespeare is presenting in Orsino a stock figure in Renaissance drama and poetry, the melancholic lover. Implicit in this depiction is the notion that love is less what moderns might consider an emotion and more what we might consider a disease. You might wish to read in class five of Thomas Wyatt's worst; almost invariably these will be the ones filled with Petrarch's images of the lover as wounded, diseased, and so on. It might be important to note that in his very first speech the name of Orsino's beloved is never spoken.

2. What does Shakespeare accomplish in juxtaposing Scenes 1 and 2?

As the answer to the preceding question suggests, Shakespeare expends a good deal of effort in establishing character in the first scene—and the second. Orsino has surrendered to fancy and suffers from an excess of what he thinks is emotion; we learn from Valentine in Scene 1 and from the Captain in Scene 2 that the woman he "loves," Olivia, has cloistered herself for seven years, avoiding the "sight/And company of men." At first glance, Olivia seems to be just the opposite of the Duke: he demands love and she rejects the possibility. But they are more alike than different, because she, too, has been swallowed up by an emotion, grief, and Valentine's metaphor—Olivia preserving the love of her dead brother with the salt of her tears—is grotesque enough for us to see clearly that Shakespeare is dropping a ponderous hint about what we are to make of Olivia's mourning.

But note Viola's response to the news that *her* brother may or not be dead; she considers both possibilities, expresses her sorrow, and moves on, hatching a scheme to ingratiate herself with the Duke. Here are no tears, no speculations about the nature of love and death—here is a woman of self-restraint and quick thought and action who adapts to her homeless state in a flash. In the first two scenes we are presented with comparisons that just cannot be missed. Shakespeare seems to be making, early in the play, a judgment that he is to underscore throughout about the dangers of a surfeit of emotions.

3. What is Malvolio's "comic flaw"?

You may not be happy with this potentially confusing term, but let me justify it. In virtually every comedy following the festive "Jack shall have Jill" pattern, at least one character has a trait or a world-view that is incompatible with the world of the "society" that exists at the end of the play. That flaw must be mended, or the character(s) must be ejected from the society. Orsino and Olivia are "corrected" at the end of the play through the machinations of the plot and the consequent circumstances that change them. They can, then, pair off with Viola and Sebastian after the potentially tragic conflicts have been resolved. Perhaps "vice" would be a better or at least more conventional term than "comic flaw," but the connotations there are even more dangerous.

Anyway, Malvolio, like Orsino and Olivia, is a dreamer capable of self-delusion. Like the Duke, Malvolio aspires to the love of Olivia, a place that by disposition and status he can never realistically hope to achieve. Like the Duke and Olivia, Malvolio would have been almost instantaneously recognized as a "humorous" character, that is, a character overcome by what we might call a chemical imbalance to the extent that he becomes dominated by a delusion. He does not, then, "know himself" any better than Orsino and Olivia, and the difference between what he is and what he thinks he is makes him ludicrous and one of Shakespeare's great comic creations. He is, as Olivia herself ironically points out, "sick of self-love."

But Malvolio has another flaw, and consequently is the most complex character in a play otherwise populated by two-dimensional figures. He is, as Maria points out, "a kind of Puritan," a killjoy who insists on forcing his will on others. He is the antithesis of the spirit of misrule and carnival that dominates Illyria and is made ample flesh in Sir Toby; we can imagine what Olivia's household might have become had Malvolio's wish come true.

4. How does Maria move the plot?

You might wish to demonstrate just how the action of the subplot is nudged along by a relatively minor character, Maria, who seems to be that subplot's stage manager or director, as well as Olivia's lady-in-waiting. She is revealed early in the play as quick-witted and a keen judge of character—she knows what Toby and Aguecheek are and how to manipulate them. It is she who gives us our first taste of what we are to expect from Malvolio, and we discover in her accurate description of the steward more than a trace of bile:

> The dev'l a Puritan that he is, or anything constantly but a time-pleaser; an affection'd ass, that cons state without book and utters it by great swarths; the best persuaded of himself; so cramm'd, as he thinks, with excellencies that it is his grounds of faith that all that look on him love him; and on that vice in him will my revenge find notable cause to work.
>
> (2.3: 128-133)

Maria is the author of the stratagems that result in the humiliation of Malvolio; she forges the "love-letter" from Olivia, and she disguises the clown as Sir Topas, exorciser of the devil tormenting the "mad" Malvolio.

Some critics have argued that Maria is "Mary" and that through her actions Malvolio, "goodman devil" to the clown, is first imprisoned and then cast out. Your class may wish to discuss the validity of this reading. Some relevant questions: Does such a reading seem in keeping with the mood of the play? With any of the major themes?

5. Do we pity Malvolio at the denouement?

I suspect that your class will be evenly divided. Those who say yes will realize that the pairing off at the end of the play includes almost all of the marriageable characters—even Maria and Sir Toby. Only Malvolio is left out in the cold. He is not permitted reconciliation with the "society" that comes together at the end of the play; he has no part in the unions and reunions that bring the play to its happy ending.

In addition, he has made mistakes that we all might. Few of us have not imagined that we are loved by someone who would find that idea laughable or pitiable. Given the evidence provided him, might not Malvolio be forgiven for jumping to his conclusions? He has been held captive in a dark room and, we are given to believe, forced to assert his own sanity in an age not renowned for enlightened treatment of the mentally ill (residents of Bedlam, London's asylum for the mad, were released regardless of their condition after one year's "treatment").

Students on the other side of the fence will argue with equal force that Malvolio's predicament and humiliation is largely his own doing. He does not love Olivia—he only aspires to high position. In addition, he is the dark spirit of this play, a man whose mean-spiritedness threatens to destroy all mirth and music and cakes and ale.

6. What does Shakespeare accomplish through the use of disguise?

As the introduction to the drama section points out, Elizabethans seemed perfectly willing to swallow dramatic conventions that might outrage modern audiences. A boy (the actor) plays a woman (Viola) who is impersonating a man (Cesario). And this disguise is so well managed that the brother (Sebastian) of the woman cannot penetrate that disguise and so must go through an elaborate identification involving their father's mole and the sister's birthdate. If your students' belief cannot remain suspended here, you might remind them that they are refusing to play the game. By this I mean that this drama (and a great many comedies of the Renaissance and Restoration) demands, through its own internal logic, that we surrender our skepticism and check our attention to the barriers between fiction and reality at the door. The disguise, after all, is no less believable than our acceptance of Orsino's rapid conversion or Olivia's marriage to Sebastian, and most students seemed to accept these improbable actions without a hitch.

Viola's disguise engages our sympathies (she has been forced by circumstance to impersonate a eunuch) and, more importantly, allows for a revelation of character (hers and others') that could be accomplished otherwise only through soliloquies. She sees the other characters in ways that she could not if she were, well, Viola. She is privy to Orsino's longings in a way she could not be if she had appeared at his court in her "woman's weeds." She becomes his confidante—and more—and certainly the object of desire for Olivia, whose icy determination to abjure the company and sight of men melts and turns to rather bald and even forward hints of her love for Cesario. Through Viola's disguise, oddly enough, we see Orsino and Olivia as they really are.

Disguise also helps establish Viola as the wisest and most admirable of the characters in the play. What I'll call the "status" of characters in comedies is determined by their ability to see themselves and other characters for what they are and by their understanding of the circumstances composing the action of the play. The Duke in *Measure for Measure*, whatever his faults, occupies a superior position in that play not because he is the Duke, but because he can see all the characters for what they are and knows all or nearly all that is going on. He can see and know all this because his disguise affords him near omniscience. Viola's disguise offers her a similar view of the action of the play, though she lacks the Duke's power to act as *deus ex machina*. She, less than any other character (excluding Feste, who is in a disguise of his own: "I wear not motley in my brain"), is susceptible to self-delusion in a play that rather straightforwardly attacks self-delusion.

7. Do the songs function other than as musical interludes?

Yes. In addition to assisting in giving us the flavor of life in Illyria, the songs underscore Shakespeare's major thematic concerns. In the second act, the clown sings a song apparently unrelated to the action:

> Come away, come away, death,
> And in sad cypress let me be laid.
> Fly away, fly away, breath;
> I am slain by a fair cruel maid.
> My shroud of white, stuck all with yew,
> O prepare it!
> My part of death, no one so true
> Did share it.
>
> Not a flower, not a flower sweet,
> On my black coffin let there be strown;
> Not a friend, not a friend greet
> My poor corpse, where my bones shall be thrown.
>
> A thousand thousand sighs to save,
> Lay me, O, where
> Sad true lover never find my grave,
> To weep there.

If you read this song to your class and then ask to whom it is sung by the Clown, almost all, without remembering specifically, will say, "To the Duke!" And when you point out that the Duke is moved by this tired and lugubrious nonsense (though some critics *have* found it moving) to reward Feste generously, all will see just how forcefully Shakespeare drives home the view of Orsino as a sop of sentiment, particularly sentiment that reveals him as the sad lover tormented and despised by la belle dame sans merci. Feste knows his audience and what that audience wants, and then delivers the goods, thus revealing Orsino's character more obliquely and yet more convincingly.

Almost all the songs in the play, excluding the song taunting Malvolio in his cell, deal with the transience of human affairs, in particular, the love between men and women. You may wish to ask your students why the Clown so often strikes this plaintive note in a play usually considered bright.

8. Does the end of this play seem forced, that is, are we prepared for reconciliations and alliances announced at the end of the play?

Yes, the end of the play is forced, and that is the great paradox of Shakespeare's middle and late comedy. Character, in order to fit the "journeys-end-in-lovers-meeting" structure, is often wrenched past the point of believability in order to suit the demands of that structure. We *are* prepared for the pairings up at the end of the play (even the unlikely marriage of Maria and Toby) because we know as certainly how this play will end as we know how *Death of a Salesman* will end. We may not know the particulars of the ending, but the pattern is so ancient and touches something in us so palpably that we feel the ah! of recognition long before the play is over.

–W.R.S.

William Shakespeare
Hamlet

There are as many approaches to *Hamlet* as there are lines in the play, and more ink has been spilt over it than any other imaginative work in Western literature. T. S. Eliot considered it "certainly an artistic failure"; Samuel Taylor Coleridge said of it that "anything finer than this conception, and working out of a great character, is merely impossible." *Hamlet* is written about and anthologized so often, of course, because Hamlet himself is so enigmatic a character, because the play presents and explores what we can only call the human condition from so many perspectives, and because the play has acquired the patina of nearly four centuries of learned debate and almost continuous production. So, for students in introductory literature courses, *Hamlet* is often the object of special reverence—and fear. Here is literature, many of them think, at its most daunting. The body of criticism is immense and diverse, the language (no matter how well glossed the text) is often impenetrable, and the themes addressed are so weighty that class discussion is often crushed beneath them. *Hamlet*, through no fault of its own, and for reasons I've enumerated above, is prone to falling into the hands of practitioners of literary gnosticism as is no other play, and students are rather easily given the impression that their own responses to the work are of little value. I like to reassure my students that, after all, every educated person should know and be equipped to talk about the play, and that they are welcome participants in a discussion already entered into by millions since 1600 or so.

One bit of background that might be helpful to your students is the note that *Hamlet* belongs to that often bad old genre, the revenge tragedy. The Elizabethans had taken Seneca and "modernized" him; instead of offstage violence and sententious speeches, there were bitten-off and spat-out tongues, stabbings, and language that was at times colloquial to the point of profanity. The Senecan hero given to Stoic restraint was replaced by an often bloodthirsty Elizabethan revenger who shouted and railed and rattled the bars of his society, and consequently sixteenth- and seventeenth-century revenge tragedy was too often merely sensational. *Hamlet* rises above all this, and a quick look at its progenitors reveals just how far. The story-line itself is immensely old, probably as old as any of the Northern sagas. Our first glimpse of it in writing is in Saxo Grammaticus' twelfth-century *Historia Danica*; in this earliest written version of the narrative, the prototype for the character of Polonius is killed, cut up, cooked, and thrown into a latrine to be eaten by pigs.

One can only imagine what such a tale might have become in the hands of an Elizabethan dramatist eager for popular success in the relatively new tradition of the grim and gory revenge tragedy. And of course there is some evidence that Thomas Kyd, author of *The Spanish Tragedy*, had written a *Hamlet* before 1589. It is almost certain that Kyd's tendency toward the melodramatic and lurid must have been fully indulged in his (apparently popular) version of *Hamlet*.

Shakespeare, then, must have had a rough-hewn and barbaric story to deal with. While one could hardly say that *Hamlet* is a return to the Stoic restraint of Seneca's creations, still the play, for all its excesses, never becomes either merely sensational or melodramatic. Hamlet himself never becomes the Machiavellian revenger that populates so many revenge tragedies; it would be difficult to imagine the protagonist of *The Spanish Tragedy*, Hieronimo, delivering Hamlet's best-known soliloquy.

That bit of background may not spark the sort of discussion one hopes for, however, when teaching *Hamlet*. I've discovered that one way to encourage discussion, particularly if you've already treated poetry at some length in your class, is to treat the play as if it were in fact a narrative poem (which, in a sense, it is). By this I mean that students will profit by looking closely at the text for patterns of imagery (a skill they may already have acquired, or one that will perhaps serve them well later in the course) that reveal, for instance, major themes. The often-quoted "Something is rotten in the state of Denmark" becomes something

more than a cliché when one puts it in the context of the images of
corruption and disease that fill the play. Such a search will take them to
the heart of the play, beginning with the Ghost's description of his
murder:

> Upon my secure hour thy uncle stole
> With juice of cursed hebona in a vial,
> , And in the porches of my ears did pour
> The leperous distillment, whose effect
> Holds such an enmity with blood of man
> That swift as quicksilver it courses through
> The natural gates and alleys of the body,
> And with a sudden vigor it doth posset
> And curd, like eager droppings into milk
> The thin and wholesome blood. So did it mine,
> And a most instant tetter barked about
> Most lazarlike with vile and loathesome crust
> All my smooth body.
>
> (1.5:61-73)

They will, of course, find *Hamlet* filled with images of disease and
death, a catalogue of the corruption afflicting Denmark and the Danes.
Naturally, since Hamlet seems to employ these sorts of images in his
speech more than any other character, your students will no doubt learn
a great deal about his character and quality of mind in particular and
the play in general.

QUESTIONS

1. How does the opening scene prepare us for the rest of the play?

As usual, Shakespeare makes good use of his opening scene. We
learn, among other things, that:

◆ the men on watch are ill at ease. Francisco, for no apparent reason, is
"sick at heart" (1.1:8), though his watch has been quiet;

◆ they have seen the Ghost, who is the mainspring of the action;

◆ that the rational Horatio thinks that the Ghost is a "fantasy" (1.1:23);

◆ that the Ghost is indeed *not* a fantasy, since it appears;

◆ that the Ghost resembles the late King, but may not be his spirit:

> Hor. What art thou that usurp'st this time of night,
> Together with that fair and warlike form
> In which the majesty of buried Denmark
> Did sometimes march? . . .
>
> (1.1:46-49)

◆ that the Ghost will not speak, and may be offended by Horatio's "By heaven I charge thee speak!" (1.1:49) [It turns out that the Ghost speaks only to Hamlet.]

◆ that Hamlet Senior had defeated the Poles and the Norwegians, and killed Fortinbras Senior, who by treaty passed his lands to the king of Denmark rather than to his own son, Fortinbras, who is stirring up rebellion (1.1:60-107).

◆ that the appearance of the Ghost might presage the fall of the state of Denmark;

◆ that Horatio is a knowledgeable man and something of a popular metaphysician, since he knows that the Ghost cannot speak after cockcrow;

◆ that Horatio is Hamlet's confidante.

[You may wish to ask Question 5, below, next.]

We learn at least this in 175 lines. While these characters are being constructed, and a great deal of exposition is adroitly handled, Shakespeare sets the mood (using the equivalent of a minor key) by communicating the uneasiness of the soldiers at the appearance of the Ghost. There are busier first scenes, but few suceed so well at creating a unified and disquieting effect.

2. How do the minor characters contribute to our understanding of the play?

I think the best way to answer this large and difficult question is to point out to your students that Shakespeare often puts minor characters in circumstances resembling those in which the protagonist can be found and then runs a sort of literary "experiment" that is designed, I'd argue, to help us make up our minds about the course that the protagonist chooses. We know, for example, that upon returning from abroad Laertes discovers that his father is dead. Like Hamlet, he suspects Claudius of murdering his father. Instead of agonizing over the question, Laertes, like the conventional revenger, goes right to work:

> How came he dead? I'll not be juggled with.
> To hell, allegiance! vows, to the blackest devil!
> Conscience and grace, to the profoundest pit!
> I dare damnation. To this point I stand,
> That both the worlds I give to negligence,
> Let come what comes, only I'll be reveng'd
> Most throughly for my father.
>
> (4.5:131-7)

Laertes is willing to relinquish both worlds, heaven and earth, in order to have his revenge. Hamlet may be willing to make the same sacrifice, but he is certainly more circumspect about it, even when through the Mousetrap play he has revealed the conscience of the King.

In Ophelia, we see Shakespeare testing out another model—how might one act upon discovering that one's father has been murdered by another loved one? Ophelia, bewildered by her treatment at Hamlet's hands and upon discovering the circumstances of her father's death, promptly goes mad—genuinely mad. Hamlet's antic disposition, on the other hand, is so transparent a stratagem that Claudius and even Polonius may see through it.

In Ophelia and Laertes, then, we see two foils for Hamlet. Instead of examining his circumstances from all perspectives, Laertes acts. Instead of feigning a madness designed to cloak her real sentiments, Ophelia falls into a frightening and pathetic insanity. Some of your students will be interested in comparing young Fortinbras' filial devotion to that of Laertes and Hamlet or in comparing Osric, Rosencrantz, and Guildenstern's subterfuges with Hamlet's.

3. Does Hamlet procrastinate in seeking revenge? If so, how does this shape our sympathies toward him? If not, why does he take so long to act?

I suspect that every reader of the play has felt some impatience with Hamlet, and a strong case could and has been made—based largely on Hamlet's self-recriminations for his own inaction—that Hamlet defers seeking his revenge until his impending death forces him to take action. Still, I think that Hamlet is his own harshest critic in this instance and that there is more evidence to support the notion that

Hamlet delays only until he is certain of Claudius' guilt. Hamlet's most famous "procrastination" occurs when he overhears Claudius alone at prayers and refuses to kill him. An Elizabethan would not have found Hamlet's rationale for sparing the King specious; to kill the King at that moment would, according to popular belief, have sent Claudius to an undeserved place in heaven. As Hamlet says, "the readiness is all," and one must be prepared, when the proper time is presented by Providence, to seize the day. He does so in the final scene.

Despite Sir Laurence Olivier's proclamation at the beginning of his film *Hamlet*, this is not "the story of a man who could not make up his mind." When, for example, Hamlet stabs Polonius, it is clear that he makes up his mind instantly to kill Claudius, who he thinks is behind the arras. Upon discovering Polonius' corpse, he says, "Thou wretched, rash, intruding fool, farewell!/I took thee for thy better" (3.4:31-32). In "thy better" Hamlet clearly refers to Claudius. It is important to note that the death of Polonius occurs in the scene immediately after the Mousetrap play; Hamlet, sure of the guilt of his uncle, has in this instance acted without deliberation.

4. Why is the exact nature of the Ghost so important to Hamlet?

The answer to this question, I think, can be found at 2.2:598-605, where Hamlet says

> The spirit I have seen
> May be a dev'l, and the dev'l hath power
> T'assume a pleasing shape, yea, and perhaps,
> Out of my weakness and my melancholy,
> As he is very potent with such spirits,
> Abuses me to damn me. I'll have grounds
> More relative than this—the play's the thing
> Wherein I'll catch the conscience of the king.

Hamlet, the scholar from Wittenberg and no slouch as a theologian, cannily takes into account the possibility that the Ghost may be a snare set for him by the Devil, and sets up the Mousetrap play as a certain means of determining the King's guilt. If, of course, the Ghost's tale is not true, then Hamlet in killing Claudius would be murdering a man at least innocent of poisoning his father, and would consequently be damned.

[I hope that this question will lead your students to examine the Mousetrap play closely. Some may object to it as a lengthy digression in a play filled with digressions. The Mousetrap is, I would argue, not merely Shakespeare having fun with theatrical conventions and theatregoers, but a sure-fire mechanism to determine the authenticity of the Ghost and the veracity of his claim.]

5. As Shakespeare often implicitly compares characters, so too does he often juxtapose scenes and invite comparisons. What are the effects of juxtaposing the first two scenes in the play?

In the first act, we discover that there is cause for uneasiness in Denmark. Even the rational and skeptical Horatio maintains that the appearance of the Ghost is

> A mote it is to trouble the mind's eye.
> In the most high and palmy state of Rome,
> A little ere the mightiest Julius fell,
> The graves stood tenantless and the sheeted dead
> Did squeak and gibber in the Roman streets.
> As stars with trains of fire, and dews of blood,
> Disasters in the sun; and the moist star
> Upon whose influence Neptune's empire stands
> Was sick almost to doomsday with eclipse.
> And even the like precure of fear'd events,
> As harbingers preceding still the fates
> And prologue to the omen coming on,
> Have heaven and earth together demonstrated
> Upon our climatures and countrymen.
>
> (112-125)

The next scene opens with a flourish of trumpets and the new King demonstrating his powers of command. He announces with equanimity that he has married his brother's widow despite his grief at the loss of his brother, then takes on and discounts the threat of young Fortinbras—"So much for him"(1.2:25). He dispatches Cornelius and Voltemand to do his kingly business, and then graciously gives Laertes leave to go to Paris after consulting with Polonius. In short, he is politic, reasonable, and powerful. His overture to Hamlet seems genuine, and his advice is sound—if Shakespeare's judgment of Olivia in *Twelfth Night* is any yardstick, it *is* possible to mourn too much for the dead.

But Shakespeare is giving us a wink and a nudge here when Hamlet says that he knows not "seems" in this scene, because, as we know from the first scene, all is not as it seems. All the pomp and circumstance inside Elsinore cannot delay the inevitable reckoning that the appearance of the Ghost and the disturbances in the heavens foretell.

6. Is there a sense that all has been made well at the end of the play?

Yes. Though some students might point out quite rightly that Denmark seems likely to be ruled by a foreigner, still, the state is out of Claudius' hands, and Hamlet, the rightful heir, has in his last moments passed the crown to Fortinbras. Fortinbras' virtues have been catalogued or demonstrated throughout the play: he is a good soldier, faithful to the memory of his father, and politically adroit. Denmark has been cleansed of the evil that Claudius represented and that Hamlet became enmeshed in; wise and loyal Horatio has been left to tell the tale.

–W.R.S.

William Shakespeare
Measure for Measure

Measure for Measure is usually cited when critics talk about the problem of problem plays. "Problem play" is such a nebulous term and usually demands so much explanation in introductory literature classes that one should use it cautiously. In the case of *Measure for Measure*, though, a bit of explanation is necessary, because the theme, plot, and characterization are, well, problematic if you attempt to place this work without reservations within the genre of comedy. The easy way out is to claim that *Measure for Measure*, since it is in all probability Shakespeare's last comedy, is a cheerless and careless farewell to a form he had grown weary of.

This play is as dark as it is not only because of what it presents, but what it doesn't. In Shakespeare's more "festive" comedies, *As You Like It*, *A Midsummer Night's Dream*, *Twelfth Night*, *Love's Labors Lost* and even *The Merchant of Venice*, there is what Northrop Frye has called a "green world," a place (often a forest or some other rural setting) where ordinary laws of behavior (and even physics) are suspended. In these places the *status quo* existing outside the green world is upset, identities become confused, and love and lovers dominate. These green worlds operate, then, as a sort of test tube in which a new order can be established, where new personalities can be tried, and where lovers can pair off. In *Measure for Measure* there is no such green world, no place to escape the dark and urban complexities of Vienna. All the conflicts must be resolved in the final scene through the equivalent of the *deus ex machina*—the last-minute intervention of the Duke.

QUESTIONS

1. Why is the play called *Measure for Measure?*

The major theme is announced in the title, which is derived from
the main action of the play and from the Sermon on the Mount: "Judge
not, that ye be not judged. For with what judgment ye judge, ye shall be
judged: and with what measure ye mete, it shall be measured to you
again." The Sermon on the Mount is largely regarded as the
cornerstone of New Testament theology, superseding for Christians the
less forgiving Mosaic law. We are certainly led by Shakespeare to watch
and approve a similar movement toward a more forgiving code as we
question Angelo's strict adherence to a brutal law and applaud the
reinstated Duke's forbearance in observing—or circumventing—that
same law.

2. How do the early scenes prepare us for the rest of the play?

Shakespeare accomplishes a good deal of exposition in the first scene.
The motif of the wise and able ruler selecting his substitute begins here,
and Escalus is established as a wise and loyal counselor. In fact, Escalus
serves, as it were, as the moral yardstick of the play; through him we
learn just how one should act when given great responsibility and
power. Angelo, to his credit, resists the burden the Duke places upon
him and asks for some lesser trial before the Duke leaves. The Duke
shows himself to be resolute in transferring all his power to Angelo.

In the second scene we are allowed to see unvarnished Vienna. Lucio
and two other gentlemen show themselves to be dissolute. The early part
of the scene is laced with images of disease, specifically syphilis.
Mistress Overdone and Pompey enter and it is revealed that Claudio has
been taken through an old law forbidding fornication and that all the
brothels in Vienna are to be torn down. Claudio appears, in custody, and
explains his circumstances. [One important note—your students may
point out that Claudio's relation to Julietta is the same as Angelo's to
Mariana. This is not the case, since the bans were not published, and
therefore Claudio and Julietta's intention to marry was not made public.
Shakespeare takes pains to make this point, one that would not have been
lost on his original intended audience.] Vienna, then, is painted as a
city perhaps irredeemably licentious.

3. Does Shakespeare's use of the "bed trick" render this play an artistic
failure or in bad taste?

The "bed trick" is an artifice that may be at least morally repugnant to some, and the plot is drawn to a close so hurriedly, and in the face of such unpleasant circumstances, that the bounds of comedy are stretched to the breaking point. One response to the first objection is that the "bed trick" *is* an artifice, but no more difficult to swallow than, for instance, the disguise of Viola and the subsequent romantic entanglements in *Twelfth Night.* The "bed trick" is an old motif in folk-tales and one that Shakespeare had used in an earlier comedy, *All's Well That Ends Well;* we should object to that no more than the failure of the other characters to penetrate the Duke's disguise. While not everyone's disbelief can be suspended to the same degree, still, to question Angelo's inability to distinguish Mariana from Isabella is to refuse to recognize the internal logic of this and many other plays of the period. The moral objections your students may have to the "bed trick" are harder to overcome, even if you feel an obligation to do so; an easy and honest route is to treat the device as a fairy-tale element of the drama that we cannot evaluate in any terms but its own. If push comes to shove, you might remind your class that in Shakespeare's day a formal betrothal like that between Angelo and Mariana was sometimes thought to constitute marriage.

4. Are the main characters the sort we expect to find in a comedy?

Most of the characters in *Measure for Measure* are unsavory or have attributes that Shakespeare has taught us to distrust in other plays. The Duke, some have argued, leaves his city in the hands of a man whom he hopes will do his dirty work, and his patching-up at the end is facile and thoughtless. Angelo, for all his qualms at blackmailing Isabella, proceeds with relish to put her in a cruelly painful predicament. Claudio begs too quickly for his sister to sacrifice her chastity, and Isabella is too shrill and inflexible (perhaps by modern standards) in refusing to save her brother's life. She and Angelo have a similar flaw: Shakespeare teaches us, in *Twelfth Night,* for example, to beware of characters who are fixed upon extremes of behavior (Ben Jonson's comedies are filled with such creatures). Isabella may be saintly, but her first appearance is a bit off-key:

Isabella:	And have you nuns no farther privileges?
Nun:	Are not these large enough?
Isabella:	Yes, truly. I speak not as desiring more, But rather wishing a more strict restraint Upon the sisterhood, the votarists of Saint Clare.

(1.5:1-5)

Isabella, not content with the restraints soon to be placed upon her by the strictest order in Europe, wishes to be curbed still more. Angelo, in his first attempt at handing out justice, claims:

> 'Tis one thing to be tempted, Escalus,
> Another thing to fall. I do not deny
> The jury, passing on the prisoner's life,
> May in the sworn twelve have a thief or two
> Guiltier than him they try. What's open made
>   to justice,
> That justice seizes. What knows the laws
> That thieves do pass on thieves? 'Tis very pregnant,
> Because we see it; but what we do not see
> We tread upon, and never think of it.
> You may not so extenuate his offense
> For I have had such faults; but rather tell me,
> When I, that censure him, do so offend,
> Let mine own judgement pattern out my death,
> And nothing come in partial. Sir, he must die.
>   (2.1:17-31)

Such a pronouncement begs for contradiction, and Shakespeare manages it by having Angelo reverse his position almost against his will. While Angelo turns out to be a monster of hypocrisy, Isabella maintains her arctic and sanctimonious resolve in the face of her brother's death. In both instances the rigidity of a character's world-view makes him or her detestable or unlikable and ripe for correction or education at the end of the play. Only then do we find Angelo palatable and then only because he freely admits his guilt and his wife-to-be sees the promise within him:

> Mariana: They say best men are moulded out of faults,
>   And for the most, become much more the better
>   For being a little bad; so may my husband.
>   (5.1:439-441)

Isabella, whom we find pitiable but can never warm to, may at last be said to have an "educated heart," that is, she is now capable of giving measure for measure in a different sense: her forgiveness is equal to the crimes against her.

5. How do the minor characters contribute to our understanding of the play?

Here as elsewhere Shakespeare runs a subplot dominated by characters of lower estate parallel to the main plot. These characters deal with some of the same questions and circumstances that confront the characters of the main plot: How does one harness natural impulses when society forbids them? How should transgressors of an unreasonable law be treated?

We can see how the minor characters inform our opinion of Angelo and the law in his hands in the first scene of Act 2, when he and the clownish Elbow are revealed as knee-jerk sticklers for the law. Early in the scene Angelo withstands Escalus' attempts to have him pardon or at least lessen the penalty for Claudio. The next case on the docket is that of Froth and Pompey. The law is enforced and represented by Elbow, who, through malapropisms and ineptitude, demonstrates that in this case the law is indeed an ass. Froth, Elbow, and Pompey become tangled in the case of the missing prunes and Angelo leaves, hoping that all will be whipped. Escalus, however, cuts to the heart of the matter eventually and shows mercy and a sense of humor in administering justice. Pompey is forced to leave a job in which he profited through the sexual appetites of others.

We are almost forced to make a number of comparisons here. Angelo's insistence on the letter of the law places him in the same camp as the dim-witted Elbow, though the consequences of Elbow's accusation are inconsequential. Escalus, on the other hand, shows himself to be evenhanded and gentle in administering justice. When he is asked by Pompey, "Does your worship mean to geld and splay all the youth of the city?" Escalus replies "No, Pompey." I think we can surmise that Angelo's answer, had he entertained the question, might have been different.

6. Is Isabella to be blamed for her unwillingness to sacrifice her virginity? Is Claudio to be blamed for his willingness to sacrifice his sister's virginity?

The heated answers to these questions will probably take up most of the class periods you devote to *Measure for Measure*. Is Claudio's life worth Isabella's degradation? What a thing to refuse a brother! What a thing to ask of a sister! It seems to me that the most fruitful discussions will move toward an understanding of the insoluble dilemma both Claudio and Isabella face and a further understanding that this is a deeper issue than is ordinarily addressed in works that we call comedies. Claudio's plea seems unnatural after Isabella is baited and leered at by Angelo; Isabella's refusal seems unnatural when we hear Claudio voice his fears:

Ay, but to die, and go we know not where;
To lie in cold obstruction, and to rot;
This sensible warm motion to become
A kneaded clod; and the delighted spirit
To bathe in fiery floods, or to reside
In thrilling region of thick-ribbed ice;
To be imprison'd in the viewless winds
And blown with restless violence about
The pendant world; or to be worse than worst
Of those that lawless and incertain thought
Imagine howling—'tis too horrible!
The weariest and most loathed worldly life
That age, ache, penury, and imprisonment
Can lay on nature is a paradise
To what we fear of death.
. . . .
Sweet sister, let me live.

(3.1:117-133)

7. Readers and viewers have often maintained that in the last scene Shakespeare forces his characters into the obligatory marriages we often find in comedies and the action to a forced and hollow happy ending. Do you think the rest of the play supports such an ending?

The end of the play does leave a bad taste in almost every reader's mouth. The tying-together of loose ends seems more forced than in any other of Shakespeare's comedies, and for good reason. Angelo has done little to deserve mercy, and the Duke's advances to Isabella, who is a novitiate, are not prepared for. For that matter, the skeleton of the plot, with a lecherous and hypocritical judge using his position to force a young would-be nun to his bed or lose her brother, is hardly the stuff of which comedy is often made. A great deal of the action takes place in a prison (no "green world" there), and there are a great many references to death, disease, and punishment in this comedy. After all, the most memorable prop in *Measure for Measure* is the severed head of Ragozine.

–W.R.S.

Henrik Ibsen
Hedda Gabler

Norwegian dramatist Henrik Ibsen shocked and outraged Victorian audiences by presenting realistic plays about contemporary social problems. *A Doll's House* (1879) illustrates the dilemma of nineteenth-century women denied educational and economic opportunities by their male-dominated society. The play ends with Nora, the heroine, leaving her husband. *Ghosts* (1881), which deals with venereal disease, was even more scandalous. After its first performance in London in 1891, reviewers clamored their moral indignation: "An open drain; a loathsome sore unbandaged; a dirty act done publicly; a lazar house with all its windows open."

With *Hedda Gabler* (1890) Ibsen shifted his focus slightly, away from the problems caused solely by a repressive society and toward the problems arising out of complex interactions between social forces and individual temperaments. Hedda, an intelligent, aristocratic woman, marries a middle-class man she neither loves nor respects, and—much to her dismay—she becomes pregnant. Angry with the world, Hedda destroys others and herself. To some extent *Hedda Gabler* is a problem play. We feel that Hedda, much like Nora in *A Doll's House,* would have fared better if society had offered her more options. (She would have made a formidable general, C.E.O., or courtroom attorney.) But *Hedda Gabler* is more than a narrow attack on the social and moral forces that inhibit individual growth, and Ibsen does not portray Hedda as a helpless victim of society. We have the impression that Hedda might have been more successful and powerful in a different society, but not that she would have been morally "better."

This play requires your students to consider an important question: Is the fall of an unlikeable protagonist tragic? Some people find Hedda absolutely contemptible. George Bernard Shaw, who championed Ibsen's drama, wrote that the trouble with women such as Hedda is that they *don't* ordinarily kill themselves. Students who share that view may feel that Hedda's suicide is cause for celebration. Others will consider Hedda an intelligent and courageous woman whose character is flawed by her overwhelming need to control others. Those students will mourn the destruction of a potentially admirable woman and applaud the dignity with which she ultimately gains control of her own destiny.

QUESTIONS

1. How is Hedda's character established in the first scene? What important aspect of her character does Ibsen hide from the audience until Act 2?

Before Hedda walks onto the stage, three different characters have offered their impressions of her. The maid, Berta, is somewhat intimidated by Hedda, a woman she characterizes as "ever so particular." Berta confides in Miss Tesman, her former mistress, "I'm really so scared I'll never give any satisfaction to the young mistress" (p. 2).

Miss Tesman, a kind woman who sees good in everyone, excuses Hedda by reminding Berta of Hedda's high social status. Miss Tesman offers us this picture of Hedda: "General Gabler's daughter. The way she was used to having things in the General's time. Do you remember her riding along the road with her father? In that long black habit? And with a feather in her hat?" (p. 2). Miss Tesman considers Hedda quite a catch for her nephew, and she says to Tesman, "And to think that you'd be the one to walk off with Hedda Gabler. The lovely Hedda Gabler. Imagine it! So many admirers she always had!" (p. 5). Tesman is obviously enchanted by Hedda and considers himself extremely fortunate to be married to her: "Yes, I dare say there are one or two of my good friends who wouldn't mind being in my shoes. Eh?" (p. 5). Tesman and his aunt then continue a conversation which illustrates that both have willingly made significant financial sacrifices so that Hedda, "a lady," could have the honeymoon and fine home she expected and—in their opinions—deserved.

When Hedda appears, she is not as advertised. Although she is beautiful, she is also haughty, peevish, inconsiderate, and demanding, a woman whose behavior toward her husband and his aunt suggests contempt rather than affection, gratitude, or even civility. When Hedda complains that Berta "left her old hat lying on the chair there" (p. 9), the audience, who knows the hat is one Miss Tesman just purchased, squirms uncomfortably, expecting Hedda to be mortified when she realizes she has insulted her guest. Hedda is surprisingly nonchalant when she learns the truth. She doesn't bother to apologize, but merely remarks, "I really didn't look at it very closely, Miss Tesman" (p. 9). As soon as Tesman and his aunt go out of the room, Ibsen relies on stage action to suggest that Hedda is deeply disturbed. Hedda "walks about the room, raises her arms and clenches her fists as though in a frenzy" (p. 10). The audience is left to speculate about the cause of her emotional turmoil.

Although that early scene prepares us to believe Hedda is self-centered and indifferent to the feelings of others, Ibsen hides one important dimension of Hedda's character. Not until Act 2 does he reveal (in Hedda's conversation with Brack) that she knew the hat was Miss Tesman's and only pretended to believe it was the maid's (p. 29). When we discover that Hedda was not merely thoughtless but deliberately cruel, we are prepared to believe her capable of almost anything.

2. Is *Hedda Gabler* a well-made play? (See Handbook entry "Well-made Play.")

Probably few if any of your students will have read or attended a well-made play, but if they've ever watched a soap opera, they should have a fairly good notion of the beast. The well-made play or *piéce-bien-faite* was introduced by two French dramatists, Scribe and Sardou, who developed a formula that guaranteed popular success. The formula requires an exciting plot (complete with cliff-hangers, twists, surprises, coincidences, and a happy ending), stock characters, sentimentality, and theatrical devices (such as letters, wills, or diaries) that serve a deus-ex-machina function. Typically, such plays lack serious themes and rely heavily on plot. In fact Scribe once commented, "When my story is right, when I have the events of my play firmly in hand, I could have my janitor write it."

Because Ibsen directed more than twenty Scribe plays in Norway, it is not surprising to find that the plots of many of his plays demonstrate characteristics of the well-made play. For example, each of the first three acts of *Hedda Gabler* ends with a cliff-hanger. At the end of Act 1 we, along with Tesman, worry about Hedda's decision to "pass the time" with General Gabler's pistols. At the conclusion of Act 2 we wait anxiously for Lovborg to return at ten o'clock "with vine leaves in his hair." Act 3, which ends with Hedda burning Lovborg's manuscript, leaves us speculating about the dire consequences of her rash behavior. In addition, the plot is heavily dependent on coincidence and the use of theatrical devices: Lovborg loses his manuscript, Tesman happens to find it and take it home for safekeeping, a letter arrives informing Tesman that Aunt Rina is dying, Tesman rushes off, and Hedda is alone with the manuscript.

But the similarities between Ibsen's drama and the well-made play are merely superficial. Few of Ibsen's plays have anything remotely resembling happy endings, almost all deal with serious social or philosophical questions, and—for Ibsen—character, not plot, is paramount. As the Counterpoint demonstrates, Ibsen's approach to the writing of a play was diametrically opposed to Scribe's get-the-story-right formula. Ibsen explains, "Before I write one word, I have to have the character in mind through and through. I must penetrate into the last wrinkle of his soul."

3. We might classify the characters in this play according to the kind of intelligence they display: academic, creative, or practical (understanding how the world works). Who belongs in which class? Does Ibsen suggest that one type of intelligence is preferable to another?

Tesman is clearly an academic in the worst sense of the word. Hedda claims that he is "absolutely in his element if he's given leave to grub around in libraries" (p. 26), and Tesman concedes that he is especially suited for "putting other people's papers in order" (p. 68). Tesman admits his lack of creative intelligence to Lovborg: "It just wouldn't enter my head to write a book like that" (p. 34). He clearly has no practical intelligence; he is oblivious to Hedda's pregnancy and her unhappiness, he fails to recognize the precariousness of his financial situation, and he never suspects that his friend Brack intends to have an affair with Hedda.

Hedda and Brack display practical intelligence that has been warped into Machiavellian ruthlessness. They are students of human nature who demonstrate a remarkably clear view of the needs that motivate others and themselves, an insight they unfortunately use to manipulate others rather than to lead them.

Thea is an example of creative intelligence. Thea credits Lovborg with the awakening of her intellect. She tells Hedda that Lovborg "[t]aught her to think...and to understand quite a lot of things" (p. 18). She suggests that her contributions to "Lovborg's book" involved more than taking dictation ("When he wrote anything, we always had to do it together"—p. 19), a claim born out by her conviction that she can recreate the book from her notes. Like Tesman, Thea lacks practical intelligence. Or perhaps it would be more accurate to say that she is not cynical enough to suspect Hedda's treachery.

The only character in the play who displays all three kinds of intelligence is Lovborg. Tesman's praise of Lovborg's recently published book ("soberly argued"—29) establishes his academic capability. Lovborg's comment that he intentionally "wrote a book that nobody could disagree with" (a position Brack admires as "sensible") because he is "trying now to build up a position for [himself]" (pp. 33-34) demonstrates his political astuteness. And Lovborg's decision to write his next book "about the future course of civilization" (p. 34) proves his creativity. Surely Ibsen wants us to conclude that Lovborg, a character the audience is likely to admire, suggests the ideal, a person who does not force his intelligence into a single narrow channel. Sadly, Lovborg willingly abandons his intelligence by yielding to Hedda's entreaties to take a drink. After that, his ignoble end is assured. In this play Ibsen presents no single character who is absolutely correct, no one who can serve as a model for right thinking, but—through Lovborg—Ibsen at least holds out the hope that such a person might exist.

4. Why does Hedda burn Lovborg's manuscript?

Although Hedda tells Tesman that she did it for his sake (p. 61), neither Hedda nor the audience believes that for even three seconds. Hedda
burns the manuscript because she is jealous of Thea's relationship with
Lovborg, and the manuscript symbolizes that relationship. Hedda recognizes that motive when she tosses the pages in the fire and whispers to
herself: "Now I am burning your child, Thea! With your curly hair!
Your child and Ejlert Lovborg's. I'm burning...burning your child (Act
3, final page). But it is not Thea's romantic relationship with Lovborg
that Hedda resents (after all, Lovborg makes it plain that he has never
stopped loving Hedda—p. 38); it is Thea's influence over Lovborg's life.
While he was composing *Hedda Gabler*, Ibsen wrote the following
notebook entry: "The demonic thing about Hedda is that she wants to
exert influence over another person." Hedda articulates her need to
dominate at the end of Act 2, when she explains to Thea why she
persuaded Lovborg to attend Brack's party:

Mrs. Elvsted:	You've got some reason for all this, Hedda!
Hedda:	Yes, I have. For once in my life I want to control a human destiny.
Mrs. Elvsted:	But surely you do already.
Hedda:	I don't, and I never have done.
Mrs. Elvsted:	But what about your husband?
Hedda:	Yes, that would really be something, wouldn't it? Oh, if only you knew how destitute I am. And you're allowed to be so rich. I think I'll burn your hair off after all.

By burning the manuscript, Hedda destroys the evidence that "the
silly little fool [Thea] has had her fingers in a man's destiny" (p. 56),
and gains control herself over Lovborg's fate. Hedda does not care that
such control will destroy Lovborg as well as his manuscript.

5. How do Aunt Julle and Thea add to our understanding of the roles
available to women in Ibsen's society?

Hedda Gabler is not primarily a diatribe lambasting those who persist
in treating women as inferior beings. Nevertheless, Ibsen manages to
show that the society Hedda inhabits is as seriously flawed as she is.
Through Aunt Julle and Thea, Ibsen demonstrates the narrow range of
roles available to nineteenth-century women. Aunt Julle, a woman who
never married, has spent her life happily sacrificing herself for her

male relatives, first for her "sainted brother" (p. 3) and now for her
nephew, "sainted Joachim's little boy" (p. 4). Aunt Julle voluntarily
mortgages her and Rina's annuity as security for the furniture and
carpets for Tesman's home, and although Tesman gallantly protests, he
is easily persuaded that Aunt Julle's sacrifices on his behalf are "the only
joy [she has] in this world" (p. 7). Although we approve of Aunt Julle's
generous spirit, we can't help but feel that life should have offered her
more.

Thea suggests that married life is no more fulfilling. Although Thea
goes to Elvsted's house to be a governess (a position that generally com-
manded little prestige and less salary), she finds that she is required to
look after the house as well. After Elvsted's wife dies and Thea marries
Elvsted, a man twenty years older than she, her role apparently changes
little. Thea confides to Hedda, "I think he just finds me useful. And
then it doesn't cost much to keep me. I'm cheap" (p. 17).

Thea then turns to Lovborg for emotional fulfillment. Although
Lovborg gladly accepts her assistance with his book and candidly admits
that he could not have written it without her, Thea neither expects nor
receives public recognition for her efforts. In fact, once she has
guaranteed Lovborg's success, he returns to his hometown, apparently
unconcerned about her future. Even after Lovborg betrays her by losing
"their child" (p. 57), Thea remains devoted to him and offers to "help"
Tesman (a man who does not appear to be her intellectual equal)
recreate Lovborg's book. After Hedda's death, there is little doubt that
Thea will marry Tesman and spend the rest of her life contributing to
books that will not bear her name.

Although we want to believe that a woman of Hedda's intelligence
could have found an alternative to suicide, through Aunt Julle and Thea
Ibsen candidly reminds us that Hedda's society expected little of a
woman except that she be a pleasant martyr, a prospect we can hardly
blame Hedda for declining.

6. Does the end of the play make us feel that the world has been set
right?

If you ask your students to compare the ending of this play with that of
Antigone or *Hamlet*, they should notice a significant difference. Even
though a Greek or Elizabethan tragedy ends with the death of the
protagonist, we are not left with a sense of despair. Instead, we feel that
the protagonist's suffering has ennobled him or her, that order has
been restored, and that the characters who remain and the audience
have gained insights that will—at least temporarily—enable us to
maintain that order. When *Antigone* ends, Creon's defiance of religious

duties has been punished and the harmonious relationship between the gods and the state reestablished. When *Hamlet* closes, there is no longer "something rotten in the state of Denmark."

In contrast, the ending of *Hedda Gabler* is bleak. At best, we may feel that Hedda achieves dignity through her courageous decision to die nobly rather than exist under intolerable conditions. That's precious little to cheer about. And there's absolutely no indication that Hedda's death will somehow enlighten the survivors or effect improvements in society. In fact, we are certain that Tesman, Thea, and even Brack will be puzzled by her suicide. Perhaps the emotional impact of a Greek or Elizabethan tragedy is not possible in a domestic tragedy that focuses on an ordinary individual. Whether Hedda shoots herself, lives a long and miserable life trapped in a ménage à trois with Tesman and Brack, or miraculously escapes both fates, the social order around her will be unchanged.

—M.R.D.

Anton Chekhov
The Three Sisters

If you are treating the plays in *The Riverside Anthology* chronologically, then you might have moved from one of Shakespeare's dramas to this, a jump of some three hundred years. You may have used *Hamlet* to inform your class's notion of tragedy; if you used *Twelfth Night* in constructing a definition of comedy (and did not confront the difficulties in categorizing *Measure for Measure*), then your students may have difficulties in determining to what genre *The Three Sisters* belongs. If so, then you might find it useful to remind them that they share that confusion with the players of the Moscow Art Theatre, who interpreted what Chekhov felt to be a comedy as a tragedy. Resolving that confusion is a tricky business, and the Handbook in this or any other text may not be of sufficient service. It is plain that we feel no sense of *catharsis* at the end of *The Three Sisters*—in fact, locating one's feelings at the end of this play may be a bewildering affair—and we can hardly call the longing for Moscow and what it represents or the ennui shared by the sisters a frailty or tragic flaw in the conventional sense. We can, then, be fairly certain that *The Three Sisters* is not a tragedy. Similarly, no matter what Chekhov might have felt, it is difficult to place this play in our comedy pigeonhole with *Twelfth Night*; Olga's final speech, delivered with her arms around her sisters, is in a minor key:

Oh, my God! Time will pass, and we shall be gone forever, they
will forget us—they'll forget our faces, our voices, and how many of
us there were, but our sufferings will turn into joy for those who
live after us, happiness and peace will come on earth, and they'll be
reminded and speak tenderly of those who are living now, they
will bless them. Oh, dear sisters, our life isn't over yet. We shall
live! The music is playing so gaily, so joyfully, and it seems as
though a little more and we shall know why we live, why we suffer
. . . If only we knew, if only we knew!

Yes, there is an affirmation of the lives the sisters have led and will
be living, and yes, this millennialist view promises well for the future,
but the *felix culpa* motif that in part drives this play just does not fit into
the narrow definition of comedy that most of us are forced to lean upon
in the classroom. Those Procrustean twin beds of comedy and tragedy
cannot accommodate *The Three Sisters*, but it might be a useful exercise
(since the attempt will allow you to retrace some important steps) to try
to squeeze *The Three Sisters* into one or the other. Your class discussion
will probably coalesce into a working definition much like the one in
The Riverside Anthology: tragicomedies are "plays which balance tragic
and comic elements so closely that neither clearly predominates." (It is
worth noting in class that Chekhov is really that rarest of literary
artifacts—a "transition figure." No earlier playwright had produced
drama that could not be rather easily categorized as a tragedy or a
comedy. *Measure for Measure*, for instance, may strike us at times as
hardly comic, but Shakespeare at the last wrenches character and plot to
fit the comedic mold.)
   Chekhov's success in the theatre can be attributed to his own genius
and to the perspicacity of Constantin Stanislavsky and Nemirovich-
Danchenko, who founded the Moscow Art Theatre and convinced
Chekhov to revive *The Seagull*. The result of that production was a revolution in modern theatre; like most revolutions, it made new and hard
demands upon its partisans. Chekhov, who wrote that "in real life
people don't spend every minute shooting each other, hanging
themselves and making confessions of love . . . They're more occupied
with eating, drinking, flirting and talking stupidities—and these are
the things which ought to be shown on the stage," was faced with the
technical difficulty of presenting a realistic slice of life, in all its
apparent formlessness, on stage—and not losing his audience in the
process. When one looks at the melodramatic tradition popular on stage
when Chekhov's career began, and then takes into account the human

appetite for spectacle and sensation, the playwright's success and achievement become all the more remarkable.

QUESTIONS

1. How would you describe the mood of this play? How is this mood established early in the play?

Most readers and audiences will agree that the play is dominated by a sense of loss, unfulfilled wishes, and impending troubles. At the very opening Olga describes the funeral of their father and remarks that few were at his funeral. Irina tells us that it is her birthday and looks back upon her childhood with a passionate nostalgia. Both she and Olga express a desire to leave their home and go to Moscow.

Vershinin reminds the three sisters of the vanity of human wishes:

> Yes. They'll forget us. That is our fate, there is nothing we can do about it. Everything that seems to us serious, significant, profoundly important—the time will come when it will be forgotten or will seem unimportant . . .

Tuzenbach, in an often-quoted passage, has already predicted social change that will sweep away the remnants of the idle aristocracy:

> The time has come: a thundercloud is hanging over us all, a great healthy storm is gathering; it's coming, it's already almost upon us, and is going to sweep out of our society the laziness, the indifference, the contempt for work, the rotten boredom.

Some of your students may point to this passage as evidence of Chekhov's vision of the Russian Revolution of 1917; this is unlikely— Chekhov scoffed in the year of his death (1904) at the possibility of revolt, though in 1905 Russia's humiliation in the Russo-Japanese war sparked unrest and reform.

In any event, virtually everyone will agree that this play is a real departure from, say, *Twelfth Night* or even *Measure for Measure*. In Chekhov's play we have characters uttering explicit social criticisms and seriously expressing their disillusionment; very little of the fairy tale or saturnalian comedy remains here. If we can imagine Vershinin's speech or something like it in a Shakespearean comedy, it would undoubtedly be spoken by a figure of fun, a melancholic or humorous (in the

Elizabethan sense) character like Jacques, Thersites, or perhaps even
Malvolio.

2. We might expect comedy to deal with love and marriage. How are
they treated in *The Three Sisters?*

This play plainly does not conform to the old comedic form in which
all conflicts end through the integration of all the characters into a new
"society," whose creation is signaled by a festive ritual like a marriage.
The new "society" in place at the end of this play is announced in quite a
different way. But marriage and love are among Chekhov's most important subjects here, as well as the source of many of the play's conflicts.

Irina—Tuzenbach—Solyony

The union of Irina and Tuzenbach is an odd one. We learn that Irina
is marrying a man she does not love:

> It isn't in my power! I'll be your wife, I'll be faithful and obedient,
> but it's not love, oh, what is there I can do? (She cries) I never have
> been in love in my life, not even once. Oh, I've dreamed so about
> love, dreamed about love so long now, day and night, but my soul's
> like some expensive piano that's locked and the key lost.

On the advice of Olga, however, she has agreed to marry him, not out
of love, but because "he's such an honest man, such a good man" (p. 56?).
He, on the other hand, is passionately and affectionately in love with
her. The abrasive and brooding Solyony, who douses himself with
perfume and imagines that his looks and disposition match
Lermontov's, declares himself and is rejected; his response to that
rejection is to declare war on his rivals:

> Well, it doesn't make any difference. I can't make you love me, of
> course . . . But rivals, happy rivals—I can't stand those . . . can't
> stand them. I swear to you by all that is holy, I shall kill any rival
> . . . Oh, wonderful one!

That declaration foreshadows and makes inevitable the duel between
the Baron and Solyony. One could hardly call the wooing of Irina a love
triangle, since she loves neither of her suitors, the Baron, who insists
on making her his, and Solyony, who insists on making her no one's if
not his.

Masha—Vershinin—Kulygin

Masha has married a man she once feared and admired for his intellect.

> They married me when I was eighteen, and I was afraid of my husband because he was a teacher and I was barely out of school. He seemed terribly learned to me then, intelligent, and important. It's different now, unfortunately.

Kulygin is a teacher who knows virtually nothing, least of all his wife's real sentiments toward him:

> Our principal is fond of saying that the most important thing in any life is its routine. . . That which loses its routine loses its very existence—and it is exactly the same in our everyday life. (He takes Masha by the waist, laughing.) Masha loves me. My wife loves me. And the curtains too, along with the carpets.

His passion for the trivial stands in opposition to the visionary Vershinin, whose concern for the future and insistence on laboring in its behalf makes it difficult for him to enjoy the present. His present, of course, seems particularly unpleasant because of his suicidal and demanding wife. He and Masha are forced to separate when his company leaves town, never, we understand, to reunite.

Andrei—Natasha—Protopopov

Andrei, whose career as a scholar is blunted, finds that his domestic life is no rosier. Natasha gradually erodes whatever will and authority Andrei might have held. Her love seems given completely to her children and to her lover Protopopov. Our attitude toward this adulterous alliance is likely to be different from our view of the relationship of Vershinin and Masha, who are seeking refuge from unhappy marriages.

3. How would you assess Natasha's character? What does she represent?

You are likely to get mixed responses to this question. Some students may find her single-mindedness and devotion to her children admirable. These same students may also assert that adultery is no more to be censured than Masha's affair with Vershinin. In addition, she is a woman who shows the sort of single-mindedness and ambition most of us might admire, particularly when she is compared to the Prozorovs, who wring their hands and long for a past now gone or celebrate a future that is likely to have little use for them.

On the other hand, there is much to dislike in Natasha. Unless we feel that only the strong should survive, we are unlikely to admire her dismantling of the Prozorovs and her off-stage infidelity. At the end of Act 2, when she levers Irina out of her room and then calmly goes off to an assignation with Protopopov, we may see her at her worst:

> Natasha: It seems to me that it's so cold and damp for Bobik in the nursery he has now. And your room is simply ideal for a child. My darling, my precious, do move in with Olga for a while!

> Irina: (Not understanding) Where?

> [A troika with bells is heard driving up to the house]

> Natasha: You and Olga will be in one room, for the time being, and your room will be for Bobik. He's such a little dear, this morning I said to him, "Bobik, you're mine! Mine!" and he looked up at me with those darling little eyes of his. (A ring) That must be Olga. How late she is!

> [A Maid comes in and whispers in Natasha's ear]

> Natasha: Protopopov! What a funny man! Protopopov's here and wants me to go for a ride in his troika with him.

While she may have married into property and gentility (if not money), Natasha treats the servants with a coolness that reveals her own origins—she feels no sense of *noblesse oblige,* a sentiment useless in a new age where landed gentry need feel no loyalty to those they once owned.

> Natasha: . . . (To Anfisa, coldly) Don't you dare sit down in my presence! Get up! Get out of here! (Anfisa goes out. A pause) What you keep that old woman for I simply do not understand!

> Olga: (Taken aback) I beg your pardon, I don't understand either . . .

> Natasha: She's around here for no reason whatsoever. She's a peasant, she ought to be in the country where she belongs . . . It's simply spoiling them! There ought not to be these useless people cluttering up the house.

We have seen Irina fold before the manipulation and bullying of Natasha; even Olga, the oldest and perhaps strongest of the three sisters, is helpless in resisting her. Soon Olga and Masha will be driven from their family home and Irina will seek refuge in a loveless marriage.

4. What attitude do the characters hold toward work? Why is work of such importance in this play?

It may be important to point out to your students that a commonplace of Russian historiography (right or wrong) is to assert that feudalism survived in that country until well into the 19th century. Whether or not that is true, Ferapont and Anfisa are relics of an earlier time, when Russian aristocratic families relied on the labors of serfs to support their way of life. Chekhov, who came from serf stock, devotes a great deal of his drama to the unproductive lives of the ineffectual ruling class.

In the face of Olga's complaint that her work as a schoolteacher makes her head ache and is robbing her of her youth, Irina claims that

> A man must work, must make his bread by the sweat of his brow, it doesn't matter who he is—and it is in this alone that he can find the purpose and meaning of his life, his happiness, his ecstasies. Oh, how good it is to be a workman who gets up at dawn and breaks stones in the street, or a shepherd, or a schoolteacher who teaches children, or a locomotive engineer! My God, it's better to be an ox, it's better to be a plain horse, and *work*, than to be a girl who wakes up at twelve o'clock, has coffee in bed, and then takes two hours to get dressed . . . Oh, how awful that is! Sometimes I—I *thirst* for work the way on a hot day you thirst for water.

Irina, we learn, does like to awaken at seven—and remain in bed until nine. We learn in Act 2 that her work is not the salvation she had hoped: "I must try to find some other job, this one's not right for me. What I longed for so, what I dreamed about, is exactly what's missing. It's work without poetry, without sense . . . "

The Baron, too, feels the importance of work and has done as little of it as Irina:

> That thirst for work—good God, how well I understand it! I've never worked a day in my life. I was born in Petersburg, cold, lazy Petersburg—born into a family that never knew what work or worry meant . . . I've been sheltered from work.

The Baron is the distillation of the displaced aristocracy that wanders *The Three Sisters* and other Chekhov dramas looking for some meaning, some purpose in life. This is a social criticism one finds in almost all of Chekhov, who held the view that men and women are defined to a large extent by the work that they do. Irina is disappointed to discover that the daily grind of work is not as stimulating and romantic as she had imagined it to be; though she complains, she is much more admirable than when she battened on others' efforts. Gorky quotes Chekhov as maintaining that "If one wants to lead a good life, a human life, one must work," and testifies that he "never met anyone who felt the importance of work as the basis of culture so profoundly and diversely" as Chekhov. In pointing out the disparity between what Irina and the Baron wish for and what they do, Chekhov is poking rather gentle fun. One of the sources of Chekhov's wistful humor is his constant reminder that we often fail to live up to our stated ideals.

5. Does this play have a climax? Where is it?

If one can say that there is a scene or point in this play where the complications reach a point where tension must be released and the action begins to "descend," it might be the ordeal of the fire in the third act. One could argue reasonably that this play, despite Chekhov's flouting of conventional comic structure, has a certain symmetry. The fire, both cleansing and destructive, signals a crisis for virtually every major character in the play, and signals as well the beginning of the end of the Prozorovs' hopes.

Olga, so weary she cannot stand, must defend Anfisa against Natasha, who insists on the old woman's dismissal. This brings about a confrontation with Andrei, who, in defending his wife, admits defiantly that he has given up his hope of an academic career and mortgaged the family house. The ordinarily cheerful Chebutykin despairs because he has killed a patient and reveals to Kulygin that his wife is having an affair with Protopopov. Irina, too, despairs, convinced that "everything's getting farther away from any real life, beautiful life, everything's going farther and farther into some abyss"; Olga suggests that the remedy is a marriage with the dull Baron. Shortly after Masha announces her love for Vershinin, we learn that his brigade, the source of civility and entertainment in the town, has been ordered to leave the town. The breaking of the clock by Chebutykin signifies pretty clearly that time is up for the way of life enjoyed by the Prozorovs.

—W.R.S

Samuel Beckett
Krapp's Last Tape

Krapp's Last Tape is a drama stripped to its barest essentials—one character, one nearly empty room, no plot in the traditional sense, and very little action. It is, of course, a great example of Beckett's definition of art: "The expression that there is nothing to express, nothing with which to express, nothing from which to express, no power to express, no desire to express, together with the obligation to express."

Students who expect conventional drama will be befuddled by *Krapp's Last Tape*. If you ask your class what they thought of the play, at least one brave soul will volunteer, "It didn't make any sense to me. Some old man listens to tapes he made when he was younger and makes some new ones. And he drinks a lot and eats bananas." A perfectly legitimate response. In fact, what occurs on stage during *Krapp's Last Tape* could be summed up with a line spoken by another of Beckett's characters in the play *Waiting for Godot*: "Nothing happens, nobody comes, nobody goes, it's awful."

The challenge of teaching absurdist drama is to persuade your students that such a situation is acceptable, that a dramatist can discard storyline, character development, and rational dialogue and still create something of merit. I have sometimes begun class discussions on absurdist drama with the following remarks: "Pretend you are a playwright who believes that life is basically meaningless; that people are born for no reason, live for no reason, and then die for no reason; that life is merely a series of senseless incidents. How would you present your view on stage?" Once I have stacked the deck, someone quickly draws the right card and suggests that the ordinary conventions of drama might be too orderly and logical to dramatize that perspective. Then the class is ready to examine *Krapp's Last Tape*.

A person who is reading the play rather than watching it may have trouble distinguishing between the recorded passages and the spoken passages. You can save your students some confusion by recommending that—before they begin reading—they highlight the words that would be spoken by Krapp onstage.

QUESTIONS

1. What are the comic elements in the play?

Any discussion of absurdist drama is likely to lead to depressing conversations about the dramatist's vision of life as ultimately meaningless.

You may need to remind your students that this play, like many of Beckett's, has its funny moments. Unfortunately, comedy that would be obvious to a person watching a stage production can be missed by someone who is reading the play. If you or one of your students will act out the opening scene (the part that occurs before Krapp says anything), you won't have to convince your class that the play is funny. All the business with the banana is pure slapstick: Krapp fishing around in a drawer of tape reels and pulling out a banana; Krapp standing at the front of the stage—banana in mouth—staring out toward the audience; Krapp slipping on a banana peel; Krapp pushing the banana peel over the edge of the stage into the pit; Krapp sticking a peeled banana into his waistcoat pocket. Add to that Krapp's name, his penchant for popping corks in the back room, his strange attire, his delight in drawing out the word "spooool," and his obsession with tapes, and you have all the ingredients for a great comedy—all, that is, except a comic vision.

2. How is this play typical of absurdist drama?

If you have to give a mini-lecture on theater of the absurd to help your students with this question, you might explain that absurdist drama takes up where existential drama leaves off. In plays such as Sartre's *No Exit*, existentialists present carefully structured plots and serious dialogue meant to convince the audience that life has no meaning unless we make one for it. Absurdists go a step further by rejecting the rationality implicit in plots predicated on the assumption that characters' actions lead to predictable consequences. In their form-follows-function plays playwrights of this school dramatize rather than articulate absurdity. Consequently, absurdist plays usually have the following characteristics:

◆ Unrealistic settings with few props
◆ One-dimensional, sometimes comic, characters who are the same at the end of the play as at the beginning.
◆ Disjointed and seemingly pointless dialogue that often involves wordplay
◆ No plot
◆ Conscious efforts to remind the audience that the play is a play
◆ Outlook—bleak

Obviously *Krapp's Last Tape* demonstrates many of these features. (1) The setting, Krapp's den, is suggested by a chair and a table with a tape-recorder and cardboard boxes on top of it. The table area is in strong white light. (2) There is no plot with a clearly defined beginning, middle, and end; no rising action, climax, falling action, and denouement; no feeling that one event is causally linked to another. There is only Krapp aimlessly munching bananas, drinking, and listening to tapes. (3) When Krapp pushes the banana peel off the stage into the pit, Beckett is reminding us that the stage is after all a stage. (4) It is difficult to imagine a drearier vision than that presented by this play. If Krapp, a bitter old man shut off from all contact with other people, is a symbol of the human condition, there is indeed cause for despair.

3. What technical problem does Beckett solve with the use of the tape recordings?

Even if your students never become enthusiastic admirers of this play, they should appreciate Beckett's stagecraft. He offers a brilliant solution to a tough technical problem: How to create a situation where it seems plausible that a character alone on a stage would talk out loud. Elizabethans accepted the soliloquy as a matter of course; modern audiences find such ploys artificial and contrived, but we are quite willing to believe that a man might record his thoughts about life and listen to those recordings later.

In addition, Beckett's use of the tape recorder makes it possible for the older Krapp to encounter his younger self, if not face to face, then voice to voice. Ask your class to suggest other methods of achieving the same goal and they will soon understand the difficulty of the task. If Krapp were to reminisce aloud about his earlier life, we would have to trust that his memories have not been distorted by the intervening years. If the young Krapp had written his thoughts rather than recorded them, and the older man read them aloud, we would not have the contrast between the strong, young, pompous voice and the old cracked voice, a contrast the older man cannot ignore. I suppose Beckett could have resorted to appearances by "Ghosts of Krapps Past," but that would be hokey rather than absurd. Besides, it would require more than one actor.

Finally, this solution to a technical problem also enables Beckett to create the kind of suspense necessary to capture an audience's attention. In most plots suspense is created by a conflict between two or more characters, a conflict that is usually resolved at the end of the play. Beckett, who has chosen to abandon traditional plot structure, creates suspense and tension through Krapp's confrontation of his earlier views of life. Although Krapp jeers at the voice of his past, he feels compelled to listen to the tapes over and over again. Once we find ourselves wondering why he listens to them, which tape he will listen to next and how he will respond to the words he hears, Beckett has guaranteed that we won't leave the theater until the play is over.

4. Is this play absolutely bleak?

Critics disagree on this issue and so, I am sure, will your students. Certainly Krapp's present life is grim, and there is nothing in the play to suggest that his future will be brighter. But if we can believe that Krapp's existence didn't have to be as hopeless as it obviously is, then the play might make us feel sorrow or pity for Krapp but not despair over the human condition. If there is an optimistic note in the play, it is the tape that describes Krapp's boat ride thirty years earlier with the woman he loved. At the time of that incident, their affair had just ended. Three times during the play Krapp listens to his lyrical description of that afternoon:

> I lay down across her with my face in her breasts and my hand on her. We lay there without moving. But under us all moved, and moved us, gently up and down, and from side to side (pp. 5, 6, 7).

After playing that tape twice, Krapp records his reflections for the present year. He begins by scoffing at the man who had been in love: "Just listening to that stupid bastard I took myself for thirty years ago, hard to believe I was ever as bad as that. Thank God that's all done with anyway" (p. 6). But then he goes on to wonder aloud whether he made the right decision. "Could have been happy with her, up there on the Baltic, and the pines, and the dunes. (Pause.) Could I? (Pause.) And she?" (p. 7). Abruptly, the bitterness returns. He records a few caustic remarks and then "wrenches off the tape, throws it away, puts on the other, winds it forward to the passage he wants, switches on, listens staring front" (p. 7). For the third time he listens to the description of his last moments of love. This time the tape plays further and concludes with words the audience has not heard before:

> Here I end this reel. Box—(pause)—three, spool—(pause)—five. (Pause.) Perhaps the best years are gone. When there was a chance of happiness. But I wouldn't want them back. Not with the fire in me now. No, I wouldn't want them back (p. 8).

Krapp remains "motionless staring before him. The tape runs on in silence. CURTAIN."

Krapp's earlier decision to reject the "chance of happiness" continues to haunt him. With his replaying of the tape Krapp tacitly admits that the chance did exist and—we suspect—that he regrets the choice he made so long ago. We sympathize with Krapp, but we are encouraged by the hope that love might have made a difference. That is a view suggested in other of Beckett's plays. In *Waiting for Godot* two tramps, Vladimir and Estragon, find ways to entertain themselves while waiting for Godot, a mysterious figure whose arrival is supposed to give their lives direction; at the end of the play they are still waiting. Their situation, which is a metaphor for all lives, is absurd, and yet the affection the two men feel for each other makes their existence bearable. In another play, *Endgame*, one of the characters walks to the front of the stage and orders the audience to "[g]et out of here and love one another."

Your students might be interested to learn that there is some question as to whether the final lines ("Perhaps my best years are gone. When there was a chance of happiness. But I wouldn't want them back. Not with the fire in me now. No, I wouldn't want them back.") are spoken in Krapp's present voice or played as part of the previous tape. Stage productions apparently differ because a number of critics have based their interpretations of the play on the assumption that those lines are spoken by the old man. You may want to ask your students how that change in the script would influence their answer to this question.

5. Is Krapp tragic? If he is not, can the play be a tragedy?

In "The Myth of Sisyphus" existential writer Albert Camus explains his view of tragedy in the modern world. In Greek mythology, Sisyphus was the man condemned for eternity to endlessly rolling a stone to the top of a mountain, knowing that it would then fall back down and he would be forced to repeat his labors. According to Camus, Sisyphus is the absurd hero:

> If this myth is tragic, that is because its hero is conscious. Where would his torture be, indeed, if at every stop the hope of succeeding upheld him? The workman of today works everyday in his life at the same tasks, and this fact is no less absurd. But it is tragic only at the rare moments when it becomes conscious. Sisyphus, proletarian of the gods, powerless and rebellious, knows the whole extent of his wretched condition: it is what he thinks of during the whole descent. The lucidity that was to constitute his torture at the same time crowns his victory. There is no fate that cannot be surmounted by scorn.

If, as Camus argues, a person does not achieve tragic stature unless he or she is conscious of the absurdity of existence, then Krapp may not be tragic. Perhaps he is merely pathetic.

In the Counterpoint, however, Arthur Miller offers a slightly
different definition of tragedy. Miller concludes that tragedy "brings us
[apparently the audience] not only sadness, sympathy, identification,
and even fear; it also, unlike pathos, brings us knowledge or
enlightenment." He goes on to define such enlightenment as "a more
exalted kind of consciousness . . . because it makes us aware of what the
character might have been."

Using this definition, we may well decide that *Krapp's Last Tape* is a
tragedy. Even if Krapp never attains the consciousness that might have
elevated him to the level of tragic "hero," the audience does gain
enlightenment. Perhaps we learn what Krapp might have been.
Perhaps we learn, as Sisyphus did, that life is meaningless. In either
case, it seems that in modern drama it is the audience rather than the
protagonist who is ennobled by facing truth.

—M.R.D.

Arthur Miller
Death of a Salesman

An early critic of *Death of a Salesman* said that the play achieved little
more than a "down in the mouth feeling." Lodged in that colloquial expression we find the issue that has surely arisen every time this play has
been taught as literature. Can a play that violates the *de casibus virorum il-
lustrium* (the fall of great men) pattern evoke the emotions we expect
from tragedy?

Some of the corollary questions are likely to be just as thorny. How *do*
we know a tragedy when we have seen and heard one? The answer to
this question, when it has been asked in literature courses, has been provided most authoritatively by Aristotle. Tragedy, Aristotle maintains,
aims to exhibit humans better than we find them; it imitates an action
that is important, complete, and of a proper magnitude; it excites terror
and pity in its audience, and those incidents most terrible and piteous
are those that involve conflicts between friends and family members.
Finally, the person who is the subject of the tragedy must be of noble
birth and neither exceedingly virtuous nor exceedingly evil, and he
must fall out of error, not out of vice. It would certainly be useful to hold
Death of a Salesman up to Aristotle's light to see how well the modern play
conforms to the description the ancient Greek provides. Your students
will discover that Miller's work is not informed by the *Poetics* except
insofar as it is at times a reaction to Aristotle; they will also find that as
far as Euripides and Sophocles are from Arthur Miller in some matters,
the ancient dramatists might agree with the modern that "in the tragic

view the need of man to wholly realize himself is the only fixed star"
(Miller, "Tragedy and the Common Man").

A second corollary question is more likely to be asked profitably right
after a performance than after a treatment in class. What emotions *do*
we discover in ourselves as a result of viewing or reading what we think
is tragedy? Few spectators of a modern production of *Antigone* or even
Hamlet, I suspect, would say that they were overcome by pity or terror or,
for that matter, felt *catharsis*. If the introduction to the Drama section of
The Riverside Anthology has done its work, some students will be quick to
point out that the drama held a place in Aristotle's culture that it may
not hold in ours, and so might be expected to evoke different emotions;
if, for example, we do not accept the premise that some form of
retributive justice awaits evil men and women, then the appearance of
the Furies onstage may strike us not as affirmation of a world-view in
which the supernatural was active in human affairs, but as a laughably
quaint and even optimistic view of the nature of things. So the question
becomes not *do* we feel pity and terror during our reading or hearing of
Death of a Salesman, but *ought* we feel pity and terror during the play?
What emotions does it evoke in us?

To return to the very first question, it might be useful to remind your
students that Aristotle is almost entirely descriptive in his *Poetics* and
very rarely prescriptive. It might be important as well to emphasize that
when Aristotle wrote about tragedy he was treating an art form with a
"tradition" in a sense hard for us to understand; Greek tragedy, for reasons social as well as aesthetic, was expected to adhere to what would be
by modern estimation a very rigid pattern. Miller inherited quite
another form. In short, the case could be made (and Miller makes one
like it in "Tragedy and the Common Man") that we should no more
expect *Death of a Salesman* to deal with the fall of a great man in order to
achieve the status of tragedy than we should expect *Hamlet* to rely on a
chorus.

Finally, then, we must examine Miller on his own terms and *Death
of a Salesman* on its own terms, and even this is tricky business. Miller
says in "Tragedy and the Common Man" that

> the possibility of victory must be there in tragedy. Where pathos
> rules, where pathos is finally derived, a character has fought a
> battle he could not possibly have won. The pathetic is achieved
> when the protagonist is, by virtue of his witlessness, his
> insensitivity, or the very air he gives off, incapable of grappling
> with a much superior force.

Most students will be eager to forgive Miller for not following the Aristotelian formula. Some, however, will maintain that Willy Loman has fought a battle he could not possibly have won, and will not forgive Miller for violating his own principle. For those students, *Death of a Salesman* is likely to achieve only the pathetic—if Miller is correct in his definition of the pathetic and his description of its effect—and evoke only a "down in the mouth" feeling.

QUESTIONS:

1. Is Willy Loman's story pathetic or tragic? If you find Willy pathetic, does this weaken the force of the play?

These questions alone will probably provide enough fuel to drive a class for at least an hour. I don't think I could resist (and I haven't, ever) reading Miller's definition (see above) of the pathetic. I've found that most students claim that that definition fits Willy snugly; he does not, they claim, have a prayer against the forces that crush him, and his end arouses only pathos. Other students claim that Willy, because of his delusions, is solely responsible for his own fate and struggles against himself, rather than an invulnerable and impersonal antagonist—that argument is often refuted by students who assert that the opening stage directions let us know clearly that Willy is menaced by forces not of his creation. Some even go so far as to say that if Willy's family receives the twenty thousand dollars, then he has "won," and Happy is correct when he says, "Willy Loman did not die in vain"; their opponents often maintain that to hold that opinion is to hold the same notion of the significance of money as Happy and Willy.

Whether the play's force is diluted by Miller's apparent foray into the pathetic is a question that may not be answerable. I would, oddly enough, be tempted to apply Aristotle's notion of pity and terror as the natural emotional products of tragedy to *Death of a Salesman*. If I read Aristotle correctly, he claims that we feel pity and terror because, as social and self-interested creatures, we evaluate the tragic hero's condition in terms of our own experience and shudder in sympathy. And we do, I think, see enough of ourselves in Willy Loman so that our sympathies become attached to him. We may even feel pity and terror, for if Willy has no chance of victory and is thus in Miller's terms pathetic, then, by definition, the pathetic arouses pity in us. It would be difficult for late-twentieth-century Americans not to feel terror when contemplating the effects that the forces that threaten and then destroy Willy Loman might have upon us. The play, then, may evoke the sentiments Aristotle claims for tragedy without observing the form that Aristotle may have insisted upon.

2. What major theme or themes in the play are emphasized through the setting provided on the first page?

The opening description may be a real lever into the play. Willy seems throughout to be dwarfed and trapped by forces much too large for him to contend with. His small house, with the "air of the dream" about it, is surrounded by threatening and "towering, angular shapes"—the world outside Willy's castle, where the world of commerce awaits the Salesman. The house, "small, fragile-seeming," is surrounded by "a solid vault of apartment houses." The adjectives say it all; we are given to understand that Willy's home is to be poor shelter against that outside world.

Miller often represents Willy's struggle against the forces represented by apartment complexes and urban sprawl as a struggle between what we might call (inelegantly) organic and inorganic principles. By this I mean that Willy's home seems to be a place where one could plant vegetables, grow daffodils and wisteria, and string a hammock between elm trees. We learn later in the play that the construction of the apartments has resulted in the destruction of those two elm trees—Chekhov has taught us about the significance of cutting down trees—and Linda is forced to remind Willy that their land will no longer support a vegetable garden. As Willy says,

> The street is lined with cars. There's not a breath of fresh air in the neighborhood. The grass don't grow any more, you can't raise a carrot in the back yard. They should've had a law against apartment houses. Remember those two beautiful elm trees out there? When I and Biff hung the swing between them?
>
> (p. 73)

We recognize Willy's bond to this organic principle whenever he and Ben talk about their father; Miller tells us that the flute music tells of "grass and trees and the horizon," of a place where carpentry and other kinds of manual labor are valued as evidence of self-reliance, a virtue Willy cannot, literally, afford. When we hear Willy's and Ben's reminiscences about how their family moved the plains in a wagon, we are reminded of a vision of the American dream entirely different from the version of that dream represented by the angular shapes and angry orange glow. Miller's choice of grass, trees, and horizon is not arbitrary or merely for poetic effect; we are shown in the first three minutes of the play that the inorganic is encroaching to the extent that the grass will not grow, that the trees have been cut down and that the horizon can no longer be seen.

3. Can we say that Willy comes to any self-knowledge at the end of the play?

Almost certainly not. He goes to his death deluded still by the notion that money—the twenty-thousand-dollar insurance benefit—will make Biff a success. When Biff thinks he has forced Willy to abandon his "phony dream" and runs upstairs, he has exhumed that dream instead. Willy, mistaking Biff's grief for submission to his (Willy's) hopes for him, delivers the line that proves to us that the "phony dream" is intact and indestructible: "That boy—that boy is going to be magnificent!." Willy, certain now of Biff's filial love, is easy prey for Ben's (perhaps, if we take Ben to be merely a creation of Willy's mind, Willy's own) call to suicide, to "fetch the diamond out."

Some students may argue that Miller makes a mistake in this play that Shakespeare avoids in *King Lear*. He has Willy die when he is mad. Lear understands his own folly and that he is not "ague-proof" by the end of that play; one could argue that such an understanding is impossible when one is raving on a moor. We might say that Willy, under the influence of his own delusions (Ben), rushes off to die without realizing, as Biff says in the Requiem, that "he never knew who he was."

4. What does money mean to Willy Loman?

It is a truism—and thus true—to say that money is for Willy Loman a symbol of independence, of greatness of spirit, of, well, magnificence. Though money is a sort of Grail for Willy, Miller has not made the mistake of giving us in the Salesman a monster of acquisitiveness—in that regard, Willy Loman is closer to Jay Gatsby than to Shylock.

Money has a talismanic power in this play. If you don't have it (and Willy doesn't), then it is a constant reminder of your impotence in staving off a world that demands it from you. When Linda catalogues their debts—they must make payments on the washing machine, the vacuum cleaner, the roof, the carburetor, the house—and reminds him of their financial condition, Willy is driven almost to despair. It is no coincidence that Linda, at the end of the play, seems to feel that one of Willy's triumphs is the paying-off of their mortgage after twenty-five years.

Money, too, is at the center of Willy's dream of success. But there are two kinds of success. Being "well-liked" is the key to having "contacts," which results in the sort of prestige and power held by Dave Singleman, whose example proves to Willy that "selling [was] the greatest career a man could want." But relying on personal magnetism and building a good territory is one thing; being fabulously and independently wealthy through a kind of courage and self-reliance is quite another and more romantic thing. In his less lucid moments Willy's idol is his brother Ben, who claims, "when I was seventeen I walked into the jungle, and when I was twenty-one I walked out . . . And by God I was rich." For Willy, Ben and American near-mythological figures like J.P. Morgan, Edison, and B. F. Goodrich represent the ability to wrest wealth from whatever the force is that withholds it from the rest of us. They are the keepers of the mystery that Willy seeks to understand when he meets up with Bernard, who also has, according to Willy, penetrated the secret:

Willy, (after a pause): I'm—I'm overjoyed to see how you made the grade, Bernard, overjoyed. It's an encouraging thing to see a young man really—really—Looks very good for Biff—very—(He breaks off, then): Bernard—(He is so full of emotion, he breaks off again.)

Bernard: What is it, Willy?

Willy, (small and alone): What's—what's the secret?

Bernard: What secret?

Willy: How—how did you?

At the end, Willy's only hope of learning that secret is to commit suicide; his dream of success is represented here not by sales calls, or being well-liked or magnificent, but by a more palpable symbol:

Ben: It's called a cowardly thing, William.

Willy: Why? Does it take more guts to stand here the rest of my life ringing up a zero?

Ben, (yielding): That's a point, William . . . And twenty thousand—that *is* something one can feel with the hand, it is there.

Willy, (now assured, with rising power): Oh, Ben, that's the whole beauty of it! I see it like a diamond, shining in the dark, hard and rough, that I can pick up and touch in my hand. Not like—like an appointment!

5. Why do you think Miller employed the Requiem?

Guessing authorial intention is always a risky business, but the following suppositions may be useful:

a.) All the major conflicts of the play are presented, if not resolved. We are reminded by Biff that Willy was never happier than when he worked away from the grind that killed him—the organic vs. inorganic conflict. We are also reminded by Biff that Willy's dream of success was unrealistic and destructive, and that Willy died to fulfill that dream without knowing better: "He had the wrong dreams. All, all wrong . . . Charley, the man didn't know who he was."

b.) Biff and Happy are revealed as they are likely to remain. Biff has withstood the moment of recognition that we expect of tragic heroes: "I know who I am, kid." Happy, on the other hand, demonstrates that he has bought into his father's notion of success completely and is likely to keep buying:

I'm not licked that easily. I'm staying right in this city, and I'm gonna beat this racket! . . . All right, boy. I'm gonna show you and everybody else that Willy Loman did not die in vain. He had a good dream. It's the only dream you can have—to come out number-one man. He fought it out here, and this is where I'm gonna win it for him.

c.) Charley delivers Miller's manifesto dedicated to elevating the modern and common man to heroic status. The salesman, we and Biff are told, runs greater risks than we know and dreams dreams greater than we suspect, and is noble because he does. He rides "on a smile and a shoeshine," and "is got to dream, boy. It comes with the territory." Miller forces us to identify with Willy/Modern Everyman by making the edge of the apron of the stage the edge of Willy's grave (note where Linda places the flowers and in what direction the mourners face), thus putting us in the position of the Salesman.

d.) Despite Willy's grandiose vision of his own funeral, none of his friends on the road come. Unlike Dave Singleman, who died "the death of a salesman" with hundreds of mourners, Willy's death attracts only his immediate family and his next-door neighbors. Willy, ironically, turns out to be anything but "well-liked," and Miller demonstrates one last time how blurred Willy's view of himself was.

e.) Miller refuses to let us know whether the insurance company pays off or not. In fact, he teases us with a masterful ambiguity by allowing Linda to let us know that she has paid off the mortgage but does not tell us just how she managed it.

—W.R.S.

Harold Pinter
The Dumb Waiter

The Dumb Waiter demonstrates why Pinter's plays have been called "comedies of menace." The play is both wildly funny and terribly frightening. When we can manage to keep a safe distance from the characters by persuading ourselves that they are merely actors on stage, we can laugh uproariously at their predicaments. But when we recognize the universality of their absurd situation, when we remember that all of us exist in a violent and incomprehensible world, our laughter is silenced. As Pinter observed of another of his plays, "[It] is funny, up to a point. Beyond that point it ceases to be funny, and it was because of that point that I wrote it."

In this one-act play two comical yet menacing hired guns, Gus and Ben, wait in a basement room in a deserted building for their next victim. They don't know who their victim will be or why the organization that employs them wants this person killed. They know only that the phone will ring, their employer Wilson will tell them it's time, they will get their guns ready, and they will shoot the first person who walks through the door into their room. It is obvious that Gus and Ben have performed this humdrum task many times before.

But on this occasion something unusual occurs. Suddenly a dumb waiter at the back of the room descends with a clatter and a bang. When the two men peer into the box, they discover a written order: "Two braised steak and chips. Two sago puddings. Two teas without sugar." The men frantically attempt to fill the mysterious order, sending up all the food they have with them—biscuits, a bar of chocolate, a half pint of milk, a packet of tea, one Eccles cake, and some crisps. The powers above are not appeased. The dumb waiter comes back down, bearing orders for complicated Greek and Chinese dishes. The men find a speaking-tube, call upstairs, and explain that they have no more food to send. An unidentified person at the other end of the line complains that the cake was stale, the chocolate melted, the milk sour, and the biscuits moldy. The conversation ends, and Ben and Gus continue their wait. When Gus goes into the kitchen for a drink, Ben hears the whistle of the speaking tube, listens, and is told that the victim "will be coming in straight away." The outer door opens, and Gus, "stripped of jacket, waistcoat, tie, holster, and revolver" stumbles in. Gus is the intended victim.

QUESTIONS

1. How is this play typical of absurdist drama?

For a brief description of absurdist drama and a list of characteristics of such plays, see question 2 of the comment on Beckett.

If you give your students a list of the characteristics of absurdist drama, they will discover that this play can't be fitted neatly into the pigeonhole labeled Theater of the Absurd. The setting is realistic—a basement room somewhere in England; the two characters, hired killers, are as believable as most characters on television crime series; the play does have a plot complete with rising action, suspense, and a climax; the dialogue (though often pointless) is firmly rooted in real speech; and there are no deliberate attempts to remind the audience that the play is a play. Nevertheless, the play is absurdist in that it presents the view that life is nothing more than a series of meaningless acts performed by bewildered actors: Gus and Ben, two men operating in a dark and threatening world, suddenly receive mysterious orders to perform impossible tasks. For no apparent reason, they desperately try to comply but, of course, fail. Minutes later, the gunmen discover that Gus has just been given a new role in this drama; inexplicably he has been recast as victim.

2. How does this play reflect the view of dominance and subservience Pinter articulates in the Counterpoint?

In the Counterpoint Pinter explains his short story "The Examination": "That short story dealt very explicitly with two people in one room having a battle of an unspecified nature, in which the question was who was dominant at what point and how they were going to be dominant and what tools they would use to achieve dominance and how they would try to undermine the other person's dominance." That description is equally appropriate for *The Dumb Waiter*. Ben, "the senior partner here," is the dominant character during most of the play. He tells Gus to make tea, he orders Gus to try to catch the person who slipped matches under the door, he forces Gus to send his snack food up in the dumb waiter, and he gives Gus his instructions for the murder.

But Gus does not accept subservience easily. In one of the major confrontations between the two men, Gus corrects Ben's usage:

Ben: Go and light it.
Gus: Light what?
Ben: The kettle.
Gus: You mean the gas.
Ben: Who does?
Gus: You do.

This skirmish over an apparently inconsequential question quickly escalates into a major battle over dominance. Gus stands his ground for some time, arguing the logic of his position. Only after Ben grabs him around the throat with both hands does Gus concede defeat. Taking Ben's hands from his throat, Gus mutters, "All right, all right."

Gus does not openly challenge Ben again, but he continues to question his authority in more subtle ways. At one point, for example, Gus sits on Ben's bed. Ben asks, "What are you sitting on my bed for?" Gus, who does not answer Ben's question, remains on Ben's bed, and Ben does not force him to move. Later, when Ben asks Gus what he has in his bag, Gus fails to mention the Eccles cake and the crisps. Ben finds the food, and his angry response shows that he understands the significance of such insubordination:

Ben (hitting him on the shoulder): You're playing a dirty game, my lad!

Gus's most effective tool for subtly undermining Ben's authority may be his habit of asking questions. It might seem that Gus is recognizing Ben's dominance when he turns to him for answers. On one level that may be true. But at the same time Gus as interrogator is assuming command, in effect ordering Ben to supply him with information. Sometimes his questions are easy to answer: "Have you noticed the time it takes the tank to fill?" "What town are we in?" At other times he raises questions Ben will not or cannot answer: "Why did you stop the car this morning, in the middle of the road?" "Who clears up after we've gone?" "If [the people who ran this place] moved out, who's got it now?" "What's going on here?" Ben is undeniably threatened by those questions. In one scene Gus becomes more and more agitated, bombarding Ben with questions Ben doesn't want to think about: "What's he doing all this for? What's the idea? What's he playing these games for?" To halt the onslaught of questions and regain dominance, Ben again resorts to violence:

Ben seizes the tube and flings Gus away. He follows Gus and slaps him hard, back-handed, across the chest.

Ben: Stop it! You maniac!

Throughout the play Gus, who is inquisitive and perhaps more intelligent than Ben, attempts to use his mind to achieve dominance. Ben, who never wins a battle of wits, always regains control through violence or the threat of violence. Given that pattern, we have little doubt about who will dominate their final encounter.

3. How do Gus and Ben differ from our stereotype of hired killers? What effect does that difference have on the audience?

This play would be far less unnerving if we could persuade ourselves that Gus and Ben are aberrations—either textbook examples of abnormal psychological development such as "The Misfit" we meet in Flannery O'Connor's "A Good Man Is Hard to Find" or thoroughly evil or demonic figures like Arnold Friend in Joyce Carol Oates' "Where Are You Going, Where Have You Been?" We finish those stories frightened by the possibility that we might encounter such people but convinced that we would recognize them anywhere. In contrast, we leave *The Dumb Waiter* knowing that if we met Gus or Ben on the street we would never suspect them of being professional killers.

Throughout the play Pinter insists that, except for their occupation, Ben and Gus are ordinary people, two men on a routine business trip. Gus hopes that this "won't be a long job"; Ben reads the newspaper to pass the time. In a scene reenacted countless times in countless hotel rooms across the country, Gus complains about their working conditions, and Ben reminds him of their job benefits:

Gus: I like to get a look at the scenery. You never get a chance in this job.

Ben: You get your holidays, don't you?

Gus: Only a fortnight.

Ben: (lowering the paper) You kill me. Anyone would think you're working every day. How often do we do a job? Once a week? What are you complaining about?

Gus: Yes, but we've got to be on tap though, haven't we? You can't move out of the house in case a call comes.

A world in which seemingly ordinary people casually discuss holidays, newspaper articles, crockery patterns, and football games while they wait to murder an unidentified victim is menacing indeed.

4. Are Gus and Ben realistic characters?

The point of this question is to make your students question what we mean by the term "realistic." Ordinarily, we label a character realistic or believable when the dramatist reveals the character's background and motives, and that character then acts in a way that is consistent with the information we have been given. In Ibsen's *Hedda Gabler*, for example, we know that Hedda has an overwhelming desire to influence the destiny of another person, and we are not surprised when she decides to gain control over Lovborg's life by burning the manuscript of his book. If that is what we mean by realistic, then neither Ben nor Gus qualifies. We know almost nothing about the lives they lead outside the basement room, and Pinter never gives us a clue about why they became professional killers.

But Pinter would argue that his decision not to give us background information about his characters makes them more, not less, realistic. In fact, he claims that the playwright who forces his characters to explain themselves to the audience is engaged in a form of cheating. As Pinter explained to an interviewer, we know as much about the characters in his plays as we know about the people we meet outside the theater:

> When the curtain goes up on one of my plays, you are faced with a situation, a particular situation, two people sitting in a room, which hasn't happened before, and is just happening at that moment, and we know no more about them than I know about you, sitting at this table. The world is full of surprises. A door can open at any moment and someone will come in. We'd love to know who it is, we'd love to know exactly what he has on his mind, but how often do we know what someone has on his mind or who this somebody is, and what goes to make him what he is, and what his relationship is to others?

For a parody of the kind of exposition Pinter calls cheating, you can direct your students to the conversation between Simon Gascoyne and Mrs. Drudge (pp. 162-169 of *The Real Inspector Hound*, by Tom Stoppard), two characters who explain themselves at length.

5. What does Pinter achieve with his use of the dumb waiter?

Pinter's use of this stage prop is ingenious. First, and most obviously, the dumb waiter sets the plot in motion by introducing a conflict. When the play opens, the situation is basically static. Although Ben and Gus periodically tussle over power, the status quo remains unchanged. Then the dumb waiter begins to deliver orders, and Ben and Gus scurry about, scrounging up food. For the rest of the play they attempt to propitiate the powers above.

The dumb waiter is also a great comic device. After its initial descent, the dumb waiter continues to rise and fall erratically. Sometimes it moves a bit, then pauses, apparently teasing Ben and Gus, who are eyeing it nervously. Each time it comes crashing down, the two men start with alarm, and the audience laughs. The orders delivered by the dumb waiter are also hilarious, the first because it is so unanticipated, the second and third because they are so ridiculously impossible.

Finally, the dumb waiter, the ultimate deus ex machina, allows Pinter to ask a serious philosophical question in the most absurd manner possible: Who is upstairs sending messages, and what do those messages mean? At first the orders delivered by the dumb waiter seem to indicate that the person upstairs is not aware of Ben's and Gus's limitations and simply doesn't realize that they can't make the cup of tea he orders because they have no money for gas. If Gus and Ben are meant to represent the universal human condition, it's far from encouraging to think that the power that controls us expects performance far beyond our capability. The other possibility feared by Gus and supported by the play's ending is even worse. Gus suspects that the person upstairs is merely playing games with them, that he understands that his demands are impossible but enjoys tormenting the men. It is a view as bleak as that offered in Mark Twain's "Mysterious Stranger."

—M.R.D.

Athol Fugard
"Master Harold"...and the Boys

This play, by South African Athol Fugard, is a *Bildungsroman* with a twist. In the play seventeen-year-old Hally becomes a white "man" in South Africa, a country where apartheid is more than a set of laws. Because Hally's alcoholic father is an embarrassment to Hally, Hally has turned to Sam for the father-son relationship he longs for. Sam, a black man of forty who works in the tea room operated by Hally's mother, has become the man Hally can go to whenever he needs help. It was Sam who went with the humiliated little boy to carry home Hally's father after he passed out drunk on the floor of the Central Hotel Bar, Sam who then made Hally a kite so that he "could look up, be proud of something," and Sam who tried to teach Hally "what being a man means."

The play is set in the tea room, and the only people onstage are Hally, Sam, and Willie, another black man who works there. The conflict arises when Hally talks with his mother on the telephone and learns that his father, who has been hospitalized, is coming home. When he hangs up, Hally is furious because "the peace and quiet" he and his mother have enjoyed will soon be ended. He vents his anger by yelling insults about his father. Sam sternly rebukes him: "No, Hally, you mustn't do it. Take back those words and ask for forgiveness! It's a terrible sin for a son to mock his father with jokes like that." Hally goes "rigid with shame" but then "his shame turns to rage at Sam," and he lashes out with the weapons his society has provided. He viciously reminds Sam that he "is only a servant," requests that Sam address him as "Master Harold" rather than Hally, and repeats an ugly racial joke that is apparently one of his father's favorites. When all that fails to convince Sam of Hally's innate superiority, Hally spits in Sam's face. It is a moment that brings audible gasps from the audience. Hally has indeed become a "man" in white South Africa.

This play will give your students an opportunity to see how an incident from a dramatist's life can be reshaped through art. In the Counterpoint to this story, an entry from one of Fugard's notebooks, Fugard describes the event in his own life that inspired this play. One day ten-year-old Fugard quarreled with Sam, a black man he describes as "the most significant—the only—friend of [his] boyhood years." A few minutes later, Fugard was biking home and saw Sam walking ahead of him. Fugard writes, "[A]s I rode up behind him I called his name, he turned in mid-stride to look back and, as I cycled past, I spat in his face. Don't suppose I will ever deal with the shame that overwhelmed me the second after I had done it." Your students will be relieved to learn that in real life Fugard and Sam made up the next day and remained lifelong friends.

QUESTIONS

1. Why does Sam wait until after Hally spits in his face to explain why Sam couldn't stay with Hally on the hill to fly the kite?

When Hally first recalls the day of the kite, he remembers that Sam tied the kite to a bench so Hally could sit and watch it, and then Sam went away. Hally remarks, "I wanted you to stay, you know. I was a little scared of having to look after it by myself." Sam quietly responds, "I had work to do, Hally." Only after Hally spits in Sam's face does Sam tell Hally, "I couldn't sit down there and stay with you. It was a 'Whites Only' bench. You were too young, too excited to notice then. But not anymore. If you're not careful . . . Master Harold . . . you're going to be sitting there by yourself for a long time to come, and there won't be a kite in the sky."

Sam, a loving father, had protected Hally from the truth for as long as possible. Sam knew that while Hally was a child, he would not be required to play the role of white racist. The child Hally was free to spend happy afternoons in Sam's room because friendships among white children and blacks are socially acceptable in South Africa. Early in the play, however, Fugard hints that those treasured days of innocence have already ended. Hally, without understanding the full significance of his words, says, "I almost wish we were still in that little room....It's just that life felt the right size in there...not too big and not too small. Wasn't so hard to work up a bit of courage. It's got so bloody complicated since then." Sam knew that once Hally became an adult, he would have to make hard choices, that Master Harold cannot have an adult friendship with a black man unless he is willing to reject the role his society has assigned him. Like a father reluctant to tell his child that Santa is a myth, Sam had tried to prolong Hally's innocence. After Hally spits in his face, however, Sam knows that Hally's childhood is behind him. It is time for Hally to face the truth.

2. What is the significance of the dance scenes in the play?

When your students are reading rather than watching the play, they may fail to realize how often the stage directions call for dancing. You may want to direct their attention to those passages and point out that Fugard, who is an actor and director as well as a playwright, is a master of stagecraft. Although readers often find the first few pages of the play slow moving, most viewers are thoroughly entertained by the sensational dancing on stage. In addition, the dance scenes lend visual support to Sam's theory that dance is a symbol of life as it should be lived.

3. Can this play or any other work of art bring about social change?

In the play Sam argues that art can and should improve the world, not by criticizing society but by providing us with an ideal that we will strive to attain. For Sam, dance is the art that best symbolizes life as it should be lived. When Sam describes the New Brighton ballroom dance contest, he tells Hally that "[t]o be one of those finalists on that dance floor is like...like being in a dream about a world in which accidents don't happen." Hally questions the value of the symbol, but Sam valiantly defends it.

> Hally: But is that the best we can do, Sam...watch six finalists dreaming about the way it should be?
>
> Sam: I don't know. But it starts with that. Without the dream we won't know what we're going for. And anyway I reckon there are a few people who have got past just dreaming about it and are trying for something real. Remember that thing we read once in the paper about the Mahatma Gandhi? Going without food to stop those riots in India?

Fugard is less certain that art can change society. He writes,

> The most my plays do is to sustain a measure of hope and faith in the dignity of people—in the face of a system that denies it. As to whether they do any good, I am totally without an answer...Sometimes I'm convinced that I'm just preaching to the converted. Theater can be a civilizing influence, but it is a second-degree experience. People can change, but it takes a first-degree experience to bring it about.

Ultimately, the question of how art affects society is unanswerable; it is, nonetheless, a question every student should ponder. Because there is no way to objectively measure the impact of art on society, we can't know whether the world was improved by Swift's *A Modest Proposal*, Harriet Beecher Stowe's *Uncle Tom's Cabin*, or Picasso's *Guernica*. But most of us can name at least one work of art that presented us with an image, an idea, or a vision that changed our lives, and like Sam, we choose to believe "[i]t starts with that."

4. What is the value of this play or any other work of art if it does not
succeed in improving society?

I ask this question so students won't be left with the impression that
art is valuable only to the extent that it brings about social change. If that
were true, how could we explain why we cherish Shakespeare's sonnets,
Gershwin's *Rhapsody in Blue,* or Leonardo's Mona Lisa? Even art that is
intended to improve society has a value independent of that goal: Few of
the modern readers who enjoy Dickens' *Bleak House* judge that novel by
its impact on the reformation of Chancery Court. Neither should the
value of this play be assessed by its effect on South Africa's policy of
apartheid.

Even Sam, our proponent of art as tool for social reform, would not
suggest that art has no value apart from its success in improving society.
Whether dance changes the world or not, Sam will continue to dance
because he recognizes (and the play demonstrates) that art can make the
life of the individual better even in an unreformed society. The character
in the play whose life is clearly bettered by art is Willie. At the
beginning of the play we learn that Willie hits his dance partner Hilda
"every time she makes a mistake in the waltz." But Sam's "dancing
lessons" transform Willie's approach to dance and to life. At the end of
the play Willie describes the transformation:

> Willie: I think about it and you right. Tonight I find Hilda and
> say sorry. And make promise I won't beat her no more. You hear
> me, Boet Sam?
>
> Sam: I hear you, Willie.
>
> Willie: And when we practice I relax and romance with her from
> beginning to end. Non-stop! You watch! Two weeks' time: "First
> prize for promising newcomers:
> Mr. Willie Malapo and Miss Hilda Samuels."

Art changes Willie's life, not by changing society, but by creating a
separate and more beautiful world where he can see himself in a different role, a role that requires both personal dignity and responsibility.

5. Is the ending of the play optimistic or pessimistic?

Fugard might have ended the play with Hally walking out of the tea
room. Instead, the curtain closes with Sarah Vaughan singing "Little
man, you've had a busy day" while Sam and Willie dance together

around the room. Because that final visual image is deliberately ambiguous, your students will disagree about whether it is a symbol of hope or of despair. Viewers who believe that Hally has made an irrevocable decision to pattern himself after the white racist father he despises see the dance as nothing more than Sam's and Willie's attempt to escape, at least momentarily, from the bitterness of reality. Other viewers are optimistic that Hally will eventually decide "to stand up and walk away from [the 'Whites Only' bench]." They note that when Sam asks, "So what do we do? Hope for better weather tomorrow?" Hally doesn't say, "No." He says, "I don't know." Those who are encouraged both by Hally's reluctance to abandon all hope for a better tomorrow and by Sam's example of how a man should behave see the final dance as an inspirational vision of the world as it may yet become, a place where people move with beauty and grace and don't bump into one another.

—M.R.D.

Wole Soyinka
The Swamp Dwellers

The Swamp Dwellers, one of the earliest plays written by Nigerian playwright, poet and novelist Wole Soyinka, is more accessible to non-African audiences than his later drama. The play was first presented at the Student Movement House, London, in 1958 as an entry for the University of London Drama festival. A year later its highly successful performance at the Arts Theater in Ibadan, Nigeria, launched Soyinka's dramatic career in his homeland.

The Swamp Dwellers dramatizes a conflict central to many of Soyinka's works—the conflict between past and future, between rural and urban, between traditional beliefs in tribal gods and modern faith in technology. Soyinka, who was born of the Yoruba-speaking peoples of Western Nigeria in 1934, has witnessed this conflict first hand. After attending the University College in Ibadan in Nigeria, he went on to the School of English at Leeds University where he studied classical and modern European drama and took an honors degree in English in 1957. As a student he had not yet begun to write for the stage, but he was an avid theatergoer. After he received his degree, Soyinka began writing his own plays and working for the Royal Court theater in London as a script-reader, a position that enabled him to observe the rehearsals and productions of plays by dramatists such as Samuel Beckett. Soon after *The Swamp Dwellers* opened in Nigeria, Soyinka received a research fellowship in African traditional drama. In 1960 he returned to Nigeria and traveled widely, observing and recording the ceremonial songs, dances and masquerades of his country. With his later plays, such a *A Dance of the Forest,* Soyinka develops a "total theater" of West Africa, a theater that connects Africa and European cultures by combining a dramatic text with music, dance, masquerade, and mime.

The Swamp Dwellers is a one-act play about the disintegration of a rural community whose young people reject the hardships of life in the swamp and flee to the city where their belief in tribal gods and their ties to their families are soon destroyed. The setting is a hut on stilts, the home of Alu and Makuri, an old couple who have lived in the swamp all their lives. When the play opens they are quarreling and waiting anxiously for the return of their son, a young man who has come home after eight months in the city only to discover that the swamp has flooded and destroyed his crops. During the play three visitors arrive at the home: a blind Beggar who tells Alu and Makuri about the drought and locust in the North; Kadiye, Servant and Priest of the Serpent of the Swamp, who announces that the rains and flooding have stopped; and their son, Igwezu, who reveals how he has been betrayed by his twin brother in the city and by the Serpent here in the swamp. Each visitor further illuminates the tensions that threaten to devastate the community and this family.

QUESTIONS

1. How do Makuri's and Alu's attitudes toward the swamp and toward the city differ?

Makuri and Alu represent radically different positions. Makuri is a traditionalist who faithfully worships the Serpent of the swamp. For Makuri, the Serpent, though far from benevolent, is a known danger, a familiar adversary who can be propitiated by prayers and offerings. Makuri seems content with this arrangement. He tells the Beggar, "There are little bits of land here and there where a man can sow enough to keep his family, and even take to the market." Makuri blames all of life's problems on the city which has made young people dissatisfied with the old ways. He complains that "[t]his younger generation is...soft," and he tells Alu, "The city ruins them. What do they seek there except money?" He is convinced that the past was better than the present: "Those were the days . . . those days were really good. Even when times were harsh and the swamp overran the land, we were able to laugh with the Serpent . . . but these young people . . . They are no sooner born than they want to get out of the village as if it carried a plague.

Alu, who also worships the Serpent, is not persuaded that the old ways are best. For her the swamp is a dark and dangerous place. She worries about Igwezu "missing his foothold and vanishing without a cry, without a chance for anyone to save him." She insists that her other son "Awuchike was drowned" and that Gonushi's son, who left his wife and children without a word, was also lost in the swamp: "It was the swamp . . . He went the same way as my son . . .". Initially, at least, Alu is willing to believe that the young people may be right and that a city life may be preferable to a precarious existence in the swamp. Apparently, her optimistic view of city life is based on little more than a fond hope that things must be better elsewhere. Nothing in the play suggests that she has ever visited a city herself. Alu's sympathy for the younger generation is evident in several of her conversations with Makuri: When Makuri makes light of Igwezu's crop loss by noting, "We've had worse years before this" (p. 7), Alu angrily replies, "But you haven't journeyed three days only to be cheated of your crops" (p. 7). At another time Makuri says of the young men, "I bet none of them has ever taken his woman into the swamps," and Alu responds, "They have more sense than that." (p. 6).

Your students may notice that although the setting is Nigeria, the bickering between an advocate of traditional ways and a proponent of change has a familiar ring. The problem that confronts Makuri and Alu is universal.

By the end of the play the worst fears of both Makuri and Alu have been realized: Awuchike has been destroyed by the city and Igwezu by the swamp. In the conflict between the old ways and the new, fatalities run high.

2. What is the significance of the chanting and drumming in the play?

The Beggar's chanting is not explained in the play. The drumming that accompanies the entrances and exits of Kadiye, the Servant and Priest of the Serpent of the Swamp, is apparently a ritual intended either to praise or to appease the Serpent. The real purpose of the question is to draw your students' attention to these somewhat unorthodox elements. You might want to mention that Soyinka's later plays include long segments of ceremonial dance, music, masquerade, and mime and, in that respect, have much in common with Greek plays such as *Antigone*. As Aristotle reminds us, spectacle—song and dance—is a major element of traditional drama.

3. How do you think Soyinka would have us understand the Serpent?

The characters in the play offer different understandings of the Serpent. Makuri believes the Serpent is a powerful god who is easily angered, and Makuri is shocked by the Beggar's suggestion that he might redeem part of the swamp and farm it. He asks incredulously, "You wish to rob the Serpent of the Swamp? You wish to take the food out of his mouth?" Igwezu, who once worshiped the Serpent god and made all the offerings required of believers, has lost his faith. He threatens and mocks Kadiye, the Serpent's priest, and accuses him of exploiting the people. After Kadiye huffs out, Igwezu sadly states his new credo: "I know that the floods can come again. That the swamp will continue to laugh at our endeavors. I know that we can feed the Serpent of the Swamp and kiss Kadiye's feet—but the vapors will still rise and corrupt the tassels of corn." It is not clear whether Igwezu no longer believes in the existence of the Serpent god or whether he refuses to pay tribute to a malevolent and capricious god.

The Beggar, who is a worshiper of Allah, has yet another interpretation of the Serpent. As a polite guest, the Beggar does not challenge the existence or power of the Serpent. He tells Makuri, "I have not come to question your faith." The Beggar does, however, doubt the holiness of Kadiye. He pointedly asks Igwezu, "Does the priest live well?" and "How does the Serpent [meaning the priest] fare in time of death?" It seems that the Beggar thinks of the Serpent as the spirit of the swamp, a natural force with which people can establish a harmonious relationship—without the intervention of a greedy priest. The Beggar tells Igwezu that he wants to know the bounds of his master's kingdom and then asks, "I know that the Serpent has his share, but not who sets the boundaries . . . Is it the priest, or is it the master?" We have no doubt about how the Beggar would answer that question.

Although we don't know how Soyinka expects us to interpret the Serpent, it seems that the dramatist uses the Serpent as a symbol of the evil that exists in the world. The characters then represent classic answers to an age-old question: How should we respond to evil? For Alu, and perhaps for Awuchike, evil is something to be avoided; for Makuri, evil is to be accepted; for Kadiye, it is to be exploited for personal gain; and for the Beggar, it is to be combatted.

4. What is the significance of the blind Beggar?

The Beggar is both a human and a symbolic figure who adds to our understanding of the play in a number of ways. As a realistic character, he serves to remind the other characters and the audience that misfortune is not confined to the swamp—that in other parts of the world fly sickness causes children to go blind, drought destroys vegetation and hope, and crops prosper only to provide feasts for locusts.

At the same time the Beggar adds a mythic dimension to an otherwise realistic play. Like the blind prophet Teiresias in *Antigone,* the beggar sees without eyes. He asks if Kadiye is fat and explains, "When he spoke, I detected a certain bulk in his voice." He senses the end of the rains: "Yes, I could feel the air growing lighter, and the clouds clearing over my head. I think the worst of your season is over" (p. 15). And he finds his way safely through the perilous swamp. His vision in those instances makes us hope that he is correct when he predicts that he "can make the land yield in [his] hands like an obedient child" (p. 18).

Perhaps the Beggar is meant to show us that—with courage, dignity, wisdom, and faith—a person can prevail even in a hostile universe. Here is a man whose sufferings rival Job's. At least twice in his life he has been the victim of a cosmic joke. As a child he lost his sight and happily concluded that he had died and gone to paradise:

> Those few moments were the happiest in my life. Any moment, I thought, and my eyes would be opened to the wonders around me. I heard familiar voices, and I rejoiced, because I thought they were dead also, and were in paradise with me . . . And then slowly, the truth came to me, and I knew that I was living—but blind.

After he became an adult, the rains came to his drought-stricken country, and the land that "had lain barren for generations" blossomed with life and hope. "But," he relates, "it turned out to have been an act of spite. The feast was meant not for us,—but for locusts." Either incident— the blindness or the locusts——would have driven most people to despair or rage. Not the Beggar. He maintains his faith in Allah and in himself, and he goes forth to make a new life. Although "even the least devout lives under the strict injunction of hospitality" toward him (p. 9), the Beggar refuses to accept charity and chooses instead to "work on the soil." He does not, however, set himself the impossible task of farming "dry crumbs of dust." Instead he vows "to tread only where the soil is moist,"and he follows the river until he arrives at the swamp.

The Beggar, the only character on stage when the curtain closes, speaks the final line of the play: "I shall be here to give account." His words are deliberately ambiguous. Is he promising to provide a description of all that has transpired, a financial reckoning, or an explanation of life? We are almost certain that he will do all three.

—M.R.D.

Tom Stoppard
The Real Inspector Hound

The Real Inspector Hound should be a natural in class because it delights and instructs. It delights because the wordplay is adroit, the scenes are busy, and the characters are engaging and familiar. It instructs because it is skillfully self-conscious; Stoppard caricatures the conventions of the genre he is working in and lampoons those who make their livings evaluating plays. *The Real Inspector Hound* is—excuse me—a "meta-who-dunit." Treating this play in class, then, is liable to be most instructive because Stoppard takes the back of the watch off and lets us see the works in action in the same way Beaumont and Fletcher do in *The Knight of the Burning Pestle* or Pirandello does in *Six Characters in Search of an Author.*

QUESTIONS

1. What type of play is Stoppard satirizing in *The Real Inspector Hound?* What are the distinguishing characteristics of these plays?

Almost everyone in your class will surely have seen or read or acted in something like Agatha Christie's *Mousetrap.* Whodunits, "thrillers," as Birdboot calls them, have been as popular on stage this century as almost any other type of drama; *Deathtrap* (which in its own way is as self-conscious about the conventions of the thriller as *The Real Inspector Hound*) was performed on Broadway almost 1800 times—Agatha Christie's *Mousetrap* (one of Stoppard's main targets here) is still running in London.

These plays rely on withholding the identity of the killer until the very end of the drama and an invitation to guess the murderer is implicitly extended to the audience; the characters, of course, make the same attempt in order to avoid becoming the next victim. Corpses and murder weapons are often-used stage properties. The characters are uniformly flat but dynamic to the extent that we almost invariably discover skeletons in their closets. Setting varies; it is not unusual to find the action occurring in a Gothic mansion cut off from the authorities, though drawing rooms and vacation resorts seem to be favorite spots for murder and intrigue as well—all three settings, by the way, are likely to include a butler. Sometimes the murderer is exposed by another character, often an amateur detective; equally often the authorities arrive and poke about until the murderer reveals himself or herself.

At the outset of *The Real Inspector Hound* Moon reads the program—the setting is a theatre-within-a-theatre, appropriate for a play-within-a-play—while Mrs. Drudge obliviously cleans around a corpse on the floor. The setting-within-the-setting is Muldoon Manor, which is surrounded by "old smugglers' paths through the treacherous swamps that surround this strangely inaccessible house." (Stoppard forces the most compressed and ungainly exposition and heavy-handed scene-setting down our throats with Mrs. Drudge's first speech, delivered by way of the time-honored telephone monologue:

> Mrs. Drudge. (Into phone.) Hello, the drawing-room of Lady Muldoon's country residence one morning in early spring? . . . *Hello!*—the draw—Who? Whom did you wish to speak to? I'm afraid there is no one of that name here, this is all very mysterious and I'm sure it's leading up to something, I hope nothing is amiss for we, that is Lady Muldoon and her houseguests, are here cut off from the world, including Magnus, the wheelchair-ridden half-brother of her ladyship's husband Lord Albert Muldoon who ten years ago went out for a walk on the cliffs and was never seen again. Should a stranger enter our midst, which I very much doubt, I will tell him you called. Goodbye.

Stoppard piles parody upon parody when Mrs. Drudge notes that "many visitors have remarked on the topographical quirk in the local strata whereby there are no roads leading from the Manor, though there *are* ways of getting *to* it, weather allowing." One can imagine that a dark and stormy night will soon fall. Stoppard continues to stockpile clichés for us: a radio announces a mad killer on the loose in the neighborhood, Felicity Cunningham is revealed as a woman scorned ("I'll kill you for this, Simon Gascoyne!" the crippled brother, Magnus, inexplicably goes to oil his gun, Cynthia Muldoon is revealed as an adulteress ("If I find that you have been untrue to me—if I find that you have falsely seduced me from my dear husband Albert—I will kill you, Simon Gascoyne!" and we are reminded repeatedly of the loneliness of Muldoon Manor. The body, by the way, remains undiscovered as the first act ends.

Having pinned it, Stoppard refuses to let the whodunit up. In the second act of the play-within-a-play the muddled events reach a crescendo relieved by the dramatic and hilarious appearance of Inspector Hound, who has by superhumanly ridiculous efforts reached Muldoon Manor by crossing the deadly swamp wearing pontoons on his feet. The undiscovered corpse is finally discovered by Hound, and Simon Gascoyne, prime suspect, is killed—as prime suspects almost always are. Hound, Stoppard's version of the plucky and canny detective who brings killers to bay, ends this second act with the melodramatic and tendentious "And now—who killed Simon Gascoyne? And why?"

Students fond of whodunits may complain that Stoppard just doesn't play fair. The play-within-a-play is just awful. I would remind them that Stoppard's purpose (see the Counterpoint) is less to satirize the thriller—an inoffensive and entertaining genre—than it is to play with the conventions of drama itself. The thriller, then, is a sort of innocent bystander, and, in fact, one could argue that Stoppard demonstrates a fondness for the genre he parodies.

2. What does this play have to say about drama criticism and critics?

The Counterpoint is helpful here as well. As Stoppard says, "I was aware that I was parodying critics, but this simply because I had two critics on stage." Once again, this parody is more or less incidental. If the characters in the play-within-a-play spout the chestnuts we expect of a melodramatic whodunit, so too do Moon and Birdboot produce during the first two acts of the-play-within-a-play the kind of lingo we expect to find in newspaper drama reviews.

> Birdboot. (Clears throat.) It is at this point that the play, for me, comes alive. The groundwork has been well and truly laid, and the author has taken the trouble to learn from the masters of the genre. He has created a real situation, and few will doubt his ability to re-solve it with a startling denouement. Certainly that is what it lacks, but it has a beginning, a middle and I have no doubt it will prove to have an end. For this let us give thanks, and a double thanks for a good clean show without a trace of smut . . .

> Moon. If we examine this more closely, and I think close examination is the least tribute that this play deserves, I think we will find that within the austere frame work of what is seen to be on one level a country-house week-end, and what a useful symbol that is, the author has given us—yes, I will go so far—he has given us the human condition—

Both assessments of the play are flat-out wrong—worse yet, they are dishonest. Birdboot praises the play because his latest flame plays a lead-ing role; even poor Aristotle is brought to bear on this play that has a be-ginning, a middle, and "will prove to have an end." Unconscious of his hypocrisy, Birdboot praises the play for containing no smut—and shortly afterwards praises the performance of his mistress. Moon's evaluation is the sort of stuff bad journal articles are filled with; this pitiful thriller cannot bear the weight of his ponderous analysis. His judgment wrecked because of his obsession with his rivals Higgs and Puckeridge, he compares the potboiler on stage to the works—to name a few—of Shakespeare, St. Paul, Sartre, Pirandello, Dante, and then finishes off with Dorothy Sayers (the translator of Dante and author of the Lord Peter Wimsey mystery novels).

The critics, in short, come off poorly in *The Real Inspector Hound*, Birdboot because in his obsession with his dalliance with Cynthia he proves himself to be a hypocrite and a fool, and Moon because his obsession with playing second fiddle to Higgs forces him into mean-spiritedness and self-pity. Their obsessions lead them to be inaccurate and dishonest critics.

3. In the Counterpoint, Stoppard says that he "was after constructing this magic box which unfolded and had insides which unfolded, and trying to make it explode at the end." What do you think Stoppard means by "the magic box"? In what sense does it "explode at the end"?

Most will take "the magic box" to mean the play and the way it turns in upon itself. At the end of the second act of the play-within-a-play, the boundaries that separate the audience composed of Moon and Birdboot and the players dissolve, and the critics become lost in the funhouse. Birdboot takes the stage to answer a phone call that we learn is from his wife and is caught up in the play-within-a-play, which suddenly resumes—but back in Act 1. Birdboot's passion for the actress who plays Cynthia is now transformed, since he has taken the role of Gascoyne, into Simon's love for the *character* Cynthia. Birdboot is drawn into the melodrama completely, and the action becomes hopelessly muddled as a result of his participation. The reprise of the bridge game in the "first" first act is mere chaos, and we feel Birdboot has given over to madness when he begins "making erratic neurotic journeys about the stage." Moon, too, is drawn into the play-within-a-play when Birdboot discovers that the unidentified corpse onstage since the beginning of *The Real Inspector Hound* is Higgs, Moon's rival. The play-within-a-play by now has almost completely folded in upon itself, and the process becomes complete when Birdfoot is shot and killed, Hound and Simon occupy the critics' seats, and Moon adopts the role of Inspector Hound. The critics have now been completely subsumed into the world of the play-within-a-play.

But just when we think that Stoppard has made the rules of the game he is playing with the critics and players clear to us, he changes them by mixing the world of the critics and the players—again. Magnus puts yet more spin on the ball when he announces that Moon, a natural suspect in the murder of his rival Higgs in the world of the critics, is

posing as Inspector Hound—just as the murderer in Agatha Christie's
Mousetrap poses as a policeman. He, Magnus, is the Real Inspector
Hound. Not content with this, Stoppard reveals that Magnus/Inspector
Hound—a character in the-play-within-a-play—is as well Puckeridge,
Moon's fellow-critic and rival.

By this time few dramatic conventions are intact. The play stops, resumes without dropping a stitch in scenes already presented with new
actors in old roles (Birdboot as a character already killed), and
concludes. The critics become the players, the players become the critics,
and then the distinctions between the two become indecipherable. Moon
and Birdboot are overtaken by their obsessions, act them out on stage,
and are killed—hardly the stuff of comedy until one considers the
context. Stoppard has nested and confused fiction and reality to the extent
that neither we nor the players nor the critics can distinguish them.

—W.R.S

Tina Howe
Painting Churches

Tina Howe finds drama in unexpected places. Her play *Museum*
features characters strolling through a museum and commenting on art.
In *The Art of Dining*, a play about a young couple who operate a restaurant
in New Jersey, Howe builds her scenes around the guests who dine at
the restaurant. In an interview for *Contemporary Authors* Howe explained
her penchant for writing about apparently unpromising topics:

> I find enormous pleasure in making playwriting as difficult as pos-
> sible. I go out of my way to look for unlikely settings and situations;
> art museums, restaurants, fitting rooms, places that are basically
> predictable and uneventful. Nothing is more theatrical than putting
> the unexpected on stage. Because the theatre is a palace of dreams,
> the more original the spectacle the better. I'm hopelessly drawn to
> digging out the flamboyant in everyday life.

In *Painting Churches*, a tragicomedy in two acts, Howe again digs out
the flamboyant in everyday life. In the play, a young artist, Mags
Church, goes home to Boston to paint a portrait of her elderly parents,
Fanny and Gardner, who are in the process of moving from their
Beacon Hill mansion to a cottage at Cape Cod. At first Mags'
preconceptions about her parents make it impossible for her to see that
they have changed—that her father, a world-famous poet, has lapsed into
helpless senility and her mother has become his nursemaid. A series of

incidents, some comic, some painful, forces Mags to open her eyes and see her parents clearly, precisely what a portrait painter must do.

QUESTIONS

1. How does the setting change from scene to scene? How do those changes reflect the changes occurring in the lives of the characters?

The entire play is set in the living room of the Church's townhouse on Beacon Hill, but the room's appearance changes from scene to scene as the packing progresses. The stages of physical disorder apparent in the room clearly mirror the changes occurring in the characters. At first the packing and the interactions between Mags and her parents are conducted on a somewhat superficial level, but as the family members sort through their most intimate personal belongings, they also pull out old memories which they re-examine. At the end, some possessions and some ideas have been discarded and others have been repacked.

When the curtain rises, the packing is in its preliminary stages. "Empty packing cartons line the room and all the furniture has been tagged with brightly colored markers." Fanny is still in the easiest phase of moving; she is deciding the relatively trivial question of which valuable but unnecessary silver items to keep and which to sell. Mags is in the preliminary stage of getting to know her subjects/parents. She is so unaware of their financial straits that she can innocently ask, "Why move now?" and then add, "You can't move. I won't let you!"

Two days later, in Scene 2, the disorder has increased dramatically: "Half of the Church household has been dragged into the living room for packing. Overflowing cartons are everywhere. They're filled with pots and pans, dishes and glasses, and the entire contents of two linen closets." Fanny is now sorting through more personal items. She decides to keep the wornout galoshes Gardner wore years earlier when they were sledding on the Common." Mags pulls out an old but still distressing memory of Fanny's embarrassing behavior when she attended Mag's first group show in Soho.

In Scene 3, twenty-four hours later, the room is in utter chaos. "The impact of the impending move has struck with hurricane force. Mags dredges up her most painful memory—that of the crayon-covered radiator—the masterpiece she created at age nine after her parents had sent her away from the dinner table for six months.

At the beginning of Act 2, Scene 1, the room is tidier: "Miracles have been accomplished. Almost all of the Churches' furniture has been moved out, and the cartons of dishes and clothing are gone. All that remains are odds and ends." But the orderliness is both deceptive and

short-lived. Fanny has not yet tackled the most difficult moving task—
Gardner's "God-awful study"—and Mags has not yet faced the truth about
her father's senility. Fanny begins to carry in armloads of books and papers which she drops in the middle of the floor, Gardner berates her for
throwing his valuable manuscript "into a box like a pile of garbage,"
and Mags flies to her father's defense. Even after Mags learns that Gardner's manuscript is incoherent and that he is incontinent, she accuses
Fanny of treating Gardner cruelly. In the emotional climax of the play,
Fanny calmly explains how she is sacrificing herself "to be Daddy's
nursemaid out in the middle of nowhere."

Scene 2 "The last day. All the books and boxes are gone. The room is
completely empty except for Mag's backdrop." Fanny and Mags have rid
themselves of false notions and useless possessions. They take with them
more honest portraits of each other.

2. Choose five incidents that illustrate the emotional range of the play
and describe the emotional response evoked by each.

This exercise will illustrate how rapidly Howe's roller coaster of a
play rushes us from one emotion to another.

The Saltine cracker scene is outrageously funny. At that time neither
the audience nor Mags knows that Gardner's eccentric behavior goes
beyond endearing absentmindedness, and our laughter is unrestrained.
In the Counterpoint, Gerald Weales suggests "that this scene should be
as horrifying as it is funny and the seeds for the later harsher tone
planted here . . . ." You might ask your students whether there is
something dark under the comedy here that might be lost if the scene is
played just for laughs.

The mood is nostalgic when Fanny recalls romantic sled rides with
Gardner: "Then Daddy would lie down on the sled, I'd lower myself on
top of him, we'd rock back and forth a few times to gain momentum and
then . . . WHOOOOOOOOOSSSSSSSHHHHH . . . down we'd plunge like a
pair of eagles locked in a spasm of lovemaking. God, it was wonderful!"

Another recollection evokes quite different emotions. In a scene
charged with repressed anger Mags reminds her parents of an incident
they had apparently forgotten. When she recounts her unjust
banishment from the dinner table, her paralyzing fear of "losing
control" and "making a mess" at the table, her parents' failure to notice
that she had stopped eating, she is accusing them of failing to love her,
understand her, and appreciate her. Fanny characterizes this exchange
as "the most distressing conversation [she's] ever had." Viewers squirm
uncomfortably, embarrassed to have witnessed this airing of private
family matters.

The climax of the play (Act 2, Scene 1) takes us to the brink of tragedy. Like Mags we move from despair (when she reads Gardner's introduction and discovers that "[i]t doesn't make sense"), through anger over Fanny's laughter, to respect for Fanny's courageous self-sacrifice.

In Act 2, Scene 2, yet another mood is created with the hauntingly beautiful description of "that summer when the ocean was full of phosphorus." Mags recalls swimming with her father: "As you dove into the water, this shower of silvery green sparks erupted all around you. It was incredible! I thought you were turning into a saint or something . . . . And then she remembers one special evening:

> We were chasing each other under water. At one point I lost you, the brilliance was so intense . . . but finally your foot appeared . . . then your leg. I grabbed it! . . . I remember wishing the moment would hold forever; that we could just be fixed there, laughing and iridescent. . . .Then I began to get panicky because I knew it would pass; it was passing already."

3. What is the significance of Fanny's and Gardner's ridiculous poses as famous paintings?

Unfortunately readers of this play miss the visual parodies Fanny and Gardner find so amusing. To compensate you might bring in pictures of Grant Wood's *American Gothic,* Michelangelo's *Pietà,* Michelangelo's *The Creation* (p. 20), and Renoir's *Le Moulin de la Galette* and ask your students to pose for tableaux vivants. That should set the tone for this class discussion.

In addition to providing comedy, the poses reveal a great deal about Fanny and Gardner—that they are witty and "cultured," that they are a bit self-conscious about posing for their portrait, that they are in the habit of having fun together, and that—as Mags suspects—they find it difficult to take their daughter's work seriously.

4. How does the portrait Mags completes on the final day of her visit home differ from the portrait she would have painted on the first day?

Although the audience never sees Mag's portrait of her parents, we do know that Fanny and Gardner like it and that it is more realistic than it could have been before Mags had worked up the courage to open her eyes and really *see* her parents. When Mags first arrives at her childhood home, she "sees" her parents as they were (or as she thought they were) when she was a child. In Mags' mind, her father is still a Pulitzer Prize-winning poet, a scholar at work on a precious manuscript;

her mother a flamboyant, slightly dotty, and somewhat tyrannical woman who fails to take her husband or her daughter seriously.

In the opening scene Fanny tries to give Mags a more accurate picture of reality by making her "face the facts around here." She tells her daughter that Daddy "is getting quite gaga," that his new book "doesn't make one word of sense," and that "[t]hings are getting very tight around here, in case you haven't noticed. Daddy's last Pulitzer didn't even cover our real estate tax, and now that he's too doddery to give readings anymore, that income is gone . . .". At first Mags refuses to see the unpleasant truths her mother paints for her. She defends her father: "There's nothing wrong with him! He's just as sane as the next man. Even saner if you ask me." She insists that he is the same as always. "He's abstracted . . . . That's the way he is." But by the end of the play, after she's seen her father overwhelmed by the difficulty of hanging his coat in the closet, shaken by his inability to find the ice for their drinks, and delighted by the childish game Fanny invents to help him pack his manuscript, Mags can no longer pretend that he is unchanged. Mags' picture of her mother is also transformed. By the end of the play she sees Fanny as a brave woman willing to give up her home, her friends, and even the easy solution offered by a bullet through the head so that she can continue to care for the man she loves.

5. Is the happy ending of this play believable?

At the end of the play Fanny and Gardner, in their final tableau vivant, become a waltzing couple from Renoir's *Le Moulin de la Galette*. Some viewers consider that ending a false note, an inappropriately cheerful close for a play about aging, senility, self-sacrifice, and the inability of family members to understand each other. Others consider it a perfect symbol of Fanny's love for Gardner and her determination to "exit with a little flourish; have some fun." If your students find this ending unsatisfactory, you might ask them to suggest alternatives. That exercise should demonstrate the difficulty of selecting the "correct" emotional tone for the final scene of a tragicomedy.

—M.R.D

Sam Shepard
Fool for Love

Some of your students may be offended by *Fool for Love*. The language is salty, and some of the action is so mysteriously symbolic and apparently unmotivated that eyebrows may be raised. The Counterpoint may help clear things up. In the excerpt from the interview there, Shepard announces a surprising influence:

> And I read most of the Greek guys—Aeschylus, Sophocles . . . I studied up on those guys, and I'm glad I did. I was just amazed by the simplicity of the ancient Greek plays, for instance—they were dead simple. Nothing complex or tricky . . . which surprised the hell out of me, because I'd assumed they were beyond me . . . They're [the Greek dramas] about destiny! That's the most powerful thing. Everything is foreseen, and we just play it out . . . I've noticed that even with the Greek guys, especially with Sophocles, there's a very simple, rawboned language. The choruses are poetic, but the speech of the characters themselves is terse, cut to the bone and pointed to the heart of the problem.

If you have treated *Medea* or *Antigone* in class, there are some useful comparisons to be made with Shepard's work. As Shepard points out, the motivations of his characters—once we have discovered them—and those, say, in *Antigone,* are simple. Antigone wants her brother to be buried and at rest; Eddie is interested in cowboying (and all that connotes) and May. The issue in the plays, classical and contemporary, is uncomplicated but hard: Should one indulge one's will no matter the cost to others?

Shepard's answer seems to be yes. Despite the fun May pokes at Eddie's view of himself as the Marlboro man, the fact is that Eddie continues his callous treatment of May and patches together his tired old image of himself as a man whose bootheels must be a-wanderin'. We know his type; here is the late-20th-century version of the Byronic hero, carrying a torch for that one woman he hates and loves, a two-fisted drinker, mysterious, man of outdoor action, moodily sensitive when he finds it picturesque and seductive—in short, a man fated to be sixteen until his body fails him—"Everything's foreseen, and we just play it out."

Some students may wonder if this cowboy is a fit character for tragedy—or, if indeed *Fool for Love* is a tragedy. Eddie, as Aristotle would have it, is "a character neither eminently virtuous or just, nor yet involved in misfortune by deliberate vice or villainy, but by some error of human frailty." Eminently virtuous Eddie is certainly not, but he preserves a grand passion for May, and we must admire grand passion. He also has a wit and a sharpness that we might admire; he holds his own in his exchanges with May and offers an intelligence that Martin cannot muster. He crosses over, however, the line separating wit and cruelty in tormenting May and baiting Martin, and, when he covers his abandonment with a transparent lie, "I'm only gonna' be a second. I'll just take a look at it and I'll come right back." we are sure, if we did not know before, that he is a small-spirited man forever fixed upon a romantic view of himself—surely an error of human frailty when it results in this sort of destruction of happiness—that forces him to leave May and that will force him to return to her.

QUESTIONS

1. What concerns does Shepard reveal in his descriptions of the set and of his *dramatis personae?*

Your students, even if they haven't seen Shepard where he is most visible (acting in *Country* or in *The Right Stuff*, most notably, at this writing), will recognize an actor's director at work here. The opening description is devoted entirely to illustrating the characters of Eddie, May, and The Old Man, because little else is of importance to this play.

The motel room is "stark," "low-rent," and the motel is, appropriately enough, at the edge of the Mojave—what better place for Shepard to explore the myth of the American West as it is represented by Eddie? The Old Man's chair is, after all, upholstered with a horse blanket. Merle Haggard's "The Way I Am" announces the same sentiment as Sinatra's "My Way": rugged individualism makes a man a man. Perhaps the most important detail we are given is that a table should be "set extreme down left (*from actor's p.o.v.*)" [emphasis only in part mine].

In the opening tableau we learn that The Old Man is to function in a fashion unlike any of the other characters, because "He exists only in the minds of MAY and EDDIE, even though they might talk to him directly and acknowledge his physical presence." He does not literally "exist in the same time and place" as the others. We learn little of May except how she is dressed and how old she might be, and those details offer little insight into her character. Of Eddie we learn a good deal more. We discover that he is a cowboy, or at least affects being a cowboy. His clothing is worn and threadbare, like The Old Man's, and his body is getting that way:

> When he walks, he limps slightly and gives the impression he's rarely off a horse. There's a peculiar broken-down quality about his body in general, as though he's aged long before his time.

We are given to understand pretty clearly that some sort of conflict is about to begin—"This play is to be performed relentlessly and without a break." You may wish to ask your class what view of the relationship of Eddie and May is being suggested in the stage directions following:

> On the floor, between his feet, is a leather bucking strap like bronc riders use. He wears a bucking glove on his right hand and works resin into the glove from a small white bag. He stares at MAY and ignores THE OLD MAN. As the song nears the end of its fade, he leans over, sticks his gloved hand into the handle of the bucking strap and twists it so that it makes a weird stretching sound from the friction of the resin and leather.

[It may interest your students to know that in *Contemporary Authors*, some of Shepard's interests are listed as "Greyhound racing, pool, rock and roll . . . Wyoming, the Sioux Nation, guns, '57 Chevrolets, sheep-dogs, highways, buffalo, knives, horse racing, fast women, and various personalities associated with the American West." The source of the list is not given.]

2. How does The Old Man function in the play? What does he symbolize?

Since he comments on the action, some might conclude that he acts in a fashion similar to that of the Greek chorus. One could make a case for that, but one important difference exists. The Old Man's remarks are "personal" in a way that no chorus's are; in his commentary he chides May and Eddie for misrepresenting his/their history, commiserates with Eddie about how difficult women are to deal with ("I wanna' hear the male side a' this thing," or rhapsodizes about the loves he has known or created, rather than exploring the relative merits of the "arguments" presented by the principals.

Determining what The Old Man symbolizes is tricky business. It is important, of course, to discourage your class from deciding upon the "correct" answer, but the following possibilities may stimulate discussion:

◆ The Old Man represents what Eddie will become. If he is literally Eddie's father, then it does not seem completely unlikely that there is a sort of predisposition in Eddie, born of nature and nurture, that forces him into destructive romantic attachments. The Old Man's reminiscences are, then, a type of "flash-forward," during which we see quite clearly what Eddie's fate will bring him to.

◆ The Old Man operates as a kind of muse for the romantic delusions we find in Eddie.

> The Old Man: I thought you were supposed to be a fantasist, right? Isn't that basically the deal with You? You dream things up. Isn't that true? . . .
>
> Take a look at that picture on the wall over there. (He points at wall stage right. There is no picture but Eddie stares at the wall.) Ya' see that? Take a good look at that. Ya' see it?
>
> Eddie: (staring at wall) Yeah.
>
> The Old Man: Barbara Mandrell. That's who that is. Barbara Mandrell. You heard a' her?
>
> Eddie: Sure.
>
> The Old Man: Well, would you believe me if I told ya' I was married to her?
>
> Eddie: (pause) No.
>
> The Old Man: Well, see, now that's the difference right there. That's realism. I am actually married to Barbara Mandrell in my mind. Can you understand that?

In fact, the line between what the characters believe to be fact and fiction is often blurred in this play. After Eddie spins the yarn to Martin of his incestuous and persistent love for May, she picks up the thread of the tale. After denying her blood relationship with Eddie, she promptly turns around and confirms that they shared a father—The Old Man— and that Eddie's mother had killed herself when confronted with Eddie and May's incestuous relationship. Eddie corroborates the story of his mother's suicide.

◆ The Old Man serves through his reminiscences as the embodiment of the destructive nature of the love between men and women that Shepard insists upon in this play. Incapable of finding happiness with one woman, he alternately abandons and reclaims the women Eddie and May late in the play claim are their mothers. At the end of the play, he forlornly points to a picture we cannot see and says:

Ya' see that picture over there? Ya' see that? Ya' know who that is? That's the woman of my dreams. That's who that is. And she's mine. She's all mine. Forever.

This is precisely the sort of force that drives Eddie and May to search out and destroy each other.

May: It was supposed to have been true every time before. Every other time. Now it's true again. You've been jerking me off like this for fifteen years. Fifteen years I've been a yo-yo for you. I've never been split. I've never been two ways about you. I've either loved you or not loved you.

3. Is the final effect of *Fool for Love* tragic or comic?

The play has its lighter moments. The relationship between Eddie and the mysterious Countess is the stuff that bad prime-time soap operas and romance novels are made of (*The Countess and the Cowboy*), and Shepard knows it. The gunshots through the window, the Mercedes-Benz, and the burning horse-trailer are self-conscious melodrama. Shepard even has a sense of humor when it comes to his own idiom; when he has Eddie lasso a chair, for example, he seems unable to resist a send-up of himself and his often-ridden theme of the True West.

But I think it is safe to say that, while the play hardly fits Aristotle's prescriptions for tragedy, the mood evoked finally is one we associate with the tragic. Eddie abandons May after what would seem to be a reconciliation, and she leaves, undoubtedly to go through the same torment again. The ending brings with it the same sense of entrapment and despair as *No Exit*. The Old Man's final speech would indicate to most of us that Eddie's destructive vision of himself and May will continue unchanged.

—W.R.S.

Beth Henley
Crimes of the Heart

Beth Henley's Pulitzer Prize-winning play, *Crimes of the Heart*, is an outrageously funny comedy about three sisters whose lives seem anything but amusing. The youngest sister, Babe, has just shot her husband, the best attorney in town, because she "just didn't like his looks." The oldest sister, Lenny, has resigned herself to a life of loneliness because she has "that *shrunken* ovary." Meg, the middle sister who moved to Los Angeles to pursue a career in singing, has taken a job "paying cold-storage bills for a dog-food company." When these three women gather in Lenny's kitchen in the house where all three grew up, we learn that the sisters have had a lot of "real bad days," beginning with the day their mother hanged herself and the three small girls moved to this small Mississippi town to live with Old Granddaddy.

So why is this play funny? Maybe it's because in *Crimes of the Heart* as in life, comedy and tragedy keep bumping into each other. Time and time again Henley leads us to the brink of the tragic; then, in fine Southern gothic tradition, she pushes us one step further and we discover that we've just entered the realm of the ridiculous. Mama doesn't just hang herself; she also hangs the old yellow cat and consequently gets "national coverage." Babe doesn't just shoot her husband; she shoots him, fixes a pitcher of lemonade, and asks her bleeding husband if he wants some.

The ending of this play will undoubtedly remind your students of the ending of Chekhov's *The Three Sisters*. Both dramatists ignore the traditional comic pattern that requires a happy ending complete with marriages or betrothals, and end their plays with tableaux of three women united by familial love. At the end of both plays, the sisters, perhaps having realized that romantic love offers them uncertain hope, turn to each other for comfort in dealing with the past and support in dealing with the future.

QUESTIONS

1. How does Henley arouse our curiosity in the opening scene?

In most plays the opening scene provides us with background information; in *Crimes of the Heart* the first scene raises more questions than it answers. Chick immediately informs us that something disgraceful has occurred: "Well," she asks Lenny, "did you see today's paper?" After Lenny nods, Chick continues, "It's just too awful! . . .How I'm gonna continue holding my head up high in this community, I do not know." Henley then hints that Babe is involved in the scandal: Chick tells Lenny that "Babe's ready to come home" and that they must "get right over and pick her up before they change their simple minds," but we still don't know who Babe is, what she did, where she is, or who *they* are. Before Henley answers any of those questions, she poses more: What was the sordid affair between Meg and Doc Porter that left him a cripple? What are the skeletons in the MaGraths' closet? Why is Chick humiliated when someone brings up the death of Lenny's mother? What happened to the poor cat? By the close of Chick's and Lenny's brief conversation, the audience is definitely hooked.

2. What does Henley achieve by confining the action of the play to the kitchen of the MaGrath family home?

If your students have seen the movie *Crimes of the Heart* (screenplay by Henley), they may remember that the action in the film version is not restricted to the kitchen. In the movie the characters enact some of the scenes that are recounted around the kitchen table in the play; consequently, the movie characters move from one setting to another, and the movie audience sees Lenny and Meg visiting Old Granddaddy in the hospital, Babe shooting Zackery in the living room of her house, Meg and Doc going for a ride out in the country, and Lenny chasing "Chick the Stick right up the mimosa tree." Whether similar scene changes would "improve" the play is debatable.

Henley admits that her decision to set the play in the MaGrath kitchen was based on practical considerations. By confining the action to a single indoor set and limiting the cast to six characters, she hoped to make the play attractive to small regional theaters that typically operate on shoestring budgets. Her plan was successful. *Crimes of the Heart* opened in Louisville in 1981 and has since been staged by regional theaters across the country.

The kitchen setting does more, however, than merely hold down production costs; it provides us with a visual symbol of the family unit that strengthens each of the sisters. For Lenny, Meg, and Babe (and for many in the audience), the kitchen is the heart of the home, the room where family members gather for emotional as well as physical nourishment. It is clear that the sisters are comfortable in the kitchen. Although Meg and Babe have lived elsewhere for years, Meg knows she will find a Coke in the refrigerator, and Babe knows she will find the ingredients for lemonade. The three sisters' fond memories of good times shared in that kitchen are illustrated by the conversation that takes place after they decide to play cards:

Lenny: Oh, good! It'll be just like when we used to sit around the table playing hearts all night long.

Babe: I know! *Getting up*: I'll fix us some popcorn and hot chocolate—

Meg: *Getting up*: Here, let me get out that old black popcorn pot.

By the time the play ends, the kitchen and the family are synonymous. When Chick comes into the kitchen and insults Meg, Lenny chases her out, shouting, "This is my home! This is my house! Get out! Out!

3. How does each sister benefit from the bonding that takes place when they are reunited in this play?

At the beginning of the play it is clear that the sisters have been separated by more than distance. Lenny and Babe don't know that Meg spent Christmas in a psychiatric ward; Lenny and Meg don't know why Babe shot Zackery; Meg and Babe don't know why Lenny stopped seeing Charlie. Each sister has been going it alone, none very successfully. When they come together, they give each other strength and courage, and at the end of the play each sister is better off than at the beginning.

It is easy to see how Babe is helped by her sisters. Lenny and Meg keep her out of prison by hiring a lawyer and persuading her to tell Barnette why she shot Zackery. Later Meg saves Babe's life when she pulls her head out of the oven and then convinces her that she is not insane. At the end, it is clear that Babe will not attempt suicide again. She tells Meg, "And I'm not like Mama. I'm not so all alone."

The reunion also changes the course of Lenny's life. Lenny is convinced that no one will ever love her because she has an underdeveloped ovary, but Babe and Meg insist that she is wrong:

Lenny: What man's gonna love me?

Meg: A lot of men!

Babe: Yeah, a lot! A whole lot!

Meg: Old Granddaddy's the only one who seems to think otherwise.

Eventually they convince her to "take a chance" and call Charlie, something she would never have done without their encouragement. She gets her courage up, telephones him, tells him about her ovary problem, and discovers that he still wants to see her.

Meg is also changed dramatically by her visit home. For the first time since her mother died, Meg allows herself to "care about someone". The someone she admits to caring about is Doc, but her behavior toward Lenny and Babe makes it clear that she cares about them too. Meg, the most private of the three sisters (she never tells

Lenny or Babe about her emotional breakdown at Christmas time), does not admit that her relationship with her sisters transforms her. However, right after the sisters look at a newspaper photo of "Mama and the cat," remember "using up one whole big box of Kleenexes" on the day of the funeral, and laugh at their memories of Babe throwing up her banana-splits breakfast in the flower arrangements, Meg hugs her sisters and cries, "Oh, Babe! Oh, Lenny! It's so good to be home!" It is more than coincidental that immediately after that scene, Meg leaves with Doc and discovers that she can care about someone.

4. Are the characters believable?

Critics who dislike this play complain that Henley's characters are overdrawn, that they are examples of Southern grotesque, not believable human beings. In one of the Counterpoints Walter Kerr explains that he found himself "simply and flatly disbelieving" when Babe, who has just shot Zackery and mixed herself a pitcher of lemonade, calls out to her husband who lies bleeding on the floor, "Zack, I've just made lemonade, do you want a glass?" Perhaps Kerr, a New York critic, disbelieves because he's never met anyone like Babe. My husband and I live in and practice law in a small rural town, and neither of us found the incident unbelievable. But, of course, the question isn't whether such things have happened, but whether Henley convinces us that Babe would offer Zack a glass of lemonade. I'm convinced.

Let's face it, Babe is not burdened with excess intelligence. When Meg, referring to Babe's affair with a young black man, comments, "I didn't even know you were a liberal," Babe responds, "Well, I'm not! I'm not a liberal! I'm a democratic!" Nor does Babe have a clear understanding of cause and effect—she doesn't even think to remove the rack before attempting to put her head in the oven. Add to those limitations the fact that Babe had been severely depressed long before the shooting (she fell asleep at the dinner table every time Zackery began speaking), that she was undoubtedly suffering from shock, and that she had been brought up to be a polite Southern lady, and her offer of lemonade becomes almost predictable. Granted, Babe is eccentric, but her actions are always consistent with the character Henley reveals.

5. Is Henley's portrait of a family convincing?

I can think of no other play that so perfectly captures the complex relationship between sisters. Who but a sister would look you in the face and say, "My God, we're getting so old!" Who but a sister would complain, "Why, remember how you had layers and layers of jingle bells sewn on your petticoats while Babe and I only had three apiece?!"

Who but a sister would fix you a Coke and drink out of the bottle before handing it to you? Lenny, Meg, and Beth do things to each other that they would do to no one else. That is why they are so convincing as a family.

At an early age, most of us learn that, outside our family, love has to be earned, that unless our friends approve of our actions, they will withdraw their affection. Families, as Lenny, Meg, and Beth understand, don't operate that way. Lenny and Meg may disapprove of Babe's decision to shoot her husband because she "just didn't like his looks," but their disapproval has no effect on their love for Babe or on their willingness to do anything they can to help her. Lenny disapproves of Meg's lifestyle, of her treatment of Doc, and of her lying to Old Granddaddy—and she tells her so, but Lenny never stops loving Meg. All three sisters know that familial love, like grace, is a gift, not a payment for good behavior. That is the assurance that binds them and gives them strength.

6. Does the happy ending seem contrived?

Before students can answer this question, they should ask themselves whether the play's ending is indeed happy. If we define as happy an ending that assures the audience that the characters will live happily ever after, *Crimes of the Heart* doesn't qualify. At the end of the play Old Granddaddy lies dying in the hospital, and Babe, Meg, and Lenny face futures that are at best uncertain. But if we define as happy an ending that makes us feel good about the world, even though we know there will be more "real bad days," then this play's ending is both happy and believable. Henley doesn't try to convince us that these three disaster-prone sisters will never again have problems; she does persuade us that their reunion has taught them to rely on each other and that together they will "learn how to get through these real bad days." Henley's ending is convincing because she promises only that the sisters will continue to have happy moments together, moments that will give them the strength to continue. Their future is symbolized by the vision that comes to Lenny's mind when she makes her birthday wish:

Babe: A vision? What was it of?

Lenny: I don't know exactly. It was something about the three of us smiling and laughing together.

Babe: Well, when was it? Was it far away or near?

Lenny: I'm not sure; but it wasn't forever; it wasn't for every minute. Just this one moment and we were all laughing.

Babe: Then, what were we laughing about?

Lenny: I don't know. Just nothing, I guess.

Meg: Well, that's a nice wish to make.

–M.R.D.

A SELECT LISTING OF PERFORMANCES AVAILABLE ON VIDEO, FILM, AND AUDIOCASSETTE

The following listing of filmed versions of certain plays and short stories included in *The Riverside Anthology,* as well as readings and interviews on audiocassete, lays no claim to comprehensiveness. As we all know, performances are being filmed very day, films are being converted into videocassettes, and videocassettes are being released to distributors. Thus, what is not available today may very well be available tomorrow.[*] Distributors themselves are the best source of information; so, too, is the latest annual edition of the *Video Source Book,* published by the National Video Clearinghouse and available in most major libraries. The book provides a thorough, alphabetical listing of available videotapes (it may be easiest to refer to the Literature category in the index), including brief descriptions of the performances and notations of distributors from which the videos may be obtained. It also features the addresses and telephone numbers of numerous distributors across the country.

A note on our listing of distributors: first, clearly, it is not exhaustive, but it does represent, to the best of our knowledge, some major sources for the videos, films, and audiocassettes listed here. Second, you will find that it is always wise to call the distributor before making firm plans. Your university library or media center may very well have catalogs from various distributors; we give phone numbers for the distributors we include below. Availability, price, and order fulfillment are all variables: for that reason, we have given no data on them here. Further, distributors maintain sometimes curious policies with regard to rental; in some instances, particular videos may be available for purchase only (perhaps you have access to a departmental budget). But if you do want to rent, make that clear: policies do change. And by all means check with your local video stores: their holdings increase weekly, and you may very well be able to turn up some pleasant surprises.

Finally, a word about serendipity. Although it feels decidedly strange to recommend the reading (or, at least, perusing) of *TV Guide,* the fact remains that public television is constantly presenting filmed performances of literary works (on such programs, among others, as *Masterpiece Theatre, Live from Lincoln Center,* and *Great Performances.*) Of course such cable networks as Arts & Entertainment, Showtime, and Bravo are likewise potential sources.

The listings below are arranged in two categories: (a) performances of works and/or programs devoted to the work and life of a particular writer, arranged alphabetically by writer; and (b) more thematic programs, arranged alphabetically by title.

---

[*] For example, within the past couple of years we have seen on television filmed performances of Chekhov's *Three Sisters* (in a splendid production directed by Trevor Nunn), Fugard's *"Master Harold". . . and The Boys,* and Howe's *Painting Churches.* They are likly to be available on videocassetts in the near future.

DISTRIBUTORS CITED IN THE FOLLOWING ENTRIES

AAPL: The American Audio Prose Library Inc.
P.O. Box 842
Columbia, MO 65205
(314) 443-0361
Readings by and interviews with American writers. Audiocasettes.

Encyclopaedia Britannica Educational Corporation
425 North Michigan Avenue
Chicago, IL 60611
1-800-558-6968
In Wisconsin (collect): (414) 351-4488

Films for the Humanities
P.O. Box 2050
Princeton, NY 08540
(609) 452-1128
1-800-257-5126

GA: Guidance Associates
Communications Park
Box 3000
Mt. Kisco, NY 10549-0900
1-800-431-1242

Kent State University Film and Video Rental Center
Kent, Ohio 44242
216-672-3456
1-800-338-5718

LCA: Learning Corporation of America
Distributed by Simon & Schuster Comm.
108 Wilmont Road
Deerfield, IL 60015
1-800-323-6301

Penn State Audio-Visual Services
Special Services Building
University Park, PA 16802
(814) 865-6314

PMI: Public Media Incorporated
Films Incorporated
1213 Wilmette Avenue
Wilmette, IL 60091
1-800-323-4333
In Illinois: (collect) (312) 356-3200

Time-Life Distribution Center
100 Eisenhower Drive
P.O. Box 644
Paramus, NJ 07653
(201) 843-4545

PERFORMANCES AND PROGRAMS RELATED TO SPECIFIC WRITINGS

Alice Adams
Interview
DIST: AAPL

Margaret Atwood
Interview
DIST: AAPL

Toni Cade Bambara
Interview
DIST: AAPL

Jorge Luis Borges
The Inner World of Jorge Luis Borges
A tour of Borges' native city, Buenos Aires, and of his mind,
narrated by Borges and Joseph Wiseman
27 min./color
DIST: Films for the Humanities

Samual Taylor Coleridge
The Rime of the Ancient Mariner
A film by Kenneth Russell, starring David Hemmings.
52 min./color
DIST: Films for the Humanities

E.E. Cummings
e.e. Cummings
A self-portrait, created by way of the poet's reminiscences, his notebooks,
poetry, and paintings.
24 min./color
DIST: Films for the Humanities

Arthur Conan Doyle
The Speckled Band
With Raymond Massey as Holmes and Athole Stewart as Watson. Made
in 1931. British
? min./black & white
DIST: Possibly available in some video stores; possibly occasionally shown
on television

Euripides
Medea
The 1982 Kennedy Center production starring Zoe Caldwell as Medea and
Judith Anderson as the Nurse.
90 min./color
DIST: Films for the Humanities/Penn State

William Faulkner
Barn Burning
From the PBS series "The American Short Story."
With Tommy Lee Jones.
41 min./color
DIST: Penn State

Gail Godwin
Reading "Dream Children"
DIST: AAPL
Interview
DIST: AAPL

Frederico García Lorca
Frederico García Lorca: A Murder in Granada
A profile of the Spanish writer, including reminiscences by members of
his family and friends. Focuses on the themes, sources, and development
of his work; also shows his paintings. Contains documentary footage of
his murder by the Falangists in the Spanish Civil War.
64 min./color
In Spanish, with English narration and subtitles

DIST: Films for the Humanities/Penn State

Gabriel García Márquez
Gabriel García Márquez
A filmed exploration of García Márquez's world of magic realism, featuring the author.
60 min./color
Ask for the English version.
DIST: Films for the Humanities

Nathaniel Hawthorne
Rappaccini's Daughter
From the PBS series "The American Short Story"
57 min./color
DIST: Penn State

Beth Henley
Crimes of the Heart
The film (directed by Bruce Beresford, screenplay by Beth Henley) features Diane Keaton as Lenny, Sissy Spacek as Babe (the performance won her an Oscar), Jessica Lange as Meg, and Sam Shepard as Doc.
105 min./color
DIST: Available for rental in video stores; also available for purchase.

Langston Hughes
Langston Hughes
A portrait of the poet, concentrating on his role in the Harlem Renaissance.
Selections from the poetry.
24 min./color
DIST: Penn State

John Keats
John Keats: His Life and Death
Written by Archibald MacLeish.
Concentrates on Keats' love for Fanny Brawne and the final year of his life.
55 min./color
DIST: Britannica Films

Edna St. Vincent Millay
Millay at Steepletop
A portrait of the poet at her farm in upstate New York, with commentary
by her sister Norma. Features Millay reading her work; shows some
sequences from home movies.
25 min./color with black and white sequences
DIST: Penn State

Arthur Miller
Death of a Salesman
With Dustin Hoffman (as Willy) and John Malkovich
    min./color
DIST: GA (for purchase only), also check video stores

Alice Munro
Interview
DIST: AAPL

Pablo Neruda
Yo Soy Pablo Neruda
A Profile of the Chilean poet, narrated by Anthony Quayle. Features
Neruda reading his poetry.
29 min./black & white
Ask for the English version
DIST: Films for the Humanities/Penn State

Katherine Anne Porter
The Jilting of Granny Weatherall
From "The American Short Story" Series
With Geraldine Fitzgerald
57 min./color
DIST: Kent State/Penn State

William Shakespeare
Hamlet
The classic 1948 version starring Laurence Olivier
155 min./black & white
DIST: LCA/Films for the Humanities
Hamlet
From the BBC series "The Shakespeare Plays"
With Derek Jacobi
222 min./color
DIST: Time-Life/Kent State

Measure for Measure
From the BBC series "The Shakespeare Plays"
With Kate Nelligan, Tim Pigott-Smith, and Christopher Straul
145 min./color
DIST: Time-Life/Kent State
Twelfth Night
From the BBC series "The Shakespeare Plays"
With Alec McCowan, Trevor Peacock, Felicity Kendall
124 min./color
DIST: Time Life/Kent State
Rehearsing the Text
With actors from the Royal Shakespeare Company
A rehearsal of *Twelfth Night*, Act 2, Scene 4, focusing on the ways in which the text itself illuminates character, language, and staging.
53 min./color
DIST: Films for the Humanities

Sam Shepard
Fool for Love
With Sam Shepard, Kim Bassinger, Harry Dean Stanton, Randy Quaid.
DIST: MGM/United Artists Home Video 1350 Avenue of the Americas New York, N.Y. 10019

Sophocles
Antigone
With Juliet Stevenson, Justin Shrapnel, and John Gielgud
120 min./color
DIST: Films for the Humanities

Alice Walker
Interview
DIST: AAPL

Walt Whitman
Walt Whitman: Poet for a New Age
A study of Whitman's primary beliefs in democracy, comradship, passionate expressiveness.
29 min./color
DIST: Britannica Films

William Wordsworth
A dramatization of the poet's life (starring David Warner), focusing on the major poems, the Lake District, and Wordsworth's relationship with his sister Dorothy.
52 min./color
DIST: Films for the Humanities

William Butler Yeats
Yeats Remembered
A profile of the poet, featuring excerpts from interviews with Yeats and his children, reading from his poetry, period photographs, and on-location photography.
DIST: GA

THEMATIC PROGRAMS

The Negro Writes in America
James Baldwin, Lorraine Hainsbury, Langston Hughes
46 min.
DIST: AAPL

Poetry on Tape
Poet's Audio Corner
P.O. Box 50145 - Dept. N
Washington, D.C. 20004-0145
1-800-824-7888
Operator 698
Ask for catalog

The Romantic Age in English Literature
An exploration of the Romantic sensibilities through excerpts from Wordsworth, Byron, Shelley, and Keats. Features biographical notes on each poet and analysis of his work; paintings from London's National Portrait Gallery; on-location photography.
DIST: GA

The Spoken Arts Treasury of 100 Modern American Poets
464 poems on 18 cassettes or LP disks, read by the poets themselves.
Includes Robert Frost, Wallace Stevens, William Carlos Williams, Ezra Pound, Marianne Moore, T.S. Eliot, Archibald MacLeish, Dorothy Parker, e.e. cummings, Louise Bogan, Langston Hughes, Countee Cullen, Richard Eberhart, W.H. Auden, Theodore Roethke, Elizabeth Bishop, Muriel

Rukeyser, Randall Jarrell, John Berryman, Robert Lowell, Gwendolyn Brooks, May Swenson, Richard Wilbur, Anthony Hecht, Denish Levertov, Allen Ginsberg, Robert Bly, Galway Kinnell, Adrienne Rich, Sylvia Plath
DIST: Spoken Arts, Inc.
Dept. PML7
P.O. Box 289
New Rochelle, NY 10802
(914) 636-5482

A Survey of English and American Poetry
A sixteen-part series on video, offering both a history and anthology of English-language poetry. As well as presenting readings of works, each program provides historical and critical commentary and visuals that illustrate the eras and places in which the poems were written.
Sir John Gielgud is the series host; among the performers are Sir Ralph Richardson, Dame Peggy Ashcroft, Stacy Keach, Cyril Cusack, and Lee Remick.

All programs are 28 minutes long and are in color. The titles and brief descriptions are given below; for further details call the distributor, *Films for the Humanities*.

Introduction to English Poetry
Excerpts from Chaucer, Shakespeare, Milton, the Romantics, Dickinson, Hardy, Yeats, etc.
Old English Poetry
"The Seafarer," "Dream of the Rood," and *Beowulf*.

Chaucer
Prologue to The Canterbury Tales; the pardoner's Tale acted out.

Medieval to Elizabethan Poetry
Skelton, Wyatt, Marlowe, Drayton, Spenser, Shakespeare's Sonnet 129.

The Maturing Shakespeare
Excerpts from *Romeo and Juliet, Twelfth Night, Hamlet, Lear, Antony and Cleopatra, Tempest*. Filmed in a 16th-century house.

Metaphysical and Devotional Poetry
Donne, Herbert, and Marvell.

Milton
Focus on *Paradise Lost,* but also "Methought I saw my late espoused saint" as an inroads to the poet's character.

Restoration and Augustan Poetry
Rochester, Dryden, Swift, and Pope.

Romantic Pioneers
Smart, Blake, Coleridge ("Kubla Khan"), and Wordsworth.

William Wordsworth
The major poems; photographed in the Lake District

The Younger Romantics
Shelley, Keats, Byron *(Don Juan).*

Victorian Poetry
Tennyson, Emily Bronte, Christina Rossetti, Browning, Arnold, Swinburne.

American Pioneers
Poe, Melville, Dickinson, Robinson

Romantics and Realists
Hardy, Hopkins, Housman, Kipling

The Earlier Twentieth Century
Yeats, Owen, Frost, Eliot, Auden.

The Later Twentieth Century
Thomas, Lowell, Larkin, Hughes.
DIST: Films for the Humanities